POLITICAL SCIENCE: A COMPARATIVE INTRODUCTION

COMPARATIVE GOVERNMENT AND POLITICS

Comparative Government and Politics
Series Standing Order ISBN 978–0–333–71693–9 hardback
Series Standing Order ISBN 978–0–333–69335–3 paperback
(*outside North America only*)

You can receive future titles in this series as they are published by placing a standing order. Please contact your bookseller or, in the case of difficulty, write to us at the address below with your name and address, the title of the series and one of the ISBNs quoted above.

Customer Services Department, Macmillan Distribution Ltd,
Houndmills, Basingstoke, Hampshire, RG21 6XS, UK

ROD HAGUE AND MARTIN HARROP

7TH EDITION

POLITICAL SCIENCE

A COMPARATIVE INTRODUCTION

palgrave
macmillan

First edition 1992
Second edition 1998
Third edition 2001
Fourth edition 2004
Fifth edition 2007
Sixth edition 2010
Seventh edition 2013

Published by
PALGRAVE MACMILLAN

Palgrave Macmillan in the US is a division of St Martin's Press LLC,
175 Fifth Avenue, New York, NY 10010.

Palgrave Macmillan in the UK is an imprint of Macmillan Publishers Limited,
registered in England, company number 785998, of Houndmills, Basingstoke,
Hampshire RG21 6XS.

Palgrave Macmillan is the global academic imprint of the above companies
and has companies and representatives throughout the world.

Palgrave® and Macmillan® are registered trademarks in the United States,
the United Kingdom, Europe and other countries

ISBN 978-1-137-32403-0

This book is printed on paper suitable for recycling and made from fully
managed and sustained forest sources. Logging, pulping and manufacturing
processes are expected to conform to the environmental regulations of the
country of origin.

A catalogue record for this book is available from the British Library.

A catalog record for this book is available from the Library of Congress.

10   9   8   7   6   5   4   3   2   1
22 21 20 19 18 17 16 15 14 13

Printed in China

Summary of Contents

Contents

List of illustrative material

Profiles

Spotlights

Timelines

Maps

Boxes

Tables

Figures

Preface

This edition retains the purpose of its predecessors: to provide a wide-ranging, accessible and contemporary introductory textbook for courses in comparative politics and in political science.

We retain a thematic approach, centred on liberal democracies and their institutions of government. Institutions constitute core subject-matter of political science and we seek to expound the substantial body of knowledge the discipline has developed about them. But the book's scope extends well beyond this focal point, encompassing wider political processes in addition to institutions and authoritarian regimes as well as liberal democracies. Our prime concern is substantive findings but we also include chapters on theoretical approaches and research methods.

As usual, we have significantly updated the book for this new edition. First, we have added a chapter on voters, not least to capture emerging research on comparative electoral behaviour. The predominantly behavioural approach in this chapter may provide a helpful contrast with the more institutional focus of the existing chapter on elections.

Second, we have added a dozen new sections to reflect recent developments and rectify old omissions. Among other topics, this new material includes democratization, women and political participation, election campaigns, judicial decision-making, e-government and policy diffusion. We hope these sections will refresh the book's content.

Third, we have again revisited our classification of regimes. This time, we have adopted a straightforward and, we hope, stable division between liberal democracy and authoritarianism. Competitive authoritarian regimes, which in the previous edition we labelled as 'illiberal democracies', are now treated as a type of non-democracy. This particular modification reflects the increasing implausibility of treating, say, Putin's Russia as a democracy of any kind.

In addition to these substantive changes, we have revised and edited the entire text in an attempt to keep the book clear, concise and current. Textbooks want to be longer but we have fought the good fight. By removing some older, peripheral and less interesting content, and also by relocating a fully updated chapter on political economy to the website, we have produced a slightly shorter book which, we hope, will continue to engage the reader.

We have also added to the book's pedagogical features. A short 'Studying' guide now appears near the start of each chapter signposting some of the chapter's main themes and the kinds of topics students might explore when looking further into the area (it may be worth emphasizing that these guides are not chapter summaries; précis continue to be available on our companion website).

In addition, we have included some discussion questions at the end of each chapter. These questions go beyond the material in the chapter; some are quite challenging. As their label suggests, they are intended for class discussion. Straightforward review questions are available on our website.

The original inspiration for this book came from our own student experience, long ago. We were often assigned to read books which claimed to introduce their readers to the literature on a particular topic. But many such volumes only made sense to us if we had already grasped the literature, in which case they were unnecessary. So we set out to write a com-parative politics text that would be introductory but not simplistic. And that is the test by which we would still ask to be judged.

This edition is the work of many hands. At Palgrave Macmillan, we would like to thank Helen Caunce, Steven Kennedy and Stephen Wenham for their support. Their persistent helpfulness was far more than helpful persistence. We thank Keith Povey and Marilyn Hamshere for their vigilant copy-editing; Ian Wileman for his skilful typesetting; and Benjamin Coulson for his editorial and research assistance. We owe a special debt to the publishers' anonymous reviewers for their comments both broad and detailed.

As we began work on this edition, we were sad-dened to learn of the untimely death of Peter Mair (1951–2011). Peter was the leading authority of his generation on political parties and a good friend of this book. He is sadly missed.

ROD HAGUE
MARTIN HARROP

Guide to learning features

This book contains a range of features designed to aid learning. These are outlined below.

Studying feature
A bulleted list near the start of each chapter signposts some of the chapter's major themes and also suggests some topics to explore should you wish to study the topic further. This feature also highlights any challenges which arise in researching the topic.

Country profiles
Profiles cover 15 specific countries and regions to complement our thematic approach. For each country or region covered, our profile provides:

● A standard set of demographic, economic and political indicators.
● A capsule description of the country's main political institutions.
● A short account of its overall political configuration.

Spotlights
Spotlights follow on from profiles, providing a detailed case study of how the chapter theme operates in the country profiled.

STUDYING . . .
LEGISLATURES

● Legislatures (parliaments) link society and state. They are an essential device in a representative democracy.

● The issue of whether legislatures should have one chamber or two, though seemingly technical, exposes contrasting perspectives on how democracy should be conceived.

● Representation is the most obvious function of legislatures. But how representation should be understood, and reconciled with the importance of party, is an important question.

● The contrast between debating and committee-based legislatures offers insight into how parliaments work in practice. For committee-based legislatures, we can look not only to the United States but also to Scandinavia.

● Scrutiny (oversight) is an increasingly important function of nearly all legislatures in liberal democracies. Understanding this role means looking carefully at parliamentary committees. Comparative projects here can offer practical lessons, as well as casting light on an important component of contemporary governance.

● If you are more intrigued by the members of legislatures than the institutions themselves, there are several worthwhile themes to pursue: career politicians, the political class, corruption and its impact, celebrity politicians, and political dynasties. All these areas are well-suited to comparative analysis.

● Assemblies are found in most authoritarian regimes. The initial (and quite difficult) task here is to identify what functions they serve. Case studies of such assemblies help to reveal the opportunities for, and the informal limits on, public dissent in non-democratic settings.

COUNTRY PROFILE
UNITED KINGDOM — LIBERAL DEMOCRACY

Form of government ▪ a parliamentary liberal democracy with a largely ceremonial monarchy.
Legislature ▪ the House of Commons (650 members) is the dominant chamber. The House of Lords, the composition of which has been under review since 1997, acts in a revising and restraining capacity.
Executive ▪ the Cabinet is the top decision-ratifying body; the prime minister selects and dismisses its members. Meetings of full cabinet are largely formal; its effective work is conducted in committee.
Judiciary ▪ based on the common law tradition. In 2009, the introduction of a supreme court, albeit without the authority to veto legislation, strengthened the autonomy of the judiciary.
Electoral systems ▪ the House of Commons is still elected by the single-member plurality method. A range of systems is used for elections to other bodies such as the Scottish Parliament, the Welsh Assembly, and the European Parliament.
Party system ▪ traditionally a two-party system, the dominance of the Conservative and Labour parties has been challenged by the rise of the Liberal Democrats.

Population (annual growth rate): 63.0 m (+0.5%)
World Bank income group: high income
Human development index (rank/out of): 28/187
Political rights score: ❶
Civil liberties score: ❶
Media status: free

Note: For interpretation and sources, see p. xvi.

The UNITED KINGDOM is a liberal democracy whose political system has nonetheless been in transition. Traditional models portrayed Britain as a centralized, unitary state; as a two-party system; as an exemplar of parliamentary sovereignty in which ministers were held to account by the assembly; and as a political system whose uncodified constitution offered little formal protection of individual rights. Yet, the accuracy of all these images has come under review.

The centralized and, even, the unitary character of the United Kingdom was put in question by the creation in 1999 of new assemblies for Scotland and Wales. The reform was asymmetric, with the Scottish parliament receiving more devolved powers than the Welsh

assembly. Devolution to Northern Ireland was reinstated in 2007, reflecting the ending of armed conflict between Catholic and Protestant groups and the UK government.

In the United Kingdom as a whole, the two-party system based on the Conservative and Labour parties was challenged by the rise of the Liberal Democrats. In the 2010 election, the Liberal Democrats won 6.8 million votes and 57 seats, forming a governing coalition with the Conservatives.

Parliamentary sovereignty has been dented by British membership of the European Union and a more assertive judiciary. Individual rights now receive clearer protection, exerted through the judiciary, from the incorporation into

British law in 1998 of the European Convention on Human Rights.

Ministerial accountability has been complicated by the delegation of government tasks to semi-independent agencies. In a particularly significant reform, the 1997 Labour government immediately took steps to give control of monetary policy to the Bank of England's Monetary Policy Committee.

The cumulative impact of these developments remains to be established. What is clear is that many of the old assumptions about British politics have ceased to apply; in a more complicated and fragmented polity, replacement clichés are harder to find.

SPOTLIGHT
The British Parliament

The new era in British politics has impinged on its assembly. Traditionally, Britain's Parliament mixed omnipotence and impotence in a seemingly impossible combination. Parliament was considered omnipotent because parliamentary sovereignty, allied to an uncodified constitution, meant there could be no higher authority in the land. It was considered impotent because the governing party exercised tight control over its own backbenchers, turning Parliament into an instrument, rather than a wielder, of power. How has the mother of parliaments adapted to the current period of change?

In the twenty-first century, Parliament's position has become less certain. The tired rituals of adversary politics in the House of Commons have become less convincing, not least for the new members – forming a majority of the House – elected between 1997 and 2010.

The notion that Parliament possesses sovereignty still carries weight but – as with many assemblies – Britain's legislature runs the risk of being left behind by international integration, by competition from the media as an arena of debate, and by the indifference of prime ministers who choose to spend less time in the House.

In addition, an expenses scandal which erupted in 2009 damaged the standing of the House. The fact that dubious expenses claims came to light showed that even MPs could not control the flow of information, while the subsequent reforms brought an end to self-policing of expenses by the House itself.

But not all developments are a response to crisis. MPs themselves have become more committed; the era of the amateur is over. They are predominantly drawn from professional, business, and political backgrounds. They devote time to an increasing volume of constituency casework. The number of late sittings has been cut. Select committees have established themselves in the debate over policy and contribute to scrutinizing the executive. The prime minister now appears twice a year before a select committee for a more detailed discussion than is possible during weekly Question Time.

Prior occupation of Conservative and Labour MPs, 2010		
	Conservative	Labour
Business	125	20
Law	56	26
Politics	31	52
Media	29	18
Armed services	15	1
Accountancy	13	2
Education	4	35
Civil Service/ local government	2	13
Manual work	2	22
Union official		29
Other	29	40
Total	**306**	**258**

Source: Adapted from Kavanagh and Cowley (2010), table 15.6.

Overall, Kelso (2011, p. 69) judges that 'there is now a very clear shift away from a chamber-based insti-

tion towards a committee-based institution, illustrated by the growing emphasis given to new public bill committees, select committees and committee-based scrutiny of the prime minister.'

As an upper chamber in what remains a unitary state, the House of Lords occupies an uncertain position. Its 760 members consist mainly of appointed life peers but reform, when finally agreed, is likely to involve a substantial measure of election. Such a development may well make the Lords more assertive in challenging the executive.

Yet, even as Britain's Parliament updates its skills, it will surely continue to do what it has always done best: acting as an arena for debating issues of central significance to the nation, its government, and its leaders. Even in an era of reform, the House of Commons has retained its position as a classic debating assembly.

Further reading: Bogdanor (2009), Heffernan et al. (2011), Kavanagh and Cowley (2010), Moran (2011).

Table 15.1 Selecting the second chamber, 2012

Upper chambers are usually smaller than lower chambers, with members selected for a longer tenure and by a greater range of methods

	Chamber	Members	Term (years)	Method of selection
Australia	Senate	76	6	Direct election by single transferable vote in each state
Germany	*Bundesrat* (Federal Council)	69	–	Appointed by state governments
Ireland	Senate	60	5	Appointed by the PM (11), elected from vocational panels (43), and from two universities (6)
India	*Rajya Sabha* (Council of States)	245	6	Indirectly elected through state assemblies (233), appointed by the president (12)
USA	Senate	100	6	Direct election by plurality voting in each state

Source: IPU (2012).

Tables

Tables display statistics, again usually with a comparative theme.

Definitions

The first time a technical term is used, it appears in **purple** and is separately defined nearby. In the index, these terms are also listed in **purple** so that they can be located easily. All these definitions, and many more, are available in our on-line dictionary.

Descriptive representation is present when the members of a representative body resemble the represented in given characteristics, such as ethnicity and gender. **Substantive representation** is present when representatives act on behalf of, and in the interests of, those they represent. A female legislator can reflect the substantive interests and opinions of her male constituents but cannot serve as their descriptive representative.

Figure 15.2 Selecting the second chamber, 2012

Seats in the second (upper) chamber are allocated by three main methods: direct election, indirect election, and appointment. For comparison, 95 per cent of members of the first (lower) chamber are directly elected.

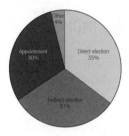

Note: Based on total number of seats (i.e. not averaged by country).
Source: IPU (2012).

Figures

Figures are used mainly to express political institutions and processes in diagrams.

Functions

Representation, we have suggested, is a key function of parliaments. But deliberation and legislation follow close behind. Other functions – crucial to some, but not all, assemblies – are authorizing expenditure, making governments, and scrutinizing the executive (Box 15.1). In discussing these roles, we will see how the significance of parliaments in liberal democracies extends well beyond the narrow task of simply converting bills into laws.

Representation

If the essence of assemblies is that they represent society to government, how can we judge whether, and how well, that function is fulfilled? What features would a fully representative assembly exhibit?

One distinction here is between **descriptive** and **substantive representation**. The idea of descriptive representation is that a legislature should be society in miniature, literally 're-presenting' society in all its diversity. Such a parliament would balance men and women, rich and poor, black and white, even educated and uneducated, in the same mix as in the population. How, after all, could a parliament composed entirely of middle-aged white men go about representing young women of colour (or, for that

matter, vice versa)? To retain society's confidence, the argument continues, an assembly should reflect social diversity, standing in for society and not simply acting on its behalf (Phillips, 1995).

The widespread introduction of gender quotas for members of parliament – or, at least, for parliamentary candidates – reflects the philosophy of

BOX 15.1

Functions of legislatures

Representation	Most members articulate the goals of the party under whose label they were elected
Deliberation	Debating matters of moment is the classic function of Britain's House of Commons
Legislation	Most bills come from the government but the legislature still approves them and may make amendments in committee
Authorizing expenditure	Parliament's role is normally reactive, approving or rejecting a budget prepared by the government
Making governments (see Chapter 16)	In most parliamentary systems, the government emerges from the assembly and must retain its confidence
Scrutiny	Oversight of government activity and policy is growing in importance and is a task well-suited to the assembly's committees

Boxes

Boxes are used mainly to define, contrast and illustrate particular political processes.

descriptive representation (Chapter 8). But considerable difficulty arises in full implementation. An exact transcript of society could best be achieved by random sampling (as with juries), dispensing with election altogether. However, if such a practice were implemented, then – for better or worse – parliaments, like juries, would contain their fair share of the addicted, the corrupt, and the ignorant.

Further, representatives selected as an accurate mirror of society would need to be replaced regularly lest they become tainted by the very experience of office – a point that led the American politician John Adams (1735–1826) to proclaim that 'where annual election ends, there slavery begins'. In reality, complete descriptive representation is an impractical and probably undesirable goal.

In the main, contemporary representation operates in a somewhat prosaic way: through political parties. Victorious candidates owe their election to their party and they vote in parliament largely according to its commands. In New Zealand, for example, Labour members must agree to abide by the decisions of the party caucus. In India, an extreme case, members lose their seat if they vote against their party, the theory being that such representatives are deceiving the voters if they switch parties after their election. The party has become the vehicle of substantive representation and the prism through which electors view candidates.

Deliberation

Many legislatures serve as a deliberative body, considering public matters of national importance. This function contrasts sharply with the descriptive view of representation, prioritizing instead substantive representation, particularly in articulating the long-term interests of society at large.

In the eighteenth and nineteenth centuries, before the rise of disciplined parties, deliberation was regarded as the core parliamentary activity. In theory, at least, members were expected to serve as **trustees** of the nation, applying exceptional knowledge and intelligence to the matters before them. What mattered was the quality of debate, not whether it reflected voters' opinions.

The Irish-born politician Edmund Burke offered the classic account of this position. Elected Member of Parliament for the English constituency of

---

Discussion questions

- Must the legislature of a true democracy be unicameral?
- Should members of the upper chamber be appointed for their experience and wisdom, or elected for their popular appeal?
- What is the most important function of the legislature in (a) contemporary liberal democracies; (b) authoritarian states?
- Does descriptive representation matter?
- What are the strengths and weaknesses of a legislature populated by professional politicians?
- Should legislators be subject to term limits?

Discussion questions

Discussion questions help consolidate knowledge by highlighting major issues and policy implications, and encourage you to apply key concepts to additional situations and countries.

Further reading

N. Baldwin, *Legislatures of Small States: A Comparative Study* (2012). An examination of the impact of small state size on the structure and functions of legislatures.

R. Corbett, F. Jacobs and M. Shackleton, *The European Parliament*, 8th edn (2011). A comprehensive guidebook to this interesting, if unusual, assembly.

M. Cotta and H. Best, eds, *Democratic Representation in Europe: Diversity, Change and Convergence* (2007). A comparative treatment of long-term changes in parliamentary careers.

L. Dodd and B. Oppenheimer, eds, *Congress Reconsidered*, 10th edn (2012). A helpful collection on the world's most intensively studied legislature: the American Congress.

S. Fish and M. Kroenig, *The Handbook of National Legislatures: A Global Survey* (2009). An extensive reference work assessing the powers of national legislatures by their autonomy, capacity, influence, and powers.

G. Loewenberg, S. Peverill and R. Kiewiet, eds, *Legislatures: Comparative Perspectives on Representative Assemblies* (2002). The essays in this volume include studies of legislative recruitment and careers, the evolution of legislatures, and the electoral systems through which legislatures are chosen.

S. Morgenstern, *Patterns of Legislative Politics: Roll-Call Voting in Latin America and the United States* (2012). A detailed analysis of voting patterns of parties, factions, and alliances in Latin America's Southern Cone, contrasted with the United States.

Further reading

An annotated list of key books is included at the end of each chapter. The citations in each chapter will guide you to more specialized material, including articles in academic journals.

Note: All the references in this book from this and the previous edition are listed by chapter on our website, offering a comprehensive guide to the topic of each chapter.

Guide to profiles

In addition to a profile on the EU, we have included 14 country profiles which contain a number of figures, rankings and scales to indicate the social and political conditions of the country. These indicators and their source are as follows.

Population (annual growth rate)

The distribution of states by population is shown in Table 2.3 and discussed on pp. 30–1. Population change is the change per year as a percentage of the initial level. A positive (negative) figure indicates a rising (falling) population. Population change is composed of births, deaths, immigration and emigration. Rapid increases in population can cause political instability; falls may reflect instability. In 2012, world population change was + 1.1 per cent. The source for population statistics is the CIA (2012), which itself bases its figures on US Bureau of the Census estimates.

Source: CIA (2012), itself based on US Bureau of the Census estimates.

Income group

The World Bank's four-fold classification of national income groups (high income, upper middle income, lower middle income, low income) is outlined in Chapter 2 (see Table 2.4).

Source: World Bank (2012)

Regime type, political rights, civil liberties

Hague and Harrop classify governments as liberal democratic, competitive authoritarian, or authoritarian. Freedom House judges political rights and civil liberties on a scale from 1 (most rights or liberties) to 7.

Source: Freedom House (2012)

Human development index (HDI)

HDI is based on averaging three dimensions: life expectancy at birth, education (mean of years of schooling for adults aged over 25 years and expected years of schooling for children of school entering age) and gross national income per head. Of 187 countries ranked in the 2011 report, based on 2011 data, Norway scored highest (rank = 1) and the Democratic Republic of Congo lowest.

Source: United Nations Development Programme (2012)

Media status

Freedom House assesses the freedom of print, broadcast and internet-based media by country, based on the legal, political and economic environment for these media. Media status is classified as free, partly free or not free.

Source: Freedom House (2012)

Hague and Harrop on the Web

The companion website is available at www.palgrave.com/politics/hague and provides:

- a dictionary of comparative politics
- debates showing both sides of major controversies
- interactive quizzes and essay questions
- a guide to comparative politics on the internet
- web links and an at-a-glance guide to chapter references
- chapter summaries

Chapter 1 Political concepts

This book examines the organization of politics in countries around the world, with a particular focus on democracies. We consider how states solve the core problem of reaching collective decisions, paying close attention to the institutions of government which serve this purpose. But, before we jump into our subject, we must explore some of the key terms used in political analysis. Fortunately, perhaps, most of the political ideas which concern us are embedded in ordinary language; politics, government, power and authority are terms familiar to us all. Even so, the exercise of seeking reasonably full and precise definitions of these everyday notions will provide a helpful introduction to the subject.

In approaching political terms, we can usefully distinguish between concepts and conceptions. A **concept** is an idea, term or category such as 'democracy', 'the state' or 'power'. Concepts are best approached with definitions restricted to their inherent characteristics. What, for example, are the features which a government must necessarily possess to qualify as a democracy? We can agree, surely, that some measure of popular control over the rulers forms part of this concept; if there were no way of holding the government to account, there could be no democracy. A good definition of a concept, in this narrow but important sense, will be clear and concise.

Conceptions build on concepts. They are understandings, perspectives or interpretations of a term. We might, for instance, conceive of democracy as self-government, as representative government or as majority rule. Conceptions build on definitions by progressing to a fuller discussion and consideration of alternative positions.

> A **concept** is a term, idea, or category. A **conception** is a broader understanding or interpretation of a concept (Gallie, 1956).

Politics

To start at the beginning: what is **politics**? We can easily list, and agree on, some examples of political activity. When the American President engages in his annual tussle with Congress over the budget, he is clearly engaged in politics. When many thousands of Israelis joined a street protest in 2011 against their government's failure to curb rising prices, they, too, were patently participating in politics. The political heartland, as represented by such examples, is clear enough.

However, the boundaries are less precise. When one country invades another, is it engaged in politics or merely in war? When a dictator suppresses a demonstration by violence, is he playing or preventing politics? When a court issues a ruling about abortion, should its judgement be con-

STUDYING . . .

POLITICAL CONCEPTS

- Even though the academic study of politics requires few technical terms, precision is gained from clear definitions. For key terms, it is useful to identify both a one-sentence definition (the concept) and any issues surrounding the term (conceptions).

- An explicit view of the nature of politics is important in approaching comparative politics. Two major views can be distinguished. Politics can be seen either as a deliberative process through which a community resolves common problems or as a competition for power and influence. A choice between these broad conceptions influences the analysis of more specific political processes.

- Power, evidently, is central to politics. But here, again, conceptions are important. If we see persuasion and manipulation (rather than just carrots and sticks) as forms of power, the range of the political expands considerably, perhaps excessively.

- The concept of 'governance' is increasingly used in political writing. This term emphasizes the activity rather than the institutions of governing, offering a distinct focus but one which should build on, rather than supplant, the more familiar notion of government. At any rate, the distinction between them is important.

- 'Nation' and 'state' are central terms in comparative politics. Although these words are sometimes used interchangeably, they denote separate entities that can overlap in several ways.

- In comparative politics, added complexity arises from the varying nuances that the same political words (e.g. state, citizen) carry in different languages, and even in separate countries using a common language. We should treat such contrasting conceptions as part of our subject matter.

---

strued as political or judicial? Is politics restricted to governments, or can it also be found in families, universities and, even, seminar groups?

A crisp definition of politics – one which fits just those things we instinctively call 'political' – is difficult. The term possesses varied uses and nuances. But three aspects of politics are clear:

- Politics is a collective activity, occurring within and between groups. A castaway on a deserted island could not engage in politics.

- Politics involves making decisions on matters affecting the group, typically to resolve disagreements about what is to be done.

- Once reached, political decisions become authoritative policy for the group, binding and committing its members. These decisions are enforced.

> **Politics** is the activity or process by which groups reach and enforce binding decisions.

Why is politics necessary? The answer is simple and compelling: the requirement for politics flows from our social nature. We live in groups that must reach collective decisions about using resources, about relating to others and about planning for the future. A country deliberating on whether to go to war, a family discussing where to take its vacation, a university deciding whether its priority lies with teaching or research – all are examples of bodies forming judgements impinging on all their members. Furthermore, the members of such groups are most unlikely to be in complete agreement on the right course to follow; they may even disagree about whether any policy is needed at all. Politics is a fundamental activity because a group which failed to reach at least some decisions would soon cease to exist. You might want to remove from office the current set of politicians in your country but you cannot eliminate the political task itself.

Once reached, decisions must be put into effect. Means must be found to ensure the acquiescence and preferably the consent of the group's members. Once agreed, taxes must be raised; once declared, wars must be fought. Public authority – ultimately, force – is used to implement collective policy. If you fail to contribute to the common task, the authorities may imprison you; at any rate, they are the only people empowered to do so. So, politics possesses a hard edge, reflected in the adverb 'authoritatively' in Easton's famous definition (1965, p. 21) of a political system:

A political system can be designated as the interactions through which values are authoritatively allocated for a society; that is what distinguishes a political system from other systems lying in its environment.

As a concept, then, politics can be defined as the process of making and executing collective decisions. But, as with many political terms, contrasting conceptions can be based on this simple definition. At this broader level, politics can be viewed, idealistically, as the search for decisions which either pursue the group's common interest or at least seek peaceful reconciliation of the varying interests present within any group of substantial size. Alternatively, and perhaps more realistically, politics can be interpreted as a competitive struggle for power and resources between people and groups seeking their own advantage. From this second vantage point, the methods of politics encompass violence as well as discussion. It is worth comparing these conceptions since they provide different starting points for understanding politics.

The interpretation of politics as a community-serving activity can be traced to the ancient Greeks. For instance, Aristotle argued that 'man is by nature a political animal' (1962 edn, p. 28). By this, he meant not only that politics is unavoidable, but also that it is the highest human activity, the feature which most sharply separates us from other species. For Aristotle, people can only express their nature as reasoning, virtuous beings by participating in a political community which seeks not only to identify the common

interest through discussion, but also to pursue it through actions to which all contribute. Thus, politics can be seen as a form of education which brings shared interests to the fore. In Aristotle's model constitution, 'the ideal citizens rule in the interests of all, not because they are forced to by checks and balances, but because they see it as right to do so' (Nicholson, 1990, p. 42). Politics is the activity through which citizens contribute to the identification and implementation of the community's goals.

A continuation of Aristotle's perspective can be found today in those who interpret politics as a peaceful process of open discussion leading to collective decisions acceptable to all stakeholders in society. Crick (2005, p. 21) exemplifies this position:

Politics, then, can be defined as the activity by which different interests within a given unit of rule are conciliated by giving them a share in power in proportion to their importance to the welfare and the survival of the whole community.

For Crick, politics is neither a set of fixed principles steering government, nor a set of traditions to be preserved. Rather, it is an activity whose function is 'to preserve a community grown too complicated for either tradition alone or pure arbitrary rule to preserve it without the undue use of coercion' (p. 24). Indeed, Crick regards rule by dictators, or by violence, or in pursuit of fixed ideologies as empty of political activity. This restriction arises because politics is 'that solution to the problem of order which chooses conciliation rather than violence and coercion' (p. 30).

The difficulty with Crick's elevated conception, as with Aristotle's, is that it provides an ideal of what politics should be, rather than a description of what it actually is. Politics can also consist in the use of the public arena to advance private interests. Narrow concerns often take precedence over collective benefits and those in authority place their own goals above those of the wider community. So, we surely need a further conception, one which sees power as an intrinsic value and politics as a competition for its acquisition and retention.

From this second perspective, politics is viewed as a competition yielding winners and losers. For example, Lasswell (1936) famously defined politics as 'who gets what, when, how'. In these conceptions, political discussion occurs in the context of fundamental differences in power, and conciliation reinforces existing inequalities. Consent is for the losers. Particularly in large, complex societies, politics is a competition between groups – ideological, as well as material – either for power itself or for influence over those who wield it. Politics is anything but the disinterested pursuit of the public interest.

Further, the attempt to limit politics to peaceful, open debate seems unduly narrow. At its best, no doubt, politics is a deliberative search for agreement, but politics as it exists often takes less conciliatory forms. To say that politics did not exist in, say, Stalin's Soviet Union would appear absurd to the millions who lived in the dictator's shadow. A party in pursuit of power engages in politics, whether its strategy is peaceful, violent or both. In the case of war, in particular, it is surely preferable to agree with von Clausewitz that 'war is the continuation of politics by other means' and with Mao Zedong that 'war is politics with bloodshed'.

What emerges, we suggest, is the multifaceted nature of politics. The subject involves shared and competing interests; cooperation and conflict; reason and force. Each conception is necessary, but only together are they sufficient. The essence of politics lies in the interaction between conceptions and we should not narrow our vision by reducing politics to either one. Laver (1983, p. 1) makes the point: 'pure conflict is war. Pure cooperation is true love. Politics is a mixture of both'.

Government, political system and governance

Small groups can reach collective decisions without any special procedures. The members of a family or sports team can reach an understanding by informal discussion. And these agreements can be self-executing: those who make the decision carry it out themselves. However, such simple mechanisms are impractical for larger units such as the states which form the units examined in this book. Countries must develop standard procedures for making and enforcing collective decisions. By definition, decision-making organizations formed for this purpose comprise the **government**: the arena for resolving political issues.

A **government** consists of institutions responsible for making collective decisions for society. More narrowly, government refers to the top political level within such institutions.

In popular use, the government refers just to the highest level of political appointments: to presidents, prime ministers and others at the apex of power. But in a wider conception, government consists of all organizations charged with reaching and executing decisions for the whole community. By this definition, the police, the armed forces, public servants and judges all form part of the government, even though such officials are not usually appointed by political methods such as election. In this broader conception, government is the entire terrain of institutions endowed with public authority.

The classic case for the institution of government was made in the seventeenth century by Thomas Hobbes (Box 1.1). He judged that government provides us with protection from the harm that we would otherwise inflict on each other in our quest for gain and glory. By granting a monopoly of the sword to a government, we transform anarchy into order, securing peace and its principal bounty: the opportunity for mutually beneficial cooperation.

In modern terms, a government offers security and predictability to those subject to it. In a well-governed society, citizens and firms can plan for the long term, knowing that laws are stable and consistently applied.

An additional argument for government, much favoured by economists, is the efficiency to be gained by establishing a standard way of reaching and enforcing decisions (Coase, 1960). If every decision had to be preceded by a separate agreement on how to reach and apply it, politics would be tiresome indeed. These efficiency gains give people who disagree on what should be done an incentive to agree on a general mechanism for resolving disagreements.

Of course, establishing a government creates new dangers. The risk of Hobbes's commonwealth is that it will abuse its own authority, creating more problems than it solves. As one of Hobbes's critics pointed out, there is no profit in avoiding the dangers of foxes if the outcome is simply to be devoured by lions (Locke, 1690). A key aim in studying politics must therefore be to discover how

BOX 1.1

Hobbes's case for government

The case for government was well-made by the English philosopher, Thomas Hobbes (1588–1679). His starting point was the fundamental equality in our ability to inflict harm on others:

For as to the strength of body, the weakest has strength enough to kill the strongest, either by secret machination, or by confederacy with others.

So arises a clash of ambition and fear of attack:

From this equality of ability, arises equality of hope in the attaining of our ends. And therefore if any two men desire the same thing, which nevertheless they cannot both enjoy, they become enemies; and in the way to their end, which is principally their own conservation, and sometimes their own delectation, endeavour to destroy or subdue one another.

Without a ruler to keep us in check, the situation becomes grim indeed:

Hereby it is manifest, that during the time men live without a common power to keep them all in awe, they are in that condition which is called war; and such a war, as is of every man, against every man.

People therefore agree (by means unclear) to set up an absolute government to escape from a life that would otherwise be '*solitary, poor, nasty, brutish and short*':

The only way to erect such a common power, as may be able to defend them from the invasion of foreigners, and the injuries of one another ... is, to confer all their power and strength upon one man, or one assembly of men, that may reduce all their wills, by plurality of voices, unto one will ... This done, the multitude so united is called a COMMON-WEALTH.

Source: Hobbes (1651).

parties and public opinion. In some low-income countries, the government may lack all autonomy, effectively becoming the property of a dominant individual or clan. One way of referring to the broader array of forces surrounding and influencing government is through the concept of a **political system**.

This phrase usefully extends our line of sight beyond official institutions, while still implying that political actors interact with each other and with government in a stable fashion, forming a distinct element or function within society (Easton, 1965). So, the 'American political system' denotes more than 'American government'; it is the space in which the activity of American politics, or at least the bulk of it, takes place.

> A **political system** consists of those interactions and organizations, including but not restricted to government, through which a society reaches and successfully enforces collective decisions.

We must introduce one more term in this section: **governance**. This old notion has undergone a recent revival. The term is nonetheless difficult to pin down; as Jordan *et al.* (2005, p. 478) observe, 'there is no universally accepted definition of governance'. In general terms, the concept of governance refers to the wide range of non-governmental actors involved in politics. But where the phrase 'political system' suggests a rather static account based on organizations, the idea of governance highlights the process and quality of collective decision-making, with a particular focus on regulation. The emphasis is on the activity of governing, rather than the institution of government. Further, the word invites us to recognize that regulation may be led by non-governmental actors: thus, we speak of the governance (rather than the government) of the Internet, because no single ministry is in charge.

> **Governance** denotes the activity of making collective decisions, a task in which government institutions may not play a leading, or even any, role. In world politics, many issues are resolved by negotiation: governance without government.

to secure the undoubted benefits of government, while also limiting its inherent dangers. We must keep in mind Plato's question of long ago: 'who is to guard the guards themselves?'

Of course, politics is far more than government. In high-income countries, government is influenced by wider forces, such as interest groups, political

So, governance directs our attention away from government's command-and-control function towards the broader task of public regulation, a role which ruling politicians in liberal democracies share with other bodies. For example, a particular sport will be run by its governing body, with the country's government intervening only in extreme situations. Hence, the need for the concept of governance as a supplement, rather than a replacement, for the notion of government.

Significantly, the notion of governance rose to prominence in discussion of the European Union, which relies almost exclusively on regulation and negotiation to influence its member states. The EU lacks many attributes of a state, such as an army, and cannot easily be understood as a government. It would be more natural to refer to the EU as a framework for governance built on its member states (Hooghe and Marks, 2001).

Because governance refers to the activity of ruling, it has also become the preferred term when examining the quality and effectiveness of rule. In this context, governance refers not to the institutions of government but to what they do and to how well they do it. For example, many international agencies suggest that effective governance is crucial to economic development in new democracies (World Bank, 1997). President Obama told Ghana's parliament in 2009 that 'development depends upon good governance' (BBC News, 2009). In this sense of governance, the focus is on government policies and activities, rather than the institutions of rule themselves.

Comparative politics

This book adopts a comparative approach, seeking to understand how particular political institutions and processes operate by examining their workings across a range of countries. Comparative analysis is well-established in the study of politics, more so than in most disciplines. This section asks, why compare? What is the value of analyzing politics in different countries? (We reserve a technical discussion of the comparative method for the final chapter). A comparative approach helps in broadening our understanding of the political world, leading to improved classifications and giving potential for explanation, and even prediction (Box 1.2). We address each purpose in turn.

BOX 1.2

The value of comparison

- Learning about other governments broadens our understanding, casting fresh light on our home nation;
- comparison permits us to classify political structures and processes;
- comparison enables us to test hypotheses about politics;
- comparison gives us some potential for prediction and control.

Broadening understanding

The first strength of a comparative approach is straightforward: it enables us to find out more about the places we know least about. This point was well-stated by Munro (1925, p. 4) in describing the purpose of his book on European governments as aiding 'the comprehension of daily news from abroad'. This ability to interpret overseas events grows in importance as the world becomes more interdependent. In an era of international terrorism, no one can afford the insular attitude of Mr Podsnap in Dickens's *Our Mutual Friend*: 'Foreigners do as they do sir, and that is the end of it'.

Understanding politics in other systems not only helps to interpret new developments, it also assists with practical political relationships. For instance, British ministers have a patchy track record in negotiations with their European partners, partly because they assume that the aggressive tone they adopt in the Commons chamber will work as well in Brussels meeting rooms. This assumption reflects ignorance of the consensual political style found in many Continental democracies. What works at home often fails when playing away.

The general point is made by Dogan and Pelassy (1990): through comparison we discover our own ethnocentrism and the means of overcoming it. In this respect, comparative politics is a virtual trip abroad – and the object of foreign travel, said the British writer G. K. Chesterton, is not so much to set foot overseas as to see one's own country as a foreign land.

Enabling classification

A second advantage of comparison is that it enables us to classify government structures and political processes. We will label countries as democratic or non-democratic, constitutions as written or unwritten and electoral formulas as proportional or non-proportional. We can then search for the factors which incline countries to one form rather than the other. We can also examine the effects of each form. For instance, once we classify governments into presidential and parliamentary systems, we can look at which type is more stable and effective.

Classification is inherently comparative, turning what is often a constant within a single country into a variable between them. In this way, it provides the raw material for explanatory projects.

Testing hypotheses

Comparative researchers seek classifications not just for their own sake, but also to formulate and test **hypotheses**. Comparative analysis enables us to develop and scrutinize such questions as: Do first-past-the-post electoral systems always produce a two-party system? Are two-chambered assemblies only found under federalism? Is parliamentary government more stable than the presidential form?

An **hypothesis** is a relationship posited between two or more factors or variables; for example, between electoral and party systems, or between war and revolution.

Confirmed hypotheses are valuable not just for their own sake, but also because they are essential for explaining the particular. Consider, for example, one specific question: Why did a major socialist party fail to emerge in the United States? An obvious answer is because the USA was built on, and retains, a strongly individualistic culture. This explanation may seem to be particular but, in fact, it is quite general. It implies that other countries with similar values would also lack a strong socialist party. It also suggests that countries with a more collective outlook will be more likely to sustain a party of the left. These hypotheses would need to be confirmed comparatively by looking at a range of countries before we could claim a full understanding of our original question about the USA. So, explaining the particular calls forth the general; only theories explain cases.

Potential for prediction

Generalizations, once validated, have some potential for prediction. Here, we come to our final reason for studying politics comparatively. If we find, say, that the introduction of proportional representation (PR) in New Zealand in 1996 did, indeed, lead to coalition government, we can reasonably suggest at least one effect of introducing PR to countries which still use the plurality method. Equally, if we know that subcontracting the provision of public services to private agencies increases their cost-effectiveness in one country, we can advise governments elsewhere that here is an idea at least worth considering.

Of course, what works in one country can fail elsewhere. In politics, predicting is an art rather than a science, and a fallible one at that. Even so, the potential for prediction provides a starting-point for drawing lessons across countries (Rose, 2005). Rather than resorting to ideology or complete guesswork, we can use comparison to consider 'what would happen if…?' questions. This function of comparative research perhaps underpinned Bryce's comment on his own study of modern democracies (1921, p. iv):

Many years ago, when schemes of political reform were being copiously discussed in England, it occurred to me that something might be done to provide a solid basis for judgement by examining a certain number of popular governments in their actual working, comparing them with one another, and setting forth the various merits and demerits of each.

Classifying governments

We turn now to the question of how governments should be classified in comparative politics generally, and in this book specifically.

We must begin with the most influential classification ever devised: Aristotle's analysis of the 158 city-states of Ancient Greece. Between approximately 500–338 BCE, these communities were small settlements showing considerable variety in their forms of rule. Such diversity provided an ideal laboratory for Aristotle to consider which type of political system provided what he looked for in a government: stability and effectiveness. His analysis

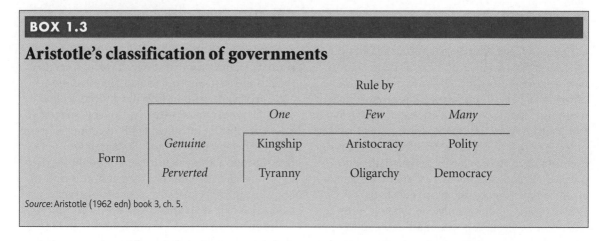

BOX 1.3

Aristotle's classification of governments

		Rule by		
		One	*Few*	*Many*
Form	*Genuine*	Kingship	Aristocracy	Polity
	Perverted	Tyranny	Oligarchy	Democracy

Source: Aristotle (1962 edn) book 3, ch. 5.

offers one of the earliest examples of comparative politics at work.

Aristotle based his scheme on two dimensions (Box 1.3). The first was the number of people involved in the task of governing: one, few or many. This dimension captured the breadth of participation in a political system. His second dimension, more difficult to apply but certainly no less important, was whether rulers governed in the common interest ('the genuine form') or in their own interest ('the perverted form'). For Aristotle, the significance of this second aspect was that a political system would be more stable and effective when its rulers governed in the long-term interests of the community.

Cross-classifying the number of rulers (one, few, or many) with the nature of rule (genuine, or perverted) yields the six types of government shown in Box 1.3. It is worth outlining each cell in this highly influential table. In the case of rule by a single person, Aristotle took kingship as the genuine form and regarded tyranny as its degraded equivalent. For government by the few, Aristotle distinguished between aristocracy (which he defined as rule by the virtuous) and its base form, oligarchy (rule by the rich). And within the category of rule by the many, he separated the ideal form, polity – broadly equivalent to rule by the moderate middle class, exercised through law – from the debased form, democracy, which he interpreted as government by the poor in their own self-interest.

Modern classifications continue to be informed by Aristotle's work. In this book, we follow convention in distinguishing between liberal democracies and

authoritarian regimes, though we also use the notion of a 'competitive authoritarian' regime to identify non-democracies with considerable if unbalanced contestation (Box 1.4).

Although the concept was unknown to Aristotle, **liberal democracy** is now a familiar term. In such a system, rulers are chosen through free, fair and regular elections. Nearly all citizens are entitled to vote and, to permit effective choice, electors can join and form political parties. Further, independent media allow electors to obtain an 'enlightened understanding' of the issues before and during election campaigns (Dahl, 1998, p. 39).

But – and, here, we reach the 'liberal' part – the government of a liberal democracy is subject to constitutional limits. Individual rights, including freedom of assembly, property, religion and speech, are effectively defended in independent courts. These rights secure opportunities to achieve Dahl's 'enlightened understanding' but are also valued in themselves. A clear boundary between public and private keeps the elected government in its place. In office, rulers are subject to explicit, constitutional limits.

So, the adjective 'liberal' in the phrase 'liberal democracy' is not used in the American sense to denote a supporter of progressive policies associated with the Democratic Party. Rather, the term refers to the philosophy of liberalism, a doctrine which regards individual autonomy as the cardinal value. In this sense, the constitution of a liberal democracy provides not only an accepted framework of political competition, but also an effective shield for defending individual rights against government excess.

BOX 1.4

A classification of governments

	Characteristics	Examples
Liberal democracy	Representative and limited government operating through law provides an accepted framework for political competition. Regular elections based on near universal suffrage are free and fair. Individual rights, including freedom of expression and association, are respected.	Affluent Western countries such as Australia, Canada, France and Germany. India is an example of a predominantly liberal democracy in what is still mainly a poor country.
Competititive authoritarian (hybrid) regime	Leaders are elected with no or minimal falsification of the count. However, the rulers exploit their position to prevent a level playing field. To keep potential opponents off-balance, rulers interfere with the rule of law, the media and the market. Individual rights are poorly entrenched and the judiciary is weak.	Many post-military states in Africa and Latin America (e.g. Venezuela). Several Asian states (e.g. Malaysia). Some post-communist states (e.g. Russia).
Authoritarian regime	Rulers stand above the law and are free from effective popular accountability. The media are controlled or cowed. Political participation is usually limited and discouraged. However, the rulers' power is often constrained by the need for tacit alliances with other power-holders such as landowners, the military and religious leaders.	Military governments, ruling monarchies and personal dictators. Authoritarian rule is the most common form of rule in history.
	In the **totalitarian states** of the twentieth century, participation was compulsory but controlled as the government sought total control of society, justified by an ideology seeking to transform both society and human nature. These regimes placed heavy reliance on party members, the secret police and other informers as agents of social control. They are often treated as a separate category from authoritarian regimes.	Communist and fascist regimes subscribed to totalitarian thinking but the model was rarely fully implemented, except for a time in the Soviet Union. More recently, Iran after the Islamic revolution of 1979 showed some totalitarian characteristics. North Korea is a further example.

We now turn to the opposite end of the spectrum. **Authoritarian regimes** are neither liberal nor democratic. Here, the population lacks any effective and regular means of controlling its rulers. Elections may not take place at all, as in military regimes; or else the choice may be artificially restricted – vote for us or go to jail. Whole swathes of the population may be excluded from voting, as with the continued denial of the ballot to women in several Middle Eastern kingdoms. Political parties may be banned altogether; or only one may be permitted; or 'independent' parties are permitted only if they accept a subordinate position. In any event, the rulers exploit the advantages of office (including influence over the media) to prevent a level playing field at elections. Communication between rulers and ruled is low in quantity and quality. Furthermore, the leaders of authoritarian regimes – unlike those of any type of democracy – are prepared to falsify the election result if necessary.

Although orthodox communist states have slipped into history and military rule is currently rare, authoritarian rule remains an important form of government. China, after all, is the world's most populous nation, while the Middle East contains a clutch of significant authoritarian regimes (and much of the world's oil reserves).

We must also note, in parentheses, the distinction often drawn between authoritarian and **totalitarian** regimes (Linz, 1975). The latter term is frequently used to denote communist and fascist states. The leaders of these systems sought tight control and total transformation of society. Most authoritarian rulers, however, seek to insulate themselves from the wider society and are rarely tyrants in the sense of possessing unlimited control. Thus, it is certainly possible to regard authoritarian and totalitarian regimes as distinct types. However, because most totalitarian regimes now belong in the past, we use the term 'authoritarian rule' to refer to all forms of non-democracy.

Finally, to the grey zone between liberal democracies and authoritarian systems. Here can be found the many **competitive authoritarian** regimes combining democratic and authoritarian elements. Numerous phrases are used to capture this form; for example, 'delegative', 'electoral', 'illiberal', 'managed' and 'sovereign' democracy (Zakaria, 2003). But our judgement is that these hybrid systems should be seen as coming closer to the authoritarian than to the democratic pole, as implied by such labels as 'electoral authoritarian' and 'semi-authoritarian' (Levitsky and Way, 2010). So, we discuss competitive authoritarian regimes in chapter sections on authoritarian regimes. Many low-income post-communist, post-military and post-colonial countries belong in this intermediate category.

Competitive authoritarian regimes are measured by political realities, rather than constitutional statements. Rulers run non-fraudulent – but yet controlled – elections; they 'make' the result, even though they do not 'steal' it (Mackenzie, 1958). In Russia, for instance, Vladimir Putin's long period in office reflects authentic popular support for a strong leader; in that sense, Russia is at least an electoral democracy. Even so, no observer in 2012 would describe Putin's Russia as a liberal democracy. As a graduate of the KGB, Putin shows a fine appreciation of the mechanics of power, dominating the broadcasting media, rewarding his friends and punishing his enemies. Because elections in a competitive authoritarian system only rarely deliver a change in government, turnover follows from resignation or – as in Russia and much of Latin America – from constitutional limits on re-election (though these are often evaded).

Competitive authoritarian regimes became more common in the 1990s, following the collapse of communist and military dictatorships. Levitsky and Way (2010, p. 3) counted 33 in 1995, characterized thus:

These post-Cold War regimes were competitive in that opposition forces used democratic institutions to contest vigorously – and, on occasion, successfully – for power. Nevertheless, they were not democratic. Electoral manipulation, unfair media access, abuse of state resources, and varying degrees of harassment and violence skewed the playing field in favour of incumbents. In other words, competition was real but unfair.

We should beware, though, of assuming that the type is wholly new. More than 40 years ago, Finer (1970) discussed the comparable notion of quasi-democracy, using Mexico as his main illustration. Although the formation itself is familiar enough, particular countries can move in and out of the category en route to fully democratic or fully authoritarian status. For instance, Mexico now qualifies as a liberal democracy, at least at national level.

Power, authority and legitimacy

Politics, we have said, is about decision-making within groups. Analysts studying the background to such decisions frequently employ the concepts of power, authority and legitimacy. So, how should we understand these terms? We examine each in turn.

The word 'power' comes from the Latin *potere*, meaning 'to be able'. One conception, then, sees power as the capacity to bring about intended effects (Russell, 1938). The greater our ability to determine our own fate, the more power we possess. In this sense, describing the United States as a powerful country means that it has the ability to achieve its objectives, whatever those may be. Conversely, to lack power is to fall victim to circumstance. Notice that the emphasis here is on power *to* rather than power *over* – on the ability to achieve goals, rather than the more specific exercise of control over other people or countries.

Power is the capacity to bring about intended effects. The term is often used as a synonym for influence, to denote the impact (however exercised) of one actor on another. But the word is also used more narrowly to refer to the more forceful modes of influence: notably, getting one's way by threats.

But most analysis of power focuses on relationships: on power over others. Here, the three dimensions of power distinguished by Lukes (2005) offer a helpful entry point (Box 1.5). Lukes's discussion helps to address the question of how we can measure a group's power, or at least ascertain whether one group is more powerful than another. As we move through these dimensions, so the conception of power becomes more subtle – but also, perhaps, somewhat stretched beyond its normal use.

The first dimension is straightforward: power should be judged by examining whose views prevail when the actors involved possess conflicting views on what should be done. The greater the correspondence between a person's views and decisions reached, the greater is that person's influence: more wins indicates more power. This decision-making approach, as it is called, was pioneered by Dahl (1961) in his study of democracy and power in New Haven, Connecticut.

Dahl's decision-making approach is clear and concrete, based on identifying preferences and observing decisions. It also links directly to the concept of politics as the resolution of conflict within groups. Even though it has now been supplemented by Lukes's other dimensions, it remains a sound initial step in studying power.

The second dimension consists in the power to keep issues off the political agenda. Bachrach and Baratz (1962, p. 948) give the example of a discontented faculty member who rails against university policy in her office but remains silent during faculty meetings, judging that an intervention there would be ineffective and even damaging to her career. Or perhaps all major parties in a particular country advocate racial tolerance, forming what amounts to an elite conspiracy to marginalize racist citizens in the wider population. In these ways, potential 'issues' (change university governance; introduce racist policies) become non-issues and the only decisions in these areas are non-decisions – successful attempts to prevent the emergence of topics which would threaten the values or interests of decision-makers.

So, this second dimension broadens our understanding of the political, taking us beyond the mere resolution of differences and inviting us to address

BOX 1.5

Lukes' three dimensions of power

	Assessing power	Proponent
First	Who prevails when preferences conflict?	Dahl (1957)
Second	Who controls whether preferences are expressed?	Bachrach and Baratz (1962)
Third	Who shapes preferences?	Lukes (2005)

their suppression. In this way, Dahl's view (1961, p. 164) that 'a political issue can hardly be said to exist unless and until it commands the attention of a significant segment of the political stratum' is rejected. Rather, the second dimension recognizes what Schattschneider (1960, p. 71) called the 'mobilization of bias':

All forms of political organization have a bias in favour of the exploitation of some kinds of conflict and the suppression of others because organization is the mobilization of bias. Some issues are organized into politics, while others are organized out.

To deal with this second dimension, Bachrach and Baratz (1962) recommend that students of power should examine which groups gain from existing political procedures, and how powerful individuals limit the political debate to safe issues. Only then should attention turn to the question of whose views prevail on those matters that are up for debate.

The third dimension broadens our conception of power still further (some say, too far). Here, power is extended to cover the formation, rather than merely the expression, of preferences. Where the first and second dimensions assume conflicting preferences, the third dimension addresses the notion of a manipulated consensus. Some examples will help to illustrate this perspective. A government may withhold information about the risks from a chemical leak, preventing those affected from taking necessary precautions to protect their health. More generally, advertising may direct people's desires towards consumption and away from non-material aspects of life which could offer deeper, or at least more natural, satisfaction of genuine needs.

Examples such as these can certainly be used to mount a case that the most efficient form of power is to shape people's information and preferences, thus preventing the first and second dimensions from coming into play. Lukes (2005, p. 28) articulates this perspective:

Is it not the supreme and most insidious exercise of power to prevent people, to whatever degree, from having grievances by shaping their perceptions, cognitions and preferences in such a way that they accept their role in the existing order of things,

either because they can see or imagine no alternative to it, or because they see it as natural and unchangeable, or because they value it as divinely ordained and beneficial?

The case for the third face of power is clearest when specific information is denied in a deliberate attempt to manipulate (Le Cheminant and Parrish, 2011). The selective briefings initially provided by the power company responsible for operating the Japanese nuclear power station which leaked radiation after the 2011 earthquake are an example.

In general, though, working with power's third dimension creates difficulties of its own. In the case of advertising, who is to say that the desire for material goods is a false need? And if a materialist culture is simply an unintended and cumulative consequence of advertising, rather than an explicit aim of specific individuals, do we have a case of power at all? In any case, does not the third face of power take us too far from the explicit debates and decisions which are the stuff of politics?

Still, power as manipulation does encourage us to recognize the centrality of attitudes and beliefs to politics. And, here, the more straightforward ideas of authority and legitimacy become relevant.

Authority is a broader concept than power. Where power is the capacity to act, authority is the acknowledged right to do so. It exists when subordinates accept the capacity of superiors to give legitimate orders. Thus, a general may exercise power over enemy soldiers but his authority is restricted to his own forces.

The German sociologist Max Weber (1922, p. 29) suggested that, in a relationship of authority, the ruled implement the command as if they had adopted it spontaneously, for its own sake. For this reason, authority is a more efficient form of control than brute power. Yet, authority remains more than voluntary compliance. To acknowledge the authority of rulers does not always mean you agree with their decisions; it means only that you accept their right to make them and your own duty to obey. Relationships of authority remain hierarchical.

Authority is the right to rule. Authority creates its own power, so long as people accept that the person in authority has the right to make decisions.

Just as there are various sources of power, so too can authority be built on a range of foundations. Almost 100 years ago, Weber distinguished three ways of validating political power: by tradition (the accepted way of doing things), by charisma (intense commitment to the leader and his message) and by appeal to legal–rational norms (based on the rule-governed powers of an office, rather than a person). Despite its antiquity, this classification remains useful, even though today legal–rational authority is pre-eminent in stable liberal democracies.

Legitimacy builds on, but is broader than, authority. Where authority inheres in a specific role, such as that of a judge, legitimacy is an attribute of the system of government as a whole. When a regime is widely accepted by those subject to it, we describe it as legitimate. Thus, we speak of the authority of an official but the legitimacy of a regime.

A **legitimate** system of government is one based on authority: those subject to its rule recognize its right to make decisions.

Although the word 'legitimacy' comes from the Latin *legitimare*, meaning to declare lawful, legitimacy is much more than mere legality. Legality is a technical matter. It denotes whether a rule was made correctly, following regular procedures. By contrast, legitimacy is a more political concept. It refers to whether people accept the authority of the political system.

Legality is a topic for lawyers; political scientists are more interested in issues of legitimacy: how a regime gains, retains and sometime loses public faith in its right to rule. As Weber suggested, a political system's legitimacy may rest on tradition, a charismatic leader, or conformity to law. But broader influences are also at work. A flourishing economy, international success and a popular governing party will boost the legitimacy of the political system, even though legitimacy is more than any of these things. In fact, one way of thinking about legitimacy is as the credit a political system has built up from its past successes, a reserve that can be drawn down in bad times. In any event, public opinion – not a law court – is the test of legitimacy. And it is legitimacy, rather than force alone, which provides the most stable foundation for rule.

The state, sovereignty and citizenship

The **state** is now the dominant principle of political organization on the world's landmass. There are, of course, some intriguing exceptions (Wilde, 2007). These include territories still under colonial control (e.g. Britain's Gibraltar), or voluntarily subject to partial external authority (e.g. Puerto Rico is affiliated to the United States), or granted substantial autonomy within a larger state (e.g. Hong Kong within China).

The **state** is a political community formed by a territorial population subject to one government.

Leaving such anomalies aside, the world is parcelled up into separate states which, through mutual recognition and interaction, form the international system (Figure 1.1). These units are the main focus of this book, and for this reason we devote Chapter 2 to conceptions of the state's evolution and significance. Here, we focus on the concept itself.

The state is a unique institution, standing above all other organizations in society. It alone claims not only the capacity, but also the right to employ force. As Weber noted, the exclusive feature of the state is precisely this integration of force with authority: 'a state is a human community that (successfully) claims the monopoly of the legitimate use of physical force within a given territory' (quoted in Gerth and Mills, 1948, p. 78). When the state's

---

Figure 1.1 Member states of the United Nations, 1945–2011

United Nations membership has now stabilized following expansion caused by decolonization and the collapse of the Soviet Union

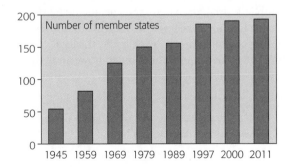

monopoly of legitimate force is threatened, as in a civil war, its very existence is at stake. As long as the conflict continues, there is no legitimate authority. In cynically describing states as nothing more than 'bodies of armed men', Lenin was only partly correct. Contrary to Lenin, a body of armed men does not constitute a state; the law of the gun is no law at all.

How does a state differ from a government? In essence, the state defines the political community of which government is the managing agent. By successfully claiming a monopoly of authorized force, the state creates a mandate for rule which the government then puts into effect. This distinction between state and government is reflected in the characteristic separation of the roles of head of state (e.g. the monarch) and head of government (e.g. the prime minister).

Since much of the theoretical justification for the state is provided by the European idea of **sovereignty**, we must unpack this related notion. As developed by the sixteenth-century French philosopher Jean Bodin, sovereignty refers to the untrammelled and undivided power to make laws. In similar vein, the eighteenth-century English jurist William Blackstone (1765–9, book 1, p. 68) argued that 'there is and must be in every state a supreme, irresistible, absolute and uncontrolled authority, in which the right of sovereignty resides'.

The word 'sovereign' originally meant one seated above. So, the sovereign body is the one institution unlimited by higher authority: the highest of the high. By definition, that body is the state. As Bodin wrote, the sovereign can 'give laws unto all and every one of the subjects and receive none from them'. Sovereignty originally developed in Europe to justify the attempt by monarchs to consolidate control over kingdoms in which authority had previously been shared with the feudal aristocracy and the Catholic Church. Indeed, monarchs and currencies are still known in some corners as 'sovereigns'. By consecrating central authority in this way, the legal concept of sovereignty contributed powerfully to the development of the European state.

Sovereignty refers to the ultimate source of authority in society. The sovereign is the highest and final decision-maker within a community.

However, as democracy gained ground, so too did the belief that elected parliaments acting on behalf of the people are the true holders of sovereignty. The means of acquiring sovereignty evolved, although the theoretical importance of Blackstone's 'supreme authority' remained unquestioned, especially in centralized European countries such as Britain and France. To this day, the notion of 'parliamentary sovereignty' remains an important theme in British politics.

Beyond Europe, the notion of sovereignty remained weaker. In the federal United States, for instance, political authority is shared between the central and state governments, all operating under a constitution supposedly made by 'We, the People' and nourished by the Supreme Court. In these circumstances, the idea of sovereignty is diluted, and so too is the concept of the state itself. Americans more often use the word 'state' to denote the 50 states of the Union, rather than the federal government in Washington. Hemmed about with checks and balances, America's central government lacks the 'absolute and uncontrolled authority' which Blackstone judged so essential to the state.

A useful distinction can be drawn between **internal** and **external sovereignty**. External sovereignty is important because it allows a state to claim the right not just to regulate affairs within its own boundaries, but also to participate as an accepted member of the international order. In this way, the development of the international system reinforces the authority of states within their domestic sphere. Thus, internal and external sovereignty are two sides of the same coin.

Internal sovereignty refers to law-making power within a territory. **External sovereignty** refers to international recognition of the sovereign's territorial jurisdiction.

Sovereignty is a theoretical concept. The formal right to make laws does not imply that the sovereign is omnipotent. All sovereigns are influenced by events beyond and within their borders. For this reason, claims that sovereignty has become a myth in an interdependent world should be treated with scepticism. Sovereignty always was an invention; that is its significance. Mexico, for instance, depends more on the United States than vice versa, but the two countries remain formally equal as sovereigns. A state's control over its destiny is a matter of degree but its sovereignty is, by its nature, unlimited. The essence of sovereignty lies exactly in an unqualified legal title:

Constitutional independence, like marriage, is an absolute condition. People are either married or not married; they cannot be 70 per cent married. The same with sovereignty: a country either has the legal title of sovereignty or it does not; there is no in-between condition. (Sørensen, 2004, p. 104)

Inherent in the notion of the state is the idea of the **citizen**. Just as the development of the state over-rode the power of the aristocracy and the Church, so the concept of the citizen betokens full and equal membership of the political community defined by the state. As Heater (1999, p. 1) notes, 'The title of citizen was adopted by the French revolutionaries [of 1789] to pronounce the symbolic reality of equality; the titles of aristocratic distinction were expunged.' To be a citizen is to possess rights (such as legal rights) as well as duties (such as military or community service) which apply to all accorded that status.

A **citizen** is a full member of a state, entitled to the rights and subject to the duties associated with that status. Citizenship is typically confirmed in a document such as a passport or identity card.

Note, however, that our mental image of a state as a container for its citizens alone is a poor guide to reality. Once condemned as political polygamy, dual citizenship is now accepted by many states (Hansen and Weil, 2002). Further, international migrants – mostly living in high-income countries – made up over 3 per cent of the world's population in 2010 (IOM, 2010). In their country of destination, legal migrants may be granted the right of permanent residence without seeking or being granted citizenship, a limitation which denies them the vote in national elections. To equate a country's adult population with its citizens is to disguise this significant inequality (Hammerstad, 2011).

Nations and nationalism

A **nation** is a more elusive concept than a state. Nations are imagined communities and a nation is often viewed as any group that upholds a claim to be regarded as such (Anderson, 1983). In two ways, though, we can be a little more precise. First, nations are peoples with homelands. As Eley and Suny (1996, p. 10) put it, a nation – like a state – implies 'a claim on a particular piece of real estate'. Here, the origin of the word 'nation', deriving from a Latin term meaning place of birth, is relevant. The link between nation and place is one factor distinguishing a nation from a tribe or ethnic group. Tribes can move home but a nation remains tethered to its motherland, changing shape mainly through expansion and contraction.

Second, when a group claims to be a nation, it professes a right to **self-determination** within its homeland. It seeks sovereignty over its land, exploiting or inventing a shared culture to justify its claim. This assertion of self-rule (not to be confused with democratic rule) gives the nation its political character. A social group becomes a nation by achieving or seeking control over its own destiny, whether through independence or devolution. Nations have either achieved statehood or are states-in-waiting.

Self-determination is the choice of acts without external compulsion. The right of national self-determination is the right of a people to possess its own government, democratic or otherwise.

So, demands for nationhood integrate territory, culture and politics. To describe French-speaking Canadians as a separate nation, as opposed to a linguistic community, indicates a claim for autonomy, if not independence, for this culturally distinct and geographically concentrated group. Similarly, the campaign for a Palestinian state since 1948 has strengthened what was previously a more amorphous Palestinian national identity.

Because the concept of nation is political, there is no necessity for nations to be united by a common language. A shared tongue certainly eases the task of cultural unification yet in Switzerland, for example, French, German and Italian are widely spoken. In India, 24 official languages are each spoken by more than one million people. Nationhood cannot be reduced to any other factor, linguistic or otherwise; rather, it is a subjective identity resulting from what the French philosopher Ernest Renan (1882) termed a 'daily plebiscite'.

Although scholars such as Smith (2009) view nations as creatures of antiquity, they are more often understood as attempts by peoples to assert their essentially modern right to self-determination. Certainly, many nations have been constructed in the course of relatively recent struggles. In the nineteenth and especially the twentieth centuries, for instance, colonial peoples marched to independence under a nationalist banner. Their assertions of national identity were often artificial but they served, nonetheless, as a fresh rallying-cry against the imperialists. It was 'the presence and power of the colonial regime that stimulated the development of a national identity as the basis of resistance' (Calhoun, 1997, p. 108). The nation was created through, not simply invoked in, the struggle for freedom.

'A portion of mankind may be said to constitute a **nationality** if they are united among themselves by common sympathies ... which make them cooperate with each other more willingly than with other people, desire to be under the same government, and desire that it should be government by themselves or a portion of themselves exclusively' (Mill, 1861, p. 391).

To view nations as modern is to suggest that they are made, rather than found. Nations assert statehood and, since states themselves are products of modernity, so too are nations. Specifically, a national identity unites people who do not know each other but who, nonetheless, find themselves yoked together under common rulers and markets. A shared nationality provides an emotional bond for an increasingly rational world. In particular, it allows the losers from the emergence of a large market economy to take comfort in the progress of their country as a whole. In a similar way, national identity provides a rationalization for participation in war, encouraging people 'to die for the sake of strangers' (Langman, 2006).

Even more than nations themselves, **nationalism** is a doctrine of modernity. Like many 'isms', nationalism emerged in the nineteenth century to flourish in the twentieth. But, unlike these other 'isms', the principle of nationalism is reassuringly straightforward. It is simply the doctrine that nations do have a right to determine their own destiny – to govern themselves. In this way, nationalism is a universal

idea, even though each individual nation is rooted in a particular place.

The United Nations Covenant on Civil and Political Rights (UNHCR, 1966) offers a succinct statement of the principle of national self-government:

All peoples have the right to self-determination. By virtue of that right they freely determine their political status and pursue their economic, social and cultural rights.

Nationalism, the key ideology of the twentieth century, is the doctrine that nations are entitled to self-determination. Gellner (1983, p. 1) writes that nationalism 'is primarily a political principle, which holds that the political and national units should be congruent'. National identity is politically vital because it answers a question beyond the reach of democracy: who are 'the people' who are to govern themselves?

Nations, unlike states, do not necessarily have tidy geographical boundaries. Some national groups are spread among several states. The Kurds, for example, are to be found in Iran, Iraq, Syria and Turkey; they form a stateless nation. Similarly, a diaspora is a group widely dispersed beyond its homeland. The Jews remain the standard case, with only a minority of the world's Jews living in the ancient homeland. At the risk of some over-simplification, however, we can draw an initial distinction between **nation-states** and **multinational** states.

A **nation-state** is a sovereign political association whose citizens share a common national identity. A **multinational state** combines a range of national identities under a single government.

An archetypal **nation-state** contains only the people belonging to its nation. The French Revolution of 1789 established the idea that the state should articulate the interests and rights of citizens bound together by a single national identity. In the nineteenth century, the British philosopher John Stuart Mill (1861, p. 392) argued that 'where the sentiment of nationality exists in any force there is a *prima facie* case for uniting all the members of the nationality under the same government, and a government to themselves apart'. In today's world,

Iceland is an example of a pure nation-state. Its population shares such a well-documented descent from within a compact island that the state's birth records provide a perfect laboratory for genetic research.

In a **multinational state**, by contrast, more than one nation is fundamental to a country's politics and assimilation to a dominant nationality is unrealistic. International migration is moving many, perhaps most, states in this direction. Even so, we should not regard the phenomenon of multinationalism as new. Britain, for instance, has long been divided between English, Welsh, Scottish and Irish nationals; Canada between English- and French-speakers; and Belgium between Dutch- and French-speakers.

Ideology, left and right

The concepts reviewed so far have mainly been *about* politics but ideas also play a role *in* politics. Political action is motivated by the ideas people hold about it. One traditional way to approach the role of ideas is via the notion of **ideology**. Our purpose here is to introduce this term, and the related concepts of left and right.

Unlike most political ideas, the term 'ideology' possesses a specific origin. The word was coined by the French philosopher Antoine Destutt de Tracy during the 1790s, in the aftermath of the French Revolution. De Tracy employed the term to denote the science of ideas: idea-ology. His notion was to found a rigorous new discipline which would create a blueprint for a just and rational society.

> **Ideology** 'is a system of collectively held beliefs and attitudes advocating a particular pattern of social arrangements, which its proponents seek to promote and maintain' (Hamilton, 1987).

The point is not so much de Tracy's detailed project but, rather, his underlying conception: that only when ideas were liberated from their moorings in religion and tradition could they acquire their proper importance. Like the French Revolution itself, the science of ideas was to be modern, secular and rational, constructed without reference to the old regime. This contrast with tradition remains central to the understanding of ideology.

Unsurprisingly, de Tracy's radical scheme soon came under attack from existing rulers. Napoleon Bonaparte (ruler of France 1804–14, 1815) sought to sustain his dictatorship with a traditional religious appeal, dismissing de Tracy's followers as windbags seeking to overturn the hallowed authority of throne and altar. Napoleon suggested that laws should be derived not from arrogant ideologists but from 'knowledge of the human heart and of the lessons of history' (Eagleton, 1991, p. 67). Napoleon wanted no truck with the 'cloudy metaphysics' of ideology. This perspective, in which a humanistic outlook based on respect for experience is contrasted with the naïve folly of forward-looking ideologies, is also still commonly encountered.

The contemporary use of 'ideology' has ceased to denote the analysis of ideas. Instead, it has come to denote packages of ideas themselves. The core modern use of ideology is to describe any system of thought expressing a view on:

- human nature;

- the proper organisation of, and relationship between, state and society;

- the individual's position within this prescribed order.

Liberalism, for instance, regards individuals as the best judges of their own interests; advocates a tolerant society which maximizes personal freedom; and favours a government which is limited but freely elected.

Which specific political outlooks should be regarded as ideologies is a matter of judgement. Marxism is surely one and fascism is usually taken as another, even though fascist leaders themselves saw their doctrine as giving priority to action, rather than reflection. It is doubtful, however, if every 'ism' should be judged an ideology. For instance, the central tradition within conservatism is sceptical of political blueprints, creating the potential paradox of an ideology against ideology. Even liberalism, the dominant outlook in the contemporary Western world, prefers to allow individuals to choose their own way of life, rather than to impose a single prescription.

In any case, the era of explicit ideology beginning with the French Revolution surely ended in the twentieth century with the defeat of fascism in 1945 and the collapse of communism at the end of the 1980s. Ideology seemed to have been destroyed by the mass graves it had itself generated. Of course, intellectual currents – such as environmental concerns, feminism and Islamic fundamentalism – continue to circulate. The United States, too, has witnessed a resurgence of intense polarized debate about the proper role of government.

Even so, it must be doubted whether the ideas, values and priorities of our century constitute ideologies in the classical sense. In particular, there seems little point in describing Islam as an 'ideology' when it can accurately be called a 'religion'. And why call 'environmental concern' an ideology when we could just term it a 'policy'? To describe any perspective, position or priority as an ideology is to extend the term in a manner that bears little relation to its original interpretation as a coherent, secular system of ideas.

Although the age of ideology may have passed, the terms **left** and **right** continue to be helpful in comparative politics.

As with ideology, the origins of these concepts lie in revolutionary France. In the legislative assemblies of the era, noble royalists sat to the right of the presiding officer, in the traditional position of honour; radicals and commoners were positioned on the left.

To be on the right implied support for aristocratic, royal and clerical interests; the left, by contrast, favoured a secular republic and civil liberties. To this day, the physical location of a party in each chamber of France's parliament reflects its ideological outlook.

> **Left** and **right** (or left-wing and right-wing) imply opposed positions on a single ideological dimension. However, the content of this dimension varies across countries and time. Broadly, the left is associated with equality, human rights and reform; the right favours tradition, established authority and pursuit of the national interest.

The words 'left' and 'right' are still commonly encountered in classifying political parties, especially in Western Europe. There remains some truth in Sartori's comment (1976, p. 78) that 'what compels us to utilize the left–right distinction is that this appears to be the most detectable and constant way in which not only mass publics but also elites perceive politics'. Surveys suggest that most electors in Western democracies can situate themselves as being on the left or right, even if many simply equate these labels with a particular party or class (Mair, 2009, p. 210). Certainly, the terms have survived the decline of the ideologies they long served to summarize.

BOX 1.6

Themes in the election programmes of left- and right-wing parties, 1945–98

Left	Right
Peace	Armed forces
Internationalism	National way of life
Democracy	Authority, morality and the constitution
Planning and public ownership	Free market
Trade protection	Free trade
Social security	Social harmony
Education	Law and order
Trade unions	Freedom and rights

Note: Based on party programmes in 50 democracies.

Source: Adapted from Budge (2006), p. 429.

They travel well throughout the democratic world, enabling us to compare parties and programmes across countries and time.

The specific issues over which these tendencies compete have naturally varied. Each disposition is often viewed in contrast to the other, rendering them difficult to pin down. 'Left' and 'right' are better seen as labels for containers of ideas, rather than as well-defined ideas in themselves.

In general, the vessel on the left is marked 'reformers and modernizers'; the one on the right, 'traditionalists and conservatives'. In Western Europe, the terms were long associated with the issue of public ownership; the left (as socialists and communists) favoured nationalization, while the right (with exceptions on the extreme) supported a free market. It is here, with the widespread acceptance of the market economy, that the concepts of left and right have lost some bite.

Even so, other contrasts continue. The left supports policies to reduce inequality; the right is more accepting, and welcoming, of natural inequalities. The left sympathizes with cultural and ethnic diversity; the right is more comfortable with national unity. We might also judge that the left is more ideological; the right, less so. It would, though, be a mistake to fix the terms with an artificial precision that denies the natural evolution of the political agenda.

Budge (2006) usefully summarizes themes in the programmes adopted by parties of the left and right in 50 democracies (Box 1.6). His analysis puts flesh on the bones of the left–right distinction. Budge notes not only the familiar contrast between support for public ownership on the left and for the free market by much of the right, he also identifies broader divisions: the left supports internationalism, while the right emphasizes a national way of life. Where the left embraces democracy, the right highlights authority and traditional morality.

The content of Box 1.6 might be quite different 50 years hence. However, the underlying contrasts in disposition – between progress and order, reform and stability, science and tradition – may well remain.

Discussion questions

- What is politics? Does the term extend to violence and war?

- How would studying the governance of your country differ from studying its government?

- Give examples of non-issues in: (a) your university, (b) your country.

- Is a happy housewife a power victim?

- Define: (a) a nation, (b) a state, (c) a nation-state, (d) a multinational state. Give an example of each.

- How far do the concepts of left and right capture the division between major parties in your country?

Further reading

B. Crick, *In Defence of Politics*, 5th edn (2005). A forceful and erudite exposition of the nature of politics that finds the essence of the subject in the peaceful reconciliation of interests.

S. Finer, *The History of Government from the Earliest Times*, three vols (1997). Offers a monumental and, in many ways, unequalled history of government.

A. Heywood, *Political Ideologies: An Introduction*, 5th edn (2012). An informative and wide-ranging textbook that successfully introduces influential political creeds and doctrines.

R. Jackson, *Sovereignty: The Evolution of an Idea* (2007). An accessible and concise introduction to the history and meaning of sovereignty.

S. Lukes, *Power: A Radical View*, 2nd edn (2005). This book introduces power's third face, offering a powerful and engaging critique of conventional interpretations.

A. Smith, *Nationalism*, 2nd edn (2010). Provides a succinct and scholarly overview of nationalism, examining conceptions, theories, histories and prospects.

ONLINE RESOURCES AVAILABLE

Visit the companion website at **www.palgrave.com/politics/hague** to access additional learning resources, including multiple-choice questions, chapter summaries, web links and practice essay questions.

Chapter 2 **The state**

Although we now take for granted the division of the world into states, we should assume neither that the state always was the dominant principle of political organization, nor that it always will be. There was a world before states and, as advocates of globalization tirelessly point out, there may be a world after them, too.

Before the modern state, government in the main consisted of kingdoms, empires and cities. These units were often governed in a personal and highly decentralized fashion, lacking the idea of an abstract political community focused on a defined territory which characterizes today's states. Even so, many of these ancient formations were substantial in area and population. For example, the ancient Chinese empire 'proved capable of ruling a population that eventually grew into the hundreds of millions over a period of millennia – albeit control was not always complete and tended to be punctuated by recurring periods of rebellion' (van Creveld, 1999, p. 36). Ancient history quickly dispels the idea that all modern states are larger and more stable than every traditional political system.

Yet the modern state remains distinct from all preceding political formations. As defined in Chapter 1, states possess sovereign authority to rule the population of a specific territory, a notion which contrasts with the more personal and non-centralized rule adopted by traditional kings and emperors. It is this contrast which enables Melleuish (2002, p. 335) to suggest that 'the development of the modern state can be compared to the invention of the alphabet. It only happened once but once it had occurred it changed the nature of human existence for ever'.

This modern idea of the state developed in Europe between the sixteenth and eighteenth centuries, with the use of the word 'state' as a political term coming into common use towards the end of this period. We begin this chapter by describing the state's development, concentrating on the powerful European form.

Emergence and expansion

The state emerged from the embers of medieval Europe (c.1000–1500). In the Middle Ages, European governance had been dominated by the transnational Roman Catholic Church and powerful feudal lords. Sandwiched between these forces, monarchs occupied a far weaker position than do today's rulers. Our initial problem, then, is to explain how modern states escaped from the dual constraints of Church and feudalism to create the core political entity of today's world.

STUDYING . . .

THE STATE

- The state is the most powerful and successful political organization that has ever existed. Understanding its evolution, and particularly its role as a war machine, is an important theme.

- Viewing the state as society's crisis manager helps in understanding its expansion and contraction. This functional perspective may be more useful in today's relatively peaceful era in which ideological debates about the state's scope have weakened.

- Terrorism and financial crises have clearly required a response from the state in its problem-solving capacity. The long-term impact of these developments on the relationship between state and society may be more apparent when you read these words than when we wrote them.

- States are formally equal in sovereignty but massively unequal in power (both domestic and international) and resources. To understand the state is in part to see how interdependence and even dependence coexist with sovereignty.

- Even among liberal democracies, conceptions of the state vary. These conceptions influence the instinctive response of state managers to what are often common problems. A comparison of France (where the state is often seen as solution) and the United States (the state seen as problem) is instructive here.

- Examining the relationship between the state and intergovernmental organizations (IGOs) helps to locate states in their international setting. One issue is whether we should see IGOs (and the EU) as an influence on states, as a product of states, or both.

Emergence

If any single force were responsible for the transition to the modern state, that factor was war. As Tilly (1975, p. 42) wrote, 'war made the state, and the state made war'. The introduction of gunpowder in the fourteenth century transformed military scale and tactics, as organized infantry and artillery replaced the knight on horseback. The result was an aggressive, competitive and expensive arms race. Between the fifteenth and eighteenth centuries, military manpower in France and England grew almost tenfold (Opello and Rosow, 2004, p. 50).

New technology forced fresh thinking from rulers. In continental Europe, kings needed administrators to recruit, train, equip and pay for standing armies, thus laying the foundation of modern bureaucracies. Reflecting the new benefits to be secured from a large army, units of rule increased in size. Between 1500 and 1800, the number of independent political units in Europe fell from around 500 to just 25 as the medieval architecture of principalities, duchies and bishoprics gave way to a more recognizable framework of larger countries. (Note, however, that two major European states, Germany and Italy, did not unify until the second half of the nineteenth century.)

With the growth of bureaucracy, local patterns of administration and justice became more uniform. As feudal ties decayed, standard rules applying throughout a country eased the growth of commerce, especially in cities. In addition, rulers began to establish formal diplomatic relations with their overseas counterparts, a central feature of the modern state system. The outcome of these changes was the more centralized monarchies which developed in England, France and Spain in the sixteenth century to flourish in the seventeenth. In France, for instance, Louis XIV of France (reign 1643–1715) became known as 'the Sun King': the monarch around whom the realm revolved.

Just as war-making weakened the feudal pillar of the medieval framework, so the Reformation destroyed its religious foundations. From around 1520, Protestant reformers led by Martin Luther condemned what they saw as the corruption and privileges of the organized Church. This reform movement entailed profound political consequences, shattering the Christian commonwealth as antagonism developed between Protestant and Catholic rulers, culminating in the Thirty Years' War (1618–48) in German-speaking Europe.

This conflict was finally ended by the **Peace of Westphalia** (1648), an important chapter in the book of the state. Westphalia is considered pivotal because it gave territorial rulers more control over the public exercise of religion within their kingdoms, thus rendering national secular authority superior to religious edict from Rome. As papal authority decayed, so the status of the state rose.

The **Peace of Westphalia** (1648) was a significant moment in the emergence of the state. In bringing an end to the Thirty Years' War, the peace treaties gave territorial rulers more control over the exercise of religion within their boundaries, thus confirming the diminished transnational authority of the Church.

As central authority developed in Europe, so did the need for its theoretical justification. The crucial idea here was sovereignty (see Chapter 1), as later tamed by the notion of consent. The French philosopher Jean Bodin made the key contribution to this new centralizing ideology. Bodin argued that, within society, a single sovereign authority should be responsible for five major functions: legislation, war and peace, public appointments, judicial appeals and the currency. Such a concentration of political authority was clearly far removed from the decentralized medieval framework of Christendom and feudalism.

But the sovereign still needed to be subject to limits and controls. Here, the English philosopher John Locke played a vital role. His thinking shaped the liberal vision of the Western state that underpinned the American Revolution of the 1770s. Locke's position was that citizens possess **natural rights** to life, liberty and property, and that these rights must be protected by rulers governing through law.

According to Locke, citizens consent to obey the laws of the land, even if only by tacit means such as accepting the protection which law provides. But should rulers violate citizens' natural rights, the people 'are thereupon absolved from any further Obedience, and are left to the common Refuge, which God hath provided for all Men against force and violence' – the right to resist (Locke, 1690, p. 412). So, in Locke's work we observe a modern account of the liberal state, with sovereignty limited by consent. In theory, at least, government had become servant rather than master.

Natural rights (such as to life, liberty and property) are supposedly given by God or by nature; in either case, their existence is taken to be independent of government. In seventeenth-century political thought, natural rights functioned to limit the authority of government, thus establishing the basis for the liberal component of liberal democracy.

These ideas of sovereignty and consent were reflected, in contrasting ways, in the two most momentous affirmations of modernity: the American and French revolutions. In America, the colonists established their independence from Britain and went on to fashion a new republic, giving substance to Locke's liberal interpretation of the state. Thus, the Declaration of Independence (1776) boldly declared that governments derive 'their just authority from the consent of the governed', while the American constitution (drafted 1787) famously begins, 'We, the People of the United States'. The powers delegated to the federal government were expressly limited and strictly enumerated, reflecting a liberal desire to limit the centre's scope.

But it was the French Revolution of 1789 that made the most daring attempt to reinterpret sovereignty in democratic (rather than liberal) terms. Described by Finer (1997, p. 1516) as 'the most important single event in the entire history of government', the French Revolution mapped out the contours of modern democracy. The French approach was far less liberal than its American counterpart. Where the American federal government had remained strictly limited in its authority, the French revolutionaries regarded a centralized, unitary state as the sovereign expression of a national community populated by citizens with equal rights. Where the revolution in America was built on distrust of power, the French revolutionaries favoured universal suffrage and a government empowered to pursue the **general will**.

> The **general will** is followed when citizens make decisions for the good of society as a whole, rather than for the interests of particular groups and individuals within it. The term was central to the thought of the French philosopher Jean-Jacques Rousseau.

The principles of France's modernizing revolution were articulated in the Declaration of the Rights of Man and the Citizen, a document which served as a preamble to the French constitution of 1791 and which still forms part of the country's constitution. Finer judges the Declaration to be 'the blueprint of virtually all modern states'. It pronounces that 'Men are born and remain free and equal in rights … These rights are liberty, property, security and resistance to oppression.' It continues: 'Law is the expression of the general will. All citizens have a right to participate in shaping it either in person, or through their representatives. It must be the same for all, whether it punishes or protects.' So, where sovereignty in the United States served to limit the state through the notion of consent, in France it served to empower the state through the concept of the general will.

True, the democratic pretensions of the French revolution were soon swept aside as violence, terror and war stimulated the return of authoritarian rule under Napoleon. However, the transformation of ideas was irreversible. As national identity joined forces with the state, so sovereignty – once the device used by monarchs to establish their supremacy over popes and noblemen – was decisively reinterpreted for a new democratic age.

Expansion

With the French Revolution, the theoretical foundations of the Western democratic state were, in essence, complete. The detailed construction work was completed in the nineteenth and the first three-quarters of the twentieth centuries, supported by growing nationalist sentiment.

During the nineteenth century, the cage of the state became more precise, especially in Europe. Borders slowly turned into barriers as precise maps marked out defined frontiers. Lawyers established that a country's territory should extend into the sea by the reach of a cannonball and, later, above its land to the flying height of a hot-air balloon. Reflecting this new concern with national boundaries, passports were introduced in Europe during World War I. To travel across frontiers became, as it had not previously been, a rite of passage, involving official permission expressed in a passport stamp.

Economically, too, the second half of the nineteenth century saw the end of an era of relatively liberal trade. Stimulated by economic depressions, many European states introduced protectionist trade policies. National markets gained ground against both local and international exchange, meaning that economies became more susceptible to regulation by central government. Internally, the domestic functions performed by the state began to expand. Many tasks we now take for granted as public responsibilities emerged in the nineteenth century, including education, factory regulation, policing and gathering statistics (literally, 'state facts').

For most of the twentieth century, Western states bore deeper into their societies (Box 2.1). As with the original emergence of European states, this expansion was fuelled by war. The 1914–18 and 1939–45 conflicts were **total wars**, fought between entire nations, rather than just between specialized armed forces. To equip massive forces with the industrial weapons of tanks, planes and bombs required unparalleled mobilization of citizens, economies and societies. The ability to tax effectively and systematically – described by Bräutigam *et al.* (2008, p. 137) as 'the central pillar of state capacity' – expanded further. Because total wars were extraordinarily expensive, tax revenues as a proportion of national product almost doubled in Western states between 1930 and 1945 (Steinmo, 2003, p. 213). The twentieth century was an era of the state because it, too, was an age of war.

> **Total war**, a significant driver of state expansion in the twentieth century, required the mobilization of the population to support a conflict fought with advanced weaponry on a large geographical scale. The conflicts of 1914-18 and 1939-45 were fought between countries, not just between armed forces, with citizens mobilized in the name of nationalism. Total wars required state leadership, intervention and funding.

The onset of peace in 1945 did not initially lead to a corresponding reduction in the state's role. Rather, Western governments sought to apply their

BOX 2.1

The Western state: expansion and restructuring

Aspect	Expansion (1789–1974)	Restructuring (1975–2000)
Centralization The penetration of central power over a specified territory.	● Emergence of national police forces. ● Introduction of border controls.	● Migrants and asylum-seekers loosen border controls. ● Agreed elimination of border controls within some EU states.
Standardization Greater uniformity within society.	● Common language. ● Standard weights and measures. ● Consistent time zones.	● Strengthening of regional autonomy and identities. ● Increased support for a multicultural society.
Force Strengthened monopoly of legitimate force.	● Emergence of national police forces, backed by the military.	● Military spending falls after the Cold War.
Mobilization Increased capacity to extract resources from society.	● Military conscription. ● Introduction of income tax. ● Increased public spending.	● Reduced rates of income tax. ● Tax-payers' revolts in a few countries.
Differentiation State institutions and employees become increasingly distinct from society.	● The idea of public service as the even-handed application of rules.	● The idea of governance as collaboration between state and society. ● Public employees encouraged to mimic private sector styles.
Functions Growth in the state's tasks and its intervention in society.	● War-making. ● Welfare provision.	● Privatization reduces state's direct economic role. ● Welfare provision reduced modestly; some public tasks contracted out.
Size Expansion of the state's budget and personnel.	● Growth of public sector.	● Public sector stabilizes. ● Fiscal deficits increase. ● Military spending falls.

Source: Adapted from Clark (1995), table 1, p. 12.

enhanced administrative skills to domestic needs. To secure full employment, many governments drew on the activist policies favoured by the British economist John Maynard Keynes. Throughout Western Europe, the warfare state gave way to the **welfare state**, with rulers accepting direct responsibility for protecting their citizens from the scourges of illness, unemployment and old age. In this way, the European state led a post-war settlement – termed the 'Keynesian welfare state' – which integrated full employment and public welfare with an economy in which the private sector continued to play a substantial part.

In a **welfare state**, the government is primarily responsible for the social and economic security of its citizens. This goal is achieved by public schemes to provide incomes for the unemployed, pensions for the elderly and medical care for the sick.

Restructuring

Eventually, the post-war expansion of the Western state reached its limits. Warfare states are temporary but welfare states involve long-term, increasingly expensive commitments extending across generations. By 1980, the average share of gross domestic product spent or transferred by the governments of 13 developed democracies had reached 46 per cent, a substantial increase on the proportion just ten years earlier. As public employment continued to expand, so financial pressures mounted. Following the oil crises of the 1970s, speculation even began to emerge about whether governments might go bankrupt. Rather like empires of old, no sooner had Western states reached their full extent than they began to look overstretched.

In consequence, the 1980s – and, to a lesser degree, the 1990s – witnessed a measure of restructuring. This refocusing was particularly pronounced in English-speaking countries, stimulated by the right-wing agendas of Ronald Reagan (America's president, 1981–89) and Margaret Thatcher (Britain's prime minister, 1979–90). In many liberal democracies, nationalized industries were sold; welfare provision was trimmed; the highest rates of income tax were reduced; and the state increasingly sought to supply public services indirectly, using

private contractors. Fiscal policies to contain unemployment lost ground to monetary policies aimed at limiting price increases. Military demands were, for once, consistent with a diminished state: spending on the armed forces declined after the Cold War.

This ideological transformation, it is worth noting, is barely reflected in public expenditure statistics. Since the 1980s, government spending has continued to increase in several countries, partly reflecting the in-built pressure from ageing populations (Table 2.1) (Goldstone *et al.*, 2012). The change in thinking was sharper than the change in spending.

A further caution is needed in concluding this section. We should avoid conflating restructuring with retreat. Even as the state's direct engagement in the economy declined, its role as a regulator expanded (see Chapters 17 and 18). Free markets do not maintain themselves without regulation which is in any case a relatively cheap activity for govern-

Table 2.1 Total government expenditure in selected democracies as a proportion of gross domestic product, 1970–2010 (%)

Even after the restructuring of the 1980s and 1990s, public spending continued to increase as a share of the national economy in some, though not all, democracies

	1970	1980	1990	2004	2010
Denmark	40.2	56.2	56.0	56.3	58.2
France	38.5	46.1	49.6	53.4	56.2
Finland	30.5	36.6	44.5	50.7	55.1
Belgium	36.5	50.7	50.8	49.3	53.1
Sweden	43.3	61.6	60.5	57.3	53.1
Netherlands	43.9	57.5	49.4	48.6	51.2
United Kingdom	38.8	44.8	41.9	43.9	51.0
Ireland	39.6	50.8	39.5	34.2	48.2
Germany	38.6	48.3	43.8	46.8	46.7
Norway	41.0	48.3	52.3	46.4	46.0
Canada	34.8	40.5	46.0	41.1	43.8
United States	31.6	33.7	33.6	36.5	42.3
Japan	19.4	32.6	31.3	38.2	40.7

Notes: Gross domestic product is the total value of goods and services produced within a country over a year. The figure of 48.2 per cent for Ireland is for 2009.

Source: OECD (2011).

ments. As Levy points out in *The State Also Rises* (2006, p. 2) the 'state after statism' remains active. Bell and Hindmoor (2009, back cover) even claim that 'far from receding, states are in fact enhancing their capacity to govern by exerting top-down controls and developing closer ties with non-governmental actors'. So, restructuring is best seen as a shift in the state's ruling style, rather than a fall in its reach – a partial transition from government to governance.

Contemporary challenges

Although the restructuring of the state at the end of the twentieth century was sometimes presented as an irreversible process, events have continued to intrude. Clearly, many 1990s predictions of the state's irrelevance in a peaceful world of unfettered trade have failed (Guehenno, 1995). On the contrary, the state has returned to centre stage as it has led the response to the multiple risks of the new century. We illustrate this theme through a discussion of two such dangers: terrorism and financial crisis.

Terrorism

Predictions of the state's backbone turning to jelly in a new century of peace were shattered on 11 September 2001 ('9/11') (Box 2.2). The strikes on New York and Washington were the first foreign assault on the continental United States in the modern era; they demonstrated the vulnerability of even the world's most powerful country to organized terrorism. Other attacks on Westerners, and people in low-income countries, proved that 9/11 could not be dismissed as a one-off. Yet again, international threats led to a stronger, better-organized and more assertive state in the liberal democratic world.

Consider, for example, the American response. The consequences of 9/11 included not just George W. Bush's 'war on terror' but also the passage of the Patriot Act (2001, amended 2006). This legislation gave federal law enforcement agencies considerable powers to investigate anyone thought to be directly engaged in terrorism or associated with terrorist suspects. The Act is so-called because its full title is the 'Uniting and Strengthening America by Providing Appropriate Tools Required to Intercept and Obstruct Terrorism Act'. The bill was signed into law by the president in the month following the 9/11 attacks and within 72 hours of its introduction to Congress.

The 9/11 strike also led to the creation of the Department of Homeland Security (DHS) in 2002, with a mission to 'lead the unified national effort to secure America'. By absorbing several existing agencies, the DHS became one of the largest and most expensive government departments in the world, with an authorized budget of $57 billion by 2012 (DHS, 2011; Mueller and Stewart, 2011).

Other Western states showed a heightened response to terrorist dangers. In the United Kingdom, where British suicide bombers killed 52 people in attacks on public transport in London in 2005, a series of new laws built on initiatives already implemented in response to the long-standing conflict in Northern Ireland. For example, the Terrorism Act (2006) introduced new criminal acts such as encouraging terrorism and participating in training for it.

Influenced by the London bombings, Australia responded similarly. Its government passed the Anti-Terrorism Act (No. 2) in 2005. This law provided for short-term preventative detention in the context of terrorist incidents; introduced court-approved control orders, which restricted the movement of people when such limits would help to prevent a terrorist act; and outlined a crime of **sedition** for those who urged the government's violent overthrow.

> To engage in **sedition** is to advocate insurrection or rebellion against a state. By contrast, treason is the act of violating an allegiance to a state, including aiding its enemies.

This emergence of what is sometimes called the 'security state' naturally produced a reaction. Interest groups expressed particular concerns about:

● the development of a surveillance society;

● threats to civil liberties;

● the limited accountability of intelligence services: 'Who's watching the spies?'

Monitoring by closed-circuit television, and of telephones and Internet use, offers new tools for the state to track its population, including ordinary citizens, terrorists and terrorist suspects. In the USA,

---

BOX 2.2

Some major attacks by Islamic terrorists on civilian Western targets, 2001–08

Date	Targets attacked	Approximate number killed	Perpetrators
2001 11 September	World Trade Center, New York; Pentagon, Washington, DC	2,974	19 hijackers – mainly from Saudi Arabia in an attack coordinated by al-Qaeda
2002 12 October	Nightclubs, Bali, Indonesia	202*	4 Indonesian Muslims – out of 30 people convicted were executed in 2008
2004 11 March	Commuter trains, Madrid	191	21 people – mainly from North Africa were convicted in 2007
2005 7 July	Underground trains and a bus, London	52	4 Muslims born or raised in the UK

* Mainly Western tourists.

National Security Letters (which required organizations such as Internet providers to supply the government with access to their records about individual users) came under particular attack from civil liberty organizations. Exchanges of information between the intelligence services of different countries raised further concerns. President Obama said, in his first inaugural address, that 'we reject as false the choice between our safety and our ideals' – but it is by no means clear that this dilemma can just be wished away.

Clearly, the state was back. In addition to administrative, legislative and budgetary developments, the voices of multiculturalism weakened in response to the threat of terrorism from both domestic and foreign sources. Notions of a common citizenship regained lost ground. Furthermore, the idea of security itself broadened, building on – but coming to embrace more than – terrorism. In the first decade of the current century, for example, several Western states sought to reassert their functional significance by offering a wider conception of threats to their country. A concern with **human security** supplemented the state's traditional concern with military security.

Human security exists when people can live their lives to the full, without the fear and uncertainty arising from external threats of any kind. For example, environmental dangers directly threaten human security but not military security (Kaldor, 2007).

The UK is, again, an illustration. As its National Security Strategy report stated in 2008, 'our view of national security has broadened to include threats to individual citizens and to our way of life, as well as the integrity and interests of the state' (Cabinet Office, 2008). This document, updated in 2010, identified a series of challenges which went well beyond traditional military threats from foreign powers (Box 2.3).

Of course, a list of risks is not, in itself, a strategy for dealing with them. Nonetheless, such statements show states positioning themselves as the overall risk manager for society, not least in protecting citizens from threats combining international and domestic elements.

Financial crises

Financial crises early in the twenty-first century also forced an active response from governments –

BOX 2.3

The UK government's tiered assessment of risks to its national security, 2010

Tier	Risks
One (Highest priority)	● International terrorism ● Cyber attacks ● Accidents requiring a national response ● International military crises drawing in the UK
Two	● Attacks on the UK using chemical, biological, radiological or nuclear weapons ● Overseas instability, which creates an environment favourable to terrorism ● Organized crime ● Disruption to satellite communication
Three	● Conventional military attacks by another state ● Increase in terrorists and criminals entering the UK ● Disruption to the supply or cost of oil and gas ● Radioactive release from a nuclear power station ● Attacks on another NATO or EU member to which the UK would have to respond ● Attacks on a UK overseas territory ● Disruption to supply of resources (e.g. food, minerals)

Source: HMG (2010).

including central banks – in their role as lender of last resort. In what may be a portent, here we see the state responding to a civil, rather than military, agenda.

For example, when excessive risk-taking led American investment banks towards or into bankruptcy in 2008–09, the United States federal government initiated a massive, and ultimately successful, policy response (Gamble, 2009). Cultural prefer-

ences for market solutions notwithstanding, America's government proved willing and able to take failing companies into short-term public ownership within the legal framework of conservatorship.

Similarly, **eurozone** member states were centrally engaged in the financial crisis which emerged in 2010. Here, governments were an immediate cause of the difficulties. Several member states in the currency area, notably Greece, had become so indebted that commercial lenders started to charge penal rates of interest, raising the possibility of governments defaulting on their debt and of the euro itself disintegrating (Table 2.2). Again, it was powerful states (notably France and Germany) that led the effort – in this case, halting and indecisive – to resolve the issue. Intergovernmental bodies such as the International Monetary Fund were only supporting players and were themselves influenced by their member governments.

So, once again, the 1990s' talk of the irrelevance of

Table 2.2 Central government debt as a percentage of gross domestic product in selected liberal democracies, 2000–10

Central government debt increased dramatically in many Western countries in the first decade of the twenty-first century. In Greece and Italy, it exceeded the value of a year's production of goods and services as early as 2000.

	Eurozone member	2000	2005	2010
Greece	√	108.9	110.6	147.8
Italy	√	103.6	97.7	109.0
Belgium	√	99.5	91.8	96.8
Portugal	√	52.1	66.2	88.0
United Kingdom		42.2	43.5	85.5
France	√	47.4	53.3	67.4
United States		33.9	36.1	61.3
Ireland	√	34.8	23.5	60.7
Netherlands	√	44.1	43.0	51.8
Spain	√	49.9	36.4	51.7
Germany	√	38.4	40.8	44.4
Canada		40.9	30.2	36.1
Sweden		56.9	46.2	33.8
Australia		11.4	6.3	11.0

Source: OECD (2011).

The **eurozone** consists of European Union countries using the euro as their common currency. By 2011, the zone contained 17 of the EU's 27 members. Denmark, Sweden and the United Kingdom had no plans to join.

the state in an era of unfettered capitalism was shown to belong to another century. Of course, the state cannot eliminate market pressures in the same way that it might, in theory, destroy the terrorist threat. The eurozone crisis is in part a story of financial markets bringing spendthrift governments to heel. But only states can resolve problems they themselves have created; whether the state operates from a position of strength or weakness, it remains the agent to which all eyes turn in an emergency.

The diversity of states

The enormous contrasts of population, wealth and power between countries are often underemphasized by those analysts who concentrate on either the formal equality of states (all are equally sovereign) or their form of government. But, clearly, neither sovereignty nor democracy matter for, say, small island nations at risk of disappearing into the ocean as a result of rising sea levels. Sovereignty is exercised by all states, but in varying conditions and with varying resources.

An overview of the distribution of states by population, income and their former colonial status provides insight into these divergent political realities. In particular, it shows how the strong form of the European state has not been fully replicated in a significant number of small, dependent post-colonial states. So, this section seeks to provide an assessment of the value of sovereignty in real world conditions.

Population

We begin with an obvious contrast: between states large and small. At the top end of the distribution, China's population exceeds that of the 160 smallest countries in the world combined. At the bottom end, the population of most countries in world is less than 10 million; one in five fall below 1 million (Table 2.3). In median position sits Switzerland (7.9 million) – a country usually presented as 'small' but which can only be viewed as such from the perspec-

Table 2.3 States by population, 2010

Although many studies in comparative politics examine large states, such countries are exceptional when viewed though a global lens. The population of most countries is less than 10 million. Interdependence (and dependence) was a reality for these smaller states long before globalization became a fashionable term in large Western democracies.

Population (million)	Number of states
Above 50	24
25–50	21
10–25	33
5–10	36
1–5	41
Below 1	38

Source: Adapted from UN DESA (2010).

tive of larger, usually Western, states.

Most **microstates** are islands in the Caribbean, the Pacific or off the African coast. They are, indeed, best understood as islands rather than states. Mostly, they possess limited capacity to shape their own destiny. They are what Jackson (1990, p. 1) calls quasi-states, 'lacking many of the marks and merits of empirical statehood'. In practice, microstates must seek protection from larger patrons. Their formal designation as sovereign entities is largely a tribute to the power of statehood as the world's overriding principle of political organization.

We should not, however, assume that all small

Microstates are small in population (say, below 1 million) and territory (say, less than 1000 square km). Andorra, Barbados and the Maldives are examples. The number of microstates increased sharply with decolonization.

states are dysfunctional. Newer regional groupings such as the European Union provide nests in which small countries can grow and develop. And several established microstates in Europe have combined political stability with economic success. In the 1970s, Dahl and Tufte cited democratic Luxembourg, then the fifth wealthiest country in the world by gross domestic product per head, as an example. As with many successful small states, Luxembourg secured its position through participation in military and economic alliances. Its success continues. Assisted by a rather more diversified economy, the country (population 502,000) has moved ever closer to the top of the economic rankings (IMF, 2011). Neither is Luxembourg an isolated case of affluence without scale: Norway, Singapore and Switzerland provide additional examples.

So, although the process of decolonization has deposited many quasi-states into the international system, we should be wary of dismissing all small states as irrelevant.

Income

The era in which states could be classified as 'rich' or 'poor', 'developed' or 'developing', has passed. Although economic inequalities between countries remain immense, a more nuanced picture is now required, especially to capture the growth of emerging economies beyond the West.

The World Bank offers a useful classification, dividing states (strictly, economies) into four income groups (Table 2.4). Introduced in 1988, this scheme sought to provide an economic indicator linked to measures of well-being such as poverty and infant mortality.

The *high-income* category is still led by the developed economies of Western Europe, North America, Australasia and parts of Asia. It is these countries which form the Organisation for Economic Co-operation and Development, the rich man's club which seeks to 'build a wider consensus for market economies and democracy' (OECD, 2011). The cultural, economic, political and scientific resources of OECD states remain enormous. However, their global strength was diminished by the financial crisis of 2008/09, the resulting increase in public debt and the subsequent difficulties experienced by the eurozone currency area. Furthermore, the weight of population lies elsewhere: the USA and Japan are the only two OECD members in the world's ten most populous countries. Note that the high-income category also includes some small, oil-rich, non-democratic states such as Kuwait and Qatar – confirming, again, that scale is unnecessary for wealth.

It is the *upper-middle* income category that captures the increasingly important second tier. Here, we find the large and often fast-growing Bric countries (**B**razil, **R**ussia, **I**ndia, **C**hina) as well as the emerging economies of China, South Africa, Malaysia, Mexico and Turkey. The economic dynamism and large population of some of these states has already initiated some rebalancing of world power away from the developed West.

The remaining categories in the World Bank scheme – the lower-middle and low-income countries – make up what is traditionally seen as the developing world. *Lower-middle* income countries are found mainly in Africa and Asia; they include India, Indonesia, Nigeria, Ukraine and Vietnam. Although such countries have undergone some

Table 2.4 Distribution of countries by income group, 2011

The world's countries cannot simply be divided into rich and poor, developed and developing. The World Bank's fourfold classification shows that most countries fall between these two extremes.

	Gross national income per head	Number of countries	Examples
High income	$12,476 or above	70	Germany, Saudi Arabia, USA
Upper-middle income	$4,036–$12,475	54	China, Russia, Thailand
Lower-middle income	$1,026–$4,035	56	Egypt, India, Nigeria
Low income	$1,025 or below	35	Afghanistan, Rwanda, Uganda

Source: World Bank (2011).

development, their levels of affluence and their global political weight remain limited compared to the upper-middle category. Note, however, the sheer scale of some of these countries: India, Indonesia and Nigeria are among the world's ten most populous.

Sometimes known as the 'fourth world', the *low-income* countries consist mainly of African states, together with some Asian countries; for instance, Afghanistan, Bangladesh and Burma. In 2010, the number of countries in this group exceeded the number belonging to the OECD. With average incomes barely $1000 per year (often substantially less), life for the vast majority of people in low-income countries remains challenging indeed.

In the low-income group (as, increasingly, in the high-income tier), income inequality is substantial, meaning that most people in the fourth world subsist on an income which falls well below their country's mean. In studying international politics, it is possible to focus on the absolute size of an economy or, alternatively, on national income per head; but, in comparative politics, we must recognize the domestic political impact of sharp inequality and mass poverty. Among many other effects, these factors create a dependence of the poor and powerless on the rich and powerful. As we will see in Chapter 3, such embedded inequalities still create a powerful barrier to a functioning liberal democracy.

The post-colonial state

In distinguishing between states, the final factor to consider is their relationship to the empires of old: as former colonizer, ex-colony or neither. Although the state was born in Europe, its form was then exported to the rest of the world by imperial powers; notably, Britain, France and Spain. Consequently, most states in today's world are post-colonial. As Armitage (2005, p. 3) points out, 'the great political fact of global history in the last 500 years is the emergence of a world of states from a world of empires. That fact fundamentally defines the political universe we all inhabit'. Countries without a history as a colony, leaving aside the ex-colonial powers themselves, are few and far between; they include China, Ethiopia, Iran, Japan and Saudi Arabia.

Although the term 'post-colonial' is usually con-

fined to countries achieving independence in the aftermath of World War II, settler societies such as Australia, Canada, New Zealand and the United States provide early examples of states formed from colonies. In settler societies, the new arrivals ruthlessly supplanted indigenous communities, recreating segments of the European tradition they had brought with them. Even though the standing of the state in settler countries is less elevated than in Europe, the political organization of these countries remains strong and recognizably Western. Settler societies are from, though not in, Europe (Lange, 2009). In the far larger number of non-settler colonies, by contrast, the imperial rulers sought to exploit local labour and resources without establishing new nations in the territory.

How, then, did non-settler colonies emerge into statehood? To answer this question is to cast light on the formative history of the majority of the world's states. The major part of the process took place in four waves spread over two centuries (Box 2.4). Each wave deposited particular kinds of state on the post-colonial shore but, in all cases, the results differed from the strong European states generated in earlier centuries by military and political competition.

The *first* wave of decolonization occurred early in the nineteenth century, in the Spanish and Portuguese territories of Latin America. Here, colonial settlers had dominated without eliminating indigenous peoples. These early wars of independence occurred soon after the American and French revolutions of the eighteenth century but lacked the liberal, egalitarian basis of their more famous predecessors. Rather, the Latin American wars took the form of republican movements against monarchical rule from Europe. New constitutions were produced but they were neither democratic, nor even fully implemented. Economic exploitation of native populations, the poor and descendants of slaves continued into the post-colonial era. The resulting inequalities created endemic conflicts within Latin American countries which remain important to this day. So, this first wave of decolonization made little contribution to the development of liberal democracy; rather, it reinforced authoritarian traditions.

The *second* wave of post-colonial states emerged in Europe and the Middle East around the end of World War I, with the final collapse of the Austro-Hungarian, Russian and Ottoman empires. The

BOX 2.4

States from empires: waves of decolonization

Wave of decolonization	Main imperial powers	Main locations of colonies	Approximate number of new states created by decolonization	Examples of newly-independent states
1810–38	Spain, Portugal	Latin America	15	Argentina, Brazil
After the 1914–18 war	Ottoman, Russian and Austro-Hungarian empires	Europe (beyond its Western core), Middle East	12	Austria, Finland, Poland, Turkey
1944–84	UK, France, Belgium, Portugal	Mainly Africa, Asia and the Caribbean	94	Algeria, Congo, India, Philippines
1991	Russia	Soviet Union republics in the Baltics, East Europe and central Asia	15	Kazakhstan, Latvia, Ukraine

Austro-Hungarian Empire, for instance, dissolved into five separate countries: Austria, Hungary, Poland, Czechoslovakia and Yugoslavia. Yet, with the exception of the Turkish state founded on the ruins of the Ottoman Empire, strong and stable countries again failed to develop. Rather, international politics in the shape of fascism and communism continued to intrude, preventing those countries on the European periphery from experiencing the continuous state development found in the continent's core. Only with the collapse of communism in the 1990s, and the entry of many of these post-colonial countries into the European Union in 2004, was independent statehood finally consolidated.

The *third* and largest wave of state creation occurred after 1945, with the retreat from empire by European states diminished by war. Asian countries, such as the Philippines (in 1946) and India (in 1947), were the first to achieve independence but many other colonies, in Africa, the Caribbean and the Middle East, followed suit. This wave of decolonization then grew in force. Between 1944 and 1984, over 90 independent states, almost half the world's current stock, were created; truly a rush to statehood. But here, above all, it is crucial to distinguish

between form and substance. The state form may have been successfully exported from Europe to ex-colonies but effective functioning has rarely followed. Most post-1945 countries lacked any previous experience as a coherent entity; rather, statehood was superimposed on ethnic, regional and religious groups that had previously co-existed in a looser arrangement. The state typically remains both coercive and weak, lacking the drive of its European forebears.

The *fourth* and final wave of state formation occurred in the final decade of the twentieth century, triggered by the collapse of communism. The dissolution of the communist bloc previously dominated by the Soviet Union led to independence for the Baltic States (e.g. Estonia) and for a dozen Soviet satellites in Eastern Europe (e.g. Poland). In addition, the Soviet Union itself – in effect, a Russian empire – dissolved into 15 successor states (e.g. Ukraine). The experience of these new post-communist states has, again, been mixed. The Baltic States gained economic and political stability from their proximity to, and now their membership of, the European Union. However, central Asian republics such as Uzbekistan revealed a more typical post-colonial syndrome: small size, ethnic division, a pre-industrial economy and autocratic rule. In the successor states to the Soviet Union, these problems are, again, reinforced by the absence of pre-colonial experience as an independent state.

Overall, then, the contrasts between West European parent states and their post-colonial progeny are deep-rooted. Post-colonial states rarely possess the strength and autonomy which their European predecessors acquired during their own development. Sovereignty remains important as a title, securing international recognition and access to aid. But the label's significance is sometimes symbolic, with little to prevent the movement of people, soldiers, goods and terrorists across boundaries. In extreme but still exceptional cases, the outcome is a fragile – or even failed – state which is unable to execute its core task of securing order (Table 2.5).

The state and intergovernmental organizations

We live, it is often said, in an era of globalization, during which the constraints of geography on economic, cultural and political arrangements have receded (Waters, 2000). In truth, there never was a time when states were self-contained, independent silos but that is, perhaps, all the more reason for placing states in an international context.

Intergovernmental organizations are a major mechanism through which overseas influences reach states and influence their governments. Around 250 now populate the international environment (Volgy *et al.*, 2006). Some date back to the nineteenth century (the International Telecommunication Union was founded by 20 member governments in 1865) but most were created in the twentieth century, not least in the aftermath of the world wars. So, the category is far from new, although it has become more fully populated.

IGOs include single purpose entities (e.g. the International Telecommunications Union), regional organizations (e.g. the Union of South American Nations) and universal bodies (e.g. the United Nations). The most important enjoy the membership of a majority of established states.

Table 2.5 Countries scoring highest on the fragile states index, 2010

By the Polity IV measure of fragility, which judges government legitimacy and effectiveness in such areas as security and the economy, many of the most fragile states are post-colonial countries in Africa

Rank	Country
1	Somalia
2	Sudan
3	Democratic Republic of Congo
4	Afghanistan
5	Chad
6	Burma
7	Ethiopia
8	Ivory Coast
9	Sierra Leone
10	Burundi

Note: A rank of one indicates greatest fragility.

Source: Polity IV Project (2011), table 1.

Intergovernmental organizations (IGOs) are bodies whose members include multiple states. IGOs are established by treaty, hold plenary sessions, and operate according to stated rules and with some autonomy. As organizations (as opposed to a mere coalition or alliance), they possess a permanent secretariat and legal identity.

Such bodies are an appropriate response to global problems by states operating in a world which lacks a world government. IGOs perform useful functions for states: sharing information, coordinating policies and developing international infrastructure. For instance, everyone gains from a sustainable environment, a world telephone network, and a functioning internet. Operating in an informal and flexible manner, with high levels of trust among participants, the distance of IGOs from democratic pressures within their member states may even contribute to their efficacy. In a sense, IGOs are as much an outgrowth of state power into the international realm as a constraint on individual governments; they represent a pooling of public authority as much as a threat to it.

However, our main concern here is the impact of IGOs on states themselves. At the very least, belonging to IGOs complicates the task of governance. States must arrange to pay their subscriptions, attend meetings, identify their national interest, consult with domestic interest groups, initiate some proposals, respond to others and implement agreements. IGOs bore into the daily activities of national governments, posing a particular challenge to the resources and capacities of small, low-income states.

Even for large countries, IGOs dilute the distinction between domestic and foreign policy, giving an international dimension to many, perhaps most, government activities. IGOs are often centrally involved in formulating the agreements which must then be implemented locally by national governments. It is one thing to agree to new international standards on animal welfare; it is quite another to draft, agree and enforce national regulations giving effect to the new regime. As Zelikow (2011) puts the point:

In the past foreign policy mainly consisted of adjusting relations between states – what they do with or to each other. Now foreign policy consists mainly of adjusting the domestic policies of states – of what they do with or to their own people.

In addition, IGOs have affected the balance of forces within national political systems. Specifically, they tend to fragment domestic policy-making. Slaughter (2004), in particular, has emphasized the segmenting effect of public officials communicating with colleagues from other countries. Noting how judges, administrators, regulators, central bankers, legislators, police forces and heads of state 'are all networking with their foreign counterparts', she suggests that:

the state is not disappearing; it is disaggregating into its component institutions. The primary state actors in the international realm are no longer foreign ministries and heads of state but the same government institutions that dominate domestic politics. The disaggregated state, as opposed to the mythical unitary state, is thus hydra-headed, represented and governed by multiple institutions in complex interaction with one another abroad and at home. (Slaughter, 2004, p. 190)

Figure 2.1 The segmented state: horizontal links between ministries

Intergovernmental organizations provide a forum where ministers, advisors and specialists can meet with their counterparts from other countries. Such networks blur the distinction between domestic and foreign policy.

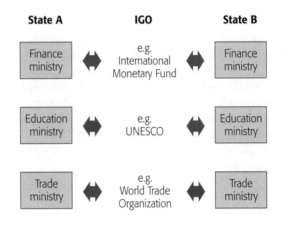

These linkages between departments in different countries deepen as a club-like spirit develops among ministers in 'their' IGO. For instance, finance ministers – never popular at home – are among friends at meetings of bodies such as the International Monetary Fund (Figure 2.1). Domestically, ministers of agriculture must defend the farmers' interests against other departments, but at IGO meetings they meet only other ministers of agriculture, all of whom agree on farming's importance (Andeweg and Irwin, 2009, p. 169).

Given such fragmentation within national political systems, we must ask which governing institutions gain, and which lose, from such interdependence. The main winners are surely the *executive* and the *bureaucracy*. These bodies provide the representatives who attend IGO meetings and conduct negotiations; they therefore occupy pole position.

The *judiciary* is also growing in significance as a result of IGO activity, partly because some influential IGOs, such as the World Trade Organization, themselves adopt a highly judicial style, issuing judgements on the basis of reviewing cases. In addition, national judges are increasingly willing to use international agreements to strike down the policies of their home government.

As for losers, the most significant are the *legislature* and *political parties*. The legislature, in particular, may only learn of an international agreement after the government has signed up to it. In some countries, Australia for one, international treaties are an executive preserve, enabling government to bypass the assembly by signing treaties on proposals opposed by parliament. In international matters, parliaments are more reactive than proactive. Similarly: 'Europeanization has strengthened the central executive at the expense of parliaments, despite the increased involvement of the latter in EU policy-making' (Börzel and Sedelmeier, 2006, p. 56). Political parties, too, seem to have lost ground under pressure from IGOs. As with assemblies, their natural habitat is the state, not the international conference.

The European Union

In a world of states supplemented by international organizations, the European Union (EU) stands alone. It is a unique hybrid blending supranational and intergovernmental elements. The EU is the world's most developed example of regional integration. It represents a deliberate attempt by European politicians to bring peace to a continent long scarred by war. As we will see in several chapters of this book, the Union has developed its institutions, acquired considerable policy-making authority, reduced national barriers to trade, established a new currency and broadened its membership. As a first look, then, we can ask: to what extent has the EU become a state in all but name?

Statistically, at least, the EU now stands comparison with the world's most powerful country: the USA (Table 2.6). It is the world's largest trading bloc and negotiates trade agreements with other countries as the external dimension of its pursuit of a coherent internal market. The world increasingly expects Europe to act as a single entity, as illustrated by its complaints in 2011 that 'Europe' was hopelessly slow in resolving the eurozone debt crisis.

The EU has certainly acquired some state-like attributes: a flag, an anthem, a mention in its citizens' passports, and its own entry in the CIA's *World Factbook*. Further, it possesses developed institutions, including an elected parliament, an influential court, and a commission to initiate policy and supervise its execution.

Table 2.6 The European Union and the USA, 2011

Less than half the area of the United States, the EU's population is substantially greater. The economies of the USA and the EU are similar in size, though EU productivity is, overall, much lower.

	European Union	USA
Area (million sq. km)	4.3	9.8
Population (million)	502	313
Member states	27	50
Median population of member states (million)	9.4	4.4
Gross domestic product (trillion $)	15.3	15.1
Gross domestic product per head ($)	34,000	48,100

Source: CIA (2012).

But, of course, the key contrast is political: the EU remains a union of states, not a state in itself. Furthermore, in some sectors the depth of integration varies between members. Britain and Ireland, for instance, have not joined the Schengen Agreement (1985) scheme to eliminate border controls, and several countries have not adopted the euro as their currency. The equivalent to this **differentiated integration** in the USA would be if some of the 50 states still required entry visas and used their own currency.

Above all, the EU neither levies personal taxes nor possesses its own armed forces. The traditional dynamic of the European state – to raise taxes so as to wage war – is therefore absent. Rather, the Union was founded as a mechanism for ensuring peace through economic integration. This underlying mission has remained broadly constant: economic integration, especially through a single market, has served to secure continental peace.

> **Differentiated integration** occurs when only some members of a community join together in a scheme to strengthen the union as a whole.

This objective has given the EU a strong regulatory character, distinguishing it from the broader functions performed by traditional states (Majone,

Map 2.1 The European Union, 2007–

Source: Adapted from Nugent (2010), Map 4.5.

THE EUROPEAN UNION

1951	Treaty of Paris signed by France, West Germany, Italy, Belgium, the Netherlands and Luxembourg. This Treaty set up the European Coal and Steel Community (ECSC) which included a supranational High Authority.
1957	The ECSC members sign the Treaty of Rome, establishing the European Economic Community (EEC) and Euratom.
1965	The Merger Treaty combines the ECSC, EEC and Euratom.
1973	Britain, Denmark and Ireland join the EEC.
1979	The European Monetary System (EMS) is agreed, linking currencies to the European Currency Unit (ECU). First direct Europe-wide elections to the European Parliament.
1981	Greece joins the EEC.
1986	Spain and Portugal join the EEC. Signing of the Single European Act, to streamline decision-making and set up a single market by 1992.
1992	Treaty of Maastricht launches provisions for Economic and Monetary Union (EMU) and replaces the EEC with the European Union (EU) from 1993.
1995	Austria, Finland and Sweden join the EU.
1997	Treaty of Amsterdam extends the Union's role in justice and home affairs, and enhances the authority of the European Parliament.
1999	Launch of (EMU), initially linking 11 national currencies to the euro. Launch of the euro as a virtual currency.
2000	Treaty of Nice agrees on institutional reforms to prepare for enlargement, including a reallocation of member states' voting power and a reduction in the issues requiring unanimity.
2002	The eurozone withdraws national currencies.
2003	Publication of a draft constitutional treaty for Europe.
2004	Cyprus, the Czech Republic, Estonia, Hungary, Latvia, Lithuania, Malta, Poland, Slovakia and Slovenia join the EU.
2005	Referendums in France and the Netherlands reject the constitutional treaty.
2007	Bulgaria and Romania join the EU.
2008	Referendum in Ireland rejects the constitutional treaty.
2009	Treaty of Lisbon, successor to the ill-fated constitutional treaty, comes into effect.
2011	Treaty agrees to admit Croatia to the EU. Entry expected in 2013.
2012	Treaty on Stability, Coordination and Governance aims to strengthen the fiscal discipline of participating governments. Agreed by all member states except the Czech Republic and the United Kingdom.

1966). Its primary mode of governance is to issue regulations, especially in areas such as trade and competition policy that facilitate its key objective of a single market. Lacking any requirement to equip and pay military personnel, the EU's budget of €129 billion for 2012 remains relatively small, historically amounting to less than 3 per cent of total public expenditure in the member states (Nugent, 2010, p. 32). The EU's funds are raised mainly by a levy on member states, not by direct taxes of persons, and are largely spent subsidizing farmers and poorer regions.

So, we should resist the temptation to assimilate the EU, as currently configured, to the more familiar and recognizable notion of the state. Rather than viewing the EU as a state in itself, it is surely preferable to interpret it as a distinctive union built on a foundation provided by strong states. Of course, as it develops, the EU may move closer to a United States of Europe. Alternatively, its intergovernmental elements may strengthen, quietening those who see the EU as a state already. In any event, the EU's current character should not be determined by placing bets on an unforeseeable future; rather, we should focus on its contemporary functioning. As such, the EU makes a unique contribution to the ecology of comparative politics.

Discussion questions

- Is sovereignty a myth?

- What is the relationship between war and the state?

- Are limits to civil liberties justified in the response to terrorism?

- 'Live long and prosper.' How would you suggest the 38 states with a population below 1 million should implement this policy?

- 'The state is not disappearing; it is disaggregating into its component institutions.' (Slaughter, 2004, p. 190). What does Slaughter mean, and how would you tell if this was true in your country?

- Is the European Union closer to an intergovernmental organization or a state?

Further reading

S. Chesterman, M. Ignatieff and R. Thakur, eds, *Making States Work: State Failure and the Crisis of Governance* (2005). An analysis not just of state failure, but also of how states can be rebuilt before they fail.

H. Lelieveldt and S. Princen, *The Politics of the European Union* (2011). An interesting and succinct account of the European Union from a comparative politics perspective.

W. Opello and S. Rosow, *The Nation-State and Global Order: A Historical Introduction to Contemporary Politics*, 2nd edn (2004). A wide-ranging introduction to the history of the state.

A.-M. Slaughter, *A New World Order* (2004). Written by the Director of Policy Planning, US Department of State, 2009–11, this book examines emerging styles of world governance

G. Sørensen, *The Transformation of the State: Beyond the Myth of Retreat* (2004). With exceptional clarity, this book locates the contemporary state in its international setting.

M. van Creveld, *The Rise and Decline of the State* (1999). A wide-ranging history of the state that also provides insight into its more recent challenges.

ONLINE RESOURCES AVAILABLE

Visit the companion website at **www.palgrave.com/politics/hague** to access additional learning resources, including multiple-choice questions, chapter summaries, web links and practice essay questions.

Chapter 3 Democracy

We live in an era of democracy; for the first time in history, most people in the world live under tolerably democratic rule. This fact reflects the dramatic transformation of the world's political landscape in the final quarter of the twentieth century. Over this short period, the number of democracies grew from fewer than 40 to about 80 (Figure 3.1). Democracy expanded beyond its core of Western Europe and former settler colonies to embrace Southern Europe (e.g. Spain), Eastern Europe (e.g. Poland), Latin America (e.g. Brazil), more of Asia (e.g. Taiwan) and parts of Africa (e.g. South Africa). Mandelbaum (2007, p. xi) goes so far as to claim that 'this global democratic surge in the last quarter of the twentieth century has a strong claim to being the single most important development in a century hardly lacking in momentous events and trends'.

Once the Cold War had passed, and the principle of unconditional state sovereignty came into question, so the promotion of democracy became a more explicit ideological objective for the West. While remaining pragmatic in its choice of allies, the United States was periodically willing to talk the talk: 'it is the policy of the United States to seek and support democratic movements and institutions in every nation and culture, with the ultimate goal of ending tyranny in our world' (White House, 2006). International law, which previously had little to say on political organization within states, also began to address the topic of democracy. Democracy promotion even became a field of academic study (Carothers, 2004).

Figure 3.1 The number of democratic countries in the world, 1800–2011

The number of democracies in the world increased dramatically after 1945. This expansion began before, but was accelerated by, the collapse of communism.

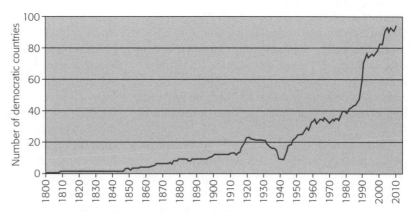

Note: Based on countries with a population exceeding 500,000.

Source: Adapted from Polity IV Project (2011), fig. 10.

STUDYING . . .

Democracy

- Despite the spread of democracy, democratic regimes are becoming thinner with the rise of expert and regulatory authority. It is in professional regulation, rather than in authoritarian ideology, that we find the contemporary challenge to democracy. In evaluating democratic governance, try comparing democracy with governance by experts, rather than with government by dictators.

- Although modern democracies are representative, studying direct democracy as in Ancient Athens offers a standard of self-rule against which, for better or worse, representative democracies are often judged. Democracy is an ideal, not just a system of government.

- The representative (indirect) character of modern democracy can be defended on the grounds of its practicality for large states. But there is a further argument which should not be evaded: that representation rightly limits the people to electing a government.

- The impact of modernization (notably, economic development) on democracy raises the question of whether liberal democracy is really a sensible short-term goal for low-income countries lacking democratic requisites. At any rate, we should avoid the easy assumption that democratic governance suits all times and places.

- A more recent approach to democracy, stimulated by recent transitions from authoritarian rule, is to study how the old order collapses and the transition takes place. Again, however, beware comfortable assumptions: the outcome of a transition from an authoritarian regime may not be a consolidated democracy. In this regard, how has the Arab Spring turned out?

Democracy and expertise

The study of democracy should avoid the comforting assumption that it is self-evidently the best system of rule. Certainly, democracy has many advantages over dictatorship – and that was the natural comparison during the Cold War. Democracy can also bring stability to historically divided societies since each group can aim to secure a share of power through elections. But, today, the more natural comparison is between democratic and expert decision-making. And here we find some important issues that should, at least, be mentioned here.

It is far from clear that policy-making by elected politicians is preferable to decision-making by experts. Expert control offers greater predictability and stability for the longer term, avoiding the danger of delaying difficult decisions before an election. It also reduces the uncertainty about the outcome (and future policy) which an election creates for potential investors. In addition, elected governments are inherently prone to underweight events occurring after the next election, leading to a concentration on the short term and an amplification of the business cycle as the economy is artificially boosted before an election. For such reasons, Bischof (2012) claimed that 'governments that have to focus on the next election date are like companies that are driven by quarterly results. Most don't succeed in the end.' In particular, the short-run focus of democracies may be inadequate for securing the long-term health of the global environment. At any rate, Dahl (1989, p. 52) was surely correct in stating that 'the idea of guardianship is democracy's most formidable rival'.

In some ways, guardianship is on the comeback trail. Schmitter (2011, p. 195) notes how 'Over the past twenty or more years – indeed, much longer in the case of the United States – "real existing democracies" have ceded control to what Dahl called guardian institutions.' Specifically, after the 1970s many Western states witnessed some thinning of democratic control as industries were privatized, as monetary policy was transferred to central banks, as judges began to step into the political arena, and as other public agencies acquired greater autonomy from elected rulers (see Chapter 17).

This quiet reduction in the scope of elected authority within Western countries has not passed by unnoticed. For example, Vibert (2007, p. 38) refers in *The Rise of the Unelected* to a 'new separation of powers' in which elected rulers increasingly share authority with unelected bodies. Olsen (2008, p. 440) reckons that the emergence of such institutions 'potentially challenges the territorial state as the key political actor'. Schmitter (2011, p. 195) considers that the outcome of this trend is 'democracy without choice'. If these authors are right, democracy triumphant may also be democracy disarmed.

Of course, authority shared between elected and regulatory authority may be an entirely appropriate format for advanced societies in which ideological conflicts have softened; certainly, Brooks (2008, p. 31) judges that a balance between technical and political authority 'has much to recommend it'. So, even if we favour democracy in the abstract, we are still left with a more specific question to which the answer is still evolving: what should democracies decide?

These points suggest that we should view democracy as a system that is flexible, rather than fixed; that responds to developments, rather than just imposing itself on them. 'What we mean by democracy changes through time; democratic institutions and ways of thinking are never set in stone', writes Keane (2009, p. xxix). Broad generalizations about the nature of democracy should invite us to ask: which democracy, when? (Box 3.1)

Direct democracy

We continue this chapter by exploring direct democracy as exemplified in the fifth century BCE in Athens. There, the Greeks invented a model of self-government which continues to shape our assessments of the less extensive liberal democracies of today.

BOX 3.1

Forms of democracy

Form	Definition
Direct (participatory) democracy	The citizens themselves debate and reach decisions on matters of common interest.
Indirect (representative) democracy	Citizens elect a parliament and, in presidential systems, a chief executive. These representatives are held to account at the next election.
Liberal democracy	A form of indirect democracy in which the scope of democracy is limited by constitutional protection of individual rights, including freedom of assembly, property, religion and speech. Free, fair and regular elections are based on near universal suffrage.

In a direct democracy, the citizens themselves are the primary agent for reaching collective decisions. Direct popular involvement – and, in particular, the open deliberation that goes with it – is judged to be educative in character, yielding confident, informed and committed citizens who are sensitive both to the public good and to the range of interests and opinions found even in small communities.

So, the core principle of democracy is self-rule; the word itself comes from the Greek *demokratia*, meaning rule (*kratos*) by the people (*demos*). From this perspective, democracy refers not to the election of rulers by the ruled but to the denial of any separation between the two. The model democracy is a form of self-government in which all adult citizens participate in shaping collective decisions in an environment of equality and deliberation. In a direct democracy, state and society become one.

Direct democracy was developed in ancient Athens. Between 461 and 322 BCE, Athens was the leading *polis* (city-community) in ancient Greece. *Poleis* were small independent political systems, typically containing an urban core and a rural hinterland. Even though Athens only comprised about 40,000 citizens, it was one of the larger examples. Especially in its earlier and more radical phase, the Athenian *polis* operated on the democratic principles summarized by Aristotle (Box 3.2). This ethos covered all the institutions of government within the community. All citizens could attend meetings of the assembly, serve on the governing council and sit on citizens' juries (Figure 3.2). Because ancient Athens continues to provide the archetypal case of direct democracy, we will focus this section on its operation, concluding with some discussion of participatory traditions in modern times.

History has judged there to be no more potent symbol of direct democracy than the Athenian *Ekklesia* (People's Assembly). Any citizen aged at least 20 could attend assembly sessions and, there, address his peers; meetings were of citizens, not their representatives. The assembly met around 40 times a year to settle issues put before it, including recurring issues of war and peace (imperial conquest by the citizen militia was a core objective). In Aristotle's phrase, the assembly was 'supreme over all causes' (1962 edn, p. 237); it was the sovereign body, unconstrained by a formal constitution or even, in the early decades, by written laws. As far as we can tell, meetings were lengthy, factional and vigorous, with the talking – and, hence, probably the subse-

BOX 3.2

Aristotle's characterization of democracy

- All to rule over each and each in his turn over all;
- appointment to all offices, except those requiring experience and skill, by lot;
- no property qualification for office-holding, or only a very low one;
- tenure of office should be brief and no man should hold the same office twice (except military positions);
- juries selected from all citizens should judge all major causes;
- the assembly should be supreme over all causes;
- those attending the assembly and serving as jurors and magistrates should be paid for their services.

Source: Aristotle (1962 edn), book VI.

quent show of hands – dominated by influential orators known as demagogues (Dahl, 1989, p. 21).

The assembly did not exhaust the avenues of participation in Athens. Administrative functions were the responsibility of an executive council consisting of 500 citizens aged over 30, chosen by lot for a one-year

Figure 3.2 **The direct democracy of Ancient Athens**

Many adult male citizens participated directly in decision-making venues though the large number of non-citizens were excluded

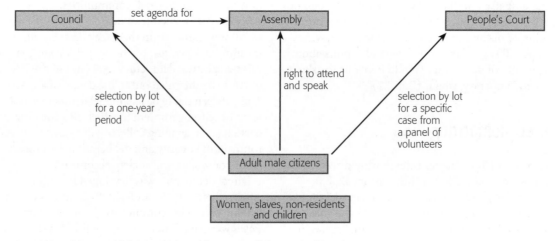

Note: citizenship was a birthright which could not normally be acquired by other means.

period. Through the rotation of members drawn from the citizen body, the council was regarded as exemplifying community democracy: 'all to rule over each and each in his turn over all'. Hansen (1999, p. 249) suggests that about one in three citizens could expect to serve on the council at some stage, an astonishing feat of self-government without counterpart in modern representative democracies.

A highly political legal system provided the final leg of Athenian democracy. Juries of several hundred people – again, selected randomly from a panel of volunteers – decided the lawsuits which citizens frequently brought against those considered to have acted against the true interests of the *polis*. The courts functioned as an arena of accountability through which top figures (including generals) were brought to book.

Thus, the scope of Athenian democracy was extraordinarily wide, providing an enveloping framework within which citizens were expected to develop their true qualities. For the Athenians, politics was intrinsically an amateur activity, to be undertaken by all citizens not just in the interest of the community at large, but also to enhance their own development. To engage in democracy was to become informed about the *polis* – and an educated citizenry meant a stronger whole.

Nevertheless, Athens's little democracy possessed serious flaws:

- Citizenship was restricted to men whose parents were themselves citizens. So, most adults – including women, slaves and foreign residents – were excluded.

- Participation was not, in practice, as extensive as the Athenians liked to claim. Most citizens were absent from most assembly meetings even after the introduction of an attendance payment.

- Athenian democracy was hardly an exercise in lean government. A management consultant would surely conclude that the system was time-consuming, expensive and over-complex, especially for such a small society.

- The principle of self-government did not always lead to decisive and coherent policy.

Indeed, the lack of a permanent bureaucracy eventually contributed to a period of ineffective governance, leading to the fall of the Athenian republic after defeat in war.

Perhaps Athenian democracy was a dead end, in that it could only function on an intimate scale which limited its potential for expansion and, worse, increased its vulnerability to larger predators. Finer (1997, p. 368) adopts just this position: 'the *polis* was doomed politically if it expanded and doomed to conquest if it did not. It had to succumb and it did.' Yet, the Athenian democratic experiment prospered for over 100 years. It provided a settled formula for rule and enabled Athens to build a leading position in the complex politics of the Greek world. Athens proves that direct democracy is, in some conditions, an achievable goal.

Modern democratic government is indirect, operating through elected representatives, rather than direct. However, the Greek inheritance can still be observed in periodic expressions of dissatisfaction with the limits of representative government. Consider, for instance, the participatory thinking of the 1960s.

This decade witnessed a resurgence of interest in participation not just in government, but also in other social institutions such as the workplace, schools and universities. The proponents of this perspective shared the enthusiasm of the Athenians for the broadening and educative effects of political participation. Significantly, though, they extended their perspective to embrace participation in the wider society. Their important starting-point was that only a participatory society could enable and sustain truly democratic politics. Carole Pateman made the case in *Participation and Democratic Theory* (1970, p. 11):

The argument of the participatory theory of democracy is that participation in the alternative areas [such as the family, the workplace, universities and local government] would enable the individual better to appreciate the connection between the public and private spheres ... In the context of a participatory society the significance of his vote to the individual would have changed: as well as being a private individual he would have multiple opportunities to become an educated, public citizen.

We observe here a response to those supporters of representative democracy who claim that ordinary people lack the interest, knowledge and skill to govern themselves. Create a more participatory social environment, the argument runs, and people will be up to – and up for – the task of self-government. Society will have schooled them in, and trained them for, democratic politics: 'individuals learn to participate by participating' (Pateman, 2012, p. 15). So, the claim that representative democracy is a practical response to the political limitations of ordinary people would be circular, if we could show that those limits resulted from existing social and political arrangements. Note, however, the large 'if' in that last sentence. (See also Box 3.3.)

Representation

At national level, all contemporary liberal democracies are **representative** (indirect). The democratic principle has transmuted from self-government to elected government, with barely a nod to ancient tradition. To the Greeks, the very idea of representation would have seemed preposterous: how can the people be said to govern themselves, if a separate class of rulers exists? As late as the eighteenth century, the French philosopher Jean-Jacques Rousseau propounded the same point: 'the moment a people gives itself representatives, it is no longer free. It ceases to exist' (1762, p. 145). In interpreting representative government as elected monarchy, the German scholar Robert Michels (1911, p. 38) argued in a similar vein:

Under representative government the difference between democracy and monarchy ... is altogether insignificant – a difference not in substance but in form. The sovereign people elects, in place of a king, a number of kinglets!

A **representative** stands for another person, group or entity. A flag represents a nation; a lawyer represents a client; and elected politicians represent their voters, districts and parties.

Yet, as large states emerged, so too did the requirement for a new way in which the people could shape collective decisions. Any modern version of democ-

BOX 3.3

Degrees of democracy: from unanimity to plurality

Unanimity   All to agree, assent or at least acquiesce

Concurrent majority   More than one majority required: for example, most voters and most provinces

Qualified majority   More than a simple majority: typically, two-thirds

Weighted majority   A majority after adjusting votes for differences in voting power: for example, shareholders may have one vote per share

Absolute majority   More than half of those entitled to vote

Majority (simple majority)   More than half of those voting

Plurality   The largest number of votes but not necessarily a majority

racy had to be compatible with massive states and an extended suffrage. One of the first authors to graft representation on to democracy was Tom Paine, a British-born political activist who experienced both the French and the American revolutions. In his *Rights of Man* (1791/2, p. 180), Paine wrote:

The original simple democracy ... is incapable of extension, not from its principle, but from the inconvenience of its form. Simple democracy was society governing itself without the aid of secondary means. By ingrafting representation upon democracy, we arrive at a system of government capable of embracing and confederating all the various interests and every extent of territory and population.

Scalability has certainly proved to be the key strength of representative institutions. In ancient Athens, the upper limit for a republic was reckoned to be the number of people who could gather together to hear a speaker. However, modern representative government allows enormous populations (such as 1.2 billion Indians and 313 million Americans) to exert some popular control over their rulers. And there is no upper limit. In theory, the entire world could become one giant system of representation. To adapt Tom Paine's phrase, representative government has indeed proved to be a highly convenient form.

As ever, intellectuals were on hand to validate this thinning of the democratic ideal. Prominent among them was the Austrian-born political economist Joseph Schumpeter. In *Capitalism, Socialism and Democracy* (1943), Schumpeter conceived of democracy as nothing more than party competition: 'democracy means only that the people have the opportunity of refusing or accepting the men who are to rule them'. Schumpeter wanted to limit the contribution of ordinary voters because he doubted their political capacity:

The typical citizen drops down to a lower level of mental performance as soon as he enters the political field. He argues and analyzes in a way that he would recognize as infantile within the sphere of his real interests. He becomes a primitive again. (1943, p. 269)

Reflecting this jaundiced view, Schumpeter argued that elections should not even be construed as a device through which voters elect a representative to carry out their will. Rather, the point of elections is simply to produce a government. From this perspective, the elector becomes a political accessory, restricted to selecting from broad packages of policies and leaders prepared by the parties. Contemporary democracy is merely a way of deciding which party will decide, a system far removed from the intense, educative discussions in the Athenian assembly, or even Pateman's participatory society:

The deciding of issues by the electorate [is made] secondary to the election of the men who are to do the deciding. To put it differently, we now take the view that the role of the people is to produce a government ... And we define the democratic method as that institutional arrangement for arriving at political decisions in which individuals acquire the power to decide by means of a competitive struggle for the people's vote. (Schumpeter, 1943, p. 270)

Support for indirect democracy does not require Schumpeter's scepticism. We might just view representation as a valuable division of labour for a specialized world. That is, a political life is available for those who want it, while those with non-political interests can confine their attention to monitoring government and voting at elections (Schudson, 1998). In this way, elected rulers remain accountable for their decisions, albeit after the event. To make the point more explicitly: how serious would our commitment to a free society be if we sought to impose extensive political participation on people who would prefer to spend their time on other activities?

Liberal democracy

Contemporary democracies are typically described as 'liberal democracies'. What does the adjective 'liberal' imply here? Liberal democracy embraces the notion of a freely elected government but adds a distinct concern with limits on the executive's scope. By definition, liberal democracy is limited government. Reflecting Locke's notion of natural rights (see Chapter 1), the goal is to secure individual liberty, including freedom from unwarranted demands by the state. A liberal democrat seeks to ensure that even a representative government bows to the fundamental principle expressed by the English philosopher John Stuart Mill in *On Liberty* (1859, p. 68): 'the only purpose for which power can be rightfully exercised over any member of a civilized community, against his will, is to prevent harm to others'. By constraining the authority of the governing party or parties, the population can be defended against its rulers. At the same time, minorities can be protected from another of democracy's inherent dangers: tyranny by the majority.

So, in place of the boisterous debates and all-encompassing scope of the Athenian *polis*, liberal democracies offer governance by law, rather than by people. Elected rulers are subject to constitutions that usually include a statement of individual rights. Should the government become overbearing, citizens can, in theory, use domestic and international courts to uphold their rights. This law-governed character of liberal democracy is the basis for Zakaria's claim (1997, p. 27) that 'the Western model is best symbolized not by the mass plebiscite but by the impartial judge'.

Of course, all democracies must allow space for political opinion to form and to receive expression through political parties. As Beetham (2004, p. 65) rightly states, 'without liberty, there can be no democracy'. But, in liberal democracy, freedom is more than a device to secure democracy; it is valued above, or certainly alongside, democracy itself. The argument is that people can best develop and express their individuality (and, hence, contribute most effectively to the common good) by taking responsibility for their own lives. By conceiving of the private sphere as the incubator of human development, we observe a sharp contrast with the Athenian notion that our true qualities can only be promoted through participation in the *polis*.

Some democracies emphasize the liberal element more than others. Here we can usefully contrast the United States and the United Kingdom. In the USA, the liberal component is entrenched by design. The Founding Fathers wanted, above all, to forestall a dictatorship of any kind, including tyranny by the majority. To prevent any government – and, especially, elected ones – from acquiring excessive power, the constitution set up an intricate system of checks and balances. Authority is distributed not only between federal institutions themselves (the executive, legislative and judicial branches), but also between the federal government and the 50 states of the Union. Power is certainly dispersed; some would say dissolved.

Where American democracy diffuses power across institutions, British democracy emphasizes the sovereignty of parliament. The electoral rules traditionally ensured a secure majority of seats for the leading party, which then forms the government. This ruling party retains firm control over its own members in the House of Commons, enabling it to ensure the passage of its bills into law. In this way, the hallowed sovereignty of Britain's parliament is leased to the party in office.

Except for the government's sense of self-restraint, the institutions that limit executive power in the United States – including a codified constitution, a separation of powers and federalism – are absent. Far more than the United States, Britain exemplifies Schumpeter's model of democracy as an electoral competition between organized parties. 'We are the masters now', trumpeted a Labour MP after his party's triumph in 1945. And his party did indeed use its power to institute substantial economic and social reforms.

But, even Britain's party-based democracy has moved in a more liberal direction. The country's judiciary has become more active and independent, stimulated in part by the European Court of Justice. Privatization has reduced the state's direct control over the economy. Also, the electoral system is now less likely to deliver a ruling majority for a single party, as reflected in the coalition established after the 2010 election. But, from a comparative perspective, a winning party (or even coalition) in Britain is still rewarded with an exceptionally free hand. The contrast with the United States remains.

To conclude this section, let us clarify the relationship between liberal democracy and representative democracy. In truth, the terms cover the same group of countries and the qualifier used is largely a matter of preference. Still, the changing popularity of the two phrases does tell a story about how democracy is implicitly conceived.

Representative democracy (also frequently described as representative government) is the older phrase, emerging at a time when indirect democracy was establishing itself as a practical alternative to the small direct democracies of the ancient world. So representative democracy was a term born from contrast with direct democracy. The phrase does not itself imply limits on elected authority, other than those needed for free and fair elections, and in the twentieth century tended to find particular favour with those favouring a strong role for party-based governments, such as socialists supporting public ownership of industry.

Liberal democracy is the more recent term, acquiring greater currency in the second half of the twentieth century and, significantly, still growing in popularity in a post-socialist era. In the name of individual liberty, it directs attention to the constitutional constraints on elected governments and hence places limits on the decision-making scope of representatives. So liberal democracy, as defined, is a more natural phrase for those who favour a market economy with its inherent limitations on the scope of government. Further, liberal democracy can be contrasted with competitive authoritarian regimes (revealingly, also called illiberal democracies) in which an elected strong-man rules as he sees fit.

Democracy and modernization

Why are some countries democratic and others not? What, in other words, are the economic and social requisites of sustainable democracy? A frequent answer is that liberal democracy flourishes in **modern** conditions: in high-income countries with an educated population. By contrast, middle-income states are rather more conducive to competitive authoritarian regimes and low-income countries to authoritarianism, pure and simple.

> A **modern** society is characterized by an industrial or post-industrial economy, affluence, specialized occupations, social mobility, and an urban and educated population. Modernization (or socio-economic development) is the process of acquiring these attributes.

Linking modernity and democracy carries important policy implications. It suggests that advocates of democracy should give priority to economic development in authoritarian states such as China, allowing political reform to emerge naturally at a later date. First get rich, then get a democracy. But if we accept this advice, controversial policy implications will follow. Should we really follow Apter (1965) in applying the notion of 'premature democratization' to low-income countries? Do we really want to encourage modernizing dictatorships?

Lipset (1959) provided the classic statement of the impact of modernization, suggesting that 'the more well-to-do a nation, the greater the chances that it will sustain democracy'. Using data from the late 1950s, Lipset demonstrated statistical relationships between affluence, industrialization, urbanization and education, on the one hand, and democracy, on the other.

The statistical relationship between affluence and democracy remains strong. Diamond (1992, p. 110) commented that this link is 'one of the most powerful and stable relationships in the study of national development'. In a study of all democracies existing between 1789 and 2001, Svolik (2008, p. 166) confirmed that 'democracies with low levels of economic development … are less likely to consolidate'. Boix (2011) concurs, with the qualification that the effect of affluence on democracy declines once societies have achieved developed status.

Inevitably, there continue to be exceptions, both apparent and real. The oil-rich kingdoms of the Middle East demonstrate that affluence, and even mass affluence, is no guarantee of democracy. But these seeming counter-examples are easily dealt with. They demonstrate only that modernity consists of more than income per head; authoritarian monarchs in the Middle East rule societies that may be wealthy, but are also highly traditional. A more important exception is India, a lower-middle-income country with a consolidated, if distinctive, democracy (see Spotlight).

So, why does liberal democracy seem to be the natural way of governing modern societies? Lipset himself judged that wealth softened the class struggle, producing a more equal distribution of income and turning the working class away from 'leftist extremism'. Echoing Aristotle, Lipset also supposed that the presence of a large middle class tempered class conflict between rich and poor. For these reasons, the rich become willing to contemplate what might prove to be just a temporary loss of power through elections.

Lipset noted further that economic security raises the quality of governance by reducing incentives for corruption. In addition, high-income countries possess more interest groups to reinforce liberal democracy. Education and urbanization – both of which are aspects of modernity – also make a difference. Education inculcates democratic and tolerant values, while towns have always been the wellspring of democracy.

Lipset's list, like the relationship between modernity and democracy itself, has stood the test of time. However, recent contributions offer a somewhat more systematic treatment (Boix, 2003). Vanhanen (1997, p. 24), for instance, suggests that a relatively equal distribution of power resources in modern societies prevents a minority from becoming politically dominant:

When the level of economic development rises, various economic resources usually become more widely distributed and the number of economic interest groups increases. Thus the underlying factor behind the positive correlation between the level of economic development and democracy is the distribution of power resources.

COUNTRY PROFILE

INDIA

LIBERAL DEMOCRACY

Form of government ■ a federal and parliamentary liberal democracy.

Legislature ■ the lower house, the Lok Sabha (House of the People), consists of 545 members, nearly all directly elected. The less significant upper chamber, the Rajya Sabha (Council of States), contains 245 members, mostly indirectly elected by state assemblies.

Executive ■ the prime minister selects and leads the large Council of Ministers (cabinet). The president, indirectly elected for a five year term, is less significant but formally asks a party leader to form the government and can take emergency powers.

Judiciary ■ the independent, respected Supreme Court defends and interprets the constitution. It consists of 31 judges appointed by the president following consultation.

Electoral system ■ elections to the Lok Sabha are by single-member plurality. The turnout in 2009 was 417 million. The powerful Election Commission of India, established by the constitution, superintends national and state elections.

Population (annual growth rate): 1,205 m (+1.31%)	
World Bank income group: lower middle	
Human development index (rank/out of): 134/187	
Political rights score: ②	
Civil liberties score: ③	
Media status: partly free	

Note: For interpretation and sources, see p. xvi.

Parties ■ The two major parties in a multiparty system are the once dominant Congress Party and the Hindu nationalist Bharatiya Janata Party. In 2009, Congress retained power as the major force in a coalition including several regional parties.

INDIA is shaped by its scale. It is the world's second biggest country by population, providing more than one in six of the world's people. It is also the world's fourth largest economy and the seventh largest country by area. It is one of the world's largest energy consumers and an increasingly important trading partner for many nations. Its economy has also experienced a phase of rapid expansion, with growth averaging seven per cent between 1997 and 2011. India's emergence is a major factor in the Asian shift which has characterized the twenty-first-century world to date.

India achieved independence from Britain as early as 1947 but economic development only began to accelerate in the 1990s. For forty years after independence, the country pursued an inward-looking strategy of economic development based on government planning, state sponsorship of heavy industry and substitution of imports by domestic products. The result was the over-regulated and corrupt 'permit/licence raj' (rule); it delivered only limited gains. The Hindu rate of growth, as it was dismissively called, fell well below that of the export-based economies of East Asia.

An important transition took place in 1991, when a newly-elected Congress government, including finance minister (later prime minister) Manmohan Singh, initiated substantial deregulation in response to a financial crisis. The rupee was devalued, foreign investment was encouraged and state involvement in industry cut back. Although labour regulation remains strong and corruption is still extensive, the reforms initiated a new phase of faster growth. In particular, the service sector expanded rapidly, notably in computing and banking. 'India Shining' became the slogan.

But it would be a travesty to end the story there. Growth is slowing once more, at a time when around a quarter of India's people still live in poverty. Almost half the country's young children are underweight – a higher proportion than in sub-Saharan Africa. India's rank in the Human Development Index remains low; almost one in three young people are functionally illiterate. The caste system continues to blight opportunities for many. Across the economy as a whole, most work is still found in the informal sector. Deprivation is even more extensive in the poorest states such as Bihar and Orissa. Because the country provides as many as one in three of the world's poor, the problem of world poverty is still first and foremost the problem of India.

Democracy in India

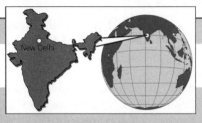

India is the great exception to the thesis that stable liberal democracy is restricted to affluent states. Notwithstanding enormous poverty and massive inequality, the formal mechanisms of democracy, including free and fair elections, are well-entrenched. So why did India succeed in consolidating liberal democracy when most other poor post-colonial countries initially failed?

Scale is again part of the answer. The complexity and sophistication of Indian society and culture offered some protection against military intervention. Coups proved more feasible in smaller ex-colonies; notably in Africa.

A more direct influence was India's experience as a British colony. Relatively speaking, democracy has fared well in the UK's ex-colonies. The British approach of indirect rule allowed local elites to occupy positions of some authority. There, they experienced a style of governance which accepted some dispersal of power and often permitted the expression of specific grievances. The resulting legacy favoured (while certainly not ensuring) pluralistic, limited government.

More important still was the distinctive manner in which the colonial experience played out in India. Its transition to independence was more gradual, considered and successful than elsewhere, avoiding the damaging rush to statehood in the 1960s stampede. The Indian National Congress, which led the independence struggle and governed for 30 years after its achievement, was founded as early as 1885. Over a long period, Congress built an extensive, patronage-based organization which

proved capable of governing a disparate country after independence. As Mitra (2011, p. 31) writes, Congress's 'legacy of direct action, mass movement and transactional politics based on patronage became an important ingredient of the political culture that sustained democratic rule in India after independence.'

In particular, Congress gained experience of elections as participation widened even under colonial rule. By 1946, before independence, 40 million people were entitled to vote

in colonial elections, providing the second largest electorate in the non-communist world (Jayal, 2007, p. 21). Their limitations notwithstanding, these contests functioned as training grounds for democracy.

But perhaps the critical factor in India's democratic success was the pro-democratic values of Congress's elite. Democracy survived in India because that is what its leaders wanted. Practices associated with British democracy – such as parliamentary government, an independent judiciary, and the rule of law – were seen as worthy of emulation. So in India, as elsewhere, the consolidation of liberal democracy was fundamentally an elite project.

The cataclysmic partition of India into the separate states of India and

Pakistan at the time of independence removed about seven million Muslims from Indian territory but surely contributed to the country's subsequent stability. Had this population transfer not occurred, violent though it was, governance in India would surely have followed a different, and possibility less democratic, course.

The quality of India's democracy is inevitably constrained by inequalities in Indian society. Political citizenship has not guaranteed social and eco-

'Social relations of domination and subordination [in India] ensure that, despite formal political equality, the interests of the powerless in society are largely ignored, while those of the powerful are not merely expressed, but often also embodied in policy. The rights of equal citizenship are, in and of themselves, necessary conditions for democracy, but the sufficient conditions require that the meaningful exercise of these citizenship rights be assured to all.'

(Jayal, 2007, p. 37)

nomic security yet such assurance is needed for democracy to deepen. But the openness of the political system at least allows low status groups to express their interests. Jayal (2007, p. 45) sums up: 'the singular merit of Indian democracy lies in its success in providing a space for political contestation and the opportunity for the articulation of a variety of claims'.

Further reading: Adeney and Wyatt (2010), Corbridge *et al.* (2012), Jayal (2007), Mitra (2011), Stepan *et al.* (2011).

We can conclude that modernity has proved to be an effective incubator of liberal democracy. However, we should remain cautious in projecting this relationship forward. Today's world contains more liberal democracies than Lipset's, suggesting that democracy can consolidate at lower, pre-modern levels of development. That threshold may continue to decrease, delivering a world that is wholly democratic before it becomes wholly modern. Alternatively, a few authoritarian regimes, such as China, may succeed in creating modern societies without succumbing to democratic pressures.

Waves of democracy

When did modern democracies emerge? As with the phases of decolonization discussed in Chapter 2, so too did contemporary democracies emerge in a series of distinct **waves** (Box 3.4). And just as each period of decolonization deposited a particular type of state on the political shore, so too did each democratic wave differ in the character of the resulting democracies.

> A **wave** of democratization is a group of transitions from non-democratic to democratic regimes that occurs within a specified period of time and that significantly outnumbers transitions in the opposite direction during that period (Huntington, 1991, p. 15).

First wave

The earliest representative democracies emerged in the 'first long wave of democratization' between 1828 and 1926. During this first period, nearly 30 countries established at least minimally democratic national institutions, including Argentina, Australia, Britain, Canada, France, Germany, the Netherlands, New Zealand, the Scandinavian countries and the United States. However, some backsliding occurred as fledgling democracies were overthrown by fascist, communist or military dictatorships during Huntington's 'first reverse wave' from 1922 to 1942.

A distinctive feature of many first wave transitions was their slow and sequential character. Political competition, traditionally operating within a privileged elite, gradually broadened as the suffrage extended to the wider population. Unhurried transi-

---

BOX 3.4

Huntington's three waves of democratization

	Period	Examples
First wave	1828–1926	Britain, France, USA
Second wave	1943–62	India, Israel, Japan, West Germany
Third wave	1974–91	Southern and Eastern Europe, Latin America, parts of Africa

Note: The first wave partly reversed between 1922 and 1942 (e.g. in Germany and Italy) and the second wave similarly between 1958 and 1975 (e.g. in much of Latin America and post-colonial Africa). Many such reversals have now themselves reversed.

Source: Huntington (1991).

---

tions lowered the political temperature; in the first wave, democracy was as much outcome as intention. In Britain, for example, the widening of the suffrage occurred gradually, with each step easing the fears of the propertied classes about the dangers of further reform (Table 3.1).

In the United States, the democratic transition was rather more rapid. There, the idea that citizens could only be represented fairly by those of their own sort rapidly gained ground against the founders' view that the republic should be led by a leisured, landed gentry. Within 50 years of independence, 'nearly all the states had achieved universal manhood suffrage' (Wood, 1993, p. 101). But women were not offered the vote on the same terms as men until 1919, and the franchise for black people was not fully realized until the Voting Rights Act of 1965. In that sense, America's democratic transition was also a prolonged affair.

Second wave

Huntington's second wave of democratization began during World War II and continued until the 1960s. As with the first wave, some of the new democracies created at this time did not consolidate. For example, elected rulers in several Latin American

Table 3.1 The expansion of the British electorate, 1831–1969

The British electorate expanded slowly, contributing to political stability

Year	Electorate (as a percentage of population aged 20+)
1831	4.4
1832	First Reform Act
1832	7.1
1864	9.0
1867	Second Reform Act
1868	16.4
1883	18.0
1884	Third Reform Act
1886	28.5
1914	30.0
1918	Vote extended to women over 30
1921	74.0
1928	Equal Franchise Act
1931	97.0
1969	Voting age reduced from 21 to 18

Source: Adapted from Dahl (1998), figure 2.

states were quickly overthrown by military coups.

But established democracies did emerge after 1945 from the ashes of defeated dictatorships, not just in West Germany, but also in Austria, Japan and Italy. These postwar democracies were introduced by the victorious allies, led by the USA, supported by local partners. The second-wave democracies established firm roots, helped by an economic recovery which was itself nourished by American aid. During this second wave, democracy also consolidated in the new state of Israel and the former British dominion of India.

How did these second-wave democracies differ from those of the first phase? Their liberal traditions were somewhat weaker, as representation through parties proved to be the stronger suit. First-generation democracies had emerged when parties were seen as a source of faction, rather than progress. For example, parties had gone unmentioned in the American constitution and George Washington (1796) had declared in his farewell address that parties were 'potent engines by which cunning

ambitions, and unprincipled men will be enabled to subvert the power of the people'.

But, by the second era of transition parties had emerged as the leading instrument of democracy in a mass electorate. As in many more recent constitutions, Germany's Basic Law (1949) went so far as to codify their role: 'the political parties shall take part in forming the democratic will of the people'. In that respect, second-wave constitutions were built in the Schumpeter mould.

In several cases, though, effective competition was reduced by the emergence of a single party which dominated national politics for a generation: Congress in India, the Christian Democrats in Italy, the LDP in Japan, Labour in Israel. Many second-wave democracies took a generation to mature into fully competitive party systems.

Third wave

The third wave of democratization was a product of the final quarter of the twentieth century. Its main and highly diverse elements were:

- the ending of right-wing dictatorships in Southern Europe (Greece, Portugal and Spain) in the 1970s;

- the retreat of the generals in much of Latin America in the 1980s;

- the collapse of communism in the Soviet Union and Eastern Europe at the end of the 1980s.

The third wave transformed the global political landscape, providing an inhospitable environment for those non-democratic regimes that survive. Even in sub-Saharan Africa, presidents subjected themselves to re-election (though rarely to defeat). With the end of the Cold War and the collapse of any realistic alternative to democracy, the European Union and the United States also became more encouraging of democratic transitions – while still, of course, keeping a close eye on their own shorter-term interests. It is possible that such factors will have inspired a fourth wave by the time you read these words.

The third wave stimulated considerable research on the mechanics of transition. Our review in the next and final section provides a way of thinking about democracy-building focused directly on the political actors involved. This emphasis on transition contrasts with the broader, sociological and more deterministic approach we addressed in the section on democracy and modernization.

Recent transitions

How did third-wave democracies make the transition from the preceding authoritarian order? What were the political processes involved? Drawing lessons from this historical experience is, again, of practical value, providing helpful background for those involved in any future transitions. Figure 3.3 summarizes the key stages, providing a template against which any particular example can be examined. We will outline these stages in general terms before reviewing the example of Spain after Franco.

However, it must be borne in mind that, as the Arab Spring confirms, a transition *from* an authoritarian regime does not entail an immediate or even medium-term transition *to* liberal democracy. Another authoritarian order, perhaps with greater freedom of speech, is an alternative outcome. In particular, Figure 3.3 reflects research on the successful transitions in Southern Europe and Latin America, rather than the more varied outcomes from the later collapse of the Soviet Union (O'Donnell *et al.*, 1986).

The *liberalization of the authoritarian regime* initiates the reform sequence. Military regimes often lose a sense of purpose once the crisis that propelled them to office is resolved; communist regimes lost the prop of Soviet support. In the more liberal environment that emerges, opportunities increase to express public opposition, inducing a dynamic of reform. For instance, as regimes decay, so the ruling coalition shrinks through defections.

The key point is that transitions are rarely initiated by mass demonstrations against a united dictatorship. Rather, democracy is typically the outcome – intended or unintended – of recognition within part of the ruling group that change is inevitable, or even desirable. As O'Donnell and Schmitter (1986, p. 19) assert:

There is no transition whose beginning is not the consequence – direct or indirect – of important divisions within the authoritarian regime itself,

Figure 3.3 Stages of democratization

Democratization can be separated into the final stages of: liberalization, transition, consolidation and deepening. However, as the notion of an unconsolidated democracy implies, reaching the fourth stage is far from guaranteed.

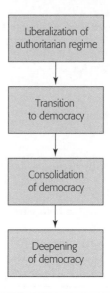

principally along the fluctuating cleavage between hardliners and softliners … In Brazil and Spain, for example, the decision to liberalize was made by high-echelon, dominant personnel in the incumbent regime in the face of weak and disorganized opposition.

In the fraught and often lengthy *transition to democracy*, arrangements are made for the new system of government. Threats to the transition from hardliners (who may consider a military coup) and radical reformers (who may seek a full-scale revolution, rather than just a change of regime) need to be overcome. Constitutions must be written, institutions designed and elections

Hardliners in an authoritarian order judge that the perpetuation of non-democratic rule is both feasible and desirable. By contrast, **softliners** in the old regime accept the inevitability or desirability of securing legitimacy for their rule through elections. Softliners and moderate reformers can constitute an influential reform coalition against hardliners.

timetabled. Negotiations frequently take the form of round-table talks between rulers and opposition, often leading to an elite settlement (pacted transition). During the transition, the existing rulers will seek political opportunities in the new democratic order. For example, military rulers may seek to repackage themselves as the only party capable of guaranteeing order and security. In any event, the current elite will seek to protect its future by negotiating privileges, such as exemption from prosecution. The transition is substantially complete with the installation of the new arrangements, most visibly through a high turnout election which is seen as the peak moment of democratic optimism (Morlino, 2012, pp. 85–96).

Though backsliding is rare, a new democracy remains fragile. *Consolidation of democracy* has only occurred when the new institutions provide an accepted framework for political competition. Przeworski's definition (1991, p. 26) is influential: 'democracy is consolidated when … a particular system of institutions becomes the only game in town and when no-one can imagine acting outside the democratic institutions'. It takes time, for example, for the armed forces to accept their more limited role as a professional, rather than a political, body.

While consolidation is a matter of attitudes, its achievement is measured through action and, in particular, by the peaceful transfer of power through elections. The first time a defeated government relinquishes office, democracy's mechanism for elite circulation is shown to be effective, contributing further to political stability. So, consolidation is the process through which democratic practices become habitual – and the habit of democracy, as any other, takes time to form (Linz and Stepan, 1996). Transition establishes a new regime but consolidation secures its continuation.

The *deepening of democracy*, finally, refers to the continued progress (if any) of a new democracy towards full liberal democracy. This term emerged as academic awareness grew that many third-wave transitions had stalled midway between authoritarianism and democracy, with accompanying popular disenchantment. As we saw in Chapter 1, in competitive authoritarian regimes 'democracy is superficial rather than deep and the new order consolidates at a low level of "democratic quality"' (Morlino, 2012, pt

III). So, the point of the term 'deepening' is not so much to describe a universal stage in transitions as to acknowledge that the outcome of a transition, especially in less modern countries, may be a hybrid regime.

Spain's transition following the death of General Franco in 1975 is an early and influential example of a successful third-wave transition. As with many other examples, the Spanish narrative was lengthy and dramatic. Consolidation was achieved only in 1982, with the peaceful transfer of power to the socialist opposition after a general election. Chapters in this transition included:

- dismantling the established institutions of the Franco regime, including the secret police;
- overcoming the suspicions of the army, the Church and the ultra-right;
- negotiating a new constitution through multi-party talks;
- securing the unreformed parliament's agreement for a constitution which involved its own liquidation;
- obtaining ratification of the constitution by referendum in 1978;
- legalizing, but also restraining, the communist party and trade unions;
- devolving power to the regions in a traditionally centralized state;
- responding to terrorism which, in 1979, killed over 100 people in the Basque country;
- surviving an attempted coup in 1981.

The story's interest is sustained by the seeming uncertainty of the outcome and the requirement for considerable political craft in achieving it. Linz and Stepan's comment about transitions (1996, p. 89) certainly fits the Spanish case: 'even the easiest and most successful transition was lived as a precarious process constantly requiring innovative political action.' Grugel (2002, p. 149) confirms the point, suggesting that, as late as 1979, 'democracy in Spain was not an inevitable outcome'. Linz and Stepan draw attention to the 'innovative leadership' of Adolfo Suárez (Prime Minister, 1976–81), while the decisive intervention of King Juan Carlos, who said after the coup attempt that he would prefer exile to the collapse of democracy, is also widely recognized. In fact, the monarch became known as *el piloto del cambio* – the pilot of change.

There is a danger, though, of seduction by compelling narrative. At least with hindsight, a consolidated democracy for Spain seems to have been by far the most likely result. Advocates of modernization as an incubator of democracy can point to extensive social development under Franco's regime, leading to a widespread cultural preference for democracy. According to Desfor Edles (1998, p. 51), democracy quickly became the country's 'new civil religion'. The neighbourhood was also supportive: Europe favoured democracy for Spain.

In these circumstances, even a successful coup in 1981 would surely only have delayed the eventual outcome, altering the route but not the destination. In transitions generally, and Spain especially, narratives of transition describe 'how', but the modernization perspective still helps with 'why'.

Discussion questions

■ What can the people decide that experts cannot decide better?

■ Is democracy an effective method of representing 'orange-bellied parrots whose habitat will be destroyed by a proposed development'? (Eckersley, 2011, p. 236) If not, how should the interests of non-human species be incorporated into political decisions?

■ Does the internet permit the recreation of Athenian-style direct democracy in today's states? If so, would such a system be desirable?

■ Do you agree with Schumpeter (1943, p. 269) that 'the typical citizen drops down to a lower level as soon as he enters the political field'? Does your answer affect your judgement of democracy's value?

■ Was Jean-Jacques Rousseau (1762, p. 145) right to proclaim that 'the moment a people gives itself representatives, it is no longer free. It ceases to exist.'?

■ Is democracy a realistic short-term aspiration for Afghanistan? If not, what political system should the international community advocate for that country?

Further reading

S. Alonso, J. Keane and W. Merkel, eds, *The Future of Representative Democracy* (2011). A wide-ranging collection of essays examining trends in representative democracy.

R. Dahl, *Democracy and its Critics* (1989). An influential prize-winning account of what democracy is and why it is valuable.

R. Dahl, *On Democracy* (1998). An accessible primer on democracy by one of its most influential proponents.

C. Haerpfer, P. Bernhagen, R. Inglehart and C. Welzel, eds, *Democratization* (2009). A comprehensive text, covering actors, causes, dimensions, regions and theories.

M. Hansen, *The Athenian Democracy in the Age of Demosthenes* (1991). An authoritative guide to democracy in Ancient Athens.

D. Held, *Models of Democracy*, 3rd edn (2006). A thorough introduction to democracy from classical Greece to the present.

L. Morlino, *Changes for Democracy: Actors, Structures, Processes* (2012). An extensive review of the academic literature on democratization, including hybrid regimes.

P. Rosanvallon, *Counter-Democracy: Politics in an Age of Distrust* (2008). An original (if abstract) interpretation viewing democracy as consisting in informal mechanisms through which the public can express confidence in, or mistrust of, its representatives. Beautifully translated from the French.

ONLINE RESOURCES AVAILABLE

Visit the companion website at **www.palgrave.com/politics/hague** to access additional learning resources, including multiple-choice questions, chapter summaries, web links and practice essay questions.

Chapter 4 **Authoritarian rule**

'The study of politics in **authoritarian** countries should be more valued by comparative scholars', writes Posusney (2005, p. 2). And the reason is straightforward: 'non-democratic government, whether by elders, chiefs, monarchs, aristocrats, empires, military regimes or one-party states, has been the norm for most of human history' (Brooker, 2009, p. 1). Certainly, the brutal twentieth century will be remembered more for the dictatorships it spawned – including Hitler's Germany, Stalin's Russia, Mao's China and Pol Pot's Cambodia – than for the democratic transitions at its close.

After the dramatic collapse of communism at the end of the 1980s and the spectacular Arab Spring of 2011, it is tempting to view any remaining non-democratic regimes as historical anomalies which will soon be vanquished by the Facebook generation. But such optimism is both sweeping and pre-mature. It fails to recognize that ousting one authoritarian leader may just lead to another – or to a failed state or invasion. The collapse of communism has not brought democracy to central Asian republics such as Uzbekistan, neither is it likely that the overthrow of authoritarian governments in Egypt, Libya, Tunisia and Yemen in 2011 will initiate stable liberal democracy in all these countries. In fact, Way (2011, p. 17) judges that a comparison with the communist collapse suggests that more Arab autocrats will hang on, 'and that those [Arab] countries which do witness authoritarian collapse will be less likely to democratize than their European counterparts were.'

Studying non-democracies is far more than a historical exercise. In 2011, 48 of the world's countries (24 per cent) were still rated 'not free' by Freedom House (2012); these countries contained 2.4 billion (35 per cent) of the world's population. Across the world as a whole, the number of authoritarian regimes has remained stable over the current century.

The most prominent authoritarian states are internationally significant, whether judged by scale (China), as incubators of terrorists (most of the 9/11 attackers came from Saudi Arabia), by oil reserves (Saudi Arabia), or by actual or intended possession of nuclear weapons (including China and Iran) (Table 4.1).

Authoritarian rule

In this section, we outline general features of authoritarian rule. We then proceed in the remainder of the chapter to discuss each of the main and highly varied bases on which non-democratic rule is founded (Box 4.1).

In approaching authoritarian rule, we should not assume that all such states place total, unlimited power in a despot seeking to control the whole population through fear and surveillance. Even in the twentieth century,

AUTHORITARIAN RULE

- Authoritarian regimes are still understudied in comparative politics. Yet, a case can be made that conflict between authoritarian and democratic states will remain an important fault line in world politics. In any case, identifying the dynamics of authoritarian regimes provides a useful contrast to our understanding of democracy.

- One key to understanding authoritarian regimes is to recognize that few are absolute tyrannies. Rather, many leaders are in a weaker political position than their equivalents in liberal democracies. The art is to identify these limitations and how such rulers seek to sustain their position.

- In particular, one skill in sustaining a non-democratic regime is for the ruling leader (or group) to maintain a political coalition strong enough to offer support but not powerful enough to pose a threat. So, ask who the other power-holders are (the army, the security services, ethnic leaders?) and to what extent the rulers are constrained by these powerful people.

- It is valuable to take a view on the effectiveness of authoritarian governance, not least for low-income countries. One (twentieth-century?) perspective is that non-democratic rule can generate the capital for economic take-off precisely because it can resist popular pressures for consumption. Here, China provides an interesting, if exceptional, case study.

- But there is also a debit list. To what extent are corruption, low economic growth, old leaders, and the absence of a succession procedure endemic weaknesses of authoritarian regimes?

totalitarian regimes demanding explicit popular support for a supreme leader were the exception rather than the rule. To be sure, elements of the totalitarian method can still be found, particularly in the widespread use of the secret police for monitoring potential opposition. But with a few exceptions, such as North Korea, totalitarian regimes are now rarely observed.

Most non-democracies are authoritarian, rather than totalitarian. That is, the rulers seek to maintain their control (and increase their wealth) by limiting mass participation, rather than by mobilizing the population. Ordinary people are unlikely to experience a knock on the door as long as they keep away from politics. In China, for instance, it is no longer necessary to show explicit support for the regime; avoiding active opposition suffices.

Authoritarian rulers operate within unspoken limits, recognizing the need to strike deals with other power-holders such as business, the Church or regional bosses. Just as democratic leaders need to retain electoral support, so too must authoritarian rulers convince their allies to continue supporting the existing regime.

Furthermore, government typically takes the form not of one single dominant leader but, rather, of an elite group – such as a military council – with considerable internal jockeying. Ideology and policy are often absent. In such a situation, governance is an uneasy combination of formally unlimited authority and considerable political vulnerability.

Since non-democratic leaders stand above the law, the constitutional architecture (if any) is a poor guide. Laws are vague and contradictory, creating a pretext for bringing any chosen troublemaker to court. Special courts, such as military tribunals, are often used for sensitive cases. Parliament and the judiciary are under-resourced, unprofessional and ineffective. Civil rights are poorly respected and the state often requires private organizations to be licensed. The absence of constitutional constraint leads to callous treatment of the powerless, including minority groups, non-nationals, prisoners, and women. With no enforceable legal frame-

Table 4.1 Some prominent authoritarian states

Some large and oil-rich countries which are important players in world politics continue to be ruled by non-democratic means

	Form of rule	Population (rank)	Gross domestic product (rank)	Oil reserves (rank)
Algeria	Presidential (strong military influence)	35	48	17
China	Communist party	1	3	14
Iran	Contested theocracy	18	18	4
North Korea	Military-backed presidential dictatorship	49	99	No known reserves
Saudi Arabia	Royal family	46	24	1
Vietnam	Communist party	14	43	45

Note: China is third, rather than second, in the CIA's ranking of countries by gross domestic product because the European Union (placed second behind the USA) is treated as a country.

Source: For rankings, CIA (2012).

work to protect private property rights, authoritarian rule is often associated with economic stagnation. The price of the rulers securing a large slice of the pie is that the pie itself fails to grow, yielding political vulnerability in the long run.

Inherited monarchies apart, the absence of a clear succession procedure is a central weakness of authoritarian regimes, providing much of their political dynamic. Because there are no competitive elections to refresh the leadership, authoritarian leaders may continue in post until well past their sell-by dates, as with the ageing autocrats finally overthrown in the Arab revolts of 2011 (Table 4.2). As those uprisings show, changing the leader in an authoritarian regime is generally a more difficult process than in a democracy. The pattern in China, where since the 1990s the Communist Party has refreshed its top leaders on a ten-year cycle, is exceptional; it surely contributes to the party's continued hold on power.

A decline into personal despotism, as with Gaddafi in Libya, is an inherent danger of authoritarian regimes. However, as Brooker (2009, p. 130) observes, 'degeneration into personal rule is common among dictatorships, particularly among party regimes, but is far from being inevitable'. A more important consequence of uncertain succession is that authoritarian rulers can be removed by upstarts at any time, meaning that they must devote constant attention to shoring up their position.

Table 4.2 Leaders overthrown in the Arab Spring, 2011

The Arab revolts toppled some (but far from all) of the elderly autocrats who had dominated their countries for decades

	Leader	Age at which overthrown	Number of years in power
Egypt	Hosni Mubarak	82	29
Libya	Muammar Gaddafi	69	41
Tunisia	Zine El Abidine Ben Ali	74	23
Yemen	Ali Abdullah Saleh	69	21

Note: Before becoming President of Yemen in 1990, Saleh was President of North Yemen for 11 years.

Identifying how authoritarian leaders respond to these inherent political uncertainties brings us to the essence of non-democratic rule. Leaders exploit three key control devices: the military, patronage and the media.

First, authoritarian rulers maintain a strong military and security presence. To sustain their position, they must be seen to be both willing and able to use this resource. The revolts in the Middle East and North Africa in 2011 generally progressed further and faster where the regime lost the support of the

BOX 4.1

Forms of authoritarian rule

	Definition	Examples
Personal despotism	A single individual owing allegiance to no institution rules though fear and rewards, relying on a personal security force to maintain power.	Dominican Republic (Trujillo), Haiti (François Duvalier)
Monarchy	A ruling sovereign emerges from the royal family, with other family members in key political and military posts.	The Gulf States: Bahrain, Kuwait, Oman, Qatar, Saudi Arabia, United Arab Emirates
Ruling parties	Rule by a single party, often combined with a strong president.	Communist states. Many African states in the decades after independence.
Ruling presidents	A president dominates politics and the media, keeping opponents off-guard and the opposition marginalized. Power may rest with the individual leader but is still exercised through the presidency.	Uzbekistan
Military rule	Government by the military, often ruling through a *junta* comprising the leader of each branch of the forces.	Many Africa, Asian and Latin American countries in the decades following World War II
Theocracy	A rare form of rule in which religious leaders rule directly.	Iran

See also: Competitive authoritarian regimes, discussed in this chapter.

organs of violence, or showed an unwillingness to use them – though government repression did not prevent violence in Libya and Syria.

High spending on the armed forces, often made possible by revenues from natural resources, is typical of authoritarian states. Such investment buys off potential opposition, permits foreign adventures, and provides the means for suppressing domestic dissent. Even when the military does not itself rule, it still provides a key support base for the political executive. Lavish treatment of the armed forces is therefore inevitable – again, producing a drag on economic performance. Authoritarian regimes lack the separation of military and political spheres which characterizes liberal democracy.

Second, authoritarian rulers maintain their position through an unofficial patronage network in which other holders of power are incorporated by providing them with resources (such as control over jobs, natural resources, and access to money-making opportunities) which they distribute, in turn, to their own supporters. In this way, allegiance to one's immediate patron, and indirectly to the regime, becomes the key to a successful career. These patron–client pyramids extend throughout society, providing a web of allegiances which overrides the public–private divide. As long as the clients are politically sound, their patrons will ignore shady behaviour, a fact which helps to explain why authoritarian governments are **corrupt**. Institutions are weak but pragmatic alliances are strong, holding the regime together. Again, however, there is a high price to pay: corruption corrodes whatever public support the regime may possess, increasing potential instability.

> **Corruption** is the abuse of office for private gain. It occurs when an official allocates a benefit in exchange for a bribe, rather than on the basis of entitlement. The bribe may persuade officials to do what they should have done anyway, or to do it promptly.

The allocation of resources such as jobs, contracts, and investment through private patronage leads to substantial misallocation of capital, a weak banking sector, reduced foreign investment, and a sharp distinction between insiders and outsiders (King, 2007). But as long as rulers continue to control key economic commodities, such as oil, they can continue to purchase political loyalty.

Third, the media in authoritarian regimes are subject to close scrutiny. Rulers ensure favourable media coverage for their own achievements; their opponents are criticized, or ignored. Censorship is implemented by catch-all offences such as threatening the dignity and effectiveness of the state. It is notable that, even as the Chinese Communist Party introduced market mechanisms to many parts of its economy, it did not privatize the mass media.

So, authoritarian politics is typically driven by fear and vulnerability. The result is a repertoire of control mechanisms in which politics comes before economics and obedience before initiative. Communication is opaque, trust is lacking, government spending is misused, corruption is endemic, laws are ignored, and foreign investors are cautious. In many cases, the outcome is a static society, an underperforming economy, and a cynical population. In the long run, such a configuration may be a poor recipe for regime stability. Still, as the English economist John Maynard Keynes said in 1923, 'this long run is a misleading guide to current affairs. In the long run, we are all dead'.

Even so, authoritarian rule can be compatible with rapid economic growth. China is the notable example: its economic growth between 1978 and 2009 far exceeded that of democratic India (Madhukar and Nagarjuna, 2011; Sen, 2011). Reasons can certainly be found for supposing that authoritarian rule can facilitate early stage development in particular. After all, industrialization requires massive investment in infrastructure, such as transport, communications, and education. Authoritarian rulers can generate the surplus for this investment by resisting short-term, electoral pressures for immediate consumption.

Simply put, they can kick-start development because they can ignore the squeals of those whose consumption is initially limited.

Although a few non-democratic regimes initiate economic take-off, most do not. Many traditional rulers, such as the ruling families in the Middle East, continue to resist modernization. Other dictators – for example, Nigeria's military 'lootocrats' – set back economic development by decades through gross mismanagement. A statistical study by Przeworski *et al.* (2000, p. 271) found that, even in those cases where authoritarian regimes did achieve growth, this increase depended primarily on expanding the labour force. Democracies, by contrast, made more productive use of their inputs, a form of growth which can, in principle, continue indefinitely.

Personal despotism

Our first form of authoritarian rule, personal despotism, is also the simplest. In its original meaning, a despot was any barbaric and arbitrary ruler who treated his subjects as little more than slaves. Here, we are concerned with a distinctive, and now rare, type of rule in which the adjective 'personal' implies that the source of power is the leader himself, together with his family, loyalists, and bodyguards.

In a personal despotism, links to a wider ideology, social forces, and an organized party were at best intermittent. The leader retained discretion in his decisions, a resource which he used to keep his opponents off-guard. He also took care to fill not only his own boots, but also those of his entourage. The despot's rule was exercised through the leader himself, rather than through institutions. Thus, personal despotism displayed, in stark and violent fashion, features found in many authoritarian regimes.

Although personal despots were most common in Central America and Africa, the syndrome was originally labelled 'sultanism' by Max Weber (1921–22, p. 231). This term was also preferred by Chehabi and Linz (1998) in their wide-ranging study of the phenomenon.

Personal despotism typically arose in small, postcolonial countries with agricultural economies, particularly during the no-questions-asked era of the Cold War. The Caribbean island of Hispaniola, divided between the Dominican Republic in the east and Haiti in the west, was an example. There, the dictatorships of Rafael Trujillo in the Dominican Republic (1930–61), and of François Duvalier in Haiti (1957–71), provided archetypal cases, illustrating many standard characteristics.

In the Dominican Republic, Rafael 'The Goat' Trujillo acquired power through a military coup in 1930. He established a brutal dictatorship, rationalized by an unsophisticated concoction of Catholic, anti-Haitian and nationalist myths. Coming from a poor background, Trujillo accumulated enormous wealth, treating sugar plantations as his own property. Torture was common. Like many despots, Trujillo was concerned with status as much as wealth. His statue was everywhere; schoolchildren prayed daily for 'God, country and Trujillo'. As the despot's abilities declined with age, so his repression became more arbitrary, the economy more impoverished, and the wealthy more resentful. His circle of supporters narrowed, eventually leading to his assassination, with American encouragement, in 1961 (Hartlyn, 1998).

The story of François 'Papa Doc' Duvalier in Haiti is fundamentally similar. Although Duvalier came to power through an election in 1957, his rule proved to be extraordinarily despotic and gruesome. He maintained a personal presidential guard and created the notorious Tontons Macoutes – the bogeymen – as an instrument of terror. Unpaid, but exempt from prosecution, the members of this militia were, in effect, invited to prey upon the population. They did so. Again, like Trujillo, Duvalier enriched himself and his family through corruption. If the government was short of money, Papa Doc would simply imprison a chosen businessman in the presidential palace until the victim provided it. Unlike many despots, Duvalier achieved his ambition of retaining power until his death, in 1971 (Girard, 2006).

Other cases of personal despotism included:

- Fulgencio Batista, Cuba, 1933–58,

- Anastasio Somoza, Nicaragua, 1936–56,

- Ferdinand Marcos, Philippines, 1965–86,

- Mobutu Sese Seko, Zaire (now the Democratic Republic of Congo), 1965–97.

Muammar Gaddafi's despotic rule of Libya (1969–2011) also showed personal features. For example, Gaddafi gave up the official position of head of state in 1977, becoming merely the 'brotherly leader' of the revolution. He was his own source of power.

Some of these dictators sought – and, for a period, succeeded in ensuring – a family successor to their own rule. In Haiti, for example, Papa Doc was succeeded by his son, Baby Doc. But the personal nature of such regimes, as well as the damage they inflicted on the economy, worked against the establishment of a dynasty. Indeed, the virtual dismantling of any government institutions can eventually produce a collapsed state. While the Cold War provided a hospitable environment for personal despots, the international environment is now less well-disposed to this crude form of authoritarian rule.

Monarchy

A ruling monarchy is a more common and stable form of rule than a personal despotism. Where a succession procedure is accepted, monarchy can provide a stable framework for the exercise of traditional authority, in which rulers show paternalistic concern for their subjects. In liberal democracies, of course, monarchs survive only as figureheads but ruling royal families remain the governing force in the oil-rich Arab states of the Persian Gulf. We will consider the monarchies in the Gulf States (Bahrain, Kuwait, Oman, Qatar, Saudi Arabia, and the United Arab Emirates) in greater detail. These Muslim countries are politically important, providing a major source of oil, gas, and terrorists.

In the Gulf, a leading tribe typically established a privileged relationship with the colonial power and exploited this connection to secure control of the Western-style state created at independence. So, although the tribe itself may be ancient, its position at the head of the state is relatively recent.

The Gulf States make few concessions to democracy. The constitution of Oman, issued by the Sultan in 1996, makes clear that the person of the Sultan 'is inviolable and must be respected and his orders must be obeyed'. Several kingdoms, notably Kuwait, have now established consultative assemblies, but this reform is unlikely to presage a transition to a constitutional monarchy (Herb, 2005).

In three ways, use of the term 'monarchy' to describe the traditional political systems found in the Gulf is imprecise. First, the titles taken by Arab 'monarchs' themselves reflect tribal or Islamic tradition: 'emir' (leader or commander), 'sheikh' (revered leader of the tribe) or 'sultan' (a leader who possesses authority). The United Arab Emirates, a federation of seven emirates, is called just that – not the United Arab Kingdom.

Second, the leading members of the ruling dynasty, rather than a single monarch, often exercise authority. Governance is by princes, rather than just the king. These countries are run by family businesses, rather than sole traders.

Third, while the king typically designates a crown prince as his preferred successor, custom requires that a clan council meets after the monarch's death to confirm, or indeed change, this appointment. Herb (1999, p. 491) judges that this element of selection is the 'glue that holds the dynastic monarchies together', enabling them to continue across the generations. In most European monarchies, by contrast, succession is based on inheritance by the first-born, a dubious procedure making no bow to competence.

Weber's notion of traditional rule captures the nature of authority in these male-dominated Arab dynasties. Authority is owed to the ruler, rather than to a more abstract entity such as a state or party. The people are subjects, rather than citizens; the ruler is constrained neither by law nor by competitive election. The emir's authority flows from the historic position of nomadic tribal leader. For example, the Al Bu Said dynasty has ruled Oman for longer than the United States has existed as an independent country.

Because the ruler is expected to take responsibility for his people, the right of ordinary people to petition on individual matters is well-established. But the petitioner requests benevolent treatment, not the implementation of constitutional rights. The abstract idea of a state linking rulers and citizens is weak, as are such modern notions as constitutions, rights, interest groups, the separation of powers, and the rule of law. Politics is based on intrigue at the palace, with little distinction between public and private sectors.

We can use Saudi Arabia – the heart of the Arab and Islamic worlds – to illustrate monarchical governance. The country's political style reflects the influence of King Abdul Aziz Ibn Saud. He led the Saudi state from its inception in 1902 until his death in 1953. In true patrimonial style, Ibn Saud ran his kingdom as a gigantic personal household, using marriage as a vital political tactic. He took several hundred wives drawn from all the powerful families in the state, a stratagem which solidified his control.

Saudi Arabia's sprawling royal family, led by an influential group of several hundred princes, still constitutes the government's core. The Basic Law promulgated in 1992 declared that Saudi Arabia is a monarchy ruled by 'the sons and grandsons of Ibn Saud'. However, the grandsons of the founding king are themselves now elderly, leading to an impending requirement to transfer power to a new generation. Succession may be smoothed by an Allegiance Council, established in 2006 and composed of representatives of the Al Saud family. Its purpose is to establish transition in the event of the incapacity or death of the King or his designated successor, the Crown Prince.

Family members occupy the key positions on the Council of Ministers, serving in particular as a bridge between the government, the military, and the active security forces. This large ruling family, itself divided into factions, populates and controls the leading institutions of state, providing a form of dispersed collective leadership and a barrier to radical change.

Although Saudi rulers have reacted firmly to the terrorist threat in their midst, the regime is more authoritarian than totalitarian. The ruling family does not monopolize wealth but, rather, leaves space for lower-tier families. There is also some separation of political and religious authority. A tradition of consultation allows the royal family to incorporate other families, as well as technical experts, within its ruling framework.

Political parties are still banned but some mechanisms of representation have emerged, adding an institutional veneer to a traditional regime. The Basic Law of 1992, an innovation in itself, introduced a Consultative Council, with a non-princely and technocratic membership, to 'advise the King on issues of importance'. The Council is a strengthened form of a body which dates back to 1927 – yet it remains, at most, a proto-parliament. Rulers also keep an eye on, and sometimes act upon, the issues raised on social media; Twitter as Consultative Council 2.

In Saudi Arabia, as elsewhere in the Middle East, ruling monarchies have proved to be resilient. In 2011, they survived the Arab Spring, though not without considerable protests in some kingdoms – notably, Bahrain. In contrast to regime-toppling rebellions elsewhere, few demonstrators in the Gulf explicitly sought political transformation. Many sought economic change (more jobs, less corruption) and political reform (widening the suffrage where representative institutions already existed), rather than abolition of the monarchy. A combination of some repression and tactical reforms, such as more hand-outs to the people, contained the protests. Times have become less certain but, so far, traditions of personal, paternalistic, and princely rule remain entrenched.

Ruling parties

Most authoritarian rulers are unconcerned with national transformation and, sometimes, even with economic development. The twentieth century, however, witnessed the birth, ossification, and disintegration of party-based dictatorships (communist, fascists, and nationalist) which monopolized public authority in the name of economic modernization, social transformation, and national revival.

The legacy of one-party rule, and especially communist party rule, remains significant. In this section, we will discuss ruling communist parties before turning to non-communist examples of party-based authoritarian rule.

Communist parties

The onset of communist party rule came with the 1917 October Revolution in Russia. This chaotic coup signalled the international advent of a regime, ideology, and revolutionary movement which sought to overthrow the capitalist democracies of the West. Until the decisive collapse of the communist order in the late 1980s and early 1990s, 23 regimes claiming Marxist inspiration ruled more than 1.5 billion people: about one in three of the world's population (Holmes, 1997, p. 4).

The communist legacy remains significant. So how should we characterize those authoritarian regimes which continue to sail under the communist banner? Reforming Cuba apart, the surviving communist party states are clustered in Asia, far from the democratic core. Even here, the North Korean tyranny is rationalized more by an idiosyncratic ideology of national self-reliance than by orthodox communist thought. However China, Vietnam, and Laos, though vastly different in size, do comprise a more coherent regional group (Box 4.2). These are traditionally poor, agricultural societies in which ruling communist parties have, from the 1970s and 1980s, loosened their direct control over the economy, while retaining a firm grip on political power.

This reform strategy has delivered substantial if uneven growth, most significant in China and Vietnam. By unleashing entrepreneurial initiative, ruling parties have averted the inertia which led to the fall of communism in the Soviet Union and Eastern Europe. As a result, Asian communist parties can still expound the nationalist agenda of catch-up with the West and, partly for this reason, their position remains intact and largely unchallenged.

China is the most importance case of Asian communism. From the beginning, communism in the People's Republic possessed distinct national characteristics. Power has certainly been exerted through the Chinese Communist Party (CCP) but the Party itself has been controlled by elite factions which have embraced nationalism. Park (1976, p. 148) goes so far as to judge that 'the success of Chinese communism lies primarily in its emphasis on nationalism'. Enhancing the country's autonomy and, subsequently, its international standing are core objectives.

Yet corruption, cronyism and cynicism remain endemic in the CCP. As a result of reform, China possesses not so much a market economy as a highly politicized economy in which not only party members, but also local bureaucrats and army officers, seek to advance themselves alongside more conventional entrepreneurs. Business people must focus not only on market opportunities, but also on creating strong ties to local officials that will provide access to those prospects. The inherent inefficiency of this corrupt system will become more damaging and visible as the economy becomes more developed.

China's reform ensemble has delivered partial industrialization, and may prove to be more successful than was the Soviet Union in meeting the demands of a more advanced economy and a more educated population. Even so, the party leaders in

Beijing face a long list of domestic challenges, including some that arise from economic development itself. These difficulties, sometimes ignored in simplistic accounts of China's rise, include:

- increasing inequality between regions and between individuals;

- inefficient allocation of capital;

- bad loans by banks;

- urban unemployment;

- environmental degradation;

- water shortages in parts of the country;

- massive population movements from the countryside;

- an unruly peasantry;

- an ageing population;

- poor social services (e.g. medical care) leading to excess savings;

- pervasive corruption;

- popular cynicism about the party;

- hostility of ethnic minorities (e.g. Tibetans, Uighurs) to Chinese rule;

- sustaining censorship in the Internet era.

BOX 4.2

Communist party states

	World Bank income group	Communist rule established	Comment
China	Upper-middle	1949	The Communist Party retains tight political control while leading substantial and successful economic reform.
Cuba	Upper-middle	1961	A military-backed regime, long dominated by Fidel Castro and now led by Raúl Castro, Fidel's younger brother. Raúl has initiated some reforms such as increasing opportunities for self-employment.
Laos	Lower-middle	1975	Laos's partly liberalized economy has grown significantly, albeit from a low base.
North Korea	Low	1948	A brutal totalitarian regime led by the Kim family for three generations. Strong military influence. The official ideology, *Juche*, stresses national independence and self-reliance.
Vietnam	Lower-middle	1976 (North Vietnam 1954)	As in China, the Communist Party has initiated economic reform while retaining a political monopoly

Note: Nepal's coalition governments have been led by Marxist parties since 2008 but the country is not a one-party communist state.

There can be no doubt that the party elite has shown exceptional skill in managing this formidable catalogue of problems. A combination of growth, propaganda, reform, and repression has forestalled mass public demands for democracy. In the absence of any indigenous democratic tradition, the nationalist narrative of China rising continues to resonate. China's very success in entering the world economy has established the world's dependence on its goods, reducing international pressures for democratization. Even though its Marxist legacy has faded, China continues to offer a model of development without democratization.

Other ruling parties

Occasionally, single ruling parties other than those that are communist provide the basis for authoritarian rule. As Huntington (1970, p. 9) pointed out, 'unless it can guarantee a low level of political mobilization, an authoritarian regime may have little choice but to organize and develop a political party as an essential structural support'.

An organized party is especially important in those authoritarian regimes permitting a measure of electoral competition; even a controlled election needs a party to control it. In Mexico, the Partido Revolucionario Institucional performed this election-winning role until the country's democratic transition in 2000. In Singapore, the People's Action Party continues to dominate elections.

Here, however, we must distinguish between the supports of power and power itself. Often, the party is the vehicle rather than the driver, with real authority resting with a dominant president, military ruler, or political elite. We find only a limited number of authoritarian regimes in which a single non-communist party sustains its position as an effective wielder of power. More often, the supposed ruling party is an arena within which more coherent actors compete.

Even when the single party does begin as an independent force, it can still be captured by a strong leader. In the Middle East, Iraq's Ba'ath party provides an example of this trajectory of decay. The Ba'ath began as a radical, secular, modernizing, pan-Arab party with a strong, cellular organization. It provided the framework within which Saddam Hussein rose to power. But, eventually, Saddam stamped his authority on the party, building what

became, in part, a personal despotism. His command was demonstrated at a party convention in 1979 when he read out the names of potential opponents and, as he did so, ordered each one to be taken out individually and shot. Those who remained applauded vigorously.

Until the Arab Spring, Egypt provided another example of the passive role which a dominant party plays in non-communist authoritarian regimes. The National Democratic Party (NDP) formed part of an established – indeed, ossified – structure of power based on a strong presidency and an extended bureaucracy. Within this framework, however, the NDP was the junior partner: 'the NDP has failed to serve as an effective means to recruit candidates into the elite. Rather, persons who are already successful tend to join the party in order to consolidate their positions' (Lesch, 2004, p. 600). With its close links to the state, the NDP was an arena for furthering political and business careers, but not a major policy-making force. Even so, its headquarters were destroyed during the Egyptian revolt of 2011 and the party itself was outlawed.

The Egyptian case thus confirms the value of distinguishing between actors and arenas. A 'dominant' party in an authoritarian state may simply be an arena within which particular elite groups express and perpetuate their control. When the elite goes, so does the party.

Ruling presidents

Many authoritarian leaders derive their power from a source external to the executive office: in a monarchy, the communist party, or even the ruler's own family. Even so, the office of president (or, less often, prime minister) can itself be the power base. Even if authority is founded elsewhere, a president in an authoritarian system occupies a unique position, possessing a visibility which can be invested in an attempt to transfer personal authority to an executive post, typically by establishing a direct relationship through the media with the people he rules. When the presidential office is itself the power base, we can speak of the presidential form of authoritarian rule.

In contrast to a personal despotism, the authority of a ruling presidency is based in a specific office which is likely to outlast its incumbent. This format is some-

COUNTRY PROFILE

CHINA

Form of government ■ communist party state.

Legislature ■ the large National People's Congress (almost 3,000 members chosen by provincial congresses and the armed forces) meets only for brief periods.

Executive ■ the State Council, headed by the premier, is the top executive body, supervising the work of the ministries. A president serves as ceremonial head of state.

Judiciary ■ rule through law has strengthened but the judicial system remains an underdeveloped branch of the administration.

Elections ■ elections have been introduced to many of China's villages since 1987 and, more recently and tentatively, to some townships. However, elected officials still operate under the party's supervision. Indirect election is usual at higher levels.

Parties ■ the Chinese Communist Party (CCP) remains the dominant political force.

Population (annual growth rate): 1,338 m (+0.47%)	
World Bank income group: upper middle	
Human development index (rank/out of): 101/187	
Political rights score: ⑦	
Civil liberties score: ⑥	
Media status: not free	

Note: For interpretation and sources, see p. xvi.

The **PEOPLE'S REPUBLIC OF CHINA** (PRC) has attracted considerable Western interest since its emergence at the start of the twenty-first century as a powerful force in the global economy. China's population is the world's largest. Its increasingly open economy has grown enormously since 1978 and, on an absolute basis, it is already the world's second largest; it may surpass that of the United States by 2050. The country is the world's largest exporter.

So, China has become a world economic force. It employs around one quarter of the world's workers, with particular strengths in manufacturing and assembly. Its international competitiveness has created an enormous trade surplus with the USA, allowing China to become the world's largest holder of US government bonds. Although the primary role of China's industry has been to serve as a low-

cost subcontractor to the West, increasing technological sophistication enables many of its producers to offer goods (if not services) of increased complexity and value. China's burgeoning industrialization has also required massive imports of raw materials, contributing to a global boom in commodity prices. Its policy-makers show little compunction in importing resources such as oil from other authoritarian regimes.

Furthermore, the country's entry into the World Trade Organization in 2001, followed by the tightly organized but successful Olympics in Beijing in 2008, demonstrated the country's more outward-facing character. In all these ways, the world has learned the wisdom of Napoleon's observation from 1803: 'China is a sickly, sleeping giant. But when she awakes the world will tremble' (Safire, 1993).

In understanding China, it is crucial to recognize its internal diversity. A destabilizing gulf exists between city and countryside; coastal zones and the underdeveloped interior; party and people; rich and poor; the corrupt and the honest; winners and losers. These inequalities have led to enormous population flows from rural areas to the cities, creating tensions within both importing and exporting regions.

Environmental problems apparent within the country itself include air pollution, water shortages, water pollution, deforestation, soil erosion, and desertification. These difficulties naturally create resentment in affected areas.

Thus far, China's cautious authoritarian rulers have ridden the country's transformation, and its effects, with both skill and difficulty. However, the political ramifications of these internal difficulties still remain to be established.

SPOTLIGHT

Authoritarian rule in China

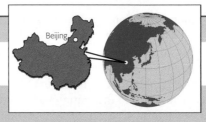

China's history differs fundamentally from both the United States, where limits on central power were built into the republic, and many Western European countries, where restraints on monarchical power were imposed gradually. China's political history is wholly non-democratic. Yet, unlike the Soviet Union, the Chinese Communist Party (CCP) succeeded in jettisoning orthodox communist policies without destroying its own hold on power. As Dickson (2007, p. 828) notes, 'China has become a prime example of how authoritarian governments can employ strategic action to survive indefinitely despite rapid economic development'. So, how has the trick been performed?

The party devotes considerable energy to maintaining its monopoly position. Even with around 80 million members, it remains an elite force, supervising the government, the justice system and the mass media. Belonging to the party involves a continuing commitment but, in exchange, membership provides access to the contacts, information, and patronage needed to acquire power and wealth. Even in the absence of ideology, ambition still glues the party together.

As governance has stabilized, so the party has become somewhat less intrusive and more supervisory. This revised role has allowed some expansion in the role of other institutions. For example, the National People's Congress remains weak but its leaders have acquired a role in supporting reform.

Similarly, the notion of a distinct legal sphere has begun to emerge. The immature judicial system still approves public executions but a measure of 'socialist legality' now prevails.

Even so, party members still occupy the key positions in all major political institutions, providing an additional mechanism of control. The media, in particular, remain tightly controlled, with many thousands of officials, supported by vigilant netizens, censoring Internet access for the world's largest body of users.

In the wider political system, the crucial reform has been the reduction of central control from Beijing. In local communities, informal networks of power-holders now determine 'who gets rich first' – a political market, rather than a free market. These collusive alliances are composed not only of well-placed men in the party, but also of officials in the bureaucracy, local government, and the army. Local officials provide favoured businesses (including their own) with contracts, land, sympathetic regulations, information, supplies, transport, and other subsidies.

Sources of legitimacy for communist party rule in China

Performance
    Central party leaders have delivered substantial economic growth

Leadership
    National party leaders are seen as wise, educated and benevolent

Nationalism
    The party is believed to be building a powerful and independent country

---

Source: Adapted from Bell (2012).

So, political and economic reform does not necessarily imply a shift towards a market economy operating within the rule of law. Reform empowers local elites to create a state-sponsored business class, whose members include public officials and party members. In this way, the newly rich remain dependent on the political system and do not seek its transformation.

The loosening of central political control has led to an explosion of corruption. In the new environment, public employees are quick to recognize opportunities to earn extra money from their official position: 'Li Gang paid 300,000 for his post but within two years netted five million. The return is 1500 per cent. Is there any other profession as profitable as this under heaven?' (an official from the Central Discipline Inspection Commission, quoted in McGregor, 2010, p. 70).

Here, perhaps, is one of the party's major dilemmas: it can only attract members by offering opportunities to acquire resources, but the dubious manner in which these are obtained increases the distance between party and society.

Like China itself, the party faces considerable challenges in the years ahead. Its prospects must depend on its ability to sustain strong economic growth and expand its international significance. Yet the possibility remains that achieving these goals will itself eventually initiate calls for a freer, and perhaps more democratic, China.

Further reading: Joseph (2010), McGregor (2010), Saich (2011).

what more institutional than a personal despotism, though still personified by the office-holder, and is better suited to larger and more complex societies.

Uzbekistan is a clear and significant case of the creeping centralization of power in the president's office. The largest of the central Asian republics, Uzbekistan formed part of the Soviet Union until the collapse of communism, becoming an independent state in 1991. The country's politics are dominated by Islam Karimov, a former first secretary of the Uzbek Communist Party. In effect, the establishment of Karimov's dictatorship in Uzbekistan was a coup against the party he once led. In 1994, Karimov resigned from the communist successor party, claiming that only a non-partisan head of state could guarantee constitutional stability. By this route, he instituted a gradual change in the nature of authoritarian rule in his country: from a party-based regime to a presidency-based regime.

To forestall opposition, Karimov regularly dismisses ministers and replaces regional leaders. He keeps tight control of the media, uses a traditional institution of local governance (the *mahalla*) as an instrument of social control, and also relies on the National Security Service for surveillance. As with other leaders of secular regimes in Islamic societies, Karimov has sought to prevent the mosque from becoming an explicit site of opposition, banning parties based on religion or ethnicity.

Although there are elements of personal despotism in Karimov's rule, his power is primarily based on the presidency. Melvin (2000, p. 34) provides a summary:

As a result of the political change since independence, a system of one-man rule has been established in Uzbekistan. The President enjoys extensive powers including appointments and he resides at the pinnacle of a system of executive power that runs throughout the country and effectively subordinates all aspects of political life to its elements. The President takes all major, and many minor, decisions.

Military rule

In the second half of the twentieth century, military government became an important form of authoritarian rule in Africa, Latin America, and parts of Asia. In most cases, the generals have now retreated to their barracks, and military coups have become rare. Today, we are more likely to speak of military influence on civilian governments rather than military rule as such. Even Burma's once repressive generals have embraced political reform, establishing a civilian government in 2011.

A **military coup d'état** (*putsch*) is a seizure of political power by the armed forces, or sections thereof. Although the term conjures up images of a violent and unwelcome capture of power against civilian rulers, many coups replaced one military regime with another, involved little loss of life, and were more or less invited by the previous rulers.

Most military coups occurred between the 1960s and 1980s, mainly in post-colonial countries where the state had failed to achieve substantial autonomy as a governing force. Sub-Saharan Africa was the major site, with 68 coups – including many counter-coups against existing military governments – between 1963 and 1987 (Magyar, 1992). Especially in smaller countries on the continent, military coups were possible precisely because the state remained simple and underdeveloped. An ambitious general just needed a few tanks, driven by a handful of discontented officers, to seize the presidential palace and begin broadcasting from the radio station.

The standard institutional form of a military regime was the *junta* (council), a small group made up of the leader of each branch of the armed forces. Within this structure, a strongman often emerged as a dominant figure. In Chile, for instance, following the coup of 1973, General Augusto Pinochet himself acted as chief executive within a classic four-man *junta* representing the army, navy, air force, and national police. He soon reinforced his dominance, becoming the country's president in 1974 and remaining in post until 1990.

Many military rulers take civilian posts in this way, merging military and political authority. Such transitions to a more civilian status may be real or purely for appearances; in either case, the armed forces usually remain a significant political actor.

Examining the role of the military in politics raises three main questions:

- Why did the armed forces enter government and then retreat from office?

- What is the legacy of military rule for today's civilian governments?

- What role does the military now play in authoritarian regimes?

First, why did military coups cluster between the 1960s and 1980s? The Cold War was of key significance. During this period, the United States and the Soviet Union were more concerned with the global chessboard than with how their client countries governed themselves. So, ruling generals could survive through the political, economic, and military backing of a superpower even though they lacked support in their own country.

As military governments prospered during the Cold War so, too, did they shrivel after its close. By the 1990s, ruling generals could no longer rely on their sponsoring superpower; instead, conditionality ruled the roost. Aid and technical assistance flowed to civilian regimes adopting democratic forms and offering at least some commitment to civil rights. The last Latin American generals were back in their quarters by 1993 (Figure 4.1), although many surviving African presidents – such as Blaise Compaoré in Burkina Faso – originally came to power via a *putsch*. In recent times, military coups have been rare and sometimes short-lived affairs in smaller countries; examples include Fiji (2006), and the West African states of Guinea (2008), Mauritania (2008), and Niger (2010).

Second, what is the legacy of military rule for civilian leaders? The inheritance is far from uniform, but many post-military regimes were characterized

by ugly birth defects which festered even as the new order matured.

The main problem was that long periods of army rule led to an interweaving of civilian and military power. In many Latin American countries, senior officers had become accustomed to such privileges as:

- guaranteed seats in the cabinet;

- a high level of military expenditure;

- sole control of the security agencies;

- personal profit from defence contracts;

- exemption from civilian justice;

- a formal role as guarantor of internal security.

The ending of military government did not eliminate these distortions. Indeed, some of these privileges had to be entrenched in new constitutions before military rulers could be persuaded to relinquish their occupancy of the state.

Chile illustrates the difficulties of full disengagement. Before returning power to civilians, General Pinochet ensured that a new constitution approved in 1980 secured military autonomy. The armed forces were granted exemption from prosecution in civilian courts, given guaranteed seats in the Senate, and retained their status as guarantors of 'institutional order' and 'national security'.

Such conditional transitions, characteristic of Latin America, helped the shift to, but weakened the depth of, the post-military democracy. As the era of military rule retreats into history, some of these con-

Figure 4.1 The ending of military rule in Latin America

Although the armed forces remain significant political actors in Latin America, military governments gave way to civilian administrations in the 1980s

ditions are being unwound but they undoubtedly left a difficult bequest for new democracies.

Third, what role does the military now play in authoritarian regimes? In most cases, it remains an important element in the civilian ruler's support base. For example, the stance of the military was decisive in determining the success of the Arab uprisings of 2011. Where the army remained loyal to the regime, as in Syria, the government could fight the disparate opposition. But where the military declined to repress protestors, as in Egypt, the regime fell.

So, the virtual disappearance of military rule does not signal the end of political influence by the armed forces. When new civilian rulers are unable to limit the generals to a professional military role, the armed forces will continue to dominate, supervise, or constrain the government, compromising its democratic credentials.

Theocracy

Its historical importance notwithstanding, government by religious leaders is now the rarest form of authoritarian rule. A religious society is one thing; a clerical government is quite another. Even Muslim countries typically separate religious and civil leadership within the context of an overall commitment to Islam. Indeed, in much of the Middle East the mosque has become a source of opposition to authoritarian rulers, a divide which would not be possible if religious and civil leadership belonged in the same hands.

At least since the end of Taliban rule in Afghanistan in 2001, the non-Arab Islamic Republic of Iran stands alone as an example of a constitutional **theocracy**. Even in Iran, rule by religious leaders (*ayatollah*s and *mullah*s) possesses limited legitimacy, especially among the young and educated. Public demonstrations in Iran disputing the result of the 2009 presidential election confirmed not only popular disaffection with the political system, but also divisions between reformers and hardliners within the ruling elite itself. However, further protests during the Arab Spring in 2011 were contained by a vigorous security response.

Iran's theocracy was a child of the 1979 revolution, the last great insurrection of the twentieth century.

Theocracy is government by religious leaders. Although most Islamic countries separate religious and political roles, the regime established in Iran after the overthrow of the Shah in 1979 is a recent example of a theocracy.

In this revolution, Ayatollah Khomeini, a 76-year-old cleric committed to Islamic fundamentalism, overthrew the pro-Western Shah of Iran. The revolutionaries advocated a traditional Islamic republic free from foreign domination; 'neither East nor West' was the slogan. In power, the *ayatollah*s created a unique Islamic state in which they governed directly, rather than under the oversight of secular rulers.

Iran's post-revolutionary constitution does incorporate a directly-elected presidency and assembly, so religious rule is indirect. Yet real power still lies with the clerics – expressed, in part, through a 12-member Council of Guardians which certifies that all legislation and candidates conform to Islamic law. In strictly enforcing traditional, male-dominated Islamic codes, the *ayatollah*s permeate society in a manner reminiscent of totalitarian regimes. The Interior Ministry still makes extensive use of informants, while the state employs arbitrary arrests as a form of control through terror.

As with many authoritarian regimes, Iran's rulers offer no clear direction on such practical matters as economic development, monetary policy, and overseas trade. Their nuclear programme and sponsorship of international terrorism attracts international sanctions. Unsurprisingly, therefore, economic growth has been limited, oil revenues notwithstanding. Instead, the clerics have grown wealthy by establishing *bonyad*s – tax-exempt 'charitable' trusts – for their own personal benefit. These foundations – and the public sector, generally – dominate an inefficient economy. Since Khomeini's death in 1989, Iran's theocratic establishment has consisted of competing factions of middle-aged to elderly men exploiting the revolutionary heritage in a successful effort to acquire and retain power and wealth. Neither a strong party nor a royal family exist to impose overall direction.

Unsurprisingly in a country where the median age was just 27 years in 2011 (ten years lower than in the USA), rule by this theocratic elite has intensified generational divisions. Well-educated young people, including many female graduates, chafe at the restrictions imposed by a hypocritical religious establishment. The young rely on the Internet, satellite television, and mobile phones to circumvent official censorship. This affirmation of freedom is not necessarily rooted in a secular outlook; rather, it reflects opposition to the cultural repression imposed by a religious leadership lacking a positive vision of the country's future (Gheissari, 2009).

Competitive authoritarian regimes

Our final category, the competitive authoritarian regime, is an authoritarian format mixed with democratic elements. As a blend, this type of government lacks the clarity of the other forms discussed in this chapter. Even so, competitive authoritarian regimes are probably the most common current form of non-democratic governance.

In a competitive authoritarian regime, the ruler – typically a president – is elected, but the contest is systematically biased towards the leading figure; for example, through manipulation of the media. Even if the count itself is honest, the ruler might still engage in ballot-stuffing if defeat were in the offing. Once elected, the government shows only a limited sense of constitutional restraint; such concepts as fair play, a loyal opposition, and individual rights barely register.

O'Donnell (1994, p. 59) describes the format well: 'whoever wins election to the presidency is thereby entitled to govern as he or she sees fit, constrained only by the hard facts of existing power relations and by a constitutionally limited term of office'.

In a competitive authoritarian system, unlike fully authoritarian regimes, electoral success forms a substantial part of the ruler's claim to authority. But election outcomes are conditioned by the ruler's influence over the media and by the use of state resources to favour his own organization. These factors exert influence long before the formal contest is under way, meaning that the campaign itself can appear free and fair.

The result is what Huntington (1991, p. 306) describes as 'democracy without turnover and competition without alternation'. Given that liberal democracy 'is a system in which parties lose elections' (Przeworski, 1991, p. 10), competitive authoritarianism is a system in which they do not. Rather,

change at the top usually results from a constitutional limit on tenure, or the occasional resignation.

Competitive authoritarian regimes are normally founded on a powerful leader, rather than strong institutions. Rather than serve as a representative agent, the president plays the part of personal ruler, taking care of the people's needs and claiming their respect, deference, and support in exchange. Having elected a saviour, the voters are expected to cheer from the stands, entering the political field at their own peril.

Because the judiciary is under-resourced, it is unable to enforce the individual rights documented in the constitution. The law is used selectively, as a tool of power. Political opponents are subject to detailed legal scrutiny but supporters find the law rarely intrudes on their activities: 'for my friends, everything; for my enemies, the law,' said Getúlio Vargas, President of Brazil, 1930–45, 1951–54. The state intervenes in the workings of the market, with political connections influencing economic rewards. Yet, in contrast to pure authoritarian regimes, the leader often does provide effective governance – thus earning, as well as manipulating, popular support.

These hybrid regimes are common in the world after the Cold War. Zakaria (2003, p. 61) notes that: 'since the fall of communism, countries round the world are being governed by regimes like Russia's that mix elections and authoritarianism'. Levitsky and Way (2010, p. 17) concur: 'Competitive authoritarianism is a post-Cold War phenomenon. Although a few competitive authoritarian regimes existed during the interwar and Cold War periods, they proliferated after the fall of the Berlin Wall.' Once communism collapsed, pressures from the West encouraged autocrats to adopt a democratic appearance, especially by holding multiparty elections, though full democratization was optional.

The form is particularly common in regimes with continuing poverty; with ethnic, religious, or economic divisions; and with real or constructed external threats. In these circumstances, a national father figure or dominant party can be presented as a protector against external threats, a bulwark against domestic disintegration, and as an engine of development. The head, it is claimed, must be allowed to rule the body politic.

For instance, many Latin American countries (including Venezuela) are characterized by extreme inequality, with the urban poor seeking salvation through a strong, populist leader. Asian regimes, such as Malaysia, combine an overriding commitment to further economic development with ethnic divisions between Chinese and Malays.

To the extent that competitive authoritarian regimes are personal in character, they might be expected to be unstable in the long run. Huntington (1991, p. 137), for example, claims 'this half-way house cannot stand'. Similarly, Levitsky and Way (2010, p. 20) note that such regimes are marked by an 'inherent tension' in which oppositions can develop a serious challenge to the existing power structure. These threats force rulers either to submit (and democratize), or to repress (and revert to cruder authoritarian rule).

Yet, we cannot wish these regimes out of existence by just deeming them to be transitional. Some (especially those far from Western zones of influence) have provided a stable method of governing poor and unequal societies, particularly since the end of communism rendered blatant dictatorship less defensible. Once set, a competitive authoritarian regime can be a strong amalgam, not least in Islamic settings where liberal democracy can be equated with Western permissiveness. For example, Crouch (1996, p. vii) shows how Malaysia's 'repressive-responsive' regime 'provides the foundation for a remarkably stable political order'. Similarly, Borón (1998, p. 43) argues that in the 'faulty democracies' of Latin America, democracy 'endures but does not consolidate'. When one strong leader departs, his regime may be replaced not by a liberal democracy but simply by another dominant leader.

Writing on sub-Saharan Africa, Herbst (2001, p. 359) judges that 'it is wrong to conclude that African states are travelling between democracy and authoritarianism simply because a majority of them belong to neither category. Rather, the current condition of African states could well prevail for decades.'

Such thinking led Case (1996, p. 464) to conclude that competitive authoritarianism is not 'a mere way station on the road to further democracy'. His prediction has proved to be sound; the number, though not the exact composition, of partly free countries in Freedom House ratings remained quite stable between 1993 and 2011.

Discussion questions

- Why are so many authoritarian regimes corrupt?

- Will China be a liberal democracy in (a) 10 years, (b) 25 years?

- 'Political power grows out of the barrel of a gun' (Mao Zedong). So, why are the armed forces not in charge everywhere?

- Would a world without dictators be a world without war?

- You can choose to be born again in authoritarian China (GDP per head $8400 in 2011: growth rate 9 per cent, about 13 per cent in poverty) or democratic India ($3700, 7 per cent growth, 25 per cent in poverty). Which country do you choose and what are the implications of your preference?

- What tests would you use to ascertain whether a regime is liberal democratic or competitive authoritarian?

Further reading

P. Brooker, *Non-Democratic Regimes: Theory, Government and Politics*, 2nd edn (2009). A comprehensive analysis of the main types of authoritarian regime.

N. Ezrow and E. Frantz, *Dictators and Dictatorships: Understanding Authoritarian Regimes and Their Leaders* (2011). A crisp summary of the academic literature on non-democratic governments.

S. Levitsky and L. Way, *Competitive Authoritarianism: Hybrid Regimes After the Cold War* (2010). A detailed account of the rise and diverging fate of competitive authoritarian regimes since 1990.

A. Saich, *Governance and Politics of China*, 3rd edn (2011). An informative guide to the world's most important authoritarian regime.

A. Schedler, ed., *Electoral Authoritarianism: The Dynamics of Unfree Competition* (2006). A collection of essays providing comparative analysis of competitive authoritarian regimes.

ONLINE RESOURCES AVAILABLE

Visit the companion website at **www.palgrave.com/politics/hague** to access additional learning resources, including multiple-choice questions, chapter summaries, web links and practice essay questions.

Chapter 5 **Theoretical approaches**

In this chapter, we introduce major theoretical approaches to the study of politics. The contemporary study of politics is marked by a variety of perspectives that developed at distinct stages in the discipline's history and which continue to be influential. By studying these approaches, we gain a sense of the different lenses through which politics can be viewed.

The focus of this chapter is academic perspectives on politics. So, although the chapter is logically positioned near the beginning of the book, in practice it may make more sense to read it after addressing later chapters. But, whatever the order, there should be a pay-off. If you can apply one or more of the perspectives we review to your own work, you will succeed in locating your project in the wider traditions of the discipline.

How should 'approaches' be defined? They are ways of understanding: 'sets of attitudes, understandings and practices that define a certain way of doing political science' (Marsh and Stoker, 2010a, p. 3). Approaches are schools of thought that influence how we go about political research, structuring the questions we ask, offering pointers on where we should search for an answer, and defining what counts as an adequate answer.

For example, in seeking to understand a political decision, are we aiming to describe how it was made or to explain why it was made? Should we begin by studying the people involved in the decision, the organizations they work for, or the wider political culture? Are we studying the decision for its own sake, or trying to use it to test some wider ideas about political decision-making? And should our answer be based on statistical data, or will qualitative sources suffice? Every study presupposes answers to these sorts of questions; the only issue is whether they are explicit or implicit.

This chapter examines five approaches: institutional, behavioural, structural, rational choice and interpretive. Our order of discussion broadly reflects the historical evolution of politics as an academic discipline though, for simplicity, we avoid the many subdivisions, crossovers and reinventions within each perspective (on which, see Lichbach and Zuckerman, 2009; Marsh and Stoker, 2010b).

We will suggest that the institutional approach continues to offer a natural route into the comparative study of government in liberal democracies; it remains the single most important perspective with which to become familiar. But the other frameworks provide additional purchase. The behavioural approach contributes useful findings, an increasing number of which are comparative, and many of these are introduced in Part II of this book. The structural approach provides a framework for comparing how political systems change over time. The rational choice and interpretive approaches, while still fundamental to political analysis, are less directly focused on comparative politics.

STUDYING . . .

THEORETICAL APPROACHES

- Theoretical approaches are ways of studying politics, aids in identifying what questions to ask and how to go about answering them.

- Adopting an explicit framework for a project such as a thesis is a challenging but valuable way of providing structure and originality, even if the subject matter itself has been examined before. Approaches are not right or wrong but more or less useful, depending on the topic and the researcher's skills and interests. But avoid pick and mix; a single framework will provide most focus.

- The institutional perspective has done most to shape the development of politics as a discipline and remains an important tradition in comparative politics.

- The behavioural approach examines politics at the level of the individual. Relying primarily on quantitative analysis of sample surveys, it contributes a growing range of findings to comparative politics.

- The structural approach, with its method of comparative history, interrogates the past to help understand contemporary outcomes. In this way, it helps to bridge politics and history (we can compare in the past as well as the present and also compare the present with the past).

- The rational choice approach, which seeks to explain political outcomes by reference to the goals and interests of the individuals involved, is a development of a perspective we naturally bring to political analysis.

- The interpretive approach, viewing politics as the ideas people construct about it in the course of their interaction, offers a fresh contrast to more mainstream approaches.

The institutional approach

The study of governing **institutions** is a central purpose of political science, in general, and of comparative politics, in particular. It provides the original foundation of the discipline and so creates a baseline against which other approaches have developed. An appreciation of institutions remains part of the tool kit of most political scientists.

> An **institution** is a formal organization, often with public status, whose members interact on the basis of the specific roles they perform within the organization. In politics, an institution typically refers to an organ of government mandated by the constitution.

An institutional approach is core to the discipline (and to this book), taking us to the area identifying politics as a distinct field of study. As Eulau (1963, p. 10) wrote:

If there is any subject matter at all that political scientists can claim exclusively for their own, a subject matter that does not require acquisition of the analytical tools of sister fields and that sustains their claim to autonomous existence, it is, of course, formal political structures.

Institutions are particularly important in liberal democracies, since they provide the framework within which decisions are reached. Any study of government and politics in a particular liberal democracy must surely cover institutions.

What is an institution? In politics, the term traditionally refers to the major organizations of national government, particularly those specified in the constitution such as the legislature, the judiciary, and the executive. Such entities often possess legal identity, acquiring privileges and duties under law; in that sense, they are treated as literal actors. Implicitly, an emphasis on institutions in political analysis affirms the origins of political studies in the examination of constitutions and the state.

However, the concept of an institution is also used more broadly to include other organizations which may have a less secure constitutional basis, such as the bureaucracy, local government, and political parties. As we move away from the heartland of constitutional structures, so the term 'organization' tends to supplant the word 'institution' (Scott, 2007).

But the term 'institution' is also used even more widely to denote any established and well-recognized political practice. For instance, scholars refer to the institutionalization of corruption in Russia, a usage implying that the abuse of public office for private gain there has become an accepted routine of political life – an institution – in its own right. This book is primarily concerned with formal institutions of government and we use words such as 'regime' or 'practices' to denote informal sets of rules. When the concept of an 'institution' is equated with any political or social practice, it risks over-extension (Rothstein, 1996).

Institutional analysis assumes that positions within organizations matter more than the people who occupy them. This axiom enables us to discuss roles, rather than people: presidencies rather than presidents, legislatures rather than legislators, the judiciary rather than judges. The capacity of institutions to affect the behaviour of their members means that politics, as other social sciences, is more than a branch of psychology.

The institutional approach offers two main reasons for supposing that organizations do, indeed, shape behaviour. First, because institutions provide benefits and opportunities, they shape the interests of their staff. As soon as an organization pays salaries, it possesses its own defence force. Employees acquire interests, such as defending their institution against outsiders and ensuring their own personal progress within the structure. March and Olsen (1984, p. 738) suggest that institutions become participants in the political struggle:

The bureaucratic agency, the legislative committee and the appellate court are arenas for contending social forces but they are also collections of standard operating procedures and structures that define and defend interests. They are political actors in their own right.

Second, sustained interaction among employees encourages the emergence of an institutional culture, or house view, which can weld the organization into an effective fighting unit. Institutions generate norms which, in turn, shape behaviour. One strength of the institutional approach is this capacity to account for the origins of interests and cultures, rather than just taking them for granted. As Zijderveld writes (2000, p. 70), 'institutions are coercive structures that mould our acting, thinking and feeling.'

In operation, institutions bring forth activity which takes place simply because it is expected, not because it has any deeper political motive. When a legislative committee holds hearings on a topic, it may be more concerned to do its job than to resolve the issue itself. The institutional approach, more than any other, suggests that much political action is best understood by reference to this **logic of appropriateness**, rather than to a **logic of consequences**.

> The **logic of appropriateness** refers to actions which members of an institution take to conform to its own norms. For example, a head of state will perform ceremonial duties because it is an official obligation. By contrast, the **logic of consequences** denotes instrumental behaviour directed at achieving a specific goal, whether self-interested or altruistic.

For instance, when a president visits an area devastated by floods, he is not necessarily seeking to direct relief operations, or even to increase his public support. He may just be doing what is expected in his job. In itself, the tour achieves the goal of meeting expectations arising from the actor's institutional position. 'Don't just do something, stand there', said Ronald Reagan, a president with a fine grasp of the logic of appropriateness. When an institution faces a requirement to act, its members are as likely to be heard asking 'What did we do the last time this happened?' as 'What is the right thing to do in this situation?' They seek a solution appropriate for the organization and its history.

This emphasis within the institutional framework on the symbolic or ritual aspect of political behaviour contrasts with the view of politicians and bureaucrats as rational, instrumental actors who define their own goals independently of the organization they represent. At the least, institutions provide the rules of the game within which individuals pursue their objectives (Shepsle, 2006).

Institutional analysis can be static, based on examining the functioning of, and relationships between, institutions at a given moment. But writers within this approach show increasing interest in institutional evolution and its effects. Institutions possess a history, culture and memory, frequently embodying traditions and founding values. In a process of **institutionalization**, they grow 'like coral reefs through slow accretion' (Sait, 1938, p. 18). In this way, many institutions thicken naturally over time, developing their internal procedures and also becoming accepted by external actors as part of the governing apparatus. In other words, the institution becomes a node in a network and, in so doing, entrenches its position.

> **Institutionalization** is defined by Huntington (1968) as 'the process by which organizations acquire value and stability' over time. An organization such as a legislature is institutionalized if it is clearly distinguished from its environment, possesses internal complexity, and follows clear rules of procedure.

As particular institutions come to provide an established and accepted way of working, they acquire resilience and persistence (Pierson, 2004). Many doubts will be expressed at a constitutional convention about the wisdom of adopting parliamentary government, but a generation later few will be found favouring a switch to a presidential system. So, as with constitutions, institutions are devices through which the past constrains the present. Thus, the study of institutions is the study of political stability, rather than change. As Orren and Skowronek (1995, p. 298) put it:

Institutions are seen as the pillars of order in politics, as the structures that lend the polity its integrity, facilitate its routine operation and produce continuity in the face of potentially destabilizing forces. Institutional politics is politics as usual, normal politics, or a politics in equilibrium.

Why are institutions so central to the functioning of liberal democracies? In addition to providing a settled framework for reaching decisions, they

enable long-term commitments which are more credible than those of any single employee, thus building trust. For example, governments can borrow money at lower rates than are available to individual civil servants. Similarly, a government can make credible promises to repay its debt over a period of generations, a commitment that is necessarily beyond the reach of any individual debtor.

Institutions also offer predictability. When we visit a government office, we do so with expectations about how the member of staff will behave, even though we know nothing about the individual employee. A shared institutional context eases the task of conducting business between strangers. So, in and beyond politics, institutions help to glue society together, extending the bounds of what would be possible for individuals acting alone.

An institutional approach, like all others, can become inward-looking. Two particular bounds should be highlighted. First, some institutions are explicitly created to resolve particular problems. We should perhaps focus more on these key historical moments which permit institutional creativity. Such periods, even though uncommon, enable us to view institutions as a product of, rather than just an influence on, political action by individuals.

Second, governing institutions rarely act independently of social forces, especially in poorer, simpler, and non-democratic countries. Sometimes, the president is the presidency and the entire superstructure of government is a facade behind which personal networks and exchanges continue to drive politics. In the extreme case of communist party states, for instance, the formal institutions of government were controlled by the ruling party. Government was the servant, not the master, and its institutions carried little independent weight.

Even in liberal democracies, it is always worth asking whose interests benefit from a particular institutional set-up. Just as an institution can be created for specific purposes, so too can it survive by serving the interests of the wealthy and powerful. For instance, the policy inertia inherent in Washington's separation of powers surely works to the advantage of those who benefit most from the existing structure of American society. In addressing the collective benefit institutions deliver, we should remember that the support of powerful interests in the wider society provides additional stability (Mahoney and Thelen, 2010, p. 8).

Overall, institutions must be seen as central to liberal democratic politics. The institutions of government are the apparatus through which political issues are shaped, processed, and sometimes resolved. They provide a major source of continuity and predictability. They shape the environment within which political actors operate and, to an extent, structure their interests, values, and preferences. The institutional approach offers no developed theory but does provide observations about institutional development and functioning which can anchor studies of specific cases.

The behavioural approach

In the 1960s, the favoured unit of analysis moved away from institutions and towards individual behaviour, particularly in American political science. The focus changed from electoral systems to voters, from legislatures to legislators, from presidencies to presidents. The central tenet of **behaviouralism** was that 'the root is man' (Eulau, 1963). This new programme invited us to study what people actually do, rather than constitutions, institutions and organization charts.

Behaviouralism was a school of thought in political science which emphasized the study of individuals, rather than institutions. The concern was not specific people but, rather, the individual as the level or unit of analysis; for example, members of parliament, rather than parliament itself. The aim was to use scientific methods to uncover generalizations about political attitudes and behaviour.

Labels notwithstanding, political behaviouralists certainly did not ignore attitudes and opinions. On the contrary, the study of elite opinion, and especially mass opinion, became an important dimension of their research. Rather than implying an exclusive concern with action, the word 'behaviour' expressed a focus on observable political reality, rather than official discourse; on individuals, rather than institutions; and on scientific explanation, rather than the loose descriptions of the institution-

alists. In these ways, behaviouralism offered a rallying cry for a new project (Farr, 1995).

Why did the agenda shift in this way? One influence was decolonization. In newly-independent countries, the institutions of government proved to be of little moment. Presidents, and then ruling generals, quickly dispensed with the elaborate constitutions written at independence. A fresher and wider approach – one rooted in social, economic and political realities, rather than constitutional fictions – was needed to understand politics in the developing world.

In the United States, furthermore, the post-war generation of political scientists was keen to apply innovative social science techniques developed during World War II – notably, interview-based sample surveys of ordinary people. In this way, the study of politics could be presented as a social science and be eligible for research funds made possible by that designation.

So, the study of assemblies, for instance, moved away from formal aspects (e.g. the procedures by which a bill becomes law) towards legislative behaviour (e.g. how members defined their job). Researchers investigated the social backgrounds of representatives, their individual voting records, their career progression, and their willingness to rebel against the party line.

Similarly, in the study of the judiciary scholars began to take judges, rather than courts, as their unit of analysis, using statistical techniques to assess how the social background and political attitudes of justices shaped their decisions and their interpretations of the constitution. As Clayton and Gillman (1999, p. 1) write, 'This level of inquiry tends to focus on the backgrounds, attitudes and ideological preferences of individual justices rather than on the nature of the Court as an institution and its significance for the political system.' In fact, the institutional setting was often just taken for granted.

Although the behavioural approach could encompass elites (Box 5.1), it earned its spurs in the study of ordinary people. Initially in the United States, and then in many other Western democracies, survey analysis yielded useful generalizations about voting behaviour, political participation and public opinion. Unlike institutional analysis of government, these studies located politics in its social setting – showing, for example, how race and class

BOX 5.1

Political behaviour in the White House: the person, not the post

In the study of political elites, Barber's *The Presidential Character: Predicting Performance in the White House* (1972) provided an influential example of the behavioural focus on individuals rather than institutions. Barber assumes that 'who the president is at a given time can make a profound difference in the whole thrust and direction of national politics'. Even superficial speculation, he suggests, 'confirms the commonsense view that the man himself weighs heavily among other historical factors' (1972, p. 3).

We can add that each president leaves his mark on the White House, so our assumptions about the office reflect the achievements (or lack of them) of its previous occupants. The office shapes the man but, over time, the men also shape the office.

Barber did not adopt the quantitative approach of most behavioural research: he treated his subjects as individuals, rather than as collections of variables. Nonetheless, his qualitative analysis was informed by a desire to understand, explain and even predict, rather than merely to describe. He examined personality but with the goal of understanding behaviour.

Specifically, Barber argued that the key differences in presidential behaviour can be predicted in advance of new incumbents taking office. Two dimensions, he suggested, are key. The first is how much energy a president invests in his work, leading to a distinction between active and passive types. The second is whether a president experiences political life as enjoyable or draining - a distinction between positive and negative presidents. Cross-classifying these factors generates a four-fold classification of presidents: active-positive, active-negative, passive-positive and passive-negative.

Barber's classification of American presidents

	Active	Passive
Positive	e.g. John Kennedy	e.g. Ronald Reagan
Negative	e.g. Richard Nixon	e.g. Dwight Eisenhower

Barber then applied his scheme to individual presidents. John Kennedy exemplified the confident active-positive: 'This is a damned good job,' said Kennedy of his office. Richard Nixon – one of Barber's most successful predictions – was the dangerous active-negative: 'he very nearly got away with establishing a presidential tyranny', claims Barber. Ronald Reagan is the genial passive-positive; as he famously said, 'It's true hard work never killed anybody, but I figure, why take the chance?" And Dwight Eisenhower is the rare passive-negative; 'a sucker for duty'.

The Presidential Character exemplifies the application of an individual-level approach to the study of elites. It examines how presidents behave in office, demonstrating that understanding politics in the White House requires more than an account of the presidency as an institution.

impinged on whether, how, and to what extent people took part in politics. In this way, the behavioural revolution broadened our outlook.

The behavioural approach constructed the research foundation for several chapters in this book. In its own terms, behaviouralism delivered: 'there are few areas in political science where schol-

arly knowledge has made greater progress in the past two generations', claim Dalton and Klingemann (2007, p. vii). Yet, as a model for the entire discipline, the behavioural revolution eventually ran its course. Its focus on individual political behaviour took the study of politics away from its natural concern with the institutions of government. Its methods became progressively more technical and its findings progressively more specialized.

Behaviouralism produced a political science with too much science and too little politics. Amid the political protests of the late 1960s, behaviouralists were criticized for fiddling while Rome burned. Rather like the institutional approach before it, behaviouralism seemed unable to address current political events. The strategy of developing generalizations applying across space and time was ill-suited to capturing the politics of any particular moment. In short, the research programme had become orthodox, rather than progressive; it was time for something new.

The structural approach

In political analysis, the **structural approach** has served, in part, as a corrective to the limitations of individual-level analysis. In downplaying the individual, structuralists resemble institutionalists. However, the notion of structure is much broader, and possibly deeper, than that of an institution. The starting point, then, is to grasp what is meant by the term 'structure'.

In politics, a **structural approach** emphasizes the objective relationships between social groups, including social classes and the state. The varying interests and positions of these leading groups shape the overall configuration of power and provide the dynamic of political change.

The dictionary defines a structure as 'the construction of a whole; its supporting framework'. Political structuralists follow this definition by focusing on the relationships between powerful groups in society, such as the bureaucracy, political parties, social classes, churches and the military. These groups possess and pursue their own interests, creating a set of relationships which forms the structure underpinning or destabilizing the institutional politics of parties and government. It is this framework which undergirds, and ultimately determines, actual politics. So, the approach is sociological, always giving due weight to class interests but, unlike much Marxism, extending its concern to non-economic groups such as the bureaucracy.

Each group within the structure seeks to sustain its political influence in a society which is always developing in response to economic change, ideological innovations, international politics and the effects of group conflict itself. Because the context and configuration of interests is always evolving, structuralists embrace change more easily than institutionalists.

A structure is defined by the relationships between its parts. The elements themselves, their internal organization and especially the individuals within them, are of little interest. For instance, what matters to the structuralist is the relationship between labour and capital in a society, not the internal organization of trade unions and business organizations. The individual leaders of such entities are of even less concern; the assumption is that 'social actors' such as capital and labour will follow their own real interests, irrespective of who happens to lead organizations formally representing their concerns.

Here, we see the contrast with the behavioural approach. As Skocpol (1979, p. 291) put it, structuralists 'emphasize objective relationships and conflicts among variously situated groups and nations, rather than the interests, outlooks, or ideologies of particular actors'. Individuals are seen as a product of, rather than prior to, their social location; they are secondary to the grand political drama unfolding around them (Box 5.2).

But 'real interests' and 'social actors' are, of course, terms imposed by the researcher. Who is to say where a group's true interests lie? How can we refer to the 'actions' of a group, rather than a person? In execution, the structural approach is broad-brush, making large if plausible assumptions about the nature of conflict in a particular society and using them to make inferences about causes without always paying great attention to the detailed historical record.

We can draw a clear contrast between structural and cultural analysis (Chapter 6). The structural perspective regards culture as a factor of little independent significance. For instance, a structural explanation of poverty would emphasize the contrasting interests and power positions of property-owners and the working-class, By contrast, a cultural explanation would place more weight on the values of poor people themselves, showing how, for

BOX 5.2

The structural approach: Skocpol on revolutions

Skocpol's account of the French, Russian, and Chinese revolutions (1979) offered an influential example of the structural approach, focused as it is not on individuals but, rather, on relationships between classes and states. Before her study, much research on revolutions had employed a behavioural perspective, seeking to understand the conditions under which people come to see themselves as deprived (Gurr, 1980). Skocpol, however, was keen to distinguish her structural approach from one focused on the perceptions of the masses and the motives of political leaders:

> The fact is that historically no successful revolution has ever been 'made' by a mass-mobilizing, avowedly revolutionary movement … As far as the causes of historical social revolutions are concerned, Wendell Phillips was quite correct when he once declared: 'Revolutions are not made; they come'. (1979, p. 17)

She quoted with approval (1979, p. 18) the structuralist observation of Hobsbawm: 'The evident importance of the actors in the drama … does not mean that they are also dramatist, producer and stage-designer'. Skocpol regarded structural conditions – the relationships between groups within a state and, equally important, between states – as fundamental to the arrival of the classic revolutions.

Specifically, she judged that regimes which were internationally weak and domestically ineffective became vulnerable to insurrection when well-organized agitators succeeded in exploiting peasant frustration with an old order to which the landed aristocracy offered only limited support.

Like other structuralists, but in contrast to traditional Marxists, Skocpol viewed the state – in its strength or its weakness – as a major factor in the overall array of forces:

> We can make sense of social-revolutionary transformations only if we take the state seriously as a macro-structure. The state properly conceived is no mere arena in which socioeconomic struggles are fought out. It is, rather, a set of administrative, policing, and military organizations headed, and more or less supported by, an executive authority. (1979, p. 29)

Skocpol's statement of her approach to revolutions provided an influential declaration of the structuralist perspective:

> One must be able to identify the objectively conditioned and complex intermeshing of the various actions of the diversely situated groups – an intermeshing that shapes the revolutionary process and gives rise to the new regime … To take such an impersonal and nonsubjective viewpoint – one that emphasizes patterns of relationships among groups and societies – is to work from what may in some generic sense be called a structural perspective on sociohistorical reality. (1979, p. 18)

Nearly 25 years later, Skocpol could look back approvingly at the achievements of the structural approach and its method of comparative historical analysis:

> Comparative historical analysis has certainly come of age over the past quarter century. By now, comparative historical analysis has claimed its proud place as one of the most fruitful research approaches in modern social science, side by side with behavioralism, rational choice and interpretive genres. (2003, p. 424)

example, limited aspirations trap the poor in a cycle of poverty that can persist across generations. For the structuralist, the important factor is social structure – specifically, the framework of inequality – not the values that confine particular families to the bottom of the hierarchy. This point, and the overall thrust of structuralism, is well-summarized by Mahoney (2003, p. 51):

At the core of structuralism is the concern with objective relationships between groups and societies. Structuralism holds that configurations of social relations shape, constrain and empower actors in predictable ways. Structuralism generally downplays or rejects cultural and value-based explanations of social phenomena. Likewise, structuralism opposes approaches that explain social outcomes solely or primarily in terms of psychological states, individual decision-making processes, or other individual-level characteristics.

The best-known structural work in politics has adopted an explicitly historical style, seeking to understand how competition between powerful groups leads to specific outcomes such as a revolution, a liberal democracy or a multiparty system. The authors of such studies recognize that, in reality, politics is struggle, rather than equilibrium. The method is comparative history, giving us another contrast with the non-historical generalizations favoured by behaviouralists and the sometimes static descriptions of the institutionalists. If an approach is known by its methods, structuralism can be seen as broad-scale comparative history.

The work which did most to shape this format of historical analysis of structural forces was Barrington Moore's *Social Origins of Dictatorship and Democracy: Lord and Peasant in the Making of the Modern World* (1966). The goal here was to understand why liberal democracy developed earlier and more easily in France, England, and the United States than in Germany and Japan. Barrington Moore suggested that the strategy of the rising commercial class was the key factor. Where the bourgeoisie avoided entanglement with the landowners in their battles with the peasants, as in the United Kingdom, the democratic transition was relatively peaceful. But where landlords engaged the commercial classes in a joint campaign against the peasantry, as in Germany, the result was an authoritarian regime which delayed the onset of democracy.

Although later research qualified many of Barrington Moore's judgements, his study demonstrated the value of studying structural relationships between groups and classes as they evolve over long periods (Mahoney, 2003). He asked important comparative questions and answered them with an account of how and when class relationships develop and evolve. Not only does Barrington Moore exemplify the structural approach, he helped to define it.

The structural approach has led to, and emerged strengthened from, wide-ranging historical studies such as Barrington Moore's and Skocpol's. It is an approach which has built on its Marxist foundations without confining itself to class analysis. It asks big questions and, by selecting answers from the past, it interrogates history without limiting itself to chronology. Many authors working in this tradition do make large claims about the positions adopted by particular classes and groups; specifically, interests are often treated as if they were actors, leading to ambitious generalizations which need verification through detailed research. Even so, the structural approach, in the form of comparative history, has made a distinctive contribution to comparative politics.

The rational choice approach

The rational choice approach stands in sharp contrast to structural analysis. It focuses on individuals, rather than social groups, modelling how people make choices. Where the structural perspective is rooted in historical sociology, the rational choice approach springs from ahistorical economics.

The starting point is often **methodological individualism**: the principle that explanations in politics must be found in the preferences and behaviour of individuals. The existence and functioning of larger units – institutions, governments, classes, and states – must, it is argued, finally be understood as the collective outcome of individuals pursuing their own interests. Even though individuals typically confront organizations they played no part in creating, such entities will change if they serve no one's interests (and everyone can agree on a replacement).

As stated by Elster (1989, p. 13), **methodological individualism** is the principle that 'the elementary unit of social life is individual human action. To explain social institutions and social change is to show how they arise as the result of the actions and interaction of individuals'.

Riker (1990, p. 171) added that consistent generalizations in the social sciences are only possible when 'the central propositions are about individuals'. 'Society, not being human, cannot have preferences', wrote Riker and Ordeshook (1973, p. 78). This determination to seek explanations of political out-

BOX 5.3

The limits of rationality: groupthink

Friedrich Nietzsche claimed that madness is the exception among individuals but the rule in groups. Janis's work (1982) on groupthink offers support to the latter part of Nietzsche's proposition, thereby encouraging us to recognize the limits of applying individual-level rational choice models to groups.

For Janis, groupthink emerges when a team's concern with maintaining internal harmony overrides its motivation to execute a realistic appraisal of alternative courses of action. The result is decisions inferior to those the group's members would have made if acting alone. This syndrome is most likely to emerge when:

- the group is under stress;
- the group is isolated from the rest of the organization;
- the group's members share a similar background and ideology.

In such conditions, the group stereotypes the opposition, becomes convinced of its own invulnerability and loses its capacity to assess risk. Later research confirmed that, even in typical conditions, group discussion tends to strengthen the predominant opinion among the members, leading to a shift to riskier decisions (Rothwell, 1986).

Groupthink is not just an academic label; it can lead to policy fiascos. Janis cites failures under five American presidents:

- Franklin Roosevelt: Pearl Harbor, 1941;
- Harry Truman: the invasion of North Korea, 1950;
- John Kennedy: the Bay of Pigs invasion, 1961;
- Lyndon Johnson: the escalation of the Vietnam War, 1964–67;
- Richard Nixon: the Watergate cover-up, 1972–74.

But these cases are well-known partly because they are exceptional. In any event, groupthink is far from inevitable even when conditions are ripe. During the Cuban missile crisis, for instance, many of the same policy-makers involved in the Bay of Pigs failure engaged in more honest and successful deliberation. Several improvements were apparent in decision-making during the missile crisis:

- Group members were charged with looking at the problem as a whole, leading to sharp discussion of all proposals;
- New members were brought in as appropriate, allowing different viewpoints to emerge;
- The president sometimes absented himself from meetings, to encourage an uninhibited debate.

Rationality in groups can be achieved, it seems, but it has to be worked at in order to overcome the negative aspects of group dynamics.

comes in individual interests and preferences provides a stark contrast with both institutional and structural approaches.

So, rational choice analysis returns us to individuals, albeit of the abstract, calculating kind found in economics. The distinctive feature of this framework is that politics is conceived as consisting of strategic interaction between individuals, with all players seeking to maximize the achievement of their own particular goals. Where behaviouralists aim to explain political action through statistical generalization, the rational choice approach focuses solely on the interests of the actors. The assumption is that people can appraise the alternatives available to them in any specific situation and can consistently choose the option that ranks highest in their order of preference.

The potential value of rational choice analysis lies in its ability to model the essentials of political action, and hence make predictions, without all-encompassing knowledge of the actors. We simply need to identify the actors' goals and how their objectives can best be advanced in a given situation. Then, we can predict what they will do. All else, including the accounts actors give of their own behaviour, is detail. The aim is to model the fundamentals of human interaction, not to provide a rich account of human motives.

Neither are rational choice analysts concerned to provide an accurate account of the mental process leading to decisions; the test is whether behaviour is correctly predicted. The underlying philosophy – that explanation is best sought in models that are both simple and fundamental – is a distinctive feature of the approach, reflecting its origins in economics. More than any other approach, the rational choice approach values parsimonious explanations – that is, those invoking as few factors as possible. To appreciate the style of rational choice thinking, it is crucial to recognize how simplifying assumptions can be seen as a strength in building models and generating predictions.

What goals can people pursue within the rational choice framework? Most analysts adopt the axiom of self-interest. As stated by John Calhoun in his *Disquisition on Government* (1851), the assumption is that each person 'has a greater regard for his own safety or happiness, than for the safety or happiness of others: and, where they come into opposition, is ready to sacrifice the interests of others to his own.'

At the cost of increased complexity, we can broaden the range of permitted goals. We can imagine that people take satisfaction in seeing others achieve their ends, or we can even permit our subjects to pursue altruistic projects. Yet, just as markets are best analyzed by assuming self-interest among the participants, so too do most rational choice advocates believe that the same assumption takes us to the essence of politics. It is rationality and self-interest in combination that facilitate prediction: 'if people are rational and self-interested it becomes possible to explain and even predict their actions in ways that would allow rational choice theorists to claim a mantle of scientific credibility' (Hindmoor, 2010, p. 42).

Rational choices are not necessarily all-knowing. Operating in an uncertain world, people need to discount the value of going for a goal by the risk they will fail to achieve it. In situations of uncertainty,

they may prefer to eliminate the risk of a bad outcome, rather than go for broke by staking all on a single bet. Thus, a rational choice needs to be distinguished from a knowledgeable one.

Consider, for instance, the task of working out for which party to vote. As voters, we might well find that the effort of full research on all the candidates exceeds the benefit gained, leading to shortcuts such as relying on expert opinion. It is not always rational to be fully informed, a fact that brings the approach closer to the real world. However, the full rational model – the version which allows us to predict most easily – takes actors to be knowledgeable, as well as rational and self-interested.

In the study of politics, the rational choice framework is often extended from the individual to the larger units that are the comparativist's stock in trade. Rational choice analysts sometimes apply their techniques to bodies such as parties and interest groups, treating them as if they were individuals.

In his analysis of political parties, for example, Downs (1957, p. 28) imagined that all party members 'act solely in order to attain the income, prestige, and power which come from being in office'. For ease of analysis, he treated parties as if they were unitary actors, in the same way that students of international politics often regard states. In both cases, the aim is accurate prediction, not a detailed reconstruction of the actual decision process. These 'as if' accounts of parties and states depart from the principle of methodological individualism, but do so in search of the simplicity and predictions which are highly prized within the rational choice approach.

A major contribution of the approach lies in highlighting **collective action** problems. These difficulties arise in coordinating the actions of individuals so as to achieve the best outcome for each person. For instance, many people persist with a polluting lifestyle, aware that their own behaviour will make no decisive difference to overall environmental quality. Yet, the outcome from everyone behaving in this way is climate change damaging to all. Individual rationality leads to a poor collective result.

Similarly, in the financial crisis of 2008–09, many investment bankers took on highly risky investments to increase their bonuses; their employers, too, were happy enough as long as their firms' profits carried on increasing. When these investments eventually turned bad, the effect was a problem not only for the original investors, but also – and more importantly – a threat to an important **public good**: the stability of the Western financial system. Some form of coordination is needed, if private actions are to be rendered compatible with a desirable collective outcome – for example, stricter regulation of banks by governments. More than any other framework, the rational choice approach encourages to us to recognize that individual preferences and collective outcomes are two different things; a government is needed to bridge the gap.

> **Collective action** problems arise when rational behaviour by each person produces an outcome which is suboptimal overall. The issue typically arises when people seek to free ride on the efforts of others in providing **public goods** – those which cannot be restricted to those who contribute to their provision. For example, the benefits of clean air, lighthouses, national defence, and public statues cannot be restricted to those willing to pay for them.

Paradoxically, the rational choice approach can be useful even when it is inaccurate. Its value lies not merely in the accuracy of its predictions, but also in identifying what appears to be irrational behaviour. If people behave in a surprising way, we have identified a puzzle in need of a solution. Perhaps we have misunderstood their preferences, or the situation confronting them. Or perhaps their actions really are irrational.

When we do fully understand how a politician seeks to gain from a particular action, our mind comes to rest. We have our explanation, an account rooted in a simple but plausible assumption about why we do what we do. In that sense, the rational choice approach is an indispensable device, advising us not only on how to go about our research, but also on when it is complete.

Yet the approach, as any other, does take rather too much for granted. It fails to explain the origins of the goals that individuals hold; it is surely here, in understanding the shaping of preferences, that society re-enters the equation. Our aspirations, our status, and even our goals emerge from our interactions with others, rather than being formed beforehand. Certainly, we cannot take people's goals and values as given.

Also, since the rational choice approach is based on a universal model of human behaviour, it possesses limited relevance in understanding variation across countries. Just as individual goals are taken for granted, so too are the varying national settings which set the choices available to individuals and within which they pursue their strategies. Guy Peters (2011, p. 42) makes the point: 'By positing common motivations for behaviour, rational choice adds less to comparative politics than to other parts of the discipline of political science.' He continues:

Comparative politics tends to be more concerned with differences among political systems than with similarities ... If, however, everyone is behaving in the same way then important differences in comparative politics such as political culture, individual leadership, ideologies and a host of others become irrelevant.

Finally, it is worth noting three areas where deviations from rationality may be systematic:

- As individuals, we must temper our rationality with the need to maintain a positive self-image. A rational analysis of the situation may take second place to the psychological requirement to see ourselves in a good light.

- Not all action is instrumental; we are not just goal-achievers and we can value behaviour for itself. By definition, spontaneity can never be planned.

- Groups sometimes make decisions which are more polarized, and less rational, than those which would have been taken by their individual members (Box 5.3).

Yet, we naturally assume that such cases are exceptional. The belief that people are fundamentally rational is one to which we are psychologically committed – perhaps beyond all reason. The rational choice approach does not always generate accurate predictions but, even so, it provides one lens, among several, for analyzing political processes.

The interpretive approach

The final framework we will address is the **interpretive approach**. The distinctive focus of this mode of analysis is the ideas and interpretations – the assumptions, codes, constructions, identities, meanings, narratives, and values – within which politics operates. This approach takes us away from the behaviouralists' search for scientific laws towards a concern with the ideas of individuals and groups, and how their constructs define and shape political activity. The starting-point is that we cannot take the actor's goals and definition of the situation for granted, as the rational actor approach does; the way those goals and definitions are constructed is, itself, the very stuff of politics.

> The **interpretive approach** assumes '(1) that the structures of human association are determined primarily by shared ideas rather than material forces, and (2) that the identities and interests of purposive actors are constructed by these shared ideas rather than given by nature' (Wendt, 1999, p. 1).

In its strongest version, the interpretive position holds that politics consists of the ideas participants hold about it. There is no political reality separate from our mental constructions, no reality which can be examined to reveal the impact of ideas upon it. Rather, politics is formed by ideas themselves. There is nothing but ideas.

In a more restrained version, the argument is not that ideas comprise our political world but, rather, that they are an independent influence upon it, shaping how we define our interests, our goals, our allies, and our enemies. We act as we do because of how we view the world; if our perspective differed, so would our actions. Where rational choice focuses on how people go about achieving their individual objectives, the interpretivist examines the framing of objectives themselves and regards such interpretations as a property of the group, rather than the individual (hence the interpretive mode is a social approach, rather than a psychological approach).

Because ideas are socially constructed, many interpretivists imagine that we can restructure our view of the world and, so, the world itself. For instance, there is no intrinsic reason why individuals and states must act (as rational choice theorists imagine)

in pursuit of their own narrow self-interests. To make such an assumption is to project concepts onto a world that we falsely imagine to be independent of our thoughts. Finnemore (1996, p. 2), for example, suggests that 'Interests are not just "out there" waiting to be discovered; they are constructed through social interaction.' Also, ideas come before material factors because the value placed on material things is itself an idea (Marxism dismissed, we might object, in one sentence flat).

For example, states are often presented as entities existing independently of our thoughts. But the state is not a physical entity such as a lake or a mountain; it is an idea built over a long period by political thinkers, as well as by practical politicians. Borders between blocs of land were placed there not by nature but by people. There are no states when the world is viewed from outer space, as astronauts frequently tell us. Or, more accurately, the maps construct their own reality. It is this point Steinberger (2004) has in mind when he says that his idea of the state is that the state is an idea. True, the consequences of states, such as taxes and wars, are real enough, but these are the effects of the world we have made – and can remake.

Similarly, the class relationships emphasized by the structuralists, and the generalizations uncovered by the behaviouralists, are based not on physical realities but, rather, on interpretations that can, in principle, be changed. For instance, a behavioural observation about women's under-representation in legislatures can generate a campaign that leads to increased female participation, thus altering the observation itself.

For this reason, interpretivists often focus on historical narratives, examining how understandings of earlier events influence later ones. Take the study of revolutions as an example. Where behaviouralists see a set of cases (French, Russian, and so on) and seek common causes of events treated as independent, interpretivists perceive a single sequence and ask how later examples (such as the Russian revolution) were influenced by the ideas then held about earlier revolutions (the French). Alternatively, take the study of elections. The meaning of an election is not given by the results themselves but by the narrative the political class later establishes about it: 'the results showed that voters will not tolerate high unemployment' (see Chapter 11).

Parsons (2010, p. 80) provides a useful definition of the interpretive approach:

People do one thing and not another due to the presence of certain 'social constructs': ideas, beliefs, norms, identities or some other interpretive filter through which people perceive the world. We inhabit 'a world of our making' (Onuf, 1989) and action is structured by the meanings that particular groups of people develop to interpret and organise their identities, relationships and environment.

The interpretive approach sees the task of explanation as that of identifying the meaning which itself helps to define action. The starting point is not behaviour but action – that is, meaningful behaviour. Geertz (1973, p. 5) judges that, since we are suspended in webs of meaning that we ourselves have spun, the academic study of social and political affairs cannot be a behavioural science seeking laws but, rather, must be an interpretive one seeking meaning. Wendt (1999, p. 105) further illustrates this notion of explanation through meaning:

If we want to explain how a master can sell his slave then we need to invoke the structure of shared understandings existing between master and slave, and in the wider society, that makes this ability to sell people possible. This social structure does not merely describe the rights of the master; it explains them, since without it those rights by definition could not exist.

In politics, as in other disciplines concerned with groups, most interpretivists consider how the meanings of behaviour form, reflect, and sustain the traditions and discourses of a social group or an entire society. The concern is social constructs, rather than just the specific ideas of leaders and elite groups as studied by Valentino (Box 5.4). For example, by acting in a world of states – by, say, applying for passports, supporting national sports teams or just using the word 'citizen', we routinely reinforce the concept of the state. By practising statehood in these ways, as much as by direct influence through education and the media, the idea itself is socially reinforced or, as is often said, 'socially constructed'. Further, these understandings can also be socially contested – 'Why should I need

a visa each time I visit this country?', leading to gradual changes in the ideas themselves.

There is a clear and useful lesson here for students of politics, and of comparative politics especially. When we confront a political system for the first time, our initial task is to engage in political anthropology: to make sense of the activities that comprise the system. What are the moves? What do they mean? What is the context that provides this meaning? And what identities and values underpin political action? Behaviour which has one meaning in our home country may possess a different significance, and constitute a different action, elsewhere. For example, offering a bribe may be accepted as normal in one place, but be regarded as a serious offence in another. Casting a vote may be an act of choice in a democracy, but of subservience in a dictatorship. Criticizing the president may be routine in one country, but sedition in another. Because the consequences of these acts vary, so does their meaning.

So far, so good. Yet, in studying politics we want to identify patterns that abstract from detail; we seek general statements about presidential, electoral, or party systems which go beyond the facts of a particular case. We want, further, to examine relationships between such categories so as to discover overall associations. We want to know, for instance, whether a plurality electoral system always leads to a two-party system. Through such investigations we can acquire knowledge which goes beyond the understandings held by the participants in a particular case.

We must recognize, also, that events have unintended consequences: the Holocaust was certainly a product of Hitler's ideas, but its effects ran far beyond the Führer's own intentions. With its emphasis on meaning, an interpretive approach misses the commonplace observation that much social and political analysis studies the unintended consequences of human activity.

In short, unpacking the meaning of political action is best regarded as the start, but not the end, of political analysis. It provides a practical piece of advice: we must grasp the meaning of political behaviour, thus enabling us to compare like with like. Yet, it would surely be unsatisfactory to regard a project as complete at this preliminary point.

Compared with the other approaches reviewed in this chapter, the interpretive approach remains more aspiration than achievement. Some studies

BOX 5.4

Ideas and politics: Valentino on mass killing and genocide

As an example of the independent impact of ideas in politics, consider Valentino's prize-winning study of mass killing and genocide in the twentieth century. Valentino suggests that the mass murder of civilians is a product of the ideas of the instigators: 'Mass killing is an instrumental policy designed to accomplish leaders' most important ideological and political objectives' (2004, p. 67). Valentino is a student of elite ideas, which he takes to encompass both goals and assessments of how to achieve them; he is less concerned with structural relationships or government institutions:

> To identify societies at high risk for mass killing, we must first understand the specific goals, ideas and beliefs of powerful groups and leaders, not necessarily the broad social structures or systems of government over which these leaders preside. (p. 66)

Specifically, Valentino contends that 'mass killing occurs when powerful groups come to believe it is the best available means to accomplish certain radical goals, counter specific types of threat or solve difficult military problems' (p. 66).

Unlike rational choice thinkers, Valentino does not assume that politicians are accurate in their perceptions of their environment. Their understandings are what matter, even if these are misunderstandings:

> An understanding of mass killing does not imply that perpetrators always evaluate objectively the problems they face in their environment, nor that they accurately assess the ability of mass killings to resolve these problems. Human beings act on the basis of their subjective perceptions and beliefs, not objective results. (p. 67)

But it is not just ideas and perceptions that are Valentino's concern. Rather, he examines how leaders are driven by actual and perceived changes in the political environment to regard mass killing as the final solution for achieving their ends. Thus, his approach is not purely interpretive but, instead, consists of a fruitful examination of the interaction over time between political realities, on the one hand, and elite ideas and perceptions, on the other.

Valentino carries through his interest in ideas to a consideration of how we can best prevent future occurrences of mass killing. He rejects the relevance of behavioural and structural generalizations suggesting that mass killings only occur in dictatorships or war. Rather, he suggests that leaders in any type of structure or political system may come to see mass killing as the best, most effective or sole method of achieving their goals. Effective prevention therefore requires us to return once more to leaders' ideas: 'if we hope to anticipate mass killing, we must begin to think of it in the same way its perpetrators do' (p. 141).

conducted within the programme focus on interesting but far-away cases when meanings really were different: when states did not rule the world; when lending money was considered a sin; or when the political game consisted of acquiring dependent followers, rather than independent wealth.

Yet, such studies do little to confirm the easy assumption that the world we have made can be easily dissolved. As the institutionalists with whom we began this chapter are quick to remind us, most social constructs are social constraints, for institutions are powerfully persistent. Our ability to imagine other worlds should not bias how we go about understanding the world as it is.

Conclusion

How can we judge the value of the various approaches reviewed in this chapter? The measure is not the conventional lens of truth or falsity; while hypotheses can be tested against evidence, approaches must be assessed in a broader way. But neither should approaches be judged against some abstract, fixed standard of philosophical adequacy.

In the final analysis, what matters is what works best in delivering new and important research findings.

In our view, the key question is whether an approach is fruitful. The cash value of a school of thought lies precisely in its ability to generate a progressive research programme – innovative studies which shape new problems and cast fresh light on old ones (Lakatos, 1978). A fertile approach will identify a manner of looking at politics which is fresh, revealing, and productive. It will generate truths, and sometimes an account of what is acceptable evidence, even though it is neither true nor false in itself (Lichbach, 2009).

As research programmes, theoretical approaches are not for all time. Rather like people, they are born, develop, tire, and decay. But each approach, as each person, leaves a legacy. Our discussion of theoretical approaches in politics has therefore introduced some themes in the history of politics as an academic discipline and has outlined some major tides that have flowed through the subject. In politics, though, established approaches tend to remain on the menu, rather than being replaced altogether, thus offering a continuing set of choices for researchers as they go about their studies.

Discussion questions

- Does studying the presidency or presidents offer more insight into American government and politics?
- Is a science of politics possible?
- Do (a) politicians and (b) voters behave rationally?
- Would you agree that since states are socially constructed, they can also be socially dissolved?
- Which of the approaches in this chapter is most useful in comparative politics?
- Suggest a topic for a dissertation and consider what would be involved in applying any two of the approaches examined in this chapter to that subject.

Further reading

R. Dalton and H.-D. Klingemann, eds, *The Oxford Handbook of Political Behavior* (2007). This comprehensive collection covers mass beliefs systems, modernization, political values, participation, public opinion, voting behaviour, and methods of comparative research into political behaviour.

D. Green, ed., *Constructivism and Comparative Politics* (2002). Examines the value of the interpretive approach in comparative politics.

D. Green and I. Shapiro, *Pathologies of Rational Choice Theory: A Critique of Applications in Political Science* (1994). Criticizes the rational choice approach for seeking universal theories of politics.

M. Lichbach and A. Zuckerman, eds, *Comparative Politics: Rationality, Culture and Structure*, 2nd edn (2009). Detailed essays on approaches to comparative politics.

J. Mahoney and D. Rueschmeyer, eds, *Comparative Historical Analysis in the Social Sciences* (2003). A thorough presentation of structural analysis as expressed in comparative history.

D. Marsh and G. Stoker, eds, *Theory and Methods in Political Science*, 3rd edn (2010). Essays on most of the approaches introduced in this chapter.

G. Tsebelis, *Veto Players: How Political Institutions Work* (2002). Uses a rational choice framework to understand political institutions.

ONLINE RESOURCES AVAILABLE

Visit the companion website at **www.palgrave.com/politics/hague** to access additional learning resources, including multiple-choice questions, chapter summaries, web links and practice essay questions.

Chapter 6 Political culture

Culture is defined by UNESCO (2002) as 'the set of distinctive spiritual … intellectual and emotional features of society or a social group. It encompasses, in addition to art and literature, lifestyles, ways of living together, value systems, traditions and beliefs.' In other words, culture is the central human characteristic, expressing our essence as aware social beings. Unlike nature (with which it is often contrasted), culture involves values, symbols, meanings, and expectations. It tells us who we are, what is important to us, and how we should behave.

A definition of **political culture** flows from this account of culture. The term refers to the overall pattern in society of beliefs, attitudes and values towards the political system. We can usefully contrast political culture with political ideology. Where an ideology refers to an explicit system of ideas, political culture comes closer to Linz's notion (1975, p. 162) of mentalities: 'ways of thinking and feeling, more emotional than rational, that provide non-codified ways of reacting to different situations.' So, political culture is the broader, more diffuse but also more widely applicable notion. With the decay of ideology, political culture is a major highway into understanding the role of beliefs and attitudes in politics.

While we can usually identify major themes in a national political culture, we must also recognize that any large country will contain a number of culturally distinctive social groups. The result may be either a national culture with one or more subcultures, or even, as for example in India, a multicultural society. In any event, cultures do not always map accurately onto countries; most religions, ethnic groups, and civilizations span national borders. So, we should always beware of reducing political culture to a stereotyped 'national character'.

In comparative politics, political culture is most often studied from a behavioural perspective, using surveys of individuals' attitudes. This approach is defensible if perhaps rather narrow. It downplays the notion of political culture as shared symbols and stories expressed in the public realm, in arenas such as advertising, art, campaigns, ceremonies, literature, museums, and television (Ross, 2009). Given that politics is a collective activity, there is certainly a case for studying political culture in its public manifestations. But public statements may not be matched by private opinion; the number of statues of the dictator is no indication of his popularity (quite the reverse, perhaps). Ascertaining what people think directly is generally a preferable strategy.

> **Political culture** denotes 'the sum of the fundamental values, sentiments and knowledge that give form and substance to political processes' (Pye, 1995, p. 965). It can be understood as either the sum of individuals' attitudes or as an attribute – the culture – of a group which gives shared meaning to political action.

STUDYING . . .

POLITICAL CULTURE

- The concept of political culture is attractive but can be misused. One risk is that a country's mix of cultures will be reduced to a single national character. Also, there is a danger of invoking cultural factors when we can think of nothing else: 'it's just part of their culture'.

- Most research on political culture is behavioural, based on sample surveys of the general public. Some ambitious concepts within the political culture literature are based on replies to a few survey questions: soft data for large claims.

- The classic concern of research in political culture has been to identify the political attitudes most supportive of stable liberal democracy. Ideas such as the civic culture, political trust, social capital, and postmaterialism have all been used, and in some cases developed, with this goal in mind.

- Although political culture is sometimes criticized for its static quality, the drift to postmaterialism – understood as part of a broad transition from survival to self-expression values as societies modernize - is an interesting attempt to understand how political cultures change.

- The idea of conflict between transnational civilizations is a controversial attempt to apply cultural analysis to a post-ideological world. Within this strand, one interesting focus is provided by studies investigating the alleged contrasts between Western and Islamic cultures.

- While most studies concentrate on mass culture, elite values possess direct political significance. The notion of consociational democracy is an attempt to capture one way in which the values of political elites engender stability in divided societies. Note also that elites are not culture victims but can exploit culture instrumentally, to further their political goals.

The civic culture

Political culture has a natural appeal for comparativists. Studying, and especially visiting, another country for the first time, we are naturally drawn to the differences with our home culture. Gabriel Almond, the father of modern studies of political culture, claimed that the sentiments and mentalities we observe are an independent force in political life: 'political values, feelings and beliefs are not simple reflections of social and political structure … the political content of the minds of citizens and political elites is more complex, more persistent and more autonomous than Marxism and liberalism would suggest' (1993, p. 14).

Yet, it is dangerously easy to use cultural contrasts as an explanation for political differences. For one thing, culture can influence how the political game is played – the rituals, the moves, the language –

without necessarily affecting the content of politics. For instance, the earthy nature of Australian political debate does not necessarily indicate the presence of sharper underlying conflict there than in a country with a more restrained political style; rather, debate by insult is the format in which the national conversation proceeds.

An additional danger in cultural analysis is that we mistake a dominant culture for a national culture. The dominant culture – as expressed in the national media to which the visitor is exposed – may reflect only the values of the political elite. The powerful usually seek to validate inequalities of power; the wealthy, to legitimize the economic system from which they benefit. Underlying this dominant discourse, but less visible to the superficial observer, we often find layers of cynicism and opposition. On closer inspection, shared understandings may turn out not to be shared at all.

We can illustrate these points about cultural differences between and within nations by considering Almond and Verba's classic study, *The Civic Culture* (1963). In this landmark project, the authors sought to identify the political culture within which a liberal democracy is most likely to develop and consolidate. Their investigation became a political science equivalent of Weber's attempt (1905) to discover the cultural source of modern capitalism. Where Weber located the spirit of capitalism in protestant values, Almond and Verba found the source of stable democracy in what they called a **civic culture**.

In a **civic culture**, many citizens are active in politics but a passive minority serves to stabilize the system, preventing it from overheating. Further, participants are not so involved as to refuse to accept decisions with which they disagree.

In thinking about liberal democracy, we would instinctively begin by imagining that a healthy political system is one whose citizens believe they can contribute to, and are affected by, government decisions. But the interest of Almond and Verba's study rested precisely in its rejection of such a proposition. The authors proposed, instead, that liberal democracy will prove most stable in societies blending different cultures in a particular mix they term the 'civic culture'. The ideal conditions for democracy, they suggested, emerge when an essentially participant culture is balanced by attitudes leading to low levels of participation. A measure of passivity provides ballast for the political system, enabling it to survive periods of stress (see also Chapter 8).

In this way, the civic culture resolves the tension within democracy between popular control and effective governance: it allows for citizen influence while retaining flexibility for the government. As Almond and Verba (1963, p. 347) summarized their perspective:

A citizen within the civic culture has, then, a reserve of influence. He is not constantly involved in politics, he does not actively oversee the behaviour of political decision makers. But he does have the potential to act if there is need ... He is not the active citizen: he is the potentially active citizen.

Armed with this theory, Almond and Verba set out to discover which countries came closest to a civic culture. In 1959 and 1960, they conducted sample surveys in Britain, Italy, Mexico, the USA, and West Germany. Of these, Britain, and to a lesser extent the United States, came closest to the civic ideal. In both countries, citizens felt they could influence the government but often chose not to do so, thus conferring on the government its required agility (Table 6.1). By contrast, the political cultures of Italy, Mexico, and West Germany all deviated in various ways from the authors' prescription.

Like most original research, Almond and Verba's study attracted considerable scrutiny. Two criticisms highlighted limitations in the concept of political culture itself. First, critics alleged that the whole notion of a national political culture was inherently vague; they suggested that the authors should have focused more on subcultures of race and class. Had they done so, suggested Macpherson (1977, p. 88), they would have discovered that the participants are the educated middle class, while those least engaged with formal politics are the poorly-educated working class. These commentators claimed that the civic culture was simply a sanitized reformulation of class rule.

Second, critics pointed out that Almond and Verba failed to offer a detailed account of the origins and evolution of political culture. Rather, political culture was largely presented as a given, raising the suspicion that the concept is little more than a sophisticated restatement of simplistic assumptions about national character. In addition, the authors

Table 6.1 Proportion of respondents saying they could do something about an unjust law at both national and local levels, by country, 1959–60 (%)

In Almond and Verba's classic study, most people in the United States and the United Kingdom, but not in Germany, Mexico and Italy, expressed a sense of civic competence

USA	66
United Kingdom	56
Germany (Federal Republic)	33
Mexico	33
Italy	27

Source: Adapted from Almond and Verba (1963), fig. VII.I.

initially had little to say about the evolution of polit-ical culture over time, a theme which, as we shall see, subsequently characterized much discussion.

Underlying these comments is the notion that a country's political culture should not be seen as fixed and stable but, rather, should be regarded as a dynamic entity which is at least partly shaped by the operation of politics itself. As we will see in the next section, later research has confirmed this position.

Political trust and social capital

Times move on. In the half century following Almond and Verba's study, many liberal democracies hit turbulent waters. Student activism, oil crises, and financial crises were interspersed with phases of growth and unparalleled prosperity. Inevitably, Western political cultures responded to these events, demonstrating the danger of drawing general con-clusions about a country's political culture from a single survey.

Much recent research has examined the evolution of one particular theme examined by Almond and Verba: **political trust**. This term refers to the belief that rulers are generally well-intentioned and effec-tive in serving the interests of the governed. The notion here is that political trust indicates diffuse support for the regime, thereby facilitating sound governance. Distrust, on the other hand, can lead to lack of compliance with government in such areas as tax collection.

> **Political trust** is the belief that the system and institu-tions of government generate competent decisions which reflect leaders' concern for those they govern (Hardin, 2006).

Especially in the 1990s and 2000s, the conventional wisdom was that political trust was decaying in many Western democracies, presaging trouble ahead. And there is certainly some evidence of such a decline. However, the fall in trust was by no means consistent across countries and may have already bottomed out. In any case, it focused more on the public's confi-dence in the performance of democratic institutions than on the principle of democracy itself.

In her initial comparative study, Norris (1999a, p. 20) demonstrated that overall public confidence in

such institutions as parliament, the civil service, and the armed forces declined between 1981 and 1991 in each of the 17 countries she examined. However, updating her analysis to include the first decade of the twenty-first century led to a more qualified interpretation (Norris, 2011, p. 82). She now chal-lenged:

the over-simple views of an inevitable downward spiral of public disenchantment and steadily growing hostility towards government actors, insti-tutions, and feelings of attachment to the nation-state ... Overall fluctuations over time usually prove far more common than straightforward linear or downward trends.

If there is a predominant pattern here, it appears to be that a decline in trust in the second half of the twentieth century gave way in the twenty-first century to event-driven fluctuations around a newly-established lower level.

Certainly, the United States illustrates this format. In 1964, around three-quarters of Americans said that they trusted the federal gov-ernment 'to do the right thing'; by 1994, at the bottom of the cycle, only about a quarter did so (Figure 6.1). Since then, trust has fluctuated in response to events. For example, despite the intelli-gence failings exposed by 9/11, Americans rallied round the flag following the attacks; faith in gov-ernment received a short-term boost (Brewer *et al.*, 2003). By 2008, however, trust had fallen back again to 30 per cent, far below the levels recorded in the late 1950s when Almond and Verba issued their broadly positive appraisal of America's civic culture. Clearly, political trust varies within coun-tries and not just between them.

A pattern of decline followed by fluctuation also characterizes some other liberal democracies. In the UK, the proportion of people saying they would 'trust a British government of any party to place the needs of this country above the interests of their own political party' more than halved from 40 per cent in 1986 to a low point of 16 per cent in 2000, before a modest recovery to 20 per cent in 2010 (BSA, 2012).

So, since Almond and Verba's study both the American and the British 'civic' cultures have wit-nessed a shift towards more sceptical and instru-

Figure 6.1 Americans' trust in the government in Washington, 1964–2008

Americans' trust in their federal government collapsed in the 1960s and 1970s but, since then, has varied around (and sometimes above) this lower base in response to economic and political conditions

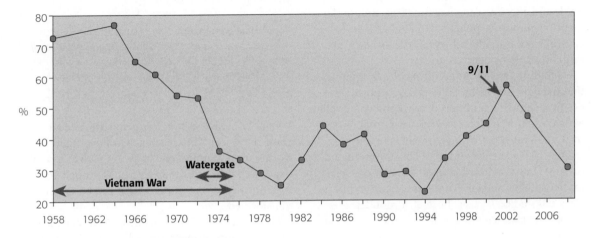

Note: Per cent trusting 'the government in Washington to do what is right' just about always or most of the time.

Source: American National Election Studies (2012).

mental attitudes but without threatening the survival of liberal democracy itself.

Putnam (2002) suggests that declining faith in government represents a deflation of the political culture, reducing the capacity of the political system to achieve shared goals. The argument here is that trust encourages cooperation, while distrust breeds political deflation. A culture of trust oils the wheels of collective action, enabling projects to be initiated which are impractical in a society where mutual suspicion prevails. But as trust in government falls, so people become less willing to believe what their leaders say, to turn out at elections, to fight wars, and to support public projects in which they do not see a sure return for themselves or their immediate circle (Hetherington, 2004).

Just as trust in others builds **social capital**, so trust in government creates political capital. Where

> **Social capital** refers to the resources embedded in human networks. The more contacts people possess, the greater the knowledge, advice, and funding on which they can draw, at least when these relationships are based on trust and cooperation, and the more effective people become (Lin and Erickson, 2008).

the bond between citizens and government is strong, the government will be granted the flexibility needed to respond effectively to shared problems. So, we have here another angle on the cultural basis of stable liberal democracy; one focused on political trust, rather than the civic culture.

It is ironic, suggest Putnam and Goss (2002, p. 3), that 'just at the moment of liberal democracy's greatest triumph, some fundamental social and cultural conditions for effective democracy may have eroded in recent decades, the result of a gradual but widespread process of civic disengagement'.

In an influential study using Italy as his laboratory, Putnam (1993) attempted to test his ideas about trust by showing how a supportive political culture directly enhances the performance of a political system. In their original work, Almond and Verba had portrayed Italy as a country whose people felt uninvolved in, and alienated from, politics. Italian culture was distinctly uncivic, lacking positive and supportive attitudes among the majority.

Putnam revisits Italy's political culture, paying more attention to diversity within the country. He demonstrates how cultural variations within Italy influenced the effectiveness of the 20 new regional governments created in the 1970s. Similar in structure and formal powers, these governments nonetheless varied greatly in performance. Some (such as Emilia-Romagna in the north) proved stable and effective, capable of making and implementing innovative policies. Others (such as Calabria in the south) achieved little. What, asks Putnam, explains these contrasts?

He finds his answer in political culture, arguing that the most successful regions have a positive political culture: a tradition of trust and cooperation which results in high levels of social capital. By contrast, the least effective governments are found in regions lacking any tradition of collaboration and equality. In such circumstances, supplies of social capital run low and governments can achieve little. National studies, such as those of Almond and Verba, are insufficiently sensitive to these regional contrasts.

But what is the source of social capital? How does a region establish a foundation of mutual trust in the first place? Putnam's answer is historical: he attributes the uneven distribution of social capital in modern Italy to events deep within each area's history. The more effective governments in the north draw on a tradition of communal self-government dating from the twelfth century. The least successful administrations in the south are burdened with a long history of feudal, foreign, bureaucratic, and authoritarian rule. Thus, Putnam's analysis illustrates how political culture can be a device through which the past influences the present. Although his interest in rebuilding trust might prompt him to disagree, the implication seems to be that social capital is largely an inherited trait. It cannot be made to order.

Generations and postmaterial values

Although some initial applications of political culture were criticized for their static quality, later advocates of the cultural approach have sought to address changes in political culture. The concept of **political generations** has proved useful here.

The idea is that each generation has the potential to develop a perspective on politics which distinguishes it both from the one before and the one after. Typically, this distinctive outlook reflects the formative experience of the cohort as it matures. For example, growing up in an environment of war or depression colours political attitudes in a manner that persists throughout life.

A **political generation** is an age cohort sharing distinctive experiences and values which shape its perspective through its life course. Generational turnover can gradually transform a political culture without any individuals changing their views.

Values can also shift across generations in a more gradual fashion. Thus, each new cohort might be slightly more sympathetic to causes such as gay marriage or environmental protection. Through generational turnover, a political culture can be slowly transformed.

There is an important technical point here. In studying political generations, life-cycle or ageing effects must be incorporated. As a generation ages, its values will inevitably adjust (becoming more conservative, for instance), so any differences between generations can only be identified by comparing two or more generations at the same life stage (Figure 6.2). The fact that the young are more left-wing than the old at a particular time does not suffice to demonstrate a generational divide. Such a contrast may reflect a life-cycle effect; it is entirely possible that a cohort of elderly conservatives might, in its youth, have been even more left-wing than the new radicals coming up behind. The lesson is that capturing a generational divide requires long-term data enabling like to be compared with like.

One factor which has been measured over a long period, and which illustrates how political scientists have sought to incorporate change into their understanding of political culture, is **postmaterialism**. As well as providing an example of political generations, this concept also addresses what many see as a transformation of the political cultures of high-income democracies.

From the late 1940s to the early 1970s, the Western world witnessed a period of unprecedented economic growth. 'You've never had it so good' became a cliché that summarized the experience of the postwar generation. This era was also a period of relative international peace, enabling cohorts to grow up with no experience of world war. In addition, an expanded welfare state (and increasing property

Figure 6.2 Political generations

The downward slopes show a life-cycle effect. The difference between the slopes shows a generational effect.

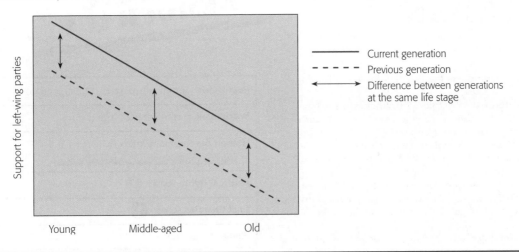

prices in some countries) offered security to many Western populations against the demands of illness, unemployment, and old age.

> **Postmaterialism** is a commitment to self-expression values, emphasizing human diversity, individual liberty, and autonomy. These values can emerge, especially among the educated young, from a foundation of personal security and material affluence. Such priorities supplant traditional survival values emphasizing physical and material security (Inglehart and Welzel, 2005).

According to Inglehart (1971), this unique combination of affluence, peace, and security led to a silent revolution in Western political cultures. Inglehart (1997, p, 28) suggested that the priority accorded to economic achievement made way for increased emphasis on the quality of life: 'in a major part of the world, the disciplined, self-denying and achievement-oriented norms of industrial society are giving way to the choices over lifestyle which characterize post-industrial economies'.

From the 1960s, a new generation of postmaterialists emerged: young, well-educated people focused on lifestyle issues such as ecology, nuclear disarmament, and feminism. Earlier generations had given priority to survival values, leading to a concern with order, security and fixed rules in such areas as religion and sexual morality. But postmaterialists gave

priority to self-expression values, emphasizing autonomy, flexibility, and tolerance, for themselves if not always for their own children. Postmaterialists were elite-challenging advocates of the new politics, rather than elite-sustaining foot soldiers in the old party battles. They were more attracted to single-issue groups than to the broader packages offered by political parties.

Based on extensive survey evidence, Inglehart showed that the more affluent a democracy, the higher the proportion of postmaterialists within its borders. Within Europe, for example, postmaterialism came first to, and made deepest inroads in, the wealthiest democracies such as Denmark, the Netherlands, and West Germany. Norway apart, the other affluent Scandinavian countries also proved receptive to these values. Postmaterialism was less common in poorer European democracies with lower levels of education, such as Greece (Knutsen, 1996).

Assuming a generational effect, postmaterial values will continue to become more prominent. When Inglehart began his studies in the early 1970s, materialists out-numbered postmaterialists by about four to one in many Western countries. By 2000, the two groups were much more even in size, a major transformation in political culture. Even allowing for some decay of radicalism with age, generational replacement will continue to work its effect. As

GERMANY

Form of government ■ a constitutional and parliamentary federal republic.

Legislature ■ the *Bundestag* (620 members) is the lower house. The smaller upper house, the *Bundesrat*, represents the 16 federal *Länder* (states).

Executive ■ the chancellor leads a cabinet of between 16 and 22 ministers. A president serves as ceremonial head of state.

Constitution and judiciary ■ Germany is a state based on law (a *Rechtsstaat*). The Federal Constitutional Court has proved to be highly influential as an arbiter of the constitution.

Electoral system ■ the *Bundestag* is elected through a mixed member proportional system. Members of the *Bundesrat* are nominated by the *Länder*.

Party system ■ the leading parties are the SPD (Social Democratic Party) and the CDU (Christian Democratic Union). Other significant parties are the Greens, the liberal FDP (Free Democratic Party) and The Left party. A CDU/FDP coalition has been in power since 2009.

Population (annual growth rate): 81.3 m (−0.2%)
World Bank income group: high income
Human development index (rank/out of): 9/187
Political rights score: ❶
Civil liberties score: ❶
Media status: free

Note: For interpretation and sources, see p. xvi.

Among all Europe's liberal democracies, **GERMANY** has experienced the most fragmented history. Although a German-speaking people has existed since time immemorial, Germany did not become a single entity until the formation of the German 'Empire' in 1871. Since then, the country's boundaries have been subject to frequent revision, with losses of territory at the end of both world wars, and a division of the remaining core into separate communist and democratic states in 1949. Germany was reunited in 1990 when the communist east was successfully absorbed into the Federal Republic.

Highly aware of its difficult history, Germany has provided a motor for post-war European integration. Its European commitment is entrenched in its constitution, while the government has so far proved willing to support the EU with hard cash.

Because Germany naturally views European developments through the lens of its own system of government, the country's political institutions are of continental significance. The framers of the post-war constitution made the chancellor the key figure in the new republic. She determines government policy, appoints cabinet ministers, heads a large staff, and can be removed from office only when the *Bundestag* simultaneously demonstrates a majority for a named successor. Within a parliamentary framework, Germany offers a distinctive form: chancellor democracy.

Germany boasts the largest economy in Europe. Its skilled employees, working in capital-intensive factories, produce premium manufactured goods for export. Germany is the world's third largest exporter, marginally behind the USA. But even the German economy experiences ups and downs. By the late 1990s, the post-war German miracle had begun to fade. As the costs of reunification mounted, unemployment grew in the west while becoming entrenched in much of the east.

However, modest reforms of the labour market under Gerhard Schröder (SPD Chancellor, 1998–2005) helped the country to re-establish its historic strength as an exporter and manufacturer.

SPOTLIGHT

Political culture in Germany

Political culture is often taken as a given but is itself shaped by a county's history. Here, the post-war division of Germany provides a rare natural experiment, allowing us to gauge how these developments affected popular thinking. How did the political culture respond?

Three main processes can be observed. The first is the positive impact of post-war economic recovery on political culture within the west. Between 1959 and 1988, the proportion of Germans in West Germany expressing pride in their political institutions increased from 7 to 51 per cent. Over a similar period, support for a multiparty system grew from 53 to 92 per cent. West Germany's experience shows that economic growth can, indeed, deliver political legitimacy. The emergence of a supportive public over this period certainly offers hope to other transitional countries seeking to build a democratic culture on an authoritarian history.

The second process is the impact of the communist German Democratic Republic (GDR) on political culture. At reunification in 1990, people in the east were significantly less trusting of parliament, the legal system and, indeed, each other than were people in western Germany. The experience of living under a communist regime, particularly one which engaged in such extraordinarily close surveillance of its population, had left its mark (Rainer and Siedler, 2006).

The third process is the impact of reunification on political culture in the former GDR. Here, there is strong evidence of declining contrasts between east and west. Trust in parliament and the legal system increased dramatically in the east following the transition to democratic rule. Among those in the east who had not experienced unemployment, trust in other people also converged towards western levels.

Ostalgie, nostalgia for the German Democratic Republic, was a German cultural phenomenon of the early 2000s. It mocked Western seriousness by presenting a rose-tinted but also self-deprecating image of life in the communist East, focusing on such GDR icons as:

■ *Ampelmänchen*: the little man on the traffic light;
■ *Trabant cars*: highly polluting, highly unreliable;
■ *Vita Cola*: communism's answer to Coca-Cola.

However, among the substantial number of easterners who had been unemployed after reunification, social trust seems to have declined. Thus, the cultural reaction of east Germans to living in a liberal democracy was not uniform but, rather, varied with personal success in coping with a market economy.

Perceptions of contrasts between east and west remain significant, even as many easterners migrate westwards. Unification without unity remains a common theme in discussions of Germany's contemporary political culture.

Certainly, 'Ossis' tend to perceive 'Wessis' as bourgeois, patronizing, materialistic, and individualistic. Conversely, many westerners seem to look down on east Germans – and certainly are perceived to do so by easterners themselves.

It is reasonable to suppose that cultural contrasts will continue to weaken if (and this is a large if) living standards in the east converge on those in the west. In such circumstances, the more materialistic culture in the east is likely to acquire the postmaterial tinge long found in the west.

Overall, the natural experiment provided by post-war Germany shows that a country's political culture is not a constant but, rather, is continually influenced by major political and economic developments.

Further reading: Conradt (2008), Green *et al.* (2011), Hancock and Krisch (2008).

Inglehart (1999, p. 247) notes, 'as the younger birth cohorts replace the older more materialist cohorts, we should observe a shift towards the postmaterial orientation'.

The never-ending expansion of education gives us one of postmaterialism's central pillars. In fact, experience of higher education is the best single predictor of a postmaterial outlook. In France, surveys conducted between 2005 and 2008 showed that 56 per cent of those with at least some university education were postmaterialists, compared with only 25 per cent among those with lower educational achievement (Dalton, 2008a, p. 91).

Postmaterialism can probably be best understood as the liberal outlook induced by degree-level education, especially in the arts and social sciences. Liberal values acquired or reinforced at college are then sustained through careers in expanding professions where knowledge, rather than wealth or management authority, is the key to success. Graduate generations are postmaterial generations. Writing on Denmark, Stubager (2010) refers to an 'educational cleavage' underpinning the division between libertarians, with their tolerance of non-conformity, and authoritarians, with their commitment to social hierarchy.

Although postmaterialism is normally interpreted as a generational value shift among the general public, its most important political effect may operate through political elites. As Inglehart's shock troops moved into positions of power, so they secured a platform from which their values could directly affect government decisions. For instance, the 1960s generation retained touches of radicalism even as it secured the seductive trappings of office. Thus, Bill Clinton (born 1946, the first president to be born after the war) offered a more liberal agenda to the American people than did his predecessor in the White House, George H. W. Bush (born 1924). These two men represented different generations, as well as different parties.

However, postmaterialism did not carry all before it. Culture may influence the agenda but it certainly does not drive it. Not only have many conservative parties continued to prosper in the current postmaterial age, but also extreme right-wing parties have emerged in European democracies, partly as a reaction against self-expression values (see Chapter 10). More broadly, the distinctive challenges of the

twenty-first century include security issues such as terrorism, energy supply, global warming, youth unemployment and pensions. These problems invite a renewed focus on the value of security, rather than self-expression. Such issues force themselves onto the political agenda with an energy that can, in the short run, overwhelm cultural change emerging gradually through the march of the generations.

Civilizations and religion

Here, we examine political culture as it operates on a global scale – drawing, in particular, on Huntington's provocative thesis of a clash of civilizations (1996). This topic raises the issue of religion, a dimension of culture that we have not yet addressed.

In an interpretation presciently published before 9/11, Huntington suggested that cultures, rather than countries, would become the leading source of political conflict in the twenty-first century. The conclusion of the Cold War did not mean the end of cultural divisions. Rather, the focus shifted from a battle of ideologies to a clash of civilizations, including conflict between Islam and the West (Box 6.1). Since such groupings are supranational, Huntington (1996, p. 20) claimed that political culture had escaped its national moorings to embrace wider identities:

A civilization-based world order is emerging: societies sharing cultural affinities cooperate with each other; efforts to shift societies from one civilization to another are unsuccessful; and countries group themselves around the lead or core states of their civilization.

Between the contradictory worldviews of these civilizations, suggests Huntington, there is little room for compromise. Economic conflicts can be bargained away but cultural differences carry no easy solutions. Huntington anticipated that, as globalization proceeded, friction and conflict would intensify, reversing the standard 'McWorld' thesis of a world converging on American norms (Barber, 1995).

Huntington noted, for example, how cultural kinship influenced the choice of sides in the wars of the 1990s: 'in the Yugoslav conflicts, Russia provided

BOX 6.1

A clash of civilizations?

Huntington defines civilizations as the broadest cultural entities in the world; they are 'cultures writ large'. He divides the world into seven or eight major civilizations:

1 Western;
2 Japanese;
3 Islamic;
4 Hindu;
5 Slavic-Orthodox;
6 Latin American;
7 Chinese;
8 African (possibly).

Source: Huntington (1996).

BOX 6.2

Relationships between states and civilizations

	Relationship to civilization	Example (civilization)
Core state	The most powerful and culturally central state in a civilization	India (Hindu)
Member state	A state fully identified with a particular civilization	UK (Western)
Lone state	A state lacking cultural commonality with other societies	Japan (Japanese)

Source: Huntington (1996), pp. 135–54.

diplomatic support to the Serbs … not for reasons of ideology or power politics or economic interest but because of cultural kinship' (1996, p. 28).

In 2006, similarly, the Russian defence minister warned the West to steer clear of Belarus, citing cultural affinities: 'Belarusians and Russians are one people' (Shepherd, 2006, p. 19). Huntington was also sceptical of states' efforts to switch civilizations, suggesting that the reason Australia had failed to reinvent itself as an Asian country was just that, culturally speaking, it was not. In a similar way, Turkey's application to join the European Union may stall because of a 'cultural chasm' (Schepereel, 2010).

How do states relate to these civilizations? Huntington provided an intriguing classification, though countries can fall into more than one category (Box 6.2). A core state leads a civilization; a member state is identified with a single civilization; while a lone state either forms its own civilization or stands, like Haiti, in a league of its own.

In addition, Huntington also discussed mixed or torn states whose leaders attempt the difficult assignment of moving their country from one civilization to another. Turkey, an Islamic society whose leaders traditionally pursued a secular Western course, is the classic case. Russia, positioned between Western and Slavic-Orthodox civilizations, provides another example of perpetual ambivalence.

Huntington drew on these civilizational themes in discussing the specific relationship between Islam and the West. The transnational character of civilizations is, indeed, exemplified by these religions, each of which predates the emergence of states. Thus, in medieval Europe, Christendom stood above kingdoms in the political hierarchy. Similarly, Muslim countries form an Islamic domain in which a shared religious commitment is supposed to transcend national divisions.

Although the origins of the conflict between Islam and the West may lie in religion, Huntington argued that the contemporary division was cultural or civilizational, rather than religious. It is no longer the West's Christian foundations which have become the target of Islamic criticism. Rather, the Muslim critique rests on the West's secular culture, particularly as exemplified by American materialism.

As would be expected for a cultural divide, differences in education and upbringing underpin these differences between civilizations. Western education is avowedly secular, allowing schooling to encompass scientific knowledge and technical training. But, in some Muslim countries, literal instruction in the Koran (Islam's holy text) remains a major theme, ill-preparing young people – male as well as female – for the modern world.

Huntington (1996, p. 217) portrayed Islam and the West as civilizations locked in permanent cultural conflict:

The underlying problem of the West is Islam, a different civilization whose people are convinced of the superiority of their culture and are obsessed with the inferiority of their power. The problem for Islam is the West, a different civilization whose people are convinced of the universality of their culture and who believe that their superior, if declining, power imposes on them the obligation to extend that culture throughout the world.

Huntington's thesis has undergone searching scrutiny. Many critics reject his essentialist reading of Islam, focused as it is on that religion's inherent characteristics. Stepan (2001, p. 234), for instance, interprets Islam as multivocal, capable of varying its voice across place and time. In similar fashion, Gregorian (2004) describes Islam as 'a mosaic, not a monolith', while Fuller (2002, p. 52) suggests that:

Islam is not a butterfly in a collection box or a set of texts prescribing a single path. The real issue is not what Islam is but what do Muslims want. People of all sorts of faiths can rapidly develop interpretations of their religion that justify practically any quest.

Consider Turkey and Saudi Arabia. Both are Muslim countries; however, Turkey's state is secular and substantially democratic, whereas Saudi Arabia's authoritarian regime leads a society constrained by a severe form of Islam. The reaction to 9/11 confirms Islam's multivocal character: the hijackers undoubtedly drew on one anti-Western dialect within Islam but most Muslims, as most Christians, regarded the attacks as morally unjustified (Saikal, 2003, p. 17).

Furthermore, any assumption of a monolithic Islam was invalidated by violent conflict between **Sunni** and **Shia** Muslims in post-invasion Iraq, and by the increasingly overt expression of this divide within Middle Eastern societies following the Arab awakening of 2011.

The political character of Islam, and its relationship with the West, varies over time. The possibility

> **Sunni** Muslims comprise the orthodox branch of Islam. This denomination founds its practices on the actions of Muhammad and accepts some separation of political and religious authority. Sunnis comprise at least 80 per cent of all Muslims. By contrast, the **Shia** branch advocates a more direct political role for religious leaders. Shia Muslims form a majority in Iran and Iraq.

of conflict with the West may be inherent but this potential often remains latent. Saikal (2003, p. 24) writes that 'since the advent of Islam in the early seventh century, relations between its domain and the largely Christian West have been marked by long periods of peaceful coexistence but also by many instances of tension, hostility and mutual recrimination.' As long as civilizations are conceived as static, it is difficult to account for variability in the relationship between them. Huntington's expansive claim (1996, p. 210) that the West's problem is 'not Islamic fundamentalism but Islam' surely involves a breathtaking dismissal of peaceful centuries.

Huntington's thesis of a divide did succeed in stimulating research examining cultural differences between Muslim and Western countries. In general, these studies demonstrate only limited differences in political attitudes between the two worlds, casting doubt on the idea of conflicting civilizations. However, larger contrasts are found on specific issues of sexuality and gender.

Norris and Inglehart's *Sacred and Secular: Religion and Politics Worldwide* is a valuable contribution here. Examining surveys conducted in over 50 countries between 1995 and 2001, these authors conclude (2011, p. 146) that 'there were no significant differences between the publics living in the West and in Muslim religious cultures in approval of how democracy works in practice, in support for democratic ideals, and in approval of strong leadership'. (Bear in mind, though, that what is understood by 'democracy' may vary between cultures).

Norris and Inglehart did find Muslim publics supporting a stronger social role for religious authorities. However, this difference proved to be a case of the West versus the rest, rather than the West versus Islam. Countries in sub-Saharan Africa (where religious, but not only Muslim, identities remain important) also sympathized with the notion of an active clergy. In this respect, the secular character of Western civilization (excluding the USA) proved to be the odd man out. It is instructive for the West, accustomed to imagining the Islamic world as an alien other, to see its own secular civilization as the exception.

But differences between Western and Islamic countries were not wholly absent. On sexual and gender issues, a distinct clash of opinions could be discerned. Norris and Inglehart (2011, p. 149) consider that:

There remains a strong and significant difference across all the social values (including approval of gender equality, homosexuality, abortion, and divorce) among those publics living in Western versus Muslim societies ... All the Western nations, led by Sweden, Germany, and Norway, strongly favor equality for women and also prove tolerant of homosexuality ... In contrast the Muslim cultures, including Egypt, Bangladesh, Jordan, Iran, and Azerbaijan, all display the most traditional social attitudes, with only Albania proving slightly more liberal.

Other scholars reach similar conclusions. Differences in public opinion between the Islamic and Western worlds are minimal on support for democracy but substantial on questions of sexuality and gender. Thus, Steven Fish (2011, p. 257), interrogating the same data source as Norris and Inglehart, concludes that some of his 'most noteworthy findings are about how different Muslims are not'. In fact, he finds that 'Muslims partake of a global consensus on keeping those who convey God's word and ways away from the realm of political decision-making.' But he, too, finds that 'being a Muslim is generally associated with stronger opposition to homosexuality, abortion, and divorce'.

The overall conclusion is, surely, that neither cultural differences nor the historical record justify the thesis of an inherent clash of civilizations between the Islamic world and the West. Political culture (and equivalent terms such as 'civilization') can only take us so far. As Roy (1994, p. viii) observes, 'culture is never directly explanatory and in fact conceals all that is rupture and history: the importation of new types of states, the birth of new social classes and the advent of contemporary ideologies'. Over time,

political debate itself shapes the political culture as leaders selectively exploit its themes in pursuit of their own goals. By themselves, concepts such as 'political culture' and 'civilization' are blanket terms, offering a seductively easy frame of comparison, but also obscuring much crucial detail.

Elite political culture

Political culture is a concept applicable not only to the mass population, but also to political elites. Even where mass attitudes to politics are well-developed, it is still the views of the elite which exert the most direct effect on political decisions. In this section, we examine **elite political culture**, focusing once more on consequences for political stability.

> **Elite political culture** consists of the beliefs, attitudes, and ideas about politics held by those who are closest to the centres of political power. The values of elites are more explicit, systematic and consequential than are those of the population at large (Verba, 1987, p. 7).

In a liberal democracy, of course, parties offer competing values and policies. But underlying these contrasts, we often uncover tacit agreements and shared understandings. And this elite culture can be more than a representative fragment of the values of the wider society. The ideas of elites are certainly distinct from, even though they overlap with, the wider political culture.

For example, an important factor in the consolidation of democracy in the unpromising conditions of post-colonial India was surely the pro-democratic values of its political elite, as channelled through the dominant Congress Party. The party's leaders, many legally trained, imbibed the British traditions of parliamentary government, an independent judiciary and the rule of law. In India, as elsewhere, the building and consolidation of democracy was driven by elites.

Or consider the post-war construction of a united Europe from the ashes of a shattered continent. A generation of statesmen designed and constructed the elaborate transnational institutions which form the European Union today. Without the sustained commitment of this cohort of leaders to what was an explicit European project, this

---

astonishing achievement would have been impossible. It was a triumph not only of interests, but also of the will.

In liberal democracies, political elites generally exhibit a more liberal and sophisticated outlook than the general population, even if differences between parties attract more attention. Education is again a factor: in most democracies, politics has become virtually a graduate profession. The experience of higher education nurtures an optimistic view of human nature, strengthens humanitarian values, and encourages a belief in the ability of politicians to solve social problems (Farnen and Meloen, 2000). Indeed, the contrast between the values of the educated elite and those of the least-educated has itself caused tension in many political systems, as seen in the emergence of far right parties (see Chapter 10).

Elite political culture bears on political stability in two main ways. The first route is through elite confidence: a political order is more likely to survive if the ruling group genuinely believes in its own right to govern. And the second mechanism is elite compromise. A willingness to compromise among the leaders representing different groups in divided societies can contain inter-group hostility, securing stability against the risk of disintegration. We examine each element in turn.

Elite confidence

The importance of elite self-confidence (or, rather, its absence) can be demonstrated with an example from authoritarian regimes. The revolutions of 1989 in Eastern Europe dramatically illustrated how a collapse of confidence among the rulers helped to precipitate major political change. As Schöpflin (1990) points out:

an authoritarian elite sustains itself in power not just through force and the threat of force but, more importantly, because it has some vision of the future by which it can justify itself to itself. No regime can survive long without some concept of purpose.

In the initial phase of industrialization, communist rulers in the Soviet Union and Eastern Europe had good reason to believe their new planned economies were producing results. By the late 1980s, however, progress had given way to decline. As any remaining support from intellectuals faded, so party officials began to doubt their own legitimacy. Communist rulers were aware that they had become a barrier to, rather than a source of, progress. Elite values had ceased to underpin the system of government.

By comparison, in China economic growth has continued apace, at least until recently, sustaining the elite's confidence in its own authority. If communist rule in China does come under threat, it could well be because a segment of the elite concludes that the party's dominance is holding back further national and economic progress, creating an opening for mass protests which would not otherwise have occurred. In China, as elsewhere, the fragmentation of elite values will be the catalyst of any regime change that takes place.

Elite compromise

The second way in which elite culture contributes to political stability is through the capacity for group leaders to engineer compromise in divided societies. The classic analysis here is by Lijphart (1968, 1977, 2002). Here, we examine Lijphart's notion of **consociational democracy**, with an emphasis on its cultural elements.

A **consociational democracy** is an arrangement in which agreements between the national leaders of separate pillars in a divided society help to secure political stability. Pillars are organized communities, typically based on religion (e.g. Catholic) or ideology (e.g. socialist).

Lijphart suggested that even a society separated into potentially hostile pillars can achieve political stability, as long as party and group leaders are willing to compromise at elite level. A culture of compromise is expressed in agreements between leaders over the distribution of state funds, with each group retaining autonomy over how it uses the resources it receives. This solution allows each community to continue to regulate itself on those matters not directly affecting other groups (Figure 6.3).

Just such an accommodating attitude, Lijphart suggests, prevailed among group leaders in European consociational democracies such as

Figure 6.3 How elite compromise can deliver political stability to divided societies

Even when the mass population is divided into separate and even hostile pillars, political stability is still possible if pillar leaders can negotiate agreements on essential matters of shared interest, including the distribution of resources

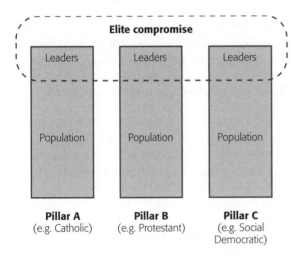

Pillar A
(e.g. Catholic)

Pillar B
(e.g. Protestant)

Pillar C
(e.g. Social Democratic)

Austria (1945–66), Belgium (from 1919), and the Netherlands (1917–67). These societies were divided by religion and ideology. In the Netherlands, for example, Catholics and Protestants constituted separate religious pillars, while the Social Democrats and Liberals formed less densely organized secular groups. Andeweg and Irwin (2009, p. 21) describe how the religious pillars structured lives in the 1950s: a typical Catholic would have been born of Catholic parents in a Catholic hospital, received a Catholic education, joined the Catholic Boy Scouts, played soccer for a Catholic team, married another Catholic, joined a Catholic trade union, read a Catholic newspaper, died in a Catholic home for the elderly, and been buried in a Catholic graveyard by a Catholic undertaker.

The leaders of the various pillars negotiated the slicing of the national pie. This elite accommodation operated on the basis of informal rules: for example, that distributions should reflect the relative population size of each group, and that each group should retain a minority veto over matters it judged vital to its own interests. Elite commitment to a policy of live-and-let-live overcame the potential instability caused by cultural conflict at mass level.

In a way, political business resembled international diplomacy, with the leaders of each pillar acting in confidential negotiations almost as if they represented a separate country. As with the international norm of non-intervention in states' domestic affairs, each pillar was left in control of the resources it was allocated. Catholic leaders might give priority to welfare within their community, Protestants might allocate more money to their schools, and the Social Democrats might choose to develop their newspapers. In what amounted to informal federalism, a culture of accommodation among the elites allowed separate communities to live together in a single state. The pillars supported the roof of the state, while the roof protected the pillars.

The pillars have crumbled as religious divisions have weakened. Nonetheless, elite compromise remains a key theme in several European democracies, not just the Netherlands. On Belgium, for instance, Deschouwer (2009, p. 7) reports that despite a 'depillarization of the minds' in a country previously divided into Catholic, socialist, and liberal segments, 'the pillar organizations are still very visible and do play a role in political decision-making'. So, Lijphart's formulation remains a practical demonstration of how elite political culture can be detached from the wider group in a way that contributes to overall stability.

Three qualifications are in order. First, the key role of elite culture means that consociational democracy is more than a matter of institutional arrangements; it cannot be expected to flourish in all conditions. In particular, what worked for the Netherlands in the 1950s will not necessarily succeed in low-income countries emerging from internal conflict. Second, elite accommodation can also be seen as an elite cartel, limiting popular influence in national politics; it is a brake on, as much as a form of, democracy. Third, there is a danger that empowering the pillars will simply reinforce them, slowing the long-term process of integration between divided groups (McGarry and O'Leary, 2006).

Political culture in authoritarian states

Just as Almond and Verba argued that stable liberal democracies are underpinned by a civic culture, so Welzel and Inglehart (2005, 2009) suggest that many authoritarian regimes are sustained by a cultural emphasis among their populations on the values of security, rather than self-expression. From this perspective, it is an error to see non-democratic rule as secured only by repression of a disaffected citizenry. Rather, authoritarian regimes can be as legitimate as democracies; it is only the basis of their authority that differs. So, we have here a cultural theory of political stability in authoritarian settings.

Specifically, Welzel and Inglehart (2009, p. 131) suggest that in low-income countries security values are to the fore: 'people give priority to authority and strong leadership over freedom and expression'. What is more, if a democracy does emerge in such unsympathetic cultures, it may be unstable: 'democracy is fragile when it is a "democracy without democrats"'.

Even if people reject the current leaders of an authoritarian government, they may simply want to replace them with another set of non-democratic rulers. In other words, Western analysts who interpret all dissent in dictatorships as a plea for democracy may simply be seeing what they wish for. Furthermore, people living under non-democratic governments who do favour democracy may interpret the term as referring not so much to self-rule as to social order, national autonomy, and a strong economy.

Some scholars suggest that Russia provides an example of an authoritarian culture centred on security and order. Its competitive authoritarian regime is buttressed by a political culture offering only limited support for democratic principles. Thus, Gitelman (2005, p. 248) writes that:

the authoritarian traditions of Russia mean that people are not used to democratic behaviours and values, such as welcoming pluralism in thinking and behaving, tolerating dissent and supporting seemingly less efficient methods of democratic decision-making. They do not easily see the advantages of debate, discussion and non-conformity, and not deferring to a class of 'superiors'.

Inglehart (2000) also judged that Russian culture was exceptionally stony ground on which to nurture a liberal democracy. Drawing on a survey conducted in 1999 and 2000, he found that Russians were less trusting, tolerant, and happy than people in most other countries – cultural features reinforced, but not created, by communist rule. His conclusion was that the prospects for a transition from a competitive authoritarian regime to a liberal democracy were, at that stage, somewhat limited.

In many non-democratic Islamic countries, too, authoritarian rulers seek to draw from the well of Islamic culture in a way that supports their hold on power. They present democracy as an alien Western concept which in practice leads to licence rather than freedom, to an emphasis on material rather than spiritual values, and to the pursuit of individual self-interest rather than social harmony.

For example, Mahathir bin Mohamad, Prime Minister of Malaysia, 1981–2003, condemned Western democracies in which 'political leaders are afraid to do what is right, where the people and their leaders live in fear of the free media which they so loudly proclaim as inviolable'. In this way, authoritarian rule can be presented as expressing an indigenous cultural tradition inherently opposed to Western liberalism.

One objection to the position that non-democratic regimes are supported by political culture is that the relationship is really the other way round. As we have already suggested, culture can reflect rather than sustain the nature of a regime. Consider Russia: the lack of political trust there may well reflect the country's non-democratic history and the corrupt nature of its contemporary governance. But were a secure liberal democracy to take root in Russia, by whatever means, the nation's political culture would probably also shift in a democratic direction. In other words, over the longer term political culture reflects the nature of the regime, rather than vice versa.

Interestingly, Welzel and Inglehart (2009, p. 136) reject this rebuttal. They insist, as did Gabriel Almond a generation earlier, that political culture is an independent force. In rejecting the view that it is merely a mirror of the current political system, Welzel and Inglehart suggest that 'high levels of intrinsic support for democracy emerged in many authoritarian societies *before* they made the transition to democracy', citing such examples as South Korea and Taiwan. Their view is that, as societies modernize, so too do its better-educated segments give more emphasis to self-expression and postmaterial values. This cultural shift then leads to pressure to democratize.

From this perspective, public protest in Russia against Vladimir Putin's manipulation of parliamentary elections in 2011, and of the presidential contest of 2012, might be seen as evidence that the country's political culture is moving in a democratic direction in response to modernization. After all, many demonstrators were younger, better-educated people in the largest cities, primarily Moscow – exactly the constituency where cultural change would be expected to arrive first.

In this line of argument, we see an interpretation of political culture as the mechanism linking modernization and democracy, a relationship we discussed in Chapter 3. Modernization supposedly initiates a transition from survival to self-expression values and this cultural transformation favours liberal democracy. To put the same point the other way around, authoritarian rule is sustained by traditional cultures focused on the need for physical and material security. Non-democratic rulers who do modernize their countries initiate a cultural transformation which becomes, in effect, their own death-warrant. China's communist leaders, beware!

As always, we must beware sweeping statements. Certainly, the culture of highly traditional, low-income countries provides stony ground for stable liberal democracy but that does not mean that all, or even many, dictatorships are legitimized by the political culture of the societies they govern.

In fact, many authoritarian rulers have ignored political culture altogether. Consider military regimes. Most generals rode to power on a tank and showed little concern for the niceties of political culture. Their task was to protect their own back against challengers seeking to supplant them and to provide money to those willing to offer political support. Far from seeking to draw support from the wider culture, military rulers typically sought to isolate the mass population from engagement with government, thus shrinking the political arena. 'We rule because we rule' remains the implicit message of some crude authoritarian regimes, civilian as well as military.

More commonly, authoritarian rulers do seek and want elaborate public justifications for their rule. These attempts (as with bin Mohamad in Malaysia) are bound to draw on cultural traditions. But whether such efforts succeed is another matter; they are typically moves in a contested and self-aware political game. Seeking to locate the survival of an authoritarian regime solely, or even primarily, in a nation's political culture is, we suggest, a doubtful strategy.

Discussion questions

- What are the main political subcultures in your country?

- Does modernization generate postmaterialism?

- What difference does it make if people trust their government?

- In your society, how, if at all, do the values of the political elite differ from those of the general public?

- Is there a clash of civilizations between the Muslim and Western worlds?

- Are authoritarian regimes sustained by cultures giving 'priority to authority and strong leadership over freedom and expression' (Welzel and Inglehart, 2009, p. 131)?

Further reading

P. Chabal and J.-P. Daloz, *Culture Troubles: Politics and the Interpretation of Meaning* (2006). An interpretive perspective on political culture which suggests that political analysis should be grounded in what makes sense to the actors involved.

S. Huntington, *The Clash of Civilizations and the Making of World Order* (1996). An original and controversial book arguing not only that civilizational clashes are a threat to world peace, but also that a world order based on civilizations is the best safeguard against war.

R. Inglehart and C. Welzel, *Modernization, Cultural Change and Democracy: The Human Development Sequence* (2005). Presents a broad intellectual framework in which modernization is seen as initiating cultural change and cultural change is seen as a driver of democracy.

P. Norris, *Democratic Deficit: Critical Citizens Revisited* (2011). Based on extensive survey analysis, this book challenges the claim that liberal democracies have experienced a continuously rising tide of public disaffection since the early 1970s.

P. Norris and R. Inglehart, *Sacred and Secular: Religion and Politics Worldwide*, 2nd edn (2011). A landmark study linking modern societies with secular values and viewing religious values as a response to insecurity.

S. Pharr and R. Putnam, eds, *Disaffected Democracies: What's Troubling The Trilateral Countries?* (2000). Reflections on why citizens of liberal democracies increasingly reported dissatisfaction and frustration with their governments at the turn of the century.

R. Putnam, ed., *Democracies in Flux: The Evolution of Social Capital in Contemporary Society* (2002). A group of scholars examine the state of social capital in eight liberal democracies.

ONLINE RESOURCES AVAILABLE

Visit the companion website at **www.palgrave.com/politics/hague** to access additional learning resources, including multiple-choice questions, chapter summaries, web links and practice essay questions.

Chapter 7 Political communication

Society – and, with it, politics – is created, sustained, and modified through communication. Without a continuous exchange of information, attitudes, and values, society would be impossible. As Williams (1962, p. 11) wrote, 'what we call society is not only a network of political and economic arrangements, but also a process of learning and communication'. It is also a technique of control: 'Give me a balcony and I will be president', said José Maria Velasco, five times president of Ecuador. Communication is a core political activity, allowing meaning to be constructed, culture transmitted, and authority exercised.

Assessments of the quality of political communication enter into the fundamental issue of classifying governments. A free flow of information is one test in discriminating between liberal democracies and authoritarian regimes. Dahl (1998, p. 37), for example, judges that a liberal democracy must provide opportunities for what he calls enlightened understanding: 'within reasonable limits as to time, each member [of a political associa-tion] must have equal and effective opportunities for learning about rele-vant alternative policies and their likely consequences'. In a competitive authoritarian regime, by contrast, dominance of major broadcasting chan-nels is a tool through which leaders maintain their ascendancy over poten-tial challengers. An authoritarian regime may permit no explicit dissent at all.

Even though much recent research in political communication focuses on the message itself and the meanings embedded within it, it is helpful to remind ourselves of the existence of receivers and, sometimes, an impact. The danger of focusing solely on content is that we learn nothing about the receivers and even less about whether the communication has the slightest effect on them. Blaming media bias for why others fail to see the world as we do can be tempting, but is usually superficial and unenlightening.

So, it is helpful to break the activity of political communication into its component parts. The transmission model (Figure 7.1) distinguishes five components:

- a sender: who?

- a message: what?

- a channel: how?

- a receiver: to whom?

- an impact: with what effect?

STUDYING . . .
POLITICAL COMMUNICATION

- Communication is a core political activity and its study should therefore form an important part of political analysis. In particular, a free flow of communication provides one test for distinguishing between liberal democracies and authoritarian regimes.

- Clichés abound regarding our media-driven world. Too often, mass media coverage is assumed to be influential without there being any evidence cited in support. To identify the effect of specific content, direct evidence of impact on consumers is needed.

- Researchers identify four classes of media effects: reinforcement, agenda-setting, framing, and priming. It is salutary to consider whether even today reinforcement (preaching to the converted) remains the most important of these effects.

- A broader perspective suggests that media provide a structure for our worldview, rather than simply an influence on it. This more interpretive account provides an alternative, if looser, framework for studying the political role of the mass media.

- Contemporary trends – including the shift to more commercial, fragmented, global, and interactive media – are reshaping the communications environment. These developments impact on politicians, on electors, and on the relationship between them (e.g. election campaigns).

- The decline of paid-for newspapers and broadcast current affairs raises an issue in need of further exploration: how can we sustain professional news-gathering and interpretation in an Internet age when consumers expect information to be free?

- In focusing on new media, there is a tendency to write off, or at least to ignore, broadcast television. Commercial advertisers never make this mistake; neither should we.

Figure 7.1 The transmission model of political communication

Any act of communication can be parsed thus: who says what to whom, through which medium and with what effects

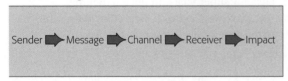

For example, a local party (the sender) might distribute a leaflet (the channel) advocating voting at a forthcoming election (the message) to its own supporters (the receivers), with the result that turnout goes up (impact).

The value of this model is that is highly specific, encouraging us to break down any communication into its specific parts and discouraging us from assuming that these parts will always operate in a uniform way.

Media development

The intimate connections between communication and politics are revealed by examining the early development of the **mass media** (see Timeline). Especially in the nineteenth and twentieth centuries, the expansion of mass media facilitated the emergence of a common national identity and the growth of the state. For the first time, the mass media delivered a shared experience for dispersed populations, providing a glue to connect the citizens of large political units. We cannot understand the development of either the media or the state without appreciating this connection between them; both are instruments of modernity. Here, we outline the emergence of the two key media of the nineteenth and twentieth centuries: the press and broadcasting.

> **Mass media** are means of communication that reach a large and potentially unlimited number of people. Television, radio, and websites are examples. Mass media are essentially one-to-many (non-interactive). **Social media**, such as Facebook and Twitter, are interactive platforms, with designated recipients, which facilitate collective or individual communication for the exchange of user-generated content. Social media bridge mass and personal communication.

Newspapers

Widespread literacy in a shared language permitted the emergence of popular newspapers in Western states, the key development in political communication during the nineteenth and early twentieth centuries (Dooley and Baron, 2001). Advances in printing and distribution, especially the railway, opened up the prospect of transforming party journals with a small circulation into populist and profitable papers funded by advertising. By growing away from their party roots, newspapers became not merely more popular but also, paradoxically, more important to politics.

In compact countries with national distribution, such as Britain and Japan, newspapers built enormous circulations. Owners became powerful political figures. In interwar Britain, for example, four newspaper barons – Lords Beaverbrook, Rothermere, Camrose and Kemsley – owned papers with a combined circulation of over 13 million, amounting to one in every two daily papers sold. Stanley Baldwin, a prime minister of the time, famously described such proprietors as 'aiming at power without responsibility – the prerogative of the harlot throughout the ages' (Curran and Seaton, 2009, p. 64).

Broadcasting

Although newspapers remain significant channels of political communication, their primacy was supplanted by broadcasting in the twentieth century. Cinema newsreels, radio, and then television enabled communication with the mass public to take place in a new form: spoken rather than written, personal rather than abstract, and, on occa-

sion, live rather than reported. Oral communication reasserted itself, though now in a form which could escape the confines of an assembled group to reach a national audience. Broadcasting was the central communications revolution of the twentieth century.

Broadcasting's impact in Western liberal democracies was relatively benign. A small number of national television channels initially dominated the airwaves in most countries, providing a shared experience of national events and popular entertainment. By offering some common ground to societies which were, in these early post-war decades, still strongly divided by class and religion, these new media initially served as agents of national integration. As John Reith, Director-General of the BBC from 1923 to 1938, claimed with some justification, in an age of broadcasting 'the nation would gather as one man' (1949, p. 4).

However, the impact of broadcasting on politicians themselves was more dramatic. Leaders had to acquire new communication techniques. A public speech to a live audience encouraged expansive words and dramatic gestures but a quieter tone was needed for transmission from the broadcasting studio direct to the living room. The task was to converse with the unseen listener and viewer, rather than to deliver a speech to a visible audience gathered together in one place. The art was to talk to the millions as though they were individuals.

President Franklin Roosevelt's fireside chats, broadcast live by radio to the American population in the 1930s, exemplified this new approach. The impact of Roosevelt's somewhat folksy idiom was undeniable. He talked not so much to the citizens but as a citizen and was rewarded with his country's trust. In this way, broadcasting – and the forgotten medium of radio, specifically – transformed not only the reach, but also the style, of political communication (Barber, 1992).

Broadcasting is also making a substantial contribution to political communication in most low-income countries, albeit for different reasons. In the developing world, broadcasting (whether radio or television) possesses two major advantages over print media. First, it does not require physical distribution to each user; second, it is accessible to the one in five of the world's population who cannot read.

THE DEVELOPMENT OF COMMUNICATION MEDIA IN THE TWENTIETH AND TWENTY-FIRST CENTURIES

Later 19th and early 20th century	Popular newspapers emerge, often with mass circulation. New railway networks allow national distribution.
1930s	Radio's golden age. For the first time, politicians broadcast directly into electors' homes.
1950s–1960s	Television becomes the most popular, and usually the most trusted, medium in Western countries. By regulation or state ownership, politicians secure access to the medium. Entertainment programmes from the USA are widely exported, diffusing American values.
1970s–1980s	The television audience begins to fragment, with an increase in the number of channels, distribution by cable and satellite, and widespread use of video.
1990s	Internet access reaches more affluent and educated groups in Western democracies, representing a further expansion of international communication. Mobile telephony emerges.
2000s	Mobile telephone access becomes standard, bringing telephony to many low-income countries for the first time. The Internet reaches the mass population in Western societies. Sharp decline in readership of printed newspapers.
2010s	Continued expansion of digital **social media**, further extending horizontal communication among citizens. In 2012, Facebook claims a billion users per month. The Internet is increasingly accessed via smartphones.

These factors initially encouraged the spread of radio. Villagers could gather round the shared set to hear the latest news, not least on the price of local crops. Today, television and mobile telephony are also accessible to many of the world's poor, expanding opportunities not only for downward communication from the elite, but also for horizontal communication between ordinary people. These developments surely mark a communications revolution.

Just as some lower-income countries have moved directly to mobile telephony, eliminating the need for an expensive fixed-wire infrastructure, so also have they developed broadcasting networks without passing through the stage of mass circulation newspapers. The capacity of ruling politicians to reach out to poor, rural populations through these radio and television networks remains an important component of governance in competitive authoritarian regimes, particularly in Latin America.

In the twenty-first century, the four major trends in communications in higher-income countries are commercialization, fragmentation, globalization, and interaction (Box 7.1). Their combined effect is that governments tend to lose control over broadcasting as consumers either choose their own polit-

Contemporary trends in mass communication

Commercialization   the decline of public broadcasting and the rise of for-profit media treating users as consumers rather than citizens

Fragmentation   more channels and an enhanced ability to download and consume programmes on demand

Globalization   improved access to overseas events and media in the global village

Interaction   increased use of interactive channels (e.g. email, social media), reducing passive top-down exposure to politics.

ical programming, or increasingly escape from politics altogether. So, if the mass media performed a nation-building function in the twentieth century, their emerging impact in the new century is to splinter the traditional national audience, fragmenting a shared experience and perhaps contributing thereby to the decline of traditional participation in formal national politics.

Commercialization

Mass communication is increasingly treated as the important business it has become. It allows media moguls such as Rupert Murdoch to build transnational broadcasting networks, achieving on a global scale the prominence which the newspaper barons of the nineteenth century acquired at national level. Even in northern and southern Europe, where the state traditionally exerted substantial influence over the media, the 1970s and 1980s saw the introduction of new commercial channels; in addition, advertising was introduced to many public stations.

Such developments threatened previously cosy links between national parties and national broadcasters. They represented a shift to seeing the viewer in less political terms – as a consumer, rather than a citizen. Parties no longer called the shots and politics had to justify its share of screen time. In an increasingly commercial environment, Tracey (1998) claimed that public service broadcasting had

become nothing more than 'a corpse on leave from its grave'.

In a similar way, McChesney argued in *Rich Media, Poor Democracies* (1999) that commercialization shrinks the public space in which political issues are discussed. Channels in search of profit devote little time to serious politics; instead, they concentrate on soft news – news you can use. Certainly, profit-seeking media have no incentive to supply public goods such as an informed citizenry and a high electoral turnout, which were traditional concerns of public media. For those who view democracy as a form of collective debate, media commercialization represents a considerable challenge.

Against this, commercial broadcasters reply that it is preferable to reach a mass audience with limited but stimulating political coverage than it is to offer extensive but dull political programming which, in reality, only ever reached a minority with a prior interest in public affairs (Norris, 2000). Specialist political programmes continue for political junkies but such broadcasts can no longer be foisted on unwilling audiences.

Fragmentation

Consumers are increasingly able to watch, hear, and read what they want, when they want, how they want. Long gone are the days when American viewers were restricted to three large networks (ABC, CBS, and NBC); young Americans are now more likely to be found using the Internet than watching TV (Murrie, 2006). Distribution by cable, satellite, the Internet and mobile devices allows viewers to receive a greater range of content – local and overseas, as well as national. Content can be accessed on demand, through a range of media, reducing reliance on what traditional broadcasters make available at a specific moment.

The outcome is a more splintered audience, with advertising revenue divided between more channels, including online. During the 1990s, the audience share of the big three American television networks dropped by over 30 per cent. Printed newspaper circulations are also plummeting in the developed world: between 2006 and 2011, by 17 per cent for dailies in the USA and by 12 per cent in Western Europe (WAN, 2011). Local and evening newspapers are closing (though some are reinventing themselves online), with some shift of printed material to generally less political free papers.

The political implications of this shift from broadcasting to narrowcasting are substantial. Governments, parties, and commercial advertisers encounter more difficulty in reaching a mass audience when viewers can defend themselves by simply choosing another channel online or via their remote control. Where earlier generations would passively watch whatever appeared on their television screen, the Internet is inherently user-driven; people select where to go. Where mass media once provided a shared experience for a national audience, the Internet encourages the formation of electronic ghettos for specialized groups, whether of the left or right, mainstream or extreme.

Overall exposure to politics falls as the electorate (especially young people) becomes harder to reach. News junkies can tune in but most people tune out. In response, political parties are forced to adopt a greater range and sophistication of marketing strategies, including the use of personalized but expensive contact techniques such as direct mail, email, social networks, and telephone – as skilfully exploited by Barack Obama in securing donations and volunteers for his successful campaigns in 2008 and 2012 (Kreiss, 2012).

In this more fragmented media environment, politicians have to communicate in a manner, and at a time, of the voters' choosing. They must continue their migration from television news to higher-rated talk shows, blurring the distinction between the politician and the celebrity in the expanding Pollywood zone where Politics meets Hollywood (Street, 2011, ch. 9). They compete for followers on Facebook and Twitter against sports personalities, movie stars and the latest TV celebrity. The sound bite, never unimportant, becomes even more vital as politicians learn to articulate their agenda in a short interview, or an even briefer commercial. Barack Obama must battle not only Mitt Romney, but also George Clooney.

Just as the balance within the media industry has moved from public service to private profit, so fragmentation has shifted the emphasis in political communication from parties to voters. Politicians rode the emergence of broadcasting with considerable success in the twentieth century, but they are experiencing a rougher ride in the new millennium of fragmented media. As Mazzoleni (1987) pointed out, the balance of power between parties and the media has switched from a 'party logic' to a 'media logic'.

Globalization

'The empires of the future will be empires of the mind', said Winston Churchill in 1943. Certainly, in the global village, the world has been compressed into a television screen. In 1776, the English reaction to the American Declaration of Independence took 50 days to filter back to the United States. In 1950, the British response to the outbreak of the Korean War was broadcast in America after 24 hours. In 2003, British and American viewers watched live broadcasts of the Iraq War at the same time. We now take for granted the almost immediate transmission of newsworthy events around the world.

It is now harder than ever for governments to isolate their populations from international developments. Even before the Internet, communist states found it difficult to jam foreign radio broadcasts aimed at their people. Discussing the collapse of communist states, Eberle (1990, pp. 194–5) claimed that 'the changes in Eastern Europe and the Soviet Union were as much the triumph of communication as the failure of communism'. Today, China's iron curtain of censorship can easily be circumvented by those of its people who take the trouble to access the range of overseas blogs and sites documenting the latest developments within their country.

Recent technological developments also facilitate underground opposition to authoritarian regimes. A small group with Internet access now has the potential to draw the world's attention to political abuses, providing source material for alert journalists. The governments of Iran and Saudi Arabia have each suffered from overseas groups in this way, though both regimes remain in place.

Interaction

A particular aspect of fragmentation is the growing exposure to interactive channels of communication. Radio phone-ins allow ordinary people to listen to their peers discussing current issues, without mediation by a politician; blogs perform the same function in electronic space. Messaging systems and social media are inherently interactive. Such media allow peer-to-peer interchanges which tend to crowd out top-down communication from politicians to voters.

m

Table 7.1 Internet use in selected countries in the Middle East and North Africa, 2000–09

In the first decade of the twenty-first century, Internet use expanded rapidly across the Middle East and North Africa from a low base. The growth of social media surely contributed to the Arab Spring of 2011.

	Internet users		Population using Internet (%) 2009	Regime overthrown in 2011?
	2000	**2009**		
Iran	250,000	32,200,000	48	No
Morocco	100,000	10,300,000	33	No
Saudi Arabia	200,000	7,700,000	27	No
Tunisia	100,000	2,800,000	27	Yes
Egypt	450,000	12,568,900	16	Yes
Algeria	50,000	4,100,000	12	No
Libya	10,000	323,000	5	Yes
Yemen	15,000	370,000	2	Yes

Source: Adapted from Wheeler and Mintz (2012), table 10.1.

The growth of interactive platforms sits uneasily alongside the reactive role expected of most voters in a representative democracy. Implicitly, a young generation schooled on interactive media is raising an important question to which politicians have yet to find an adequate answer: why should we listen to you when we have the option to interact electronically with friends of our own age who share our interests?

The use of online platforms for interaction among citizens has further weakened political control in some authoritarian regimes. The Arab Spring is a revealing illustration. As Table 7.1 shows, the Internet became a significant medium in the first decade of the new millennium in the Middle East and North Africa, allowing peer-to-peer communication among alienated urban youth, as in Iran's *Blogistan* (Srebeny and Khiabany, 2010). This growth was not confined to those countries experiencing regime change in 2011 but did become a significant factor in some overthrows, notably in Egypt and Tunisia.

Online facilities not only permitted rapid circulation of news about the latest protest venues, but also created a rare free space for social interaction – for example, between people of the opposite sex (Bayat, 2010). The word on the tweet proved harder to censor than the word on the street. In this way, social media created a model of a free and exciting democratic society against which authoritarian political systems in the Arab world seemed ever more ossified. Facebook became the freedom forum, leading Lynch (2011, p. 301) to claim boldly that 'the long term evolution of a new kind of public sphere may matter more than immediate political outcomes'. Wheeler and Mintz (2012, pp. 260–1) argue along similar lines:

Political and social change can emerge from the exchange of ideas, information and models that create and sustain an active citizenry ... The ground for significant political change in authoritarian contexts can be readied by people using new media tools to discover and generate new spaces within which they can voice their dissent and assert their presence in pursuit of bettering their lives.

Media structures

Technological innovations such as broadcasting are potentially universal, applying to all countries.

Nonetheless, the way in which the mass media has developed, and been integrated into national politics, varies significantly across liberal democracies, yielding distinctive **media structures**.

> The **structure of the media** refers to historically stable patterns of media use and, in particular, to the relationships between media, the state, and the economy. For example, the extent of newspaper circulation, the scope of public broadcasting, and the partisanship of the press are components of the media structure.

In a contribution described by de Albuquerque (2012, p. 72) as 'a turning point for comparative media studies', Hallin and Mancini (2004) distinguished between Anglo-American, northern European, and southern European media structures within the liberal democratic world (Box 7.2). Exploring these structures demonstrates the value of moving beyond a uniform characterization of the media in liberal democracies towards an appreciation of crossnational variation.

In the *Anglo-American* model, first, market mechanisms predominate and the mainly private media respond to commercial considerations. Reflecting the early achievement of mass literacy, newspaper circulation remained relatively high into the twenty-first century. The notion of journalism as a news-gathering profession is entrenched, while the media and political worlds inhabit distinct spheres, with the former acting as a watchdog over the latter. This liberal model underpins many instinctive conceptions of the proper relationship between media and politics in a free democracy.

But the Anglo-American model is not the only one on offer. In the *northern European* structure, the media are interpreted as responsible social actors with their own contribution to make to society in general, and to political stability in particular. Newspapers and even television networks represent particular groups (e.g. religions, trade unions, political parties) but do so in an environment shaped by an interventionist state. For example, public broadcasting is significant and the government subsidizes private media in support of both their information and representation functions. Regulations governing media coverage, such as the right to privacy and to reply, are also more extensive than in the Anglo-American format.

BOX 7.2

Media structures in liberal democracies

	Anglo-American structure	Northern European structure	Southern European structure
Newspaper circulation	High	High	Low
Professionalism of journalism	High	High	Low
Links between media and politics	Low	High	High
State intervention	Low	High	High
Examples	Britain, Canada, Ireland, USA	Denmark, Finland, Norway, Sweden	Greece, Portugal, Spain

Source: Adapted from Hallin and Mancini (2004), who also refer to the Anglo-American structure as 'liberal'; to the Northern European structure as 'democratic corporatist'; and to the Southern European structure as 'polarized pluralist'.

This northern European format – which to a degree extends beyond Scandinavia to Belgium, Germany, and the Netherlands – is an element of a wider settlement in which the political system emphasizes the search for accommodation between strong social groups. In this sense, the role of the media is similar to that of such mechanisms as proportional representation and coalition government: to facilitate the expression of, and encourage agreement between, potentially hostile social groups. Journalistic professionalism is fully supported, but is tempered by an awareness of the media's role as an actor in, and not merely an observer of, politics and society.

Finally, let us turn to the *southern European* structure. In some ways, this format is the opposite of the northern European model. In such Mediterranean countries as Greece, Portugal, and Spain, authoritarian regimes initially acted as a brake on the development of universal literacy, mass circulation newspapers, and a vibrant civil society. Even following the democratic transitions of the 1970s, governing parties still strongly influenced public broadcasting, while newspapers and other television stations are subject to party political influence. Television becomes a potent vehicle of popular entertainment but newspaper circulation remains low, with journalists seeing themselves as providing ideologically-loaded commentary, rather than hard news. In these party-dominated southern European countries, the political position of the media remains even more subdued than in the northern European format (see Spotlight on Spain). Elements of this format can also be found in many non-Western countries (Hallin and Mancini, 2012).

Hallin and Mancini demonstrate the danger of discussing the media in liberal democracies without reference to national – or, in this case, regional – traditions. As with many categories in comparative politics, the 'same' role is understood differently in different areas. Consider conceptions of the journalist's task. In the Anglo-American world, the journalist is a reporter: a news-gathering professional, speaking truth to power and engaged in a combative relationship with government. In northern Europe, journalists are less adversarial: they are expected to add greater sensitivity to the national interest, political stability, their newspaper's outlook and the social group it serves. In southern Europe, journalism focuses less on information and more on commentary from an ideological perspective. These varying conceptions of the journalist's role reflect and reinforce differing relationships between the worlds of media and politics.

As with any other schema, Hallin and Mancini's classification underplays variation within each category. For example, within the general Anglo-American format public broadcasting and partisan national daily newspapers remain far more significant in the UK than in the USA, where commerce dominates the media and newspapers are primarily local.

The value of Hallin and Mancini's scheme is being eroded by the contemporary media trends discussed in the previous section. Within Western liberal democracies, the tendency is to a more Anglo-American approach, especially in conceptions of the journalist's task. Still, the authors provide insight into where the media in the Western world are coming from – if less so on where they are going.

Media impact

What is the media's impact on those exposed to it? This innocent question takes us to the final element of the transmission model (Figure 7.1) and to an area where unqualified assertions of media power often remain unsupported by clear evidence.

One way of thinking about the question of impact is counterfactually. How would politics change if all mass media were suddenly abolished? Clearly, the consequences would be profound. For example, we would surely observe the denationalization of politics, with a revival of local campaigning in particular. But such mental experiments are as hypothetical as imagining a house without walls: particularly with the emergence of social media, there is perhaps more plausibility in describing the media as the structure within which many people (especially young people) live their political lives. Jones (2005, p. 17) articulates this viewpoint:

Media are our primary point of access to politics – the space in which politics now chiefly happens for most people, and the place for political encounters that precede, shape and at times determine further bodily participation (if it is to happen at all) … Such encounters do much more than provide 'information' about politics. They constitute our mental maps of the political world outside our direct experience. They provide a reservoir of images and voices, heroes and villains, sayings and slogans, facts and ideas that we draw on in making sense of politics.

For example, a clutch of American movies about Vietnam, 9/11, and the Iraq war provided political exposure to material which was, in its way, as much a form of political participation as volunteering to take part in an election campaign, or paying a subscription to an interest group. The underlying insight here – that following politics in the media is itself a form of political behaviour, rather than just an influence on it – captures the importance of the media in today's world.

Mechanisms of impact

Even so, it is well worthwhile examining how scholarly thinking about specific media effects has evolved. Box 7.3 outlines four mechanisms of influence: reinforcement, agenda-setting, framing, and priming. At various times since 1945, each of these themes has contributed to academic thinking about how we should address media impact; together, they provide a helpful repertoire in analysing the more tangible effects of the media.

In the 1950s, before television became pre-eminent, the **reinforcement** thesis – also known as the 'minimal effects model' – held sway (Klapper, 1960). The argument then was that party loyalties initially transmitted through the family acted as a political sunscreen protecting people from media effects. People saw what they wanted to see and remembered what they wanted to recall.

In Britain, for instance, where national newspapers were strongly partisan, many working-class people brought up in Labour households continued to read Labour papers as adults. The correlation between the partisanship of newspapers and their readers reflected **self-selection** by readers, rather than the propaganda impact of the press. Given strong self-selection, the most the press could do was to reinforce readers' existing dispositions, encouraging them to stay loyal to the cause and to turn out on election day. Those effects may have been significant but they hardly justified the more extreme statements about the power of the media.

Self-selection is a choice made by an individual. For example, people who are already racist may choose to visit racist websites, complicating the task of estimating the websites' impact.

The reinforcement theory proved its value fifty-plus years ago; it helped to account for stable party loyalties, and remains relevant. Consider the polarized environment in some segments of the American media. The typical viewer of Fox News is surely more

BOX 7.3

Media effects

	Definition	Comment
Reinforcement	The media strengthen existing opinions	People consume media which support their existing outlook (selective exposure). In addition, people interpret information to render it consistent with their prior opinions (selective interpretation) and forget information that runs counter to existing beliefs (selective recall).
Agenda-setting	The media influence what we think and talk about	The compressed nature of news, especially on television, means coverage is highly selective. Reported events are widely discussed by the public but non-reported events lose visibility.
Framing	How an event is narrated as a coherent story highlights its particular features	A frame focuses on particular aspects of a problem, its origins, remedies and evaluation. It encourages viewers and readers to interpret the topic in a similar way.
Priming	Media coverage influences how we interpret events beyond those in the particular story	Priming extends media impact beyond the coverage of a given story. For example, coverage of a crime story in the national media may encourage electors to judge candidates for election by their law and order policies.

likely to be a conservative drawn to that network than to be an ex-liberal converted to the right as a result of stumbling upon Fox News' coverage. To some extent, at least, Fox News – as the British newspapers of old – preaches to the converted.

Alternatively, consider the Internet. The web allows electors to seek out, and be reinforced by, any shade of opinion with which they already sympathize. In the main, opponents will chose not to go there, except if they are one of the few who wish to know their enemy. Here, too, the effect of self-selection is to facilitate reinforcement but limit conversion.

Although the reinforcement account retains relevance, it is surely past its best as a primary perspective on media effects. We can no longer imagine the typical elector as wholly contained in an information silo dominated by one political outlook. Party loyalties have weakened and the press has declined as television news (more neutral, Fox News notwithstanding) became more pervasive. There must be more to media effects than mere reinforcement. It was for such reasons that the agenda-setting view of media impact gained ground in the 1970s and 1980s.

The **agenda-setting** perspective contends that the media (and television in particular) influence what we think about, though not necessarily what we think. The media write certain items onto the agenda and, by implication, keep other issues away from the public's gaze. As Lazarsfeld and Merton (1948) pointed out in an early statement, 'to the extent that the mass media have influenced their audiences, it has stemmed not only from what is said but more significantly from what is not said.'

In an election campaign, for example, television directs our attention to major candidates and to the race for victory; by contrast, fringe candidates and the issues are often treated as secondary. Walter Lippman's widely quoted view (1922) of the press articulated the agenda-setting perspective: 'it is like a beam of a searchlight that moves restlessly about, bringing one episode and then another out of the darkness and into vision'.

Agenda-setting is forced by the limited length of news broadcasts. It is through their assumptions about newsworthiness that news editors resolve their daily dilemma of reducing a day's worth of world events to less than 30 minutes on the evening broadcast. In deciding what to cover, in what order, and

---

BOX 7.4

Some tests used by journalists to determine newsworthiness

- Will the story have a strong impact on our audience?
- Does the story involve violence? ('If it bleeds, it leads.')
- Is the story current and novel?
- Does the story involve well-known people?

---

what to leave out, programme editors set the agenda and exert their impact.

Because news programmes focus on the exceptional, their content is invariably an unrepresentative record of events. Policy fiascos receive more attention than policy successes; corruption is a story but integrity is a bore; a fresh story gathers more coverage than a new development of a tired theme. Necessarily, agenda-setting creates a warped image of the world. The shorter news bulletins become, the more selective the editor must be and the greater the distortion becomes.

But we should recognize two limitations to the agenda-setting perspective. First, editors do not select stories on a whim (Box 7.4). In deciding whether to pursue a story, they take into account their assessment of the interest their audience will show in it. Editors are highly sensitive to the item's potential impact on audience size and appreciation.

Editors are paid to demonstrate their news sense; if they consistently fail to do so, they lose their jobs. Just as we do not blame the newsreader for the news, neither should we condemn the news selector for the agenda. It is therefore naive to attribute broad agenda-setting power to editors simply because they make specific judgements about what is to appear on screen or on the front page. The wider cultural context enters into their calculation of what to cover.

A more nuanced view, that the media circulate rather than create opinions, is implicit in Newton's assessment of the relationship between journalists and society (2006, p. 215):

Implicit in many statements about media effects on society is the idea that somehow the media are quite

COUNTRY PROFILE

SPAIN

Form of government ■ a parliamentary liberal democracy, with strong regions and a hereditary monarch playing a largely ceremonial role as head of state.

Executive ■ the prime minister appoints the cabinet (typically 16–20 strong). Cabinet members need not be drawn from parliament. The monarch – Juan Carlos, since 1975 – is head of state.

Legislature ■ the bicameral legislature (Cortes Generales) consists of the Congress of Deputies (350 members) and the Senate (264 members).

Constitution and judiciary ■ The Constitutional Court consists of 12 members appointed by parliament, the government, and the judiciary itself. The legal system is based on civil law.

Electoral system ■ deputies are elected by PR with closed party lists. A small district magnitude gives large parties an advantage. For the Senate, electors can vote for up to three candidates for their province. The four winning most votes are elected.

Party system ■ the 1978 constitution placed parties at the centre of the new democracy. The Spanish Socialist Workers' Party (PSOE) and the centre-right People's Party (PP, Popular Party) together secured 73 per cent of the vote in the 2011 elections to the lower chamber. The PP won a majority of seats with 44 per cent of the vote.

Population (annual growth rate): 47.0 m (+0.7%)	
World Bank income group: high income	
Human development index (rank/out of): 23/187	
Political rights score:	
Civil liberties score: ❶	
Media status: free	

Note: For interpretation and sources, see p. xvi.

SPAIN's political transition following the death of General Franco in 1975 is one of democratization's great success stories. As Heywood (1995, p. 4) writes, 'Franco's death was followed not by bloody conflict, as many had feared, but by a remarkably rapid and skilfully engineered transition to democracy'.

Spain's delayed democratization came all the easier for its late arrival. All the power centres, such as the Catholic Church and the military, wanted to avoid reopening old conflicts, leading to the triumphant compromise of the 1978 constitution.

Spain now scores highly on the Human Development Index. It is securely integrated into Europe, joining the

European Union in 1986 and using the euro currency since its inception.

However, economic problems remain. Reflecting a highly-regulated labour market, average living standards are significantly below those of Europe's wealthiest economies; unemployment is high, especially among the young; and public debt is excessive, raising the government's cost of borrowing.

Although Spain is one of Europe's oldest states, regional divergences remain central to its politics. Specifically, the country has granted extensive (perhaps excessive) devolution to historic regions while retaining what is, in theory, a unitary rather than federal framework.

The constitution established a complex mechanism by which regions could aspire to varying levels of autonomy. The historic communities of the Basque Country and Catalonia quickly proceeded to the most autonomous level, with other regions being offered the prospect of a later upgrade, leading to *café para todos* – coffee for all. In 2006, even greater devolution was agreed for Catalonia, including recognition of its status as a distinct nationality.

But *café para todos* comes at a price: overspending by some regional governments has added substantially to the national debt. By 2012, Catalonian nationalists were agitating for independence.

The media in Spain

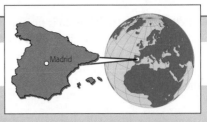

Madrid

The development of the Spanish media over the era of democratization in some ways exhibited a typical pattern. Monotonous coverage under the dictatorship gave way to a flowering of free expression, followed by a media restructuring in which broadcasting increasingly dominated the press. Spain's media structure exemplifies the southern European pattern, with extensive links between media outlets and political parties, and continuing partisan advocacy in media coverage.

Under the authoritarian leadership of General Franco, the position of the media had been wholly subservient. Rigid censorship ensured that newspapers offered only the dullest of political coverage, largely confining themselves to reprinting official press releases. The fare provided by the broadcasters was little better. Monopoly channels under state control offered an inoffensive diet of operetta, sport, and soaps. The media formed an essential part of the dictatorship's 'culture of evasion' (Heywood, 1995, p. 76).

With liberalization, independent media burst into life, offering all shades of opinion through a diverse range of publications. As in post-communist countries, television quickly established itself as the key medium. This pattern reflected not only the indifferent quality and poor reputation of the press, but also the greater accessibility of television to an electorate with variable education; until the 1990s, illiteracy remained significant.

The dominance of broadcasting over print in Spain is exceptional within

western Europe and more typical of the pattern found in Spain's former colonies in Latin America. According to a 2005 survey, 90 per cent of Spaniards watched television daily, while only 41 per cent read newspapers – and many of these confined themselves to *Marca*, a sports journal with the highest daily readership of any paper in the country. In 1996, 66 per cent of respondents said that television was their main source of political information; a mere 17 per cent mentioned the press (Gunther *et al.*, 2004, p. 146).

Media use in Spain

	Average minutes per day
Television	220
Radio	108
Internet	36
Newspapers	17
Magazines	4

Source: Adapted from WARC (2009). Data from 2007. Internet use has expanded since then (penetration grew from 44 per cent in 2006 to 63 per cent in 2010).

Reflecting the country's authoritarian and corporate traditions, membership of social organizations and political parties remains low. When combined with reliance on television, the effect is an electorate which is mobilized cognitively, rather than socially. That is, links between politicians and voters operate not so much through social networks such as trade unions and churches as through the mass media, especially television. The

result is an individualized style of politics which gives considerable weight to party leaders (Magone, 2008, p. 39).

This pattern is common among new democracies but, in Spain, it has not resulted in a competitive authoritarian regime in which one key politician dominates the airwaves. Rather, political parties now compete for influence over a pluralistic media environment in which large commercial media organizations coexist alongside diminished state channels.

The leading parties have sought influence over broadcasting, relying in part on a constitutional statement that interprets broadcasting as an essential public service requiring government regulation. In addition, anti-terror legislation and large libel awards against newspapers have placed some pressures on what are still fundamentally free media. The country ranked only 43rd in Freedom House's 2012 media freedom index.

Supporting these judgements, Hallin and Mancini (2004, p. 120) comment that, in Spain, 'intervention by the state in media markets is almost always seen – and with much reason – as a cynical attempt at political control'. Yet, these characteristics, and the excessive strength of the major parties, do not seriously threaten Spain's status as an established liberal democracy.

Further reading: Gunther *et al.* (2011), Gunther and Montero (2009), Magone (2008).

separate from society, firing their poison arrows from a distance. In fact, the media are part of society; journalists and editors do not arrive on Earth from Mars and Venus, they are part of society like the rest of us.

Second, the explosion of channels in the electronic era means that agenda control is no longer as strict as in the heyday of broadcast television. Even if people do still search for reinforcement, they can, if they wish, follow even the most specialized political interests through some media outlet somewhere. As the media become more pluralistic, so consumers acquire the capacity to follow their noses and shape their own agendas.

The **framing** of a story – the way in which reports construct a coherent narrative about an event – is a more recent attempt to understand media impact. The idea here is interpretive in character (see Chapter 5), reflecting Plato's observation that 'those who tell the stories also rule society'. The journalist's words, and the camera's images, help to interpret the story, providing a narrative which encourages a particular reaction from the viewer.

For example, are immigrants presented as a stimulus to the economy, or as a threat to society? Does the American media portray a war critically (Vietnam, in its later stages) or positively (Iraq, in the invasion phase)? Is a criminal who has been sentenced to die receiving his just deserts, or a cruel and unusual punishment? As the concept of a 'story' suggests, the journalist must translate the event covered into an organized narrative which connects with the receiver: the shorter the report, the greater the reliance on the shared, if sometimes simplistic, presuppositions which Jamieson and Waldman (2003) term 'consensus frames'.

Finally, the media's agenda and frames may exert a **priming** effect, encouraging people to apply the criteria implicit in one story to new information and topics. In a widely-cited American study, Iyengar *et al.* (1982) noted how 'problems prominently positioned in television broadcasts loom large in evaluations of presidential performance'. For example, the more the media focuses its coverage on foreign policy, the more likely it is that voters will be primed to judge parties according to their policies in this area – and perhaps even to vote accordingly. Similarly, it is possible that coverage of racist attacks

may prompt some individuals to engage in similar acts themselves, should the opportunity arise in their neighbourhood.

This indirect, cueing effect may have been understated in research focused on direct media effects. Bear in mind, however, that priming is more often asserted than demonstrated – it is, again, often claimed by those who seek to blame the media for behaviour that, in fact, has its roots elsewhere. To attribute one racist incident solely to media coverage of another is surely to ignore the underlying causes of both events.

The effects we have outlined here – reinforcement, agenda-setting, framing, and priming – are precise and, in principle, measurable. Their importance is that they offer insight into how the content and tone of media coverage can impinge on the audience. In this way, they take us beyond blanket assertions of media power to a more nuanced account of the media's role in political life.

Television and newspapers

One danger in discussing the mass media lies in treating its various channels as uniform – as though books, films, magazines, press, radio, television, and websites were identical in their partisanship and effects. True, the same content can increasingly be accessed in a variety of media – newspapers and television news can both be accessed on the Internet, for example – so we should not overstate the importance of the platform. The medium is not the message after all. Even in an era of social media, there remains value in contrasting the impact of the two key channels of the mass media age: broadcast television and newspapers.

Even in its heyday, broadcast television was far from all-powerful. By the 1980s, it had certainly become the pre-eminent mass medium in all democracies. Even today, television remains a visual, credible, and easily digested format which reaches almost every household. Consider election campaigns. Here, the broadcasting studio has become the main site of battle. The party gladiators participate through appearing on interviews, debates, talk shows, and commercials; merely appearing on television confirms some status and recognition on candidates. Ordinary voters consume the election, if at all, through watching images, whether on television, computer screens, or smartphones.

But we must be careful here. To say that the studio is the site of battle is one thing; to say that it determines the outcome is quite another. In fact, it is difficult to demonstrate a strong connection between television coverage of campaigns and the voters' response. For instance, one frequent observation about the electoral impact of television is that it has primed voters to base their decision more on personalities, especially those of the party leaders. To which an obvious riposte is: Compared to when? Before television, after all, came the now forgotten media of radio and, in some countries, cinema. Even the claim that the broadcasting media as a whole have led voters to decide on personality neglects the importance of personalized press coverage of the parties in earlier times.

To be sure, some studies have shown a modest increase in recent decades in the focus of media coverage of election campaigns on party leaders (Mughan, 2000). However, it is far from proven that votes are increasingly cast on the basis of leaders' personalities and even less clear that any such increase is attributable to broadcasting. Certainly, research does not support the proposition that television, even in the USA, has rendered the images of the leaders the key influence on electoral choice (see Chapter 12).

Where television may initially have made a broader but larger contribution is in partisan dealignment: the weakening of party loyalties among electors. Because of the limited number of channels available in television's early decades, governments required balanced and neutral treatment of politics. The result was an inoffensive style that contrasted with the more partisan coverage previously offered in many national newspapers, especially outside the USA.

In the Netherlands, for instance, television helped to break down the separate pillars comprising Dutch society in the 1950s, providing a new common ground for citizens exposed to a single national channel: 'Catholics discovered that Socialists were not the dangerous atheists they had been warned about, Liberals had to conclude that orthodox Protestants were not the bigots they were supposed to be' (Wigbold, 1979, p. 201).

Despite the primacy of television, it would be wrong to discount the political impact of the second mass medium, newspapers. Falling circulation notwithstanding, quality newspapers possess an authority springing from their longevity. In nearly all democracies, newspapers are freer with comment than is television. In an age when broadcasters still lead the provision of instant news, the more relaxed daily schedule of the press allows print columnists to offer interpretation and evaluation.

Television tells us what happened; at their best, newspapers place events in context. The press helps to frame the political narrative in a way that television finds difficulty in matching. Broadcast news can only cover one story at a time whereas newspapers (in print or online) can be scanned for items of interest and can be read at the user's convenience. Newspapers offer a luxury which television can rarely afford: space for reflection. For such reasons, quality newspapers remain the trade press of politics, read avidly by politicians themselves. In countries with a lively press tradition, newspapers retain a political significance greatly in excess of their circulation.

Newspapers also influence television's agenda: a story appearing on TV's evening news often begins life in the morning paper. This agenda-influencing role, it is worth noting, does not depend on a newspaper's circulation. But when an elector does see a story covered both on television and in the press, the

Table 7.2 The world's top 10 newspaper websites, 2011

As circulation of printed paid-for newspapers declines, many press groups have migrated to the Internet, where they have acquired a more international, if barely profitable, audience

	Number of visitors per month (million)
New York Times	62.0
Mail Online	39.6
Huffington Post (online only)	38.4
Tribune Newspapers	34.6
Guardian	30.9
USA Today	27.0
Wall Street Journal	25.3
Xinhua News Agency	23.2
Washington Post	21.8
Advance Internet (online only)	20.3

Source: Adapted from the Guardian (2012), citing Comscore.

combined impact is likely to exceed that of either medium considered alone (Miller, 1991).

Given the rise of online newspaper readership, the dramatic decline in the circulation of printed copies is an incomplete guide to the press's continuing significance. Indeed, migration to the Internet has allowed the leading newspaper groups to engage a new international audience, albeit usually with little commercial benefit (Table 7.2).

Still, the drop in both newspaper readership and viewing of television news does pose a significant threat to the quality of political communication and, hence, to the political process itself. Quality newspapers (local as well as national) and major broadcasting networks traditionally provided the means by which society gathered news about itself and the wider world. But as the advertising revenues of traditional media decline, so it becomes more difficult to maintain expensive networks of professional journalists to gather, report, and interpret the news. The danger is that the profession of journalism becomes populated with amateurs, as low-cost media look for no-cost content from readers and others.

We live, of course, in an information-rich age. But more does not always mean better. In fact, the hard news-gathering performed by many traditional media groups, whether directly or through contracts with news agencies, compares favourably with the 'comment-rich, fact-poor and analysis-thin' character of blogs, many of which just react to stories generated offline (McCargo, 2012). There is surely some truth in the comment of Brian Williams (anchor of NBC Nightly News) that 'these days he's up against a guy called Vinny who hasn't left his apartment in two years' (quoted in Fox and Ramos, 2012a, p. 10). Fox and Ramos go on to make the general point:

As traditional journalistic outlets shrink and blogs and other Internet outlets ascend to greater levels of prominence, citizens experience increasingly unfiltered news and information. Many blogs lack a traditional journalistic hierarchy in which an editor, who has the power to withhold publication, can demand writer accountability and accuracy.

If it is to be sustained, professional news-gathering and interpretation (whether by print or broadcast journalists) may need to be reinterpreted as a public good and provided with a public subsidy. In any

event, the decline of broadcast television and newspapers in the Internet age poses a challenge to the quality of political communication.

Political communication in authoritarian states

Just as democracy thrives on a flow of information, so authoritarian rulers limit free expression; this leads to media coverage which is subdued and, usually, subservient. Far from acting as the **fourth estate**, casting a searchlight into the darker corners of government, journalists in authoritarian states defer to political authority. Lack of resources within the media sector limits professionalism and increases vulnerability to pressure. Official television stations and subsidized newspapers reproduce the regime's line, while critical journalists are harassed and the entire media sector develops an instinct for self-preservation through self-censorship.

> 'Burke said there were Three Estates in Parliament; but, in the Reporters' Gallery yonder, there sat a **Fourth Estate** more important far than they all' (Carlyle, 1840).

The consequence is an inadequate information flow to the top, increasing the gap between state and society, and leading ultimately to incorrect decisions. A thoughtful dictator responds to this problem by encouraging the media to expose malfeasance at local level, thus providing a check on governance away from the centre. But there is no escape from the paradox of authoritarianism. By controlling information, rulers may secure their power in the short run, but they also reduce the quality of governance – potentially threatening their own survival over the longer term. The more developed the country, the more severe is the damage inflicted by an information deficit at the top.

How exactly do authoritarian rulers limit independent journalism? The constraints are varied and sometimes subtle. An understanding of these limitations contributes to an appreciation of authoritarian rule. In her study of sub-Saharan Africa before the wave of liberalization in the 1990s, Bourgault (1995, p. 180) identified a typical roster of mechanisms limiting media development and coverage:

- declaring lengthy states of emergency which formally limit media freedom;

- passing broad libel laws that can be selectively applied;

- threatening the withdrawal of government advertising;

- selectively restricting access to newsprint;

- requiring publications and journalists to be licensed;

- taxing printing equipment at a high rate;

- requiring a bond to be deposited with the government before new publications can launch.

As we saw in Chapter 4, authoritarian states are most often found in low-income countries. Here, limited resources undoubtedly hold back the development of the media. Restricted means stifle journalistic initiative and increase vulnerability to pressure. Sometimes impoverished journalists are reduced to publishing favourable stories (or withdrawing the threat to write critical ones) in exchange for money.

In much of post-communist central Asia, large parts of the media remain in state hands, giving the authorities direct leverage. The state also typically retains ownership of a leading television channel. The outcome is subservience:

From Kazakhstan to Kyrgyzstan and Tajikistan to Belarus and Ukraine, the story is a dismal one: tax laws are used for financial harassment; a body of laws forbids insults of those in high places; compulsory registration of the media is common. In Azerbaijan, as in Belarus, one-man rule leaves little room for press freedom. (Foley, 1999, p. 45)

The justification for these restrictions is typically an overriding national requirement for social stability, nation-building, and economic development. The subtext is that we cannot afford Western freedoms until we have caught up, and perhaps not even then. Before the Arab uprisings, for instance, the Egyptian government expected that 'the press should uphold the security of the country, promote economic development, and support approved social norms' (Lesch, 2004, p. 610). A free press is presented as a recipe for squabbling and disharmony.

Even though many of these justifications are simply excuses for authoritarian government, we should not assume that the Western idea of a free press garners universal appeal. Islamic states, in particular, stress the media's role in affirming religious values and social norms. A free press is seen as an excuse for licence. The question is posed: why should we import Western, and particularly American, ideas of freedom if the practical result is the availability of pornography? When society is viewed as the expression of an overarching moral code, whether Islamic or otherwise, the Western tradition of free speech appears alien – and even unethical.

The remaining states with a nominal communist allegiance also keep close control over the means of mass communication. In China, access to information has traditionally been provided on a need-to-know basis. The country's rulers remain keen to limit dissenting voices, even though they do now permit 'newspapers, magazines, television stations and news web sites to compete fiercely for audiences and advertising revenue' (Shirk, 2011, p. 2). In 2011, the communist party even cancelled *Super Girl*, a television talent show with a peak audience of 400 million, fearing the subversive effect of allowing the audience to vote.

Although the Chinese government is keen to promote e-commerce, Internet users who search for 'inappropriate' topics such as democracy or Tibetan independence will find their searches blocked and their access to search engines withdrawn. The government even pays selected citizens to post pro-government messages online (Fox and Ramos, 2012, p. 8). Of course, sophisticated users find a way round the regime's electronic censorship, producing a parallel communications system which may eventually prove to be politically transformative, but for now the Great Firewall of China holds.

In competitive authoritarian regimes, control over the media is far less extensive than in authoritarian states. The press and the Internet, are often left substantially alone, offering a forum for debate which perhaps offers some value, as well as danger, to the rulers.

Yet, the leading political force also dominates broadcast coverage, even where explicit or implicit censorship is absent. To some extent, such an emphasis reflects political reality: a viewer is naturally most interested in those who exert the greatest influence over his or her life. Latin America provides a good example. In many countries on the continent, a tradition of personal and populist rule lends itself well to expression through broadcasting media which reach many poor and illiterate people seeking salvation through 'their' leader.

Foweraker *et al.* (2003, p. 105) describe the origins of this tradition in the twentieth century, when 'populist leaders in Latin America made popular appeals to the people through mass media in newspapers and especially radio'. These authors comment that contemporary populism continues in the same vein, albeit now operating through television.

The political style of Hugo Chávez, president of Venezuela since 1998, is a good example. Many callers to his lengthy Sunday morning broadcast show, *¡Aló, Presidente!*, petition the president for help in securing a job or social security benefit, usually citing in the process the callousness of the preceding regime. The president has created a special office to handle these requests. The regime continues to secure privileged access to television and to intimidate critical journalists (Hellinger, 2003, p. 49). In Chávez's governing style, we see how the leader of a competitive authoritarian regime can strengthen his authority through dominance of the broadcast media even against the opposition of many media professionals themselves.

Even in many post-communist competitive authoritarian regimes, pressures on the media – from powerful business people, as well as politicians – remain intense. In Russia, for instance, this influence derives precisely from the centrality of television to political communication. As in Latin America, broadcasting is the main way of reaching a dispersed population for whom free television has greater appeal than papers for which they must pay. In a 2004 survey, 82 per cent of Russians said they watched television routinely, compared with just 22 per cent who said they were regular readers of national newspapers (Oates, 2005, p. 124). The television audience in Russia for nightly news programmes is substantial, matching that in the United States for the Super Bowl. In the size and interest of its audience, Russia's television news is the equivalent of soap operas elsewhere.

Particularly during elections, television showcases the achievements of the administration and its favoured candidates; opposition figures receive less, and distinctly less-flattering, attention. This pro-regime bias continued even during Dimitry Medvedev's more liberal tenure as president, 2008–12.

With over 100 laws governing media conduct in Russia, and the occasional journalist still found murdered by unknown assailants, self-censorship – the voice in the editor's head which asks 'Am I taking a risk in publishing this story?' – remains rife. Because editors know on which side their bread is buttered, there is no need for politicians to take the political risk involved in explicit instruction. The internal censor allows the president to maintain deniability. 'Censorship? What censorship?' he can ask, with a smile.

By comparison with television, the Internet and, even, the press are less explicitly controlled in Russia, an important change to the all-embracing censorship of the communist era. Internet access, in particular, has allowed younger people in urban areas to express and organize opposition to the distinctly authoritarian style of President Vladimir Putin. As befits a competitive authoritarian regime, dominance of the major media does not imply complete censorship.

Discussion questions

■ 'The Goliath of totalitarianism will be brought down by the David of the microchip' (Ronald Reagan, 1989). Has it? Will it?

■ Which exerts more influence on people's values: (a) the mass media, or (b) friends and family?

■ Should newspapers be kept alive by public subsidy if necessary?

■ Is broadcast television or the Internet the dominant mass medium in politics?

■ Does the media shape or reflect public opinion?

■ 'Since people can always spot propaganda, the importance of government control of the media in authoritarian states is easily exaggerated.' Do you agree?

Further reading

R. Fox and J. Ramos, eds, *iPolitics: Citizens, Elections and Governing in the Internet Era* (2012). Examines the political impact of new media, mainly in the United States, but also in Europe and the Arab world.

D. Graber, *Mass Media and American Politics*, 8th edn (2009). A text which focuses on American media coverage of politics, and its impact on both voters and political elites.

D. Hallin and P. Mancini, *Comparing Media Systems: Three Models of Media and Politics* (2004). This influential book presents an original classification of media systems.

D. Hallin and P. Mancini (eds), *Comparing Media Systems Beyond the Western World* (2012). This collection applies the classification in *Comparing Media Systems: Three Models of Media and Politics* to a wider range of countries.

H. Semetko and M. Scammell (eds) *The Sage Handbook of Political Communication* (2012). Forty-one chapters bring together a fragmented and multidisciplinary field.

S. Shirk (ed.), *Changing Media, Changing China* (2011). An interesting account of how China's rulers have reacted to the new media climate.

J. Street, *Mass Media, Politics and Democracy*, 2nd edn (2011). A thoughtful text assessing the evolving relationship between mass media and politics.

Visit the companion website at **www.palgrave.com/politics/hague** to access additional learning resources, including multiple-choice questions, chapter summaries, web links and practice essay questions.

Chapter 8 Political participation

Political participation refers to any of the many ways in which people seek to influence the composition or policies of their government. Clearly, citizens contacting their representative and activists canvassing for their favoured candidate are involved in the formal political process. But participation can also take less conventional forms – such as signing a petition, taking part in a demonstration, or even engaging in terrorist acts against the state. One distinction in the study of participation, then, is between its **conventional** and **unconventional** forms.

In a liberal democracy, people can choose whether to get involved in politics, to what extent and through what channels. But, contrary to expectation, participation is also found in some non-democratic regimes. Most communist states required citizens to engage in regimented demonstrations of support for the government, producing higher levels of participation (albeit of lower quality) than in liberal democracies. Some authoritarian regimes still demand at least a facade of engagement, manipulated so as to support, rather than threaten, the existing rulers.

> **Political participation** is activity by individuals formally intended to influence who governs or the decisions taken by those who do. **Conventional participation** takes place within formal politics; **unconventional participation** is, to a degree, outside or even against orthodox politics.

What expectations should be brought to the study of participation in liberal democracies? One perspective, dating back to Aristotle and the ancient Greeks, is that involvement in collective decision-making is both an obligation owed to the community and an exercise in personal development, broadening individual horizons and providing political education. From this standpoint, participation is beneficial both to the political system and to the individual. Non-participants are condemned as free-riding on the efforts of others. This approach finds echoes in recent writing on the duties (as opposed merely to the rights) of the citizen (Bellamy, 2008).

An alternative approach, rooted in practical realities more than high ideals, sets a lower bar. Contrary to Aristotle, the suggestion is that people are not naturally political animals; rather, we should interpret extensive participation as a sign of unresolved tensions within a political system. Demonstrations, protests, and even a high electoral turnout may indicate a system that is overheating, rather than in rude health. In normal times, limited participation may indicate the system's success in meeting popular demands, thus freeing citizens to pursue more fulfilling activities.

In such accounts, all that is required in a liberal democracy is that citizens **monitor** political events, with the realistic ability to become involved as necessary. What matters is that the channels are open, not that they are in

STUDYING . . .

POLITICAL PARTICIPATION

- Although the supposition that participation is healthy for a liberal democracy is inherently plausible, an alternative school of thought maintains that excess participation can indicate strain on a political system. It is not self-evident that the more participation, the better.

- Studies of participation in liberal democracies focus on who takes part, to what extent and through what channels. The bias in participation towards privileged social groups, reflecting inequalities of resources and interest, is a particular theme.

- An emerging issue is whether discussion and monitoring of politics, and not simply behaviour, should be viewed as a mode of participation. Some authors not only answer in the affirmative, but go on to suggest that public opinion has become the central mechanism of representation in liberal democracy. In this connection, studies comparing how younger and older people understand the nature of political participation would be useful.

- Studies of public opinion do not consist only of national opinion polls. Focus groups and citizens' juries offer opportunities for research that is both cheaper and deeper. Non-participants – the politically withdrawn or excluded – receive insufficient attention. But note that political participation may be differently understood within excluded groups (e.g. as self-help activity in the local community).

- Trends in participation by women attract attention, as do policies to increase female representation in legislatures. Gender quotas for party candidates have been adopted in many countries; their study offers a lively research area, with attention now turning to the impact of quotas.

- While much research on participation focuses on its conventional forms, the study of social movements provides an interesting contrast. Participation in movements both challenges and supplements orthodox channels. For the people involved, however, conventional and unconventional participation may be seen as a single menu of opportunities.

- Aided by modern communications, social movements can easily move across national boundaries. Their study therefore provides an opportunity to combine national, comparative and international politics.

---

constant use. Schudson (1998, p. 311) suggests that, even when citizens appear inactive, they remain poised for action when required, like parents watching their children play in the swimming pool. Especially in an age when some conventional forms of participation have declined, such surveillance can even be seen as a central mechanism of democracy: 'To be watchful, alert, and on guard are essential attributes of citizenship', suggests Rosanvallon (2008, p. 33). He insists that monitoring should be understood as itself a form of participation:

vigilance should be seen as a mode of action. Though it produces nothing by itself, it cannot be dismissed as mere passivity. It defines a particular

form of political intervention that involves neither decision-making nor exercise of the will.

> **Monitoring** (surveillance) consists in keeping an eye on political developments with the option to participate more directly in matters deemed particularly important.

Participation in liberal democracies

Although the debate about how much participation is desirable raises issues of judgement rather than fact, the findings reviewed in this section are nonetheless relevant. If we should discover, for instance, that non-participants are clustered in lower social strata, then we might well want to conclude that lack of engagement reflects political cynicism, rather than satisfaction. The positive functions of apathy, as seen from the academic's study, may be less apparent in the ghetto.

The most striking result from participation studies is the limited extent of any direct participation other than voting. In an influential analysis, Milbrath and Goel (1977, p. 11) divided the American population into three groups, a classification which has since been applied to other liberal democracies. These categories, based on involvement with conventional politics, were:

- a small proportion of gladiators (around 5–7 per cent of the population) who are active in politics – for instance, campaigners;

- a large group of spectators (around 60 per cent) who observe the contest but rarely participate beyond voting;

- a substantial number of apathetics (around 35 per cent) who are not engaged in formal politics.

Milbrath and Goel's labels were based on an analogy with Roman contests at which a few gladiators performed for the mass of spectators but with some apathetics not even watching the show (Figure 8.1).

As we have suggested, it is important not to write off the large population of spectators: those who observe politics without becoming involved other than through casting an occasional ballot. Especially among the young, political engagement may take the form of visiting websites, discussing an election with friends, or watching a film about a current issue. Political spectating may be becoming a leading and highly influential form of participation. In an age of spectatorship, suggests Green (2010a), the disciplinary gaze of the people – their eyes, rather than their voice – has become the source of their power.

Furthermore, monitoring is not, as far as we can tell, in decline. Norway is typical of a wider trend: despite a fall in turnout, 'the broader political activity of citizens has increased. The rise in political involvement is quite widespread, covering political

Figure 8.1 Patterns of participation in liberal democracies

Most people are political spectators, keeping an eye on political developments but only participating directly through voting. The apathetics, who disregard formal politics altogether, outnumber the gladiators who fight the political battle.

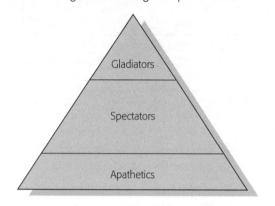

interest and political discussion' (Listhaug and Grønftlaten, 2007). In other liberal democracies, too, many citizens recognize the value of surveillance. In Britain, for instance, half the respondents to a 2008 survey claimed that it was essential, or very important, to remain informed about current affairs, higher than the proportion making the same observation about contacting politicians, or joining a party (Ipsos-Mori, 2008).

However we interpret political spectating, the most striking fact about political participation in liberal democracies is the small proportion of gladiators. Table 8.1 shows some typical findings from a British study: apart from signing a petition, participation declines rapidly once we move beyond voting at national elections. Throughout the democratic world, anything other than voting is the preserve of a minority of activists. The gladiators are, indeed, outnumbered by the apathetics: people who neither vote nor even monitor politics through the media.

It is easy to assume that different forms of conventional participation form a scale, such that those who engage in the rarer forms of participation also perform the more popular acts. In fact, however, there is some tendency for people to specialize; those who engage do so in different ways. In their classic study of political engagement in the United States, Verba *et al.* (1978) identified four types of participant:

- voters (e.g. those who participate in local as well as national elections);

- campaigners (e.g. those who engage in canvassing);

- communal activists (e.g. those who participate in organizations concerned with a particular issue);

- contactors (e.g. those who communicate – sometimes obsessively! – with officials about an individual problem).

So, participation is, to a degree, a matter of 'how?' and not simply 'how much?'. This observed division of labour suggests the value of providing a menu of participation opportunities for citizens so they can choose the channels of engagement with which they feel most comfortable.

Who then are the gladiators comprising the highest layer of the participation pyramid? These people are likely to exert political influence yet they are far from a cross-section of society. In most democracies, participation is greatest among well-educated, upper-income, white men. In addition, for all but protest behaviour (found disproportionately among the young), participation peaks among the middle-aged.

Furthermore, the highest layers of political involvement show the greatest skew. As Putnam (1976, p. 33) put it:

The 'law of increasing disproportion' seems to apply to nearly every political system; no matter how we measure political and social status, the higher the level of political authority, the greater the representation for high-status social groups.

This bias in participation towards upper social groups is significant because it suggests that apathy may not, after all, be a sign of satisfaction with the existing order. In that case, we would expect the well-heeled to be less involved in politics because they have relatively little to complain about – exactly the opposite of the observed pattern.

So, why does participation increase as we move up the social scale? Two factors seem to be particularly influential: political resources and political interest (Verba *et al.*, 1995).

Table 8.1 Political participation in Great Britain, 2011

In Britain, as in many other liberal democracies, voting in national elections is the only political activity attracting a majority of citizens. Direct involvement in political meetings, demonstrations, parties, and campaigns is the preserve of a small minority.

Which, if any, of the things on this list have you done in the last two to three years?	%
Voted in the last general election	65
Discussed politics with someone else	35
Signed a petition/e-petition	27
Presented my views to a representative	13
Boycotted certain products	10
Expressed my political views online	6
Been to any political meeting	4
Taken part in a demonstration	4
Joined or donated money to a political party	3
Taken an active part in a political campaign	2

Sources: Hansard Society (2012); turnout from Kavanagh and Cowley (2010), table A1.2.

First, consider resources. People in high-status groups are equipped with such assets as education, money, status, and communication skills. Education gives access to information and, we trust, strengthens the ability to interpret it. Money buys the luxury of time for political activity. High status provides the opportunity to obtain a respectful hearing. And communication skills, such as the ability to speak in public, help in presenting one's views persuasively. Added together, these resources provide a useful tool kit for effective political intervention; their unequal distribution helps to account for under-participation by less privileged social groups.

Second, consider political interest. High-status individuals are more likely to be engaged with formal politics. They possess the motive as well as the means to become involved. No longer preoccupied with the daily struggle, they can take satisfaction from engagement in collective activity (Inglehart and Welzel, 2010). The wealthy are also more likely to be brought up in a family, and to attend a school, where an interest in current affairs is encouraged. They will probably see how politics can impact on their own wealth. So, higher social groups possess an interest in politics – in both senses of 'interest' – and can afford to put their concerns into practice. Conversely, those in lower social strata are more likely to come from a family and community where the main focus is the challenge of daily life, rather than the remote goings-on of national politics.

The emphasis of research on political participation is on explaining what distinguishes the gladiators from the spectators. But let us not ignore the apathetics, the people who do not participate at all. This group raises the problem of **political exclusion**. As Verba *et al.* (1995) write, effectively the apathetics exclude themselves – or perhaps are excluded – from the normal means by which citizens collectively shape their society. A typical non-participant might be an unemployed young person with no qualifications, inhabiting a high-crime, inner-city neighbourhood, often from a minority culture and perhaps not even speaking the dominant language. Such a profile may encourage radical activity among a few but, in general, a preoccupation with everyday life limits or eliminates formal participation in conventional political processes.

There is an important point here. As inequality increases in some liberal democracies, so it becomes more important to avoid the natural bias in participation studies towards those who are already active. Research should encompass those who are not engaged, as well as those who are.

> **Political exclusion** refers to those people who are effectively prevented from taking part in collective decision-making because they occupy a marginal position in society. Examples include many drug users, migrant workers, prisoners, and people who do not speak the native language.

Overall, findings about conventional political participation demonstrate the tension within liberal democracy between traditional participatory principles and a distinctly prosaic reality. The aims of universal participation and political equality coexist alongside the facts of limited and unequal involvement. This gap provides room for concerned citizens to advocate measures to increase formal political activity, a theme of some importance given the concentration of disengagement among the poor. For example, Macedo *et al.* (2005, p. 9) comment that 'persistent or even increasing inequalities in participation in the United States impoverish our public life and call into question the democratic credentials of our politics'.

However, such efforts will not close the gap between democratic aspirations and achievements. Because participation in a liberal democracy is an option rather than a requirement, it is unlikely ever to be equal; and, because inequalities in participation are deeply rooted in social differences in resources and interest, so the active minority is sure to remain sociologically unrepresentative of the passive majority. Critical assessments of participation in liberal democracies may reflect inflated expectations, leading to undervaluation of its real, if limited, achievements.

Women and political participation

Participation by women is an interesting subfield within the broader field of political engagement. It is an area where significant trends are apparent within liberal democracies, reinforced by widely-adopted policies aimed at increasing the proportion of women legislators. Yet, women remain under-represented at the top tiers of government – often severely so – raising the question of whether a glass ceiling still limits women's progress, even in an era when open prejudice has waned.

In many liberal democracies, women are now as, or more, likely than men to vote. In itself, this finding represents a significant change to traditional patterns. As Norris states, 'the earliest studies of political behavior in western Europe and North America, conducted during the 1920s and 1930s shortly after the female franchise was granted in many countries, commonly observed that men were more likely to vote than women' (2009, p. 728). This particular gender gap has now closed or even reversed, helped no doubt by increased education and employment among women. Among those registered to vote in the United States, a higher proportion of women than men turned out at every presidential election between 1980 and 2008. In 2008, for instance, female turnout was 60.4 per cent, nearly five points higher than among men (CAWP,

2012). In other democracies, too (including France, Germany, and the Scandinavian countries), women now outvote men (Stevens, 2007, p. 49). Male turnout remains higher among the elderly, suggesting that women's lead may increase further as generational replacement proceeds.

Yet, men still predominate in most forms of formal political participation beyond voting, including election campaigns. As Adman (2009, p. 315) writes:

Voter turnout is generally equal among women and men in most areas of the world but other forms of political participation, such as political party activities, contact activities directed towards politicians and civil servants, and involvement in protest activities, are dominated by men.

Furthermore, those women who do occupy direct political roles are found disproportionately at local rather than national level (Stokes, 2005, pt V).

These contrasts seem to reflect political attitudes. At least in the USA and the UK, men remain somewhat more interested in and knowledgeable about politics (Norris, 2009, p. 728; Hansard Society, 2012, p. 66). In Britain, this difference in outlook has remained steady in the new millennium.

So, Putnam's law of increasing disproportion still applies; the higher the political office, the more likely we are to find a man in post. In particular, men continue to provide the lion's share of parliamentary representatives throughout the democratic world. Yet, even here, women's share continues to increase. In 2009, women made up one in five of the world's legislators, double the figure from 30 years earlier (Table 8.2).

This under-representation seems to reflect a shortage of women willing to put themselves forward, rather than direct discrimination by selectors or voters. Thomas (2005, p. 9) reports that in the United States, 'Women's share of the vote, controlling for party and incumbency, is now equal to men's. The message is increasingly clear: If women run, they win.' The problem is explaining why women are less likely to seek a legislative career in the first place. At least three factors seem to be involved:

- women are less likely than men to be found in occupations that serve as a springboard to

political careers, notably law (Darcy *et al.*, 2004);

- confidence may still be an issue: 'even among those with similar levels of experience and achievement, women tended to perceive themselves as less qualified than men' (Thomas, 2005, p. 12);

- legislatures remain, or at least are seen by many women, as **gendered institutions** – for example, by practicing irregular hours of work that are unwelcoming to women with more than their fair share of family responsibilities (Kittilson and Schwindt-Bayer, 2012).

> **Gendered institutions** operate with formal rules and informal conventions which, often unintentionally, advantage men over women. An adversarial debating style in parliament is an example. So, 'Even when women win a place in a gendered institution, they remain outsiders' (Duerst-Lahti, 2002, p. 22).

More than 100 countries have adopted gender quotas to improve women's participation in legislatures. These policies are by far the most widespread attempt to alter patterns of political participation, providing a model which could be applied to other under-represented groups, such as ethnic minorities. Although quotas for women date back to the 1930s, most countries only introduced them in the 1990s and 2000s, with the UN-sponsored Beijing Platform for Action (1995) providing momentum for what has become a global cascade.

How do quotas operate? Three main methods are used (Box 8.1). The oldest but rarest solution is **reserved seats**. Here, a proportion of seats is allocated to women; for example, by allowing a party to select women members for special seats granted in proportion to its share of the vote. So, the more seats a party wins in the general election, the more reserved seats it is allocated. In Pakistan, where this format is well-established, 60 special seats in the national assembly are reserved for women. Introduced to Asia by British colonial rulers, reserved seats ensure some female representation without typically aiming at full parity. The method is also used in Rwanda, the country with the world's

Table 8.2 Female representation in the national legislatures of some liberal democracies, 1993 and 2012

Women provide an increasing, but still minority, share of parliamentary representatives. Higher rates of female representation are associated with proportional representation.

	Electoral system	Female representation (%)	
		1993	2012
Sweden	List PR	40	45
Norway	List PR	39	40
Netherlands	List PR	31	39
Germany	MMP	26	33
New Zealand	MMP	29	32
Australia	AV	8	25
Canada	SMP	18	25
United Kingdom	SMP	18	22
Italy	List PR	15	21
France	Two-round system	6	19
USA	SMP	11	17
Ireland	STV	2	15

Note: In bicameral assemblies, the figure shown is for the lower house. AV – alternative vote; List PR – list proportional representation; MMP – mixed member proportional; SMP – single-member plurality; STV – single transferable vote. See Chapter 11.

Source: IPU (2012).

highest proportion of female legislators. There, 24 of 80 seats in the lower house are reserved for women; other female candidates are elected directly.

By far the most common method, introduced and prevalent in Europe, is the voluntary **party quota**. Typically, one party adopts a quota and others follow, not necessarily with an identical format, in order to avoid being seen as old-fashioned. The device aims to ensure that a party selects a given proportion (the quota) of either female candidates or, more neutrally, of candidates from each gender. To forestall a token effort, additional stipulations may require some women to be placed high on a party's list (in list systems), or to be selected for winnable constituencies (in plurality systems).

The final and most recent method for increasing women's representation, particularly common in Latin America, is the **legislative quota**. These operate in a similar way to party quotas except that they are mandated by law and apply to all parties.

The rules may be vague, allowing wiggle room for unenthusiastic parties, but they do enable the government to parade its commitment to gender equality.

Quotas are no cure-all. Because party and legislative quotas operate at party and candidate level, they do not deliver a predefined proportion of female members in parliament. In most cases, the percentage of women in parliament remains lower than that set in party, or even legislative, quotas. France passed an ambitious parity law in 2000; by 2012, the proportion of women in the National Assembly had only increased to 27 per cent. One reason (doubtless of several) for such discrepancies is implementation failure: not all parties deliver on the quota to which they have subscribed. In an overall assessment, Hughes (2011, p. 604) concludes that 'the quota policies in effect today rarely challenge men's majority dominance of national legislatures.'

Quotas are not the only reason why female representation is increasing; neither are they the only policy needed to ensure more diverse assemblies. They can even be seen as a remedy that fails to address the underlying causes of unequal representation. Even so, they are a widely-used device for influencing patterns of participation and have rapidly become a global standard (Dahlerup, 2006; Krook, 2009).

Just as female representation in parliaments has grown, so too has the number of women breaking though the highest glass ceiling into executive office. Indeed, one argument for legislative quotas is that the number of women in parliament seems to influence the number in executive office. By 2010, more than a dozen women served as heads of government or state, including Chancellor Angela Merkel in Germany and Prime Minister Julia Gillard in Australia. Unlike many of the early female political leaders in Asia, most of these leaders attained high office without inheriting their post from male relatives.

Globally, women's presence in cabinets has also advanced, from 9 per cent in 1999 to 17 per cent in 2010. This latter figure nearly matches the proportion of women in parliament. Several countries, including Finland, France, Iceland, Norway, Spain, South Africa, Sweden, and Switzerland have achieved – or come close to achieving – an equal number of women as men in cabinet. While women ministers

BOX 8.1

Methods for increasing female representation in parliament

	Definition	Where practised (main phase)	When introduced
Reserved seats	Some seats (typically 10–30 per cent) in the legislature are reserved for women	Parts of Asia, Africa and the Middle East	1930–70
Party quotas	A party voluntarily decides to adopt a certain proportion (typically 25–50 per cent) of female candidates	Mostly Europe	1970–90
Legislative quotas	Electoral law requires each party to adopt a certain proportion (typically 25–50 per cent) of female candidates	Particularly Latin America	1990–

Source: Adapted from Krook (2009).

are still found in the soft areas of education and social policy, they have also moved into traditionally masculine fields such as defence, finance, and foreign policy (Bauer and Tremblay, 2011). Despite this progress, it is as well to remember that the glass of participation remains four fifths empty. In a large majority of countries, most ministers and legislators – as most top business executives – are men.

Social movements

In 2011, protestors occupied Zuccotti Park in New York City's financial district to express their disapproval of growing income inequality, especially in the financial sector. Using the slogan 'We are the 99 per cent', Occupy Wall Street rapidly became not only a national, but also an international phenomenon, with tented encampments emerging in many countries. Without putting up candidates for election or engaging in conventional lobbying, the Occupy protests undoubtedly succeeded in focusing public attention on income disparities in Western, and especially English-speaking, countries.

Occupy was an example of a **social movement** – an unconventional form of participation that has come to provide a significant challenge, or at least a supplementary tonic, to standard channels. In this section, we extend our discussion of political participation by examining the nature and interpretation of these movements.

Social movements consist of people from outside the mainstream who come together to seek a common objective through an unorthodox challenge to the existing political order. Occupy was a typical example, in that many participants considered themselves to be independent of political parties. Their camps were a protest against the perceived indifference of all major parties to corporate power and economic inequality.

Social movements (also known as 'popular movements') are groups emerging from society to pursue non-establishment goals through unorthodox means. Their objectives are broad rather than sectional and their style, sometimes referred to as **new politics**, involves a challenge by traditional outsiders to existing elites.

Social movements espouse a political style which distances them from established channels, thereby questioning the legitimacy, as well as the decisions, of the government. The members of social movements adopt a wide repertoire of protest acts, including demonstrations, sit-ins, boycotts, and political strikes. Some such acts may cross the border into illegality but the actors' motives are political, rather than criminal.

To appreciate the character of social movements, we can usefully compare them with parties (Box 8.2). Movements are more loosely organized, typically lacking the precise membership, subscriptions, and leadership of parties. As with those parties whose origins lie outside the legislature, movements emerge from society to challenge the political establishment. However, movements do not seek to craft distinct interests into an overall package; rather, they claim the moral high ground in one specific area.

Movements can also be contrasted with interest groups. In a similar fashion to interest groups, social movements typically focus on a single issue: nuclear disarmament, feminism, the environment. Again, as with interest groups, social movements do not seek state power, aiming rather to influence the political agenda, usually by claiming that their voice has previously gone unheard. But the contrasts with interest groups are more important. Whereas protective interest groups seek precise regulatory objectives, movements are more diffuse, seeking cultural as much as legislative change. For example, the gay

movement might measure its success by how many gay people come out, not just by the passage of anti-discrimination legislation. Similarly, women's movements may emphasize consciousness-raising among women. By focusing on culture and identity, movements adopt a broader interpretation of politics, and of the purpose of political participation, than do protective groups.

Tilly (2004, p. 33) regards the British anti-slavery movement of the late eighteenth and early nineteenth centuries as the earliest example of a social movement as now understood. The techniques adopted in this campaign, including petitions and boycotts, established a palette of protest activities soon emulated by other reforming groups. It is clear, at any rate, that while social movements are a product of the modern era, they are neither a recent phenomenon, nor are they necessarily expanding in number: **new politics** is a label that can mislead.

Social movements may not be new but perspectives on them have certainly evolved. In the 1950s, 'mass movements', as they were then called, were perceived as a threat to the stability of liberal democracy. They were taken as a sign of a poorly functioning mass society 'containing large numbers of people who are not integrated into any broad social groupings, including classes' (Kornhauser, 1959, p. 14). Movements were judged to be supported by marginal, disconnected groups: unemployed intellectuals, isolated workers, the peripheral middle class. Goodwin and Jasper

BOX 8.2

Comparing social movements, political parties and protective interest groups

	Social movements	Political parties	Protective interest groups
Seek to influence the government?	Usually	Yes	Yes
Seek to become the government?	No	Yes	No
Focus on a single issue?	Yes	Rarely	Yes
Formally organized, led and funded?	Not usually	Yes	Yes
Tactics used	Unconventional	Conventional	Conventional
Main levels of operation	Global, national, local	National	National

Note: On protective interest groups, see Chapter 9.

(2003a, p. 5) claim that 'Until the 1960s, most scholars who studied social movements were frightened of them.'

The 1960s and 1970s saw a radical rethink. The American civil rights movement could hardly be dismissed as irrational, while Vietnam and the draft propelled parts of the educated American middle class into anti-war movements. As intellectuals became more critical of government, so their treatment of social movements became more positive. Especially in the United States, movements were judged to be engaged in 'rational, purposeful and organized action', mobilizing resources in pursuit of political goals (Tilly, 1978). As with public interest groups, they were now reinterpreted as a component of normal politics.

Reviewing this revised perspective at the end of the twentieth century, della Porta and Diani (1999, p. 10) concluded that 'it is no longer possible to define movements in a prejudicial sense as phenomena which are marginal and anti-institutional. A more fruitful interpretation towards the political interpretation of contemporary movements has been established.'

It is certainly worth noting that the movement activists of the 1960s resembled the social profile of participants in orthodox politics. In both spheres, they tended to be well-educated, articulate, young people from middle-class backgrounds: 'the higher the level of education, the higher the percentage of people who engage in protest' (Rucht, 2007, p. 715). At the level of the political system, too, modernity seems to catalyze unorthodox activism: 'protest is facilitated by a syndrome of factors found in advanced industrial democracies: affluence, open and effective political institutions, and post-material values' (Dalton and van Sickle, 2005, p. 16).

More than a few leaders of social movements switched to orthodox politics as they aged; many a protest activist of the 1960s turned into a party leader by the century's end. Prominent examples included Joschka Fischer, Germany's foreign minister 1998–2005, and Peter Hain, a minister in Tony Blair's Labour government in Britain. For all the stylistic contrast between mainstream and movement politics, one function of movements has been to provide a training ground for future national leaders. In this way, too, protest activity has entered, and helped, the mainstream.

Developments in communications have lowered the barriers to entry for new movements, facilitating their rapid emergence when ordinary politics has been deemed to fail. Take the protest in Britain in 2000 against the country's high tax on petrol (Joyce, 2002). A diverse network of British farmers and road hauliers blocked petrol refineries in a series of protests coordinated by mobile telephones. The action quickly created a national fuel crisis.

Mass communication also facilitates simultaneous global protest with virtually no central leadership at all; people in one country simply hear what is planned elsewhere and decide to join in. The international protests in a single weekend in 2003 against the invasion of Iraq provide a remarkable example. Bennett (2005, p. 207) reckons this protest, which provided a shared label for people from different backgrounds as well as countries, was 'the largest simultaneous multinational demonstration in recorded history' (Table 8.3). As Bennett (2005, p. 205) writes, 'such applications of communication technology favour loosely linked distributed networks that are minimally dependent on central coordination, leaders or ideological commitment'.

Table 8.3 Not in my name: the largest demonstrations against the Iraq War by city, 15–16 February 2003

Over a single weekend, an estimated six million people took part in demonstrations in 600 or so cities against the American-led war in Iraq. These rallies show how transnational protest can occur with minimal central leadership.

	Estimated number of protestors
Rome	Up to 3,000,000
Barcelona	1,300,000
London	1,000,000
Madrid	600,000
Berlin	500,000
Paris	200,000
Sydney	200,000
Damascus	Up to 200,000
Melbourne	160,000
New York	100,000

Source: Figures are estimates reported in the *Financial Times*, 17 February 2003.

As the rapid diffusion of the Occupy movement beyond American borders confirms, movements can expand more easily from the national to the international level than can parties and interest groups. On its eviction from Zuccotti Park in November 2011, Occupy claimed, 'This movement can't be contained in one square block in lower Manhattan. It is bigger than that. You can't evict an idea whose time has come.' Its time may have gone again, but not without a phase of rapid international replication.

The ability of social movements to mushroom in this way, without any central organization or leader, confirms their capacity to articulate authentic public concern at a transnational level. Again, however, we should retain historical perspective. As the anti-slavery movement shows, international protest is far from new. What we can say is that social movements continue to provide a form of participation well-suited to addressing global issues which national governments are judged to have failed to address (Tarrow, 2005).

Liberal democracies hold no monopoly over social movements. In the 1970s and 1980s, they also became a significant feature in many authoritarian regimes in lower-income countries. In contrast to liberal democracies, however, these movements were the territory of the poor, as people facing acute problems of daily life collaborated to improve their living conditions in a hostile political environment. The urban poor organizing soup kitchens, the inhabitants of shanty towns lobbying for land reform, groups of mothers pressing for information on their sons who had 'disappeared' under military rule – all were examples of this blossoming of popular political activity. Such movements were a response to political exclusion.

However, many community-based movements in low-income countries lacked the desire or the means to engage with national politics. A culture of anti-politics limited the movements' wider impact. Indeed, the democratic transition took some wind from their sails. In Uruguay, for example, 'democracy brought, by a curious twist, the disappearance of many grass-roots movements that had been active during the years of dictatorship' (Canel, 1992, p. 290). In and beyond the developing world, there is nothing as damaging to a protest movement as success.

Where the boundary between social movements and promotional groups is more porous, as in the United States and some other liberal democracies, social movements stand more chance of entering and influencing the mainstream. As with successful business start-ups, they can obtain a good price for their groundwork.

Public opinion

Participation, we have suggested, can take the form of monitoring political events, even if that surveillance does not lead to participatory behaviour. Given that broad approach, we can view **public opinion** as an arena of political participation. When people discuss the issues of the day in a way that shapes public opinion, they are taking part not simply in politics, but also in democratic politics.

Public opinion matters, especially, but not only, in democracies. Opinion pollsters gauge public opinion, internet research companies monitor Twitter trends, and the political class engages in a continuous debate on what the public thinks about particular issues. And this activity is for a reason: politicians do take note. Public opinion is democracy's courtroom. Stimson (2009, p. 855) demonstrates that in the USA 'governing bodies do respond to public opinion – and perhaps more important, to changes in public opinion'. A case can even be made that public opinion is a more powerful influence on political decisions than elections, given that public opinion is measured continuously and on specific issues. What applied during the French Revolution still speaks to us:

Public opinion was a power that manifested itself always and everywhere without being represented or instituted in any particular place. Hence it became the essential manifestation of the people as an active and permanent presence. (Rosanvallon, 2008, p. 31)

Defining public opinion

One common conception of public opinion is highly pragmatic: it is simply what the adult population thinks about a given issue, nothing more and nothing less. From this viewpoint, public opinion can be measured by a straightforward opinion poll surveying the adult population.

Public opinion can refer to (1) 'the range of views on some controversial issue held by some significant portion of the population', or (2) the informed judgement of a community on an issue of common concern, where that judgement is formed in the context of shared political goals (Qualter, 1991).

While this definition benefits from clarity, it fails to capture what most politicians understand by 'public opinion'. Their thinking is sensitive to structured and organized opinion as expressed through the media, or by opinion leaders. This more political perspective links the idea of a 'public' to an informed community sharing basic political principles – essentially, to what Jean-Jacques Rousseau termed the 'general will'.

The nineteenth-century British statesman W. E. Gladstone articulated this view, suggesting that 'public opinion represents the sum or balance of the abstract moral principles of the persons forming the community' (quoted in Hare, 1873, p. xix). In this conception, a community is only regarded as capable of a public opinion if its people are settled on the ends of government and the range of means for pursuing them. Within this framework, public opinion is interpreted as the considered will of a cohesive group.

Measuring public opinion

The idea of public opinion has gained further currency as opinion polls, citizens' juries, and focus groups have developed to study it. Indeed, there are few areas where a concept is so closely linked to its measurement. In liberal democracies, public opinion is both assessed by, and partly composed of, investigations into its content (Box 8.3).

Consider **opinion polls** and **sample surveys**, the most accurate methods of identifying what people profess to believe. Although the public itself remains resolutely sceptical of sample surveys, their accuracy is now well-attested, at least in predicting election outcomes. Table 8.4 shows the record in the United States; track records are similar, if only available for a shorter period, in many other democracies.

Counter-intuitive it may be, but 1,000 people carefully selected for an opinion poll can accurately represent the whole population. The key phrase here is 'carefully selected'. The procedure must be system-

Table 8.4 Share of the vote at presidential elections and in the final Gallup poll, United States, 1936–2012

Polls work. The average difference between Gallup's final survey and the winner's share of the vote in 20 American presidential elections is below 3 per cent. Even this divergence is not all error because opinions may change between the last survey and the election.

	Winner	Share of vote (%)	Final Gallup survey (%)	Difference
2012	Obama	50.9	49.0	1.9
2008	Obama	53.0	55.0	2.0
2004	Bush, G.W.	50.7	49.0	1.7
2000	Bush, G.W.	47.9	48.0	0.1
1996	Clinton	49.2	52.0	2.8
1992	Clinton	43.3	49.0	5.7
1988	Bush, G.H.W.	53.0	56.0	3.0
1984	Reagan	59.2	59.0	0.2
1980	Reagan	50.8	47.0	3.8
1976	Carter	50.1	48.0	2.1
1972	Nixon	61.8	62.0	0.2
1968	Nixon	43.5	43.0	0.5
1964	Johnson	61.3	64.0	2.7
1960	Kennedy	50.1	50.5	0.4
1956	Eisenhower	57.8	59.5	1.7
1952	Eisenhower	55.4	51.0	4.4
1948	Truman	49.5	44.5	5.0
1944	Roosevelt	53.8	51.5	2.3
1940	Roosevelt	55.0	52.0	3.0
1936	Roosevelt	62.5	55.7	6.8
			Average:	2.5

Source: Gallup (2012).

atic, such as randomly selecting telephone numbers; even then, the social composition of the sample must be compared with known figures for the population, with adjustments (known as 'weighting') for any discrepancies. Weighting is particularly important when the sample is self-selected, as with people who agree to take part in polls conducted through the Internet. Weighting or not, some self-selected samples, such as the small minority of constituents who contact their representative about their pet topic, should not be

BOX 8.3

Measuring public opinion

- An **opinion poll** is a series of questions asked in a standard way of a systematic sample of the population. The term usually refers to short surveys on topical issues for the media. Polls were traditionally conducted face to face; now, telephone interviews are customary in many countries, with online samples becoming more common.
- A **sample survey** is conducted using the same methods as an opinion poll but involves a more detailed questionnaire. Such surveys are often commissioned by governments or academic researchers.
- A **focus group** is a moderated discussion among a small group of respondents on a particular topic. It is a qualitative open-ended device used to explore the thinking and emotions lying behind people's attitudes. This technique has found favour with party strategists.
- In a **deliberative opinion poll**, or **citizens' jury**, people are briefed by, and can question, experts and politicians on a given topic before their own opinions are measured. This technique seeks to measure what public opinion would be if the public were fully informed on the issue.

A **focus group** overcomes some of these difficulties. Here, a researcher gathers a small group of people – typically eight to ten – with a common characteristic: non-voters, say, or donors to a particular party. The idea is to explore, in open-ended style, the perspectives through which participants view the issue. Unlike an opinion poll, the agenda can be at least partly driven by those taking part. A focus group is a qualitative technique, smaller in scale than an opinion poll and often self-selected, but aiming at a deeper understanding than is possible with the pre-coded answers used in most quantitative surveys.

Because opinion polls do not give respondents a chance to discuss the issue before expressing their views, their results are criticized by those who favour more ambitious interpretations of the public's role. Building on a richer view of the public's capacity, scholars have developed the idea of a **deliberative opinion poll** or **citizens' jury** (Fishkin, 2011). This technique involves exposing a small sample of electors to a range of viewpoints on a selected topic, perhaps through presentations by experts and politicians. With the background to the problem established, the group proceeds to a discussion and a judgement. Opinion is only measured when the issues have been thoroughly aired. As Fishkin (1991, p. 1) explains:

an ordinary opinion poll models what the public thinks, given how little it knows. A deliberative opinion poll models what the public would think, if it had a more adequate chance to think about the questions at issue.

Deliberative polling can therefore be used to anticipate how opinion might develop on new issues. It is also helpful on issues with a large technical content; for example, global warming or genetic testing. In such areas, expert explanation can usefully precede an expression of public opinion. Though not widely used, citizens' juries are an ingenious attempt to overcome the problem of ill-informed replies which bedevils conventional opinion polls.

The impact of public opinion

Given the importance of public opinion as a channel of political participation, how exactly does it exert

---

regarded as a valid basis for estimating public opinion at all – at least not when public opinion is equated with the whole adult population.

Yet, even when a sample is chosen systematically, it would be wrong to overstate the reliability of opinion polls in measuring the opinions of individual respondents. As with students taking a test, interviewees in a survey are answering questions set elsewhere. Polls are commissioned by journalists and party officials in the capital city, not by the ordinary people who answer the questions. They are a form of agenda-setting.

As a result, people may never have thought about a topic before they are invited to answer questions on it (Althaus, 2003). They may give an opinion when they have none, or they may agree to a statement because it is the easiest thing to do ('yea-saying') or because it is socially acceptable. Certainly, one danger of opinion polls is that they help to construct the public opinion they claim they are simply measuring.

its sway? In a sense, public opinion pervades all policy-making. It forms the environment within which politicians work, sitting in on many government meetings even though it is never minuted as a member.

In such discussions, public opinion usually performs one of two roles: acting either as a prompt or as a veto. 'Public opinion demands we do something about traffic congestion' is an example of the former; 'public opinion would never accept restrictions on car use' illustrates the latter. So, as Qualter (1991, p. 511) suggests, 'while public opinion does not govern, it may set limits on what governments do'.

Yet, public opinion is never all-powerful, even in liberal democracies. It informs agendas, rather than policy. Four limits are worth noting:

● Public opinion offers few detailed policy prescriptions. A few important objectives preoccupy the public but most policies are routine and uncontroversial. In detailed policy-making, expert and organized opinion matters more than public opinion.

● The public as a whole is often ill-informed, especially, but not only, on foreign policy. Asked before the invasion of Iraq in 2003, 'To the best of your knowledge, how many of the September 11 hijackers were Iraqi citizens?', only 7 per cent of Americans gave the correct answer: none (Pryor, 2003).

● Public opinion can evade trade-offs but governments cannot, though they sometimes try. The public may want lower taxes, more government spending, and a lower budget deficit but rulers must choose between these incompatible objectives. Further, the risks associated with a policy are poorly assessed by the public but require close attention from decision-makers (Weissberg, 2002).

● Politicians' perceptions of public opinion are often inaccurate. They are excessively influenced by personal contacts and by politicians' natural tendency to project their own views onto the wider electorate (Herbst, 1998).

Public opinion is most influential when it is seen to change. Only foolhardy politicians disregard developments in the overall climate of opinion and many politicians are sensitive to changes in the national mood (Stimson, 2004). Environmental damage can be an irrelevance one year and the topic everyone is talking about the next; a skilled politician can spot and respond to such agenda shifts. Change in public opinion matters as much as levels.

Participation in authoritarian states

The argument is sometimes made that political participation, at least as understood in liberal democracies, is an empty concept in non-democratic settings. After all, the nature of authoritarian regimes is that they must limit popular activity seeking to influence the government.

Yet, many experts on authoritarian regimes insist that participation is found in the political systems they study, even if its character is distinctive. Participation (and we will use that word) is often **mobilized**, rather than voluntary, and typically operates through informal sectors such as ethnic groups, rather than formal channels such as political parties. Writing well before the Arab uprisings, Albrecht (2008, p. 16) suggested that 'the concept of participation is not only applicable in the authoritarian states of the Middle East and North Africa, but also critical to a comprehensive understanding of state–society relationships in this region.'

Mobilized participation is elite-controlled involvement in politics designed to express popular support for the regime. Unlike voluntary (or autonomous) participation in liberal democracies, it is not designed to influence the composition or policies of the government.

In non-democracies, the limits and nature of participation are often subject to an implicit dialogue as activists test the boundaries of the acceptable. Authoritarian rulers may allow free space in those areas such as local politics which do not directly threaten the central leadership. They may permit the expression of opinion on the Internet even as they censor television broadcasts. Further, as societies grow more complex, rulers often come to realize that responding to popular pressure on non-sensitive issues can limit dissent and enhance political stability.

To illustrate these points, we will review participation in communist and post-communist states before examining one important mode of engagement found in many authoritarian systems: the patron–client network.

Communist and post-communist states

In communist regimes, participation was both more extensive and more regimented than in liberal democracies. Mobilized participation, high in quantity but low in quality, was a central feature. Under communism, it is still worth noting, citizen activity outscored the level found in liberal democracies. Ordinary people sat on comradely courts, administered elections, joined para-police organizations, and served on people's committees covering local matters.

However, the calibre of participation did not match its extent. To ensure that mass engagement always strengthened the party, communist party members guided all the avenues of political expression. Communication flowed only from top to bottom. So, people eventually behaved as they were treated: as passive, rather than active.

Eventually, some ruling parties did allow more participation, but only in areas that did not threaten their monopoly. Political participation also became more authentic on local matters. But these modest reforms were not matched in national politics. Because no real channels existed for airing grievances, people were left with two choices: to shut up and continue with life, or to air their complaints outside the system.

The trajectory of participation in China illustrates these themes. In the 1950s and 1960s, participation through accepted channels was required as a way of demonstrating active support for the party's predetermined goals. The question was not whether citizens participated but, rather, to what extent. This ritual, mobilized engagement was comparable with other communist states.

In contrast to most other communist leaders, however, Mao Zedong remained dissatisfied with the caution of the party establishment. In 1966, he launched the Cultural Revolution, encouraging the masses to turn on corrupt power-holders within the party, the workplace, and the family. The outcome was uncontrolled participation on an enormous scale; it threatened the country's social fabric and caused permanent damage to the party's reputation. In 1969, Mao called on the army to restore order; unrest continued for several years thereafter.

Following this remarkable episode, political participation in China developed along more predictable lines. After Mao's death in 1976, the leadership favoured economic reform over political purity, discouraging any form of participation which might threaten growth. Political passivity became acceptable.

More recently, the party has opened some social space in which sponsored groups can operate with relative freedom. For example, more than 150,000 civic associations were registered as early as 2007, providing an opportunity for citizen-to-citizen communication under the party's watchful eye in such areas as education and the environment (Guo, 2007). The regimented routines and the political excesses of Mao's era have been consigned to the past.

However, explicit opposition to the party remains forbidden. The topic may go unmentioned but memories remain of the Tiananmen Square massacre of 1989, when the army's tanks turned on pro-democracy demonstrators in Beijing. At local level, sometimes violent protests continue against corruption, unemployment, pollution, illegal levies, or non-payment of wages or pensions. The extent of such unconventional participation is unusual in entrenched non-democratic regimes. Demonstrations by ethnic minorities aside, these local protests do not threaten the party's dominance but are directed at local failures to implement national policies.

So, participation in China today operates within narrow channels. Passivity is acceptable, as is civic engagement of a non-political kind, but explicit opposition to the party's position as the guardian of society and the guider of economic development is still suppressed, often brutally.

Patron–client networks

A common technique for channelling, but also controlling, participation in authoritarian states is the patron–client network. **Clientelism**, as this practice is often called, is a form of political involvement which differs from both voluntary participation in liberal democracies and the mass mobilization in totalitarian states. Although patron–client relationships are found in all political systems, including liberal democracies, they are of greatest political significance in authoritarian regimes. Particularly in low-income countries, personal networks of patrons and clients can be the main instrument for bringing ordinary people into contact with formal politics; indeed, they are often the central organizing structure of politics itself (Figure 8.2). Despite their informality, these networks underpin, and often overwhelm, more formal channels of participation such as political parties.

Clientelism denotes politics substantially based on patron–client relationships. A powerful figure (the patron) provides protection to a number of lower-status clients who, in exchange, offer their unqualified allegiance and support.

So, what exactly are patron–client relationships? They are traditional, informal hierarchies fuelled by exchanges between a high-status patron and clients of lower status. The colloquial phrase 'big man/small boy' conveys the nature of the interaction. Patrons are landlords, employers, party leaders, government ministers, ethnic leaders, or anyone with control over resources. Lacking resources of their own, clients gather round their patron for protection and security.

Political patrons control the votes of their clients and persuade them to attend meetings, join organizations, or simply follow their patron around in a deferential manner. These public (on stage) affirmations of support are politically relevant, even though they often fail to reflect clients' private (off stage) opinion (Scott, 1985). Participation by clients is controlled and mobilized, as in communist states, but the patron–client relationship is based on personal exchange rather than a political party or a shared political outlook.

The patron's power, and its inhibiting effect on democracy, is illustrated in this comment by Egypt's President Abdul Nasser, interviewed in 1957 when he was still a reforming leader (Owen, 1993):

We were supposed to have a democratic system between 1923 and 1953. But what good was this democracy to our people? You have seen the landowners driving the peasants to the polling

Figure 8.2 A patronage network linking centre and periphery

Relationships between patrons and clients provide a way of organizing politics, especially in unequal societies with weak governing institutions

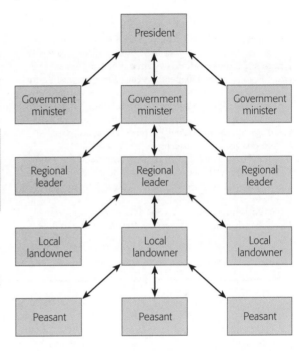

Note: Resources flow downwards, support flows upwards.

booths. There they would vote according to the instructions of their masters. I want the peasants to be able to say 'yes' and 'no' without this in any way affecting their livelihood and daily bread. This in my view is the basis for freedom and democracy.

Participation through patronage appeals in authoritarian settings because it links elite and mass, centre and periphery, in a context of inequality. Although inequality provides the soil in which patronage networks flourish, these relationships still act as political glue, binding the highest of the high with the lowest of the low.

By linking people across social levels, patron–client relationships limit the expression of solidarity among people of the same class, such as peasants. For the elite, they are a useful tactic of divide and rule. The decay of such hierarchical networks of

COUNTRY PROFILE

RUSSIA

Form of government ■ a federation of over 80 units, comprising republics, provinces, territories, districts, and cities.

Legislature and electoral system ■ the State Duma (lower house) contains 450 members elected by party list PR for a five-year term. The Federal Council (upper house) contains two members from each federal unit.

Executive ■ semi-presidential. The prime minister heads the Council of Ministers and succeeds the elected president, if needed (no vice-president).

Judicial branch ■ based on civil law and the constitution of 1993. Headed by a Constitutional Court and, for civil and administrative cases, a Supreme Court. Substantial lawlessness.

Party system ■ parties are weak and unstable – reflecting, rather than shaping, power. The leading party, United Russia, is led by Prime Minister Dmitry Medvedev.

Population (annual growth rate): 138.0 m (−0.5%)	
World Bank income group: upper-middle income	
Human development index (rank/out of): 66/187	
Political rights score: ⑥	
Civil liberties score: ⑤	
Media status: not free	

Note: For interpretation and sources, see p. xvi.

RUSSIA is a vast country with an imperial and authoritarian past: by area, it is the world's largest – almost twice the size of the United States. Russia's rulers have, in the past, been autocratic empire-builders, founding their imperial expansion on a large conscript army and control of a serf society. Thus, Russia's experience with communist dictatorship represented a culmination of a familiar authoritarian pattern.

Russia can still be conceived as an empire whose leaders are concerned to extend the country's international influence. With the collapse of the Soviet Union, 25 million Russians now live outside the country's new boundaries. This 'near abroad' is a particular foreign policy concern.

A broader objective is to restore Russia's status as a great power in what President Putin perceives as a hostile world. This goal is seemingly supported by the country's huge reserves of oil, gas, timber, and minerals. These resources comprise about 80 per cent

of Russia's exports. However, in Russia, as elsewhere, an economy based on commodity exports encourages corruption and rent-seeking, inhibiting both economic and democratic development.

The transition from communism in the 1990s was characteristically turbulent, involving a chaotic restructuring. Life expectancy and population plummeted as unemployment and alcoholism soared; even in 2012, male life expectancy remains a disappointing 16 years below that in the USA. Many state-owned entities were, in effect, stolen – creating a few wealthy oligarchs, but also a nexus between capitalism, crime, and corruption. This botched transition offers a powerful lesson: market economies must be underpinned by sound public institutions, including effective courts.

Russia is a hybrid regime but its authoritarian tendencies intensified during the first presidency of Vladimir Putin (2000–08). Exploiting the considerable

powers accorded to the presidential office under the 1993 constitution, Putin strengthened his control over television, the judiciary, and the provinces, while dealing ruthlessly with potential opponents. At the same time, his centralizing policies were at least partly directed towards producing a more law-governed society in which corruption would become less prominent and property rights more secure.

Blatant manipulation of parliamentary elections in 2011, and of the presidential contest of 2012, damaged the country's democratic claims. In addition, manoeuvring at the top exemplified Russia's top-down politics. Subject to a constitutional limit of two consecutive terms as president, Putin occupied the position of prime minister between 2008 and 2012, with his ally and former prime minister Dmitry Medvedev standing in as president. In a cynical move, both leaders returned to their previous posts in 2012.

Participation in Russia

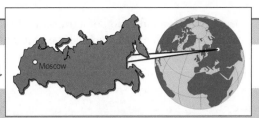

Russia presents a clear case of the limits of political participation in a competitive authoritarian regime. On the one hand, Russia is an intensely political society with an educated people fully aware of national developments. On the other hand, political participation is extremely shallow, held back by pervasive cynicism about the capacity of ordinary people to make a difference. So, how does political participation work in the setting of this iconic example of competitive authoritarianism?

Most Russians follow politics on television, and often in national and local newspapers. Two thirds of Russians say they either regularly or sometimes discuss the country's problems. They are well aware of the impact of politics on the country's development and, reflecting the communist era, are highly sophisticated in interpreting the nuances of news reports.

Yet, authoritarianism, past and present, pervades current attitudes, creating a country with a passive majority. In one survey, most Russians said that the country is not a democracy and that their vote would not change anything. In another study, 85 per cent said they had no power to influence overall government decisions (Rose, 1999).

Suspicion of organizations is endemic, with more people distrusting than trusting even the highest-rated institutions: the army and the Church. Trust remains contained within personal networks of friends and family.

Political parties come near the

bottom of the trust list, perhaps explaining why so many of them choose bland names such as 'Russia's Choice' and 'United Russia'. At just 1 per cent, membership of parties remains well below even declining Western levels. The parties themselves have proved to be unstable, with an insecure social base. They are, in the main, creatures of politicians, or even of the Kremlin itself.

Minimal membership of parties reflects limited participation in social organizations. Most Russians do not

belong to any voluntary public organizations; membership of trade unions is low; regular church attendance is uncommon. Although some organizations emerging during Mikhail Gorbachev's era of *glasnost* (openness) have survived, few have acquired large memberships and others have been incorporated into the regime. Particularly under President Putin, the government expresses suspicion of non-governmental bodies, regarding those with foreign links as engaged in espionage.

In a pattern characteristic of competitive authoritarian regimes, and also of some of the more liberal democracies in eastern Europe, mass political

participation in Russia is concentrated on national elections, with few organizations standing between citizen and state. Russia remains a distinctly uncivil society. The Russian people remain subjects, first; participants, second.

Public protest in Russia against Vladimir Putin's manipulation of parliamentary elections in 2011, and of the presidential contest of 2012, did represent an important development. Younger, better-educated people in the largest cities, notably

Moscow, demonstrated their dissatisfaction with their country's highly-managed politics. At least in the short term, however, the most concrete outcome was a new law restricting (but not banning) such protests. Also in 2012, the imprisonment of members of Pussy Riot, the feminist punk rock collective whose songs included *Putin Wets His Pants*, caused further protests, albeit internationally as much as domestically.

Civil society

The poverty of participation in Russia is often said to result from a weak civil society. Civil society consists of those groups which sit above the personal realm of the family but beneath the state. The term covers public organizations such as labour unions, interest groups and, on some definitions, recreational bodies. However, businesses are usually excluded because they are not voluntary bodies emerging from society. Developing civil society, and the social capital that grows from it, is a problem not only in Russia, but also in many other post-communist countries with a history of an over-bearing state and a legacy of distrust.

Further reading: Remington (2011), Sakwa (2011), White (2011), White *et al.* (2009).

dependence can be an indication of a transition to a more modern society in which people have acquired sufficient resources to be able to participate in an autonomous fashion. Put bluntly, security means people no longer need to trade their vote. Poverty and authoritarian rule provide a setting in which patron–client relationships flourish; affluence and democracy generate a climate in which they decay.

Discussion questions

■ Is extensive political participation a warning sign for a liberal democracy, or an indicator of its health?

■ Which groups under-participate in politics in your country and what can be done to engage those who belong to them?

■ Is public opinion a more important influence than elections on governments in liberal democracies?

■ Is it right to set quotas for female representation in parliament? If so, should the principle be extended to under-represented minorities?

■ Identify any significant social movements, past or present, in your country. Are they a challenge to establishment politics, or just another form of political participation?

■ What is a patron–client network? What are the strengths and weaknesses of such networks as a form of participation?

Further reading

R. Dalton, *Citizen Politics: Public Opinion and Political Parties in Advanced Industrial Democracies*, 5th edn (2008). This comparative text provides a wide-ranging review of political attitudes and behaviour in liberal democracies.

M. Krook, *Quotas for Women in Politics: Gender and Candidate Selection Reform Worldwide* (2009). One of the first global analyses of gender quotas for legislative office.

P. Norris, *Democratic Phoenix: Reinventing Political Activism* (2002). A widely cited study suggesting new forms of political participation have emerged to supplement traditional modes.

R. Putnam, *Bowling Alone: The Collapse and Revival of American Community* (2000). An influential assessment of the decline of social participation in the USA, with a focus on its political impact.

C. Tilly, *Power in Movement: Social Movements and Contentious Politics*, 3rd edn (2011). Focuses on the rise and fall of social movements as the outcome of political opportunities, state strategy, the mass media, and international diffusion.

P. Whiteley, *Political Participation in Britain: The Decline and Revival of Civic Culture* (2012). Reviews a range of findings about political values, participation, the media and civil society in Britain.

ONLINE RESOURCES AVAILABLE

Visit the companion website at **www.palgrave.com/politics/hague** to access additional learning resources, including multiple-choice questions, chapter summaries, web links and practice essay questions.

Chapter 9 Interest groups

Interest groups (also known as 'pressure groups') are non-governmental organizations which seek to influence public policy. Examples include employers' organizations, consumer groups, professional bodies, trade union federations, and campaigning associations. Traditionally, the term only covered bodies specifically created for lobbying purposes, excluding entities such as businesses, churches, and sub-national or overseas governments. But since much lobbying is done by organizations whose primary focus is elsewhere, this restriction is too limiting (Scholzman, 2010). In Washington, the Ford Motor Company functions as an interest 'group' alongside the Alliance of Automobile Manufacturers.

Like political parties, interest groups are a crucial channel of communication between society and government, especially in liberal democracies. However, interest groups pursue specialized concerns, seeking to influence without becoming the government. They are not election-fighting organizations; instead, they typically adopt a pragmatic, low-key approach in dealing with whatever power structure confronts them.

Although many interest groups go about their work quietly, their activity is pervasive. Their staff are to be found negotiating with bureaucrats over the details of proposed regulations, pressing their case in legislative committee hearings, and seeking to influence media coverage. As Finer noted decades ago, 'their day-to-day activities pervade every sphere of domestic policy, every day, every way, at every nook and cranny of government' (1966, p. 18). Without question, interest groups are central to a system of functional representation which supplements electoral representation, especially on detailed issues of policy implementation.

Political cultures vary in how they imagine the relationship between interest groups and the state:

●   as an essential component of a free society, separate from the state (e.g. USA);

●   as partners with the state in securing a well-regulated society (as in many smaller European democracies, e.g. the Netherlands); or

●   as organizations operating under the leadership of the state which alone defines the general will (France).

However, these broad conceptions vary rather more than the actual reality of how interest groups operate. In practice, interest group influence is universal in high-income liberal democracies.

From a historical perspective, too, interest groups developed in a rather predictable way. In the West, they emerged in a series of waves formed by

STUDYING . . .

INTEREST GROUPS

- Interest 'groups' can be a misleading label. Much lobbying is conducted directly by individual organizations, which include not only private corporations, but also other public organizations (e.g. state universities) and government bodies (e.g. local authorities).

- In liberal democracies, interest groups exert a pervasive influence over the details of public policies affecting them. But interest groups are far from omnipotent; understanding interest groups also requires an awareness of their limits as political actors.

- We can distinguish between how political systems conceive the role that interest groups should play (contrast the European Union, France, and the USA) and their actual significance in policy-making (invariably significant throughout the liberal democratic world).

- Much thinking on interest groups comes from the United States, where groups are exceptionally significant. A balanced appreciation requires an understanding of the contrasting, but still influential, position of groups in other liberal democracies.

- Pluralism, and the debate surrounding it, is a major academic interpretation of the political role of interest groups. Any evaluation of interest group activity, including a judgement on its impact on the quality of liberal democracy, requires a view about pluralism.

- Relationships between interest groups and governments change over time. Examples include the opening of the policy-making environment to a greater range of groups and the decay of peak associations as implementers of policies agreed with government. Appreciating these trends helps to prevent over-generalization.

- The growth of specialist lobbying firms raises issues of regulation and judgement: are they purveyors of sleaze or efficient intermediaries?

social change (e.g. industrialization) and the expansion of state activity (e.g. public welfare). Periods of social change raised new problems, while an active government created more incentives to lobby the administration. So, as with many other aspects of modern politics, interest group activity is a response to the growth of public regulation: 'groups are more active when and where the state is more active' (Mahoney and Baumgartner, 2008, p. 1253). Those who support pruning the interest group undergrowth would therefore be well-advised to begin by restricting the scope of government itself.

Box 9.1 summarizes the development of interest groups in the United States. Most Western nations followed a similar (if somewhat less vigorous) course, resulting in the mosaic of independent group activity found in nearly all contemporary liberal democracies.

Classifying interest groups

When we think of interest groups, the bodies which first come to mind are **protective groups** that articulate the material interests of their members: trade unions, employers' organizations, professional associations, and the like (Box 9.2). Sometimes known as 'sectional' or 'functional' groups, these protective bodies give priority to influencing government and

> **Protective groups** seek selective benefits for their members and insider status with relevant government departments. Because they represent clear occupational interests, protective associations are often the most influential of all groups. They are well-established, well-connected and well-resourced.

Waves of interest group formation in the United States

	Wave	Examples
1830–60	Founding of first national organizations	YMCA Many anti-slavery groups
1880–1900	Creation of many business and labour associations, stimulated by industrialization	National Association of Manufacturers American Federation of Labor
1900–20	Peak period of interest group formation	Chamber of Commerce American Medical Association
1960–80	Founding of many environmental and public interest groups	National Organization for Women Common Cause

Source: Adapted from Hrebenar (1997), pp. 13–15.

can invoke sanctions to help them achieve their goals. Workers can go on strike; business organizations can withdraw their cooperation with government.

But protective groups can also be based on local, rather than functional, interests. Geographic groups emerge when the shared interests of people living in the same location are threatened by plans for, say, a new highway, or a hostel for ex-convicts. Because of their negative stance – 'build it anywhere but here' – these geographical bodies are known as Nimby groups: not in my back yard. Collectively, Nimby groups can generate a Banana outcome: 'build absolutely nothing anywhere near anyone'. Unlike permanent functional organizations, however, Nimby groups come and go in response to particular threats.

A particular concern of protective groups is scrutinizing government activity; for example, by monitoring proposed regulations. A trade association will keep a beady eye on even the least newsworthy of developments within its zone of concern. A detailed regulation about product safety may be politically trivial but commercially vital for a group's members. Much activity of protective groups involves technical issues of this kind.

Many associations founded since the 1960s are promotional, rather than protective, and operate in a different way. In contrast to the more defensive stance of protective bodies, **promotional groups**

advocate ideas, identities, policies, and values. Also known as 'advocacy', 'attitude', 'campaign' and 'cause' groups, promotional organizations focus on such issues as abortion, the environment, or global development. Their members are interested in the issue concerned without, in most cases, possessing a material stake in how it is resolved.

In liberal democracies, promotional groups have undoubtedly expanded in number, significance, and recognition by government. Their growth since the 1960s constitutes a major trend in interest politics. In the United States, for example, Common Cause (2012) describes itself as a 'nonpartisan, nonprofit advocacy organization founded as a vehicle for citizens to make their voices heard in the political process and to hold their elected leaders accountable to the public interest'. Its nearly 400,000 supporters, 35 state organizations and $10 million annual budget are a tribute to the willingness of people to join an organization seeking to counter the influence of special interests.

However, even more than for members of political parties, many who join promotional groups are credit card affiliates only. To be sure, a financial contribution expresses the donor's commitment, but it also delegates pursuit of the cause to the group's leaders. For this reason, the effectiveness of promotional bodies as schools for democracy can easily be overstated (Maloney, 2009).

BOX 9.2

Protective and promotional groups

	Protective groups	Promotional groups
Aims	A group *of*: defends an interest	A group *for*: promotes a cause
Membership	Closed: membership is restricted	Open: anyone can join
Status	Insider: frequently consulted by government and actively seeks this role	Outsider: consulted less often by government; targets public opinion and the media
Benefits	Selective: only group members benefit	Collective: benefits go to both members and non-members
Focus	Group aims to influence national government on specific issues affecting members	Group also seeks to influence national and global bodies on broad policy matters

The boundary separating protective and promotional groups is poorly defined. For example, bodies such as the women's and gay movements seek to influence public opinion and are often classified as promotional. However, their prime purpose remains to promote the interests of specific non-occupational groups. Perhaps they are best conceived as protective interests employing promotional means.

Protective interest groups representing a specific industry do not only lobby government directly. Often, they will also join a **peak association**. Industrial associations and individual corporations join a wider body representing the business interests to government. Examples of peaks include the National Association of Manufacturers in the USA, the Federal Organization of German Employers, and the Confederation of British Industry (CBI) in the UK (Figure 9.1).

A **peak** (or 'apex') **association** is an umbrella organization representing the broad interests of capital or labour to government. The members of peak associations are not individuals but other organizations such as firms, trade associations, and labour unions.

Trade unions respond similarly. Despite the widespread decline in union membership and labour militancy, many trade union peaks still speak with a voice that carries weight. In 2011, the Confederation of German Trade Unions (DGB) comprised eight unions with a total of more than six million individual members. Britain's Trades Union Congress had 58 affiliated unions in 2012, representing a comparable number of working people. Such numbers usually suffice to deliver a seat at the policy table.

Peak organizations seek to influence public policy and usually succeed. They are attuned to national government, possess a strong research capacity and talk the language of policy. For example, the DGB (2012) defines its task thus:

As the trade union umbrella organisation, the DGB represents the German trade union movement in dealing with: the government authorities at state and national level; the political parties; the employers' organisations; and other groups within society. The DGB itself is not directly involved in collective bargaining and cannot conclude pay agreements. However, it is significant for its specialist competence on broader issues of a general political nature.

In some smaller West European countries, such as Austria, the peak associations became centrally involved in the post-war decades in negotiating broad policy packages with government. The content of such agreements included price controls, wage increases and welfare benefits. Here, the peaks

Figure 9.1 A peak association: Britain's CBI

Peak associations, such as Britain's CBI, seek to influence government policy at a high level. They represent, and provide services to, their corporate members.

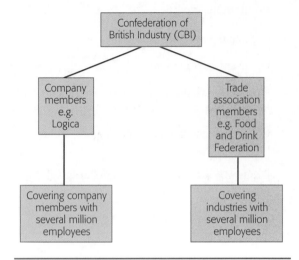

became full social partners, working alongside government and playing a key role in implementing tripartite agreements (that is, between government, capital, and labour). In a sense, the peaks formed an unofficial coalition with the government. These arrangements, known as 'societal corporatism' or 'social partnership', offered a striking illustration of how functional interests, working in conjunction with the executive, can marginalize representation in parliament (Berger and Compston, 2002).

Throughout the democratic world, the decline of trade union membership (Table 9.1, p. 164) and the rise of pro-market thinking, international markets, and smaller service companies has diminished the standing of peak associations. In response, they have tended to become policy-influencing and service-providing bodies, rather than organizations negotiating collectively with government on behalf of their members (Silvia and Schroeder, 2007). Even if individual unions and firms still join peaks, they keep their own lobbying capability.

Even so, extensive consultation – if no longer joint decision-making – continues between the peaks and government, not least in Scandinavia. And some smaller countries, including Ireland and the Netherlands, have even developed or revived social partnerships in an effort to combine social protec-

tion with improved economic efficiency. Such structured arrangements provide a contrast to the pluralist interpretation of interest groups which we discuss in the next section.

Pluralism, iron triangles and issue networks

Debate on the general role of interest groups in liberal democracies has centred on the broad concept of pluralism and we begin this section by outlining this important idea. We then turn to more detailed interpretations of interest groups' political significance, highlighting the transition from iron triangles to issue networks.

Pluralism

Pluralism is an American-inspired view that regards competition between freely organized interest groups as a form, rather than a denial, of democracy. In this way, pluralism offers not merely a claim about how interest groups operate, but also an understanding of liberal democracy itself. It gives us a model of the relationship between groups and government which is far removed from the European notion of social partnership mentioned in the previous section.

What is pluralism? It is a form of governance in which the state becomes an arena for competition between interest groups. The groups compete for influence over a government willing to listen to all the voices it discerns in the political debate. The government adds little of its own; it is an arbiter, not an initiator. For Arthur Bentley (1908), an American pioneer of this approach, 'when the groups are adequately stated, everything is stated. When I say everything, I mean everything'.

Literally 'rule by the many', **pluralism** refers to a political system in which numerous competing interest groups exert strong influence over a responsive government. The state is umpire, rather than player. Each interest group concentrates on its own sector (for example, education, health care) so that no single elite dominates the political system as a whole.

All kinds of interest have their say before the court of government. Groups compete on a level playing field, with the state showing little bias either towards interests of a particular type, or towards specific groups within that type. As new interests and identities emerge, groups form to represent them, quickly finding a place in the house of power. In a pluralist system, politics forms an open, competitive market with few barriers to entry.

Pluralism brings healthy fragmentation across the range of government activity, since most interests are restricted to a single policy sector: the influence of physicians is confined to health care; that of teachers, to education policy. Indeed, a central tenet of pluralism is that no single elite dominates the entire sphere of government. Rather, different interest groups lead the way in each area of policy. Power does not cumulate across issues. Overall, pluralism depicts a wholesome process of dispersed decision-making in which government's openness allows its policies to reflect developments in the economy and society.

The significance of pluralism lies in its implications for our understanding of liberal democracy. Pluralists accept that majority rule is an insufficient account of how democracies work in practice. Rather, pluralists judge that democracy must, in reality, include a strong element of rule by minorities, each operating in a particular policy area but subject to the informal checks and balances of other groups operating in the same sector, with the government as broker.

Pluralists invite us to recognize that for all the battle of ideas in election campaigns, most policy decisions emerge from discussion between government departments and interest groups. At the level of detail practised in executive departments, governing parties experience mandate uncertainty; their manifesto and ideology provide insufficient guidance on what to do. Interest groups fill the gap.

In weighing interests rather than votes, pluralism takes account of intensity of preferences by assuming, perhaps complacently, that organized opinion will, in the main, be strongly held. Surely, pluralists say, people living under the flight-path should have a particular say on proposals to permit more night flights. In these ways, competing interest groups become a key instrument of democracy as rule by minorities, comparable to the role played by parties in a traditional reading of democracy as majority rule.

The strengths of pluralistic governance are substantial. Dahl, for example, notes that:

groups have served to educate citizens in political life, strengthened them in their relations with the state, helped to ensure that no single interest would regularly prevail on all important decisions, and, by providing information, discussion, negotiation and compromise, even helped to make public decisions more rational and more acceptable. (1993, p. 706)

Pluralism remains an important perspective but many political scientists now accept that its original portrayal of the relationship between groups and government was one-sided and superficial (McFarland, 2010). Criticism focuses on four areas:

● Interest groups do not compete on an equal playing field. Some interests, such as business, are inherently powerful (after all, firms generate jobs, taxes, and wealth, all of which are useful to government). Other interests, such as professional groups, are central to policy implementation. In reality, groups form a stable hierarchy of influence, with their ranking reflecting their value to government.

● Pluralism neglects the bias of the political culture and political system in favour of some interests but against others. Groups advocating modest reforms within the established order are heard more sympathetically than those seeking radical change (Walker, 1991). Regulation is achievable; redistribution less so. Some groups experience difficulty in organizing at all; for example abused children, the elderly, and hospital patients.

● The state is far more than a neutral umpire. In addition to deciding which groups to heed, it may regulate their operation and even encourage their formation in areas it deems important, thus shaping the interest-group landscape itself.

● Pluralist conflict disguises interests shared by leaders of all the mainstream groups, such as their common membership of the same class and ethnic group. 'The flaw in the pluralist heaven', remarked Schattschneider (1960, p. 35), 'is that the heavenly chorus sings with a strong upper-class accent.' In similar vein, Wright Mills famously argued in *The Power Elite* (1956) that American leaders of industry, the military, and government formed an interlocking power elite, rather than separate power centres.

Both as an ideal and as a description of how politics works, pluralism draws on American experience. In the USA, interest group patterns certainly come closest to the pluralist model. As de Tocqueville (1835) wrote, 'in no country in the world has the principle of association been more successfully used, or applied to a greater multitude of objects, than in America'. Petracca (1992, p. 3) made the point succinctly: 'American politics is the politics of interests.'

Nowhere else are interest groups so numerous, visible, organized, competitive, well-resourced, and successful. One directory listed more than 27,000 organizations politically active in Washington between 1981 and 2006 (Scholtzman, 2010, p. 431). These groups, ranging from the National Association of Manufacturers to the American Association of Retired Persons, seek to influence policy at federal, state, and local levels. In addition to a full roster of protective economic interests, promotional groups are also uniquely prominent in the USA, with over 500 focusing on environmental issues and 100 on women's concerns.

Washington politics reflects the competitive spirit that is pluralism's hallmark. Most of the time, American government is too fragmented to be anything more than an umpire. The detailed party programmes of Western European parties, the social partnerships in some Western European countries between peak association and government, and the French idea of a state, which alone defines the public interest, are largely absent here. Instead, the separation of powers gives interest groups several points of leverage, particularly congressional committees, executive agencies, and the courts. Such helpful conditions mean that the constitutional right 'to petition the government for a redress of grievances' is fully exploited.

But at a price. Fragmented government entrenches the interests of those who are already wealthy and powerful, including financial institutions deemed too big to fail. In 2006, business interests provided

half – and the better-resourced half – of all the organizations registered in Washington (Scholtzman, 2010, p. 434). As many American presidents elected on a reform ticket have discovered, the voice of the status quo often sings louder in Washington than that of reform. The general interest often drowns in a sea of special pleading, certainly avoiding majority dictatorship, but substituting the risk of tyranny by minorities. So, while we can certainly use the United States to demonstrate pluralist politics in action, we can also see the country as an illustration of pluralism's weaknesses.

From iron triangles to issue networks

While the debate about pluralism provides an overall perspective on the position of interest groups in liberal democracies, we must also examine how their role has evolved over time. In the United States, this pattern can be broadly characterized as a transition from **iron triangles** to **issue networks**. This trend is also visible in most other liberal democracies.

American political scientists used the term 'iron triangle' to describe a traditional relationship between groups and government in a few policy sectors in the USA, particularly those areas where resources were available for distribution. The three points on the triangle were government departments (or agencies within them), interest groups, and congressional committees (Figure 9.2).

Such triangles became an exercise in mutual exchange and support: the committee appropriated funds which were spent by the department for the benefit of interest group members. For example, the Department of Defense would offer contracts to arms corporations setting up manufacturing facilities in the home districts of influential committee members. Or the Department of Agriculture, the relevant committees in Congress (with members drawn from rural areas), and farmers' groups would collude on larger food subsidies. Each point on the triangle benefited substantially, With neither a strong state nor disciplined parties to impose overall coherence **subgovernments** could act as policy cartels, providing exceptions to pluralist ideas of competitive policy-making.

Outside the United States, the term **policy community** was sometimes used to describe a similar pattern of inward-looking policy-making

Iron triangles, subgovernments, and policy communities are terms used to refer to inward-looking coalitions of interests, based on senior bureaucrats, interest group leaders and, sometimes, relevant legislators, that dominate policy-making in particular sectors (e.g. agriculture). In many liberal democracies, these secretive and distinctly non-pluralistic cartels have given way to looser and more pluralistic issue networks which are more open to outside organizations and considered debate.

Figure 9.2 Iron triangles: how subgovernments operated in the USA

An iron triangle described a pattern of cosy links between interest groups, government departments, and congressional committees. Such relationships facilitated policies and spending which benefited all points on the triangle by subsidizing interest group members, expanding government departments and providing resources such as jobs to the home districts of congressional representatives.

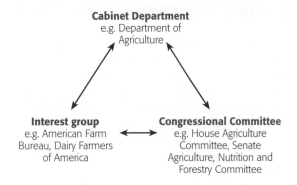

(Marsh and Rhodes, 1992). Within a particular sector, it was alleged, interest group leaders and senior civil servants (but rarely members of the legislature) formed their own small communities. All the members in the policy village knew each other and sought to remain on good terms. The participants developed a shared world view. They learned to trust and respect each other. Village business was conducted behind closed doors to prevent political posturing and to allow a quiet life for all. Insiders were sharply distinguished from outsiders. The golden rule was 'Never upset the apple cart.'

These cosy iron triangles and policy communities have decayed in many liberal democracies, contributing to a somewhat more pluralistic environment. Policies in most sectors are subject to closer scrutiny by the media, new public interest groups protest loudly when they spot the public being taken for a ride, and legislators are more willing to speak out. As issues become more complex, so more groups are drawn into the policy process, making it harder to stitch together insider deals. In the United States, where this trend has gone furthest, the committee barons who used to dominate Congress have lost much of their power. The iron has gone out of the triangle; now influence over decisions depends on what you know as much as whom you know.

Reflecting these trends, the talk now is of issue (or policy) networks. These refer to relationships between the familiar set of organizations involved in policy-making: government departments, interest groups, and legislative committees, with the addition of expert outsiders. However, the structure of an issue network is much looser than that of an iron triangle; the impact of a particular interest group varies from one topic within the field to the next, depending on its expertise. The idea of a 'network' focuses on relationships between actors; the partici-

pants themselves, and ad hoc coalitions between them, may change from topic to topic. For instance, several interest groups might form a short-term coalition to promote a particular policy on which they can agree. As Heclo (1978, p. 102) pointed out in an influential statement:

The notions of iron triangles and subgovernments presume small circles of participants who have succeeded in becoming largely autonomous. Issue networks, on the other hand, comprise a large number of participants with quite variable degrees of mutual commitment ... it is almost impossible to say where a network leaves off and its environment begins.

Clearly, the idea of issue networks enables us to portray policy-making in liberal democracies more positively. A wider range of interests participate in decisions, the bias towards protective groups is reduced, new groups can enter the debate, and a sound argument carries greater weight. Inward-looking policy villages have given way to more open policy towns. Because networks operate in a non-hierarchical way, we can portray their participants as engaged in a constructive exchange of resources – such as knowledge (e.g. academic specialists), legitimacy (elected politicians), information provision plus engagement in implementation (interest groups), and the capacity to draft bills and regulations (bureaucrats). At a minimum these networks are more pluralistic than subgovernments.

Channels of influence

We turn now to the channels of communication between interest groups and government. How do interest groups set about communicating with decision-makers? In the main, groups follow the debate to the arenas where it is resolved but there may also be opportunities for **venue shopping**, given that many detailed issues engage multiple authorities including the bureaucracy, legislative committees and the courts.

> Interest groups engage in **venue shopping** when they choose to raise their concerns in the arena where they possess the greatest leverage and are most likely to receive a positive response. For example, a group may judge that a joint government-industry committee will provide a more predictable venue than a parliamentary committee or a courtroom. It will shop accordingly.

Figure 9.3 sets out three mechanisms of interest group influence: direct interaction with people in policy-making institutions, indirect influence through political parties, and indirect influence through public opinion. We examine each channel, and also look at specialist lobbying companies which help to pilot their interest group clients through these channels.

Direct discussion with policy-makers

Those who shape and apply policy are the ultimate target of most protective and many promotional groups. So, direct conversations with the ministers who form the political *executive* are ideal if access is available. Talking with ministers before specific policies have crystallized is particularly valuable because it enables a group to enter the policy process at a formative stage. But, in many large political systems, such privileges are confined to a few well-connected individuals: the heads of the major peak associa-

Figure 9.3 Channels of interest group influence

Protective interest groups seek to influence policy though direct discussion with public servants and, on occasion, ministers. Some groups, including promotional ones, aim for indirect influence on policy through public opinion and political parties.

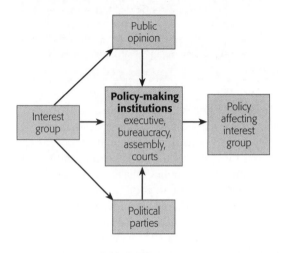

tions, say, or the chief executives of the country's largest corporations. In any case, policy decisions taken by senior ministers are likely to reflect political objectives beyond the influence of most groups. It is on details of regulation, rather than principles of high politics, that protective interest groups seek to say their piece.

In practice, most interest group activity focuses on the bureaucracy, the legislature and the courts. Of these, the *bureaucracy* is undoubtedly the main pressure point. Interest groups follow power and it is in civil servants' offices that detailed decisions are formed. As Matthews (1989, p. 217) commented:

the bureaucracy's significance is reinforced by its policy-making and policy-implementing roles. Many routine, technical and 'less important' decisions, which are nonetheless of vital concern to interest groups, are actually made by public servants.

For instance, ministers may decree a policy of subsidizing consumers who use renewable energy, a strategy that most groups must accept as given. However, the precise details of these incentives, as worked out in consultation with officials, will impinge directly on the profitability of energy suppliers.

So, shrewd protective groups focus on the small print because details are easier to modify. Access to top ministers may be difficult but most democracies follow a convention of discussion over detail with organized opinion through consultative councils and committees. Often, the law requires such deliberation. In any case, the real expertise frequently lies in the interest group rather than the bureaucracy, giving the government an incentive to seek out this knowledge. Besides, from the government's viewpoint, a policy which can be shown to be acceptable to all organized interests is politically safe.

While the bureaucracy is invariably a crucial arena for groups, the significance of the *assembly* depends on its political weight. A comparison between the United States and Canada makes the point. The American Congress (and, especially, its committees) forms a vital cog in the policy machinery. Members of Congress realize they are under constant public scrutiny. In the House, especially, a two-year election cycle means that politicians must be constantly aware of their ratings by interest groups. The ability of groups to endorse particular candidates – and, indirectly, to support their re-election campaigns – renders legislators sensitive to group demands (Cigler and Loomis, 2012). So, representatives are open to interest groups, especially those which resonate in their home districts, because this responsiveness contributes to their re-election prospects.

But the USA is a unique case. In Canada, as in most democracies, parliament is more reactive than proactive; as a result, interest groups treat its members as opinion-formers (if that), rather than policy-makers. Party voting is entrenched in Canada's House of Commons, extending beyond floor votes to committees and, in any case, 'committees seldom modify in more than marginal ways what is placed before them and virtually never derail any bill that the government has introduced' (Brooks, 2012, p. 257). Such a disciplined environment offers few opportunities for influence. As Landes (2002, p. 488) comments on Canada:

interest groups have an acute sense of smell when tracking the scent of power. Interaction with the bureaucracy and not with members of parliament is the goal of most groups and one reason why interest group activity is not highly visible to the untrained eye.

If interest groups feel slighted in the policy-making process, they may still be able to seek redress through the *courts*. In the United States, business corporations routinely subject government statutes and regulatory decisions to legal challenge. Within the European Union, an interest group that is unsuccessful at home can take its case to the European Court of Justice.

But, just as the USA is exceptional in the powers of its legislature, so too is it unique in its reliance on courts to resolve disputes. Elsewhere, the judicial system is certainly growing in importance; in Canada, for instance, Ecojustice seeks to hold 'governments and corporations accountable to nature' specifically through court actions. In general, though, the courts remain a venue of last resort. Judicial action is expensive, time-consuming, uncertain, and disruptive of established relationships.

Indirect influence through political parties

In the past, many interest groups sought to use a favoured political party as a channel of influence, with group and party often bound together as members of the same family. For instance, Britain's labour movement historically regarded its industrial wing (the trade unions) and its political wing (the Labour Party) as elements of a single drive to promote broad working-class interests. In a similar way, the environmental movement spawned both promotional interest groups and green political parties.

However, such intimate relationships between interest groups and political parties have become exceptional. Roles have become more specialized as interest groups concentrate on their members' specific concerns, while parties develop broader agendas. For instance, the religious and class parties of Western Europe have broadened their appeal in the post-war era, seeking to be viewed as custodians of the nation as a whole. The distinction between parties bent on power and interest groups focused on influence has sharpened as marriages of the heart have given way to alliances of convenience. As a result, most interest groups now seek to hedge their bets, rather than to develop close links with a political party. Loose, pragmatic links between interests and parties are the norm.

In the United States, this pattern is well-established. Business and organized labour gravitate

PROFILE

EUROPEAN UNION

Form of government ■ a unique hybrid body in which policy is made partly by European Union institutions and partly through negotiations among the 27 member states.

Executive

- The powerful *European Commission*, arranged into directorates, general departments and specialized service units, initiates many proposals and oversees their implementation. It is a cross between an executive and a bureaucracy, representing the common European interest.
- The *Council of the European Union* ('Council of Ministers') is the meeting place for ministers from national governments. Because it must approve Commission proposals before they become law, the Council is a legislative upper chamber as well as an executive body.
- The separate *European Council* is the EU forum for meetings of heads of government from the member states (the *Council of Europe* is a separate body again, unconnected with the EU).

Parliament ■ the members of the large, multi-site *European Parliament* are directly elected from each country for a five-year term. The number of MEPs from each country

Area (sq. km): 4.3m	
Member states: 27	
Population (annual growth rate): 504m (+0.2%)	
Gross domestic product (billion $): 15,390	
Gross domestic product per head: $34,000	

reflects its population, but with over-representation of smaller states. Given the legislative role of the Council of the European Union, the European Parliament is, in effect, the lower chamber of a bicameral legislature. Its standing has increased substantially since the 1970s, though its scope still does not cover all areas of EU responsibility.

Judiciary ■ the influential *European Court of Justice*, composed of one judge from each member country, has developed the EU's strong legal foundations, supporting the drive for European integration, especially in the final decades of the twentieth century.

The **EUROPEAN UNION**'s emergence owes much to the continent's history of conflict. After World War II, many European leaders set out to create a unified continent within which war would no longer be feasible: a United States of Europe. However, economic factors were also fundamental. European economies needed to be rebuilt after 1945 and then, in order to achieve the benefits of scale, integrated into a large, single market.

Some later members, notably Britain, emphasized the economic basis of the Union, while rejecting its federal vision. Margaret Thatcher said, in 1988, that 'willing and active cooperation between independent sovereign states is the best way to build a successful European Community'. Even on the continent, some publics have grown sceptical of

further integration. Proposals for a European constitutional treaty, expressing a commitment 'to forge a common destiny', were defeated by referendums in France (2005), the Netherlands (2005), and Ireland (2008). So, the notion of an explicit constitution has been abandoned and the EU's basis still lies in treaties.

In addition, the euro currency is currently confined to 17 countries, reflecting an increasingly variable geometry in which integration proceeds at a different pace among particular groups of members. In 2011, for example, Britain vetoed a plan to enforce greater fiscal discipline on all member states, forcing eurozone members to seek a separate intergovernmental solution.

Future developments in the EU remain uncertain. On the one hand, pressures to resolve the eurozone crisis, complete the single market, provide an effective response to environmental and terrorist threats, and counter American and Asian influence in the world will surely continue, providing strong ammunition to those committed to further deepening.

On the other hand, sceptical national leaders (mindful of their often cynical electorates) will continue to suggest that such matters can be adequately addressed through intergovernmental means. Indeed, national governments (rather than the EU itself) took the lead in responding not only to the eurozone crisis of 2011, but also to the global financial crisis of 2008–09.

Interest groups and the EU

One European Commission official said, 'My division is responsible for 44 directives and 89 regulations. And I have about nine staff to deal with all of this. The corresponding administration in the US has 600 people' (Greenwood, 2011, p. 6). It is no surprise, therefore, that the Commission not only encouraged relevant interest groups to develop but also remained accessible to them. How, then, do interest groups operate in the unique hybrid that is the European Union?

Reflecting the European tradition of social partnership, the EU has encouraged interest groups. Around 3,000 such bodies, including about 1,000 business associations, maintain an EU presence, rendering Brussels the European equivalent of Washington, DC. The main peak associations are BusinessEurope (40 full-time staff) and the European Trade Union Federation (ETUC) (58 staff). Influential sectoral groups include COPA-COGECA (European Farmers/European Agri-Cooperatives) (over 50 staff).

Although the strengthened authority of the European Parliament has extended the scope for lobbying, most activity still focuses on the Commission, which has established an extensive system of consultative committees with members drawn from organized interests. Even more than national governments, the Commission depends on interest groups – not only for information, intelligence, and advice, but also to back its proposals. As a regulatory body, it is difficult to envision how the Commission could function without specialist input from interest groups.

Originally, the Commission preferred to deal with groups organized on a Europe-wide basis. However, these federations proved to be slow-moving and under-resourced. So, the Commission has turned to more effective operators: national peak associations and individual companies capable of communicating current market developments. In their turn, many companies, including multinational corporations

How the European Trade Union Federation defines its task

'The process of European integration, with the euro, the European Constitution, and the growing impact of EU legislation on daily life, has changed the setting in which trade unions operate. To defend and bargain for their members effectively at national level, they must coordinate activities and policies across Europe … This is the challenge that the European Trade Union Confederation has taken up. The ETUC's objective is an EU with a strong social dimension that safeguards the wellbeing of all its citizens.' (ETUC, 2012)

based outside the EU, have become more willing to lobby the Commission directly.

Compared with the lobbying of national governments, interest representation in the European Union differs in three main respects:

- Policy is more frequently revised or dropped as it passes through the complex filters of the Union's institutions. For this reason, any initial agreements reached with the Commission retain a conditional quality.
- Brussels remains at one remove from the glare of national politics. The focus is interest groups, rather than social movements; quality information and reasoned argument, but not political grandstanding, are valued. Effective

lobbying depends on developing long-term relationships of trust combined with sensitivity to the Commission's agenda. Reflecting this policy style, lobbying is less conspicuous than in the USA.

- Because the European Union is a union of states, groups retain the option of seeking influence through their national governments. Similarly, the Commission must depend on national governments for implementation – and on its interest group partners to monitor whether member states are, in fact, complying with EU rules.

Here, then, we see the complex reality of multilevel governance which allows skilled interest groups to influence the development of EU policy.

Further reading: Beyers *et al.* (2009), Greenwood (2011), Hix and Hoyland (2011), Lelieveldt and Princen (2011), Nugent (2010).

towards the Republican and Democratic parties, respectively, but these have always been partnerships of convenience, not indissoluble marriages. In Germany, the powerful Federation of German Industry certainly enjoys close links with the conservative Christian Democratic Union. However, it wisely remains on speaking terms with the more left-wing Social Democrats. The rule is simple: protective interests follow power, not parties.

Indirect influence through public opinion

Press, radio, and television provide an additional resource for interest groups engaged with a broader constituency than specific decision-makers. This wider audience can be attacked by focusing on paid advertisements (advocacy advertising), or by promoting favourable editorial coverage (public relations).

The media are a central concern for promotional groups as they seek to steer public opinion and recruit a mass membership. Many promotional groups lack both substantial resources and access to decision-makers, so public opinion becomes a venue of necessity. In contrast to protective groups, cause groups view the media as sympathetic, rather than as a threat – and they may, indeed, be justified in their assumption (Dalton, 1994).

Traditionally, the media are less important to protective groups with their more specialized and secretive demands. What food manufacturer would go public with a campaign opposing nutritional labels on foods? The confidentiality of a government office is a more appropriate arena for fighting rearguard actions of this kind. Keen to protect their reputation in government, protective groups steer away from disruption; they want to be seen as reliable partners by the public servants on the other side of the table.

But even protective groups are now seeking to influence the climate of public opinion, especially in political systems where legislatures help to shape policy. In the United States, many protective groups understand that the surest route to the hearts of members of Congress is through their constituents. Especially when groups sense that public opinion is already onside, they increasingly follow a dual strategy, going public and going Washington. The risk lies in upsetting established relationships with bureaucrats; however, this danger has declined com-

pared with the era of iron triangles. In Denmark, for instance, 'decision makers seem to accept that groups seek attention from the media and the general public without excluding them from access to making their standpoint heard in decision-making' (Binderkrantz, 2005, p. 703). Slowly and cautiously, even protective groups are emerging from the bureaucratic undergrowth into the glare of media publicity.

Lobbyists

Although interest groups are usually their own best **lobbyists**, our focus in this section turns to companies whose aim is to open the doors of government to their interest group clients. These lobbying firms, sometimes known as contract or consultant lobbyists, are technicians of influence: hired guns in the business of interest group communication. Such services are offered not only by specialist government relations companies, but also by divisions within law firms and management consultancies. These operations are growing in number in liberal democracies, with some companies operating internationally. Because popular suspicion of lobbying feeds into scepticism about government generally, this expanding profession merits attention.

> A **lobbyist** is defined in the United States Legislative Reorganization Act (1946) as any person or organization that receives money to be used principally to influence legislation before Congress. The term derives from the hall or lobby of Britain's House of Commons where people approach members of parliament to plead their case.

Why is lobbying an expanding profession? Three reasons suggest themselves:

- Government regulation continues to grow, often impinging directly on companies, interest groups and trade unions. A specialist lobbying firm working for a number of interest groups can often monitor proposed regulations more efficiently than would be the case if each interest group undertook the task separately.

- Public relations campaigns are becoming increasingly sophisticated, often seeking to influence interest group members, public opinion and the government in one integrated project. Professional agencies come into their own in planning and delivering multifaceted campaigns, which can be too complex for an interest group client to manage directly.

- Many firms now approach government directly, rather than working through their trade association. Companies, both large and small, find that using a lobbying company to help them contact a government agency or a sympathetic legislator can yield results more swiftly than working through an industry body.

The central feature of the lobbying business is its intensely personal character. A legislator is most likely to return a call from a lobbyist if the caller is a former colleague. Lobbying is about who you know. For this reason, lobbying firms are always on the look-out for former legislators or bureaucrats with a warm contact book. However, regulations (where they exist and are implemented) typically specify a time gap before former government employees can take up a lobbying job (Box 9.3).

The key question, though, concerns the political impact of lobbying companies. Is it now possible for wealthy interest groups and corporations simply to pay a fee to a lobbying firm to ensure that a bill is defeated or a regulation deferred? Is lobbying just a fancy word for bribery? On the whole, the answer is 'no'. Lobbyists are inclined to exaggerate their own impact for commercial reasons but, in reality, most can achieve little more than access to relevant politicians and, perhaps, bureaucrats. Often, the lobbyist's role is merely to hold the client's hand, helping an inexperienced company find its way around the corridors of power when it comes to town.

Shaping the policy-maker's response to the message is a far greater challenge. Allegations of sleaze notwithstanding, influence can rarely be purchased through a lobbyist but must come, if at all, from the petitioning group itself. And, first and foremost, impact depends on the intrinsic strength of the case. To the experienced politician, a convincing case direct from a petitioner sings louder than yet another rehearsed presentation delivered by a lobbying firm.

Rather than viewing professional lobbying in a negative light, we should recognize its contribution

---

BOX 9.3

Regulating lobbyists

One way of securing the advantages of lobbying while reducing the risk of corruption is through public regulation. Several democracies – including Australia, Canada, the European Union, Germany, and the United States – have now adopted formal rules. Typical requirements are that:

- lobbyists register as individuals on a public list;
- expenditure on lobbying is disclosed and made public;
- a public agency audits the spending of lobbying firms;
- a cooling-off period is imposed on former legislators before they can become lobbyists.

Source: Chari *et al.* (2010).

---

to effective political communication. It can focus the client's message on relevant decision-makers, ensuring that the client's voice is heard by those who need to hear it. Furthermore, lobbyists spend most time with sympathetic legislators, contributing to their promotion of a cause in which they already believe. Crossick, quoted in Thomas and Hrebenar (2009, p. 138), said that 'successful lobbying involves getting the right message over to the right people in the right form at the right time on the right issue'. In that respect, at least, it enhances the efficiency of governance.

Of course, not everything in the lobby is rosy. Even if a company achieves no more for its fee than access to a decision-maker (and even if that meeting would have been possible with a direct approach), perhaps such exchanges in themselves compromise the principle of equality which underpins democracy. Because buying access and buying influence are rarely distinguished in the public's mind, meetings arranged through lobbyists damage the legitimacy of the political process and generate a need, only now being met, for effective regulation. But as long as petitioning the government is a right rather than a requirement, it is difficult to see how inequalities in interest representation can be avoided.

Ingredients of influence

There is no doubt that some interest groups exert more influence over government than others. So, what is it that gives particular groups the ability to persuade? Much of the answer is to be found in four attributes, ranging from the general to the specific: legitimacy, sanctions, membership, and resources.

First, the degree of *legitimacy* achieved by a particular group is clearly important. Interests enjoying high prestige are most likely to prevail on particular issues. Professional groups whose members stand for social respectability can be as militant on occasion, and as restrictive in their practices, as blue-collar trade unions once were. But lawyers and doctors escape the public hostility that unions continue to attract. Similarly, the intrinsic importance of business to economic performance means that its representatives can usually obtain a hearing in government.

Second, a group's influence depends on its *membership*. This is a matter of **density** and commitment, as well as sheer numbers. For example, the declining density of trade union membership in the final quarter of the twentieth century, especially in the private sector, undoubtedly weakened labour's bargaining power (Table 9.1). Influence is further reduced when membership is spread among several interest groups operating in the same sector. For instance, American farmers are divided between three major organizations with lower total coverage than Britain's National Farmers' Union. To be sure, the larger American food producers are politically well-connected, but the interests of agriculture as a whole would be better served if all farmers belonged to a single national association.

> **Density** of membership refers to the proportion of all those eligible to join a group who actually do so. An encompassing membership enhances a group's authority and strengthens its bargaining position with government.

The commitment of the membership is also important. For instance, the four million members of America's National Rifle Association (NRA) include many who are prepared to contact their congressional representatives in pursuit of the group's

Table 9.1 Density of trade union membership in selected democracies, 1980–2010 (%)

The proportion of employees belonging to trade unions fell in nearly all liberal democracies between 1980 and 2010, weakening labour's bargaining power with government, as well as employers. Except for Scandinavia, union members are now a minority of the workforce. In a few democracies, they always have been.

	1980	1990	2000	2010
Finland	69	72	75	70
Denmark	79	75	73	69
Sweden	78	81	79	68
Norway	58	59	54	54
Italy	50	39	35	35
Ireland	57	51	37	34
Canada	35	33	28	28
United Kingdom	51	39	30	26
New Zealand	69	51	23	21
Germany	35	31	25	19
Netherlands	35	24	23	19
Australia	50	41	25	18
Japan	31	25	22	18
United States	20	16	13	11

Source: OECD (2011).

goal of 'preserving the right of all law-abiding individuals to purchase, possess and use firearms for legitimate purposes'. Their well-schooled activism led George Stephanopoulos, spokesman for President Clinton, to this assessment: 'let me make one small vote for the NRA. They're good citizens. They call their Congressmen. They write. They vote. They contribute. And they get what they want over time' (NRA, 2012).

Third, the financial *resources* available to an interest group affect influence. Here, money talks but not always loudly. Take the NRA, once more. With an annual budget of $40 million, the NRA can afford to employ 275 full-time staff. Certainly, the coalition of gun control groups cannot match the NRA's fire power. Yet, it would be naive to suppose that the cause of gun control in the USA is held back solely by the NRA's bank balance. The wider political environment also matters – including the extent of gun ownership and an ambiguous constitutional reference to the 'right of the people to keep and bear arms'. It would be simplistic to conclude that any existing public policy favourable to an interest group must be a product of that group's resources.

Fourth, the ability of a group to invoke *sanctions* is clearly important. A labour union can go on strike, a multinational corporation can take its investments elsewhere, a peak association can withdraw its cooperation in forming policy. As a rule, promotional groups (such as environmental movements) have fewer sanctions available to use as a bargaining chip; their influence suffers accordingly.

Interest groups in authoritarian states

The role played by interest groups in non-democratic states provides a sharp contrast to their position in liberal democracies. Authoritarian rulers see freely-organized groups as a potential threat to their own power; hence, they seek either to repress such groups, or to incorporate them within their power structure. In this section, we will examine the workings of these strategies in non-communist authoritarian regimes before turning to communist China.

In the second half of the twentieth century, many authoritarian rulers had to confront the challenge posed by new groups unleashed by economic development, including labour unions, peasant leagues, and educated radicals. How did rulers respond to these new conditions? One strategy was to suppress such groups completely. Where civil liberties were weak and groups were new, this approach was feasible. For example, a strategy of repression was adopted by many military regimes. Military leaders often had their own fingers in the economic pie, sometimes in collaboration with overseas corporations; the rulers' goal was to maintain a workforce that was both compliant and poorly paid. Troublemakers seeking to establish labour unions were quickly removed.

Long-term military rule in Burma demonstrated this syndrome of forced exploitation. The military *junta* outlawed independent trade unions, collective bargaining, and strikes; imprisoned labour activists; and maintained strict control of the media. This repressive environment enabled the regime to use forced labour, particularly from ethnic minorities, to extract goods such as timber, which were exported through the black market for the financial benefit of army officers. Fortunately, governance in Burma softened considerably as military rulers relaxed their hold on power in 2011.

Alternatively, authoritarian rulers could seek to manage the expression of new interests created by development. That is, they could allow interests to organize, but seek to control them – a policy of incorporation rather than exclusion. By enlisting part of the population, particularly its more modern sectors, into officially sponsored associations, rulers hoped to accelerate the push towards modernization. This approach was common in Latin America, where the state licensed, funded, and granted a monopoly of representation to favoured groups, reflecting a Catholic, corporatist tradition inherited from colonial times (Wiarda, 2004).

Before the democratic and economic reforms of the 1980s and 1990s, Mexico offered a particular working of this format. Its governing system was founded on a strong ruling organization: the Institutional Revolutionary Party (PRI). This party was itself a coalition of labour, agrarian, and 'popular' sectors (the latter consisting mainly of public employees). Favoured unions and peasant associations within these sectors gained access to the PRI. Party leaders provided state resources, such as subsidies and control over jobs, in exchange for the political support (not least in ensuring the PRI's re-election) of incorporated groups. The system was a giant patron–client network. For the many people left out of the organized structure, however, life was extremely hard.

But Mexico's system has also declined. It was over-regulated, giving so much power to government and PRI-affiliated sectors as to deter business investment, especially from overseas. As the market sector expanded, so the patronage available to the PRI diminished. In 1997, an independent National Workers Union emerged to claim that the old mechanisms of state control were exhausted, a point which was confirmed by the PRI's defeat in a presidential election three years later (the PRI regained the presidency in 2012 though its victorious candidate claimed there would be no return to the past.)

The position of interest groups in communist states was even more marginal than in other non-democratic regimes. This dependent position also provides a complete contrast to pluralism. For most

BOX 9.4

Examples of social organizations in contemporary China

	Type	Comment
All-China Federation of Trade Unions	Mass organization	A traditional transmission belt for the party
All-China Women's Federation	Mass organization	Traditionally a party-led body, this federation has created some space for autonomous action
China Family Planning Association	Non-governmental organization	Sponsored by the State Family Planning Commission, this association operates at international and local level
Friends of Nature	Non-governmental organization	Operates with some autonomy in the field of environmental education

Source: Adapted from Saich (2011), pp. 216–21.

of the communist era, there were no independent interest groups. Interest articulation by freely-organized groups was inconceivable. Communist rulers sought to harness all organizations into transmission belts for party policy. Trade unions, the media, youth groups, and professional associations were little more than branches of the party, serving the cause of communist construction.

Elements of this tradition can still be found in contemporary China. The ruling Communist Party continues to provide the framework for most formal political activity. 'Mass organizations' – such as the All-China Federation of Trade Unions and the Women's Federation – are led by party officials and continue to transmit policy downwards, rather than popular concerns upwards.

However, a new breed of non-governmental organization did emerge in China in the 1980s, strengthening the link between state and society. Examples include the China Family Planning Association, Friends of Nature, the Private Enterprises Association, and the Federation of Industry and Commerce (Box 9.4). Typically, only one body is officially recognized in each sector, indicating the state's continuing control. The limited status of these new entities is reflected in their title: government-organized non-governmental organizations (GONGOs). So, we have witnessed what Frolic

(1997) calls a 'state-led civil society' in China. But civil society serves as an adjunct, rather than an alternative, to state power.

In competitive authoritarian regimes, as we might expect, the position of interest groups resides somewhere between their comparative autonomy in liberal democracies and their marginal status in authoritarian states. The borders between the public and private sectors are poorly policed in hybrid regimes, allowing the president and his allies to intervene in the economy so as to reward friends and punish enemies. But this involvement is selective, rather than comprehensive, occasionally overriding normal business practices but not seeking to replace them.

At least in the more developed competitive authoritarian states, the result can be a dual system of representation, combining some role for interest groups on routine matters, with more personal relationships, nurtured by patronage, on matters that are of key importance to the president and his ruling group. In the most sensitive economic areas (control over energy resources, for example), employer is set against employer in a competition for political influence, leaving little room for the development of influential business associations. The general point is that, even though competitive authoritarian regimes allow some interests to be expressed, interest groups, as such, are far less significant than in a liberal democracy.

Russia, as always, is an interesting case. Certainly, the separation between public and private sectors, so central to the organization of interests in the West, has not fully emerged. Particularly in the early post-communist years, ruthless business executives, corrupt public officials, and jumped-up gangsters made deals in a virtually unregulated free-for-all. Individual financiers pulled the strings of their puppets in government but the politics were personal, rather than institutional. In such an environment, interests were everywhere but interest groups were nowhere. Comrade Criminal was disinclined to join trade associations.

As Russian politics stabilized and its economy recovered, so some business associations of a Western persuasion emerged, even if they have not yet secured extensive political influence. As early as 2001, Peregudov (p. 268) claimed that 'in Russia a network of business organizations has been created and is up and running'. He suggested that this network was capable of adequately representing business interests to the state. However, this network received limited attention from Vladimir Putin during his tenures as president. At a strategic level, he continued to reward his business friends and, on occasion, to imprison his enemies. Top-level relationships are still between groups of powerful individuals, not institutions.

We must be wary of assuming that Russia will eventually develop a Western system of interest representation. Certainly, pluralism is not currently on the agenda. Evans (2005, p. 112) even suggests that President Putin 'sought to decrease the degree of pluralism in the Russian political system; it has become increasingly apparent that he wants civil society to be an adjunct to a strong state that will be dedicated to his version of the Russian national ideal'. In a manner resembling China's GONGOs, the state sought to collaborate with favoured groups, while condemning others to irrelevance.

The Russian government's strong nationalist tone led to particular criticism of those groups (such as women's associations) which depended on overseas support to survive in an unsympathetic domestic environment. Few promotional groups in Russia possess a significant mass membership; most groups operate solely at grass-roots level, working on local projects such as education or the environment. As in China, these groups operate under state supervision. So Russia's combination of an assertive state and a weak society continues to inhibit interest group development.

Discussion questions

■ Do you see interest groups as a part of, or a threat to, liberal democracy?

■ Which groups in your country are inadequately represented though interest groups and what can and should be done about it?

■ How, if at all, does the role of interest groups in your country differ from that assumed by pluralism?

■ Is business the most powerful interest in your country? And how would you tell?

■ This chapter suggests that, rather than viewing professional lobbying in a negative light, we should recognize its contribution to effective political communication. What case can you mount against this proposition and how convincing is your rebuttal?

■ As chief executive of the University Lecturers' Association in your country, explain how you will set about influencing the government's policy towards higher education. Where precisely will you direct your efforts?

Further reading

J. Beyers, R. Eising and W. Maloney, eds, *Interest Group Politics in Europe: Lessons from EU Studies and Comparative Politics* (2012). A collection analyzing interest group politics in the European Union.

C. Cigler and B. Loomis, eds, *Interest Group Politics*, 8th edn (2012). Provides a wide range of material on interest groups in the United States.

J. Greenwood, *Interest Representation in the European Union*, 3rd edn (2011). This book provides a detailed assessment of the important role played by organized interests in the European Union.

L. Maisel and J. Berry, eds, *The Oxford Handbook of American Political Parties and Interest Groups* (2010). This extensive handbook includes several reviews of research on interest groups in the United States.

G. Wilson, *Business and Politics: A Comparative Introduction*, 3rd edn (2003). Offers a clear comparative assessment of an important, but still understudied, topic.

ONLINE RESOURCES AVAILABLE

Visit the companion website at **www.palgrave.com/politics/hague** to access additional learning resources, including multiple-choice questions, chapter summaries, web links and practice essay questions.

Chapter 10 Political parties

'In this book I investigate the workings of democratic government. But it is not institutions which are the object of my research: it is not on political forms, it is on political forces I dwell.' So did the nineteenth century Russian-born political thinker Moisei Ostrogorski begin his pioneering comparison of party organization in Britain and the United States. Ostrogorski was one of the first to recognize that **political parties** were becoming vital in the new era of democratic politics: 'wherever this life of parties is developed, it focuses the political feelings and the active wills of its citizens' (1902, p. 7).

Ostrogorski's supposition that parties were growing in importance proved to be fully justified. In Western Europe, mass parties battled for the votes of enlarged electorates. In communist and fascist states, ruling parties monopolized power in an attempt to reconstruct society. In the developing world, nationalist parties became the vehicle for driving colonial rulers back to their imperial homeland.

> Sartori (1976, p. 63) defines a **political party** as 'any political group identified by an official label that presents at elections, and is capable of placing through elections candidates for public office'. Unlike interest groups, serious parties aim to obtain the keys to government; in Weber's phrase, they live 'in a house of power'.

So, parties proved to be a key mobilizing device of the twentieth century, drawing millions of people into the national political process for the first time. Parties jettisoned their original image as private factions engaged in capturing, and even perverting, the public interest. Instead, they became accepted as the central representative device of liberal democracy.

Reflecting this new status, in the second half of the twentieth century, parties began to receive explicit mention in new constitutions. Some countries went so far as to ban non-party candidates from standing for the legislature, or even prevented members from switching parties once elected (Reilly, 2007). Such restrictions were judged necessary for implementing party-based elections. By the century's end, most liberal democracies offered some public funding to support party work. Parties had become part of the system.

Therein rests the problem. No longer do parties seem to be energetic agents of society, seeking to bend the state towards their supporters' interests. Rather, they appear to be at risk of capture by the state itself. No longer do parties provide a home for the politically engaged; instead, social movements, promotional groups and political discussion possess greater appeal for younger generations. Western publics still endorse the principle of democracy, but they seem to be increasingly disillusioned with the means of

STUDYING . . .

POLITICAL PARTIES

- The dilemma of parties is that they appear to be poorly rated by the public yet they remain an essential device of liberal democracy. How this quandary might be resolved is an urgent question.

- Charting the decline in party membership, and its implications for how parties operate, has occupied some research effort. But no trend continues forever and updating is always helpful.

- The historically strong parties of Western Europe mean that the region has served as a research laboratory for this topic. Both parties and party systems are often weaker elsewhere. That said, American parties are exceptional in gaining organizational strength and ideological coherence at a time when parties are in some ways losing ground elsewhere.

- The transition of major parties from agents of society (e.g. representing a particular class) to agents of the state (e.g. receiving public funding) has attracted attention. In studying the ties now binding party and state, we should ask Lenin's question: 'Who, whom?'

- The extent and basis of public funding for parties is a comparative topic with potential for lesson-drawing.

- The widening selection process for party candidates and leaders is a confirmed trend – though its causes, and the effects on candidate quality, are less clear. Whether we can see this trend as a transition towards democracy within the party is also debatable.

- Carty (2004) draws a comparison between contemporary parties and franchise organizations such as McDonald's. His analysis could usefully be tested against a wider range of parties and franchises.

- Understanding the role of parties involves looking at party systems, not simply individual parties. The major theme here is the decline of dominant party and two-party systems, and the rise of multiparty systems.

achieving it: competing parties. With many parties now seen as self-serving and corrupt, Mair (2008, p. 230) could speculate, contra Ostrogorski, that parties are in danger of ceasing to be a political driving force.

But we should not write parties off just yet. In the United States, exceptionally, the major parties have gained organizational strength and ideological coherence. And throughout the democratic world, major parties continue to perform essential functions:

- Ruling parties offer direction to government, pursuing the vital task of steering the ship of state.

- By allowing voters to choose between parties with different teams of leaders and sometimes with contrasting policies, a system of competing parties gives effect to liberal democracy.

- Parties function as agents of political recruitment, preparing and recruiting candidates for the legislature and the executive.

- Parties aggregate (combine) interests, filtering a multitude of specific demands into manageable packages of proposals. Parties select policies and prioritize them in an overall programme.

Party origins

In examining party origins, it is helpful to distinguish between cadre parties – with their origins in parliament – and mass parties created to achieve parliamentary representation for a particular social group; notably, the working class.

Cadre (or elite) parties are formed by members within an assembly – the cadres – joining together to reflect common concerns and then fighting effective campaigns in an enlarged electorate. The earliest nineteenth-century parties were of this type; for example, the conservative parties of Britain, Canada, and Scandinavia. The first American parties – the Federalists and the Jeffersonians – were also loose elite factions, based in Congress and state legislatures. Cadre parties are sometimes known as 'caucus' parties, the caucus denoting a closed meeting of the party's members of parliament. Such parties remain heavily committed to their leader's authority, with ordinary members playing a supporting, but not sovereign, role.

By contrast, mass parties are a later innovation. They originate outside the assembly, in social groups seeking representation in the legislature as a way of achieving policy objectives. The working-class socialist parties that spread across Western Europe around the turn of the twentieth century, such as the German Social Democratic Party (SPD), epitomized these externally-created parties. These mass socialist parties exerted tremendous influence on European party systems in the twentieth century, stimulating many cadre parties to copy their extra-parliamentary organization. Mass parties acquired an enormous membership organized in local branches. Unlike cadre parties, they aimed to keep their representatives in parliament on a tight rein. In their discourse, at least, mass parties continue to revere their members.

As cadre and mass parties matured, so they tended to evolve into catch-all parties (Kirchheimer, 1966). The catch-all party responds to a mobilized political system in which electoral communication takes place through television, bypassing the membership. Such parties seek to govern in the national interest, rather than as representatives of a social group: 'a party large enough to get a majority has to be so catch-all that it cannot have a unique ideological program' (Kirchheimer, quoted in Krouwel, 2003, p. 29). Catch-all parties seek electoral support wherever they can find it; their purpose is to govern, rather than to represent.

The broadening of Christian Democratic parties (such as the CDU in Germany) from religious defence organizations to broader parties of the centre-right is the classic case of the transition to catch-all status. The subsequent transformation of several mass socialist parties into leader-dominated social democratic parties, as in Spain and the United Kingdom, is another example.

While most major parties are now of the catch-all type, their origins inside or beyond parliament continue to influence party style, the autonomy of their leaders, and the standing of ordinary members.

Party organization

Large political parties are multilevel organizations, with their various strata united by a common identity and, sometimes, shared objectives. As Duverger (1954, p. 17) noted, long ago, 'a party is not a community but a collection of communities, a union of small groups dispersed throughout the country and linked by co-ordinating institutions'. A major party's organization will include staff or volunteers operating at national, regional, and local levels (in countries belonging to the European Union, at the European level, too). Where assemblies exist at a given tier, the party will be represented in them. And the party will aim to populate national, regional, and local governments. This complexity means that any large party is decentralized. While references to 'the party' as a single entity are unavoidable, they clearly simplify a highly fragmented reality. As Bolleyer said (2012, p. 316), without fear of contradiction, 'parties are not monolithic structures'.

Party 'organization' is sometimes too grand a term. Below the centre, and especially in areas where the party is electorally weak, the party's organization may be little more than an empty shell. And coordination between levels is often weak. Some authors even draw a comparison between parties and franchise organizations such as McDonald's (Carty, 2004). In a franchise structure, the centre manages the brand, runs marketing campaigns, and supports the operating units. Within that framework, local units act with considerable autonomy.

Similarly, it is said, the party at the centre loans the brand to its local branches. Party leaders set policy priorities, develop their organization's image, and provide material for election campaigns. But, as with McDonald's franchises, local agents are left to get on with key tasks: selecting candidates, for example, or implementing election strategy at local level. This comparison with commercial franchises is intriguing, even if it does place local parties rather closer to centre stage than is really the case.

It is natural to ask where authority within parties really resides. Who truly commands the party? The answer is far from clear, reflecting the blunt nature of the question. American parties, in particular, are sometimes seen as empty vessels waiting to be filled by fresh ideas and ambitious office-seekers. The American party is not controlled from any single point; no one pulls the levers, no one rules the party.

Yet, much European research on parties does suggest that authority within the party flows from the top down, with the leaders who represent the party to the public playing a key role. In 1911, the German scholar Robert Michels (1875–1936) published *Political Parties*, certainly the most influential work on leadership within parties. Michels argued that even organizations with democratic pretensions become dominated by a ruling clique of leaders and supporting officials. Using Germany's SPD as a critical case, Michels suggested that leaders develop organizational skills, expert knowledge, and an interest in their own continuation in power. The ordinary members, aware of their inferior knowledge and amateur status, accept their own subordination as natural, even in an externally created party such as the SPD. Michels's pessimism about the possibility of democracy within organizations such as political parties was expressed in his famous **iron law of oligarchy**.

> Michels's **iron law of oligarchy** states that 'to say organization is to say a tendency to oligarchy' (often reproduced as, 'who says organization, says oligarchy'). Michels argued that even parties formally committed to democracy become dominated by a ruling elite ('oligarchy' is rule by and for the few).

Party members

Between the 1960s and the 1990s, party membership declined dramatically (Table 10.1). In Denmark, for instance, membership collapsed from one in every 5 people to one in every 20. The general drop seems to have continued into the 2000s, with membership of

Table 10.1 Party membership, 1960s–1990s

In most countries, the proportion of the electorate belonging to a political party more than halved in the latter part of the twentieth century

	Total party membership as a percentage of the electorate		
	Beginning of 1960s	Beginning of 1980s	End of 1990s
Austria	26	22	18
Finland	19	13	10
Belgium	8	9	7
Norway	16	14	7
Denmark	21	8	5
Italy	13	10	4
Germany	3	4	3
Netherlands	9	3	3
New Zealand	23	9	3
UK	9	3	2

Note: Party membership in New Zealand is expressed as a proportion of votes cast, not the whole electorate.

Sources: Adapted from Mair (1994), table 1.1; Mair and van Biezen (2001), table 1; Sundberg (2002), table 7.10; Miller (2005), table 1.1.

Sweden's Social Democrats falling from 177,000 in 1999 to just 125,000 in 2005 (Möller, 2007, p. 36). Voerman and van Schurr's verdict (2011, p. 93) on the Netherlands resonates widely: 'We must regard the era of the mass party as over'. Across the democratic world, millions of party foot soldiers have simply given up.

Furthermore, many new members do not engage with their party beyond paying an annual subscription; these credit card supporters tend to be fairweather supporters, resulting in increased turnover. Their commitment to the party is often no greater than to other voluntary groups to which they donate. Seyd and Whiteley's assessment (2002, p. 169) of trends in Britain's Labour Party is applicable elsewhere:

Whatever activity one focuses on, participation has been declining over the past 10 years. The extent of the commitment of the average member is increasingly merely one of paying a yearly subscription and occasionally donating money to the party when asked to do so.

Lacking a steady flow of young members, the average age of members has gone up. Nearly everywhere, those who belong to a party are older than those who vote for it. By the late 1990s, the average age of members of Canada's main parties was 59. Fewer than 1 in 20 members of Germany's Christian Democratic Union (CDU) are aged under 30. Belonging to a party, like attending church, is increasingly a hobby for the middle-aged and elderly (Scarrow and Gezgor, 2011).

However, we should locate this recent decline in a longer perspective. If statistics were available for the entire twentieth century, they would probably show a rise in membership over much of the century, followed by a fall in the final third. The recent decline is from a peak only reached, in many countries, in the 1970s. In other words, it is arguably the bulge in membership after World War II, rather than the later decline, which requires explanation.

The recent reduction in membership has occurred in tandem with dealignment among electors and surely reflects similar causes. These include:

- the weakening of traditional social divisions such as class and religion;

- the loosening of the bond linking trade unions and socialist parties;

- the decay of local electioneering in an era of media-based campaigns;

- the greater appeal of social movements and more informal modes of political engagement to younger generations;

- the declining standing of parties, often linked to cases of corruption;

- the perception of parties as forming a single structure of established authority with the state (Whiteley, 2011).

How should we appraise this fall in membership? As we suggested in discussing political participation generally (Chapter 8), we should not automatically assume that less is worse. Specifically, the fall may indicate an evolution in the nature of parties, rather than a weakening of their significance in government. Crotty (2006, p. 499), for one, notes how 'the demands of society change, and parties change to meet them'. Too often, perhaps, models of what parties ought to be like are drawn from the narrow experience of Western Europe in the decades following the war. It is unrealistic to expect the rebirth of mass membership parties with their millions of members and their supporting pillars of trade unions and churches. Social and political change has destroyed this format.

In its stead comes the modern format of parties found in new democracies: lean and flexible, with communication from leaders through television and the Internet. Rather than relying on a permanent army of members, such parties mobilize volunteers for specific, short-term tasks – notably, election campaigns. This approach is long familiar in the United States, where parties lack a membership base but, instead, are invigorated anew at each election by volunteers and donors. The multitude of supporters mobilized through the Internet by Barack Obama in his 2008 and 2012 campaigns is a sophisticated application of this flexible model (Kreiss, 2012).

Selecting candidates and leaders

Elite recruitment is a vital and continuing function of parties. Even as parties decline in other ways, they continue to dominate elections to the national legislature from which, in parliamentary systems, most of the nation's leaders are drawn. Given that candidates nominated for safe districts, or appearing near the top of their party's list, are virtually guaranteed a place in parliament, it is the **selectorate**, not the electorate, which makes 'the choice before the choice'. The nominators open and close the door to the house of power (Rahat, 2007).

> The **selectorate** consists of those who nominate a party's candidates for an election. This group often plays a more critical role than the electorate in determining who will represent the party in office.

How, then, do parties select their candidates and leaders? In answering this question, we will observe an increasing role for ordinary members, a finding suggesting that Michels's iron law is corroding as parties seek to retain members by giving them a greater if still limited voice in party affairs (Cross and Katz, 2013).

Candidates

A range of options is available for selecting parliamentary candidates, from exclusive (selection by the leader) to inclusive (an open vote of the entire electorate) (Figure 10.1). Reflecting the complexity of party organization, the nomination process is generally decentralized. In Western Europe, certainly, a few parties do give control to the national leadership, though even here the leaders usually select from a list generated at lower levels. More often, local parties are the active force, either acting autonomously or putting forward nominations to be ratified at national level. Small and extreme parties, and those in Scandinavia, are the most decentralized in their selection procedures (Lundell, 2004).

The nomination task is constrained by three wider features of the political system:

● The electoral system: choosing candidates for individual constituencies in a plurality system is naturally a more decentralized task than preparing a single national list in a party list system (see Chapter 11).

● Incumbents: current members of parliament possess an advantage almost everywhere, usually achieving reselection without much ado. Often, candidates are only truly 'chosen' when the incumbent stands down.

● Rules: nearly all countries impose conditions such as citizenship on members of the legislature while many parties have adopted gender quotas for party candidates (see Chapter 8).

Consider how the electoral system affects the nomination process. Under the list form of proportional representation, parties must develop a ranked list of candidates to present to the electorate. This requirement forces central coordination, even if candidates are suggested locally. In the Netherlands, for example, each party needs to present a single list of candidates for the whole country. The major parties use a nominating committee to examine applications received either from local branches, or directly from individuals. A senior party board then produces the final ordering.

In the few countries using the plurality method, the nomination procedure is typically more decentralized. Candidates must win selection by a local party in a specific district, though often they must pre-qualify by gaining inclusion on a central master list of approved candidates. Local bodies are invariably keen to guard their autonomy against further encroachment from headquarters. In Canada, for instance, constituency parties show little concern for national needs; they seek candidates with an attractive local profile (Carty, 2002).

The USA has gone furthest in opening up the selection process. There, **primary elections** enable a party's supporters to choose their candidates for a particular office. In the absence of a tradition of direct party membership, a 'supporter' is generously defined in most states as anyone who declares, in advance, an affiliation to that party.

Figure 10.1 Who selects candidates for legislative elections?

Methods for selecting parliamentary candidates vary widely, from narrow reliance on the party leader to an open vote of the entire electorate

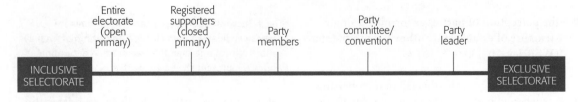

Source: Adapted from Hazan and Rahat (2010), fig. 3.1.

The remarkable procedure of an **open primary** extends the choice still further: to any registered elector.

> A primary election is a contest in which a party's supporters select its candidate for a subsequent general election (a direct primary), or choose delegates to the presidential nominating convention (a presidential primary). A **closed primary** is limited to a party's registered supporters but any registered elector can participate in an **open primary**, though only for one party. Primaries are firmly established in the United States.

An increasing number of countries operate a mixed electoral system, in which electors vote for both a party list and a district candidate. These circumstances complicate the party's task of selecting candidates, requiring a national or regional list, plus local constituency nominees. In this situation, individual politicians also face a choice: should they seek election by means of the party list, or through a constituency? Many senior figures ensure they appear on both ballots, using a high position on the party's list as insurance against restlessness in their home district.

Leaders

The method of selecting the party leader merits (but too rarely receives) special attention. In most cases, the person selected becomes the party's nominee for prime minister or president, fronting its election campaign.

Note, however, that in some countries and parties, including many in continental Europe, the party chairperson may not be the same individual as the party's nominee for the top post in government (Cross and Blais, 2012a, p. 5). In Germany, for instance, the party's candidate for chancellor is appointed separately from the party leader and need not be the same person. Belgium goes further: party statutes normally preclude the party president from becoming a government minister; even so, the party president typically remains the key figure. In the USA, too, the presidential candidate and chair of the party's national committee are separate; indeed, the former usually chooses the latter. But it is usually clear which is the top post and this position is the one on which our discussion of leadership selection centres.

In the same way that many parties afford their ordinary members a greater voice in candidate selection, so too has the procedure for selecting the party leader become more inclusive. As Mair (1994) notes, 'more and more parties now seem willing to allow the ordinary members a voice in the selection of party leaders'.

One factor here is the desire to compensate members for their declining role in what have become media-driven election campaigns; after all, party volunteers, unlike paid employees, can just walk away if they are given nothing interesting to do. The catalyst for reform is often an electoral setback or a desire to be seen as inclusive (Cross and Blais, 2012b).

At the century's start, the most common way to choose the leader was still by a special *party congress* or convention (Box 10.1). American parties have long selected their presidential candidates through such conventions but these meetings are no longer the effective site of decision. The real choice is made by voters in the primaries, with elected delegates tied to particular candidates. Since the 1970s, the convention itself has become a media event for the party to sell its anointed nominee.

A ballot of *party members* is an alternative and increasingly popular method of selecting leaders. Such elections, often described as OMOV (one member, one vote) contests, provide an incentive for people to join the party, and can also be used to limit the power of entrenched factions within it. In Belgium, for example, all the major parties have adopted this approach to choosing their party president. In Canada, too, all major parties (except the Liberals) have adopted OMOV.

Election by the *parliamentary party* is the traditional method, especially for cadre parties with their assembly origins. The device is still used in several parliamentary systems, including Australia, Denmark, and New Zealand. Interestingly, several parties give a voice to both members of parliament and ordinary members – either through a special congress, or a two-stage ballot. For instance, the British Conservatives offer ordinary members a choice between two candidates chosen by the parliamentary party. Cross and Blais (2012a, p. 174) favour this dual approach: 'we believe that the ideal leadership selectorate is one that includes both a party's parliamentary wing and its rank-and-file members'.

BOX 10.1

Selection of party leaders in liberal democracies

	Countries in which most major parties use this method	Total number of parties using this method
Party congress or convention	Finland, Norway, Sweden	37
Rank-and-file members	Belgium	19
Members of the parliamentary party	The Netherlands, New Zealand	17
Party committee	Italy	8

Note: Analysis based on 16 democracies.

Source: Adapted from Hazan (2002), p.124.

A vote of the party's members of parliament alone is, of course, a narrow constituency. And the ability of potential leaders to instil confidence in their parliamentary peers may say little about their capacity to win a general election fought on television. Even so, colleagues in the assembly will have a close knowledge of a candidate's abilities; they provide an expert constituency for judging the capacity to lead not only the party, but also – more importantly – the country. Members of parliament appear to be more influenced by experience than are ordinary party members. It is perhaps for this reason that many parties still permit the parliamentary party to remove the leader, even if the initial selection now extends to other groups (Cross and Blais, 2012a).

Party finance

Falling membership implies a smaller subscription income for parties in an era when party expenses (not least for election campaigns) continue to rise. The problem of funding political parties has therefore become highly significant (Box 10.2). Should members, donors, or the state pay for the party's work? Should private donations be encouraged (to increase funds and encourage participation), or restricted (to maintain fairness and reduce scandals)? Do limits on contributions and spending

interfere with free speech? Whichever is the case, some method of funding parties must be found while also minimizing the danger of corruption.

In the main, the battle for public funding has been won. State support for national parties is now virtually universal in liberal democracies (Figure 10.2). On a global level, 68 per cent of 180 countries made provision for public funding of parties by 2011; a similar proportion offer free or subsidized access to the media (IDEA, 2012). As Fisher and Eisenstadt (2004, p. 621) comment, 'public subsidies have replaced private sponsorship as the norm in political finance'. State subsidies have also developed quickly in the new democracies of Eastern Europe, where party memberships are far smaller than in the West.

What forms does public funding take? Typically, support is provided for parliamentary groups, election campaigns, or both. Campaign support, in turn, may be offered to parties, candidates, or both. In an effort to limit state dependence, public funding may be restricted to matching the funds raised by the party from other means, including its members. In any case, most funding regimes only reimburse a specified amount of party spending.

Altering the sources of any organization's funds is always consequential; state funding of parties is no exception. Three points are crucial here. First, public financing reduces a party's incentive to attract members. When party leaders know that their

Figure 10.2 Introduction of public subsidies for parties' extra-parliamentary work, Western Europe, 1959–90

West Germany was the first Western European country to introduce public subsidies for political parties, but the practice had become widespread by the 1990s

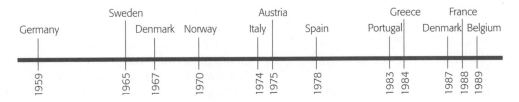

Source: Adapted from Scarrow (2006), table 1.

funding comes from the state and that they can appeal to the electorate directly through the mass media, they place less value on a subscribing membership army. Thus, the evolution of party funding contributes to a move away from mass parties and to a partial recovery of the old cadre format.

Second, public funding tends to reinforce the status quo. Subsidies are usually restricted to parties gaining seats in the assembly; often, the more votes won in the previous election(s), the greater the payout. Thus, large established parties have an advantage over new ones. Some authors have developed this point by suggesting that the transition to public funding has led to a convergence of the state and major parties on a single system of rule. Governing parties, in effect, authorize subsidies for themselves, a process captured by Katz and Mair's idea (1995) of **cartel parties**: 'colluding parties become agents of the state and employ its resources to ensure their own survival'. The danger of cartel

---

BOX 10.2

Public funding of political parties: for and against

FOR	AGAINST
Parties perform a public function, supplying policies and leaders to the state.	Public funding is creeping nationalization, creating parties that serve the state, not society. Also, it requires a new regulatory body.
Parties should be funded to a professional level and not appear cheap. Marketing should match private-sector standards.	Public funding favours established and large parties, encouraging a cartel.
Public funding creates a level playing field between parties.	To maintain a level playing field, spending should be capped, rather than subsidized.
Without public support, pro-business parties gain access to greater funding.	Why should taxpayers fund parties against their wishes? A tax credit for voluntary donations is a preferable compromise.
Relying on private donations encourages corruption.	Corruption can be reduced by banning anonymous donations, rather than adopting public funding.

parties is that they become part of the political establishment, weakening their historic role as agents of particular social groups and inhibiting the growth of new parties in the political market.

> **Cartel parties** are leading parties that exploit their dominance of the political market to establish rules of the game, such as public funding, which reinforce their own strong position.

Third, public funding gives governments a device for influencing parties: those who pay the piper call the tune. The state may wish to use this lever in future in any number of ways: perhaps to promote democracy within parties, perhaps to encourage particular types of candidate, perhaps to discourage platforms judged unacceptable. To a degree, public funding is bound to turn parties into public utilities.

Issues of party finance extend beyond the provision of subsidies. What of donations: who can give how much and with what reporting requirements? This topic has become newsworthy as a result of scandals in which cash-hungry parties have raised funds from private sources perceived by the public as seeking a payback.

On a worldwide basis (including, here, authoritarian regimes in which parties are permited), nearly all countries now regulate donations in some way. The vast majority ban political donations by government and its agencies to parties and candidates (other than through regulated public funding); most also disallow donations from overseas parties and candidates. However, only a minority of countries currently place limits on the size of donations to parties or candidates; just one fifth ban corporate donations altogether. As IDEA (2012, p. 51) points out, even these limits can be ineffective – either because financial reports are inadequately monitored, or because restrictions on donations to parties are circumvented by aiding candidates directly, or because the limits are ignored.

The issues involved in controlling political finance – both donations and spending – emerge from considering the main outlier: the United States. American campaigns are uniquely expensive. For example, in 2008 the Democratic and Republican parties raised a total of over \$2 billion; presidential candidates raised a total of \$1.1 billion in additional support for their own campaigns (O'Connor *et al.*,

2011, p. 346). The total cost of the 2012 presidential election cycle, including spending by presidential and congressional candidates, political parties, and interest groups, was projected at \$5.8 billion (Center for Responsive Politics, 2012). Such massive figures are beyond compare.

Detailed regulation of campaign *contributions* has proved ineffective in the USA, and with no cap on campaign *spending* (except for presidential candidates unwise enough to accept public funding), campaign costs continue to escalate. Campaign advertising by groups which are independent of candidates is also unrestricted.

The extraordinary sums involved in American elections reflect the near absolute priority accorded to free speech in the United States, for corporations as well as individuals. The Supreme Court remains keen to enforce the first amendment: 'Congress shall make no law … abridging the freedom of speech'. For the Court, the thought of a government regulator banning excessive campaign advertising by particular groups (and perhaps seeking to prosecute them for expressing their views if they do exceed their limits) is a no-go area, violating an explicit constitutional principle which is fundamental to free elections. The Court may well be right on the constitution – but, if so, the constitution may well be wrong when applied literally to contemporary campaigns.

Social cleavages

Every political party draws its electoral support from a particular demographic; none appeals to a perfect cross-section. But, in countries with a presidential system, including the USA, parties must assemble a broad coalition of demographic categories to secure a majority. Thus, we can speak of Obama's diverse winning coalition in 2008, composed of blacks, city-dwellers, Hispanics, infrequent churchgoers, Jews, low-income earners, single people and women (Brewer, 2010).

By contrast, in the parliamentary systems of Western Europe (mostly based on proportional representation), parties historically concentrated on maximizing their support from a narrow social base, typically defined by class or religion. Traditionally, parties were linked not only to a social category, but also to one side of a social **cleavage**. Although there divisions have weakened, their analysis has preoccupied European political scientists. We consider their conclusions, and the base of newer political parties, in this section.

> A **cleavage** is a social division creating a collective identity among those on each side of the divide. These interests are expressed in such organizations as trade unions, churches and parties (Mair, 2006).

In a renowned analysis, Lipset and Rokkan (1967) showed how critical moments on the journey to the modern, West European state created cleavages which provided a long-term foundation for political parties. In historical order, the divisions of centre versus periphery, Church versus state, agriculture versus industry, and employer versus industrial worker led to the emergence of parties defending the interests of groups on a particular side of each cleavage. Not all the parties envisaged by this scheme emerged or survived in every West European country; cleavage structures varied from country to country.

However, the authors did claim that, in the 1960s, West European parties still remained largely unchanged, reflecting the cleavages created by their country's national development. Even though the underlying cleavages had already begun to fade, the parties based on them remained secure. This, then, was Lipset and Rokkan's much-quoted thesis of frozen party systems.

However, considerable thawing has undoubtedly now taken place. For instance:

● many Catholic parties repositioned themselves as catch-all parties of the centre-right;

● most agrarian parties became broader centre parties;

● working-class socialist parties adopted a milder social democratic programme.

The more open conditions resulting from cleavage dilution permitted the emergence and strengthening in many West European countries of new **niche parties**, such as far right and green parties, appealing to narrow – and, to some extent, newly-defined –

segments of the electoral market. By the mid-2000s, these 'outsider' parties had participated in coalitions in several countries (Box 10.3). Prominent examples were the German Greens and extreme right parties such as Austria's Freedom Party, and Switzerland's People's Party (Ignazi, 2006). Whatever the limits to their own support, both green and far right parties succeeded in influencing the agenda of mainstream parties.

> **Niche parties** appeal to a narrow section of the electorate. They are positioned away from the established centre and highlight one particular issue. Unlike mainstream parties, they rarely prosper by moderating their position but, instead, achieve most – but still inherently limited – success from exploiting their natural support group (Meguid, 2008). Far right, green, and regional parties are examples.

Parties of the extreme right, in particular, are an exception to the thesis that parties emerge to represent well-defined social interests. So, where exactly do far right parties gain their votes? Evidence from many West European countries suggests they draw

---

BOX 10.3

Participation by far right and green parties in the governments of some West European democracies at some point between 1994 and 2008

	Green parties	Far right parties
Austria		✔
Belgium	✔	
Finland	✔	
France	✔	
Germany	✔	
Ireland	✔	
Italy	✔	✔
Netherlands		✔
Portugal		✔

Note: ✔ indicates participation in government. Support parties (see Chapter 15) excluded.

Source: Adapted from Bale and Dunphy (2011), table 1.

heavily on the often transient support of uneducated and unemployed young men. Disillusioned with orthodox democracy and by the move of established conservative parties to the centre, this constituency is attracted to parties that blame immigrants, asylum seekers, and other minorities not only for crime in general, but also for its own insecurity (cultural, as well as economic) in a changing world (Kitschelt, 2007). Far right voters take solace in a strong and exclusive nationalism, forming a cultural counter to the educated, cosmopolitan postmaterialists we encountered in Chapter 6 (Lucassen and Lubbers, 2011). Far right supporters, it is said, are the ugly sisters of the greens.

It is tempting to identify a new, post-Lipset and Rokkan cleavage here: between the winners and losers from contemporary labour markets. In the winner's enclosure stand well-educated, affluent professionals, proudly displaying their tolerant postmaterial liberalism. But in the shadows we find another group. Labour market losers are without qualifications, without jobs, and without prospects in economies where full-time unskilled jobs have been exported to lower-cost producers.

This economically insecure group constitute globalization's darker side. Where some professionals benefit from globalization, finding opportunities to ply their trade in foreign lands, the poorly-educated white underclass finds itself locked into a peripheral position in increasingly demanding national labour markets. In this context, the perceived economic success of immigrants, especially those of a different colour, is easily seen as globalization's dagger.

Such analysis is plausible, but we should note that the division between labour market winners and losers is not a social cleavage in the classic sense. The traditional industrial working class was supported by an organizational infrastructure of trade unions and socialist parties. But far right parties are supported by alienated individuals, rather than by social and political institutions. So, in considering the far right it may be preferable to speak not of a new cleavage but, rather, of post-cleavage analysis – of what Betz (1994, p. 169) called 'political conflict in the age of social fragmentation'.

We should not be carried away. Many right-wing movements have proved to be short-lived flash parties whose prospects are held back by inexperienced leaders with a dubious background who have proved to be inept participants in coalition governments (Akkerman, 2012). As niche organizations, many protest voters might cease to vote for them if they became leading parties, thus creating a natural ceiling to their support. Even joining a coalition dilutes the party's outsider image. So, in this sense, far right parties may lack the potential of those based on a more secure and traditional cleavage (McDonnell and Newell, 2011).

Although party systems have thawed, the plain fact is that in the political market (as in many others) the major players have retained their leading position. The emergence of new niche parties has not led to the collapse of the established players. In New Zealand, for instance, 'despite the array of parties represented in parliament, the two major parties have continued to attract the lion's share of the vote' (Miller, 2005, p. 5). Sundberg (2002, p. 210) offers a similar appraisal of the situation in Northern Europe:

Parties in Scandinavia remain the primary actors in the political arena. To be old does not automatically imply that the party as a form of political organization is obsolete. The oldest car makers in the world are more or less the same age as the oldest parties in Scandinavia, yet nobody has questioned the capacity of these companies to renew their models. The same is true for political parties. They have developed their organizations and adapted their policies to a changing environment.

Party systems

To understand the significance of parties, we must move beyond an examination of them individually. Just as the international system is more than the states that comprise it, so too is a **party system** more than its individual elements. A party system refers to the overall pattern formed by the component parties, the interactions between them, and the rules governing their conduct. Parties copy, learn from, and compete with each other, with innovations in organization, fundraising, and campaigning diffusing across the system. By focusing on the relationships between parties, a party system denotes more than just the parties themselves. The United States, for instance, has a strong party system even

BOX 10.4

Party systems in liberal democracies

	Definition	Example
Dominant party system	One party is constantly in office, governing alone or in coalition	South Africa (African National Congress)
Two-party system	Two major parties compete to form single-party governments	Great Britain, at least until 2010 (Conservative and Labour)
Multiparty system	The assembly is composed of several minority parties, leading to government by coalition or a minority party	Scandinavia

though the parties themselves were historically weak by West European standards.

As with parties, structures of party competition persist over time, forming part of the operating procedures of democratic politics. We can distinguish three overlapping formats: dominant, two-party, and multiparty (Box 10.4). Note that both dominant and two-party systems are in decline; multiparty systems have become the most common configuration in the democratic world.

Dominant party systems

In a dominant party system, one party outdistances all the others and becomes the natural party of government, albeit sometimes governing in coalition with junior partners. In practice, such dominant parties use their control of the state to reward their supporters, thus building a more secure base, but also rendering themselves vulnerable in the long term to corruption and decline. For this reason, sustaining a dominant position over the longer term is a considerable challenge.

A **party system** denotes the overall configuration of parties, as shown in the number of parties, their relative importance, and the interaction between them. Legal regulation, applying across the board, is also an attribute of a party system.

One of the few contemporary examples of a dominant party is South Africa's African National Congress (ANC). This party has multiple strengths,

benefiting not only from cultural memories of its opposition to apartheid and from its strong position among the black majority, but also from its use of office to reward its own supporters. In the 2009 elections to the National Assembly, the party secured 66 per cent of votes and seats, a remarkable achievement. However, factions and corruption are emerging; eventually, they may threaten the ANC's supremacy.

Dominant parties do fall victim to their own success. Figure 10.3 shows the decline in electoral support for India's Congress Party, Japan's Liberal Democrats (ejected from office in 2009 only to return in 2012) and Sweden's Social Democrats (out of office since 2006). To avoid the mistake of discussing only survivors, we should also note that other dominant parties, notably Italy's Christian Democrats, have disappeared entirely. The very strength of a dominant party means that factions tend to develop within it, leading to an inward-looking perspective, a lack of concern with policy, excessive careerism, and increasing corruption.

India provides us with a diminished 'dominant' party. From independence in 1947, the country's politics was led by the Congress Party, an organization which under Mahatma Gandhi had provided the focus of resistance to British colonial rule. To maintain its leading position, the party relied on a patronage pyramid of class and caste alliances to sustain a national organization in a fragmented and religiously divided country. For two decades, Congress dominated national elections, drawing support from

COUNTRY PROFILE

ITALY

LIBERAL DEMOCRACY

Form of government ■ a parliamentary republic, with an indirectly-elected president who can play a role in government formation.

Legislature ■ the Chamber of Deputies (630 members) and the Senate (321) are elected simultaneously by popular vote for a maximum of five years. A bill must receive the positive assent of both houses and (as in Australia) the Cabinet is equally responsible to both chambers.

Executive ■ the prime minister formally appoints, but cannot dismiss, the members of the Council of Ministers.

Judiciary ■ based on the civil law tradition, Italy has both ordinary and administrative judicial systems. A 15-member Constitutional Court possesses the power of judicial review.

Electoral system ■ (Chamber of Deputies) party list 'proportional' representation with the winning coalition guaranteed at least 340 seats.

Party system ■ the leading parties are the centre-right People of Liberty and the centre-left Democratic Party.

Population (annual growth rate): 61.3 m (+0.38%)	
World Bank income group: high income	
Human development index (rank/out of): 24/187	
Political rights score:	
Civil liberties score: ❶	
Media status: partly free	

Note: For interpretation and sources, see p. xvi.

ITALY was late to join the club of states, forming only in 1861. Statehood was established in the absence of a common national identity – a case of unification without unity. For example, the powerful Catholic Church organized itself outside – and, to an extent, against – the new state. And acute regional contrasts, particularly between the more modern north and the underdeveloped south, remain important.

Since unification, Italy has experienced three systems of rule:

■ a constitutional monarchy, which continued until 1922;

■ the fascist regime of Benito Mussolini, overthrown by an Allied invasion in 1943;

■ a parliamentary and republican democracy established in 1946.

The post-war constitution established a liberal democracy with a strong emphasis on checks and balances. The safeguards included two legislative chambers of equal status; a constitutional court; an independent judiciary; proportional representation; and provision for referendums and regional government. As a concession to the left, the constitution also emphasized social and economic rights, and placed the state under an obligation to address inequality.

The most obvious feature of the new republic was its instability, with 63 governments by 2011 – an average of one per year. Coalitions emerged and collapsed, limiting not only the authority of the prime minister, but also the standing of government as a whole. Yet, after an administration fell, the same ministers (and occasionally even the same parties) would return (Giulio Andreotti was prime minister seven times). So, public policy was rather more stable than government turnover might imply.

Government instability also proved compatible with social modernization. As with other European countries, Italy underwent enormous development in the post-war decades. The economy became more industrial and open, though contrasts persisted between a few large industrial companies (often, politically well-connected) and a throng of smaller, family firms operating independently of the state.

The overall environment for business remains difficult by the standards of high-income countries. Regulation is extensive, the non-wage costs of employment are high, and the legal system remains extremely slow.

The disparity between an increasingly sophisticated private sector and a spendthrift state with an inefficient bureaucracy provided part of the backdrop to the party transformation of the 1990s.

Parties in Italy

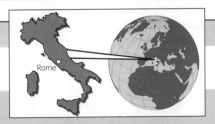

Rome

The recent history of Italian politics is, first and foremost, a story about the fall of parties. In the 1990s, a dominant party system collapsed with astonishing speed, to be replaced after an interregnum by a more bipolar, but still not completely stable, system. Then, in 2011, Italy adopted a remarkable technocratic cabinet of unelected professionals to address the state's considerable debt.

Until 1992, Italy was a leading example of a dominant party system, with the Christian Democrats (DC) the leading player in all post-war governments. A patronage-based, Catholic catch-all party that derived its political strength from serving as a bulwark against Italy's strong communist party, the DC slowly colonized the state, with particular ministries becoming the property of specific factions. The party used its control of the state to reward its supporters with jobs and contracts, creating a patronage network that spanned the country.

Between 1992 and 1994, this party system disintegrated. Still the largest party in 1992, the Christian Democrats had ceased to exist two years later. Its old sparring partner, the communists, had already given up the ghost, largely reforming as the Democratic Party of the Left (PDS) in 1991.

Why did this party-based system collapse? Catalysts included the interna-tional collapse of communism; referendums on electoral reform in the early 1990s, which revealed public hostility to the existing order; vivid attacks by President Francesco Cossiga on the patronage power of the leading parties; and the success of a newly-assertive judiciary in exposing corruption. As with many other dominant parties, the DC's reliance on patronage was also threatened by the demand for greater transparency.

Prime Minister's Mario Monti's cabinet of technocrats, 2011–13

- Seven academics
- Five physicians
- Two lawyers
- One admiral
- One ambassador

Source: Watson (2011).

Although the collapse of the old system was decisive, Italy's new order remained unconsolidated. The election of 1994, the first fought under a new electoral system designed to reduce fragmentation, fell apart after seven months. It was replaced by a crisis government of technocrats containing no parliamentary representatives whatsoever. The next election, in 1996, did produce signs of consolidation. Two major alliances emerged: the centre-left Olive Tree Alliance and the more right-wing Liberty Pole.

But it was not until 2001, when Silvio Berlusconi's House of Freedom coalition won a majority in both legislative chambers, that stable government seemed to become a serious possibility. However, consolidation remained insecure – partly as a result of Berlusconi's own volatile temperament. He lost and then regained power, resigning in 2011 as Italy's public debt came into focus during the eurozone crisis.

Whatever the future may bring, Italy's old mass parties have disappeared, replaced by the looser, leader-dominated parties which characterize the new democracies of the 1990s. Indeed, after Berlusconi's departure in 2011, another technocratic non-party administration took office under Mario Monti, seeking to make and implement the difficult economic decisions which had eluded previous party-based coalitions.

Monti's effective but short-term government continued until 2013 when a fresh election was fought between Monti (now leading a centrist alliance), the more left-wing Democratic Party and the right-of-centre People of Freedom party, led by the irrepressible Berlusconi.

Further reading: Cotta and Verzichelli (2007), Mammone and Veltri (2010), Newell (2010), Shin and Agnew (2008).

Figure 10.3 The decay of some dominant parties, 1976–2012 (share of vote, %)

Dominant parties lost substantial electoral support in India, Japan, and Sweden in the final quarter of the twentieth century

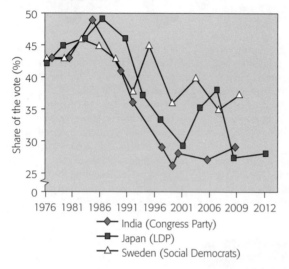

Note: Where assemblies are bicameral, data given are for the lower house.

Source: IPU (2012).

all social groups. Lacking access to the perks of office, no other party could challenge its hegemony.

But authoritarian rule during Indira Gandhi's State of Emergency (1975–77) cost Congress dear. The party suffered its first defeat at a national election in 1977 and has received less than 30 per cent of the vote at every election since 1996. It remains the largest party, and the lead party in a minority coalition, but its glory days are gone.

Two-party systems

A two-party system is as it says: two major parties of comparable size compete for electoral support, providing the framework for political competition. The other parties exert little, if any, influence on the formation and policies of governments. Neither major party dominates by itself but, in combination, they form the pillars of a strong party system.

Rather like dominant parties, the two-party format is rare – and becoming rarer. The United States is the surest example. Although American parties may lack the stable social foundations of their West European counterparts, a two-party

system has been a constant feature of American history. The Republicans and Democrats have dominated electoral politics since 1860, assisted by the high hurdle that plurality elections set for minor parties. In particular, winning a presidential election is a political mountain which can only be climbed by major parties capable of assembling a broad national coalition.

Legal regulation provides additional reinforcement. The country's regulators view parties as utilities performing the collective service of selecting candidates for public office. This perspective encourages sympathetic oversight of the major parties; minor parties, unable to present winning candidates, even confront difficulties in placing their party on the ballot (Lowenstein, 2006). So, the position of the Republicans and Democrats is heavily entrenched. In the country of the free market, the two leading parties form a powerful cartel which is strengthened by judicial policy.

Unusually, too, America's major parties have revived, rather than weakened, since the 1980s, offering further ballast for the two-party system. National party organizations have gathered new impetus as fund-raisers; ideological differences have sharpened between the parties, while diminishing within them; and party voting has intensified in Congress, and even in the electorate. No longer can books be published with such titles as *The Party's Over* (Broder, 1972). Instead, as Stonecash (2010a, p. 3) proclaims, 'partisanship is on the rise!'

Note that the trends here may well be specific to the USA, partly reflecting a decline in what were once exceptional levels of ideological diversity within each major party. A revival of parties, and a resulting deepening of two-party systems, is unlikely elsewhere (Adams *et al.*, 2012).

Apart from the USA, Britain is often presented as an emblem of the two-party pattern. However, its contemporary politics barely pass the two-party test. Certainly, the Conservative and Labour parties regularly alternate in office, offering clear accountability to the electorate. However, third parties have gained ground; far more so, indeed, than in the United States. In 2010, the centre Liberal Democrats won 57 seats in a parliament of 650 members, forming a coalition with the Conservatives after no party won an overall majority. The Liberal Democrats have also progressed in local government and in the new

BOX 10.5

Major party families in Western Europe

	Level of support	Examples	Comment
Far Left	Low	Communist Party (France). Left Party (Sweden).	Once a strong force in Finland, France and Italy, most communist parties have now reformed or decayed. New left parties have emerged since the 1960s.
Green	Low	Alliance '90/The Greens (Germany). Green League (Finland).	Green parties emerged from the late 1970s to become a significant if small minority in many countries.
Social Democrat	High	Social Democratic Workers' Party (Sweden). Social Democrats (Finland).	Originally created to represent the working class, trade unions and socialist values, most such parties no longer challenge the free market.
Christian Democrat	High	Christian Democratic Appeal (Netherlands). Christian Democratic Union (Germany).	Mainly Catholic in origin but with some Protestant cases. Christian Democratic parties now mainly represent the centre-right.
Conservative	High	Conservative Party (Britain, Norway).	These parties emphasize shared national loyalties and class unity, advocating a strong state as well as a market economy.
Centre	Medium	Centre Party (Finland, Norway, Sweden).	Farmers' parties by origin, these parties have moved to the centre while often retaining traditional moral values.
Liberal	Medium	Liberal Party (Netherlands). Venstre (Denmark).	Early advocates of universal suffrage, liberal parties favour individual rights and decentralization.
Far Right	Low	Flemish Block (Belgium). National Front (France).	These racist anti-immigration parties possess a strong nationalist and anti-establishment flavour.

Note: Level of support is assessed for countries in which a relevant party exists. Regional parties are also significant in some states.

Source: Adapted from Gallagher *et al.* (2011), ch. 8.

assemblies in Scotland and Wales. Britain is effectively a multiparty system.

As with dominant party systems, the two-party format is in decline, with even the prop of the plurality electoral method (itself becoming less popular) proving insufficient to keep the format alive. Even where a favourable electoral regime continues, as in Canada, India, and the UK, the two-party system has buckled.

Multiparty systems

In multiparty systems, several parties – typically, at least five or six – achieve significant representation in parliament, becoming serious contenders for a place in a governing coalition. The underlying philosophy is that political parties represent specific social groups (or, increasingly, opinion constituencies such as environmentalists) in what were divided societies. Parliament then serves as an arena of conciliation between parties, and hence cleavages, with coalitions forming and falling in response to often minor changes in the political balance. This emphasis on the representative and consensus-seeking function of parties contrasts sharply with the American notion of parties as post-fillers. The smaller European democracies, such as the Benelux countries and Scandinavia, exemplify this multi-party pattern.

In multiparty systems, the familiar competition between a social democratic party of the left and either a Christian Democratic or a conservative party of the right is supplemented by parties drawn from other families (Box 10.5). These additional parties are rarely large but their representation in parliament, facilitated by proportional representation, suffices to yield a multiparty system.

The exact configuration of parties in a multiparty system varies by country. Typically, parties will be drawn from some, but not all, of the eight major party families. In the left bloc, we find far left parties (some with a communist origin), the greens, and the social democrats. The centre and right bloc contains what are sometimes called the 'bourgeois' parties (Christian Democratic, conservative, centre, and liberal) plus, as a distinct element, the far right.

Denmark provides a clear example of a full multiparty system. Here, no party has held a majority in the unicameral People's Diet since 1909. The country's complex party system has been managed through careful consensus-seeking but this practice has come under some pressure from the rise of new parties. In an explosive election in 1973, three new parties achieved representation and, since then, a minimum of seven parties have won seats in parliament. The centre-left coalition that followed the 2011 election comprised four of these, supported in parliament by the Red–Green Alliance.

Parties in authoritarian states

'Yes, we have lots of parties here,' says President Nazarbaev of post-communist Kazakhstan. 'I

created them all' (quoted in Cummings, 2005, p. 104). This quotation indicates the secondary character of parties in most authoritarian settings. The party is a means of governing, rather than a source of power. As Lawson (2001, p. 673) says of parties under dictatorships, 'the party is a shield and instrument of power. Its function is to carry out the work of government as directed by other agents with greater power (the military or the demagogue and his entourage).'

A few authoritarian states, mainly ruling monarchies in the Middle East, get by with no parties at all. However, most civilian authoritarian rulers have found a single party useful as a disguise for personal rule and as a technique for distributing patronage. In post-independence Africa, for example, the heroes of the nationalist struggle soon put a stop to party competition. With independence achieved, one-party systems were established, with the official party serving as the leader's personal vehicle. In defence of the one-party system, the tradition of the benevolent chief was skilfully exploited by dictators such as President Mobutu of the Congo:

In our African tradition, there are never two chiefs; there is sometimes a natural heir to the chief, but can anyone tell me that he has known a village that has two chiefs? That is why we Congolese, in the desire to conform to the traditions of our continent, have resolved to group all the energies of the citizens of our country under the banner of a single national party. (Quoted in Meredith, 2006, p. 295)

But these single parties proved to be weak, lacking autonomy from the national leader. As with government itself, they lacked presence in the countryside and showed little concern with policy. True, the party was one of the few national organizations and proved useful in recruiting supporters to public office but these functions could not disguise a lack of cohesion, direction, and organization. Indeed, when the founder-leader eventually departed, his party would sometimes disappear with him. When a coup overthrew President Kwame Nkrumah in Ghana in 1966, his Convention People's Party also collapsed.

Cases of authoritarian rule where the political party, rather than a dominant individual, is the true source of power are few and far between. One such is

Figure 10.4 Organization of the Chinese Communist Party

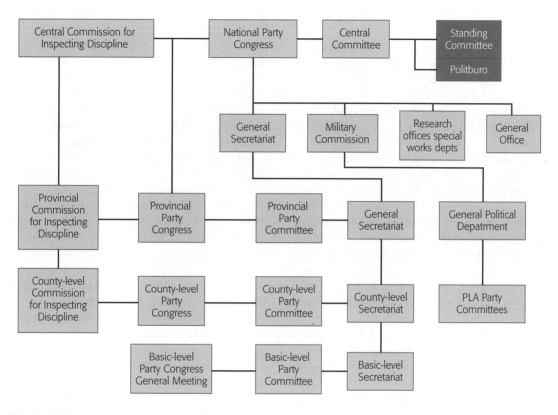

Note: PLA – People's Liberation Army.

Source: Saich (2011), fig. 5.1.

Singapore. There the People's Action Party (PAP) maintains a close grip despite permitting a modest, and perhaps increasing, level of opposition. Lee Kuan Yew, the island's Prime Minister from 1959 to 1990, acknowledged that his party post, rather than his executive office, was the real source of his authority: 'all I have to do is to stay Secretary-General of the PAP. I don't have to be president' (Tremewan, 1994, p. 184). Tremewan (p. 186) went on to refer to the 'PAP-state', in which the party uses its control of public resources to ensure citizen quiescence:

It is the party-state with its secretive, unaccountable party core under a dominating, often threatening personality which administers Singaporeans' housing, property values, pensions, breeding, health, media, schooling and also the electoral process itself.

Parties may be mainly an instrument of power in most authoritarian states but they are, of course, the leading institution in communist regimes. Reforms notwithstanding, the Chinese Communist Party (CCP) still illustrates the elaborate internal hierarchy of ruling communist parties. At its base stand 3.5 million primary party organizations, found not only in local areas such as villages, but also in factories and military units. As shown in Figure 10.4, these units have their own congresses, committees, and secretariats. At the top, at least in theory, is the sovereign National Party Congress, a body of around 2,200 people which meets infrequently and for short periods. In practice, the Congress delegates authority to its 370-member Central Committee and, through that body, to the 25-strong Politburo ('political bureau') and its Standing Committee. This intricate pyramid allows the seven men on the

Politburo's Standing Committee to exert enormous influence over the political direction of the most populous country on earth – in itself, an astonishing political achievement.

The party is massive. In 2011, its membership reached 83 million, exceeding the population of the United Kingdom. And unlike most parties in the democratic world, the CCP's membership, at around 6 per cent of the population, is still growing. Women, in particular, remained heavily under-represented (ChinaToday.com, 2009).

What accounts for the party's continuing control? The answer can hardly be ideology, for the CCP's communist commitment is now nominal. Indeed, Saich (2011, p. 95) reports that, on his travels, he has met 'party members who are Maoists, Stalinists, Friedmanites, shamans, underground Christians, anarchists, and social and liberal democrats'. Nearly 3 million members work in the private sector, while 800,000 are self-employed. The emergence of red capitalists is one of the many paradoxes of China in an era of reform.

Party members are united by ambition, rather than ideology. The CCP remains an important academy for go-getters. A business route to worldly success has now emerged, but even the most apolitical entrepreneurs still find value in close party links. Members are prepared to undergo a searching entry procedure, and the continuing obligation to participate in dull party tasks, in order to secure privileged access to information, contacts and the resulting opportunities to acquire wealth.

Those members who are particularly determined will seek out a patron to help them ascend the party hierarchy. Within the party's formal structure, it is these patron–client networks – not political ideologies or policy differences – that provide the integrating force. Factions both divide and unite the party.

We turn finally to the position of parties in competitive authoritarian regimes. Here, too, parties are more often a political form than a political force. They are shells for ambitious politicians (and powerful presidents), rather than disciplined actors in their own right. The result is a democratic gloss applied to a substantially authoritarian structure.

Post-communist Russia provides an example of ineffectual parties in a hybrid regime. The Russian party system is unstructured and free-floating, with parties playing second (or even third) fiddle in the

president's orchestra (Rose, 2000). At national level, power is focused on the political elite and is, at most, confirmed by the *Duma* (lower chamber of the legislature). The party composition of the *Duma* is therefore only of secondary political interest.

In any case, the choice on offer in *Duma* elections is limited by the rapid turnover and limited coherence of parties. Where major Western parties developed a recognized brand over the course of a century, Russian parties come and go. For instance, most parties competing in the 2003 parliamentary elections, a decade after the end of communist rule, were fighting their first campaign. What is more, these new parties succeeded in winning a majority of the list vote, showing the lack of entrenched party loyalties in the electorate. Clearly, when parties cease to exist from one election to the next, it is impossible for them to be held to account. Not surprisingly, they are the least trusted public organizations in a suspicious society (White, 2007, p. 27).

Far more than in the United States, voters in Russia's presidential elections are choosing between candidates, not parties. The party is vehicle, rather than driver. President Vladimir Putin did not even deign to belong to United Russia, an organization with no vision other than to support him. United Russia is what Russians term a 'party of power', meaning that the Kremlin uses threats and bribes to ensure it is supported by powerful ministers, regional governors and large companies. The equivalent in the USA would occur if the president were to start a new party just before his re-election campaign, dragooning state governors and the chief executives of the biggest corporations into supporting his new entity.

Given the weak position of Russia's parties, it is not surprising that they are poorly organized, with a small membership and minimal capacity to integrate a large and diverse country. In a manner typical of competitive authoritarian regimes, the rules concerning the registration of parties, the nomination of candidates, and the receipt of state funding are skewed in favour of larger parties. In post-communist Russia (as in the communist era), there is only one party of power. Minor parties are trapped: they cannot grow until they become more significant but their importance cannot increase until they are larger (Kulik, 2007, p. 201).

Discussion questions

■ Are you more likely to join a party, an interest group, or a social movement? Why?

■ Why has party membership fallen, and what can and should be done to reverse this trend?

■ 'If the main reason we need political parties at all is in order for them to facilitate democracy in the government of the country, then might not parties that are internally oligarchic serve that purpose just as well, or maybe better than, parties that are internally more or less democratic?' (Dahl, 1970, p. 5). What is your answer to Dahl?

■ Which method of selecting party leaders produces the best leaders of a country?

■ Three in 10 countries in the world limit the amount of money political parties are allowed to spend during election campaigns while 4 in 10 apply such limits to candidates (IDEA, 2012). If you support free speech, must you oppose such restrictions? If you support such limits, would you also apply them to other areas of public debate (e.g. pro-choice/pro-life)?

■ Why have previously dominant parties declined in liberal democracies?

Further reading

P. Brooker, *Non-Democratic Regimes: Theory, Government and Politics*, 2nd edn (2009). This wide-ranging examination of authoritarian rule includes a chapter on one-party rule.

W. Cross and R. Katz, eds, *The Challenges of Intra-Party Democracy* (2013). This book considers the principal issues that parties and the state must address in introducing greater democracy within parties.

M. Gallagher, M. Laver and P. Mair, *Representative Government in Modern Europe*, 5th edn (2011). An informative source on European politics, this text includes extensive material on political parties.

R. Hazan and G. Rahat, *Democracy within Parties: Candidate Selection Methods and Their Political Consequences* (2010). A comparative analysis of candidate selection methods which concludes by recommending a particular format.

S. Scarrow, ed., *Perspectives on Political Parties: Classic Readings* (2002). An interesting and unusual collection of primary documents, from various countries, revealing changing understandings of party politics in the nineteenth century.

J. Stonecash, ed., *New Directions in American Political Parties* (2010). This volume brings together assessments of the changing significance of American parties, including the impact of social change, the sources of increasing political divisions and the impact of changes in the parties on institutions and policy.

ONLINE RESOURCES AVAILABLE

Visit the companion website at **www.palgrave.com/politics/hague** to access additional learning resources, including multiple-choice questions, chapter summaries, web links and practice essay questions.

Chapter 11 **Elections**

'Elections are the defining institution of modern democracy', wrote Katz (1997, p. 3). For the brief moment of an election campaign, voters are the masters and are seen to be so. As liberal democracies grow in number, so elections become more widespread, with the annual number of votes cast exceeding one billion by 2004 (Muñoz, 2006, p. 1).

Clearly, one function of elections is to provide a competition for office and a means of holding the government to account. But that is not their only role. An election campaign also permits a dialogue between voters and parties, and so between society and state: 'no part of the education of a politician is more indispensable than the fighting of elections', claimed Winston Churchill. As with coronations of old, competitive elections also endow the new office-holders with authority, contributing thereby to the effectiveness with which leaders can perform their duties. In short, competitive elections facilitate choice, accountability, dialogue, and legitimacy – a rich bounty for what is, after all, only an occasional event.

Scope and franchise

One rather neglected question about elections in liberal democracies concerns their scope. The number of offices subject to election varies considerably between, say, the United States and Europe. At one extreme, the USA possesses more than 500,000 elected posts, a figure reflecting a strong tradition of local self-government. At the other extreme, many democracies in Europe traditionally confined voting to national assemblies and local government, with regional and European elections added more recently. To illustrate the contrast, Dalton and Gray (2003, p. 38) calculate that 'between 1995 and 2000 a resident of Oxford, England, could have voted four times; a resident of Irvine, California, could have cast more than 50 votes in just the single year of 2000'.

There are dangers in too many elections. One is voter fatigue, leading to a fall in interest, turnout, and quality of choice. Estimates from the USA suggest that five additional trips to the polls over a five-year period are likely to depress turnout by around 4 per cent (Dalton and Gray, 2003, p. 39).

Another side-effect of electionitis is the emergence of **second-order elections**: contests whose outcomes reflect the popularity of national parties, even though they do not install a national government. These

Second-order elections are heavily influenced by the results of first-order contests, often occurring at the same time. For example, a party's votes at local contests may reflect its popularity at national level, thus degrading the link between local governance and local elections.

STUDYING . . .

ELECTIONS

- Although the issue of who can vote is usually regarded as settled, some interesting questions remain. Sixteen and seventeen year olds? Non-citizen residents? Prisoners? Academic research here could surely offer more support to policy-makers as they address these questions.

- In research on electoral systems , the politics of electoral reform has attracted recent attention. These studies invite us to think about the origins of electoral systems, not merely their effects.

- Recent developments in electoral systems include the rise of mixed electoral systems and the declining ability of the plurality method to deliver a majority of seats for the winning party. Both points encourage us to move on from the traditional debate between supporters of plurality and pro-portional systems.

- Studies of electoral systems concentrate on legislative elections. By comparison, the systems used for presidential elections receive insufficient attention.

- Election campaigns are not usually decisive for the result. So, we must ask what other functions they perform. They are learning opportunities – but who learns what about whom with what long-term effects?

- The political impact of an election depends on the narrative established about it soon after the results are in. This topic raises the issue of the mandate. The interpretive approach is ideally suited to studies in this area.

- Direct democratic mechanisms such as the referendum, the initiative and the recall increasingly sup-plement elections. The quality of these devices, including their impact on representative democracy, is a significant issue.

second-order contests – which include many regional and local elections, and those to the European Parliament – weaken the link between the representative's performance and the voters' response. For instance, a competent local adminis-tration might find itself dismissed for no other reason than the unpopularity of its party at national level. The perverse effect of too many elections is that they hinder accountability.

The franchise (who can vote) is another under-emphasized aspect of contemporary elections. In most democracies, the voting age was reduced to 18 in the 1960s and 1970s. Even so, some issues remain. Votes at 16, as in Austria and Brazil? (Folkes, 2004). Votes for prisoners, as in most liberal democracies? Votes at national elections for non-citizen residents? Let us consider these last two cases.

In a few countries, many convicted criminals are still denied the vote; the USA is the prime exhibit.

The number of disenfranchised felons and ex-felons there exceeds five million; about one in seven black men cannot vote for this reason. Britain also takes a tough line, resisting rulings from the European Court of Human Rights to grant the vote to pris-oners. David Cameron, Britain's Prime Minister (2010–), even claimed that the prospect of inmates voting made him 'physically sick'.

Although Weale (2007, p. 157) suggests that 'there are probably as many arguments against depriving prisoners of the right to vote as there are in favour', not everyone accepts that being locked up should also mean being locked out. Canada's highest court has ruled that prisoner disenfranchisement 'has no place in a democracy built upon the principles of inclusiveness, equality and citizen participation'. Israel's Supreme Court even restored the right to vote to the assassin of the country's prime minister, declaring that 'we must separate contempt for his act from respect for his right' (Manza and Uggen, 2008, p. 232).

There also remains a question about non-citizen residents. Should such people be granted the vote in the country where they live, work, and pay taxes alongside citizens? If so, should they also retain the vote in their home country? The slow trend here is to greater inclusiveness. Around 40 countries have now approved some form of non-citizen voting rights (Immigrant Voting Project, 2012). Within the European Union, all EU citizens residing in a country of which they are not a national can vote and can stand as a candidate at local elections. This policy is a tangible step towards maintaining voting rights in an age of mobility.

Electing legislatures

Most discussion of **electoral systems** centres on the rules for converting votes into seats. Such rules are as important as they are technical. They form the inner workings of democracy – often little understood by voters, but essential to the system's operation and never, ever, ignored by politicians themselves (Box 11.1). In this section, we examine the rules for translating votes into seats in parliamentary elections, leaving presidential systems to the next section.

The key characteristic of an **electoral formula** is whether the parliamentary seats obtained by a party are directly proportional to the votes it receives. Proportional representation (PR) simply means that a mechanism to achieve this goal is built into the allocation of seats. In non-proportional systems, by contrast, parties are not rewarded in proportion to the share of the vote they obtain; instead, 'the winner takes all' within each electoral district.

> In a broad sense, an **electoral system** denotes all the rules governing an election. However, the term is usually restricted to three aspects: first, the **structure of the ballot** (e.g. how many candidates are listed per party); second, the **electoral formula** (how votes are converted to seats); third, **districting** (the division of the territory into separate constituencies).

Plurality system

In the single-member plurality (also called 'first-past-the-post') format, the winning candidate is simply the one receiving the greatest number of votes in a particular electoral district. A party's representation in the legislature consists of those of its candidates winning constituency contests.

Despite its antiquity and simplicity, the plurality system is becoming less common. It survives principally in Britain and British-influenced states such as Canada, India, and the United States. However, because India and the USA are so populous, the largest share of the world's people living under democratic rule still votes by this method.

The crucial point about the plurality system is the bonus in seats it can offer to the party leading in votes. To see how this bias operates, consider an example in which just two parties, the Reds and the Blues, compete in every constituency. Suppose the Reds win by one vote in each district. There could hardly be a closer contest, yet the Reds sweep the board in seats.

The political significance of this amplifying effect lies in its ability to deliver government by a single majority party. In parliamentary systems with dominant national parties, the plurality method can function as a giant conjuring trick, pulling the rabbit of majority government out of a hat containing only minority parties. This amplifying characteristic is crucial for those who consider that the function of an electoral system is to deliver decisive majority government by a single party.

For example, 16 of the 18 general elections in Britain between 1945 and 2010 yielded a majority in the House of Commons for a single party, even though no party secured a majority of votes in any of these contests. A similar pattern holds for some, but not all, federal elections in Canada. In 2011, for instance, the Conservatives won a majority of seats with a minority of votes (Table 11.1).

Note, however, that this amplifier only works its magic when two dominant parties compete throughout the country, as in some contests in Bangladesh. In other plurality systems, the decline of two-party systems, and the retreat of major parties into regional strongholds, mitigates against a parliamentary majority for the leading party.

Thus, no party has won a majority of seats in India's strongly regional system since 1984. Of the four general elections in Canada held between 1994 and 2011, only one delivered a majority. Even in Britain, the 2010 result required a coalition between

BOX 11.1

Electoral systems: legislatures

PLURALITY AND MAJORITY SYSTEMS

Single-member plurality: first-past-the-post

Procedure The candidate securing most votes (not necessarily a majority) is elected on the first and only ballot within each single-member district.

Examples Bangladesh, Canada, India, UK, USA.

Two-round system

Procedure If no candidate wins a majority on the first ballot, the leading candidates (usually the top two) face a second, run-off election.

Examples Iran, Mali, Vietnam.

Absolute majority: alternative vote (AV)

Procedure Voters rank candidates. If no candidate wins a majority of first preferences, the bottom candidate is eliminated and his or her votes are redistributed by second preferences. This process continues until a candidate has a majority of votes.

Examples Australia, Papua New Guinea.

PROPORTIONAL SYSTEMS

List system

Procedure Votes are cast for a party's list of candidates, though in some countries the elector can also express support for individual candidates on the list.

Examples Brazil, Czech Republic, Israel, Netherlands.

Single transferable vote (STV)

Procedure Voters rank candidates in order of preference. Any successful candidate needs a set number of votes – the quota. All candidates who exceed this quota on first preferences are elected. Their surplus votes are then distributed according to second preferences. When no candidate has reached the quota, the bottom candidate is eliminated and these votes are transferred. This process continues until all seats are filled.

Examples Ireland, Malta.

Mixed member proportional (MMP)

Procedure Electors usually have two votes. One is for the district election (which typically uses the plurality method), and the other is for a PR contest (usually party list). The two tiers are linked so as to deliver a proportional outcome overall. The party vote determines the number of seats to be won by each party. Elected candidates are drawn, first, from the party's winners in the district contests, topped up as required for proportionality by candidates from the party list.

Examples Germany, New Zealand.

PARALLEL SYSTEM

Mixed member majoritarian (MMM)

Procedure As for MMP, except that the two tiers are separate, with no mechanism to achieve a proportional result overall.

Examples Japan, Thailand.

Table 11.1 The Canadian federal election, 2011

In 2011, Canada's single-member plurality system allowed the Conservative Party to secure a majority of seats despite winning only a minority of votes.

	Votes (%)	Seats (%)
Liberal	18.9	11.0
Conservative	39.6	54.2
New Democratic Party	30.6	33.1
Bloc Québécois	6.0	1.3
Green	3.9	0.3

Source: Psephos (2012).

Conservatives and Liberal Democrats to secure a working majority. So, the plurality system is now as likely to deliver a **hung parliament** as a single party majority, a point rarely recognized by the system's defenders.

A **hung parliament** is a British term for a situation in which no party wins a majority of seats in parliament, thus complicating the task of forming and maintaining a government.

Because the plurality system is based on the representation of districts, it offers no guarantee that the party which leads in votes nationally will secure most seats in the legislature. The second party in votes may achieve such an efficient distribution of votes that it wins a parliamentary majority. The bizarre situation of coming first in seats but second in votes has arisen twice in post-war British general elections, in 1951 and February 1974.

For Lijphart (1999, p. 134), the possibility of 'seat victories for parties that are mere runners-up in vote totals is probably the plurality method's gravest democratic deficit'. In a democratic era, the expectation is that votes, rather than seats, should count. An election resulting in a government formed by the

Tactical voting occurs when electors vote instrumentally for a party or candidate other than their preferred choice. In plurality electoral systems, voters sometimes support their second preference because their favoured party has no chance of winning in their local district.

party coming second in votes is regarded as delivering the wrong winner. Certainly, if we were designing an electoral system from scratch, we would surely reject a method in which the party securing most votes can come second in seats.

Three other weaknesses of the plurality method deserve mention:

● It encourages **tactical voting** when electors feel their favoured party stands no chance of victory in their particular district. No electoral formula should encourage voters to disguise their true preferences.

● The plurality method treats minority parties inconsistently, according to the geographical concentration of their support. Small parties with even support are hit badly (e.g. the Liberal Democrats in the UK) but regional parties with their concentrated vote can secure a nice bonus.

● The importance of constituency **districting** gives incentives for **gerrymandering**. In the United States, partisan districting has become a fine art in elections to the House of Representatives and state legislatures, enabling incumbents to choose their voters, rather than the other way round.

Gerrymandering is the art of drawing seat boundaries to maximize the efficiency of a party's support. The term comes from a constituency designed by Governor Gerry of Massachusetts in 1812. It was so long, narrow and wiggly that it reminded one observer of a salamander – hence 'gerrymander'.

Majority systems

The plurality system is not the only form of non-proportional representation. There are other less common but perhaps more democratic versions based on the majority method. As its name implies, this formula requires the winning candidate to obtain a majority of votes. This outcome can be achieved through the alternative vote (Box 11.1) or, more commonly, a two-round system. In the latter case, if no candidate wins a majority on the first round, an additional ballot is held, usually a run-off between the top two candidates – of whom one will win a majority.

Many countries in Western Europe used two-round majority voting before switching to PR early in the twentieth century. The system remains significant in France and its ex-colonies. It was also used to elect some members of both legislative chambers in Egypt in 2011. The democratic argument for a majority system is quite strong; namely, that no candidate should be elected without being shown to be acceptable to a majority of voters.

Proportional representation

We move now from non-proportional systems to proportional representation. PR is more recent than non-proportional systems. It emerged in Continental Europe towards the end of the nineteenth century, stimulated by associations dedicated to electoral reform. PR is now more common than plurality and majority systems, becoming the method of choice for most democratic countries since the early 1920s. PR is the norm in Europe, both West and East, and in Latin America.

The underlying principle is straightforward. PR is party-based, aiming to achieve equitable representation for parties, rather than to elect representatives for a given territory. In a perfectly proportional system, every party would receive the same share of seats as of votes: 40 per cent of the votes would mean 40 per cent of the seats. By definition, PR systems are designed with this principle in mind but, in practice, most PR systems fall short. They usually offer at least some bonus to the largest party, though less than most non-proportional methods, and they also discriminate by design or practice against the smallest parties. So, it is a mistake to assume that any system labelled 'proportional' must be completely so.

The key point about PR is that a single party rarely wins a majority of seats. Hence, majority governments are unusual and coalitions become standard. Because PR usually leads to post-election negotiations in parliament about which parties will form the next government, it is best interpreted as a method of electing parliaments, rather than governments.

How does PR achieve its goal? The most common method, first introduced in Belgium in 1899 and still used there, is the party list system. In a pure list system, an elector votes for a slate of the party's candidates, rather than for a single person. The number of votes won by a party determines how many candidates are elected from that party's list, while the order in which candidates appear on the list (decided by the party itself) governs the order in which they are elected.

Suppose a party wins 10 per cent of the vote in an election to a 150-seat assembly. Assuming perfect proportionality, that party will be entitled to 15 members and those will be the first 15 candidates on its list. If winners withdraw, candidates further down the list can serve instead.

List systems vary in their **ballot structure** and, specifically, in how much choice they offer between candidates on a party's list. Many countries – such as Belgium, South Africa, and Spain – employ closed-party lists; electors vote only for a party. In this format, party officials exert enormous control over political recruitment, including the ability to include women and minorities near the top of the list. However, most list systems in Western Europe give voters at least some choice between candidates. This option, known as preference voting, allows or requires voters to select one or more candidates from the party list. The total of votes cast for a given list still determines the party's overall representation, but a candidate's preference votes influence (to varying degrees) the order of appointment.

As with all forms of PR, list systems require multi-member constituencies. Usually, the country is divided into a set of multimember districts and seats are allocated separately within each district. Employing constituencies in this way preserves some territorial basis to representation but reduces the proportionality of the overall outcome. This bias arises because, when only a few seats are on offer per district, the least popular parties may not receive any seats at all. In an extreme case, if only three seats are on offer, the party coming fourth in votes will be left empty-handed.

The number of members returned per district is known as its **district magnitude**. This figure – which varies between countries, and usually also between regions within a country – is a critical influence on how proportional PR systems are in practice. As Farrell (2011, p. 79) observes, 'the basic relationship for all proportional systems is: the larger the constituency size, and hence the larger the district magnitude, the more proportional the result'. For example, Spain is divided into over 50 districts, returning an average of just seven members each. This small magnitude means that minor parties can be denied seats; in consequence, large parties receive an artificial boost.

District magnitude refers to the number of representatives chosen for each electoral district. The more representatives to be elected for a district, the more proportional the electoral system can be and the less the discrimination against minor parties.

Many countries have introduced a compensating mechanism by which some seats are held back from the district allocation to be reallocated at regional and/or national level. These seats go to parties with votes remaining after the initial distribution at the lower level. These additional tiers achieve greater proportionality at the cost of additional complexity.

However, in the Netherlands, Israel, and Slovakia, the whole country serves as a single large constituency, eliminating the need for compensating tiers and extending proportionality even to small parties. The Israeli election of 2009, for example, saw a total of 12 parties winning seats in the 120-member Knesset. Seven of these parties each secured less than 5 per cent of the vote.

Most PR systems add an explicit threshold of representation. If a party's vote share falls below the threshold, it receives no seats, whatever its entitlement under the list formula. The threshold varies, from just 2 per cent in Denmark and Israel to an excessive 10 per cent in Turkey. Operating at district or national level, thresholds help to protect the legislature from fragmentation and extreme parties. As Kostadinova (2002) observes, 'the threshold is a powerful mechanism for reducing fragmentation in the assembly. It can be and is manipulated by elites to cut off access to parliament for smaller parties'. But the effect can be brutal: one third of the voters in the Kyrgyzstan legislative election of 2010 supported parties receiving no parliamentary representation.

Mixed systems

Plurality and PR systems are usually considered alternatives; however, a hybrid form has emerged that combines geographical representation and party representation. The best-known blend – mixed member proportional (MMP) – retains a mechanism for achieving overall proportionality and is,

indeed, a form of PR. Awareness of MMP enables debates about electoral reform to move beyond the issue of whether plurality or proportional systems are preferable.

Germany is the inspiration for MMP. Here, electors have two votes: one for a district candidate, and the other for a regional party list. Half the seats in the *Bundestag* (lower house) are filled by candidates elected by plurality voting within single-member districts: as with any other plurality election, the results here can be extremely disproportional, as in 2009 (Table 11.2). But the list vote rides to the rescue; candidates from the party's list are used to top up its directly-elected candidates until proportionality is achieved. So, the list vote is more important because it determines how many seats are awarded to each party. Should a party win more district seats in a region than its entitlement under the party vote, it retains the extra seats for that region and the *Bundestag* expands in size.

A few countries have adopted the idea of parallel district and party list votes without any top-up to achieve a proportional outcome overall. This non-proportional mixed member majority (MMM) system can result in what amounts to two separate campaigns. White (2005b, p. 324) notes that, when Russia used this method, 'the two contests could be separately organized, with different headquarters and campaign headquarters and campaign staff even in the case of candidates from the same party'. Many independent candidates, often drawn from local elites or reflecting local concerns, were elected through the districts. It was a desire to reduce the number of independents that led to a decision in 2007 to replace MMM with party-based list PR.

Electoral systems and party systems

The relationship between electoral systems and party systems has proved a source of controversy. The question is whether a technical feature such as the formula for converting votes into seats nonetheless exerts a strong influence on the system of parties. In a classic work, Duverger (1954, p. 217) answered in the affirmative. He argued that 'an almost complete correlation is observable' between the plurality method and a two-party system; indeed, he suggested that this relationship, based on **mechanical** and **psychological** effects, approached that of 'a true sociological law'.

Table 11.2 How the mixed member proportional system works: the German federal election, 2009

Although the Christian Democrats won most of the district seats (B), the allocation of list seats (C) served to restore considerable proportionality in the overall outcome (compare D and A)

	A Party list vote (%)	B Number of district seats won	C Number of list seats awarded (to bring D closer to A)	D Seats won in the Bundestag (%)
Christian Democrats/ Christian Social Union	33.8	218	21	38.4
Social Democrats	23.0	64	82	23.5
Free Democrats	14.6	0	93	15.0
Left Party	11.9	16	60	12.2
Green Party	10.7	1	67	10.9
Others	6.0	0	0	0.0

Note: Total number of seats is 622.

Source: Álvarez-Rivera (2009).

Duverger (1954) distinguished two effects of electoral systems. The **mechanical** effect arises directly from the rules converting votes into seats. Example: the threshold for representation used in many proportional systems. The **psychological** effect is the impact of the rules on how electors cast their votes. Example: tactical voting in plurality systems when the voter's first choice party has no prospect of winning in the elector's own district.

But a reaction set in against attributing weight to political institutions such as electoral systems. Writers such as Rokkan (1970) adopted a more sociological approach, pointing out that social cleavages produced multiparty systems in Europe long before the introduction of PR. Jasiewicz (2003, p. 182) makes the same point about post-communist Europe: 'political fragmentation usually preceded the adoption of a PR-based voting system, not vice versa'. Miller (2005, p. 13) adopts a similar position in discussing New Zealand's move away from the plurality method in 1996: 'the fracturing of the two-party system occurred long before the advent of PR'.

So, it appears that electoral systems result from a party system to a greater degree than they influence it. The lesson of this debate is that we should ask not only about the impact of an electoral system, but also about the political calculations that lead to its adoption in the first place (Renwick, 2010).

Electing presidents

Electoral systems for choosing presidents receive less attention than those for electing legislatures. Yet, most presidents in democracies are elected, whether the system of government is presidential (e.g. the USA), semi-presidential (e.g. France), or parliamentary with a presidential figurehead (e.g. Ireland).

In one sense, the rules for electing presidents are straightforward. Unlike seats in parliament, a one-person presidency cannot be shared between parties; the office is indivisible. So, PR is impossible, and the main choice is between the plurality and the majority methods. However, in another sense, presidential electoral systems are more complicated since many, including the USA's, are still based on **indirect election** through a special college.

Indirect election occurs when office-holders are elected by a body which has itself been chosen by a wider constituency. The device is employed in some presidential elections and for some upper houses of parliament.

Figure 11.1 Methods for selecting presidents

Most presidents are directly elected, usually by a two-round system. However, indirect election is still used in some countries.

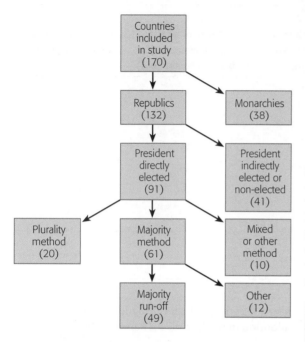

Source: Adapted from Blais *et al.* (1997).

We begin with directly-elected presidents. As Figure 11.1 shows, in the mid-1990s, most directly-elected presidents were chosen by a majority system. This number is increasing as countries dispense not only with indirect election, but also with the plurality method, matching the trend in parliamentary elections (Negretto, 2008). The reason for the pre-eminence of the majority system in presidential elections is that it is more important to confirm majority backing for a single president than for every single member of a legislature. Plurality contests, in which the candidate with most votes wins on the first and only round, can lead to victory with an unacceptably small share of the vote. For example, Fidel Ramos became president of the Philippines in 1992 with just 24 per cent of the vote – hardly a resounding endorsement with which to send the winner to the highest executive office in the land.

Most majority elections for presidents employ a run-off between the top two candidates, assuming neither wins a majority on the first round. France is an influential case; French voters, it is said, choose in the first count and decide in the second. By their nature, run-offs create a possibility that the leading candidate in the first round fails to win election in the second; this outcome occurred in one third of the run-offs in Latin America between 1979 and 1992 (Peréz-Liñán, 2006). Most often, however, the winner leads in both rounds, as in France in 2012 (Table 11.3).

Given that most presidential elections are by national ballot, it is possible to require the winning candidate to obtain a certain level of support in the regions, as well as nationally. Such **distribution requirements** are still uncommon but they do encourage candidates to broaden their support. This virtue is important in regionally divided societies. In Indonesia, for instance, a first-round victory requires at least 20 per cent of the vote in a majority of provinces. However, distribution rules introduce their own dangers, including the possibility of a **failed election**.

> **Distribution requirements** set out how a winning candidate's votes must be arranged across different sections of the electorate. The most common (but still unusual) requirement is for a minimum level of support in a certain number of provinces. Such requirements can lead to **failed elections** in which no candidate succeeds in jumping through all the hoops.

We turn now to indirect election of presidents. As Figure 11.1 shows, almost one third of presidents manage to avoid the perils of direct election altogether. Many of these are chosen via indirect election in which a special body (which may itself be elected) supposedly acts as a buffer against the whims of the people. In the United States, for example, the Electoral College is still technically used to elect an incoming president. But the College survives only as a procedural and pre-democratic relic mandated by the constitution. Delegates to the College still assemble but, with the odd exception, they conscientiously follow the verdict of the state they represent.

Three other features of presidential elections, whether direct or indirect, are worthy of note. These are the length of term, the possibility of re-election, and the link with other elections (Box 11.2).

Table 11.3 A two-round system: the French presidential election, 2012

François Hollande, the Socialist candidate, led narrowly on both rounds. However, without a run-off (and assuming an unchanged first round result), he would have been elected with less than one third of the overall vote.

		First round (22 April) %	Second round (6 May) %
Nathalie Arthaud	*Workers' Struggle*	0.6	
François Boyou	*Democratic Movement*	9.1	
Jacques Cheminade	*Solidarity and Progress*	0.3	
Nicholas Dupont-Aignan	*Arise the Republic*	1.8	
François Hollande	*Socialist Party*	28.6	52.0
Eva Joly	*The Greens*	2.3	
Marine le Pen	*National Front*	17.9	
Jean-Luc Mélenchon	*Left Front*	11.1	
Philippe Poutou	*New Anticapitalist Party*	1.2	
Nicolas Sarkozy	*Union for a Popular Movement*	27.2	48.0
Turnout		*79.5*	*80.3*

Source: Psephos (2012).

On the first point, the presidential term is sometimes longer, and usually no shorter, than for legislators. The longer the term, the easier it is for presidents to adopt a broad perspective free from the immediate burden of re-election. At just four years, the term of office of American presidents is perhaps rather short. The danger is that the first year is spent acquiring experience and the fourth year campaigning, leaving only the middle phase for real accomplishments.

Second, term limits are often imposed, restricting the incumbent to just one or two periods in office. The fear is that without such constraints presidents will be able to exploit their unique position to secure re-election without end. Thus, the USA introduced a two-term limit after Franklin Roosevelt won four elections in a row between 1932 and 1944. Mexican presidents (and its legislators) cannot stand for re-election.

As with many institutional fixes, term limits bring unintended consequences. Clearly, a president who cannot be re-elected is no longer directly accountable to the voters – an important, if not necessarily undesirable, limitation on democracy. Also, presidents lose political clout as their term nears its end. And popular presidents, replete with confidence and experience, may be debarred from office at the peak of their careers.

Third, the timing of presidential elections matters. When they occur at the same time as elections to the assembly, the successful candidate is more likely to be drawn from the largest party in the legislature. Without threatening the separation of powers, concurrent elections limit fragmentation, increasing the likelihood that president and congress will be of similar mind. Such thinking lay behind the decision in 2000 to reduce the French president's term to five years, the same tenure as that of the assembly. In the United States, by contrast, presidential and congressional elections are only weakly aligned, complicating the president's job (see Chapter 16).

Electoral systems: design and reform

In the nineteenth and twentieth centuries, by far the most common reform of electoral systems was from a majority or plurality system to PR (Colomer, 2004b). That direction of travel was for a reason. Because PR is not a winner-takes-all system, it is always a safe option for parties negotiating electoral reform. In the discussions preceding suffrage exten-

BOX 11.2

Electing presidents: some examples

	Method of election	Term (years)	Re-election permitted?
Argentina	Two round	4	One term out required after two consecutive terms
Brazil	Two round	4	Two-term limit
Finland	Plurality	6	Yes
France	Two round	5	Two-term limit
Mexico	Plurality	6	No
Russia	Two round	5	One term out required after two consecutive terms
United States	Electoral college	4	Two-term limit

sion in Europe early in the twentieth century, conservative and liberal parties felt that a shift from a majority system to PR would at least guarantee their own survival into the new era of mass suffrage. At the same time, socialist parties, still uncertain of their electoral potential, also judged that PR would at least remove the bias of the majority system against them. So, for all the major players, PR proved to be the least bad option – a risk-averse strategy in the face of uncertainty (Lewin, 2004).

Similar calculations applied in the wave of democratic transitions in the final quarter of the twentieth century. With memories of communist and military dictatorship still fresh, reformers were keen to see a wide range of interests represented in the assembly. PR will usually provide at least some representation for parties based on minority groups and ideologies, typically leading to coalitions

offering further protection against domination by a single ruling party. Explicit thresholds and small district magnitudes can limit fragmentation and discord by excluding small anti-system parties. Because there are no wasted votes, PR also leads to higher turnouts than the plurality system (IDEA, 2006).

Yet, an electoral system cannot be expected by itself to resolve underlying social conflicts. In general, a method of election is performing its function if it proves to be widely acceptable and, therefore, stable over time. Its purpose is to deliver an equilibrium such that no party with the power to change the rules feels it will obtain a long-term benefit from doing so. If the winners do not seek to modify the system to their own advantage, and the losers do not blame the election rules for their own defeat, then the electoral system has done its job. It has become, as it should be, taken for granted – a part of the political furniture.

Election campaigns

We move now from the rules governing elections to election campaigns themselves. In the **short campaign**, we expect voters to compare, decide and deliver their verdict. But expectations must be tested against reality. We will suggest here that national election campaigns in liberal democracies are often notable for what they do not achieve: they rarely bring about decisive changes in party support; straight conversions among voters from one major party to another remain unusual; and advertising, for all the attention it is given, rarely makes a great difference.

But none of that is to say that campaigns are irrelevant. Rather, one of their positive functions is to provide an intense political seminar for the country as a whole, and to advance elite political debate in particular. In practice, campaigns are as much about what they do for politicians as for voters.

The **short campaign** is the period from the announcement of the election to election day. Where election dates are fixed, there is no specific starting point; the **long campaign** begins whenever electioneering starts. The **permanent campaign** is a phrase suggesting that electioneering never stops.

Figure 11.2 Proportion of voters deciding which party to support during the election campaign: Australia, Britain and the USA, 1948–2010

The proportion of electors deciding how to vote during the campaign increased substantially during the second half of the twentieth century, but late deciders remain a minority

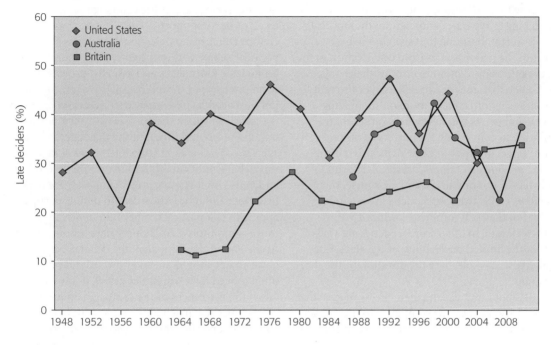

Sources: Updated from the sources in McAllister (2002), fig. 2.1.

Campaigns do not usually deliver decisive changes in parties' shares of the vote. As Wlezien (2010, p. 114) notes, they typically only have small to modest effects on net voter preferences in national elections. Even today, many voters have decided how to vote before the campaign begins (Figure 11.2). Neither are these findings especially surprising: elections are, in part, referendums on government performance and this record (though not its interpretation) is fixed by the start of the short campaign.

When a party's support does change during a campaign, it often just takes the form of returning a party's support to its natural share as underlying predispositions reassert themselves (Holbrook, 1996). To be sure, Hillygus's review of American elections (2010, p. 326) concludes that 'campaign efforts can have a significant impact on voters' turnout and candidate choice'. Even so, few would argue that such impact is routinely decisive. It is surely more accurate to agree with Butler (1989, p.

116) that 'the function of elections is to record the decisions of individuals rather than to create them'.

Two points are helpful in understanding why most campaigns only exert limited effects. The first is the difference between **gross** and **net** effects. Voters who change their preference from party X to Y may be cancelled out by those moving from Y to X, limiting net impact.

> **Gross** change refers to the proportion of electors changing their preference between two points in time. **Net** change denotes the overall change in levels of party support between two points in time. To some extent, gross change cancels out, reducing net change.

The second point is the short-run nature of many campaign effects. Some events – often including leader debates, for example – produce a temporary bounce in a party's support, a fillip which nonetheless decays before the election arrives. Events with effects continuing to election day are less common (Wlezien, 2010, p. 111). The import of campaigns is often overstated by journalists who assume or pretend (to puff up their story) that short-term bounces will translate into long-term consequences.

In seeking to separate campaign myths and realities, it is worth observing that switches between supporters of the major parties from one election to the next are often only a minor source of the change, gross or net, that does occur. Reflecting this reality, party strategies often focus more on mobilizing existing supporters and new voters rather than attempting to convert the supporters of other parties. Target groups typically include first-time electors, previous abstainers, previous defectors, supporters of minor parties, and, of course, the undecided. Collectively, such niche groups are significant but they still comprise a minority of the whole electorate. In other words, parties are well-aware of the limited malleability of the electorate, considered as a whole, over the duration of the short campaign.

Doubts about overall campaign effects suggest that we should also apply some scepticism to the impact of paid advertising, a form of campaign communication which is permitted in most liberal democracies (de Vreese, 2010). Certainly, advertising can provide valuable information about candidates and their positions, at least in subnational contests receiving little news coverage. Attack advertisements and those making emotional appeals appear to be particularly memorable (Corrigan and Brader, 2011). But, as with campaigns, so too with advertising: when resources are roughly equal, any effects tend to cancel out. Although the impact of advertising is difficult to measure, it is hard to find evidence that parties or candidates can advertise themselves to victory in high-stimulus national contests.

Still, let us not conclude that campaigns are full of sound and fury, signifying nothing. At a minimum, they provide a final examination which candidates and parties must pass if they wish to proceed to office: in that sense, campaigns always have the potential to be decisive. And in a close contest, the campaign, as any other influential factor, can be judged crucial.

Even when campaigns do not change the result, they provide a national political seminar, enlightening many voters about parties, candidates, and

policies. They also educate many politicians about the electorate – either through public opinion research, or direct encounters on the campaign trail (Schmitt-Beck and Farrell, 2002). These effects operate irrespective of the campaign's impact on levels of party support.

Above all, perhaps, election campaigns advance political debate within the elite. For a short period, politicians, journalists, and assorted experts engage in an intense, public and competitive scrutiny of the political agenda. Of course, parties seek to focus on the issues on which they possess a natural advantage but, in the cut and thrust of the dialogue, complete agenda control is rarely possible. In the course of this debate, political reputations are made and lost and, more importantly, policy proposals are floated, dissected, and often discarded. In public, parties may appear to talk past each other but, in private, every move is monitored and appropriate lessons drawn. At the end of the campaign, the debate about what government should do, and how it should do it, has often moved forward. Butler (1989, p. 116) again: 'often the utterances of the campaign educate the voters and the participants to new expectations about what politics should yield over the coming years.' Election campaigns are politics speeded up.

Messages and mandates

An election does not end when the results are declared. Far from it. After the declaration comes the construction of the message about the real meaning of the results. In the immediate aftermath, journalists and politicians establish a shared understanding which rapidly hardens to resist later change. In part, this interpretation shapes the election's impact on the politics that follows. A mandate for change? An instruction to end the war? A referendum on the economy? Support for 'steady as she goes'? When the results are in, the people have, indeed, spoken but they remain mute as their message is dissected.

Here, then, we can see the relevance of an interpretive approach to politics (Chapter 5). The election narrative can influence later politics, even if the party composition of the government remains unchanged.

Political scientists have given insufficient attention to how an election's meaning is constructed (but see

Kelley, 1983; Conley, 2001; Peterson *et al.*, 2003). Clearly, a transaction takes place between media and politicians: the journalists need a straightforward interpretation and the winners, in particular, are happy to supply one.

The primary focus is on the victor: everyone loves a winner, everyone forgets a loser. The larger and more unexpected the winner's margin, the greater the demand for a narrative giving positive reasons for the victor's triumph. Claiming that Party X won because of Party Y's unpopularity rarely fits the bill. One benign effect of this search for the winning party's merits is to add to its authority as it begins to govern.

Interpretations of election results centre on the distinctly opaque notion of a **mandate**. The winner claims a mandate from the people to do X, Y, and Z, and the media can often be persuaded to agree. However, rarely is adequate evidence available to support such assertions. Only individual voters, not the electorate as a whole, have reasons for their decisions. Even so, editorials can be found after every campaign explaining what the electorate intended by its collective judgement (even if, as in the occasional plurality election, the winner actually came second in votes). In any case, voters respond to multiple factors in reaching their verdicts: parties, leaders, policies, and records. Isolating a specific proposal, and claiming a mandate for it, is rarely justified. If we want to know whether the public favours a particular proposal, we should conduct a sample survey, not inspect election results.

> A **mandate** is a commission to act on another's behalf in a specific area. It implies more discretion than serving as a delegate, but less than working as a representative. An election mandate is an authorization from the people for the government to follow a particular course.

Mandate claims treat the voters as accomplices: proposal X was in our manifesto, you voted us in, therefore we have a mandate to implement X. Your approval of the proposal is shown by your failure to take your chance to reject us. The comparison is with a company which invokes a highly specific contractual obligation on the grounds that it was in the small print all along.

Ronald Reagan's victory in the American presidential election of 1980 is a classic illustration of these points. Reagan won only 51 per cent of the popular vote, securing the backing of barely one quarter of the electorate. And some of this support was motivated by a desire to unseat the incumbent president, Jimmy Carter. Yet, because Reagan dominated the Electoral College after a race many had judged too close to call, the result was interpreted as a landslide victory giving the president-elect a clear mandate to pursue the explicit conservatism he had espoused during the campaign.

For example, *Time* magazine declared a 'Landslide. Yes, landslide – stunning, startling, astounding, beyond the wildest dreams and nightmares of the contending camps.' Even though the proportion of electors considering themselves right of centre was no greater in 1980 than in 1976 or 1968, Lewis asserted in the *National Review* that 'What happened in the 1980 election reflected a profound and general turn to conservatism in the country' (quotes from Kelley, 1983, pp. 168, 183). The illogic was clear: Reagan was a conservative; Reagan won; therefore Reagan must have won because he was a conservative.

Inevitably, mandate claims followed, not least from vice-president-elect George H. W. Bush. He declared on election night that Reagan's victory was:

not simply a mandate for a change but a mandate for peace and freedom; a mandate for prosperity; a mandate for all Americans regardless of race, sex or creed; a mandate for leadership that is both strong and compassionate.'

As Kelley comments (1983, p. 217), 'this set of mandates, surely, is an odd mixture of the specific, the sweeping, the vacuous, and the far-fetched'. Most mandate claims are almost as dubious. Even so, they can be politically consequential and their consolidation in the weeks immediately after the result deserves more frequent study.

The referendum, initiative, and recall

Elections are instruments of representative democracy; the role of the people is only to decide who will decide. But devices such as the **referendum**, the **initiative**, and the **recall** have now been introduced to many liberal democracies, supplementing elections

BOX 11.3

The referendum, initiative and recall

Referendum	A vote of the electorate on an issue of public policy such as a constitutional amendment. The term is usually applied to ballots called by government or parliament.
Initiative	A procedure which allows a certain number of citizens either to initiate a popular vote on a given proposal (a referendum initiative) or to place it on the legislature's agenda (an agenda initiative).
Recall	A popular vote on whether an elected official should be removed from office during normal tenure.

Table 11.4 Western democracies holding most national referendums, 1940–2006

Most liberal democracies held at least one referendum in the final quarter of the twentieth century, with the heaviest use in Europe, especially Switzerland, Australia, and New Zealand

	Number of referendums
Switzerland	396
Italy	63
New Zealand	29
Ireland	28
Australia	27
Denmark	16
France	14
Sweden	5
Spain	4

Source: Adapted from Morel (2007), table 1.

(Box 11.3). Experience with these mechanisms allows us to judge the practical effectiveness of direct democratic forms in the setting of representative democracy.

Referendums

Referendums are the most important mechanism of direct democracy. The term implies a reference from another body – typically the government, or legislature – to the people. A referendum initiated by the people themselves is usually classed as an initiative.

Referendums may be mandatory (meaning that they must be called on specified topics, such as constitutional amendments), optional, or even constitutionally forbidden on a few reserved subjects such as taxation and public spending. Their outcome may be binding – as with constitutional amendments requiring popular approval, or merely consultative – as with Sweden's vote in 1994 on membership of the European Union.

Referendums are growing in frequency (Table 11.4). Switzerland heads the list, holding 396 referendums between 1940 and 2006 on a range of issues including nuclear power, same sex partnerships, and immigration. However, few other countries have made more than occasional use of the device.

The United States federal constitution makes no provision for national referendums at all; Germany's constitution bans them entirely at federal level.

What is the contribution of referendums to democracy and governance? How desirable is it to transform citizens into legislators? On the plus side, referendums do seem to increase voters' understanding of the issue, their confidence in their own political abilities, and their faith in government responsiveness (Bowler and Donovan, 2002). As with elections, referendums help with an important objective of any democracy: to educate the people.

Similarly, referendums can also inform the politicians. For instance, the rejection of the proposed European constitutional treaty by French and Dutch voters in 2005 taught the European Union elite that national electorates had grown weary of grand European projects. Referendums educate the rulers, as well as the ruled.

Referendums provide a safety valve, allowing governments, particularly coalitions, to put an issue to the people when it is incapable of reaching a decision itself. Like a plumber's drain-rods, referendums resolve blockages. In this way, they supplement representative democracy (Qvortrup, 2005).

But there are also reasons for caution. As with elections, a surfeit of referendums can tire the voters, depressing turnout. In addition, a referendum treats an issue in an isolated way, ignoring the implications for other areas. The parlous state of California's public finances, for example, owes something to the tendency of voters there to support not only referendums involving extra spending, but also those setting a cap on state taxes. There is no mechanism for ensuring consistency in referendum decisions; neither is it always clear for how long the results should be considered decisive.

Also, voters' judgements are often informed by wider considerations than the specific proposition on the ballot. 'The answer was "Non" but what was the question?' asked one analyst after the French rejection of the European treaty in 2005 (Ivaldi, 2006).

Optional referendums are ad hoc in character, with the government picking and choosing topics on which it feels a ballot would be to its political benefit. Specifically, the outcome can be influenced by government control of timing. In 2003, the European Union commenced a sequence of referendums in Eastern European states to establish whether their people wished to join the Union. It began the series in Hungary, judging that a positive result there would influence the outcome in other Eastern European states where public opinion was more doubtful. The tactic worked: all the accession countries holding referendums voted in favour.

More crudely, rulers can simply ignore the result of a referendum. In 1955, Swedes voted decisively to continue driving on the left; eight years later, the parliament passed a law introducing driving on the right. Alternatively, a referendum can be repeated until the desired outcome is obtained. Irish voters only ratified the Nice Treaty on the European Union in 2002, and the Lisbon Treaty in 2009, in each case at the second time of asking.

In addition to these difficulties, referendums can easily be hijacked by:

- wealthy companies waging expensive campaigns on issues in which they have an economic interest;

- government control over the precise wording of the question to be put to the voters;

- intense minorities seeking reforms to which the majority is indifferent.

Initiative

As its name suggests, the initiative allows the people to take the lead in calling for a referendum on, or requiring the legislature to discuss, a particular topic. By giving the power of initiative to the population, this device is more interesting for students of direct democracy than referendums sponsored by the government.

A *referendum initiative* allows a certain number of citizens to initiate a popular vote on a given proposal. In Switzerland, for example, 100,000 electors can propose a new law at canton level, or an amendment to the constitution at federal level. The government offers advice, usually to reject, before the ballot. Elsewhere, referendum initiatives can be employed more broadly, for ballots on proposed or existing policies.

The referendum initiative is a legal possibility in 37 countries, mostly in Europe or Latin America. It is commonly included in post-authoritarian constitutions in an attempt to prevent a return to dictatorship. The technique has also been adopted by many western states in the USA; notably, California.

Agenda initiatives are more closely integrated into existing representative institutions. They function as a petition to the legislature, requiring it to discuss a particular topic if the required number of electors' signatures is reached. One advantage of this technique is that it allows minorities to place their concerns on the table.

This mechanism was introduced to the constitutions of several European countries (e.g. Austria and Spain) after World War I and has been extended to a number of other states (e.g. Poland and Thailand) since 1989 (IDEA, 2008). Agenda initiatives are particularly well-established in Austria (Giese, 2012). In 2006, for example, over 250,000 signatories requested a national referendum in the event that Turkey be proposed for European Union membership by the EU, a demand accepted by Austria's Prime Minister. In Britain, a petition obtaining at least 100,000 signatures must now be considered by the House of Commons for debate, provided at least one member speaks in support of a debate.

COUNTRY PROFILE

UNITED STATES

LIBERAL DEMOCRACY

Form of government ■ a presidential republic comprising a federation of 50 states.

Legislature ■ the 435-member House of Representatives is the lower house. The 100-member Senate contains two directly-elected senators from each state.

Executive ■ the president (who can serve a maximum of two four-year terms) is supported by a massive apparatus, including the Executive Office of the President and the White House Office. However, the Cabinet is far less significant than in parliamentary systems.

Judiciary ■ a dual system of federal and state courts is headed by the Supreme Court, with the authority to nullify laws and actions running counter to the constitution. Many political issues are resolved through the courts.

Electoral system ■ the USA is one of the few large countries still employing the plurality method. Formally, the president is elected indirectly through an electoral college. Re-election rates in Congress are exceptionally high.

Party system ■ the Democratic and Republican parties show great resilience, despite periodic threats from third parties. The survival of the major parties reflects an entrenched position in law and the bias of plurality elections against minor parties.

Population (annual growth rate): 313.8 m (+0.9%)	
World Bank income group: high income	
Human development index (rank/out of): 4/187	
Political rights score:	
Civil liberties score: ①	
Media status: free	

Note: For interpretation and sources, see p. xvi.

With the end of the Cold War, the **UNITED STATES** became the world's one remaining superpower. This unique status was based partly on the country's hard power: a large population, the ability to project military force anywhere, growing awareness of enormous energy reserves ('Saudi America'), and a dynamic market economy. But America's soft power is also significant. Its leading position in the media, medical, technology, and telecommunications sectors is underpinned by a strong base in science and university education. Its culture, brand names, and language carry universal appeal.

Yet, hardly had commentators begun to refer to the emergence of an American 'empire' than the global reputation of the United States began to decay:

■ The invasion of Iraq in 2003 was widely condemned;

■ Images of the initial reaction to Hurricane Katrina in 2005 reminded the world of poverty within the country;

■ The country's failure to lead on environmental issues was judged a dereliction of its global duty;

■ A fragmented political system seemed incapable of solving high levels of government debt;

■ Ageing infrastructure, massive health care costs, an obesity epidemic, and growing economic inequality amid static incomes for the middle class all contributed to a sense of a country failing to grapple with its difficulties;

■ The emergence of China threatened American hegemony.

Domestically, the world's No. 1 country operates a political system intended to frustrate decisive policy-making. By constitutional design, power is divided between federal and state governments. The centre is itself fragmented between the executive, the legislature, and the judiciary. American politics is extraordinarily pluralistic; reforms are more easily blocked by interest groups than carried through by the executive.

Although President Obama did eventually succeed in passing a substantial health care reform package, all presidents finds their plans obstructed at some stage by a legislature which is the most powerful, and among the most decentralized, in the world. Typically, Washington politics is a ceaseless quest for that small amount of common ground on which all interests can agree. Compromise is especially elusive when, as in the twenty-first century, ideological differences between the two dominant parties are sharp and explicit.

Elections in the United States

The United States is unique in its massive range of elected offices. At federal level, Americans can vote for the president and vice-president, two senators per state, and their member of the House of Representatives. An even greater range of positions is subject to election at state and local level. These posts include auditors, judges, members of school boards, sheriffs, treasurers and, in North Dakota, the soil conservation supervisor. So, why does the USA possess so many elected offices? And how successful has its national experiment with selection through election proved to be?

The exceptional array of elected posts in the USA reflects not only the practical requirements of governing a large, frontier society, but also a culture that emphasizes equality, competence, and a belief that administration is a practical matter. The task of those elected was, and is, to get the job done.

America played a pioneering role in extending the franchise for white men. As early as 1830, property qualifications for voting had been withdrawn and almost all states selected members of the Electoral College by direct popular ballot. In addition, traditions of direct democracy live on. Images of town meetings in New England are etched into the political culture, while most western states continue to employ some direct democratic devices such as the referendum, initiative, and recall. Further, the distinctly American institution of primary elections opens up the selection of a party's candidates to a remarkably wide proportion of the population.

Yet, American experience with elections is far from an unconditional celebration of democracy. Southern blacks were effectively denied the vote until the Voting Rights Act of 1965. Felons and ex-felons are unable to vote in many states. The log cabin to White House ideal is widely accepted, but money is increasingly necessary – though insufficient – for electoral success. In many elections, advertising by interest groups overwhelms candidates' voices. The many confusions of the 2000 presidential election hardly contributed to the authority with which the eventual winner entered the White House. This election also drew attention once more to the fact that, under the cumbersome Electoral College procedure, American presidents are still not elected by a direct national ballot.

By contrast, the 2008 presidential election demonstrated the authority which can flow from a successful campaign. Barack Obama gained a convincing 68 per cent of the votes in the Electoral College, despite winning just 53 per cent of the popular vote. Obama's ethnicity, together with the expense and technological sophistication of his campaign, stimulated interest in and beyond the United States.

In a relatively close contest between two non-incumbents, turnout reached 62 per cent of eligible voters, high by recent American standards. The success of the 2008 election gave the youthful president considerable governing authority, though high expectations were soon frustrated by a political system riddled with veto points. Nonetheless, a slowly improving economy and another sophisticated campaign allowed Obama to secure re-election in 2012, albeit on a reduced turnout.

Further reading: Lewis-Beck *et al.* (2008), McKay (2009), Schmidt *et al.* (2012)

Figure 11.3 Turnout at American presidential elections, 1948–2012

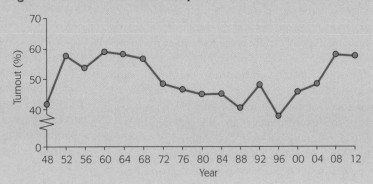

Note: Base is population of voting age.

Sources: 1948–2008: Adapted from McKay (2009), table 6.2. 2012 (estimated): Bipartisan Policy Center (2012).

Recall

The recall, finally, is a ballot on whether an elected official should be removed from office during normal tenure. A vote is initiated by a petition signed by a minimum proportion (typically, around 25 per cent) of the votes cast for that office at the previous election (so, the recall is a form of popular initiative). Unlike impeachment, the recall is a political rather than legal device, a modern equivalent of the old device of denunciation (Rosanvallon, 2008, p. 207). Where first election is a vote of confidence, the recall is a vote of no confidence. It seeks to improve governance by removing incompetent and corrupt incumbents before their normal term is up.

At national level, one of the few countries to employ the recall is Venezuela. There, a recall vote can be held on any elected official, including the president, on the initiative of 20 per cent of the relevant electorate. Some 15 American states also make provision for recall elections for all state officials; more allow the recall of local officials. However, the device has rarely been used – though Arnold Schwarzenegger did become governor of California following the successful recall of the incumbent in 2003.

It is worth noting that electronic communication eases the task of generating the required number of signatures for an initiative or recall. Here, perhaps, is one of the few examples of the Internet delivering on its democratic potential as imagined in its early days (McLean, 1989). Of course, the integrity of the sign-up process needs to be maintained for e-petitions, as much as for petitions.

Elections in authoritarian states

Most non-democratic rulers recognize that elections can be a useful political device. Internationally, they please donors who are often happy enough if it is only the facade that is democratic. Domestically, they create friends for the ruling elite by establishing a pool of successful candidates who can be given access to resources to distribute to their own supporters in their home districts (Blaydes, 2011). But the outcome is usually predetermined. We begin this section by looking at elections in communist states before turning to their functions in other authoritarian regimes.

Elections in communist states made little pretence of offering choice. There was no possibility that the ruling party could be defeated, or even opposed, through elections. In the Soviet Union, for instance, the official candidate was simply presented to the electorate for ritual endorsement. The voting act itself discouraged dissent; in Mao's China, voting was in public.

Some communist states in Eastern Europe eventually introduced a measure of choice to their elections by allowing a choice of candidates from within the ruling party. Central rulers found these candidate-choice elections useful in testing whether local party officials retained the confidence of their communities.

This local monitoring is one reason for the gradual introduction of such elections to many of China's one million or so villages since 1987 and, more recently and tentatively, to some townships. The aim of these elected committees is to limit corruption in the villages and to reduce what are often violent conflicts between leaders and peasants.

However, even in contemporary China no explicit opposition to the party's policy platform is permitted. In many villages, real authority still resides with the local party official, who may also serve as chair of the village committee. In fact, a revision to the election law in 1997 explicitly affirmed the party's supervisory role.

Neither in the countryside nor in the towns are there many signs of elections threatening the party's control. The remarkable free election in Wukan village in 2012, agreed by the party after extensive local protests against corrupt land sales, is an exception. In general, tight limits on what elections can achieve dashed expectations raised by the original reform, thereby increasing popular frustration. In that respect, manipulated elections are worse than no elections at all.

Elections in non-communist authoritarian regimes exhibit a different character. Here, competition is usually constrained, rather than eliminated. Some opposition victories may be permitted, but too few to affect the overall result. Independent candidates find themselves operating in a threatening environment. The secret police follow them around, breaking up some of their meetings. Using arbitrary registration rules, independent politicians may be banned from standing. Control over the media, the electoral system, and the government is exploited to favour the ruling party. Through its conduct of campaigns, the regime projects both the illusion of choice (not least for outsiders) and the reality of power (for the domestic population). It usually secures its victory without needing to falsify the count – though this option remains, if all else fails.

Until the Arab uprisings, Egypt provided an example of such manipulated elections. From 1976, numerous parties competed for seats in the People's Assembly, offering the appearance of a vigorous multiparty system. But President Hosni Mubarak's party retained its dominant position throughout. These 'contests' contributed to public cynicism and, eventually, to the regime's overthrow.

In competitive authoritarian regimes, elections play a more important part in confirming the authority of the ruler; indeed, they are central to its democratic pretensions. The election outcome is more than just a routine acceptance by the people of the realities of power. Explicit vote-rigging is avoided, some candidates from non-governing parties gain election, and the possibility of a low turnout, and even defeat, cannot be entirely dismissed.

But elections do not operate on as free and fair a playing field as in a liberal democracy. In particular, the leading figure dominates media coverage, using television to trumpet his often real achievements in office. In contrast to authoritarian regimes, the emphasis is as much on the carrot (providing reasons for voting for the dominant figure) as on the stick (threatening opposition supporters).

Incumbents in hybrid regimes can exploit unique resources. They are well-known to voters, draw on the state's coffers for their campaign, implement a favourable electoral system, lead extensive patronage networks, give hand-outs to their election districts, and call in political credits carefully acquired while in office. Anticipating the president's re-election, underlings currying favour will seek to help the campaign. Credible opponents will be deterred from embarking on a hopeless fight: why annoy the candidate who is sure to win? Bratton (1998, p. 65) summarizes the position in many African countries: 'in a "big man" political culture, it is unclear whether

the re-election of an incumbent constitutes the extension of a leader's legitimacy or the resignation of the electorate to his inevitable dominance'.

In Russia's competitive authoritarian regime, President Vladimir Putin proved to be a skilled exponent of election management in a hybrid regime. Indeed, Russians employ a special term for these dark arts: political technology. McFaul (2005) describes how Putin moved early to neutralize potential threats in the media, the regions, and business. In each sector, a few opponents were removed from office, yielding the desired servility among the remainder. McFaul's summary of the Russian president's electoral strategy could be applied to many other competitive authoritarian regimes:

The effect of these reforms occurred well before the votes were actually cast. The absence of independence within media, regional elite and oligarchic ranks reduced the freedom of manoeuvre for opposition political parties and candidates. At the same time, the state's larger role gave incumbents enormous advantages, be it national television coverage, massive administrative support from regional executives or enormous financial resources from companies like Gazprom. (McFaul, 2005, p. 77)

Such techniques presuppose weaknesses in the rule of law, the market economy, and civil society in general. These deficits are not easy to measure, making the task of effective election monitoring extremely difficult. If the political technologists have done their job, the election is over by election day.

But by 2012, when Putin secured his return to the Kremlin after a term out, such deficits had become more visible. In the context of an increasingly sophisticated urban citizenry, and a decline in Putin's own popularity and aura of invincibility, blatant manipulation of the count attracted considerable protest. The result stood but the climate changed. Even in Russia's hybrid regime, the presidential election (as with parliamentary elections the previous year) had sent a message. So elections in hybrid or even fully authoritarian settings always possess the potential to serve as catalysts of change when the existing regime is already weakened.

Discussion questions

- Which, if any, of these groups should be entitled to vote in national elections: (a) non-citizen residents, (b) prisoners, (c) 16–17-years-olds?

- What is the best electoral system for choosing (a) a parliament, and (b) a president?

- What functions do election campaigns perform?

- Did the last general election in your country deliver a mandate? If so, to whom and to do what?

- What role, if any, should referendums play in a liberal democracy?

- Why do authoritarian regimes hold elections?

Further reading

D. Farrell, *Electoral Systems: A Comparative Introduction*, 2nd edn (2011). This text provides a helpful and accessible guide to electoral systems.

M. Gallagher and P. Mitchell, eds, *The Politics of Electoral Systems* (2005). Through four general chapters and 22 country essays, this volume seeks to apply themes in the study of electoral systems to particular liberal democracies.

L. LeDuc, R. Niemi and P. Norris, eds, *Comparing Democracies 3: New Challenges in the Study of Elections and Voting* (2010). This comparative review of elections and voting includes chapters on electoral systems, parties, campaigns, the media, participation, the economy, and women in elections.

S. Medvic, ed., *New Directions in Campaigns and Elections* (2011). Surveys the changing character of elections in the USA, including financing, polling, mobilization, parties, media, voting, and election administration.

B. Geissel and K. Newton, eds, *Evaluating Democratic Innovations: Curing the Democratic Malaise* (2012). This comparative volume analyzes and evaluates devices of direct and deliberative democracy.

ONLINE RESOURCES AVAILABLE

Visit the companion website at **www.palgrave.com/politics/hague** to access additional learning resources, including multiple-choice questions, chapter summaries, web links and practice essay questions.

Chapter 12 **Voters**

Given that voters have a choice, how do they decide for which party to vote? Although this is the most intensively studied question in all political science, there is no single answer. Still, extensive research has established a set of broad themes which are of undoubted value in providing a context for examining voting behaviour in any particular liberal democracy.

These academic studies are focused on broader questions than the often small shifts in party support between elections, which are the natural concern of journalistic commentary. The academic approach seeks to understand electoral stability, as well as change, and focuses rather more on how voters decide than on election results, as such.

It is useful to distinguish between long-term and short-term forces shaping electoral choice. We begin this chapter with the long-term forces: specifically, party identification as supported by its social base. As we will also show, these pillars of electoral stability are weakening, allowing more room for shorter-term influences to affect voting choices. We will address three of these more short-term factors: political issues, the economy and leaders' personalities.

We will also examine two further topics. The first is rational choice analysis of voters and parties, a topic which gives us a case study of one of the broad theoretical approaches we introduced in Chapter 5. And, in the final section, we will discuss the more specific question of turnout, a topic which crosses over to the field of political participation (Chapter 8).

Party identification

The starting point for any discussion of voting in liberal democracies is *The American Voter* (Campbell *et al.*, 1960). This book established a way of studying voters, and a way of thinking about how voters decide, which remains influential not just in the United States but also in other liberal democracies. The method employed by Campbell *et al.* was to obtain national sample surveys of individual voters and their focus was the attitudes expressed in these polls. The task is judged to be one of objective investigation into subjective states – the behavioural approach at work. Other traditions, notably those placing the individual voter in the social and spatial context provided by family, friends, neighbours, workmates, electoral district, and regions lost ground.

At the centre of many voters' political minds lies **party identification** – a commitment to a particular party which not only solves the problem of knowing which party to vote for but also provides electors with a lens for interpreting the remote world of politics. As with many other identities, a primitive party allegiance emerges in childhood and early adolescence,

STUDYING . . .

VOTERS

- Voting is most often studied through national sample surveys. Such an approach emphasizes the individual's attitudes but perhaps understates the immediate social environment within which these attitudes are at least partly formed. Party identification is the core concept in the leading approach to understanding voters (the social psychological or attitudinal approach). However, it is important to address doubts about the applicability of party identification beyond American borders.

- Partisan dealignment is clearly an important and widespread trend. But, as with other political trends, always aim to bracket any discussion with dates: when did it start and, in the USA and perhaps elsewhere, end?

- The social bases of voting have weakened since the 1960s, and continue to do so, but we should avoid over-generalization. Class, yes; but religion? Employment sector (public/private)?

- The performance of the economy is an important factor in explaining electoral change. Here, much research seeks to correlate economic fluctuations with movements in government popularity. The statistical techniques may be complex but the findings are accessible and significant in most countries.

- A wider issue, with implications for how we assess liberal democracy, concerns the quality of the choices made by voters and – a distinct issue – the electorate as a whole. Here, early conclusions about voters' limitations have been modified as a result of an increase in issue voting. Furthermore, the electorate is sometimes portrayed as more effective than the voters who comprise it.

- The rational choice approach offers a radically different way of looking at voters and parties. It raises intriguing theoretical puzzles, such as the apparent irrationality of turning out to vote.

- The decline in turnout has clearly been important but this trend, too, may now be ending. In any event, political science has generated clear findings about the features of both the individual elector and the electoral system that encourage turnout. In contrast to some other topics in voting studies, turnout does raise a policy issue: what is to be done?

influenced by parents and peer groups, and then deepens as a person moves through adulthood, reinforced by the predominant allegiance of social groups to which that person belongs. In a circle that substantially immunizes older voters against vote-switching, the more often electors vote for the party with which they identify, the stronger their allegiance becomes.

Party identification is a long-term attachment to a particular party which provides a filter for understanding political events. Party identification predicts electoral choice but voters often retain an allegiance to their party, even if they fail to support it in a particular contest.

This cueing effect of party identification helps to distinguish it from other models of voting, particularly those that see electors voting instrumentally for the party that comes closest to their own policy preferences. Party identification is the engine of the voter's political belief system, driving attitudes to leaders and policies. So, the best leaders must be those that lead one's own party and the best policies must be those that one's own party supports.

In the USA, party identification is measured by the question, 'Generally speaking, do you think of yourself as a Republican, a Democrat, an Independent, or what?' Those who express a party preference are asked, 'Would you call yourself a strong Republican/Democrat or a not very strong Republican/Democrat?' Independents are asked 'Do you think of yourself as closer to the Republican or Democratic Party?' The result is a seven-point scale covering strong and weak identifiers for each party, those who lean to each party and independents. In 2004, to take a typical result, 33 per cent of Americans were strong identifiers, 28 per cent were weak identifiers, 29 per cent were leaners and 10 per cent were independents.

So, strong allegiants are only in a minority. We need not imagine that all Americans identify with a party with the same intensity that sports fans claim to apply to their particular team. Rather, we can interpret party identification as consisting, for many, in an underlying disposition to support a particular party. Just as regularly buying Toyota cars pragmatically short-circuits the need to make a full-scale assessment of automobile engineering with every purchase, so voting for a given party becomes a standing commitment which precludes the need to look under the political bonnet at each election. For many, voting for a given party is simply a pragmatic, long-term brand choice. Occasionally, special circumstances might lead the Toyota buyer to choose a Ford, and a Democrat to vote Republican, but the homing tendency will do its job and normality will be restored next time.

It is important to note that distinctive features of American politics provide fertile ground for party identification. These are: an entrenched two-party system, the requirement to register as a supporter of a party to participate in closed primaries, and the ability to vote a party ticket for the exceptionally large number of offices subject to election. In a comparative setting, these characteristics are wholly exceptional.

So, it is perhaps unsurprising that the notion of party identification is not the best traveller. In at least some countries in Western Europe, party identification does not seem to be much more stable than electoral choice, diminishing the concept's utility (Franklin and Webber, 2010, p. 673). Historically, European voters' identities were bound up with class and religion, and the labour unions and churches which expressed these affiliations. Parties formed part of such networks, rather than free-standing entities. In addition, the concepts of left and right provide alternative reference points, notably in countries such as France and Italy where

parties are, or have become, weak. Also, there are few signs of strong party loyalties emerging in the more fluid party systems found in the newer democracies of Eastern Europe and beyond.

Still, the political market – as with most others – retains considerable stability in most liberal democracies. Very broadly, a party's share at a previous election is usually a good predictor of its support at a current election. And at the individual level, too, stability of electoral choice remains substantial. Before we can explain electoral change, we must understand this continuity. Party identification, the habit of voting for the same party, ideological labels, and group loyalties all fit the bill, even if the balance between them varies across countries and, as we will now see, over time.

Partisan dealignment

The measurement of party identification over time allows us to track trends in its prevalence and strength. And, here, **partisan dealignment** is a clear and widespread trend. The ties which once bound voters and parties have loosened but not disappeared. In the United States, where measurement of party identification began, this trend was concentrated on the 1960s and 1970s. But dealignment is clearly a much wider phenomenon:

Among the nineteen advanced industrial democracies for which we have long-term survey data, seventeen show a drop in the percentage of partisans. Furthermore, the *strength* of partisanship has decreased in all nineteen nations. In countries as diverse as Austria, Canada, Japan, New Zealand, and Sweden, the pattern is the same: the partisan attachments of the public weakened during the latter half of the twentieth century (Dalton, 2008a, p. 183).

Britain is a striking case of declining intensity of partisanship. Between 1964–6 and 2010, the proportion of British electors identifying with a party fell from 90 to 82 per cent – a decline but a modest one. But over the same period, the proportion of respondents with a 'very strong' allegiance collapsed from 40 to 11 per cent. Denver *et al.* (2012, p. 71) remark that strong Conservative and Labour identifiers are 'now something of an endangered species'.

Partisan dealignment refers to the weakening bonds between electors and parties. It can take the form of a fall in the proportion of voters identifying with any party or, more often, a decline in the strength of allegiance among those retaining a party loyalty.

What caused dealignment? Although commentators within a country often concentrate on national factors, the prevalence of the trend points firmly to common causes. Box 12.1 suggests the political and sociological factors at work.

Politically, the role of parties changed dramatically in the final third of the twentieth century (see Chapter 10). Their funding increasingly came from the state, rather than their own members. Election campaigning now operates through the media (the air war) as well as, or in place of, local parties (the ground war). Members drifted away to the warmer waters of single-issue groups. Major parties became increasingly indistinct in their programmes and their social base. Now viewed as part of the system, rather than as expressions of social interests, parties in many countries faced the same loss of trust as other state institutions. Partisan dealignment is surely a part of these broader trends.

Sociologically, the weakening of historic social divisions and the expansion of education contributed to a thinning of political identities. Dalton (2008a, pp. 187–9) suggests that what he calls 'cognitive mobilization' is an increasingly common way in which citizens connect themselves to politics. By this, he means that educated and politically-interested electors can orient themselves to politics on their own, using the media for information and their own understanding to interpret it. Political vision has improved and the spectacles of party identification are no longer required.

It is possible, of course, that the political factors behind dealignment will cease to operate, or even go into reverse. Indeed, they already have done so in the USA. At elite level, the Democratic and Republican parties have rediscovered their taste for ideological conflict, leading to some recovery in partisanship among the electorate. At mass level, too, the parties have become more cohesive, as white conservatives previously incorporated into the Democratic New Deal coalition moved to their natural Republican home (Abramowitz,

BOX 12.1

Factors contributing to partisan dealignment

Disillusionment with party politics	Events such as Watergate, and more recent publicity about corruption, reduce popular trust in parties
Convergence of party policies	If policies diverge again, party loyalties may also recover
Decay of social divisions	As the class cleavage weakens, so too do loyalties to parties based on it
Rising education	Educated voters can interpret events with less need for party cues
Television becomes the dominant medium	Supplants the more partisan coverage in many newspapers

2010). As a result of these trends, ideology, partisanship, and vote have come into closer alignment, enabling many commentators to locate partisan weakening in the United States within a specific period:

Partisan dealignment is a historic episode, however traumatic, essentially a closed chapter of American electoral history, bracketed by the elections of 1964 and 1976 ... There are strong signs that the process of dealignment was halted and even reversed after 1976, with the electorate growing more polarized along party lines (Lewis-Beck *et al.*, 2008, p. 157).

Will partisan recovery follow elsewhere? Possibly, for no trend continues forever, and we are entitled to be suspicious of explanations that presume they will. Still, the forces at work in the United States, including the decay of the New Deal coalition, do seem to be specific to that country.

Politically, the consequences of dealignment are more important than their causes. The impact has been substantial:

- new parties such as the Greens and the far right gained ground;

- turnout and active participation in campaigns fell;

- electoral volatility increased;

- **split-ticket voting** increased;

- more electors decided how to vote closer to election day;

- issue voting increased.

> **Split-ticket voting** occurs when electors vote for candidates from more than one party in an election covering several offices. In the United States, ticket splitting in voting for president and members of the House of Representatives increased markedly between the 1950s and the 1980s (Lewis-Beck *et al.*, 2008, p. 157).

The social base

'A cross on the ballot is an implicit statement of social identity' (Harrop and Miller, 1987, p. 173). Party activists campaigning in a neighbourhood can usually sense from its sociological character whether it will be for or against them even before they start knocking on doors. Yet, electoral research is no longer as concerned with the sociological foundations of voting preferences as it was in the age of alignment.

This shift in focus is understandable but, in some ways, undesirable. For instance, understanding the origins of party identification must surely take us back to the critical junctures when links between social groups and parties were established. So, let us restore the balance somewhat. In this section, we focus on the changing electoral impact of the two most important components of the social base: class and religion.

Social class

Since the industrial revolution, social class has exerted some influence on electoral choice in all liberal democracies. Often, however, it was not the most powerful force. Of few countries could it be

said, as Pulzer said of Britain in the 1960s, that 'Class is the basis of British party politics; all else is embellishment and detail' (1967, p. 98). But, everywhere, there was the same tendency – the working class was prone to support parties of the left; the middle-class, parties of the right.

In analysing class voting, the early comparative research drew a simple but convenient distinction between manual (blue-collar) and non-manual (white-collar) workers. The extent of class voting was measured by the **Alford Index**. Scores on this scale show the percentage difference between the working class and the middle class in their support for parties of the left. There is no question that on this measure class voting has declined substantially across the democratic world since the 1960s. In Britain, for instance, the index plunged from 43 in 1966 to 17 in 2010 (Denver *et al.*, 2012, p. 67). In some countries, including the USA, scores are in single digits.

> The **Alford Index** of class voting assumes two classes and divides parties into those on the left and those on the right. The measure is calculated by taking the percentage of the working class voting for left parties and subtracting the percentage of the middle class voting left. So, if all working-class but no middle-class voters vote left, the index reaches its maximum of 100. But if the middle class is as likely to vote left as the working class, the index returns its minimum value of 0.
>
> Example: In Britain in 2010, 44 per cent of the working class and 27 per cent of the middle class voted Labour. The Alford index is (44 − 27) = 17. In 1964, the index was (64 − 22) = 42.

But some scholars, including a redoubtable group of British sociologists, resisted the thesis of a declining class alignment (Goldthorpe, 1999). They introduced a more sophisticated measurement of classes, known as the Goldthorpe scheme (Box 12.2). In this system, the self-employed are separated from employees, as Marx would have wished; and managers, administrators, and professionals are characterized as the salariat or service class.

Within the service class, we can distinguish further between professionals (such as doctors and teachers) and employees in direct managerial positions. Professionals whose authority rests on specialized knowledge and qualifications are generally less conservative than the managerial group.

BOX 12.2

The Goldthorpe class scheme

Class	Definition
Salariat (service class)	Managers, administrators, professionals, supervisors of non-manuals
Routine non-manual	Rank-and-file white-collar employees
Petty bourgeoisie	Own-account workers, small proprietors, farmers
Foremen and technicians	Supervisors or technicians; or those with discretion at work
Working-class	Skilled, semi-skilled and unskilled manual workers

Naturally, this more elaborate and convincing class scheme delivers a higher measured level of class voting. But the trend remains intact and largely unreduced. Using the new scheme, Knutsen (2006) found a decline of about half in class voting in eight Western European countries between the mid-1970s and the late 1990s, with the largest falls in Denmark, the Netherlands, and Britain. In general, class voting declined the most where it was previously highest (notably, in the Nordic countries), producing some convergence across democracies on a new, lower level.

So, the fall in class voting is consistent and substantial. What accounts for it? We can distinguish – if not wholly separate – political and sociological factors. At a political level, the collapse of socialism initiated a march to the centre by many left-wing parties. In their new location, they played down traditional class themes; Old Labour became New Labour. This diminished class rhetoric is likely to dampen class voting (Evans and de Graaf, 2012). Thus, Knutsen (2006) finds in a comparative analysis that 'the political strategies of the major leftist parties showed a consistent pattern where a decisive move towards the centre was accompanied by a decline in class voting'.

But familiar sociological processes are also at work. As the service sector replaces manufacturing within the economies of liberal democracies, so large unionized factories disappear to be replaced by smaller service companies offering more diverse work to qualified staff. These skilled employees derive their power in the labour market from their individual qualifications, experience, and ability; unlike manual employees performing similar tasks, they are not drawn to labour unions promoting collective solidarity. In this way, the foundations on which class parties were based began to erode. And, indeed, comparative evidence suggests that the smaller the size of the working class in a country, and the lower the proportion of its workforce employed in industry, the greater the decline in class voting (Knutsen, 2006).

Growing income inequality in some liberal democracies, notably the United States and Britain, may represent an off-setting trend. Resentment against what were seen as excessive earnings by the best-paid workers in the financial sector fuelled considerable popular resentment in the wake of the financial crisis of 2008–09 (Hacker and Pierson, 2010). In the USA, Barack Obama's hostility to the fat cats of a winner-take-all economy certainly did no harm to his presidential campaigns in 2008 and 2012. Still, even in America individual income is not a dominant influence on how people vote. In any case, this theme of resentment against the highest earners lacked the same resonance in other liberal democracies, such as the Nordic countries, where inequality remained less pronounced.

Class interests are not the only interests derived from the workplace. Employment in the public sector gives employees a direct interest in sustaining an expansive government. For instance, accountants working in government departments may well be more inclined to support non-conservative parties than their colleagues working in the private sector. This difference has not necessarily increased but its political importance grew as public sector employment expanded in the decades following World War II.

Knutsen (2007, p. 464) reports: 'In Scandinavia, sector of employment has a large impact on voting, and the division within the service class in particular is substantial. The service class in the public sector is more likely to support left-wing parties than the service class in the private sector.' In an era of much diminished class voting, the public sector offers a foothold not only for traditional left-wing parties, but also for new formations such as the Greens.

Religion

'Want to know how Americans will vote next Election Day? Watch what they do the weekend before … If they attend religious services regularly, they probably will vote Republican by a 2–1 margin. If they never go, they likely will vote Democratic by a 2–1 margin' (newspaper story, 2003, quoted in Green, 2010b, p. 433). Leaving the exact figures to one side, what became known in the USA as the 'God Gap' illustrates the continuing relevance of religion (as indicated here by church attendance) to voting behaviour. The example is from America but religion's electoral influence remains widespread in liberal democracies, offering a contrast to the fall in class voting.

Religion is not a single variable. Rather, it can be studied from three main angles. First, we can distinguish between religious and secular voters, putting all denominations into the religious category. In general, broad religious values encourage voters to the right, while secular voters incline to the left.

Second, within the religious category we can separate voters by religiosity (the importance of religion to the individual). Religiosity can be measured directly by questions in sample surveys, or indirectly through church attendance. Typically, it is the distinction between the religiously committed and the rest which produces the largest contrasts in voting choice and also in electoral participation (with churchgoers more likely to turn out).

Third, we can examine the impact of specific denominations, noting for example how Jewish voters are inclined to the left. Such studies can be extended to examine the electoral impact of other religions and denominations, including Islam and evangelical movements.

Comparative research has long recognized the electoral importance of religion, broadly interpreted. Rose and Urwin (1969, p. 12) concluded from a study of 16 Western democracies that 'religious divisions, not class, are the main social bases of parties in the Western world today'. Examining voters rather than parties, Lijphart (1979) judged from a study of countries where both class and religion play a political role that 'religion tends to have a larger influence on party choice'. Head to head, religion matters more than class.

So, in a sense, class mattered only when religion did not. Thus, traditionally high levels of class voting in Scandinavia can be seen as reflecting the absence of religious conflict there once national Lutheran churches were established in the Reformation.

Just as industrial change has contributed to the decline of class voting, so **secularization** might be expected to lead to a fall in religious voting. Norris and Inglehart (2011) maintain that religious belief is a response to human insecurity. As societies modernize, so they naturally become more secular. And, certainly, church attendance and religious belief continues to decline in many liberal democracies, not least in Europe (and perhaps now among young Americans) (Esmer and Pettersson, 2007, table 25.2).

> **Secularization** refers to the declining space occupied by religion in political, social, and personal life. Whether the process continues is matter of debate (Norris and Inglehart, 2011).

Yet, even if this broad thesis of a secular transition is correct, it is difficult to find evidence that religious voting has declined to the same extent as class voting. Some reduction is apparent but, overall, the religious base of electoral behaviour demonstrates considerable staying power. For instance, Esmer and Petterson (2007, p. 409) find that 'religiosity still significantly shapes electoral choice in most European countries' – noting, in particular, that 'the devout and the pious are more likely to vote for the political right and the Christian Democrats'. The exceptions are all in Northern Europe: Denmark, Estonia, Norway, Sweden, and the United Kingdom.

To the extent that moral issues such as abortion and gay marriage retain their salience, the conflicting values of religious- and secular-minded voters might even increase in electoral importance. At the very least, God has outlasted Marx and continues to provide some support for the partisan alignment of most liberal democracies.

The rational voter

The social psychological account with which we began this chapter is not the only approach to understanding voters. A contrasting perspective, drawing on the rational choice approach we reviewed in Chapter 5, is to assume that voters are rational participants in the political market. As with other consumers, they seek to maximize their utility. Within this framework, electors' mental states are of no particular significance. Rather, the task is to deduce how voters (and parties) will behave, given the assumption of rationality, and to compare these predictions with what happens. We have here a distinct approach which stands apart from the predominantly behavioural tone of this chapter. Still, rational choice has become part of the vocabulary within electoral studies and certainly merits a visit.

Within this framework, the most influential study by far is Downs's *An Economic Theory of Democracy* (1957). Because this book has influenced political science generally, its intellectual significance exceeds that of *The American Voter*. Downs is concerned not merely with voters, but also with parties – and even more with the relationship between the two. In that sense, his analysis is more dynamic than that of the social psychological approach.

Downs defines a party as 'a team of people seeking to control the governing apparatus by gaining votes in a duly constituted election'. We are asked to imagine that parties act as if they are motivated by power alone. Voters, too, are assumed to want only a government which reflects their self-interest, as represented in their policy preferences. Downs's question is: Given these assumptions, what policies should parties adopt to maximize their vote?

Downs assumes that voters' policy preferences can be shown on a simple left–right scale. He treats the left end as representing full government control of the economy; the right end, a completely free market. In his best-known scenario, Downs further imagines that public opinion forms a symmetrical, bell-shaped distribution around the midpoint (Figure 12.1). Again, this assumption is simple but plausible: except in polarized societies, more people are probably found at the centre than anywhere else.

The crucial result, now grandly known as the **median voter theorem**, is that vote-maximizing parties in a two-party system will converge at the midpoint of the state. So, the position of the **median voter** is the critical one in a Downsian democracy. The reasoning is straightforward. A party may start at one extreme but it will move towards the centre because there are more votes to be won there than

are likely to be lost to abstention at the extreme. In driving to the centre, the party remains closer to voters at its own extreme, thus retaining their support. But it also attracts middle-of-the-road voters who were previously closer to the competitor. Once parties have converged at the position of the median voter, they reach a position of **equilibrium** and have no incentive to change their position.

> The **median voter** has an equal number of voters on either side when voters are positioned on a dimension such as left and right. When this dimension is the sole cleavage, the **median voter theorem** states that parties will converge on the position represented by the median voter. So, under these assumptions, elections will deliver the policy supported by the median voter.

Our concern here, though, is with voters, rather than parties. What should we make of Downs's assumption that electors behave rationally by voting for the party closest to their policy preferences on a single left–right scale? To say that this approach is simplistic misses the point; as we noted in Chapter 5, parsimony is the name of this particular game. Even so, Downs's view of the voter does encounter substantial difficulties. We discuss three objections (Ansolabehere, 2006).

> **Equilibrium** is a position of balance. A political equilibrium exists when no significant actors feel they would gain appreciably from changing the current position. For example, an electoral system is in equilibrium if no significant party prefers any alternative.

First, why would Downs's self-interested voters turn out to vote at all, given the vanishingly small possibility of a single ballot determining the outcome? On any plausible calculation, the cost of voting exceeds the likely benefit (which is the voter's utility of government by a given party discounted by the possibility of his or her vote deciding whether that party governs). So, the very notion of a rational voter seems to dissolve in its own contradiction; we can only find rational abstainers and irrational voters.

The only solution to this problem appears to be to allow electors to value the act of voting positively, rather than negatively. And this move is eminently plausible. Many people do want to perform their

Figure 12.1 Parties converge at the centre

Downs's model locates electors on a single left–right dimension, with a bell-shaped distribution. In these circumstances, vote-maximizing parties will 'converge rapidly at the center' (Downs, 1957, p. 118).

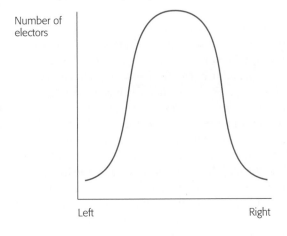

duty, to express their preference on national issues, to play their part in a democracy, to go with the flow and to avoid free-riding on the efforts of others. In this way, we can move people to the polling place while still, perhaps, maintaining the proposition that narrow self-interest reappears there (we can also add that, since most electors in most democracies do not vote at most elections, rational abstention does appear to be widespread).

The second objection proceeds along similar lines. Since no single ballot is likely to be decisive, why should Downs's voters go to the expense of acquiring the information needed to cast a rational vote? A full understanding of party programmes requires time and effort. Certainly, Downs's assumption that voters are perfectly informed seems particularly unrealistic, given the avalanche of polls revealing the limits of voters' understanding of parties, candidates, and the national political process. This ignorance may be rational, or simply ignorance, but surely our starting point should be what voters do not know, rather than what they do (Green and Shapiro, 1994).

Studies of voters' use of information offer a little solace. It does appear that many electors in liberal democracies are effective in interpreting the information that does come their way. They focus on essentials, discount information from biased sources, and listen to experts. As with many students taking an examination, they are pragmatic and intelligent users of the limited information they have acquired (Kuklinski and Peyton, 2007). They are shrewd, if not knowledgeable.

It is also worth noting that small shifts in election results, initiated by a minority of attentive voters, can send messages to rulers even if most voters are unaware of current developments. For example, judgements of a government's record do show up in changes in party support from one election to the next. As Erikson *et al.* (2002, p. 5) teach us, this miracle of aggregation means that the electorate as a whole can, in a sense, be judged more rational than the average voter. Referring to the USA, they write:

One can agree that the average citizen is not particularly informed, not particularly thoughtful, and not particularly attentive, but still find these characteristics emerge in the aggregate ... Those at the low end of the scale have little input on aggregate movement; those at the high end have major input. The net result is that the more informed, thoughtful and attentive citizens contribute disproportionately to aggregate movement.

The third objection to Downs's view of the voter is more fundamental. We can question the assumption that elections are best understood as debates over policies on which voters adopt different positions, as suggested by Figure 12.1. Often, in fact, the objectives are agreed and the main difference between parties – and the factor which shapes the outcome – is their perceived competence at delivering these goals. For example, everyone wants peace, prosperity, and a government that can handle the unexpected. The question is which party is best at execution, a question that raises issues of skill, integrity, experience, unity, and leadership.

Recognizing the importance of **valence** (or **performance**) **issues** leads to a challenge for the median voter theorem. As Ansolabehere (2006, p. 33) says, when performance issues matter, 'some voters will choose a more competent candidate, even if the other is ideologically closer to those voters' ideal points'. A competent party can secure the support of rational voters even if its location on position issues is away from the median voter.

Indeed, exploiting a reputation for effective governance is exactly the strategy adopted by some conservative parties whose right-wing policies are treated with suspicion: 'you may not agree with us but at least we know how to govern'. Voting for competence is far from irrational; indeed, we might well judge that it reflects wisdom. But incorporating valence issues into models of voting does involve an extension to Downs's original assumptions.

> **Position issues** are those on which parties offer different policies. Examples include abortion or government intervention in the economy. **Valence (or performance) issues** are those on which the goal is agreed and parties compete only on their capacity to deliver. Examples include economic growth and a low crime rate.

Overall, Downs's influential theory leads us to some interesting paradoxes. His axioms of self-interest and rationality, while standard for rational choice thinking, appear to result in ignorant electors who fail to vote and in parties that adopt virtually indistinguishable policy positions. Still, as we have seen, the very process of comparing predictions with reality does generate puzzles whose resolution creates insight. And that is how deductive approaches, such as rational choice, earn their spurs.

Issue voting

Let us return to position issues. Performance may be primary but it is not everything. So, what exactly is the electoral importance of policies towards such topics as abortion, defence, the environment, foreign affairs, gay marriage, public spending, and taxation? These are, after all, the kinds of topics we have in mind when we discuss the 'issues' of a campaign. To what extent do electors vote on such issues?

Here, it is important for us, as politics students, to avoid projecting our interests and knowledge onto the wider electorate. There are a number of rivers to cross before an elector can be described as an issue voter:

- the voter must be aware of the issue;

- the voter must have an opinion on the issue;

- the voter must believe the parties differ on the issue;

- the voter must vote for the party closest to his or her position.

These barriers are considerable. Studies conducted during the era of alignment judged that only a minority of voters passed them all. Writing of Britain, and using an English metaphor, Denver *et al.* (2012, p. 96) write that 'when aligned voting was the norm, relatively few voters fulfilled the conditions for issue voting. As in the Grand National, large numbers fell at every fence.' *The American Voter* was equally sceptical, classifying no more than one third of the electorate as passing the first three of the four conditions listed above on each of a long list of issues. Note, too, that gross voting on a particular issue will exceed its net impact on the result.

Even in these early studies, issue voting was far from negligible. Higher estimates could be obtained by looking at the issue of most importance to each voter, rather than taking issues one by one. Still, policy voting was lower than most researchers had anticipated. The glass of issue voting was seen to be half empty, rather than half full.

More recent studies show that voting on the basis of specific policies (and also broader ideologies) has increased. As early as 1992, Franklin concluded from a study in 17 liberal democracies that the rise of issue voting matched more or less precisely a decline in voting on the basis of social position. Lewis-Beck *et al.* (2008, p. 425) reach a similar conclusion for the United States, where comparable information is available for the longest period:

> The level of education within the American electorate has increased sharply since the 1950s, and this is reflected in more frequent issue voting, greater overall clarity in the structure of mass issue attitudes, and enhanced salience of ideological themes within the public's political thinking.

Wisely, Lewis-Beck *et al.* advise us not to fall too easily into the tempting narrative, 'from party identification to issue voting'. They tell us that the peripheral nature of politics to most Americans continues to create a ceiling to policy voting. The barriers remain in place in the USA, and surely in other democracies too. And the nature of the political times is an understated factor: a return to the quiescence of the 1950s, when the initial studies were conducted, might lead to a reduction in issue voting, even as education levels continue to rise. Position issues are far from irrelevant but they remain only a partial explanation for why people vote as they do.

The economy

We turn now to a factor that possesses undoubted potential in explaining movements in party support over time: the economy. Of course, linking government popularity to economic performance is hardly a new idea. In 1814, the British MP Henry Brougham wrote that 'A government is not supported a hundredth part so much by the constant, uniform, quiet prosperity of the country as by those damned spurts which Pitt used to have just in the nick of the time' (quoted in Butler and Stokes, 1971, p. 468). James Carville, lead strategist for Bill Clinton's 1992 presidential campaign, put the point more succinctly in a notice he posted at campaign headquarters listing key themes for the election: 'The economy, stupid.'

Clearly, the overall relationship between the economy and political support is an important theme. With data on economic performance and political popularity available for most liberal democracies, we also encounter here a topic well-suited to comparative analysis.

Conclusions, first. The economy does matter, just as Brougham and Carville thought it did. It affects not only government popularity, as recorded in opinion polls, but also how people behave in the polling booth ('the economic vote'). Although this result is robust, most estimates suggest the measured effect is perhaps smaller than we might have anticipated, given the centrality of economic issues to election campaigns. Paraphrasing Churchill's view of democracy, the economy is the worst explanation of election results we have – except for all the others (Hellwig, 2010, p. 200). Here, we review some of the detailed findings supporting this assessment.

One obvious question is: which aspect of the economy matters, electorally speaking? Just as it is unwise to discuss media effects without specifying a particular medium, so too should we avoid discussing economic effects without specifying a particular component. Three variables often emerging as significant are trends in:

- real disposable personal income (i.e. after taxes and inflation);

- unemployment;

- inflation.

Personal income appears to be particularly important, especially in the USA. In the second half of the twentieth century, the growth of personal income over an electoral cycle predicted the vote share of American presidents with remarkable accuracy. One analysis suggested that 'each percentage point increase in per capita real income [averaged across a presidential term] yielded a four per cent increase of the incumbent party's vote share from a constant of 46 per cent' (Hibbs, Jr, 2006, pp. 576–7). In other words, a president who achieves an annual average of 1 per cent growth in personal income over his term should score 50 per cent of the vote; 2 per cent growth is rewarded with 54 per cent of the vote; and so on. (Put differently, the advantage of incumbency is such that presidents need achieve only modest economic growth to stack the deck further in favour of their own re-election.)

Whether measured directly, or indirectly (through figures for gross domestic product), personal incomes appear in most American presidential election forecasting models (Box 12.3). But presidents are well advised to save the best for last: 'per capita real income growth rate in the last full quarter before an election has almost four times the electoral impact of income growth in the first full quarter of the term' (Hibbs, Jr, 2012, p. 5). In this respect, at least, voters have short memories, creating the potential for damaging amplification of the normal business cycle and thus identifying a weak spot in liberal democracy.

Still, we see in such findings the force of the question Ronald Reagan put to American voters during the 1980 campaign: 'Ask yourself, "Are you better off now than you were four years ago? Is it easier for you to go and buy things in the stores than it was four years ago? Is there more or less unemployment in the country than there was four years ago?"'

Studies of the impact of the incumbent's actual economic record dominated early research into economic voting. In recent decades, attention has shifted to how these effects operate. In particular, researchers have investigated how electoral choice varies with voters' own assessments of how the economy has performed. After all, voters will vary in how they judge the economic record; some will see inflation where others perceive stable prices. Such opinions provide a channel through which the objective economy affects votes.

Studies here strongly confirm the presence of an economic vote. For example, Hellwig (2010) combined the results from surveys conducted in 28 countries between 1996 and 2002 to examine the electoral effect of respondents' perceptions of whether 'over the last twelve months, the state of the economy in [country] has got better, stayed about the same, or got worse.' As Table 12.1 shows, the results were striking. A positive view of the economy helps incumbent parties.

Of course, those who already support the governing party are inclined to view the economy through rose-tinted glasses, exaggerating the real economic vote. Partisanship is at work here, as everywhere. Even so, the observed relationship between economic assessments and electoral choice appears to reflect more than simply the projections of the partisans (Lewis-Beck *et al.*, 2008, table 13.8).

By examining electors' attitudes, we can consider the effect not just of actual economic performance (**retrospective voting**) but also of voters' assessments of future economic prospects under different governing parties (**prospective voting**). In other words, we can move from examining sanctioning (elections as referendums on actual economic performance) to discussing selecting (elections as a valence choice between different parties as managers of the economy).

> **Retrospective voting** means casting one's vote in response to the record; **prospective voting** occurs when voters take future prospects into account.

The evidence suggests that the economic vote is at least partly prospective. Lewis-Beck and Stegmaier (2007, p. 522) observe that 'In American presidential elections, it appears that economic voting can be prospective as well as retrospective', especially when

Table 12.1 Perceptions of the economy and electoral choice across 28 countries, 1996–2002

In this large study, those electors who believe the economy had improved over the last 12 months were twice as likely to vote for the party of the incumbent president or prime minister, as were those who thought the economy had got worse

Perception of the economy over the past 12 months	Voting for the party of the incumbent president or prime minister (%)
Has got better	46
Has stayed the same	31
Has got worse	23

Source: Adapted from Hellwig (2010), table 9.1, rebased to 100 per cent.

the sitting president is not standing for re-election. Within and beyond the United States, retrospective plus some prospective appears to be a fair reading of the balance between the two.

Are retrospective voters more concerned with the performance of the economy as a whole or with their own material well-being? Here, we can be decisive: it is the national economy that matters most. An analysis of surveys from six countries 'found that evaluations of the national economy, but not individuals' assessments of their own finances, strongly and consistently affected vote choice' (Hellwig, 2010, p. 189).

This result is intriguing in that it might be seen as suggesting, contrary to the rational choice approach, that voters are motivated by altruism, rather than self-interest. But such an interpretation would be premature. People receiving family bequests might find their own finances transformed but would surely be unlikely to attribute their good fortune to the government. Electors appreciate that the government's responsibility is confined to the national economy.

One final point. The extent of economic voting in a country varies with its institutional arrangements. In particular, the economy is more influential when a single party can be held accountable for economic performance, as in parliamentary systems with

BOX 12.3

Forecasting the American presidential election of 2024

Abramowitz's early model (1988) for forecasting American presidential election results a few months in advance was:

$$V = 50.75 + .107P + .818E - 5.14T$$

where

V = incumbent's vote share;

P = presidential popularity (approval minus disapproval) in the final Gallup poll in June of election year;

E = annualized real gross domestic product growth rate over the first two quarters of election year;

T = time of president's party in office (1 if more than one term, 0 otherwise) ('time for a change').

In 2024, President Maria Sanchez is standing for re-election, having won convincingly in 2020. In a Gallup poll conducted on 30 June 2024, 60 per cent approved of the job the president was doing; 30 per cent disapproved. The economy, faltering from intense African competition, was static in the first two quarters of 2024.

What share of the vote will President Sanchez obtain, according to Abramowitz?

The answer is at the end of this chapter.

single party government. By contrast, accountability is diffused by coalitions and by presidential systems when the chief executive's office and the legislature are controlled by different parties (that said, American presidents do seem to be held primarily accountable for economic performance). Clarity of responsibility helps to explain why, for example, economic voting in the second half of the twentieth century was higher in the United Kingdom and New Zealand than in countries where coalitions are normal, such as Belgium and the Netherlands (Duch and Stevenson, 2008, figure 3.3).

So, the lesson is clear: look at the economy first. Political events and leaders come and go but the economy is always there. It is the constant that varies. Consider a salutary example. In 1983, Mrs Thatcher was re-elected prime minister of the United Kingdom after a remarkable political recovery widely attributed to success in the Falklands war. But later analysis suggested the Falklands factor was distinctly feeble. According to controversial estimates by Sanders *et al.* (1987, p. 281), 'the Falklands war produced a boost to Conservative popularity of at most three percentage points for a period of only three months'. Expectations of economic recovery after a fearful recession seem to have been a more important if less visible influence on the Conservative Party's triumph (but see also Norpoth, 1992).

Leaders' personalities

In seeking to understand electoral change, party leaders provide an additional focus of interest. Leaders are, naturally, politically important, with some reshaping their party and its policies. But, here, we examine specifically the electoral impact of a leader's character and personality.

There is a familiar, if usually untested, narrative here. It is that, in a televisual and less partisan age, voters have come to base their decisions on a leader's character, and even appearance, rather than the party to which he or she belongs. Did not Richard Nixon's stubble count against him in 1960 in that famous televised debate against a relaxed and tanned John Kennedy? Was not Mrs Thatcher encouraged by her spin doctors to convey greater authority by lowering her tone of voice? Were not François Hollande and Barack Obama successful in presidential elections in 2012 because they were seen as more likable than their competitors, Mitt Romney and Nicolas Sarkozy? The proposition is that we have witnessed the triumph of style over substance, of how things are said over what is said, of the leader over a group of leaders. The growing focus of the media on leaders' personalities means that even parliamentary systems have, effectively, become presidential.

There are obvious weaknesses in this tale. Even if it could be shown that character is now all important, that proof would not itself demonstrate any change over time; some past leaders, from Franklin Roosevelt to Winston Churchill, were hardly anony-

COUNTRY PROFILE

VENEZUELA

COMPETITIVE AUTHORITARIAN

Form of government ■ a federal and presidential republic with 23 states.

Legislature ■ the 165 members of the National Assembly are elected for a five-year term.

Executive ■ the president, directly elected by plurality for a six-year term, heads both the state and government, and chooses the members of the Council of Ministers.

Constitution and judiciary ■ the constitution dates from 1999, with later amendments abolishing term limits for all elected officials. The judiciary is headed by the Supreme Tribunal of Justice whose members are elected by the National Assembly for a 12-year term. Considerable political intervention.

Electoral system ■ Mixed member majoritarian, with most seats awarded in the district contests, favouring the PSUV. Voting is legally required but abstention is common.

Party system ■ President Hugo Chávez's party is the United Socialist Party of Venezuela (PSUV), formed in 2006 by a merger of existing parties supporting the president.

Population (annual growth rate): 28.0 m (+1.4%)	
World Bank income group: upper middle	
Human development index (rank/out of): 73/187	
Political rights score: ⑤	
Civil liberties score: ⑤	
Media status: not free	

Note: For interpretation and sources, see p. xvi.

When Columbus arrived on the northern shores of Latin America in 1498, he was so impressed by the local buildings, constructed elegantly on stilts, that he was reminded of Venice – hence **VENEZUELA**. In 2012, a visitor to Caracas, the country's capital city, confronts a modern but dilapidated city surrounded by ever-expanding *barrios* (shanty towns) climbing almost vertically on the ravines around.

This contrast expresses the fundamental fact about Venezuela and many other countries on the continent: inequality. In a country with an upper-middle income economy, over one quarter of the population live in poverty. The rich possess considerable wealth, displayed through European cars, manicured suburbs, gated communities, and private planes.

Yet, private affluence coexists with public squalor. Crime is endemic in most of this highly urban country, including Caracas. McCaughan (2004, p. 2) reports that 'the capital is literally falling apart as thieves filch metal from metro elevators, remove street lamps, dismantle apartment intercoms, steal electricity cables and even pickaxe cement barriers separating car lanes'.

As part of Gran Colombia, full independence from Spain was achieved in 1819, with Venezuela becoming an autonomous country in 1830. 'The liberator' Simón Bolívar was the hero of this movement. Aspiring to create a Latin American federation which would entrench individual rights, Bolívar's revolutionary spirit and unfinished project are still frequently invoked by Latin America's left; the country's formal title is the Bolivarian Republic of Venezuela.

Oil was discovered in Venezuela in 1914 and has proved to be the dominating feature of its economy and politics. In 2012, the country's oil reserves were the second largest in the world. Oil accounts for nearly all the country's exports and for around 40 per cent of government revenues.

The ability of the regime to distribute some of its oil revenue to the poor is the foundation for the populist leadership of Hugo Chávez. However, the price is considerable: a distorted economy, demonization of opponents and a ceaseless, tiresome emphasis on the primacy of politics.

Further reading: Brewer-Caríos (2010), Gates (2010), Gott (2011), Smilde and Hellinger (2011).

Voting in Venezuela

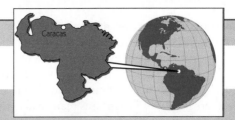

'Venezuela is not an electoral democracy. While the act of voting is relatively free and the count is fair, the political playing field favors government-backed candidates, and the separation of powers is nearly nonexistent.' This judgement by Freedom House (2012) is just the assessment we should expect of the role of elections in a competitive authoritarian system. So, we can use voting in Venezuela as a case study of how elections in hybrid regimes can be free but not fair.

Former paratrooper Hugo Chávez launched his remarkable 'Bolivarian revolution' when he won the presidential election of 1998; he has since been re-elected three times. Chávez promised to bring social justice and clean government to the *barrios*: 'this is a different Venezuela, where the wretched of the earth know they can free themselves from their past. And this is a different Latin America.'

The Chavistas cheered him on, especially from the *barrios*. A charismatic and intensely political figure, the president has retained considerable popular support among the dispossessed. The votes of the poor provide a large, and largely authentic, electoral base for Chávez and his programme of 'twenty-first century socialism'.

The regime's support in the shanty towns has been reinforced by generous social programmes delivered there. Doctors have been imported from Cuba to supply medical care, teachers have been drafted in to reduce illiteracy, residents' committees have sought to establish local property rights, and identity documents have given status to people previously denied any formal recognition. These programmes are imbued with a communal ethos, allowing sympathetic

commentators to regard them as a contribution to participatory democracy.

Sustained by faith in his cause, Chávez has energetically manipulated the political environment to bias the electoral process in his favour, without interfering with the count itself. He dominates the powerful medium of television, intimidates journalists, pressures public employees, uses state resources for political ends, and manipulates both the constitution (e.g. abolishing term limits) and the electoral system used

for parliament. With the judiciary under-funded and non-governmental organizations subject to legal restraints, political opponents experience difficulty in gaining traction.

In pursuing these tactics, Chávez takes advantage of enormous oil revenues and increasingly direct control of an under-performing economy. In these respects, his economic base and political strategy resemble those of another leader of a competitive authoritarian regime in a petrostate: Vladimir Putin.

▶ TIMELINE

HUGO CHÁVEZ

1954	Born in Sabaneta, Venezuela
1975	Graduates from the Academy of Military Sciences
1992	Leads a failed coup
1994	Released from prison, where he studied Simón Bolívar
1998	Elected president (56 per cent of the vote)
1999	Referendum ratifies new constitution
2000	Re-elected president (60 per cent)
2001	National strike against decree laws
2002	Removed from power by coup but returns two days later after street protests
2004	Wins recall vote. Announces alliance with Cuba
2006	Wins all seats in the National Assembly after opposition boycott. Re-elected president (63 per cent)
2007	Defeated in a referendum to amend constitution (including abolition of term limits)
2009	Term limits abolished after another referendum
2012	Re-elected president (54 per cent)
2013	Dies of cancer

mous drones. In any case, discussion of leaders often reveals a selection bias, focusing on the characterful while forgetting the anonymous. And, as with other factors affecting electoral choice, the net effects of a leader's character may be limited, even if gross effects are large. For instance, as many voters may be repelled as attracted by a particular candidate's personality, resulting in no net impact.

In understanding the electoral impact of leaders, it helps to distinguish between candidate-centred and personality-centred politics. As the American experience demonstrates most sharply, the former does not entail the latter. Wattenberg (2011, pp. 76–8) points out that 'the American electoral system has led to a system of candidates, for candidates, and by candidates'. He notes, in particular, how 'the election of Ronald Reagan in 1980 brought forth a new era in American politics in which the presidential candidate has virtually become the embodiment of the political party'.

But Wattenberg goes on to say that 'candidate-centred politics in the United States is NOT simply a personality contest'. He observes that 'despite common-place assertions from pundits that the most appealing candidate is bound to be victorious, data show this was not the case in a number of presidential election contests'. Stubble notwithstanding, Nixon was better-liked in 1960 than Kennedy (Stokes, 1966). Kennedy won because of his party, rather than his personality (King, 2002b, p. 214).

Rather, 'what has become most candidate-centred in the United States have been the issues'. In judging presidential candidates, American voters have come to rely more on aspirants' issue stance than on their personal qualities (Wattenberg, 2011, table 5.4). In that sense, purely personal ratings have declined, rather than increased, in importance. American presidential candidates are now known primarily by what they stand for; so supporting one rather than another can be viewed as a form of issue voting. It is just that the candidate, rather than the party, is the carrier of issue preferences.

Evidence that evaluations of leaders' personalities play a determining, or even increasing, role in shaping electoral choice is hard to come by. In and beyond the United States, we are entitled to doubt the thesis of a transformation from a golden age of parties to a current bronze age of personality-centred electoral appeal.

In the first comparative study linking leaders' characters to election outcomes, King (2002) attempted to judge whether leaders' personalities determined the winning party in 52 elections held between 1960 and 2001 in Canada, France, Great Britain, Russia, and the USA. His conclusions? His answer was mainly, but not wholly, negative: 'no' in 37 cases; 'possibly' in 6; 'probably' in 5, and 'yes' in just 4 (Harold Wilson, Great Britain, 1964 and February 1974; Charles de Gaulle, France, 1965; and Pierre Trudeau, Canada, 1968).

King's general conclusion (2002, p. 221) is that 'most elections remain overwhelmingly political contests, and political parties would do well to choose their leaders and candidates in light of that fact'. This judgement is surely sound, but we must qualify it a little. By examining whether leaders' personal traits change election outcomes, King mixes the effect of the leader with the closeness of the contest.

Still, much subsequent research that has sought to examine the impact of leaders' personalities on votes, rather than the overall election winner, has confirmed King's views. These studies typically examine the correlation between leader ratings and voting intentions in sample surveys. Not least in parliamentary systems, the difference that leaders' characters make is typically, but not always, shown to be modest, with but limited evidence of an increase over time.

For instance, a statistical study edited by Aarts *et al.* (2011, back cover) and covering nine liberal democracies 'shows, in contrast with popular wisdom, how unimportant [are] characteristics of the leaders themselves'. As part of this study, Holmberg and Oscarsson (2011, p. 51) conclude that 'the argument that leaders, over time, have become a greater influence on the vote is simply not substantiated'. Aardal and Binder (2011, pp. 122–3) agree, judging that their 'findings represent an important correction to the widespread assumption that political leaders have become more important for the voters than parties and politics'.

Reviewing studies from several countries, Bittner (2011, pp. 94) comes to rather more positive conclusions. She suggests that 'the results of these analyses indicate that leaders' personality traits can have a [net] impact anywhere from 0 to 8 per cent', consistent with Stokes's (1966) early finding from the USA that the impact of candidates led to a net partisan advantage ranging from 2 to 8 per cent. Bittner's own findings do suggest a substantial role for leader traits. Still, even these findings are consistent with the view that leaders' characters are only a part, and often a minor part, of the factors shaping individual votes and overall election results.

Where leader traits do make a difference, which attributes matter most? The key characteristics appear to be those directly linked to performance in office. By comparison, purely personal characteristics, such as appearance and likeability, are unimportant. Specifically, the two main desiderata for candidates are competence and integrity. In the United States, 'there is broad agreement on two core traits [used in evaluating candidates' personal qualities]: one, ability to do the job well, based on performance in office (incumbency) or a previous record of accomplishment; and two, a reputation for honesty' (Lewis-Beck *et al.*, 2008, pp. 55–6).

Extending the analysis to Australia, Germany, and Sweden, Ohr and Oscarsson (2011, p. 212) reach similar conclusions, judging that 'politically relevant and performance-related leader traits are important criteria for voters' political judgements'. They conclude that 'leader evaluations and their effect on the vote in the electorate are firmly based on politically "rational" considerations – be it in a presidential or in a parliamentary system'. If personal traits matter, it is because they are judged to be relevant to government performance.

In general, leaders are higher in visibility than in impact. There is also a wider lesson here for students of electoral behaviour. As Key (1966, p. 7) pointed out long ago, 'voters are not fools' and little insight is gained from treating them as such. Before dismissing voters as dupes, remember that you, too, are or might become one (Goren, 2012).

Turnout

Our concern thus far has been with the forces shaping electoral choice and change. But the topic of turnout must also be addressed. We examined contrasting views on the importance of political participation in Chapter 8. Here, our approach is more specific. We address the recent decline in turnout, the factors distinguishing voters from abstainers, and the measures that might increase turnout.

Despite rising education, turnout fell in most of the democratic world in the second half of the twentieth century. In 19 liberal democracies, it declined on average by 10 per cent between the 1950s and the 1990s (Wattenberg, 2000). Figure 12.2 shows the trend for one high-turnout country (Sweden), one traditionally middle-turnout country (the United Kingdom), and one low-turnout country (Switzerland). The pattern is clear, with the fall concentrated in the 1990s. In many countries, abstainers remain in the majority at regional and local contests.

It is possible that the main fall in turnout has already taken place, at least for national contests. As Figure 12.2 shows, participation increased modestly in the 2010 elections in Switzerland and the United Kingdom. In the USA, too, turnout among the eligible population has recovered in the closer presidential elections of this century (see Spotlight, Chapter 11). However, prudence suggests that we should avoid dismissing low turnout as yesterday's problem.

Why the fall? The decline surely forms part of a wider trend in the democratic world; namely, a growing distance between voters on the one hand, and parties and government on the other. It is

---

Figure 12.2 Turnout at parliamentary elections in three liberal democracies, 1970–2010

Turnout trended down in the final decades of the twentieth century in Sweden, Switzerland, and the United Kingdom but some recovery occurred subsequently

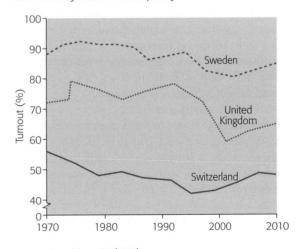

Source: Adapted from IPU (2011).

BOX 12.4

Features of the political system and of individuals which increase turnout

Features of the political system	Features of individuals
Compulsory voting	Middle aged
Automatic registration	Home owner
Voting by post and by proxy permitted	Strong party loyalty
Advance voting permitted	Extensive education
Weekend polling	Attends church
Election decides who governs	Belongs to a trade union
Cohesive parties	Higher income
Proportional representation	Has not changed residence recently
Close result anticipated	Voted in previous elections
Small electorate	
Expensive campaigns	
Elections for several posts held at the same time	

Sources: Endersby *et al.* (2006), Geys (2006), IDEA (2012).

surely no coincidence that turnout reduced as partisan dealignment gathered pace, as party membership collapsed, and as the class cleavage which sustained party loyalties in the early post-war decades decayed.

In an influential analysis, Franklin (2004) linked the decline of turnout to the diminishing significance of elections. He suggested that the success of many democracies in sustaining welfare states and full employment in the post-war era resolved long-standing conflicts between capital and labour. With class conflict disarmed, electors possessed fewer incentives to come out and vote on election day. As Franklin (2004, p. 174) wrote, 'elections in recent years may show lower turnout for the simple reason that these elections decide issues of lesser importance than elections did in the late 1950s'. As Downs would predict, when less is up for grabs, people are more likely to stay at home.

But declining satisfaction with the performance of democratic governments has surely also played its part. Especially in the 1980s, popular trust in government and parties fell in many democracies. Even though mass support for democratic principles remains strong, rising cynicism about government performance in the final two decades of the twentieth century probably encouraged more people to stay away from the polls (see Chapter 6).

Turnout varies not only over time, but also between countries. How can we explain these cross-national differences? Here, a Downsian cost-benefit analysis is useful. Turnout tends to be higher in those countries where the costs or effort of voting are low and the perceived benefits are high. On the cost side, turnout is reduced when the citizen is required to take the initiative in registering as an elector, as in the USA. It is also lower when electors must vote in person and during a weekday (Box 12.4). So, voting can be encouraged by allowing voting at the weekend, by proxy, by mail, by email, and at convenient locations such as supermarkets (Blais *et al.*, 2003). The ability to vote in advance is also helpful; it is notable that over 30 million votes in the US presidential election of 2012 were cast before election 'day' (United States Elections Project, 2012).

On the benefit side, the greater the impact of a single vote, the more willing voters are to incur the costs of voting. Thus, proportional representation enhances participation because each ballot affects the outcome. Participation is about 8 percentage points higher among countries employing party list PR than in those states using the plurality method (IDEA, 2012).

At the level of the individual, variations in turnout reflect the pattern found with other forms of polit-

BOX 12.5

Compulsory voting: for and against

FOR

- A full turnout means the electorate is representative;
- Disengaged groups are drawn into the political process;
- The authority of the government is enhanced by a full turnout;
- More voters will lead to a more informed electorate;
- People who object to voting on principle can be exempted;
- Blank ballots can be permitted for those who oppose all candidates;
- Parties no longer need to devote resources to encourage their supporters to vote.

AGAINST

- The freedom to abstain should be part of a liberal democracy;
- Compulsory voting gives influence to less informed and less engaged electors;
- Abstention may reflect contentment and is not necessarily a problem;
- In practice, turnout remains well below 100 per cent even when voting is mandatory;
- Voting (and deciding who to support) takes time;
- The better policy is to attract voters to the polls through their own volition.

ical participation. Specifically, high turnout reflects political resources and political interest (see Chapter 8). Thus, those most likely to vote are educated, affluent, married, middle-aged citizens with a job and a strong party loyalty, who belong to a church or a trade union, and are long-term residents of a neighbourhood. These are the electors with both resources and an interest in formal politics. By contrast, abstention is most frequent among those with fewer resources and less reason to be committed to formal party politics. Such people include young, poorly-educated, single, unemployed men belonging to no organizations, lacking party ties, and newly moved to their current address.

Attempts to boost turnout must remain sensitive to political realities. Conservative parties have reason to be cautious about such schemes, given their belief that abstainers would vote disproportionately for the left. Increased participation may benefit the system as a whole but impact unequally on the parties within it, thus delaying or preventing reform. So, has the time come to consider the most effective solution of all: compulsory voting? Because mandatory voting is usually only lightly enforced, it does not guarantee a full turnout. Still, it does make a difference: when the Netherlands made voting optional in 1970, turnout fell considerably.

There are arguments for and against compulsion (Box 12.5). On the one hand, most citizens acknowledge obligations to the state, such as paying taxes, serving on juries, and even fighting in war. Why should we reject what Hill (2002) calls the 'light obligation and undemanding duty' of voting at national elections? Abstainers take a free ride on the efforts of the conscientious.

On the other hand, mandatory voting denies the liberty which is an essential part of liberal democracy. Requiring people to participate is a sign of an authoritarian regime, not a democracy. Paying taxes and fighting in battle are duties where every little helps and where numbers matter. In all democracies, elections still attract more than enough votes to form a decision. There appears to be no evidence that high turnout increases the intrinsic quality of choices made. Why not continue to rely on the natural division of labour between interested voters and indifferent abstainers?

Answer to question in Box 12.3

$V = 50.75 + 0.107P + 0.818E - 5.14T$
$V = 50.75 + 0.107(30) + 0.818(0) - 5.14(1)$
$V = 48.8$ per cent.

Discussion questions

- Do most voters in your country support the same party at general election after general election in your country? If so, why?

- How likely is the recovery of partisanship in the United States to spread to other liberal democracies?

- Is it irrational to vote?

- Did the personality of the party leaders exert significant influence on voting in the last general election in your country?

- Should voting be compulsory?

- Your government has requested advice on how to increase turnout at (a) national and (b) local elections. What are your recommendations?

Further reading

K. Aarts, A. Blais and H. Schmitt, eds, *Political Leaders and Democratic Elections* (2011). This volume assesses the role of political leaders in the vote decision in nine democracies, suggesting that characteristics of leaders are less important than conventional wisdom imagines.

D. Denver, C. Carman and R. Johns, *Elections and Voters in Britain*, 3rd edn (2012). A clear and concise textbook.

R. Duch and R. Stevenson, *The Economic Vote: How Political and Economic Institutions Condition Election Results* (2008). An authoritative analysis of economic voting in liberal democracies.

C. van der Eijk and M. Franklin, *Elections and Voters* (2009). A well-informed, comparative textbook including chapters on voter orientations, public opinion, and voters and parties.

M. Franklin, *Voter Turnout and the Dynamics of Electoral Competition in Established Democracies* (2004). An influential comparative study of turnout and its decline.

L. LeDuc, R. Niemi and P. Norris, eds, *Comparing Democracies 3: New Challenges in the Study of Elections and Voting* (2010). This valuable series offers comparative reviews of elections and voting. The third edition includes chapters on ideology, partisanship, and economic voting.

ONLINE RESOURCES AVAILABLE

Visit the companion website at www.palgrave.com/politics/hague to access additional learning resources, including multiple-choice questions, chapter summaries, web links and practice essay questions.

Chapter 13 Constitutions and law

The academic study of politics began as a branch of law and, belatedly, these friends have renewed their old acquaintance. Four factors were involved in this rebirth of interest in the legal dimension of politics:

● the late twentieth century witnessed an explosion of constitution-making among post-authoritarian states, with 85 constitutions introduced between 1989 and 1999 (Derbyshire and Derbyshire, 1999);

● stimulated by the legal character of the European Union and by judicial activism in the USA, judges in many liberal democracies have become more willing to step into the political arena, not least in investigating corrupt politicians;

● the growing emphasis on human rights lends itself to judicial engagement;

● the expanding body of international law increasingly impinges on domestic politics, with judges called on to arbitrate between the conflicting claims of national and supranational law.

In connecting law and government, the idea of the **rule of law** offers a useful entry point. In liberal democracies, the rule of law has succeeded in ensnaring rulers in the threads of legal restraint. In the words of the nineteenth-century English jurist, A. V. Dicey (1885, p. 27), the purpose of the rule of law is to substitute 'a government of laws' for a 'government of men'. When rule is by law, governors cannot exercise arbitrary power and the powerful are subject to the same laws as everyone else. More specifically, the rule of law implies that laws are general, public, prospective, clear, consistent, practical, and stable (Fuller, 1969).

> The **rule of law** is a Western and primarily Anglo-American term. Its varied dimensions include consistent application of the law, one law for all, and **due process** (respect for an individual's legal rights) (Kleinfeld, 2006).

The gradual implementation of the rule of law and **due process** is an accomplishment of liberal politics, providing a basis for distinguishing liberal democracies from authoritarian regimes. That success, however, is never completely secure. The American constitution did not alter on 11 September 2001, but the rights of immigrants who found themselves imprisoned for several months without charge suddenly became less certain. As with all countries facing external threats, the rule of law takes second place to national security and needs to be rebuilt subsequently through the courts.

STUDYING . . .

CONSTITUTIONS AND LAW

- Understanding liberal democracy requires an appreciation of the constitutions on which they are at least partly based. Constitutions are not just statements of human rights; they also set out the distribution of powers within and between levels of government.

- In comparing constitutions and law across countries, the distinctions between common and codified law, and between supreme and constitutional courts, are central starting points.

- The judiciary is a rising political profession. Senior judges are increasingly willing to use their position as guardians of the constitution to pronounce on issues of public policy. So, it is essential for students of politics to appreciate the nature of judicial decision-making.

- Given the political relevance of judicial decisions, questions of judicial recruitment (e.g. appointment or election?) and independence also acquire significance.

- The European Court of Justice is a remarkable, if exceptional, case of a court contributing to the development of a transnational political system.

- In understanding judicial decision-making, the legal, attitudinal, and strategic models developed from studies of the American Supreme Court provide helpful perspective.

- Administrative law, which sets out principles for decision-making by public bodies, is a branch of law of particular relevance to students of politics.

Common law and civil law

In liberal democracies, the two fundamental legal systems are **common law** and **civil law**. It is impossible to understand the differences in the political role of the judiciary in Anglo-American and continental European democracies without some appreciation of this distinction.

Common law is used mainly in the United Kingdom and its former colonies, including the USA. It consists of judges' decisions on specific cases. Originally based on custom and tradition, judges' decisions were first published as a way of standardizing legal judgements across a state's territory. Because judges abided by the principle of *stare decisis* (stand on decided cases), their verdicts created precedents and established a predictable legal framework, contributing thereby to economic exchange and nation-building.

Common law, then, is judge-made law. Of course, explicit statutes (laws) are also passed by the legislature in specific areas but these statutes usually build

on case law and are themselves refined through judicial interpretation. The political significance of common law systems is that judges constitute an independent source of authority. They form part of the governance, but not the government, of society. In this way, common law systems contribute to political pluralism.

> The **common law**, found in England and many of its former colonies, consists of judicial rulings on matters not explicitly treated in legislation. Common law is based on precedents created by decisions in specific cases. In the more widespread **civil law** system, judges reach decisions by applying extensive written codes, rather than by comparing cases. Civil law derives from the original Roman law codes (civil law is unconnected with a 'civil case' – a term used to indicate a non-criminal action).

Civil law springs from a different well. It is founded on written legal codes which seek to provide a single overarching framework for the conduct of public affairs, including public administration and business contracts. The original codes were developed under Justinian, Roman Emperor between 527 and 565. This system of Roman law has evolved into distinct civil codes, seen in contrasting codes in France and Germany. These codes are then elaborated through laws passed by the national parliament. Civil law has shaped the legal character not only of continental Europe, but also of Latin America, the European Union and, reflecting Spanish and French influence, Louisiana.

In civil law, judges (rather than juries) identify the facts of the case; often, indeed, judges direct the investigation. They then apply the relevant section of the code to the matter at hand. The political importance of this point is that judges are viewed as impartial officers of state, engaged in an administrative task; they are merely *la bouche de la loi* (the mouth of the law). The courtroom is a government space, rather than a sphere of independent authority; judge-made law would be viewed as a threat to legislative supremacy.

The underlying codes in civil law systems often emphasize social stability as much as individual rights. The philosophy is one of state-led integration, rather than pluralism. Indeed, the codes traditionally functioned as a kind of extensive constitution, systematically setting out obligations as well as freedoms. However, the more recent introduction of distinct constitutions (which have established a strong position in relation to the codes) has strengthened the liberal theme in many civil law countries. In addition, judges have inevitably found themselves filling gaps in the codes, providing decisions which function as case law, even though they are not acknowledged as such. These developments dilute, without denying, the contrast between civil law and common law (Stone Sweet, 2000).

Constitutions

We can look at **constitutions** in two ways. The first reflects their historic role as a regulator of a state's power over its citizens. For the Austrian philosopher Friedrich Hayek (1899–1992), a constitution was nothing but a device for limiting the power of government, whether unelected or elected. In similar vein, Carl Friedrich (1901–84) defined a constitution as 'a system of effective, regularized restraints

---

BOX 13.1

The arrangement of constitutions

- A *preamble* seeks popular support for the document with a stirring declaration of principle and, sometimes, a definition of the state's purposes;
- An *organizational section* sets out the powers of government institutions;
- A *bill of rights* covers individual and, often, group rights, including access to legal redress;
- *Procedures for amendment* define the rules for revising the constitution.

---

upon government action' (1937, p. 104). From this perspective, the key feature of a constitution is its statement of individual rights and its expression of the rule of law. In this sense, constitutions express the overarching principles within which non-constitutional law – and the legal system, generally – operates.

A bill of rights now forms part of nearly all written constitutions (Box 13.1). Although America's Bill of Rights (1791) confines itself to such traditional liberties as freedom of religion, speech, and assembly, recent constitutions are more ambitious, often imposing duties on rulers such as fulfilling citizens' social rights to employment and medical care. The Mexican constitution of 1917 was the first to introduce such expansive provisions. Several post-communist constitutions have extended rights even further, to include child care and a healthy environment. In consequence, the documents are expanding: the average length (including amendments) is now 29,000 words, compared with only 7,400 for the elegant American constitution (Lutz, 2007).

The second, more political and more fundamental role of constitutions is to specify a power map, defining the structure of government, articulating the pathways of power, and specifying the procedures for law-making. As Sartori (1994, p. 198) observes, the key feature of a constitution lies in this provision of a frame of government. A constitution without a declaration of rights is still a constitution, whereas a document without a power map is no constitution at all. A constitution is therefore a form of political engineering – to be judged, like any other construction, by how well it survives the test of time. From this perspective, the American version, still standing after more than 200 years, is a triumph.

Much is made of the distinction between written and unwritten constitutions. Yet, no constitution is wholly unwritten; even the 'unwritten' British and New Zealand constitutions contain much relevant statute and common law. A contrast between **codified** and **uncodified** systems is more helpful. Most constitutions are codified; that is, set out in detail within a single document. By contrast, the uncodified constitutions of Britain and New Zealand are spread out among several sources. But such distinctions are rarely neat and tidy. Sweden, for example, falls in between: its constitution comprises four separate acts passed at different times.

> A **constitution** sets out the formal structure of the state, specifying the powers and institutions of central government, and its relationship with other levels. In addition, constitutions express the rights of citizens and, in so doing, create limits on government. A **codified** constitution is set out in a single document; an **uncodified** constitution is spread among a range of documents and is influenced by tradition and practice.

Amendment

Procedures for amendment are an important building block of the constitutional structure. **Rigid constitutions**, with their demanding amendment criteria, offer the general benefit of a stable political framework. For rulers, a rigid framework limits the damage should political opponents obtain power, for they, too, would face the same barrier to change. Political enemies, coming together to agree a new constitution, thus find security in entrenchment. Put differently, a rigid constitution can deliver a political equilibrium.

Flexible constitutions, though rare, do offer the advantage of ready adaptability. In New Zealand, this flexibility permitted a recasting of the country's electoral system and government administration in the 1980s and 1990s. Similarly, the United Kingdom

> **Flexible constitutions** can be amended in the same way that ordinary legislation is passed; the United Kingdom is the major example. **Rigid constitutions** are entrenched, ring-fenced by a more demanding amendment procedure such as a super- or concurrent majority.

was able to devolve significant powers to Scotland and Wales in 1999 without much constitutional ado.

Constitutions are entrenched by setting a higher level and wider spread of support for amendments than for ordinary bills. Typically, modification requires both a two-thirds majority in each house of parliament and additional endorsement from a broader constituency. In a federation, this extra ratification is from the component states; unitary countries usually employ a referendum (Box 13.2).

The most extreme form of entrenchment is a clause that cannot be amended at all. For example, the French and Turkish constitutions secure the republican character of their regimes in this way. Such statements set out to enforce a break with the old regime, but they also provide ammunition to those who see constitutions as the dictatorship of the dead over the living. In new conditions, past solutions have a way of turning into current problems.

The amendment procedure shapes the status of the constitution in relation to the legislature. When modifications cannot be approved by the legislature alone, the constitution stands supreme over parliament. In Australia, for example, amendments must be endorsed not only by the national parliament, but also by a referendum achieving a concurrent majority – in most states and in the country as a whole.

In a few countries, however, special majorities within the legislature alone are authorized to make amendments. In such a situation, the status of the constitution is somewhat reduced and that of the assembly increased. This approach is found in European countries with a strong commitment to parliamentary supremacy. Germany is a partial example: amendments (where permitted at all) require only a two-thirds majority in both houses. Flexible constitutions, of course, are at the mercy of the assembly.

Although rigid constitutions may appear to be incapable of coping with change, in practice they adapt through judicial interpretation. As we will see, the American Supreme Court has shown particular skill at adjusting an old document to fit new times. It has reinterpreted a constitution designed in the eighteenth century for the fresh challenges of later eras. Thus, one contrast between rigid and flexible constitutions is that, in the former, the judiciary manages evolution; in the latter, politicians take the lead.

BOX 13.2

Entrenching the constitution: some examples

	Amendments require the approval of
Australia	Both houses of parliament, then a referendum achieving a concurrent majority both overall and in a majority of states
Canada	Both houses of parliament and two-thirds of the provinces containing at least half the country's population
Germany	A two-thirds majority in both houses of parliament[1]
India	A two-thirds majority in both houses of parliament and a majority of the total membership of each house[2]
Sweden	Majority vote by two successive sessions of parliament with an intervening election[3]
USA	A two-thirds majority in both houses of Congress and approval by three-quarters of the states[4]

Notes:
1. The federal, social, and democratic character of the German state, and the rights of individuals within it, cannot be amended.
2. Some amendments, such as those changing the representation of states in parliament, must also be approved by at least half the states.
3. Sweden has four fundamental laws which comprise its 'constitution'. These include its Instrument of Government and Freedom of the Press Act.
4. An alternative method, based on a special convention called by the states and by Congress, has not been used.

Origins

In the main, constitutions are a deliberate creation, designed and built by politicians. As the English political theorist John Stuart Mill wrote, constitutions 'are the work of men … Men did not wake up on a summer morning and find them sprung up' (1861). How, then, do constitutions come into being? What conditions create the founding moment in which societies set about reconstructing their political order?

New constitutions typically form part of a fresh start after a period of disruption. Such circumstances include:

- regime change: for example, the collapse of communist rule;

- reconstruction after defeat in war: for example, Japan after 1945;

- achieving independence: for example, much of Africa in the 1950s and 1960s.

Constitutions experience a difficult birth. Often, they are compromises between political actors who have merely substituted distrust for conflict. In Horowitz's terms (2002), constitutions are built from the bottom up, rather than designed from the top down. For instance, South Africa's post-apartheid settlement of 1996 achieved a practical accommodation between leaders of the white and black communities against a backdrop of near slavery and continuing racial hostility. Acceptability was everything; elegance was nothing.

As vehicles of compromise, most constitutions are vague, contradictory, and ambiguous. They are fudges and truces, wrapped in fine words (Weaver and Rockman, 1993). As a rule, drafters are more concerned with a short-term political fix than with establishing a resilient structure for the long run. In principle, everyone agrees with Alexander Hamilton (1788b, p. 439), that constitutions should 'seek merely to regulate the general political interests of the nation'; in practice, they are lengthy documents reflecting an incomplete settlement between suspicious partners.

The lauded American constitution of 1787, though shorter than most, is no exception. Finer (1997, p. 1495) makes the point: 'the constitution was a thing of wrangles and compromises. In its completed state, it was a set of incongruous proposals cobbled together. And furthermore, that is what many of its framers thought.'

The main danger of a fresh constitution is that it fails to endow the new rulers with sufficient authority. Too often, political distrust means the new government is hemmed in with restrictions, limiting its effectiveness. The Italian constitution of

1948 illustrates the underpowered character of many new settlements. Its hallmark is *garantismo*, meaning that all political forces are guaranteed a stake in the political system. Thus, the document establishes a strong bicameral assembly and provides for regional autonomy. Intended to prevent a recurrence of fascist dictatorship and to accommodate the radical aspirations of the political left, *garantismo* led to ineffective governance.

The courts and judicial review

Constitutions are no more self-implementing than they are self-made. Some institution must be found to enforce its provisions, striking down offending laws and practices. This review power has fallen to the judiciary. With a capacity to override decisions and laws produced by democratic governments, unelected judges occupy a unique position both in and above politics. India's Supreme Court is even empowered to override any constitutional amendments which it deems to violate the basic structure of the constitution (Mitra, 2011, p. 79). Through their power of review, high courts express a liberal conception of politics, restricting the power of elected rulers. In this way, **judicial review** both stabilizes and limits democracy.

In reality judicial review empowers senior judges to address a range of moral predicaments, political controversies and public policy issues. Hirschl (2008, p. 119) makes the point:

Armed with judicial review procedures, national high courts worldwide have been frequently asked to resolve a range of issues, varying from the scope of expression and religious liberties, equality rights, privacy, and reproductive freedoms, to public policies pertaining to criminal justice, property, trade, and commerce, education, immigration, labor, and environmental protection.

Given the length of this list, Hirschl (2004) even refers to the rise of juristocracy – government by judges.

The function of judicial review can be allocated in two ways (Box 13.3). The first and more traditional method is for the highest or supreme court in the ordinary judicial system to take on the task of con-

> **Judicial review** empowers ordinary or special courts to nullify not only legislation, but also executive acts that contravene the constitution. **Abstract review**, practised by constitutional courts only, is an advisory but binding opinion on a proposed law. **Concrete review**, practised by both constitutional and supreme courts, arises in the context of a specific legal case.

stitutional protection. A supreme court rules on constitutional matters, just as it has the final say on other questions of common and statute law. Australia, Canada, India, the USA, and much of Latin America provide examples of this approach. Because a supreme court heads the judicial system, its currency is legal cases which bubble up from lower courts.

A second and more recent arrangement for judicial review is to create a special constitutional court, standing apart from the ordinary judicial system. This approach originated with the Austrian constitution of 1920 and is now widely used. By 2005, almost half the world's constitutions made provision for such a body (Horowitz, 2006). Constitutional courts are much favoured in Western and Eastern Europe. Given the importance of this distinction, we will examine supreme and constitutional courts separately.

Supreme courts

The United States is the prototypical case of the supreme court approach. America's constitution vests judicial power 'in one Supreme Court, and in such inferior Courts as the Congress may from time to time ordain'. Although the Court possesses **original jurisdiction** over cases to which an American state or a representative of another country is a party, its main role is **appellate**. That is, constitutional issues can be raised at any point in the ordinary judicial system and the Supreme Court selects for **concrete review** only those cases with broad significance. Most petitions for the Court to review a case are turned down, allowing the justices to set their own agenda by focusing on the issues they regard as crucial.

Although many founders of the American constitution supported judicial review, the constitution does not explicitly specify the Court's role in adjudicating constitutional disputes. Rather, this function was acquired by the justices themselves, with *Marbury v Madison* (1803) proving decisive. In this

BOX 13.3

Judicial review: supreme courts versus constitutional courts

	Supreme court	Constitutional court
Form of review	Concrete	More abstract
Relationship to other courts	Highest court of appeal	A separate body dealing with constitutional issues only
Recruitment	Legal expertise plus political approval	Political criteria more important
Normal tenure	Until retirement	Typically one non-renewable term (between six and nine years)
Examples	Australia Canada United States	Austria Germany Russia

case, Chief Justice John Marshall struck down part of the Judiciary Act (1789) as unconstitutional. 'To what purpose are powers limited', asked Marshall, 'and to what purpose is that limitation committed to writing, if these limits may, at any time, be passed by those intended to be restrained?' The court, Marshall added, possesses the power to 'say what the law is'. President Jefferson expressed his displeasure, claiming that the judgement ran the danger of 'placing us under the despotism of an oligarchy'. But, whatever the constitutional basis of Marshall's decision, the principle of judicial review was established.

Stare decisis notwithstanding, the Supreme Court does occasionally strike out in new directions. This 'inconsistency' has proved to be a source of strength,

---

Original jurisdiction entitles a court to try a case at its first instance. **Appellate jurisdiction** authorizes a court to review decisions reached by lower courts.

---

enabling the Court to adapt the constitution to changes in national mood. For example, after its rearguard struggle against the New Deal in the 1930s, the Court conceded the right of the national government to regulate the economy.

At other times, the Court has sought to lead, rather than follow. The most important of these initiatives, under the leadership of Chief Justice Earl Warren, concerned black civil rights. In its unanimous decision in *Brown v Topeka* (1954), the Court outlawed racial segregation in schools, dramatically reversing its previous policy that 'separate but equal' facilities for black children fell within the constitution. Implementation proved to be tortuous, requiring many more interventions by the Court, but the decision itself was path-breaking. It demonstrated the capacity of a united court to drive public policy (Riches, 2010).

Constitutional courts

Continental Europe, both West and East, favours constitutional courts, rather than supreme courts. In Western Europe, such courts were adopted after 1945 in, for instance, West Germany and France (Figure 13.1). In this system, ordinary courts are not empowered to engage in judicial review, with appeals to the supreme court; rather, this review function is exclusive to a separate constitutional authority.

As with the constitutions they nurture, these courts represented a general attempt to prevent a revival of dictatorship, whether of the left or the right. More recently, new democracies have created constitutional courts, separate from the ordinary judicial system, for a similar reason: to overcome the inefficiency, corruption, and opposition of judges from the old order who remain in post.

Where a supreme court is a judicial body making the final ruling on all appeals (not all of which involve the constitution), a constitutional court is more akin to an additional parliamentary chamber. Hans Kelsen (1881–1973), the Austrian inventor of constitutional courts, argued that these courts should function as a negative legislator, striking down unconstitutional bills but leaving positive legislation to parliament.

Certainly, this approach is more political, flexible, and less legal than that of supreme courts. Constitutional courts practise **abstract review**,

Figure 13.1 Establishing constitutional courts in Europe

Constitutional courts became established in continental Europe, both West and East, after World War II. The success of Germany's Federal Constitutional Court encouraged other countries to follow this model.

* These countries also possessed similar, but somewhat ineffective, courts in the interwar period.

Source: Adapted from Stone Sweet (2000, p. 31).

judging the validity of a law, or issuing advisory judgements on a bill at the request of the government or assembly, often without the stimulus of a specific case. Judgements are often short and are usually unsigned, lacking the legal argument used by supreme courts. Unusually, France's Constitutional Council can only practise abstract review. That is, it can only advise on the constitutionality of a bill before it becomes a law; it cannot invalidate bills once they have been enacted.

Just as the USA illustrates the supreme court tradition, so Germany has become the exemplar of this newer constitutional court approach. Its Federal Constitutional Court (FCC) provided an influential model for all post-communist countries in Eastern Europe (Kühn, 2006). Germany's Basic Law (constitution) gives the FCC duties that overlap with, but also go beyond, those of America's Supreme Court. It is assigned the functions of judicial review, adjudication of disputes between state and federal political institutions, protection of individual rights, and responsibility for protecting the constitutional and democratic order against groups and individuals seeking to overthrow it (Conradt, 2008, p. 253). While decisions of America's Supreme Court can be overturned by constitutional amendment, the **eternity clause** in Germany's Basic Law means that the Federal Court's judgements in key areas of democracy, federalism and human rights are absolutely the final word.

The FCC consists of 16 members appointed by the legislature for a non-renewable term of 12 years. The Court is divided into two specialized chambers, of which one focuses on the core liberties enshrined in the Basic Law. The Court's public reputation has

> The **eternity clause** in Germany's constitution states that 'an amendment of this Basic Law affecting the division of the federation into *Länder* (states), the participation in principle of the *Länder* in legislation, or the basic principles laid down in Articles 1 and 20, is inadmissible' (Articles 1 and 20 cover the dignity of man, human rights, democracy, the rule of law, and the 'social federal' character of the German state).

been enhanced by the provision of constitutional complaint, an innovative device permitting citizens to petition the Court directly once other judicial remedies are exhausted.

The Court actively pursued its duty of maintaining the new order against groups seeking its overthrow; for instance, by banning both communist and neo-Nazi parties in the 1950s. For this reason, among others, Kommers (2006) describes the Court as the 'guardian of German democracy'. It has continued in this role by casting a careful eye on whether European Union laws and policies detract from the autonomy of the country's parliament. The Court's engagement here is potentially a powerful constraint on the development of both the EU and the euro.

The Court has proved to be active in many other areas of policy. Its decisions have impinged on topics such as abortion, election procedures, immigration, party funding, religion in schools, and university reform. Between 1951 and 1990, the Court ruled that 198 federal laws (nearly 5 per cent of the total) contravened the constitution.

Conradt (2008, pp. 253–4) offers an overall assessment of the Court's achievements:

More than any other postwar institution, the Constitutional Court has enunciated the view that the Federal Republic is a militant democracy whose democratic political parties are the chief instrument for the translation of public opinion into public policy. The court has become a legitimate component of the political system, and its decisions have been accepted and complied with by both winners and losers.

European Court of Justice

In discussing the judiciary, we must acknowledge the special case of the European Union. The Court of Justice of the European Communities (ECJ) provides us with an influential constitutional court operating on a transnational basis.

Just as Germany's Federal Constitutional Court helped to shape the development of the postwar republic, so too has the European Court of Justice contributed to building the European Union. From the 1960s to the 1980s, in particular, it was the decisive actor in expanding the EU's legal order, developing a regime that remains fundamental to the Union's functioning. The cumulative impact of the ECJ's decisions amounted to what Weiler (1994) termed a 'quiet revolution' in transforming the founding treaties into something closer to a European constitution. Alter (2008) describes the Court's early decisions as 'audacious' and its overall development as 'incredible'.

The Court's formal purpose is to ensure that those aspects of the Union's treaties subject to its jurisdiction, and the provisions concerning EU institutions, are correctly interpreted and applied. European law is generally less specific than national legislation, leaving many gaps for the Court to fill. Cases can be brought by member states, or by other institutions of the Union. Reflecting its role as a constitutional court, the ECJ also responds to requests from national courts for preliminary rulings. Based in Luxembourg, the ECJ is unconnected with the European Court of Human Rights in Strasbourg.

The Court of Justice consists of one judge appointed from each member state for a renewable six-year term, with broad experience more important than specialized judicial expertise. Many cases are dealt with by small chambers of three to five judges; support is provided by eight advocates-general whose function is to make an initial recommendation on most cases coming before the Court. Even though a General Court (previously known as the Court of First Instance) was established in 1988 to process routine cases, judgements are still slow to emerge: the time between lodging a case and final decision averages almost two years (Nugent, 2010, p. 218).

In its early decades, the Court's decisions consistently and creatively strengthened the authority of central institutions (see Timeline, p. 243). It achieved this goal in three ways, insisting that European law:

- applies directly within member states (direct applicability);

- must be enforced by national courts (direct effect);

- takes precedence over national law (primacy).

In the 1990s, however, some member states began to question both the ECJ's procedures and the further expansion of its authority. Some slippage occurred in implementing the Court's decisions and a few national courts grew restive. In particular, Germany's Federal Constitutional Court showed itself keen to retain jurisdiction over whether European treaties violated Germany's own constitution – an issue that continues to be troublesome.

Even so, the ECJ remains the pre-eminent example of a judicial contribution to the emergence of a new transnational political order, fully justifying Shapiro's comment (1987, p. 1007) that 'no other court has ever played so prominent a role in the creation of the basic governmental and political process of which it is a part'. Other courts, including America's, have strengthened the central authority; the European Court helped to create one.

Judicial activism

Perhaps with the exception of Scandinavia, judicial intervention in public policy has grown throughout the liberal democratic world since 1945, marking a

COUNTRY PROFILE

SOUTH AFRICA

Form of government ■ a liberal democracy with an executive president and entrenched provinces.

Legislature ■ the National Assembly, the lower house, consists of 400 members elected for a five-year term. The president cannot dissolve the assembly. The smaller, weaker upper house, the National Council of Provinces, contains 10 delegates appointed from each of the nine provinces.

Executive ■ a president heads both the state and the government, ruling with a cabinet. The National Assembly elects the president after each election.

Judiciary ■ the legal system mixes common and civil law. The Constitutional Court decides constitutional matters and can strike down legislation.

Electoral system ■ the National Assembly is elected by proportional representation using closed party lists.

Party system ■ the African National Congress (ANC) (264 seats and 66 per cent of the vote in 2009) has dominated the post-apartheid republic. The more liberal Democratic Alliance (67 seats), now the leading party in the Western Cape, forms the official opposition.

Population (annual growth rate): 48.8 m (–0.41%)

World Bank income group: upper middle

Human development index (rank/out of): 123/187

Political rights score:

Civil liberties score: ❷

Media status: partly free

Note: For interpretation and sources, see p. xvi.

SOUTH AFRICA was shaped by two groups of settlers: the Boers (farmers), descended from Dutch-speaking colonists of the seventeenth century, and a smaller group of British colonists. The discovery of diamonds and gold in the late nineteenth century consolidated a reliance on migrant labour, providing the economic foundation for the ruthless system of apartheid (apartness) institutionalized after 1945.

Apartheid defined white, coloured, and black races, controlled the relationships between them, and secured white dominance. Apartheid's survival into the 1990s showed that governments based on brute power can last a long time. Yet, change was eventually induced by three main factors:

■ the collapse of communism which destroyed the regime's bogeyman;
■ the imposition of sanctions by the EU and the United States;

■ black opposition which began to encompass armed resistance.

As so often, initial reforms merely stimulated demands for more and faster change. In 1990, ANC leader Nelson Mandela was released from prison after 26 years, symbolizing recognition by the white rulers that the time had come to negotiate their own downfall. Four years later, the ANC won the first multi-racial elections with 63 per cent of the vote. Mandela became president of a government of national unity, including the white-led National Party. South Africa returned to the family of nations, a transition later exemplified by holding the soccer World Cup there in 2010.

The ANC has retained its hegemonic position though, as occurs with all dominant parties, cracks are beginning to appear. It remains the natural party of the black majority and has proved

adept at incorporating a range of other organizations, including trade unions, into its fold. Unlike many other liberation movements, the cohesiveness of the party survived the transition from opposition to government and the retirement of its hero-leader. But leadership conflicts, corruption, and ineffective governance pose substantial challenges.

The ANC provides a measure of order in a country beset with social problems. These difficulties include not only the sensitive legacy of apartheid, but also crime (including extensive sexual violence), inequality, poverty, unemployment, corruption, emigration, HIV/Aids, inadequate infrastructure, and limited education. In a democratic country, the ANCs long-term future surely depends on its ability to meet popular expectations of progress in such areas.

The constitution and the legal framework in South Africa

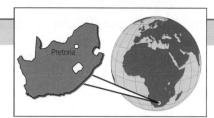

South Africa's transformation from a militarized state based on apartheid to a more constitutional order based on democracy was one of the most remarkable political transitions of the late twentieth century. What was the nature of the political order established by the new constitution?

In 1996, after two years of hard bargaining between the ANC and the white National Party (NP), agreement was reached on a new 109-page constitution to take full effect in 1999. The NP expressed general support despite reservations that led to its withdrawal from government.

In a phrase reminiscent of the American constitution, South Africa's constitution declares that 'the Executive power of the Republic vests in the President'. As in the USA, the president is also head of state. Unlike the United States, though, the president is elected by the National Assembly after each general election. He can be removed through a vote of no confidence in the assembly (though this event would trigger a general election), and by impeachment. The system is therefore fundamentally parliamentary in character. The president governs in conjunction with a large cabinet.

Each of the country's nine provinces elects its own legislature and forms its own executive headed by a premier. But far more than in the USA, authority and funds flow from

the top down. In any case, the ANC provides a glue linking not only executive and parliament, but also national, provincial, and municipal levels of government. So far, at least, the ruling party has dominated the governing institutions whereas, in the USA, the institutions have dominated the parties.

2009 elections has exerted a moderating effect, reducing the ANC's desire and capacity to amend the constitution in its favour. But the country's politics, more than most, should be judged by what preceded it. By that test the achievements of the new South Africa are remarkable indeed.

Preamble to the South African constitution, 1999

We, the people of South Africa,
Recognise the injustices of our past;
Honour those who suffered for justice and freedom in our land;
Respect those who have worked to build and develop our country; and
Believe that South Africa belongs to all who live in it, united in our diversity.
We therefore, through our freely elected representatives, adopt this Constitution as the supreme law of the Republic so as to

- Heal the divisions of the past and establish a society based on democratic values, social justice and fundamental human rights;
- Lay the foundations for a democratic and open society in which government is based on the will of the people and every citizen is equally protected by law;
- Improve the quality of life of all citizens and free the potential of each person; and
- Build a united and democratic South Africa able to take its rightful place as a sovereign state in the family of nations.

May God protect our people.

South Africa's rainbow nation faces some difficulties in reconciling constitutional liberal democracy with the political dominance of the ANC. The modest reduction in the size of the ANC's parliamentary majority in the

Further reading: Sparks (2009).

transition from **judicial restraint** to **judicial activism**. Judges have become more willing to enter political arenas that would have once been left to elected politicians and national parliaments; for instance:

- the Australian High Court under Sir Anthony Mason (Chief Justice, 1987–95) boldly uncovered implied rights in the constitution which had remained undetected by its predecessors (Pierce, 2007);

- India's Supreme Court has 'appointed itself as the guardian of vulnerable social groups and neglected areas of public life, such as the environment' (Mitra, 2012, p. 587).

- Israel's Supreme Court addressed such controversial issues as the West Bank barrier, the use of torture in investigations by the security service, and the assassination of suspected terrorists (Hirschl, 2008).

Judicial activism refers to the willingness of judges to venture beyond narrow legal reasoning so as to influence public policy. **Judicial restraint**, a more conservative philosophy, maintains that judges should simply apply the letter of the law, leaving politics to elected bodies.

What explanation can we offer for this significant judicialization of politics, a trend which Herschl (2008, p. 119) regards as one of the most significant phenomena of government in the late twentieth and early twenty-first centuries? Four reasons suggest themselves, the first of which is historical but the remainder of which are of continuing significance.

First, the decay of explicit left-wing ideology enlarged the judiciary's scope. Socialists were suspicious of judges, believing them to be unelected defenders of the status quo, and of property specifically. Now, the left has changed its tune, discovering in opposition that the courtroom can be a venue for harassing governments of the right. As political ideology waned, so professional (including legal) authority has waxed.

Second, the increasing reliance on regulation as a mode of governance encourages court intervention.

A government decision to deny gay partners the same rights as married couples is open to judicial challenge in a way that a decision to go to war or raise taxes is not.

Third, international conventions give judges an extra lever they can use to break free from the shackles of national law. Documents such as the United Nations Universal Declaration of Human Rights (1948) and the European Convention on Human Rights (1950) provide a base on which judges can construct what would once have been viewed as excessively political statements. The emergence of international courts such as the International Court of Justice (2007) has also encouraged national courts to become more assertive.

Fourth, the continuing prestige of the judiciary encouraged some transfer of authority to its domain. The judicial process in most liberal democracies has retained at least some reputation for integrity and impartiality, whereas the standing of many other institutions – notably, parties – has declined. Judicial status was reinforced when, as in Italy in the 1990s, civil law judges were seen to be investigating corrupt politicians.

Whatever the factors lying behind the expansion of judicial authority, the process seems to reinforce itself. Stone Sweet (2000, p. 55) makes the point: 'as constitutional law expands to more and more policy areas, and as it becomes "thicker" in each domain, so do the grounds for judicialized debate. The process tends to reinforce itself'. Sensing the growing confidence of judges in addressing broader political issues, interest groups, rights-conscious citizens, and even political parties have also become more willing to continue their struggles in the judicial arena.

Of course, judicial activism has proceeded further in some democracies than in others. In comparative rankings of judicial activism, the United States invariably comes top. America is founded on a constitutional contract and an army of lawyers forever quibbles over the terms. The USA exhibits all the features contributing to judicial activism. These include a written constitution, federalism, judicial independence, no system of separate administrative courts, a legal system based on judge-made case law, and high esteem for judges. The influence of the Supreme Court on American public policy has led one critic of 'government by judges' to dismiss it as 'a nine-man, black-robed junta' (Waldron, 2007, p. 309).

▶ TIMELINE

THE COURT OF JUSTICE OF THE EUROPEAN COMMUNITIES (ECJ)

1952	*Court of Justice of the European Communities* established as part of the European Coal and Steel Community.
1957	*Treaty of Rome*: the Court's jurisdiction extends to the new European Economic Community and Euratom treaties.
1963	*Van Gend en Loos*: European laws apply directly to individuals, creating rights and obligations that national courts must implement.
1964	*Costa* v. *Enel*: European law takes priority over national law.
1979	*Cassis de Dijon*: a product sold lawfully in one member state must be accepted for sale in other member states ('mutual recognition').
1987	*Foto-Frost*: national courts cannot invalidate EU measures but must refer their doubts to the ECJ for resolution.
1988	*Court of First Instance* established to reduce the ECJ's workload and to improve its scrutiny of factual matters.
1992	*Francovich and Bonifaci* v. *Italy*: when member states breach EU law, they must compensate those affected.
1992	*Maastricht Treaty* clarifies the ECJ's jurisdiction: for example, to include treaty provisions for closer cooperation between member states but to exclude the Common Foreign and Security Policy.
2003	*Constitutional Treaty* for Europe published in draft.
2005	*Commission* v. *Council*: the Community can require member states to adopt criminal legislation.
2005	*Constitutional Treaty* rejected in referendums in France and the Netherlands.
2008	*Constitutional Treaty* rejected in a referendum in Ireland.
2009	The *Treaty of Lisbon*, a weaker replacement of the failed Constitutional Treaty, comes into effect.

Further reading: Alter (2009), Hartley (2010).

Fewer conditions of judicial autonomy are met in Britain – a country in which parliamentary sovereignty traditionally reigned supreme. Lacking the authority to annul legislation, judicial review in the British context normally refers to the capacity of judges to review executive decisions against the template provided by administrative law.

Even in Britain, however, judicial activism has increased, reflecting European influence. British judges were willing accomplices of the European Court of Justice as it established a legal order applying to all member states. The country's belated adoption of the European Convention on Human Rights in 1998, and the decay of the royal prerogative which once allowed the state to stand above the law, also encouraged judicial assertiveness. The establishment of a Supreme Court in 2009 reinforced the notion of judicial autonomy (previously the Law Lords, as they were called, sat as part of Parliament's upper chamber, the House of Lords).

Formal statements of rights have also encouraged judicial expansion in other English-speaking countries. In Canada, a Charter of Rights and Freedoms was appended to the constitution in 1982, giving judges a more prominent role in defending individual rights. Similarly, New Zealand introduced a bill of rights in 1990, protecting 'the life and security of the person' and also confirming traditional, but previously uncodified, democratic and civil rights.

Judicial independence and recruitment

Given the growing political authority of the judiciary, the question of maintaining its independence gains in importance. Liberal democracies accept judicial autonomy as fundamental to the rule of law, but how is this independence to be achieved in practice?

Security of tenure is, of course, important. In Britain, as in the American federal judiciary, judges hold office for life during 'good behaviour'. America's constitution is not the only one to stipulate that judges' pay 'shall not be diminished during their Continuance in Office'. Although the justices of Europe's constitutional courts are usually limited to a single term of between seven and nine years, their position remains secure during this period.

But judicial autonomy depends on recruitment as well as on security of tenure. Were the selection of judges on the highest court to be controlled by politicians who appointed their own placemen, the

judiciary would simply reinforce partisan authority, providing an integration (rather than a separation) of powers. This danger is particularly acute when judicial tenure is short, limiting the period in which judges can develop their own perspective on the cases before them. Political systems have developed varying solutions to the issue of judicial selection; the main methods are shown in Figure 13.2.

At one extreme comes democratic election. This method is practised in some American states; it is certainly responsive, perhaps excessively so, to popular concerns (Bonneau and Hall, 2009). At the other extreme, co-option by judges already in post offers the surest guarantee of independence but can lead to a self-perpetuating elite. The danger is that the existing judges will seek out new recruits with an outlook resembling their own.

In between these extremes come the more conventional methods: appointment by the assembly, by the executive, and by independent panels. The British government, for example, recently ceded power of appointment to an independent commission, a decision justified by the relevant minister in the following way:

In a modern democratic society, it is no longer acceptable for judicial appointments to be entirely in the hands of a government minister. For example the judiciary is often involved in adjudicating on the lawfulness of actions of the executive. And so the appointments system must be, and must be seen to be, independent of government. (Falconer, 2006)

In practice, many countries now combine these orthodox methods, with the government choosing from a pool of candidates prepared by a professional body. In South Africa, for instance, the President of the Republic appoints senior judges after consulting

Figure 13.2 Methods of appointing judges to the highest court

Methods for appointing senior judges range from popular election (a device which encourages responsiveness to the public) to co-option by existing judges (a method which secures judicial independence – albeit at the risk of entrenching judicial conservatism)

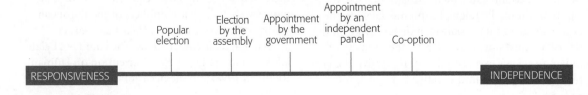

a Judicial Services Commission which includes representatives from the legal profession as well as the legislature. India's President appoints Supreme Court judges after consulting such judges as he may deem necessary.

Alternatively, and more traditionally, some judges on the senior court can be selected by one method, while others are chosen by a different method. Thus, one third of the members of Italy's Constitutional Court is appointed by parliament in joint sitting, one third is nominated by the president, and one third is selected by the judiciary itself.

For most courts charged with judicial review, selection still involves a clear political dimension. For example, the stature of America's Supreme Court is such that appointments to it (nominated by the president but subject to Senate approval) are key decisions. Senate ratification can involve a set-piece battle between presidential friends and foes. In these contests, the judicial experience and legal ability of the nominee may matter less than ideology, partisanship, and a clean personal history. Even so, Walter Dellinger, former acting US Solicitor General, argues that 'the political appointment of judges is an appropriate "democratic moment" before the independence of life tenure sets in' (Peretti, 2001).

A political dimension is also apparent in selection to constitutional courts. Typically, members are selected by the assembly in a procedure that can involve party horse-trading. For instance, 8 out of the 12 members of Spain's Constitutional Court are appointed by the party-dominated parliament. In both America and Europe, then, political factors influence court appointments.

Below the level of the highest court, judicial autonomy raises the issue of **internal independence**. The judiciary is more than the highest court of the land; it is an elaborate, multi-tier structure encompassing ordinary courts, appeal courts, and special bodies such as tax and military courts. Whether justices at lower levels are inhibited or empowered shapes the effectiveness of the judicial system as a whole in resolving conflicts in a fair, effective and predictable fashion.

Guarnieri (2003, p. 225) emphasizes the importance of internal independence. Noting that 'judicial organizations in continental Europe traditionally operate within a pyramid-like organizational structure', he argues that 'the role played by organiza-

tional hierarchies is crucial in order to highlight the actual dynamics of the judicial corps'. This issue arose in acute form in some Continental European countries after 1945, when judges appointed under right-wing regimes continued in post, discouraging initiative by new recruits lower in the pyramid.

> The **internal independence** of the judiciary refers to the autonomy of junior judges from their senior colleagues, who often determine career advancement. Where this autonomy is limited, judicial initiative may be stifled.

Guarnieri concludes that promotion and salary progression within the judiciary should depend solely on seniority, noting that such reforms were needed in Italy before younger 'assault judges' became willing to launch investigations into government corruption. Guarnieri's blanket solution may be extreme but it is important to recognize that the decisions of judges lower in the hierarchy will be influenced by anticipated effects on their career prospects.

Judicial decision-making

The thrust of this chapter is that senior judges must be seen as performing a broadly political function; they are undoubtedly important actors in shaping the contemporary regulation of liberal democracies. So, it is important to ask how judges go about reaching their decisions.

Research here has focused primarily, but not exclusively, on the American Supreme Court. There, the Court's opinion is typically signed by all the justices who agree with it. Verdicts are given in the form of unanimous or majority opinions, with dissenting opinions often also produced. These open procedures allow researchers to assess whether, across a series of cases, a particular justice can be classified as consistently liberal or conservative, and to relate his or her ideological profile to such factors as the justice's social background.

The behavioural focus of studies of individual judges contrasts with the predominantly institutional tone of this chapter. Still, it is useful to highlight the three accounts that have emerged from these studies (Box 13.4). They are surely applicable beyond America's Supreme Court. In practice, of course, judges will base their judgements on a range of considerations.

The **legal model** is the most traditional. It assumes that judges draw on legal considerations in reaching their judgements. Of course, the fact that an issue has reached the highest court means that it is legally uncertain; otherwise, it would not have been referred. So, the law itself is not wholly deter-mining. Even so, judges are likely to bear in mind precedent, legal principles, and the implications of their judgement for the future development of the law. They can hardly reach a particular decision unless they can wrap it in at least some legal cov-ering. Students of politics are unwise to dismiss this model completely (Graber, 2008).

The **attitudinal model** suggests that judges' deci-sions on constitutional and policy issues reflect their political ideology. On America's Supreme Court, cer-tainly, a justice's decisions are often consistently liberal or consistently conservative. Differences in political attitudes between judges surely help to explain why they often reach contrasting conclu-sions on the same case. If justices' decisions were not broadly political, their appointment would not arouse so much public interest. It seems highly likely that this attitudinal model is also relevant beyond the United States (Segal and Spaeth, 2002).

The **strategic model**, finally, regards judges as sensitive to the likely reactions of other political actors and institutions to their pronouncements. As with any other institution, the highest courts (and often lower ones, too) act so as to maintain their standing, autonomy, and impact. Accordingly, judges will think hard before courting controversy or making decisions that will be ignored, or even reversed through constitutional amendment. Courts would surely be unique organizations if institutional interests did not form part, and an important part, of their decision-making calculus (Spiller and Gely, 2008). So, this strategic model invites us to think of judges on the highest court as full players in the game of elite politics. They, too, must abide by the rule of anticipated reactions.

For example, Germany's constitutional court is certainly concerned to sustain democracy by defending the autonomy of its country's parliament. Nonetheless, it will think long and hard before declaring that European plans to resolve the euro

---

BOX 13.4	
How judges decide	
Model	Description
Legal	Judges' decisions reflect their under-standing of what the law requires
Attitudinal	Judges' decisions reflect their liberal or conservative ideology
Strategic	Judges' decisions take into account the likely reaction of other political actors to their judgements

---

debt crisis run counter to national sovereignty. As Darnstädt (2012) succinctly pointed out, 'The Karlsruhe-based institution will not stop European integration because it can't.' In general, courts are reluctant to pick fights, especially those they are likely to lose. So, judicial influence on politics also implies political constraints on the judiciary.

Administrative law

Where constitutional law sets out the fundamental principles governing the relationship between citizen and state, administrative law covers the rules governing this interaction in detailed settings. If a citizen (or other affected body) is in dispute with a public agency over a specific issue – such as obtaining a passport, or eligibility for a welfare benefit – some standards must be developed enabling allegations of maladministration to be resolved. This task, too, has fallen to the judiciary; it is a role that grew massively in importance with the expansion of government in the twentieth century.

Administrative law sets out the principles governing decision-making by public bodies and the remedies for breaching such rules. For example, America's Administrative Procedure Act (1946) requires courts to hold unlawful any agency action that is 'arbitrary, capri-cious, an abuse of discretion, or otherwise not in accor-dance with law'.

The issues involved here concern public law and have no clear analogy in the private sector. Typical questions asked in the area concern:

● competence: Is an official authorized to make a particular decision?

● procedure: Is the decision made in the correct way (e.g. with adequate consultation)?

● fairness: Does the decision accord with natural justice?

● liability: What should be done if a decision were incorrectly made, or led to undesirable results?

How can administrative justice be realized? Liberal democracies handle the problem of legal regulation of the administration through either a separatist or an integrationist approach, with the chosen method reflecting and reinforcing differing conceptions of the state.

The first solution, common in codified legal systems, is to establish a separate system of administrative courts concerned exclusively with legal oversight of the bureaucracy. This **separatist approach** marks out a strong public sphere operating within a civil law framework. Where this approach is used, the work of civil servants is seen as legal in character, based on the uniform application of codes and leading naturally to judicial oversight.

> The **separatist approach** to administrative justice (as in France) is to establish special courts and laws to review the interaction between citizen and state. By contrast, the **integrationist approach** (as traditionally favoured in the United Kingdom) seeks to control the bureaucracy by reviewing disputes in ordinary courts, relying in large part on the ordinary law of the land.

France is the most influential example of the separatist model. The country has developed an elaborate structure of administrative courts, headed by the *Conseil d'État*, founded in modern form in 1799 but with roots in the thirteenth century (Figure 13.3). The Council is the final court of appeal within the hierarchy, and also assesses administrative decisions taken by government ministers and their offi-

Figure 13.3 Administrative courts in France

France's elaborate system of administrative courts illustrates the principle that legal issues involving the public sector should be resolved outwith the ordinary judicial system

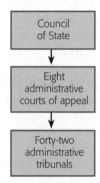

Note: Separate courts exist for constitutional cases and for civil and criminal law.

Source: Adapted from Elgie (2003).

cials as part of its original jurisdiction. By developing its own case law, the Council has established general principles regulating administrative power. The Council's prestige, which exceeds that of the ordinary courts, expresses the autonomy of the public realm and reinforces its capacity to check the executive.

The separatist solution speaks directly to the specific problems arising in public administration but raises difficulties of its own. These include boundary disputes over whether a case should be processed through administrative or ordinary courts. Such debates can be especially awkward when, as is increasingly the case, a public task has been outsourced to a private contractor. In addition, special administrative courts reinforce a legalistic interpretation of public service which can lead to inflexible and unresponsive decision-making (as those with experience of the French bureaucracy will testify).

The second solution, favoured in Anglo-American countries with a common law tradition, reflects a less exalted view of public authority. The **integrationist approach** asserts that one set of courts should address legal issues arising in both the public and the private sector. The philosophy here is 'one law for all'. That is, the same principles should span both sectors: for instance, employment in the public sector should be regulated by the same rules applying to private firms. Ordinary courts should be able to arbitrate disputes between bureaucrats and citizens; no council of state is required.

Two strengths of this integrationist philosophy are that it prevents boundary disputes and simplifies the judicial system. Above all, the integrationist philosophy affirms a modest aspiration for the public realm; the state must abide by the same laws as its citizens. A. V. Dicey (1885) was the strongest exponent of this approach; his thinking was that special laws and courts for public business would, in practice, serve to advantage the government against the citizen.

In reality, special courts are rarely avoided entirely, even in the English-speaking world. The United States, for instance, has developed administrative courts dedicated to tax, military, bankruptcy, and patent issues. Influenced by the strong public law tradition in the European Union, the United Kingdom introduced an Administrative Court in 2001. Dicey lost this particular battle, defeated by the relentless expansion of regulation.

Note, however, that judicial review is only the final court of appeal for citizens protesting against an administrative decision. Normally, panels and tribunals closer to the decision offer an easier route of appeal. Thus, the first level of complaint is typically to an appeals panel operating within the department making the original decision. The complainant can then appeal to an external tribunal, rather than a law court. These panels and tribunals review the substantive decision reached by the official, allowing the appellant to argue that the decision was wrong under the rules, even if the correct rules were applied. By contrast, judicial review will normally focus solely on process – on whether the decision was reached by a competent official following the correct procedure.

Tribunals do have strengths: they are inexpensive, cheap, flexible, substantive, informal, and often speedy. They can also focus more on mediation and can redress the imbalance of legal knowledge between a government agency and a citizen, thus countering Dicey's concern about inequality of expertise. So, in theory at least, the work of tribunals and courts should be complementary, with judicial intervention serving only as a final court of appeal on matters of procedure.

However, tribunals themselves need to be seen to operate in a fair and consistent way; so, just like the courts, they tend to develop their own standards and rules. In effect, they too become governed by administrative law, leading to complaints that they have become too formal and expensive to serve the practical purpose for which they were originally designed. We observe here another illustration of how judicial processes are inherently prone to expand.

In some countries, citizens also have access to an ombudsman, a public official who can investigate a complaint about inadequate, if not illegal, behaviour by public authorities (see Chapter 18).

Administrative law seeks to ensure that public agencies do not abuse their power. The risk is that this goal will be achieved in such a way as to discourage agencies from using their authority in a decisive and constructive fashion. We want agencies to exercise discretion not only fairly, but also effectively. As Rodriguez comments (2008, p. 341), 'the tension between governance and legality has grown over the last hundred years'; it is unlikely to go away.

Law in authoritarian states

In authoritarian regimes, constitutions are feeble. The nature of such states is that restraints on rule go unacknowledged; power, not law, is the political currency. As guardian of the law, the status of the judiciary is similarly diminished. In fact, it is often only in the transition to democracy that the old elite empowers the courts, seeking guarantees for its own diminished future (Solomon, 2007).

Non-democratic rulers follow two broad strategies in limiting judicial authority. One tactic is to retain a framework of law, but to influence the judges indirectly. Recruitment, training, evaluation, promotion, and discipline procedures provide many opportunities for the regime to influence judges even while maintaining a facade of judicial independence.

More crudely, unsatisfactory judges can simply be dismissed. Egypt's President Nasser adopted this strategy with vigour in 1969. He got rid of 200 in one fell swoop: the 'massacre of the judges'. In Uganda, an extreme case, the killing was real rather than metaphorical; President Amin had his Chief Justice shot dead.

A second strategy, more subtle but nonetheless effective, is to bypass the judicial process. For instance, many non-democratic regimes use Declarations of Emergency as a cover to make decisions which are exempt from judicial scrutiny. In effect, a law is passed saying there is no law. Once introduced, such 'temporary' emergencies can drag on for decades.

Alternatively, rulers can make use of special courts that do the regime's bidding without much pretence of judicial independence; Egypt's State Security Courts were an example. Military rulers frequently extend the scope of secret military courts to include civilian troublemakers. Ordinary courts can then continue to deal with non-political cases, offering a thin image of legal integrity to the world.

Communist states offered a more sophisticated downgrade of constitutions and the judiciary. In Marxist theory, courts were viewed not as a constraint upon political authority but, rather, as an aid to the party in its overriding mission of building socialism.

Echoes of this perspective can still be found in official Chinese thinking. As in the Soviet Union, China has regularly introduced new constitutions, the fourth and most recent dating from 1982. Even though the current version begins by affirming the country's socialist status, it is the least radical of the four (Box 13.5). It seeks to establish a more predictable environment for economic development and to limit the ruling party's historic emphasis on class conflict, national self-reliance, and revolutionary struggle. The leading role of the party is now mentioned only in the preamble, with the main text even declaring that 'all political parties must abide by the Constitution'. Amendments in 2004 gave further support to private property and human rights. In the context of communist states, such liberal statements are remarkable, even if they remain a poor guide to reality.

In addition to moderating the content of its constitution, contemporary China also gives greater emphasis to law in general. There were very few laws at all in the early decades of the People's Republic, reflecting a national tradition of unregulated power. The judiciary was, essentially, a branch of the police. However, laws did become more numerous, precise, and significant after the hiatus of the Cultural Revolution. In 1979, the country passed its first

BOX 13.5

Article I of the Chinese constitution, 1982

1. The People's Republic of China is a socialist state under the people's democratic dictatorship led by the working class and based on the alliance of workers and peasants.
2. The socialist system is the basic system of the People's Republic of China. Sabotage of the socialist system by any organization or individual is prohibited.

Source: Tschentscher (2004).

criminal laws; later revisions abolished the vague crime of counter-revolution and established the right of defendants to seek counsel. Law could prevail to the benefit of economic development. For law-abiding citizens, life became more predictable.

Judges, too, have become more professional. By 2005, most judges in China were graduates, compared with only 7 per cent 10 years earlier (Liebman, 2007). In forming their verdicts, judges now look to other legal decisions, and not always to the party elite.

Reform notwithstanding, Chinese politics remains deeply authoritarian. 'Rule by law' still means exerting political control through law, rather than limiting the exercise of power. The courts are regarded as just one bureaucratic agency among others; legal judgements are not tested against the constitution and many decisions are simply ignored. Rulings are unpublished and difficult cases are often left undecided. In comparison with liberal democracies, legal institutions remain less specialized, and legal personnel less sophisticated. Trial procedures, while improving, still offer only limited protection for the innocent. The death penalty remains in use, the police remain largely unaccountable, political opponents are still imprisoned without trial, and party officials continue to occupy a protected position above the law. Because the party still rules, power continues to trump the constitution and human rights.

Constitutions and the law also play second fiddle to elected authority in competitive authoritarian regimes. There, the leader is elected within a constitutional framework but that environment has been shaped by the leader. More important, the exercise of power is rarely constrained by an independent judiciary. Rather, it is the president who occupies the highest ground, defining the national interest under the broad authority granted to him by the voters:

How could it be otherwise for somebody who claims to embody the nation? In this view other institutions – such as congress and the judiciary – are nuisances that come attached to the domestic and international advantages of being a democratically elected president. Accountability to these institutions appears as an unnecessary impediment to the full authority that the president has been delegated to exercise (O'Donnell, 1994, p. 63).

Put differently, presidential accountability in a hybrid regime is vertical (to the voters), rather than horizontal (to the judiciary). In contrast to a liberal democracy, where the main parties have concluded that being ruled by law is preferable to being ruled by opponents, under competitive authoritarianism the commanding figure still sees the constitution, the law, and the courts as a source of political advantage. Legal processes operate more extensively than in pure authoritarian regimes but remain subject to political manipulation.

In Latin America, where hybrid regimes are common, several elected presidents have treated the constitution as a flexible document to be adapted to their own political needs. Many have sought to abolish term limits so that they can stand for re-election, providing a recurring source of tension between politics and the constitution.

Other constitutions in the region have retained privileges for departing generals, thus perpetuating a sense of an additional institution remaining above the law. For instance, Chile's armed forces were initially granted immunity from prosecution in civilian courts, a tactic that effectively enabled former generals to escape justice for political murders committed during their tenure.

In addition to the difficulties of establishing the constitution as an effective political framework, the rule of law has long been held back throughout Latin America's hybrid regimes by deep-seated weaknesses in the judiciary. Prillaman (2000) enumerates the problems:

- chronic inefficiency within the judicial system;

- the vulnerability of judges to political pressure;

- inadequate and outdated laws;

- insufficient resources and training;

- the public's lack of trust in legal remedies;

- judgements are often ignored.

As judicial professionalism increases, so too will the judiciary's standing, generating a positive feedback loop. But the journey will surely be long. For example, the Russian experience shows that law can gain ground – if only slowly and with difficulty – in at least some competitive authoritarian regimes. Russia's post-communist constitution of 1993 set out an array of individual rights (including that of owning property); proclaimed that 'the individual and his rights and freedoms are the supreme value'; and established a tripartite system of general, commercial, and constitutional courts. The Constitutional Court, in particular, represented a major innovation in Russian legal thinking.

Since 1993, the government has established detailed and lengthy (if not always well-drafted) codes appropriate for a civil law system. From 1998, criminal defendants who have exhausted all domestic remedies have even been able to appeal to the European Court of Human Rights (Sharlet, 2005, p. 147). More prosaically, tax law and business law have been modernized.

But in Russia, as in other hybrid regimes (and some liberal democracies), 'there has been and remains a considerable gap between individual rights on paper and their realization in practice' (Sharlet, 2005, p. 134). For instance:

- the conviction rate in criminal cases remains suspiciously high;

- expertise and pay within the legal system are low, sustaining a culture of corruption;

- violence by the police is common;

- politics overwhelms the law on sensitive cases (such as the imprisonment of business oligarch, Mikhail Khodorkovsky);

- legal judgements, especially against the state, can be difficult to enforce;

- the public still shows little faith in the legal system (Smith, 2010, p. 150).

So, Russia's competitive authoritarian regime has made more progress towards achieving the rule of law than has China's fully authoritarian state. But assuming that law in Russia will eventually acquire the status it possesses in liberal democracy still involves drawing a cheque against the future. Smith (2010, p. 135) sums up:

Since the enactment of the new constitution of the Russian federation, substantial progress has been made in establishing a workable and independent judiciary and legal system. Many new laws have been enacted and important legal reforms have been undertaken. At the same time, the enforcement of laws has been uneven and at times politicised, which erodes public support and belief in the courts.

Discussion questions

■ Why has the standing of the judiciary remained high while that of parties and politicians has declined?

■ Are codified constitutions a desirable component of, or an undesirable constraint upon, liberal democracy?

■ How would American government and politics differ if the United States introduced a European-style Constitutional Court?

■ Do you find the legal, attitudinal, or strategic model of judicial decision-making more convincing?

■ Should judges be elected and, if not, who should appoint them?

■ Is the European Union primarily a legal order?

Further reading

K. Alter, *The European Court's Political Power: Selected Essays* (2009). Analysis of the European Court of Justice.

J. Calleros-Alarcón, *The Unfinished Transition to Democracy in Latin America* (2008). The difficulties of entrenching a professional judiciary in Latin America.

C. Guarnieri and P. Pederzoli, *The Power of Judges: A Comparative Study of Courts and Democracy* (2002). A cross-national study of the judiciary.

W. Sadurski, *Rights before Courts: A Study of Constitutional Courts in Postcommunist States of Central and Eastern Europe* (2005). A discussion of constitutional courts in Eastern Europe.

A. Stone Sweet, *Governing with Judges: Constitutional Politics in Europe* (2000). An examination of constitutional politics in five European political systems.

K. Whittington, R. Kelemen and G. Caldeira, eds, *The Oxford Handbook of Law and Politics* (2008). American scholars' reflections on legal themes with political relevance.

ONLINE RESOURCES AVAILABLE

Visit the companion website at **www.palgrave.com/politics/hague** to access additional learning resources, including multiple-choice questions, chapter summaries, web links and practice essay questions.

Chapter 14 **Multilevel governance**

Governance always incorporates a spatial dimension. Rulers need to extract resources from their territory while also retaining the willingness of the population to remain within the state's orbit. To achieve these ends, the modern state consists of an intricate network of organizations, typically consisting of:

● the central government;

● its offices and representatives in the field;

● regional governments;

● local authorities.

For its member countries, the European Union provides an additional tier of governance above the national level. In examining these layers, and the relationships between them, we can put flesh on the bones of the governance concept (Chapter 1).

Multilevel governance

Multilevel governance is the term used to describe how policy-makers and interest groups in liberal democracies find themselves discussing, persuading, and negotiating across multiple tiers, seeking to deliver coherent policy in specific functional areas such as transport and education. Where multilevel governance predominates, a policy-maker in a central department of education will spend more time on vertical relationships (talking to people from different tiers within the same field) than on horizontal coordination (engaging in discussion with people at the same level but working in a different policy area) (Figure 14.1).

> **Multilevel governance** emerges when practitioners from several levels of government share the task of making regulations and forming policy, usually in conjunction with relevant interest groups (Hooghe and Marks, 2001). The term is often used in discussing the European Union, whose presence adds a supranational tier to existing governance networks within member states.

Communication is not confined to officials working at the same or adjacent levels. Rather, international, national, regional, and local officials in a given sector will form their own policy networks, with interaction across all tiers. Thus, the leaders of major cities within EU countries will negotiate

STUDYING . . .

MULTILEVEL GOVERNANCE

- Multilevel governance is a popular framework for examining the relationships between levels of administration (supranational, national, regional, local) in liberal democracies. The assumptions underpinning this term can be usefully compared with those expressed in pluralist thinking (see Chapter 9).

- Although multilevel governance emphasizes relationships of persuasion, it is important to be aware of the constitutional, financial and political realities which underpin negotiations between different levels of government. To understand relationships, first understand the players.

- The constitutional contrast between unitary and federal systems remains important. However, unitary states are just as tiered as federal states – and often more so. The strengthening of regional government is a significant trend within unitary states.

- Federations cover around 40 per cent of the world's population. Traditionally associated with large countries, federalism also bears an interesting relationship to multiculturalism. It can both stabilize and reinforce ethnic divisions.

- The concept of multilevel governance emerged from research on the relationship between the European Union and tiers of government in member states. The status of the European Union itself - supranational, confederal, or federal – is itself something of a puzzle.

- In an urban world, providing effective governance of metropolitan areas cutting across traditional boundaries is a challenge. Capital cities, especially when they claim the mantle of 'world city', display an ambivalent relationship with national authority.

- Local government is still the place where the citizen meets the state. Too often understudied (at least, outside Scandinavia), its organization and functioning raise some interesting current questions, including the enabling authority and elected mayors.

directly with the European Commission, as well as with and through their national governments. The use of the term 'governance' instead of 'government' directs our attention to these relationships between institutions, rather than simply the organizations themselves.

The idea of multilevel governance carries a further implication. As with pluralism, it recognizes that actors from a range of sectors – public, private, and voluntary – help to regulate contemporary societies. In education, for example, the central department will want to improve educational attainment in schools; but, to achieve its target, it will need not only to consult lower tiers within the public sector (such as education boards), but also wider interests such as parents' associations, teachers' unions, private sector suppliers, and educational researchers.

In fact, the multiple tiers of government involved in policy-making give more points of access and influence for these private groups. So, the concept of multilevel governance denotes a pluralistic pattern of policy-making whose participants include relevant interest groups. The resulting networks resist purely hierarchical political control; they respond more to persuasion, leadership, and resource allocation.

In common with pluralism, multilevel governance can be portrayed in a positive or negative light. On the plus side, it implies a pragmatic concern with finding solutions to shared problems through give-and-take among affected interests. On the negative side, it points to a complicated, slow-moving form of regulation by insider groups, a form which resists both democratic control and penetration by less mainstream groups and thinking. Multilevel gover-

Figure 14.1 Coordination within and across tiers of government

Much negotiation in the public sphere is across different levels or government, all dealing with the same topic. In getting things done, coordination across tiers is as important as coordination at the same level.

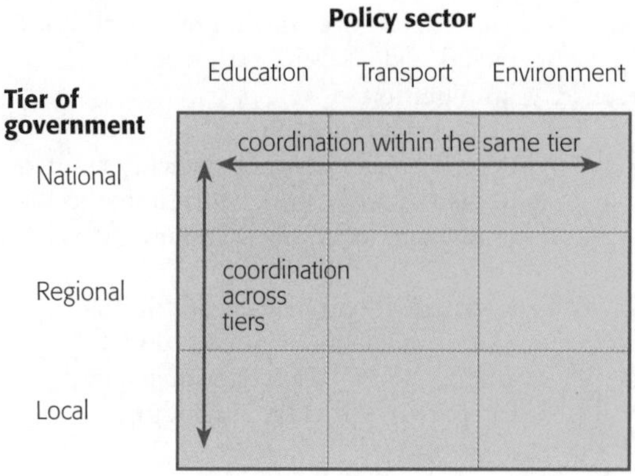

Federalism

Federalism is a form of multilevel governance which shares sovereignty, and not just power, between governments within a single state. It is a constitutional device, presupposing a formal political agreement establishing both the levels of government and their spheres of authority. As Brooks (2012, p. 196) writes, 'federalism is chiefly a property of constitutions not societies'. So, **federations** are always a deliberate creation. In such a system, legal sovereignty is shared between the federal (or national) government and the constituent subunits (often known as 'states' or 'provinces').

> **Federalism** (from the Latin *foedus*, meaning 'treaty') is the principle of sharing sovereignty between central and state (or provincial) governments; a **federation** is any political system that puts this idea into practice. A **confederation** is a looser link between participating countries which retain their separate statehood.

nance may be a fashionable term but its popularity should not lead us to assume that the form of rule it describes is optimal.

Understanding multilevel governance requires an appreciation of the resources all tiers bring to the table. Typically, the national level possesses political visibility, large budgets and strategic objectives. But, just like interest groups, officials from lower levels will possess their own power cards: detailed knowledge of the problem and the ability to judge the efficacy of the remedies proposed. If lower tiers are both resourced and enthused, they are in a position to make a difference; if not, they may lose interest, limiting the ability of the centre to achieve its policy goals.

It would be wrong to infer that power in multilevel governance is merely the ability to persuade. Communication still operates in a constitutional framework that provides both limits and opportunities for representatives from each tier. If the constitution allocates responsibility for education to central government, local authorities are unlikely to build new schools unless the Ministry of Education signs the cheque. Thus, the formal allocation of responsibilities remains the rock on which multilevel governance is constructed. Multilevel governance develops from, without replacing, multilevel government.

The key point about a federal partnership is that neither tier can abolish the other. It is this protected position of the states – not the extent of their powers – that distinguishes federations (such as the USA and Canada) from unitary governments (such as the UK and France). Multiple levels of government are integral to a federation whereas, in a unitary system, sovereignty resides solely with the centre, with lower levels existing at its pleasure. So this section on federalism should be read alongside the later section on unitary governance.

The constitution of a federal state allocates specific functions to each tier. The centre takes charge of external relations – defence, foreign affairs, and immigration; and some common domestic functions – such as the currency. The functions of the states are more variable but typically include education, law enforcement, and local government. As in Germany, residual powers often lie with the states, not the centre (Box 14.1).

In nearly all federations, the states have a guaranteed voice in national policy-making through an upper chamber of the assembly. In that chamber, each state normally receives equal, or nearly equal, representation. The American Senate, with two senators per state, is the prototype.

BOX 14.1

The allocation of functions in the Canadian and German federations

	Canada	Germany
Exclusive jurisdiction (federal level)	The federal government exclusively controls 29 functions, including criminal law, the currency, and defence.	The federal government's responsibilities include defence, citizenship and immigration.
Exclusive jurisdiction (provincial level)	The provinces control 'all matters of a merely local or private nature', including local government.	Few specific powers are explicitly granted to the *Länder* (states), which nonetheless implement federal laws 'in their own right'.
Concurrent jurisdiction (functions shared between levels)	Both the national and provincial governments can pass laws dealing with agriculture and immigration.	Concurrent powers include criminal law and employment. A constitutional amendment in 1969/70 created a new category of joint tasks, including agriculture.
Residual powers (the level responsible for functions not specifically allocated by the constitution)	The national parliament can make laws for the 'peace, order and good government of Canada'.	Any task not otherwise allocated remains with the *Länder*.

The natural federal structure is for all the states within the union to possess identical powers under the constitution. However, some federations are less balanced. Asymmetric federalism arises when some states within a federation are given more autonomy than others, typically in response to cultural differences. In Canada, notably, Quebec nationalists have long argued for special recognition for their French-speaking province; they view Canada as a compact between two equal communities (English- and French-speaking), rather than as a contract between 10 equal provinces.

Although asymmetric federalism is an understandable response to differences in power and culture between regions, the solution carries its own danger. A spiral of instability can develop as the less-favoured states seek the status already granted to more privileged provinces.

Federations must be distinguished not only from unitary states, but also from a less common format: confederation. In a confederation, the central authority remains the junior partner and acts merely as an agent of the component states, which retain their own sovereignty. A confederation is more than an alliance but less than a federation. The classic case is the short-lived system adopted in 1781 in what is now the United States. The weak centre, embodied in the Continental Congress, could neither tax nor regulate commerce, and lacked direct authority over the people. It was the feeble nature of the Articles of Confederation that led to the creation of the federal United States in 1787. In the contemporary world, the European Union is sometimes interpreted as a confederation. It, too, suffers from slow policy-making.

Federalism is a recognized solution to the problem of organizing the territorial distribution of power. Elazar (1996, p. 426) counted 22 federations in the world, containing 40 per cent of the world's population (Table 14.1). Sheer size is a motivating force, though China is unitary. In India, the population of 8 out of 28 provinces exceeds that of the United Kingdom; a federal arrangement is probably the only way to integrate what is not only a large country, but also one which is far more diverse than China.

Table 14.1 Some major federations in liberal democracies

Federalism is particularly common in large countries, whether size is measured by area or population. Examples include Australia, Canada, India, and the United States. Some small multinational states, such as Belgium and Switzerland, are also federal.

	Year established as a federation	Area (rank in world)	Population (rank in world)	Number of states in federation
United States	1789	9	3	50
Switzerland	1848	143	96	26
Canada	1867	8	36	10
Brazil	1891	11	5	26
Australia	1901	6	54	6
Germany	1949	69	16	16
India	1950	14	2	28
Belgium	1993	147	82	3

Note: Reflecting practice in India, we regard India as a federation, even though the word 'federation' does not appear in its constitution.

Source: CIA (2012).

There are two routes to a federation: first, by creating a new central authority ('coming together'); second, by transferring sovereignty from an existing national government to lower levels ('holding together'). In practice, federalism almost always emerges as a compact between previously separate units combining to pursue a common interest. The United States, for instance, emerged from a meeting of representatives from 13 states in 1787. Similar conventions, strongly influenced by the American experience, took place in Switzerland (1848), Canada (1867) and Australia (1897/98).

The second route, restructuring as a federation to hold a divided country together, is rare. Belgium is the main example. First established in 1830, Belgium has been beset by divisions between its French-speaking region and a larger, wealthier, Dutch-speaking region. After constitutional revisions in 1970 and 1980, which devolved more power to these separate groups, the country finally proclaimed itself a federation in 1993. It comprises three main parts:

- predominantly French-speaking Wallonia (which includes a small German-speaking community);

- Dutch-speaking Flanders;

- the Brussels region, centred on the bilingual but mainly French-speaking capital (Map 14.1).

To date, the Belgian experience suggests that federation can be an alternative to disintegration, a lesson of value to other states confronting internal divisions with a spatial dimension (Brans *et al.*, 2009).

What, then, provokes distinct peoples to set out on the journey to a federation? Motives are more often negative than positive; fear of the consequences of remaining separate must overcome the natural desire to preserve independence. Thus, Rubin and Feeley (2008, p. 188) suggest that federalism becomes a solution when, in an emerging state, 'the strong are not strong enough to vanquish the weak and the weak are not strong enough to go their separate ways'.

Historically, the main incentive for coming together has been to secure the military and economic bonus of size, especially in response to strong competitors. Riker (1996) emphasized the military factor, arguing that federations emerge in response to an external threat. The American states, for instance, joined together partly because they felt vulnerable in a predatory world.

However, economic factors also encourage a federal formation. Both Australian and American

Map 14.1 Regions of Belgium

federalists believed that a common market would promote economic activity. Currently, however, straightforward free trade areas (FTAs) between neighbouring countries are a more convenient device for securing gains from trade. Unlike federations, FTAs – such as the North American Free Trade Agreement – entail no loss of sovereignty.

Military and economic arguments for forming new federations may have weakened but interest in ethnic federalism has grown. The Belgian experience shows that federations are useful for bridging ethnic diversity within a divided society; they are a device for incorporating such differences within a single political community. Thus, Switzerland integrates 26 cantons, four languages (German, French, Italian, and Romansh), and two religions (Catholic and Protestant) into a stable federal framework.

Yet, there is a danger in ethnic federations; namely, that they merely reinforce the divisions they were designed to accommodate. This risk is particularly acute when only two communities are involved. In these conditions, the gains of one group are the visible losses of another and the majority community may be able to impose its will, defeating the original object of diffusing power. Citing Czechoslovakia, Watts (2005, p. 234) suggests that 'bipolar federations have invariably experienced serious tensions, instability and a high failure rate'.

Even in Belgium, usually judged to be a federal success story, Deschouwer (2012, p. 105) reports that

'the granting of autonomy to the language groups ... has increased and deepened the differences between both communities and regional entities'. Federations are more effective when they cut across (rather than entrench) ethnic divisions, and when they marginalize (rather than reinforce) social divisions.

Dual and cooperative federalism

In developing an understanding of federalism, it is helpful to distinguish between dual and cooperative forms. The former represents the federal spirit and remains a significant theme in American culture; the latter is an important ideal within European thinking and moves us closer to the contemporary realities of multilevel governance.

Reflecting the original federal principle as conceived in the United States, **dual federalism** implies that national and state governments operate independently, each tier acting autonomously in its own sphere, and linked only through the constitutional compact. Bryce (1919, p. 425) offered the image of two sets of machinery working well precisely because they avoided contact – the exact opposite of multilevel governance. In the circumstances of eighteenth-century America, such separation was a plausible objective; extensive coordination between federal and state administrations was judged to be neither necessary, nor feasible.

Perhaps always a myth, dual federalism has disappeared, overwhelmed by the demands of an integrated economy, world war, and terrorism. Even so, it expresses an implicit if unrealizable strand in federal thinking. Just as democracies are often judged against an unrealistic model of direct self-government, so contemporary federations are often found wanting against the unattainable and backward-looking ideal of independent tiers.

The second approach is **cooperative federalism**. This interpretation is favoured by some European

> As originally envisaged in the USA, **dual federalism** meant that national and state governments retained separate spheres of action. Each level independently performed the tasks allocated to it by the constitution. **Cooperative federalism**, as in Germany, is based on collaboration between levels. It is a version of multilevel governance in which national and state governments are expected to work together as partners in pursuing the interests of the whole.

federations, especially Germany and German-influenced Austria. Where the American federation was based on a contract in which the states joined together to form a central government with limited functions, the European form rests on the idea of cooperation between levels. Such solidarity expresses a shared commitment to a united nation, binding the participants together. The moral norm is solidarity and the operating principle is **subsidiarity**: the idea that decisions should be taken at the lowest feasible level. The central government offers overall leadership but implementation is the duty of lower levels: a division, rather than a separation, of tasks.

> **Subsidiarity** is the principle that no task should be performed by a larger and more complex organization if it can be executed as well by a smaller, simpler body. The tenet emerged from Catholic social thought, where it functioned as a defence for the continuing role of the Church and voluntary associations against the encroachments of the welfare state.

Consider, for example, the German federation. From its inception in 1949, the Federal Republic of Germany was based on interdependence, not independence. All the *Länder* (states) are expected to contribute to the success of the whole; in exchange, they are entitled to respect from the centre. The federal government makes policy but the *Länder* implement it, a division of administrative labour expressed in the constitutional requirement that 'the *Länder* shall execute federal laws as matters of their own concern'. Further, the constitution now explicitly defines some 'joint tasks', such as higher education, where responsibility is shared (Box 14.1). We can hardly be further removed from the original American spirit of separate spheres.

Although the German federation remains far more organic than its American equivalent, its cooperative ethos came under pressure early in the twenty-first century from a growing perception that decision-making had become cumbersome and opaque. Accordingly, constitutional reforms finalized in 2006 sought to establish clearer lines of responsibility between Berlin and the *Länder*; for example, by giving the states more autonomy in education and environmental protection. Although this package represents a move away from cooperative federalism towards greater subsidiarity, consultation remains embedded in German political practice. Multilevel governance cannot be legislated away.

An evolving balance

In most federations, the central government gained influence for much of the twentieth century. Partly, this trend reflected the centre's financial muscle. The flow of money became more favourable to the centre as income tax revenues grew with the expansion of both the economy and the workforce. Income is mainly taxed at national level because, otherwise, people and corporations could move to low-tax states. For their own independently raised revenue, the states had to depend on sales and property taxes, a smaller and less dynamic revenue base.

Federal governments now receive the lion's share of total public revenue, redistributing some of this money to the provinces through grants of various kinds (Box 14.2). In the USA, for instance, the centre's share of total government spending grew from 17 per cent in 1929, before the depression, to an estimated 60 per cent in 2012 (usfederalbudget, 2012).

BOX 14.2

Financial transfers from the federal government to states

Type of transfer	Comment
Categorical grant	For specific projects (e.g. a new hospital).
Block grant	For particular programmes (e.g. medical care).
Revenue-sharing	General funding which places few limits on the recipient's use of resources.
Equalization grant	Used in some federations (e.g. Canada and Germany) in an effort to harmonize economic conditions between the states. Can create resentment in the wealthier states.

COUNTRY PROFILE

CANADA

Form of government ■ a federal parliamentary democracy with 10 provinces. Most Canadians live in Ontario or Quebec. A governor general serves as ceremonial figurehead.

Legislature ■ the 308-seat House of Commons is the lower chamber. Unusually for a federation, the 105 members of the Senate, the upper chamber, are appointed by the prime minister, rather than selected by the provinces.

Executive ■ the prime minister leads a cabinet whose members are selected with regard for provincial representation.

Judiciary ■ Canada employs a dual (federal and provincial) court system, headed by a traditionally restrained Supreme Court.

Electoral system ■ a plurality system with single-member districts.

Party system ■ the major parties are traditionally the Conservatives and Liberals. The Conservatives have governed since 2006, securing a majority in 2011. At this election, the left-wing New Democratic Party (NDP) won more votes and seats than the Liberals.

Population (annual growth rate): 34.3 m (+0.8%)	
World Bank income group: high income	
Human development index (rank/out of): 6/179	
Political rights score: **1**	
Civil liberties score: **1**	
Media status: free	

Note: For interpretation and sources, see p. xvi.

CANADA is a large country with a relatively small population. Its land mass is the second largest in the world but its population is little more than one tenth of its powerful American neighbour. Most Canadians live in urban settlements in a 100-mile strip bordering the United States. The country's economy depends heavily on the USA, a relationship reinforced by the signing of the North American Free Trade Agreement in 1994.

The United States therefore provides a natural contrast. Although both countries are settler societies, Canada never experienced America's radical break with colonial power. The basis of its constitution remains the Constitution Act (1867). Not until the Constitution Act (1982) was authority to amend the constitution returned to Canada; indeed, the country's governor general still formally

represents the British monarch. Where the American constitution is based on a philosophy of limiting government to protect the liberty of states and individuals, Canada's federation is more centralized and, unusually, operates within a parliamentary system in which members of the upper chamber are appointed by the prime minister, rather than elected by the provinces. The country has experienced neither slavery nor civil war; it has also followed a more orthodox path in policy development, with extensive public services premised on the principle of equality.

In common with both the USA and Britain, Canada uses a single-member plurality electoral system. However, the traditional major parties (Liberal and Conservative) are more American than British in organization and philosophy: they are election-fighting entities

lacking a mass membership and strong central organization. They never acquired the sharp ideological differences which once characterized Britain's Conservative and Labour parties; as in the USA, the spoils of office were the prize for which the parties competed.

Yet, Canada's major parties receive less legal protection than their American equivalents and, during periods of unpopularity, can be punished by the electoral system. Thus, the Conservatives were reduced to a low ebb in the 1990s as the regional dimension intruded, with a populist party gaining seats from the concentrated support of dissatisfied voters in the resource-rich west. Similarly, the Liberals suffered badly in 2011, winning a mere 34 seats in the House of Commons.

Federalism in Canada

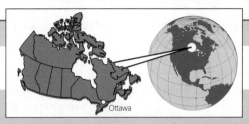

Ottawa

The federal constitution of 1867 gave priority to Canada's national government, reserving to the provinces 'matters of a merely local or private nature'. As this phrase suggests, the document's authors thought of the provinces as little more than glorified municipalities. Since then, however, 'Canada has moved from a highly centralized political situation to one of the most decentralized federal systems in the world' (Landes, 2002, p. 102). What explains this transformation?

Canada's decentralizing trend, perhaps unique among federations, reflects the central issue of its politics: the place within it of French-speaking Quebec. From the sixteenth century, France and then Britain colonized the territories of Canada, with Britain finally defeating the French in 1763. The francophone population in Canada has declined since them, falling to 22 per cent by 2006.

In contrast to the racial division in the USA, where blacks do not comprise a majority in any state, more than 85 per cent of Canada's francophones live in Quebec and about 80 per cent of Quebec's population speaks French as a mother tongue (Lachapelle, 2009). Canada therefore provides a test case of federalism's ability to integrate a geographically concentrated minority.

For many francophones, Canada consists of two founding peoples – the British and French – whose status should be equal. The assumption is that the country is a compact between two cultures, rather than 10 provinces. The inference is that Quebec, as a representative of one of

the founding cultures, should receive special recognition within the federation.

From the 1960s, a revived nationalist party in Quebec sought to implement this vision. However, the federal response has been to decentralize power to all 10 provinces, not merely to Quebec. In Quebec itself, the Parti Québécois (PQ), elected to power in 1994, held a referendum in 1995 on 'sovereignty association' for the province. This scheme would have combined political sovereignty for

phases of intense debate over the position of French-speaking Canada. As Brooks (2012, p. 220) puts it, 'divided jurisdiction has given rise to a sprawling and complicated network of relations linking the federal and provincial governments. This network is often compared to an iceberg, only a small part of which is visible to the eye'.

Although multilevel governance is often viewed favourably in the European Union, its secrecy and unclear accountability in Canada has

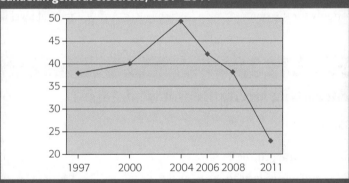

Figure 14.2 Bloc Québécois share of the vote (%) in Quebec: Canadian general elections, 1997–2011

Quebec with continued economic association with Canada. The proposal lost by the narrowest of margins. Subsequently, the issue of constitutional reform declined in intensity, with the PQ voted out of provincial office in 2003. The share of the vote obtained by the Bloc Québécois (which runs candidates at federal elections) also plummeted in the 2000s (Figure 14.2).

Multilevel governance, known in Canada as executive federalism, continued to operate even during these

sparked significant criticism. In the context of a state with clear democratic traditions, executive federalism lacks any explicit base in law and the constitution. Even so, the practices of multilevel governance are surely an inherent feature of Canada's distinctive but long-lasting federation.

Further reading: Brooks (2012), Inwood (2012), Stevenson (2009).

But the enhanced authority of the centre was far more than a financial matter. It also reflected the emergence of a national economy demanding overall coordination. Clearly, national planning is needed to forestall the absurdity of highways ending at a state's borders. or villains just being expelled from a state, rather than arrested there.

Over the twentieth century, the broader expansion of public functions also worked to the centre's advantage. Wars and depressions invariably empowered the national government. Additional powers, once acquired, tended to be retained. In European federations, the post-1945 drive to complete a uniform welfare state based on national citizenship enhanced the national government still further.

From the 1980s, however, the trends became less clear-cut. On the one hand, big projects run by the centre went out of fashion, partly because national governments found themselves financially stretched in eras of lower taxation and, latterly, financial crisis. Reflecting this trend, the judiciary in many federations also made some effort to encourage greater autonomy for the states.

On the other hand, the centre still sought to provide overall direction. Most obviously, early in the twenty-first century national governments led the response to the terrorist threat. In the USA, 'national control of domestic security eliminates a great deal of the discretion available to state and local government in areas that have previously been left free of federal interference' (Albritton, 2006, p. 14). Times of crisis overwhelm the niceties of federalism (Benz and Broschek, 2012).

Assessing federalism

What conclusions can we reach about the federal experiment (Box 14.3)? The case for federalism is that it offers a natural and practical arrangement for organizing large states. It provides checks and balances on a territorial basis, keeps some government functions closer to the people, and allows for the representation of ethnic differences.

Federalism reduces overload in the national executive, while the existence of multiple provinces produces healthy competition and opportunities for experiment. States can move ahead even when the federal level languishes: early in the twenty-first

---

BOX 14.3

Federalism: strengths and weaknesses

Strength	Weakness
A practical arrangement for large countries	May be less effective in responding to security threats
Provides checks and balances	Decision-making is slow and complicated: 'trouble, expense and delay' (Bryce, 1919, p. 341)
Allows for the recognition of diversity	Can entrench divisions between provinces
Reduces overload at the centre	The centre experiences greater difficulty in launching national initiatives
Provides competition between provinces and allows citizens to move between them	How citizens are treated depends on where they live
Offers opportunities for policy experiments	Complicates accountability: who is responsible?
Allows small units to cooperate in achieving the economic and military advantages of size	May permit majorities within a province to exploit a minority
Brings government closer to the people	Basing representation in the upper chamber on states violates the principle of one person, one vote

century, for example, California and some other American states showed more concern with climate change than did the federal government in Washington.

Citizens and firms also have the luxury of choice: if they dislike governance in one state, they can always move to another. Above all, federalism reconciles two modern imperatives: securing the economic and military advantages of scale, while retaining – indeed, encouraging – cultural diversity.

But a case can also be mounted against federalism. Compared with unitary government, decision-making in a federation is complicated, slow-moving, andhesitant. When a gunman ran amok in Tasmania in 1996, killing 35 people, federal Australia experienced some political problems before it succeeded in tightening gun control uniformly across the country. By contrast, unitary Britain acted speedily when a comparable incident occurred in the same year at a primary school in Dunblane, Scotland.

Federalism can place the political interests of rival governments above the resolution of shared problems. Fiscal discipline becomes harder to enforce; for instance, several Latin American federations have struggled to control their free-spending (and free-riding) provinces. Extravagant spending by provinces – aware that they will be bailed out, if necessary, by the centre – can dent the fiscal strength of the state as a whole (Braun *et al.*, 2003).

Any final judgement on federalism must take a view on the proper balance between the concentration and diffusion of political power. Should it rest with one body in order to allow decisive action? From this perspective, federalism is likely to be seen as an obstacle and impediment – and, even, as an anti-democratic device. Alternatively, should power be dispersed so as to reduce the danger of majority dictatorship? Through this lens, federalism will appear as an indispensable aid to liberty.

The European Union

Our understanding of federalism can be usefully tested against the challenging case of the European Union. Leaving aside opinion on whether the EU ought to develop as a federation, to what extent can this singular entity already be regarded as possessing a federal, rather than simply intergovernmental, character?

The case for admitting the EU to the federal family is certainly substantial. Shared sovereignty is the core feature of federalism and, by this test, the Union already possesses a broadly federal status, as a comparison with the USA shows. As with the United States, the European Union has a strong legal basis in the treaties on which it is founded. The European Court of Justice, like America's Supreme Court, adjudicates disputes between levels of government. In both cases, court decisions apply directly to citizens, must be implemented by member states, and take priority over state laws.

In both the EU and the USA, citizens of the component parts are also citizens of the whole. British passports, for instance, are adorned with 'European Union' as well as 'United Kingdom'. Externally, the EU is directly represented in international bodies such as the United Nations; it maintains delegations to more than 100 countries. A directly-elected parliament exercises increasing influence in EU affairs. As with the American federal government, the Union has specific policy responsibilities, notably for the single market. These are hardly signs of a mere intergovernmental organization.

In short, in the European Union – as in America – sovereignty is already pooled. It is only UK intransigence that insisted on the name 'European Union' rather than 'European Federation'. McKay's judgement from 1999 (p. 220) is certainly still relevant: 'we can conclude that although, after the implementation of Maastricht (1992), the EU remains an unusual and still evolving political entity, it also qualifies as a species of federal state'.

Yet, the points against interpreting the EU as a federation are also substantial. Contrasts with the American exemplar remain clear:

- the USA possesses a single currency and freedom of movement, but these goals have only been partly achieved within the EU;

- the EU is still governed by treaties between states, whereas the United States was founded on a constitution;

- where the USA was designed as a federation from the start, the EU was built on agreeing concrete policies, particularly for a single market, with federation as a faded aspiration;

- where the USA fought a civil war to preserve its union, the EU has not faced this vital test nor, without its own military force, is it in any position to do so;

- the EU possesses a unicameral parliament, whereas the USA, as with the legislatures of other federations, is bicameral;

- national identities remain far more important to EU citizens than state loyalties are to Americans.

In addition, we should note three additional points against a federal interpretation of the Union. First, the EU does not tax its citizens directly. Its main revenue source is a levy on the gross national income of member states.

Second, member states have retained substantial control of the vital areas of foreign and defence policy, including the use of armed force. The Common Foreign and Security Policy (established in 1991 to build on earlier cooperation in this area) remains a work in progress.

Third, member states retain individual membership of intergovernmental bodies, such as the United Nations.

Overall, we can conclude that the EU represents some pooling of its members' sovereignty and consists of institutions through which sovereignty is exercised. In these respects, the Union is certainly more than an alliance yet, as in the early decades of the United States, its members retain much of their traditional autonomy. Fundamentally, the members are still separate states and are recognized as such in the international system. If the EU is to be seen as a federation, it is certainly unique in its distribution of powers between the centre and its members.

One possible compromise is to interpret the Union as confederal in character (Warleigh, 1998). Nugent (2010, p. 425) provides a summary of this position:

Insofar as the EU is a union of previously sovereign states created by treaty in which supranational institutions exist but whose range of powers fall short of the powers exercised by their counterparts in federal systems, it may be thought of as displaying distinctive confederal traits.

Unitary states

Academic interest in federalism notwithstanding, we should remember that most states are unitary, meaning that sovereignty lies exclusively with the central government. In this hierarchical arrangement, the national government possesses the theoretical authority to abolish lower levels. Subnational administrations, whether regional or local, may both make and implement policy, but they do so by leave of the centre. Reflecting central supremacy, the national legislature in most unitary states has only one chamber, since there is no need for a second house to represent entrenched provinces.

Unitary frameworks emerge naturally in societies with a history of rule by sovereign monarchs and emperors, such as Britain, France, and Japan. In such circumstances, authority radiates from a historic core. Unitary structures are also the norm in smaller democracies, particularly those without strong ethnic divisions. In Latin America, nearly all the smaller countries (but none of the larger ones) are unitary.

The countries of Eastern Europe have also chosen a unitary structure for their post-communist constitutions, viewing federalism as a spurious device through which Russia sought to obscure its dominance of the Soviet Union.

After the complexities of federalism, a unitary structure may seem straightforward and efficient. However, the location of sovereignty is rarely an adequate guide to political realities; unitary government is often decentralized in its operation. Indeed, in the 1990s many unitary states attempted to push responsibility for more functions to lower levels. In practice, just like federations, unitary states are best viewed through the lens of multilevel governance.

We can distinguish three broad ways in which unitary states disperse power from the centre: deconcentration, decentralization, and devolution (Box 14.4). The first of these, **deconcentration**, is purely an administrative matter, denoting a relocation of central government employees from the capital. The case for deconcentration is that it spreads the work around; reduces costs by allowing activities to move to cheaper areas; and frees central departments to focus on policy-making, rather than execution. Routine tasks such as issuing passports

---

BOX 14.4

Methods for distributing power away from the centre

	Definition	Example
Deconcentration	Central government functions are executed by staff in the field	Most US federal civilian employees work away from Washington, DC
Decentralization	Central government functions are executed by subnational authorities	Local governments administer national welfare programmes in Scandinavia
Devolution	Central government grants some decision-making autonomy to lower levels	Regional governments in France, Italy and Spain

Note: Deconcentration and decentralization occur in federal as well as unitary states.

---

can be deconcentrated to an area with higher unemployment and lower costs.

The second, and politically more significant, way of dispersing power is through **decentralization**. This term means that policy execution is delegated to subnational bodies, such as local authorities. Scandinavia is the classic example. There, local governments put into effect many welfare programmes agreed at national level. In a similar way, local government in the UK serves as the workhorse of central authority, implementing plans formed at the centre.

The third and most radical form of power dispersal is **devolution**. This occurs when the centre grants decision-making autonomy (including some legislative powers) to lower levels. Spain is an example here. Its regions were strengthened in the transition to democracy following General Franco's death in 1975, and devolution has continued apace since, with Catalonia's status as a distinct nationality recognized in 2006. Although Spain is often treated as a *de facto* federation, in theory its framework is devolved but unitary.

In the UK, too, the contrast with federations remains even after devolution. Britain remains a unitary state because the devolved assemblies introduced in Scotland and Wales in 1999 could be abolished by Westminster through normal legislation. As the English politician Enoch Powell observed, 'power devolved is power retained'.

Regional governance

The creation and expansion of the middle tier of government – the regional level standing between central and local authority – was an important trend in many unitary states in the second half of the twentieth century. In a study of 42 mainly high-income countries over this period, Hooghe *et al.* (2010, p. 54) found that 29 witnessed an increase in regional authority compared with only two showing a decline. The larger the country, the more powerful this middle level tended to be. As a result of these developments, unitary states such as France, Italy, and Poland now possess three levels of subnational government: regional, provincial, and local (Table 14.2).

Complexity is increased by the fact that, in several countries, lower levels are not accountable to the next level up. The result is a multilevel system that is even more intricate than federations in which local governments are typically nested within, and a responsibility of, each state.

In origin, many regions were merely spatial units constructed by the centre to present figures on inequalities within a country and policies to reduce them. Regional planning of this kind became common in Western democracies in the 1950s and 1960s, initially as part of post-war reconstruction (Bickerton and Gagnon, 2011, p. 286).

Table 14.2 Subnational government in some unitary liberal democracies: number of units by tier

Large unitary states in Europe typically possess three tiers of subnational government. However, the lowest tier sometimes consists of minute communes with few functions.

	France	Italy	Netherlands	Poland	Sweden
Highest tier (region)	22	20	–	16	–
Middle tier (province)	100	103	12	314	20
Lowest tier (municipality)	36,568	8,101	408	2,478	290

Source: Updated from Loughlin *et al.* (2011), appendix 1.

In most large unitary states, however, specific regional organizations were soon established. They became an administrative vehicle through which the centre could decentralize planning, with regional bodies taking responsibility for economic development and related public infrastructure; notably, transport. These bodies were not always directly elected; indeed, they were typically created by a push from the centre, rather than a pull from the regions.

In many large European unitary states, the coordinating function of administrative regions has advanced considerably. Regions provide a valuable **mesolevel** perspective below that of the country as a whole but above that of local areas. Amalgamation of local governments can achieve some of the same effect but often at greater political cost, given the importance of traditional communities to many inhabitants.

A key factor influencing the development of regional institutions is whether they are, or become, directly elected. Election enhances visibility but, for better or worse, political and partisan factors come to intrude more directly into their operations.

> The **mesolevel** is the intermediate, typically regional, layer of government located between national and local levels. 'Meso' comes from the Greek *mésos*, meaning middle.

France is an example of this transition. The 22 regional councils established there in 1972 initially possessed extremely limited executive powers. However, their status was enhanced by a decentral-

ization law passed in 1982 providing for direct election. The first round of these elections took place in 1986. Even though French regional bodies continue to operate with small budgets, they have acquired greater visibility and authority.

The case for direct election is perhaps strongest where regions are already important cultural entities, providing a focus for citizens' identities. In the United Kingdom, for example, attempts by the Labour government to create elected regional assemblies in England foundered on public apathy. But assemblies were successfully introduced to Scotland and Wales, where national loyalties were well-established.

The European Union has encouraged the development of a regional level within its member states. The European Regional Development Fund, established in 1975, distributes aid directly to regions, rather than through central governments. The notion, somewhat exaggerated but significant at the time, was that the EU and the regions would gradually become the leading policy-makers, outflanking central governments which would be left with less to do in this new disposition.

The EU furthered such aspirations by introducing a Committee of the Regions and Local Communities in 1988. This body, composed of subnational authorities, proved to be merely consultative, however. National executives remain more central to the policy process than the more committed proponents of regional governance in the EU had envisaged.

Even so, the complexities of multilevel governance in unitary states mean that the exclusive focus of sovereignty at the national level is an increasingly poor guide to the realities of making and implementing coherent public policy.

Local governance

Local government is universal, found in federal and unitary states alike. It is the lowest level of elected territorial organization and it is 'where the day-to-day activity of politics and government gets done' (Teune, 1995b, p. 16). For example, 9/11 was certainly a global event, but it was officials in New York City who faced the immediate task of providing emergency services. Given its role in service delivery, local government should not be what it tends to be: the forgotten tier.

At their best, local administrations express the virtues of limited scale. They can represent natural communities, remain accessible to their citizens, reinforce local identities, offer a practical education in politics, provide a recruiting ground to higher posts, serve as a first port of call for citizens, and distribute resources in the light of specialist knowledge. Yet, local governments also have characteristic weaknesses. They are often too small to deliver services efficiently, lack sufficient fund-raising powers to set their own priorities, and are easily dominated by traditional elites.

> **General competence** is the authority of a local government to make regulations in any matter of concern to its area. Where general competence is lacking, local authorities are restricted to those tasks expressly mandated by higher authority. Any additional acts would be *ultra vires* – beyond the powers.

The balance struck between intimacy and efficiency varies over time. In the second half of the twentieth century, local authorities were encouraged to become more efficient, leading to larger units. For example, the number of Swedish municipalities fell from 2,500 in 1951 to 274 in 1974 (Rose, 2004, p. 168). In Britain, where efficiency concerns have been a high priority, the average population served by local authorities reached 142,015 by 2007, the highest in Europe (Loughlin *et al.*, 2011, appendix 1).

Towards the end of the twentieth century, signs emerged of a rebirth of interest in citizen involvement, stimulated by the need to respond to declining turnout at local elections. In New Zealand, successful managerial reforms introduced in 1989 were followed by the Local Government Act (2002). This law outlined a more expansive, participatory vision for local authorities.

Similarly, 'in the early 1990s, Dutch local government was preoccupied with a concern for effectiveness and efficiency. During the 1990s, however, the

---

BOX 14.5

Exploring the status of local government

Higher	Lower	Comment
In European democracies	In New World democracies (e.g. Australia, USA)	In Europe local governments often represent historic communities, but in the New World local government is more utilitarian in character
In Northern Europe (e.g. Scandinavia)	In Southern Europe (e.g. France, Italy)	Local governments administer the extensive welfare states found in Northern Europe but perform fewer functions in Southern Europe
When local governments possess **general competence** to represent their community	When local governments cannot act *ultra vires* ('beyond the powers')	General competence allows local authorities to take the initiative whereas *ultra vires* restricts them to designated functions

emphasis switched to the issue of public responsive-ness' (Denters and Klok, 2005, p. 65). In 1995, Norway resolved that 'no further amalgamations should be imposed against the wishes of a majority of residents in the municipalities concerned' (Rose, 2004, p. 168). This cycling between efficiency and participation concerns suggests not only a real trade-off between the two, but also the difficulty of arriving at a stable balance between them.

Status

The status of local government varies markedly across countries (Box 14.5). Consider, first, the con-trast between European and New World democra-cies. In most of Europe, local authorities represent historic communities that predate the emergence of strong national governments. The origins of many Italian communes, for instance, can be dated back to the twelfth century. Reflecting this position, European constitutions normally mandate some form of local self-government. Sweden's Instrument of Government roundly declares that Swedish democracy 'shall be realized through a representative and parliamentary polity and through local self-gov-ernment'.

In the New World, by contrast, local government reflected more pragmatic, utilitarian concerns. Local authorities were set up as needed to deal with 'roads, rates and rubbish'. Special boards (appointed or elected) were added to deal with specific problems such as mosquito control, harbours, and land drainage. The policy style was apolitical: 'there is no Democratic or Republican way to collect garbage'. Indeed, special boards were often set up precisely to be independent of party politics.

Second, the standing of local government varies within Europe on a broad north–south axis. In the northern countries, local authorities became impor-tant delivery vehicles for the extensive welfare states that matured after 1945. Services such as social assis-tance, unemployment benefit, and education were funded by the centre but provided locally, giving rise to such phrases as the 'welfare municipality' and the 'local welfare state'. In effect, local authorities became the government's front office, employing about one in four of the total workforce in Nordic countries (Rose, 2004, p. 169). In some countries, including Denmark, local authorities also act as tax collectors for the centre.

In southern Europe, by contrast, welfare states remain less extensive, with the Catholic Church playing a greater role in providing care, while public services such as education remain under the direct control of central government. In Italy, for instance, teachers are civil servants, rather than employees of local councils. Also, communes in Southern Europe have remained small, especially in France where some are longer on history than people (Figure 14.3). Limited scale precludes an extensive adminis-trative role.

Third, **general competence** enhances both the authority and the standing of local authorities. Germany's Basic Law, for instance, gives local com-munities 'the right to regulate [all local matters]

Figure 14.3 Average population of municipalities (lowest tier) in selected European liberal democracies, 2007

Municipalities in many European democracies remain remarkably small. They represent historic communities but must often join consortia for the supply of services.

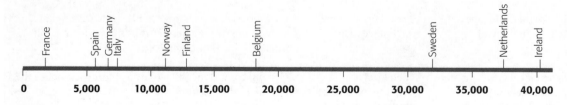

Note: Not shown: Denmark (56,239), UK (142,015).

Source: Adapted from Loughlin *et al.* (2011), appendix 1.

under their own responsibility and within the limits of the law'. Similarly, the Dutch constitution states that local communities have 'autonomous' powers to regulate their own affairs.

But in other countries, including the United Kingdom, councils could traditionally only perform those tasks expressly designated by the centre; any other act would be *ultra vires*. In the United States, Dillon's Rule (1872) similarly restricts local governments to tasks delegated by their particular state. Some countries in which *ultra vires* applies, including the United Kingdom and New Zealand, did establish a more liberal legal framework at the start of the twenty-first century but without granting the full power of general competence (Bush, 2005).

Structure

The structure of local government has recently attracted attention as attempts are made to render decision-making more visible to local electorates in an era of falling turnout. One particular goal has been to repackage mayors as public figureheads of the districts they represent. Just as political parties have sought to reverse a decline in membership by giving their supporters more say in the selection of candidates and leaders, so local governments in such countries as Italy, the Netherlands, and the United

Kingdom have encouraged turnout by introducing direct mayoral elections. A high profile mayor, such as Boris Johnson in London, can enhance the district's visibility not only within the area but also, and equally importantly, among potential visitors and investors. We see here a relationship between institutional design and the marketing of place.

There are, in fact, three broad ways of organizing local government: the council, mayor–council, and council–manager formats (Box 14.6). We outline each in turn.

The *first* and most traditional method is the council system, as used in Sweden and, traditionally, in England. This arrangement concentrates authority in a college of elected councillors which is formally responsible for overseeing the organization's work. This council often operates through powerful committees covering the main local services. The mayor is appointed by the council itself, or by central government. Whatever virtues this format may have, its collegiate character presents an opaque picture to residents and the wider world.

Accordingly, a *second* method of organization, known as the 'mayor–council' system, has attracted attention. This model is more presidential than parliamentary. It is based on a separation of powers between an elected mayor and an elected council. The mayor is chief executive; the council possesses

---

BOX 14.6

Structures for local government

	Description	Examples
Council system	Elected councillors form a council which operates through a smaller subgroup or through functional committees. The unelected mayor is appointed by the council, or by central government.	Belgium, Netherlands, Sweden
Mayor–council system	An elected mayor serves as chief executive. Councillors elected from local wards form a council with legislative and financial authority. This format is subdivided into strongly-mayoral and weakly-mayoral systems.	About half the cities in the USA, including Chicago and New York
Council–manager system	The mayor and council appoint a professional manager to run executive departments. The mayor has no executive powers.	Almost half the cities in the USA, including Dallas and San Antonio

legislative and budget-approving powers. Used in many large American cities (such as New York), this highly political format permits a range of urban interests to be represented within an elaborate framework. The mayor and council often disagree, just as at national level the president is frequently in conflict with Congress. Again, as at national level, the mayor is usually elected at large (from the entire area), while councillors represent specific neighbourhoods.

The powers awarded to the mayor and council vary considerably. In the 'strong mayor' version, the mayor is the focus of authority and accountability, with the power to appoint and dismiss department heads without council approval. New York City is an example. In the 'weak mayor' format, the council retains both legislative and executive authority, keeping the mayor on a closer leash. London's mayor – directly elected since 2000 – is a classic weak mayor. Whether strong or weak, an elected mayor does at least offer a public face for the area.

The *third* structure for local government is the council–manager system. This intriguing arrangement seeks to depoliticize and simplify local government by separating politics from administration. This distinction is achieved by appointing a professional city manager, operating under the elected council, to administer the authority's work. Emerging in the USA early in the twentieth century in an attempt to curb corruption, the council–manager format has been widely adopted in the American west and south-west. The council–manager model has corporate overtones, with the voters (shareholders) electing councillors (board of directors) to oversee a city manager (chief executive) who is responsible for cost-effective service delivery. As in the council system, the mayor's position is largely ceremonial. This format does allow the manager to focus on efficient service delivery, free from political interference, but the distinction between politics and administration is often difficult to maintain in practice.

Functions

What is it that local governments do? Broadly, their tasks are twofold. First, they provide an extensive and, for residents, significant range of local public services. These include libraries, local planning, primary education, provision for the elderly, refuse collection, and water supply. The second task, more important in some countries than others, is to implement national welfare policies. However, a static description of functions fails to reveal how the role of local government has evolved since the 1980s, particularly in those countries where large local authorities perform significant functions.

One important trend, especially prominent in the English-speaking world and Scandinavia, has been for municipal authorities to reduce their direct provision of services by delegating tasks to non-government organizations, both profit-making and voluntary. This transition from local government towards local governance reflects the emergence of new public management at national level (see Chapter 17). In theory, most local government services – from libraries to street-cleaning – can be outsourced, with potential gains in efficiency and service quality. But in practice these benefits are not always achieved, creating some risk in the transfer, and there remains the broader issue of whether direct provision of services by a local authority to the citizen is intrinsically preferable to delivery by a contractor to a consumer.

Delegation of services represents an evolution from providing to enabling. The enabling authority does not so much provide services as ensure that they are supplied. In theory, the authority becomes a smaller, coordinating body, more concerned with governance than government. In addition to outsourcing, a greater number of organizations can become involved in local policy-making, many of them functional (e.g. school boards), rather than territorial (e.g. county councils). This more coordinating and strategic approach is often linked to a growing concern among local governments with economic development, especially in attracting inward investment.

Relationships with the centre

We must ask an additional question about local government: how is it integrated into the national structure of power? The answer depends partly on whether the system is federal or unitary. In federations, local authorities tend to be subordinate to the states, creating organizational diversity but also reducing overall coherence. For example, none of the American, Australian, or Canadian constitutions mention local government; it is the creature of the provinces and can be modified, or even abolished, as they wish. Inevitably, though, important cities do develop direct relationships with the central government, to some extent bypassing their provincial authority.

In unitary states, relationships with the centre are variable, depending on whether local governments are seen as an agent of a single, undivided state structure (see definitions below). In a **dual** approach, local government is seen as an organization separate from the centre: public authority is divided rather than integrated. It is as if there were two spheres of authority, connected for practical reasons only – an equivalent to dual federalism but in a unitary setting. Local governments retain free-standing status, setting their own internal organization and employing staff on their own conditions of service. Employees move horizontally (from one local authority to another), rather than vertically (between central and local government). Ultimate authority rests with the centre, but local government employees do not regard themselves as working for the same employer as central civil servants. National politicians rarely emerge from local politics.

Traditionally, Britain was regarded as the classic example of this dual system. Even though the country is unitary, with sovereignty focused on the centre, local government is seen as more than a sub-branch of national authority. This separation reflects history. Before the rise of the modern state, local magistrates had administered their local communities. The spirit of self-government survives in a perception that central and local government are distinct, if intensely interdependent, spheres.

In the Nordic countries, too, local authorities are still viewed as self-governing units operating with discretionary authority within a unitary framework, even though much of their detailed work involves implementing national policy.

A **dual** system of local government (as in Britain) maintains a formal separation of central and local government. Although the centre is sovereign, local authorities are not seen as part of a single state apparatus. In a **fused** system (as in France), municipalities form part of a uniform system of administration applying across the state's territory.

Under a **fused** system, by contrast, central and local government combine to form a single sphere of public authority. Both levels are expressions of state authority. In some European countries, such as Belgium and the Netherlands, the local mayor is even appointed by the national government, and is responsible to the centre for maintaining law and order. In addition, central authority is represented locally in the office of the **prefect**. In theory, a prefectoral system signals central dominance by establishing a clear hierarchy running from national government through the prefect to local authorities.

A **prefect** is an official appointed by the central government to oversee the implementation of national policy in a particular area. The prefectoral system was originally designed to encourage policy uniformity and to enforce local allegiance to central authority.

France is the standard example of this fused approach. Established by Napoleon early in the nineteenth century, the system consists of 96 *départements* in mainland France, each with its own prefect and elected assembly. Napoleon called prefects 'emperors with small feet' but, in practice, the prefect must cooperate with local and regional councils, rather than simply oversee them. The prefect has ceased to be the local emperor and is instead an agent of the *département*, representing interests upwards as much as transmitting commands downwards. The French model remains influential, however. Many other countries have adopted it, including all France's ex-colonies and several post-communist states.

One expression of a fused system is the ease with which politicians move between, and frequently straddle, national and local government. In Belgium, two out of three members of the National Assembly also hold local political office (Winter and Brans, 2003, p. 51). In France, too, national politicians often become or remain mayor of their home town. This simultaneous occupancy of posts at different tiers is known in France as the *cumul des mandats* (accumulation of offices). Even after the rules were tightened in 1985 and 2000, the most popular *cumul* – combining the office of local mayor with membership of the National Assembly – is still permitted. It is an entrenched tradition reflecting the fused character of French public authority even in an era of decentralization.

Cities

As most of the world's people live in cities, the governance of large urban areas has emerged as an issue complicating multilevel governance in both federal and unitary states. The interdependence of cities and suburbs means that both need to be treated as a single metropolitan area – a city region. But this goal has proved difficult to achieve, given traditional boundaries.

Cities possess distinctive problems. Typically, rich and poor, as well as native and immigrant, coexist uneasily within city boundaries. Poverty and ethnic diversity create a strong need for public policy.

Just as the need for planning stimulated the emergence of regional government in the second half of the twentieth century, so it has come to drive the development of techniques for governing large city regions. Large, integrated urban areas do not match traditional local government units. Bull and Newell (2005, p. 158) note that Italy provides an example of one response to this problem:

Urbanization and industrialization over the postwar decades led to an increasing concentration of population and economic activity in a small number of urban areas, giving rise to strategic needs not always met by existing divisions of competence. Law no. 142 (1990) thus denoted specific large cities as 'metropolitan areas', and made it possible for the communes within such areas to come together to form metropolitan cities.

Not all countries have made a success of metropolitan governance. Australia illustrates the failure to develop effective mechanisms (Gleeson and Steele, 2012). Australia is a nation of cities, with the five largest state capitals – Adelaide, Brisbane, Melbourne, Perth, and Sydney – accommodating most of the country's people. These urban areas are inadequately governed in the existing, three-tier (national, state, local) federation. National involvement in running cities is limited by the constitution; state administrations must also confront other pressures (including those from rural areas); and local government itself is subordinate and fragmented, with 34 local authorities operating in Sydney alone.

A federal structure does not mesh well with a population concentrated in a few large cities.

In the governance of cities, the capital occupies a special place. As an important component of the national brand, the capital's leaders merit regular communication with the central government. For instance, how well Sydney, Beijing, and London deliver the Olympics is a matter of concern for the national government as well as for the host cities themselves.

However, the capital's international connections mean it can become semi-detached from its national moorings, as implied by the notion of a world city. Here, we see substance to the notion that the relationships between levels of government within a country depends partly on their position in the international order. Located in the same country, the interests of the centre and the capital can nonetheless diverge. Inevitably, the capital is treated somewhat differently from other cities, producing a further complexity to multilevel governance.

Central–local relations in authoritarian states

Studying the relationship between centre and periphery in authoritarian states confirms the relative insignificance of institutions in non-democracies. In these regimes, the distinction between local government and local power is fundamental. The former is weak: authority flows from the top down, and bottom-up institutions of representation are subordinate. When national power is exercised by the military or a ruling party, these bodies typically establish a parallel presence in the provinces, where their authority overrides that of formal state officials. For a humble mayor in such a situation, the main skill required is to lie low and avoid offending the real power-holders. Little of the pluralistic policy-making suggested by the notion of multilevel governance takes place and the more general description 'central–local relations' is preferable.

But it would be wrong to conclude that authoritarian regimes are highly centralized. That position would represent a somewhat stereotyped view of dictatorships. Rather, central rulers – just like medieval monarchs – often depend on established provincial leaders to sustain their own, sometimes tenuous, grip on power. Central–local relations therefore tend to be more personal and less structured than in a liberal democracy. Particularly in smaller countries, the hold of regional strongmen on power is not embedded in local institutions; such rulers command their fiefdoms in a personal fashion, replicating the authoritarian pattern found at national level. Central and local rulers are integrated by patronage: the national ruler effectively buys the support of local bigwigs who, in turn, maintain their position by selectively distributing state resources to their own supporters. Patronage, not institutions, is the rope that binds.

In larger authoritarian states, we can observe more structure to central–local relations. Consider China and Russia. In China, despite its vast scale, we find a unitary state centred on Beijing. With some exceptions, including 'autonomous' regions such as Tibet which are ruled in imperial fashion from Beijing, subnational government takes the form of 22 provinces (five of which contain over 70 million people). There are further subdivisions into either counties and townships, or cities and districts. These provinces have gained substantial practical autonomy as the moral authority of, and funding from, the centre has declined. Provincial and city governments have spearheaded local economic development, stimulated by the desire of local political elites not simply to achieve personal wealth, but also to improve the resource base of their administrations. This effective decentralization allows provinces to become laboratories for new policies but simultaneously accentuates inequalities between them, leading to occasional expressions of concern about the possibility of the country disintegrating.

However, as in the Soviet Union, the party itself provides a method of integrating centre and periphery. In particular, the circulation of party leaders between national and provincial posts helps to connect the two tiers, providing China's equivalent to the European *cumul des mandats*. Several provincial leaders serve on the party's central politburo; further, most members of this key body have worked in top provincial posts at some point in their career. It is these party linkages that provide the key channel through which Beijing maintains a measure of control over the country.

In Russia, by contrast, we find a federation, rather than a unitary state. The federation of over 80 units comprises republics, provinces, territories, districts, and cities. But, as we might expect in a competitive authoritarian regime, the theory of federalism is overcome by the realities of power. Unlike China, there is no party with the capacity to integrate

> The **power vertical** is a Russian phrase denoting central control over lower levels of government within the federation.

centre and periphery. Rather, the **power vertical** operates from the Kremlin.

Although Russia experienced the most remarkable decentralization of power under Boris Yeltsin (President, 1991–99), this experiment was followed by considerable recentralization under Vladimir Putin. He achieved his goal in three main ways:

- by establishing a uniform system which sought to eliminate special deals his predecessor had established with many regions;

- by acquiring the power of appointment and dismissal over regional governors;

- by creating, in 2000, seven extra-constitutional federal *okrugs* (districts) to oversee lower-level units. Each *okrug* is responsible for between 6 and 15 regions. These overlords ensure that branches of the federal government in the regions remain loyal to Moscow.

Through these devices, Putin increased the capacity of the central state to govern the Russian people. Ross (2010, p. 170) even concludes that 'Russia is now a unitary state masquerading as a federation.' Certainly, Putin's reforms contributed to his project of creating what he termed a 'sovereign democracy' in Russia. In Putin's eyes, a sovereign democracy is not built on the uncertain pluralistic foundations of multilevel governance. Rather, it gives priority to the interests of Russia herself, interests which include an effective central state capable of controlling its population. On that foundation, the Russian state seeks to strengthen its position in what it sees as a hostile international environment.

Discussion questions

■ What is multilevel governance and does it exemplify or limit liberal democracy?

■ In what circumstances is a federation an appropriate form of government?

■ Is the European Union a federation?

■ Should local governments be headed by elected mayors?

■ Should local authorities enable, provide, or both?

■ To what extent has the capital city in your country become detached from its national moorings, as implied by the notion of a world city?

Further reading

I. Bache and M. Flinders, eds, *Multi-level Governance* (2004). Examines multilevel governance and applies the notion to specific policy sectors.

M. Burgess, *In Search of the Federal Spirit: New Theoretical and Empirical Perspectives in Comparative Federalism* (2012). Classic treatments of federalism applied to contemporary examples.

B. Dollery, J. Garcea and E. LeSage, Jr, eds, *Local Government Reform: A Comparative Analysis of Advanced Anglo-American Countries* (2008). A discussion of local government reform in Anglo-American countries.

J. Loughlin, F. Hendriks and A. Lidström, eds, *The Oxford Handbook of Local and Regional Democracy in Europe* (2011). Surveys subnational democracy in 29 countries and assesses the Anglo, French, German, and Scandinavian state traditions.

J. Pierre, *The Politics of Urban Governance* (2011). Assesses four models of governance against the challenges facing cities.

R. Watts, *Comparing Federal Systems*, 3rd edn (2008). Considers the design and operation of a wide range of federations.

ONLINE RESOURCES AVAILABLE

Visit the companion website at **www.palgrave.com/politics/hague** to access additional learning resources, including multiple-choice questions, chapter summaries, web links and practice essay questions.

Chapter 15 **Legislatures**

Legislatures are symbols of popular representation in politics. They are not governing bodies, they do not take major decisions and, usually, they do not even initiate proposals for laws. Yet, they remain a foundation of both liberal and democratic politics. This significance arises from their representative role: 'legislatures join society to the legal structure of authority in the state. Legislatures are representative bodies: they reflect the sentiments and opinions of the citizens' (Olson, 1994, p. 1). As the English political theorist John Locke observed:

It is in their legislative, that the members of a commonwealth are united, and combined together into one coherent living body. This is the soul that gives form, life, and unity, to the commonwealth: from hence the several members have their mutual influence, sympathy, and connexion: and, therefore, when the legislative is broken, or dissolved, dissolution and death follows. (Locke, 1690, sec. 212)

In short, legislatures help to mobilize consent for the system of rule. As liberal democracy spreads throughout the world, so a greater number of legislatures are gaining the political weight which comes from performing this function of standing for the people.

> A **legislature** is a multimember representative body which considers public issues and 'gives assent, on behalf of a political community that extends beyond the executive authority, to binding measures of public policy' (Norton, 1990, p. 1). The words used to denote these bodies reflect their original purpose: assemblies gather, congresses congregate, diets meet, dumas deliberate, legislatures pass laws, and parliaments talk.

How did legislatures acquire this significance? In brief, the origin of parliaments lies in the ancient royal courts of Europe. There, monarchs would judge important legal cases and meet with noblemen of the realm. Gradually these assemblies became more settled, coming to represent the various estates – the clergy, the nobility, and the towns – into which society was then divided. In the thirteenth and fourteenth centuries, kings began to consult estate leaders more consistently on issues of war, administration, commerce, and taxation. These early European assemblies were viewed as possessing a right to be consulted long before they became modern legislatures with the sovereign authority to pass laws.

Where European parliaments accumulated powers gradually and with difficulty, most modern constitutions celebrate the importance of the legislature. In the debates surrounding the American constitution, for instance, James Madison declared that 'in republican government, the legislative

STUDYING . . .

LEGISLATURES

- Legislatures (parliaments) link society and state. They are an essential device in a representative democracy.

- The issue of whether legislatures should have one chamber or two, though seemingly technical, exposes contrasting perspectives on how democracy should be concevied.

- Representation is the most obvious function of legislatures. But how representation should be understood, and reconciled with the importance of party, is an important question.

- The contrast between debating and committee-based legislatures offers insight into how parliaments work in practice. For committee-based legislatures, we can look not only to the United States but also to Scandinavia.

- Scrutiny (oversight) is an increasingly important function of nearly all legislatures in liberal democracies. Understanding this role means looking carefully at parliamentary committees. Comparative projects here can offer practical lessons, as well as casting light on an important component of contemporary governance.

- If you are more intrigued by the members of legislatures than the institutions themselves, there are several worthwhile themes to pursue: career politicians, the political class, corruption and its impact, celebrity politicians, and political dynasties. All these areas are well-suited to comparative analysis.

- Assemblies are found in most authoritarian regimes. The initial (and quite difficult) task here is to identity what functions they serve. Case studies of such assemblies help to reveal the opportunities for, and the informal limits on, public dissent in non-democratic settings.

power necessarily predominates' (Hamilton, 1788d, p. 265). A leading role for the assembly was judged to be an essential defence against executive tyranny; in consequence, the list of powers awarded to Congress was longer and more detailed than that given to the president. Few other legislatures are as important as the American Congress, but the principle of expressing the popular will through an assembly has become a fundamental tenet of liberal democracy. In theory, only the constitution (and the judiciary which interprets it) stands above Locke's legislative.

Contemporary legislatures contribute to detailed governance as well as to broad expressions of the popular will. Indeed, one purpose of this chapter is to show how a modern assembly – one with a well-resourced committee system and professional members with some autonomy from party – can improve the quality of legislation, scrutinize the actions of the executive, and hold influential hearings

on matters of public concern. It is in these specific ways, as much as through general representation, that the contemporary assembly confirms its mettle.

Structure

Only two things can be said with certainty about every assembly in the world: how many members it has and the number of chambers of which it is comprised. In this section, we examine these aspects of assembly structure.

Size

The size of an assembly, as indicated by the number of members in the more important lower chamber, reflects a country's population (Figure 15.1). In China, the world's most populous country, the cumbersome National People's Congress has almost 3,000 members. By contrast, the assembly in the

Figure 15.1 Population and assembly size, 2012

The larger a country's population, the greater the size of its legislature. However, assembly size plateaus once population exceeds the range of this graph.

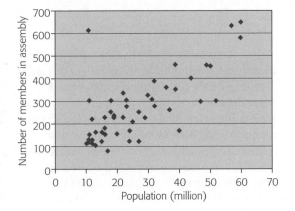

Notes: For bicameral assemblies, the size of the lower chamber is used. Analysis is confined to countries with populations in the range 10–60 million.

Sources: CIA (2012); IPU (2012).

South Pacific island of Tuvalu (population 12,373) contains just 15 representatives.

However, size is a poor measure of strength. On the contrary, giant assemblies are rendered impotent by their inability to act cohesively. They are in constant danger of being taken over by more coherent actors – such as political parties, or even their own committees. Ruling communist parties, as in China, prefer a large legislature precisely because it is easier to control.

By contrast, a very small chamber – numbering, say, under 100 – offers opportunities for all deputies to have their say in a collegial environment. An exceedingly small chamber may be entirely appropriate for island communities such as Tuvalu. In practice, as Figure 15.1 illustrates, few lower houses possess more than 500–600 members, and this is probably a fair estimate of the maximum size for an effective body.

Number of chambers

Should a legislature have one chamber, or two? If two, what role should the second chamber play and how should its members be selected? These traditional questions acquired new significance in the 1990s as a fresh wave of democratization raised anew issues of institutional design.

Unicameral legislatures are the contemporary norm. Their number increased in the second half of the twentieth century as several smaller democracies abolished their second chamber, including Sweden (1971) and Iceland (1991). Many smaller post-colonial and post-communist states also embraced a single chamber. By 2012, 115 of the world's 193 national parliaments (60 per cent) possessed only one chamber (IPU, 2012).

By contrast, **bicameral** legislatures are most often found in larger countries and in democracies; they are universal in federations, where the second chamber typically expresses the voices of the component states. Note, however, that the separation of chambers is incomplete. Many bicameral legislatures do occasionally meet in common session, not least for ceremonial purposes such as swearing in the head of state.

> Although some European assemblies originally contained multiple chambers, one for each feudal estate, parliaments today are **unicameral** (one chamber), or **bicameral** (two chambers). The first (or lower) chamber is typically known as the 'chamber of deputies', 'national assembly' or 'house of representatives'. The second (or upper) chamber is usually known as the 'senate'.

The choice between one and two chambers is not simply a technical matter of institutional design. Fundamentally, the decision reflects contrasting visions of democracy. Unicameral parliaments are justified by a majoritarian reading of popular control. The proposition is that an assembly based on direct popular election reflects the popular will and should not be obstructed. The radical French cleric Abbé Sieyès (1748–1836) put the point well: 'if a second chamber dissents from the first, it is mischievous; and if it agrees, it is superfluous' (Lively, 1991). Also, a single chamber is more accountable, economical, and decisive; it lacks the petty point-scoring which becomes possible as soon as two houses with distinct interests are created.

But the defenders of bicameral parliaments reject both the majoritarian logic of the Abbé and the penny-pinching of accountants. Bicameralists stress the liberal element of democracy, arguing that the upper chamber offers checks and balances. It can defend individual and group interests against a potentially oppressive majority in the lower house.

The second chamber can also serve as a house of review, revising bills (proposed laws), scrutinizing constitutional amendments, and eliminating intemperate legislation: in short, a second chamber for second thoughts. To adopt the terms used by the British statesman Edmund Burke (1729–97), the upper house can be a 'deliberative assembly of one nation', rather than a mere 'congress of ambassadors'.

For these reasons, the upper chamber's power to delay can be presented as a positive virtue. For example, James Madison, one of America's founding fathers, suggested that an upper house afforded protection against 'an excess of law-making' (Hamilton, 1788e). It can offer a modern approximation to the traditional idea of a council of elders, often debating in a less partisan style than the lower house.

A second house can also share the workload of the lower chamber, conduct detailed committee work, and assist with appointments (e.g. to the judiciary). In performing these detailed tasks, it can contribute to the effective functioning of a modern legislature and thereby pay its way.

Where legislatures do consist of two chambers, the question arises of the relationship between them. Usually, the lower chamber dominates. This format of **weak bicameralism** is typical of parliamentary government. In this system, after all, the government's survival depends on maintaining the assembly's support, and for clarity one chamber must (or should) become the focus of such accountability. The task of sustaining or voting down the government falls naturally to the lower house, with its popular mandate.

The dominance of the first chamber can also be seen in other ways:

- it is usually the larger house, averaging 254 members compared with 95 in the upper house (IPU, 2012);

- it often has special responsibility for the budget;

- it is the forum where major proposals are introduced;

- it is entitled to override vetoes or amendments proffered by the second chamber.

> **Weak bicameralism** arises when the lower chamber dominates the upper house, providing the primary focus for government accountability, as in most parliamentary systems. In **strong bicameralism** – found in a few federations with presidential government, such as the USA – the two chambers are more balanced.

In presidential systems, by contrast, the president is directly elected and his continuation in office does not depend on the legislature's confidence. This independent survival means that there is no need for the executive's accountability to focus on a single chamber. **Strong bicameralism** can emerge in these conditions, especially when combined with federalism. The American Congress is the best illustration of this more balanced arrangement. With its constitutional position as representative of the states, the Senate plays a full part in the country's governance.

Selection of the second chamber

A bicameral structure raises the question of how members of the second chamber should be chosen. Some divergence with the lower house is needed to avoid mirroring the party balance in the first chamber. The three main methods are direct election, indirect election, and appointment (usually by the government) (Figure 15.2).

Even when members of the upper chamber are directly elected, a contrast with the lower house is still normally achieved by offering its members a longer tenure: typically five or six years compared with four or five in the lower chamber (Table 15.1). To sharpen the contrast, the election cycle is often staggered. For instance, American senators are granted a six-year term, with one third of the seats up for election every two years.

A federal structure also produces a natural divergence between chambers. This contrast arises because, except in Canada, elections to the federal upper chamber are arranged by state, with smaller states deliberately over-represented. For instance, the American Senate contains two members for each of 50 states, meaning that California (population 37.2 million) has the same representation as Vermont (626,000). By contrast, electoral districts for the House of Representatives (the lower chamber) are designed to be equal in population. The result is that each house can check the other, especially when different parties control each chamber.

Table 15.1 Selecting the second chamber, 2012

Upper chambers are usually smaller than lower chambers, with members selected for a longer tenure and by a greater range of methods

	Chamber	Members	Term (years)	Method of selection
Australia	Senate	76	6	Direct election by single transferable vote in each state
Germany	*Bundesrat* (Federal Council)	69	–	Appointed by state governments
Ireland	Senate	60	5	Appointed by the PM (11), elected from vocational panels (43), and from two universities (6)
India	*Rajya Sabha* (Council of States)	245	6	Indirectly elected through state assemblies (233), appointed by the president (12)
USA	Senate	100	6	Direct election by plurality voting in each state

Source: IPU (2012).

Figure 15.2 Selecting the second chamber, 2012

Seats in the second (upper) chamber are allocated by three main methods: direct election, indirect election, and appointment. For comparison, 95 per cent of members of the first (lower) chamber are directly elected.

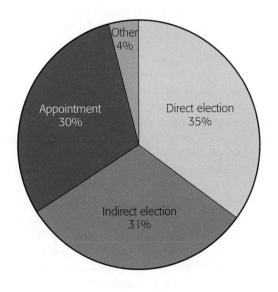

Note: Based on total number of seats (i.e. not averaged by country).

Source: IPU (2012).

Functions

Representation, we have suggested, is a key function of parliaments. But deliberation and legislation follow close behind. Other functions – crucial to some, but not all, assemblies – are authorizing expenditure, making governments, and scrutinizing the executive (Box 15.1). In discussing these roles, we will see how the significance of parliaments in liberal democracies extends well beyond the narrow task of simply converting bills into laws.

Representation

If the essence of assemblies is that they represent society to government, how can we judge whether, and how well, that function is fulfilled? What features would a fully representative assembly exhibit?

One distinction here is between **descriptive** and **substantive representation**. The idea of descriptive representation is that a legislature should be society in miniature, literally 're-presenting' society in all its diversity. Such a parliament would balance men and women, rich and poor, black and white, even educated and uneducated, in the same mix as in the population. How, after all, could a parliament composed entirely of middle-aged white men go about representing young women of colour (or, for that

Descriptive representation is present when the members of a representative body resemble the represented in given characteristics, such as ethnicity and gender. **Substantive representation** is present when representatives act on behalf of, and in the interests of, those they represent. A female legislator can reflect the substantive interests and opinions of her male constituents but cannot serve as their descriptive representative.

matter, vice versa)? To retain society's confidence, the argument continues, an assembly should reflect social diversity, standing in for society and not simply acting on its behalf (Phillips, 1995).

The widespread introduction of gender quotas for members of parliament – or, at least, for parliamentary candidates – reflects the philosophy of

BOX 15.1

Functions of legislatures

Representation	Most members articulate the goals of the party under whose label they were elected
Deliberation	Debating matters of moment is the classic function of Britain's House of Commons
Legislation	Most bills come from the government but the legislature still approves them and may make amendments in committee
Authorizing expenditure	Parliament's role is normally reactive, approving or rejecting a budget prepared by the government
Making governments (see Chapter 16)	In most parliamentary systems, the government emerges from the assembly and must retain its confidence
Scrutiny	Oversight of government activity and policy is growing in importance and is a task well-suited to the assembly's committees

descriptive representation (Chapter 8). But considerable difficulty arises in full implementation. An exact transcript of society could best be achieved by random sampling (as with juries), dispensing with election altogether. However, if such a practice were implemented, then – for better or worse – parliaments, like juries, would contain their fair share of the addicted, the corrupt, and the ignorant.

Further, representatives selected as an accurate mirror of society would need to be replaced regularly lest they become tainted by the very experience of office – a point that led the American politician John Adams (1735–1826) to proclaim that 'where annual election ends, there slavery begins'. In reality, complete descriptive representation is an impractical and probably undesirable goal.

In the main, contemporary representation operates in a somewhat prosaic way: through political parties. Victorious candidates owe their election to their party and they vote in parliament largely according to its commands. In New Zealand, for example, Labour members must agree to abide by the decisions of the party caucus. In India, an extreme case, members lose their seat if they vote against their party, the theory being that such representatives are deceiving the voters if they switch parties after their election. The party has become the vehicle of substantive representation and the prism through which electors view candidates.

Deliberation

Many legislatures serve as a deliberative body, considering public matters of national importance. This function contrasts sharply with the descriptive view of representation, prioritizing instead substantive representation, particularly in articulating the long-term interests of society at large.

In the eighteenth and nineteenth centuries, before the rise of disciplined parties, deliberation was regarded as the core parliamentary activity. In theory, at least, members were expected to serve as **trustees** of the nation, applying exceptional knowledge and intelligence to the matters before them. What mattered was the quality of debate, not whether it reflected voters' opinions.

The Irish-born politician Edmund Burke offered the classic account of this position. Elected Member of Parliament for the English constituency of

A **trustee** is responsible for protecting the property and interests of another. To view political representatives as trustees, rather than mere delegates, is to emphasize substantive representation, broadly defined.

In a **debating legislature**, such as the British House of Commons, floor debate is the central activity; it is here that major issues are addressed and parties gain or lose ground. By contrast, in a **committee-based legislature**, such as the American Congress, most work takes place in committees. There, members engage in the specialized skills of transforming bills into laws, conducting hearings, and scrutinizing the executive.

Bristol in 1774, Burke admitted in his victory speech that he knew nothing about his constituency and had played little part in the campaign. But, he continued:

Parliament is not a congress of ambassadors from different and hostile interests; which interests each must maintain, as an agent and advocate against other agents and advocates; but Parliament is a deliberative assembly of one nation, with one interest, that of the whole; where, not local purposes, not local prejudices, ought to guide, but the general good, resulting from the general reason of the whole. You choose a member indeed; but when you have chosen him, he is not a member for Bristol, but he is a member of Parliament. (Burke, 1774)

The deliberative style of contemporary parliaments is distinctly varied. The main contrast is between **debating** and **committee-based legislatures**. In a debating legislature, such as that of Britain, deliberation takes the form of general discussion in the chamber. Key issues eventually make their way to the floor of the House of Commons where they are discussed with passion, partisanship, and sometimes flair. Floor debate is the arena for national political discussion, forming part of a continuous election campaign. The mood of the House, as revealed in debate, is often more significant than the vote which follows. One of the achievements of the Commons is precisely this ability to combine effective deliberation, at least on vital issues, with strong partisanship.

Appropriately, it was the nineteenth-century English political philosopher John Stuart Mill who made the case for a debating assembly:

I know not how a representative assembly can more usefully employ itself than in talk, when the subject of talk is the great public interests of the country, and every sentence of it represents the opinion either of some important body of persons in the nation, or of an individual in whom such bodies have reposed their confidence. (Mill, 1861, p. 353)

By contrast, in committee-based assemblies (such as the American Congress and the Scandinavian parliaments) deliberation is less theatrical, taking the form of policy discussion in committees. The practical task is to assess the government's proposals, while also providing measured scrutiny of its actions. This deliberative style makes its own contribution to governance: less dramatic than a set-piece debate but often more constructive.

Legislation

Naturally enough, most constitutions explicitly assert the legislative function of parliaments. The end of absolute executive power is affirmed by giving to parliament, and to it alone, the right to make laws. Arbitrary government is replaced by a formal procedure for law-making. The painstaking process for passing bills into law signals the importance attached to government by rules, rather than by individuals. Where authoritarian rulers govern by decree, in a democracy bills are scrutinized and authorized by a national congress operating in accord with formal procedures (Figure 15.3).

We must be careful here, however. Legislation is rarely the function in which 'legislatures' exert the greatest influence. In most liberal democracies, effective control over legislation rests with the government. Bills pass through the assembly without being designed, or even transformed, there.

In party-dominated Australia, for instance, the government treats the legislative function with virtual contempt. On a single night in 1991 it sought to put 26 bills through the Senate in three hours. Before New Zealand adopted proportional representation, one prime minister boasted that if an idea came to him while shaving, he could have it on the statute book by the evening: truly a case of slot-machine law. The result, almost certainly, was too many laws.

Figure 15.3 Typical stages in making a law

The overall procedure is explicitly deliberative, involving several readings (debates) as the bill moves from the floor to committee and back again. In bicameral legislatures, differences in the versions of the bill passed by each chamber must be reconciled.

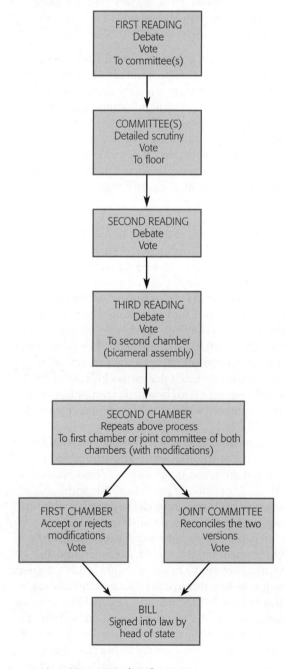

Source: Adapted from Mahler (2007), table 4.9.

In Britain, similarly, the governing party has historically dominated law-making. As Moran (2011, p. 157) points out:

The House of Commons is misunderstood if viewed as a legislator. Virtually all legislative proposals originate from, and are shaped by, the executive. Nor are the Commons' extensive debates on legislative proposals of great significance in shaping the law: secure government majorities (which up to now have been the usual state of affairs) mean that legislative proposals are hardly ever overturned wholesale, and detailed amendments are usually the result of concessions by ministers.

In the party-dominated parliaments of Britain and some of its ex-colonies, the legislative function is reduced to quality control: patching up errors in bills prepared in haste by ministers and civil servants. In legislation, at least, these assemblies are reactive.

By contrast, committee-based parliaments in continental Europe do play a more positive role in law-making. Coalition governments, influential committees, and an elite commitment to compromise combine to deliver laws acceptable to all sides.

But it is in presidential systems, including the United States, that the assembly achieves the greatest autonomy in law-making. The separation of powers and personnel inherent in a presidential regime limits executive influence over the legislature. This institutional separation is often reinforced by divided government. That is, the party in the White House may lack a majority in at least one chamber of Congress, further reducing the legislature's willingness to convert the administration's proposals into laws.

Yet, even in presidential systems the initiative in framing bills usually lies with the executive. Certainly, in the American Congress only members of the House of Representatives can formally introduce bills. But the executive can easily find a friendly representative to initiate a bill on its behalf. The political reality is that bills are developed by the administration and then transformed in Congress – if they do not expire in its maze of committees. 'You supply the bills and we work them over', one member of Congress reportedly said to an administration official. The executive proposes, as in most

BOX 15.2

Resolving differences in the versions of a bill passed by each chamber

	Description	Example
Conference or mediation committee	A joint committee of both chambers negotiates a compromise version which is then voted on by each house	Many countries, including France, Germany, Switzerland and the USA
Lower house is decisive	The lower house decides whether to accept or reject amendments from the upper house	Czech Republic, Spain, United Kingdom
Vote of a joint session of both chambers	The larger lower chamber exerts more weight in a joint vote	Australia, Brazil, India, Norway
Indefinite shuttle	Amended versions continue to shuttle between chambers until agreement is reached (if ever)	Italy is the main example of this rare procedure

Source: Adapted from Tsebelis and Money (1997), table 2.2a.

political systems, but Congress disposes, usually by saying 'no'.

Inevitably, this pluralistic process reduces the coherence of any overall legislative programme. As President Kennedy said, 'it is very easy to defeat a bill in Congress. It is much more difficult to pass one' (Eigen and Siegel, 1993, p. 82). The difficulty American and other presidents experience in securing approval for their bills stands in marked contrast to the much tighter control over the legislative programme exerted by the ruling party or coalition in parliamentary systems.

Bicameral legislatures face an additional hurdle in realizing the legislative function. What if the second chamber amends a bill passed by the lower house? There must be some means of resolving such discrepancies. In almost all countries, the initial step is for the amended bill to return to the lower chamber for further discussion. But if the bill continues to shuttle between houses in this way until an agreed version emerges, as in Italy's strongly bicameral legislature, the danger is that it will be delayed, or never become law at all. In Italy, for instance, a bill on rape introduced in 1977 did not become law until 1995.

To resolve this problem, most legislatures develop a procedure for short-circuiting an endless shuttle

(Box 15.2). The most popular arrangement – used for example in France, Germany, and the USA – is to employ a special conference committee, comprising an equal number of members from each chamber, to produce an agreed bill. Conference committees are sometimes described as third chambers, for it is here that the final deals are struck and the decisive compromises made. They are frequently a vital arena for resolving, or at least reaching a compromise on, important national issues.

Authorizing expenditure

This is one of the oldest functions of parliament, and of the lower house in particular. The origin of European assemblies, after all, lay in the monarch's requirement for money. Since, as Spencer Walpole (1881, p. 4) wrote, the necessities of kings are the opportunities of peoples, assemblies were able to establish the right to raise grievances before granting supply (that is, revenue). In Britain, this tradition continued until 1982 in the use of the term 'supply days' to describe opportunities for the opposition to raise any issues it wished.

The power to authorize spending may be one of parliament's oldest functions but, in many democracies, it has become nominal. Even more than the law-making role, control of the budget forms part of the myth of parliamentary authority. In truth, lack of real impact on government spending is a major weakness of the modern assembly. Typically, the overall executive prepares the budget, which is then reported to parliament but rarely modified there.

For the legislature to possess the power of the purse, suggests Wehner (2006), several conditions must be fulfilled:

- the assembly must be able to amend the budget (as opposed, say, to simply being authorized to make cuts);

- the assembly must possess an effective committee system;

- the assembly must be granted sufficient time to consider the budget in detail;

- the assembly must have access to background information underlying the budget;

- the executive must be limited in its ability to alter budget allocations during implementation;

- the **reversionary budget** must differ from the government's own proposals.

Inevitably, few countries meet all these conditions. In general, parliamentary approval is after the fact, serving to confirm compromises worked out between government departments. In many democracies, the budget is a done deal once it reaches the assembly. If parliament began to unpick any part of a complicated package, it would fall apart.

The United States is the clearest exception to the thesis of executive control of the purse. Congress

A **reversionary budget** is the default (typically, the previous year's) budget which takes effect should the legislature fail to approve a new one in time.

remains central to the confused tangle that is American budget-making. Under the constitution, all money spent by executive departments must be allocated under specific expenditure headings approved by Congress. No appropriations by Congress means no government programme. As

Flammang *et al.* (1990, p. 422) wrote, 'without the agreement of members of Congress, no money can be doled out for foreign aid, salaries for army generals or paper clips for bureaucrats'.

The result is that the annual American budget has become an elaborate game of chicken. The executive and the legislature each hopes the other side will accede to its own proposals before the money runs out. Every year between 1978 and 1996, Congress failed to pass a complete budget by its own deadline, forcing government agencies to operate under a reversionary budget.

Furthermore, Congress must also approve revenue-raising proposals. Yet, it prefers to spend money rather than to raise it and shows no inclination to run a balanced budget. The result is a massive and growing public debt which, at some point, will impose greater discipline on Congressional extravagance. In sum, the American experience offers convincing support for the proposition that financing the modern state is too important to be left to the legislature's many hands.

Scrutiny

The final function of legislatures is scrutiny (oversight) of the executive. John Stuart Mill emphasized this role as early as 1861:

The proper office of a representative assembly is to watch and control the government: to throw the light of publicity on its acts, to compel a full exposition and justification of all of them which any one considers questionable; [and] to censure them if found condemnable. (1861, p. 258)

However, in many countries such activity has only been growing in significance and value in recent decades.

To emphasize the scrutiny function is to acknowledge that the executive, not the legislature, must govern. But given adequate resources and professional support, the assembly can restate its key role as representative of the people by acting as a watchdog over the administration. Effective monitoring can compensate for the downgrading of the assembly's legislative and expenditure functions, providing a new direction to parliament's work. Scrutiny appeals in particular to younger cohorts of educated and professional members.

A modern assembly possesses three potential instruments with which to monitor the executive: first, questions and interpellations; second, emergency debates and confidence votes; and, third, committee investigations. However the separation of powers means that only the third instrument is available in presidential systems (Chapter 16). We consider questions, interpellations, emergency debates, and votes of confidence here, reserving committee investigations to the next section.

Questions refer to direct queries of ministers. In many parliamentary systems, oral and written questions are mainstays of oversight. In Britain, for example, members of the House of Commons ask over 500 questions per day, keeping many civil servants busy as they prepare answers for their ministerial masters (House of Commons Procedure Committee, 2009). Prime Minister's Question Time, a weekly event, remains a theatrical joust between the PM and the leader of the opposition. In other parliaments, however, questions are accorded lower status. French ministers often fail to answer them at all.

Interpellations provide an alternative form of interrogation in some European assemblies including Finland, France, and Germany. An interpellation is a substantial question demanding a prompt response which is followed by a short debate and usually a vote on whether the government's answer is deemed acceptable. This technique, which is a form of confidence motion, felled several governments in the French Third (1870–1940) and Fourth (1946–58) Republics. It became a weapon in parliamentary guerrilla warfare.

An **interpellation** is an enquiry of the government, interrupting normal business, which is followed by a short debate and usually a vote on the assembly's satisfaction with the answers given.

Emergency debates are a further and higher-profile way in which parliaments can call the executive to account. Typically, a minimum number of members, together with the Presiding Officer (Speaker), must approve a proposal for an emergency debate. The discussion usually ends with a government win; however, the significance lies in the debate itself and the fact of its having been called. An emergency debate creates publicity and demands a considered response from the government's spokesperson.

Votes of confidence or censure motions are the ultimate test which a legislature can pose to the executive in a parliamentary system. Such motions are not so much a form of detailed scrutiny as a decision on whether the government can continue at all. Again, special rules may apply: in France and Sweden, a majority of all members (not only those voting) is required to demonstrate the legislature's loss of confidence. In other cases, a confidence motion is not specifically designated but is simply any vote on which the government would feel obliged to resign if defeated. Defeat on a motion to approve the budget would be a typical example. In some countries, again including Sweden, votes of confidence can be directed against individual ministers as well as the government as a whole.

Committees

Committees have grown in number and significance. They have become the workhorses of effective legislatures, offering detailed scrutiny of both the executive and its bills. Even though committee operations in debating legislatures lack the profile accorded to meetings of the whole chamber, their activities merit scrutiny. So, what purposes do committees serve? And what makes them effective?

Committees are small workgroups of members, created to cope with the volume and detail of parliamentary business, particularly in the larger and busier lower chamber. They take the form of standing, select, or conference committees (Box 15.3). Standing committees offer line-by-line examination of bills, while select committees monitor the main executive departments and hold hearings on matters of public concern. Whatever the committee type, members are usually allocated in proportion to overall party strength. In operation, however, partisanship is often held in check, yielding a more cooperative outlook than on the floor.

The American Congress is the classic example of a committee-based legislature. Although unmentioned in the constitution, committees rapidly became vital to the work of Congress. 'Congress in session is Congress on public exhibition, whilst Congress in its committee rooms is Congress at work', wrote Woodrow Wilson (1885, p. 79). Bryce (1921, p. 68), a nineteenth-century British observer

UNITED KINGDOM — LIBERAL DEMOCRACY

Form of government ■ a parliamentary liberal democracy with a largely ceremonial monarchy.

Legislature ■ the House of Commons (650 members) is the dominant chamber. The House of Lords, the composition of which has been under review since 1997, acts in a revising and restraining capacity.

Executive ■ the Cabinet is the top decision-ratifying body; the prime minister selects and dismisses its members. Meetings of full cabinet are largely formal; its effective work is conducted in committee.

Judiciary ■ based on the common law tradition. In 2009, the introduction of a supreme court, albeit without the authority to veto legislation, strengthened the autonomy of the judiciary.

Electoral systems ■ the House of Commons is still elected by the single-member plurality method. A range of systems is used for elections to other bodies such as the Scottish Parliament, the Welsh Assembly, and the European Parliament.

Party system ■ traditionally a two-party system, the dominance of the Conservative and Labour parties has been challenged by the rise of the Liberal Democrats.

Population (annual growth rate): 63.0 m (+0.5%)

World Bank income group: high income

Human development index (rank/out of): 28/187

Political rights score: ①

Civil liberties score: ①

Media status: free

Note: For interpretation and sources, see p. xvi.

The **UNITED KINGDOM** is a liberal democracy whose political system has nonetheless been in transition. Traditional models portrayed Britain as a centralized, unitary state; as a two-party system; as an exemplar of parliamentary sovereignty in which ministers were held to account by the assembly; and as a political system whose uncodified constitution offered little formal protection of individual rights. Yet, the accuracy of all these images has come under review.

The centralized and, even, the unitary character of the United Kingdom was put in question by the creation in 1999 of new assemblies for Scotland and Wales. The reform was asymmetric, with the Scottish parliament receiving more devolved powers than the Welsh

assembly. Devolution to Northern Ireland was reinstated in 2007, reflecting the ending of armed conflict between Catholic and Protestant groups and the UK government.

In the United Kingdom as a whole, the two-party system based on the Conservative and Labour parties was challenged by the rise of the Liberal Democrats. In the 2010 election, the Liberal Democrats won 6.8 million votes and 57 seats, forming a governing coalition with the Conservatives.

Parliamentary sovereignty has been dented by British membership of the European Union and a more assertive judiciary. Individual rights now receive clearer protection, exerted through the judiciary, from the incorporation into

British law in 1998 of the European Convention on Human Rights.

Ministerial accountability has been complicated by the delegation of government tasks to semi-independent agencies. In a particularly significant reform, the 1997 Labour government immediately took steps to give control of monetary policy to the Bank of England's Monetary Policy Committee.

The cumulative impact of these developments remains to be established. What is clear is that many of the old assumptions about British politics have ceased to apply; in a more complicated and fragmented polity, replacement clichés are harder to find.

The British Parliament

The new era in British politics has impinged on its assembly. Traditionally, Britain's Parliament mixed omnipotence and impotence in a seemingly impossible combination. Parliament was considered omnipotent because parliamentary sovereignty, allied to an uncodified constitution, meant there could be no higher authority in the land. It was considered impotent because the governing party exercised tight control over its own backbenchers, turning Parliament into an instrument, rather than a wielder, of power. How has the mother of parliaments adapted to the current period of change?

In the twenty-first century, Parliament's position has become less certain. The tired rituals of adversary politics in the House of Commons have become less convincing, not least for the new members – forming a majority of the House – elected between 1997 and 2010.

The notion that Parliament possesses sovereignty still carries weight but – as with many assemblies – Britain's legislature runs the risk of being left behind by international integration, by competition from the media as an arena of debate, and by the indifference of prime ministers who choose to spend less time in the House.

In addition, an expenses scandal which erupted in 2009 damaged the standing of the House. The fact that dubious expenses claims came to light showed that even MPs could not control the flow of information, while the subsequent reforms brought an end to self-policing of expenses by the House itself.

But not all developments are a response to crisis. MPs themselves have become more committed; the era of the amateur is over. They are predominantly drawn from professional, business, and political backgrounds. They devote time to an increasing volume of constituency casework. The number of late sittings has been cut. Select committees have established themselves in the debate over policy and contribute to scrutinizing the executive. The prime minister now appears twice a year before a select committee for a more detailed discussion than is possible during weekly Question Time.

Prior occupation of Conservative and Labour MPs, 2010

	Conservative	Labour
Business	125	20
Law	56	26
Politics	31	52
Media	29	18
Armed services	15	1
Accountancy	13	2
Education	4	35
Civil Service/ local government	2	13
Manual work	2	22
Union official	-	29
Other	29	40
Total	**306**	**258**

Source: Adapted from Kavanagh and Cowley (2010), table 15.6.

Overall, Kelso (2011, p. 69) judges that 'there is now a very clear shift away from a chamber-based institution towards a committee-based institution, illustrated by the growing emphasis given to new public bill committees, select committees and committee-based scrutiny of the prime minister.'

As an upper chamber in what remains a unitary state, the House of Lords occupies an uncertain position. Its 760 members consist mainly of appointed life peers but reform, when finally agreed, is likely to involve a substantial measure of election. Such a development may well make the Lords more assertive in challenging the executive.

Yet, even as Britain's Parliament updates its skills, it will surely continue to do what it has always done best: acting as an arena for debating issues of central significance to the nation, its government, and its leaders. Even in an era of reform, the House of Commons has retained its position as a classic debating assembly.

Further reading: Bogdanor (2009), Heffernan *et al.* (2011), Kavanagh and Cowley (2010), Moran (2011).

BOX 15.3

Parliamentary committees

Standing committee	Considers bills in detail.
Select committee	Scrutinizes the executive, ideally with one committee for each main government department.
	Ad hoc temporary committees investigate particular matters of public interest.
Conference or mediation committee	In bicameral legislatures, a joint committee usually reconciles differences in the versions of a bill passed by each chamber.

of American politics, described the House of Representatives as 'a huge panel from which committees are selected'. Despite a resurgence of partisanship since the mid-1990s, Bryce's comment still applies. In the 112th Congress (2011–13), there were 20 standing committees in the House and 16 in the Senate. These bodies spawned multiple subcommittees: around 90 in the House and 70 in the Senate.

Committees draw on the power granted to Congress by the American constitution. Exceptionally, Congress (rather than the executive) is responsible for such important matters as commerce, the currency, defence, and taxation. Of course, Congress does not carry out these functions itself; it delegates the task to the bureaucracy. But, because of its constitutional position and the budgetary authority flowing from it, Congress possesses inherent powers of oversight. Because the floor is an inappropriate venue for detailed scrutiny, committees are of key importance to oversight.

Through its committees, Congress achieves a unique level of involvement with the executive. Much committee work is as a partner, rather than an overseer, but a few investigative committees have achieved national status. The House Committee on Un-American Activities in the 1940s and 1950s, and the Senate Watergate Committee in the 1970s, are the best-known examples.

Even in the USA, however, committee oversight is limited. It can only cast light on a few corners of a vast bureaucracy; Congress sometimes seeks to micromanage departments, rather than setting broad targets; and reports can quickly be forgotten as the political spotlight shifts. Even though Congress is the world's best-resourced legislature, the government's big battalions outnumber its limited forces.

In addition to its scrutiny function, Congressional committees also decide the shape and fate of most bills. Here, we observe the strengths and weaknesses of American pluralism in tangible form. Committee hearings allow interest groups to express their views, while committee members take care not only of the interests of their constituents, but also of those groups offering support, including campaign contributions, to the legislator. **Logrolling** is also widespread. The whole business is just that – political business. But, especially in the House, party leaders are also important in driving the legislative process; we should not overestimate the autonomy of House committees from parties and interest groups.

Logrolling is vote trading of the form 'you scratch my back and I'll scratch yours'. For example, Congressman Brown agrees to vote as Congresswoman Green wishes on a particular bill of importance to Green but not Brown. Green then reciprocates on another bill which is vital to Brown (in olden days, neighbours joined together to move each others' logs).

Committees are generally less influential in the more party-dominated parliaments found in most parliamentary systems. In Britain's House of Commons, for instance, government bills are examined by standing committees which largely replicate party combat on the floor of the chamber. These committees, unlike those of Congress, do not challenge executive dominance in framing legislation. They are unpopular, unspecialized, and underresourced. However, like many other legislatures, the Commons has expanded its system of select committees of scrutiny. Since 1979, select committees have shadowed all the main government departments, probing government policy and monitoring its implementation. Their reports contribute to governance and sometimes attract wider interest. In 2011, for example, a committee interrogation of

Rupert Murdoch (as part of a phone-hacking scandal) attracted international attention. The following year, the interrogation of the former head of Barclays Bank (as part of an investigation into rate-fixing) also received considerable publicity.

Scandinavia, however, provides cases of influential committees operating in the context of both strong parties and parliamentary government. Scandinavia's main governing style, sometimes known as 'committee parliamentarianism', is one in which influential standing committees negotiate the policies and bills on which the whole parliament later votes. In Sweden, for instance, committees modify about one in three government proposals and have the right, sometimes exercised, to put their own proposals (including bills) to the assembly as a whole. Parliamentary committees are partners in a remarkably deliberative law-making process (see Spotlight, Chapter 18).

The influence of committees depends, first and foremost, on the strength of the legislature in the political system. But internal organization is also important and, here, three major factors are expertise, intimacy, and support:

- Expertise emerges over time from committees with specialized responsibilities and a clear field of operation. Expertise is most likely in permanent committees with continuity of operation and membership. Detailed knowledge is further encouraged if legislators are limited to a few committee memberships.

- Intimacy emerges from small size (perhaps no more than a dozen members) and is, again, reinforced by stable membership. Particularly when meetings take place in private, a small group can encourage cooperation and consensus, overcoming adversarial relationships between political parties.

- The use of qualified staff to advise committees is essential. Expert researchers can assist politicians in producing credible recommendations, to a degree countering the wall of knowledge available to the executive.

Significantly, all three factors are present in the American Congress.

Members

Who are the members who populate the legislature? And how do they go about their work? Answering these behavioural questions offers additional understanding to that provided by an institutional approach to legislatures. At the level of the individual member, three themes emerge: career politicians, celebrity politicians, and political dynasties.

Career politicians

In liberal democracies, the most important development is the rise of the **career politician**: the degree-educated legislator with limited experience outside politics who expects politics to provide a full-time, fulfilling profession. The amateurs of yesteryear – local landowners representing 'their' territory, ageing trade unionists rewarded with a seat in the assembly for their final years, lawyers seeking some short-term political experience – have given way to career politicians who know no other job. In politics, as elsewhere, specialization is now necessary for success. Even when politicians have experience of other careers such as law, the earlier occupation is often chosen as a pathway to politics.

Particularly in Europe, the rise of the professional has led to speculation about the growth of a **political class** with a background and interests removed from the people it represents. As with any other occupational group, legislators from all parties share a concern with improving their conditions such as hours of work, research support, pay, and pensions.

In Weber's renowned distinction (1918), **career politicians** live off, and not merely for, politics. They are full-timers requiring an appropriate income, support, career development, and pension. Professional politicians are sometimes said to form a **political class**, implying the existence of a group that possesses, and can act on, its shared interests (Mosca, 1896).

But parliamentarians are in a unique position to act on their common interests by simply voting themselves an enhancement. Reports of corruption in a number of assemblies offer further support to the notion of a horizontal 'class' division between legislators and electors which supplements the traditional vertical distinction between parties. An example here is the damaging expenses scandal which engulfed Britain's House of Commons in 2009. Members of all parties, it turned out, had been claiming on the public purse for supposed expenses such as cleaning moats and tuning pianos. Members of the mother of parliaments were in a position to dip their fingers in the pie – and did so.

More importantly, incumbent members from all parties typically seek re-election. To achieve this goal, they supply themselves with campaign resources (e.g. free mail) unavailable to their challengers, thus creating a powerful cartel against newcomers. Viewing politics purely as a clash between parties often leads to inadequate emphasis on this distinction within parties between incumbents and challengers. As in any other established class, politicians in post – of whatever party – are reluctant to upset the apple cart that has served them so well. Indeed, the greater the proportion of professional politicians in an assembly, the more likely it is that incumbent candidates will be re-elected (Berry *et al.*, 2000).

Politics as a profession implies a distinct view not only of representation, but also of politics. It rejects the notion that governance is a task which Athenian-style citizen-legislators can undertake. It implies dissatisfaction with the idea that an assembly should draw together a representative sample of citizens 'different in nature, different in interests, different in looks, different in language' (Bagehot, 1867, p. 155). Rather, politics as a profession implies an emphasis on training, knowledge, experience, and skill. Politics becomes a job, in the same way as law, medicine, and teaching.

Within the broad category of professional politician, the main contrast is between American political entrepreneurs and the more party-based careerists found in the parliaments of other liberal democracies. In Congress, candidates must compete against opponents from their own party in a primary; in office, they must build a personal profile and record of achievement which protects them from challenge, and offers insurance should their party fall on hard times. And they must raise money for their campaign – which, for members of the House of Representatives, takes place every two years. Members of Congress must nurture their personal brand.

In most other liberal democracies, strong parties at both parliamentary and electoral level leave less room for independent action, resulting in loyal backbenchers, rather than political entrepreneurs. Even when partisanship is important, however, younger and better-educated members are keen to express their professionalism by making a difference. Although the French National Assembly remains a weak institution, Kerrouche (2006, p. 352) reports that even here 'deputies want to criticize, to attract media attention and to put forward alternative policies'. These aspirations are reflected in a substantial number of private members' bills and legislative amendments.

Of course, career politicians can only flourish in parliaments where re-election prospects are good. Generally, re-election is the norm in liberal democracies. Typically, most sitting legislators return for a new term (Figure 15.4). The question of the ideal level of turnover is difficult to answer with precision. On the one hand, the return rate should be high enough to sustain professionalism, allowing the

Figure 15.4 Incumbent return rates to legislatures

Most legislators are re-elected in most liberal democracies. A high return rate encourages professionalism but can also indicate an uneven playing field favouring incumbents and encouraging the emergence of a political class.

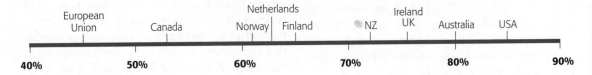

Note: Based on elections between 1979 and 1994 to the lower chamber (European Union: 1989, 1994).

Sources: Adapted from Matland and Studlar (2004); Nugent (2010, p. 199).

development of experience and expertise. On the other hand, it should not be so high as to create the 'three As' which Jackson (1994) associated with a surfeit of incumbency: arrogance, apathy, and atrophy.

Turnover is greater in countries employing party-list proportional representation, a format that allows party leaders to manage the order of candidates on the list so as to ensure at least a trickle of fresh blood. In countries employing plurality elections, the extent of turnover is less predictable and return rates can become indefensibly high. For instance, in the United States between 1982 and 2010, the proportion of incumbent candidates securing a further term never fell below 85 per cent in the House and 75 per cent in the Senate (Schmidt *et al.*, 2012, table 12.4). The **incumbency effect** is particularly striking in the USA, where members of Congress are world experts in securing their own continuation in office. They can, and do, exploit such resources as voters' recognition, public subsidies, financial backing, constituency service, their own experience, and even (in the House of Representatives) the ability to manipulate the boundaries of their electoral districts. For these reasons, fresh candidates stand the greatest chance when an existing representative stands down, creating an **open seat**.

> The **incumbency effect** refers to the electoral bonus accruing to sitting members when they stand for re-election. In the United States, where this effect is large, an **open seat** is defined as one in which the existing representative has stood down, creating a more even contest.

Term limits provide a blunt solution to this incumbency effect. In Mexico, for example, members of the Chamber of Deputies are restricted to one three-year tenure. Term limits are also now employed widely in states of the USA, although the Supreme Court declared in *U.S. Term Limits, Inc.* v. *Thornton* (1995) that states cannot impose term limits on their federal representatives.

> **Term limits** restrict elected politicians to a maximum number of periods in office, or ban re-election without a break. They enforce turnover at the risk of reducing professionalism.

Although popular with the public, term limits may create more problems than they solve. When members are automatically removed after each election, no parliamentary career is possible. The outcome is lame duck legislators lacking electoral accountability and concerned mainly with their next job. Carey *et al.* (2006) find that term-limited legislators in American states are, in fact, less responsive to their constituents. Ideally, turnover of legislators should be encouraged by levelling the playing field between incumbents and challengers, not by banning all experienced players.

Celebrity politicians

Professional politicians are the leading category in most contemporary legislatures but they do not have it entirely their own way. One group, in particular, stands out in contrast. **Celebrities-turned-politicians** exploit their fame in other fields to leapfrog into the legislature or (as with former Governor Arnold Schwarzenegger of California) direct to executive office (Box 15.4).

> **Celebrities-turned-politicians** exploit the fame they have acquired in non-political arenas to ease their entry into political office, including the legislature. Such characters are distinct from **politicians-as-celebrities** whose style is to present themselves to the electors as though they are famous stars of stage and screen.

It is tempting to regard celebrities-turned-politicians as an emerging group of post-professional politicians who exploit both their media-generated fame and their status as clean political outsiders to achieve quick political success (Beckman, 2007). Certainly, their presence in the assembly seems to convey a message that voters want to judge politicians by what they stand for, not simply by their technical competence. Professional politicians are not universally admired.

But we should avoid easy generalization about trends. In particular, the celebrity-turned-politician is far from new. For example, American actress and singer Helen Gahagan Douglas was elected to the House of Representatives as early as 1944. Rather, the appeal of celebrities-turned-politicians seems to lie partly in their outsider status and their very rarity, suggesting a natural limit to their ability to colonize the legislature.

BOX 15.4

Actresses, athletes and astronauts: some celebrities in national legislatures

	Year of birth	Country	Source of celebrity
Helen Gahagan Douglas	1900	USA	Actress
John Glenn	1921	USA	Astronaut
Melina Mercouri	1925	Greece	Actress
Sonny Bono	1935	USA	Singer
Glenda Jackson	1936	UK	Actress
Bill Bradley	1943	USA	Basketball
Imran Khan	1952	Pakistan	Cricket
Sebastian Coe	1956	UK	Athletics
Govinda Arun Ahuja	1963	India	Actor
Tanja Saarela	1970	Finland	Beauty queen

Further reading: Corner and Pels (2003), Jones (2005), West and Orman (2003).

In an era in which electors have become less partisan and are less likely to watch television news, politicians as a class may find themselves driven to compete in the celebrity space (e.g. talk shows), rather than for the diminishing media coverage set aside for politics exclusively. The incumbency effect encourages even professional politicians to develop a high-profile image based on character and individuality – in other words, to adopt the mantle of the **politician-as-celebrity**. These trends suggest that many liberal democracies may be witnessing a transition in the nature of the professional representative, from party loyalist towards a more entrepreneurial style.

Political dynasties

One final group of representatives is worthy of note: offspring who follow a parent into the legislature. In Asia, political families often represent lineages with an established national reputation, or at least tight control over a particular electoral district. In India, for example, the Nehru-Gandhi dynasty goes back to the nineteenth century. Before the 2009 election, more than one third of the members of the Japanese Diet were second-generation law-makers, often inheriting the same seat as their family predecessor (Martin and Steel, 2008).

Beyond Asia, the phenomenon of second-generation legislators may simply reflect socialization: children growing up in a family where politics is viewed as an achievable career are more likely to enter the profession themselves. This effect surely helps to explain why as many as one quarter of the candidates standing in the Australian election of 2001 had a close family member who had also stood for elected office (McAllister, 2003).

From one perspective, political families may be no more disturbing than family lines of physicians. Yet, just as the notion of the professional politician gave rise to the concept of a political class, so too does the idea of the political family encourage us to think in terms of a political caste. Both ideas imply a measure of closure in political recruitment; they rest uneasily alongside the traditional interpretation of democracy as government by the people.

The European Parliament

As with other European Union institutions, the European Parliament (EP) is an unusual entity worth special attention. It is that rarest thing: a supranational entity which is directly elected. Its 736 members are chosen every five years by proportional representation, with smaller states over-represented. The Parliament is the only directly elected organization in the EU; the Council of the European Union, which also possesses legislative powers and is effectively an upper chamber, comprises government ministers from the member states. The EP's primary base is Brussels but, rather absurdly, it also holds monthly plenary sessions in Strasbourg and maintains its secretariat in Luxembourg.

The Parliament has enormously expanded its authority within the EU since it was first constituted (see Timeline). As with all established assemblies, it has developed elaborate internal procedures with a particular focus, in the EP's case, on considering draft legislation in committee.

THE EUROPEAN PARLIAMENT

1952	Assembly of the European Coal and Steel Community established as an instrument of scrutiny, with the right to dismiss the Commission in some circumstances. Assembly members are drawn from national legislatures.
1962	The Assembly is renamed the European Parliament (EP).
1970	The EP gains more influence over the budget.
1975	The EP wins the right to propose modifications in areas where expenditure is not mandated by previous agreements.
1979	First direct elections. Average turnout 62 per cent.
1980	Isoglucose judgement by the European Court requires the EP to be consulted on proposed laws.
1986	The Single European Act initiates cooperation and assent procedures which give the EP more influence over legislation.
1992	The Maastricht Treaty requires members of the Commission to be approved by the EP. A new co-decision procedure gives the EP some veto authority over legislation.
1997	The Treaty of Amsterdam extends the co-decision procedure and formalizes the EP's right to veto the nominee for Commission president.
1999	All 20 commissioners (the Santer Commission) resign rather than face dismissal by the EP for mismanagement. Fifth direct elections. Average turnout 50 per cent.
2004	Sixth direct elections. Average turnout 45 per cent.
2009	Seventh direct elections. Average turnout 43 per cent.
2009	The Treaty of Lisbon further extends the co-decision procedure (now known as the 'ordinary legislative procedure').

Further reading: Corbett *et al.* (2011), Judge and Earnshaw (2008), Nugent (2010).

Just as national parliaments operate through political parties, so too is the EP structured by political groups. These groupings receive subsidies and guaranteed representation on committees, providing incentives for them to form. As with parties in many European countries, the left–right dimension is the main ideological axis along which these groups form, but support or opposition to deeper European integration provides a secondary dimension of division.

Yet, as Lelieveldt and Princen (2011, p. 70) comment, 'the EP's powers are similar to, but in all cases less extensive than, those of national parliaments'. The EP is relatively youthful but its growth is constrained by the intergovernmental component of the EU.

To assess the EP's weight, Box 15.5 judges its performance against the six functions we have attributed to national legislatures. As a *deliberating* and *scrutinizing* body, the EP perhaps comes closest to an effective national legislature. In the other areas, its authority is more limited.

As a *representative* body, the Parliament suffers from its remoteness from electors, a low turnout (which is typically 20 per cent below that at national

---

BOX 15.5

The functions of legislatures and the European Parliament

	European Parliament
Representation	MEPs are further removed from constituents than MPs. Turnout at European elections is lower. European elections reflect national politics.
Deliberation	Consists mainly of considering draft legislation in committee. Plenary sessions less significant.
Legislation	Can amend and must approve most (not all) legislation. Can request but not initiate legislation.
Authorizing expenditure	Can alter specific allocations within a long-term budget set by member governments.
Scrutiny	Can question the Commission and other bodies. Can investigate the implementation of laws but not compel witnesses to attend.
Making governments	Approves (but does not propose) and can dismiss the College of Commissioners.

Note: MEP – member of the European Parliament; MP – member of national parliament.

---

elections), and the dominance of national factors in European elections.

The EP still does not possess *legislative* power in all areas of EU policy. For example, social security and police cooperation remain excluded. The fact that the Parliament is not required to approve all European legislation further diminishes its standing compared with national assemblies.

Although the EP can influence specific allocation of funds within the budget, it does not approve the overall budget itself. If only symbolically, this inability to *authorize overall expenditure* is an additional weakness.

Finally, the Parliament's role is also limited in *making governments* – in the EU's case, the College of Commissioners. Where the government in a national parliamentary system emerges from the assembly, the EP only approves, without proposing, the team of commissioners. The Parliament does, however, possess the right to dismiss the College, a power akin to that of impeachment in a presidential system.

Legislatures in authoritarian states

Since assemblies are symbols of popular representation in politics, their significance in authoritarian regimes is inherently limited. Such parliaments generally function only as shadow institutions. Sessions are short and some members are appointed by the government. Members concentrate on raising grievances, pressing constituency interests, and sometimes lining their own pockets. The rulers regard these activities as non-threatening because the real issues of national politics are left untouched.

Yet, legislatures are difficult to extinguish. Except for a few traditional and dictatorial regimes, most authoritarian regimes possess an assembly of some description. So, why do non-democratic rulers bother with them at all? Their value is fourfold:

● A parliament provides a fig leaf of legitimacy, both domestic and international, for the regime. The ruler can say to visiting dignitaries and donors, 'Look! We too have an assembly, just like the British House of Commons and America's Congress!'

- The legislature can be used to incorporate moderate opponents into the political system, providing a forum for negotiating matters that do not threaten rulers' key interests.

- Raising constituents' grievances and lobbying for local interests provide a measure of integration between centre and periphery, and between state and society. Such activity oils the political wheels without threatening those who control the machine.

- Assemblies provide a convenient pool of potential recruits to the elite. Behaviour in parliament provides a useful initial test of reliability.

Gandhi (2008, p. 181) offers a useful summary of the functions of parliaments in authoritarian regimes:

Legislatures under dictatorship serve as a controlled institutional channel through which outside groups can make their demands and incumbents can make concessions without appearing to cave in to popular protest.

Consider China. It illustrates the trend in communist states for assemblies to acquire modest significance as such regimes become a little more pluralistic. In the 12 years before Mao Zedong's death in 1976, the National People's Congress (NPC) did not meet at all. However, in the subsequent era of economic reform, the NPC began to acquire some authority. A growing emphasis on the rule of law raised the status of the legislature, which has now also begun to express popular hostility to corruption. Many votes are no longer unanimous, proceedings are less easily choreographed, committees are growing in authority, some professional support is available, and the party must anticipate the NPC's reaction to its proposals.

Senior figures drafted into the assembly have skilfully strengthened the NPC's position in Chinese governance, not by confrontation with the ruling party but, rather, by assisting the growth of the private sector and by making efforts to encourage national integration through links with subnational congresses (O'Brien, 2008).

However, the NPC, still the world's largest legislature with members indirectly elected through subnational governments and the military, remains strongly hierarchical. It meets only once a year for a session lasting about two weeks. Even more than in committee-based assemblies in democracies, the NPC's influence operates through smaller subgroups. The most important of these is the Standing Committee, a group of about 150 members which meets regularly throughout the year. These subgroups remain sensitive to the party's interests; most members of the Standing Committee – as of the wider NPC – also belong to the party, giving the leadership an additional mechanism of control.

Of course, party domination of legislative proceedings is also found in parliamentary systems in liberal democracies, but there the party in command varies with the election results. Although the NPC and its subgroups have become part of the Chinese power network, the party's supremacy is such that these bodies still cannot be understood through Western notions of the separation of powers and parliamentary sovereignty.

In competitive authoritarian regimes, by contrast, legislatures are certainly an essential part of the political furniture. Their position can be significant in areas that do not threaten the realities of presidential leadership: in representing local districts, for instance, and in passing routine legislation.

However, such assemblies still operate in the shadow of executive authority. A nose for power will lead us away from parliament and towards the presidential office. There, we may discover an incumbent who governs by decree as well as by law and who may, in extremis, simply dissolve a recalcitrant legislature in search of more congenial arrangements.

The political environment of competitive authoritarian regimes is particularly hostile to the notion that assemblies can hold the government to account through detailed scrutiny. On the contrary, the national leader considers himself responsible to the whole nation, not to what he sees as corrupt, partisan, and parochial representatives in the assembly.

In addition, many competitive authoritarian systems are either new regimes, or located in relatively poor countries; both factors militate against the development of a professional legislature with a stable membership, extensive research support, and a well-developed committee system.

In Russia's competitive authoritarian regime, parliament (the Federal Assembly) occupies a secondary position. Certainly, the communist era of mute and meek assemblies has withered. Russia's post-communist constitution (1993) created a significant bicameral legislature which is now well-established. Laws take precedence over presidential decrees.

The weaknesses of the Federal Assembly lie more in its relationship with the executive. In the United States, the balance between Congress and president is one of mutual checks; in Russia, authority is tilted to the Kremlin. Where America sought to limit presidential authority, the Russian tradition emphasizes strong government. Thus, the 1993 constitution states that Russia's president is not only 'guarantor of the constitution', but is also required to 'ensure the coordinated functioning and collaboration of bodies of state power'. So far, presidents have performed this role with no great regard for the legislature.

As in other competitive authoritarian regimes, the exact political weight of Russia's parliament is subject to change. During the 1990s, the Duma (lower house) became a site of resistance to President Yeltsin's reforms, producing vigorous debate. In the current century, however, President Putin's United Russia party has dominated the Duma, reducing parliament to subservient status. Still, President Putin himself claims to find value in legislative institutions: 'today, we can justifiably call this period a time of strengthening the country's parliamentary and legal culture. One can speak about a modern State Duma as a working instrument of power' (quoted in Donaldson, 2004, p. 249). In Russia's hybrid regime, the legislature is expected to make itself useful in supporting state projects.

Discussion questions

- Must the legislature of a true democracy be unicameral?

- Should members of the upper chamber be appointed for their experience and wisdom, or elected for their popular appeal?

- What is the most important function of the legislature in (a) contemporary liberal democracies; (b) authoritarian states?

- Does descriptive representation matter?

- What are the strengths and weaknesses of a legislature populated by professional politicians?

- Should legislators be subject to term limits?

Further reading

N. Baldwin, *Legislatures of Small States: A Comparative Study* (2012). An examination of the impact of small state size on the structure and functions of legislatures.

R. Corbett, F. Jacobs and M. Shackleton, *The European Parliament*, 8th edn (2011). A comprehensive guidebook to this interesting, if unusual, assembly.

M. Cotta and H. Best, eds, *Democratic Representation in Europe: Diversity, Change and Convergence* (2007). A comparative treatment of long-term changes in parliamentary careers.

L. Dodd and B. Oppenheimer, eds, *Congress Reconsidered*, 10th edn (2012). A helpful collection on the world's most intensively studied legislature: the American Congress.

S. Fish and M. Kroenig, *The Handbook of National Legislatures: A Global Survey* (2009). An extensive reference work assessing the powers of national legislatures by their autonomy, capacity, influence, and powers.

G. Loewenberg, S. Peverill and R. Kiewiet, eds, *Legislatures: Comparative Perspectives on Representative Assemblies* (2002). The essays in this volume include studies of legislative recruitment and careers, the evolution of legislatures, and the electoral systems through which legislatures are chosen.

S. Morgenstern, *Patterns of Legislative Politics: Roll-Call Voting in Latin America and the United States* (2012). A detailed analysis of voting patterns of parties, factions, and alliances in Latin America's Southern Cone, contrasted with the United States.

ONLINE RESOURCES AVAILABLE

Visit the companion website at **www.palgrave.com/politics/hague** to access additional learning resources, including multiple-choice questions, chapter summaries, web links and practice essay questions.

Chapter 16 The political executive

The political executive is the core of government, consisting of political leaders who form the top slice of the administration: presidents and ministers, prime ministers and cabinets. The executive is the regime's energizing force, setting priorities, mobilizing support, resolving crises, making decisions and overseeing their implementation. Governing without an assembly or judiciary is perfectly feasible, but ruling without an executive is impossible.

The political executive (which makes policy) must be distinguished from the bureaucracy (which puts policy into effect). Unlike appointed officials, the members of the executive are chosen by political means, most often by election, and can be removed by the same method. The executive is account-able for the activities of government; it is where the buck stops.

Democratic and authoritarian regimes are defined by the operation of their executive. Liberal democracies have succeeded in the delicate and difficult task of subjecting executive power to constitutional constraint. The government is not only elected, but remains subject to rules which limit its power; it must also face regular re-election. In an authoritarian regime, by contrast, constitu-tional and electoral controls are absent or ineffective. The scope of the execu-tive is limited not by the constitution but, rather, by political realities.

The executives of liberal democracies fall into three main groups: presiden-tial, parliamentary, and semi-presidential. In all three types, power is dif-fused. In presidential and semi-presidential regimes, the constitution sets up a system of checks and balances between distinct executive, legislative and judicial institutions. In parliamentary systems, the government is constrained in different ways. Its very survival depends on retaining the confidence of the assembly. Typically, its freedom of action is limited by the need to sustain a coalition between parties that have agreed to share the task of governing.

Presidential government

The world contains many presidents but fewer examples of **presidential government**. The distinction is important. First, any dictator can style himself 'president' and many do so. Second, many parliamentary systems possess a president who serves only as ceremonial head of state. For these

Presidential government
- The elected president steers the government and makes appointments to it;
- Fixed terms of offices for the president and the assembly, neither of which can ordinarily bring down the other;
- Less overlap in membership between the executive and the legislature than in parliamentary systems;
- The president serves as head of state.

STUDYING . . .
THE POLITICAL EXECUTIVE

- The political executive is the top tier of government. In liberal democracies, its understanding begins with the study of institutional arrangements. In authoritarian regimes, the executive tends to be more fluid, patterned by informal relationships, rather than formal rules.

- The three institutional forms of the executive – presidential, parliamentary, and semi-presidential – can be understood as contrasting methods for dividing and controlling executive authority. These arrangements can be tested against their contributions to political stability and effective governance.

- Understanding the presidential system involves looking at examples from Latin America, not just at the somewhat atypical case of the USA. One issue which has been debated, and which could be explored further through non-American case studies, is whether the format is (was?) inherently unstable.

- If the USA continues to encounter governance problems such as an expanding public debt, we can expect more debate on whether its presidential system offers a form of governance in which 'everyone is in check, but no-one is in charge' (Senator William Cohen, quoted in Cronin and Genovese, 2012, p. 161). Rightly or wrongly, America's decline as the world's hegemon will also lead to more criticism of the checks and balances built into its political system.

- Parliamentary government is often studied through the British example. Here, it is important to be aware of the decay of the two-party system in the United Kingdom, as well as the emergence there of coalitions, both at national level and in devolved assemblies.

- In any case, parliamentary government is more accurately represented through the established multi-party coalitions of Western Europe. The smaller countries, in particular, provide opportunities to address issues concerning the origins, stability, and effectiveness of different types of coalition. Here, there is a considerable research literature to consider and to apply to new coalitions and under-studied countries.

- In addition, the nature and effectiveness of the process for forming governments, including pre-election agreements and post-election negotiations, is an issue which can be examined through the extensive West (and East) European experience.

- In the study of the executive in competitive authoritarian regimes, Vladimir Putin's transition in Russia from president to prime minister (and back) surely provides a natural experiment for comparing the importance of institutions and leaders.

reasons, the existence of a president is an insufficient sign of a presidential system.

Similarly, the frequent assertion that prime ministers in parliamentary systems are becoming 'presidential' is strictly incorrect. It is merely a metaphor – and a misleading one because, as we will see, presidents often experience more difficulty than prime ministers in achieving their goals.

Presidential government is a form of constitutional rule in which a single chief executive governs using the authority derived from popular election, with an independent legislature (Figure 16.1). Usually, this election takes the form of a direct vote of the people, with a limit on the number of terms a president can serve (see Chapter 11). The president directs the government and, unlike most prime ministers in parliamentary government, also serves as ceremonial head of state. Because both president and legislature are elected for a fixed term, neither can bring down the other, giving each institution some autonomy.

This separation of powers is the hallmark of the presidential system and is typically reinforced by a separation of personnel. Members of the executive cannot sit in the assembly, creating further distance between the two institutions. Similarly, legislators must resign their seats if they wish to serve in the government, meaning the president's ability to buy members' votes with the promise of a job is self-limiting.

Contrasting methods of election create a natural difference of interests. Legislators depend only on the support of voters in their home district, while the president (and the president only) is elected by a broader constituency – typically, the country at large. This divergence generates the political dynamic whereby the president pursues a national agenda against special and local interests in the legislature.

Figure 16.1 Presidential government

Presidential government divides power between president and legislature. This distinction is achieved by separate election, as shown, and also by separate survival – the president cannot dissolve the legislature and the legislature can only remove the president through impeachment.

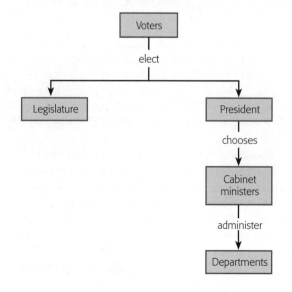

So, despite the focus on a single office, presidential government divides power. The system creates a requirement for the executive to negotiate with the legislature and, by this mechanism, seeks to ensure the triumph of deliberation over dictatorship.

Presidential government predominates in the Americas. It is entrenched not only in the United States, but also throughout Latin America. We must begin with the USA, where the format emerged, but we will then turn to Brazil as a more typical example.

United States

When the framers of the American constitution met in Philadelphia in 1787, the issue of the executive created a dilemma. On the one hand, the Founding Fathers wanted to avoid anything that might prove to be a 'foetus of monarchy'. After all, the American Revolution had just rid the new nation of England's George III. On the other hand, many delegates agreed with Founding Father Alexander Hamilton that a single executive was needed for 'decision, activity, secrecy and dispatch'. Eventually, the founders settled on the presidency, an office capable of providing prompt action for a republic in which Congress was, nonetheless, expected to play the leading role.

But how should the occupant of this new, non-monarchical chief executive be selected? Here, the delegates were less clear. Somewhat late in the proceedings, they agreed to select the president through an Electoral College whose members would be appointed by state legislatures. So, the framers had stumbled across an essential feature of presidential government: separate election of executive and legislature.

The founders were not, however, prepared to embrace direct election. On the contrary, one purpose of the Electoral College was to insulate the choice of president from influence by the 'excitable masses'. It is somewhat ironic, therefore, that the national vote has become far more important than the delegates intended. The College has become a mechanical device for allocating College votes; each state has a specific number of College votes which, Maine and Nebraska excepted, go to the leading presidential candidate in that state's election. So, the College is not the site of decision imagined by the framers. Still, it remains possible to win the popular vote but lose in the College, as Al Gore discovered in his defeat by George W. Bush in 2000.

The constitution also ensures that the president, once selected, remains secure in office, thus establishing the separate survival of executive and legislature which is a hallmark of presidential government. The president can only be dismissed by Congress through 'Impeachment for, and on Conviction of, Treason, Bribery, or other high Crimes and Misdemeanors'. So far, just two – including Bill Clinton in 1998 – have been impeached, though neither was convicted (Richard Nixon, however, resigned in 1974, anticipating conviction). Just as Congress cannot normally remove the president, neither can the president dissolve Congress and call new elections.

The constitution states that 'The executive power shall be vested in a President of the United States of America'. In addition to a general obligation to 'take Care that the Laws be faithfully executed', the president is given explicit duties, such as commander-in-chief. These express powers have been interpreted over time as giving the president further implied powers – those without which he could not fulfil his constitutional duties. For instance, presidents can claim executive privilege: the right to withhold information from Congress and the courts which, if released, would damage the president's capacity to 'faithfully execute' the laws. The president possesses further powers explicitly granted by Congress and can also engage in actions on his own initiative, such as issuing executive orders, statements, and proclamations (Mayer, 2011). So, the president's tool kit is far from empty.

Even so, the office was originally designed in a concerted effort to limit executive pretension. And it is equally clear that these restrictions continue. Lyndon Johnson offered this advice to his successor Richard Nixon:

Before you get to the presidency you think you can do anything. You think you're the most powerful leader since God. But when you get into that tall chair, as you're gonna find out, Mr. President, you can't count on people. You'll find your hands tied and people cussin' you. The office is kinda like the little country boy found the hoochie-coochie show at the carnival, once he'd paid his

dime and got inside the tent: 'It ain't exactly as it was advertised.' (Quoted in Cronin and Genovese, 2012, p. 108)

President Kennedy agreed. In less home-spun language, he observed that 'the president is rightly described as a man of extraordinary powers. Yet it is also true that he must wield those powers under extraordinary limitations'. For instance, many of the president's most important powers are shared with Congress:

● the president is commander-in-chief but Congress retains the power to declare war;

● the president can make government appointments and sign treaties, but only with 'the advice and consent' of the Senate;

● the president 'recommends to Congress such measures as he shall judge necessary and expedient', but is offered no means to ensure his proposals are accepted;

● the president can veto legislation, but Congress can override his objections;

● Congress, not the president, controls the purse strings.

Two points flow from the president's constitutional position. First, describing the relationship between the president and Congress as a separation of powers is misleading. In reality there is a separation of institutions, rather than of legislative and executive powers. President and Congress share authority: each seeks to influence the other, but neither is in a position to dictate. The two institutions are connected by a metaphorical rubber band that responds flexibly to political developments (Rottinghaus, 2011). The system is subtle, intricate, and balanced.

The tension within the system, it is important to note, continues even when the same party controls both the White House and Congress. Whatever their party, members of Congress have different electoral interests from the president. In contrast to the president's national constituency, legislators are elected without term limits from local areas for terms of two years in the House and six years in the Senate (Box 16.1). The divergent interests resulting from these distinct constituencies mean that party cannot integrate executive and legislature in the manner of a parliamentary system. This point, frequently mis-understood by foreign observers, was well-stated by Mayhew in *Divided We Govern* (1991, p. 135): 'to suppose that an American party winning Congress and the presidency thereby wins the leeway of a British governing party is to be deluded by the elec-tion returns'.

Second, in a system of shared control presidential power becomes the power to persuade (Neustadt, 1991). As President Truman said, 'the principal power that the president has is to bring people in and try to persuade them to do what they ought to do without persuasion'. In this task, the contempo-rary president can follow two strategies: **going Washington** and **going public**.

> **Going Washington** means the American president engages in wheeling and dealing with members of Congress, assembling majorities for his legislative pro-posals. **Going public** occurs when the president exploits his access to the mass media in an attempt to influence public opinion and so persuade Washington indirectly (Kernell, 2006).

Lyndon Johnson, a former leader of the Senate Democrats who succeeded to the presidency fol-lowing President Kennedy's assassination in 1963, was a master of the Washington strategy. To secure his bold domestic reforms, he leant heavily on members of Congress, using a potent combination of bullying, flattery, and persuasion. 'There is only one way for a President to deal with Congress', he said, 'and that is continuously, incessantly and without interruption' (Kearns, 1976, p. 226). The Great Cajoler was, however, less successful with the wider public, lacking sparkle in front of a television camera.

By contrast, the Great Communicator Ronald Reagan (President, 1981–89) adopted the wider approach, seeking to communicate his policies to the public and, indirectly, to influence Congress through his domination of the agenda. However, the evidence that presidents can actually shape the public's preferences and priorities is distinctly thin. Reagan himself wisely employed experienced aides to keep the pressure on key legislators – in effect, fol-lowing a dual strategy (Wood, 2011).

The paradox of the American presidency – a weak governing position amid the trappings of omnipotence – is reflected in the president's support network. To meet presidential needs for information and advice, a conglomeration of sup-porting bodies has evolved, including the White House Office, the National Security Council, and the Office of Management and Budget. Collectively known as the Executive Office of the President, these bodies provide far more direct support than is available to the prime minister in any parliamentary system, forming what is some-times known as the 'institutional presidency' (Burke, 2010). The days have long passed (they did once exist) when presidents secured secretarial support by asking family members to volunteer their help.

BOX 16.1

Separate election in the United States

	How elected	Length of term	Limit on re-election
Presidency	A national vote, aggregated by state in an Electoral College	4 years	Maximum of two terms
Senate	Direct popular vote in each of 50 states	6 years	No limit
House of Representatives	Direct popular vote in each of 435 districts	2 years	No limit

BOX 16.2

Comparing presidential powers in Brazil and the USA

	Brazil	USA
Can the president issue decrees?	Yes, in many areas. Valid for 60 days	No
Can the president initiate bills?	Yes, exclusively in some areas	No
Can the president declare bills urgent?	Yes	No
Can the president veto legislation?	Yes, in whole and part	Yes, but no **line-item veto**
How can Congress override a veto?	Absolute majority in joint meeting of both houses	Two-thirds majority in each house
President's control over the budget	Stronger	Weaker
Party system	Multiparty	Two-party
Does the president's party possess a majority in Congress?	No	Occasionally in both houses (12 years between 1969–2012)
Party discipline in Congress	Weak	Stronger

Yet, the massive apparatus of advice available to presidents has often proved to be a weakness. Many advisers are political outsiders, appointed by the president at the start of his tenure before his eye for Washington's politics is set. Far from helping the president, advisers sometimes end up undermining his position. The Watergate scandal in the 1970s destroyed the presidency of Richard Nixon; the Iran–Contra scandal in the 1980s, involving secret arms sales to Iran, laid siege to the reputation of Ronald Reagan. In both cases, over-zealous officials formed at least part of the problem.

One consideration here is that the presidential system lacks a strong cabinet to offer a counterbalance to personal advisers. In the USA, the cabinet goes unmentioned in the constitution; its meetings are little more than a presidential photo opportunity. Cabinet members often experience difficulty in gaining access to the president through his thicket of advisers. Unlike some parliamentary systems, presidential government is never cabinet government.

A **line-item veto** is the ability to override a part – a line – of a bill without rejecting it in its entirety. Congress granted American presidents this power in 1996 but the Supreme Court declared the law unconstitutional two years later, stating that the constitution made no provision for the president to amend statutes.

Brazil

With democracy now established in parts of Latin America, students of presidential government must broaden their horizons beyond the USA. The United States remains the prototype but most working examples are now found to the south, where the experience is somewhat less positive. This mixed performance reflects the difficulties of integrating a presidential system with two common features, proportional representation and a multiparty system, which are absent in the USA. In short, comparative analysis shows that the American presidency is both prototypical and untypical.

A comparison between the USA and Brazil is particularly useful in widening our perspective. Where the American president is hemmed in with restrictions, the Brazilian constitution appears to offer the country's president an arsenal of weapons (Box 16.2). Brazil's president can:

- issue decrees – provisional regulations with the force of law – in specified areas;

- declare bills to be urgent, forcing Congress to make a prompt decision;

- initiate bills in Congress – in some areas, the president alone is empowered to do this;

- propose a budget which goes into effect, month by month, if Congress does not itself pass a budget.

The combined effect of these entitlements would appear to give Brazil's president ample means to govern.

Yet, despite their panoply of formal powers, Brazilian presidents face the same problem as their colleagues to the north: legislators who know their own interests. Indeed, Brazilian leaders experience much greater difficulty in bending Congress to their will. The explanation for this contrast lies in Brazil's fragmented multiparty system. In 2010, as many as 13 parties won more than 10 seats in the Chamber of Deputies.

Furthermore, party discipline within Brazil's Congress is exceptionally weak, reflecting the use of preference votes in the list electoral system. Deputies often switch party in mid-term, and are more concerned to obtain resources for their district than to show loyalty to their party. In Brazil, parties are not only more numerous, but also less cohesive than in the USA – a contrast which complicates the president's task.

In responding to this partisan fragmentation, Brazil's presidents build informal coalitions. This requirement takes the form of appointing ministers from a range of parties in an attempt to extract loyalty from them. For instance, nine parties were represented in the governing coalition after the 2010 election. It is as though a Republican president in the United States, confronting a hostile Congress,

could bolster his support by appointing Democratic legislators to his cabinet.

In forming coalitions, Brazilian presidents are assisted by a more flexible interpretation of the separation of institutions than is found in the USA. The United States is, in fact, exceptional within presidential systems in insisting on a strict separation of personnel between government and assembly. For instance, we certainly could not substitute 'the United States' for 'Brazil' in this quotation:

In Brazil, ministers will occasionally resign their government positions just before an important vote in the assembly, resume their legislative seats, vote and then resign their legislative seats and resume their ministerial posts again. (Cox and Morgenstern, 2002, p. 459)

Thus, Brazil shows that the executive in presidential government does not need to be drawn from a single party. As with some other chief executives in the region, Brazilian presidents rely on a multiparty governing coalition as a technique for influencing the legislature. However, these coalitions are more informal, pragmatic, and unstable than the carefully crafted inter-party coalitions which characterize parliamentary government in Western Europe. In presidential systems, after all, the collapse of a coalition does not mean the fall of a government, reducing the incentive to sustain a coalition.

So, although Latin American constitutions appear to give the chief executive a more important political role, appearances are deceptive. The Latin American experience confirms that presidents operating in a democratic setting confront inherent difficulties in securing their programme.

Assessing presidential government

In assessing the presidential system, we must begin by acknowledging its strengths:

- the president's fixed term provides continuity in the executive, avoiding the collapse of governing coalitions to which parliamentary governments are prone;

- winning a presidential election requires candidates to develop broad support across the country;

- elected by the country at large, the president rises above the squabbles between local interests represented in the assembly;

- a president provides a natural symbol of national unity, offering a familiar face for domestic and international audiences alike;

- since a presidential system necessarily involves a separation of powers, it should also encourage limited government and thereby protect liberty.

But presidential government also carries inherent risks. Only one party can win the presidency; everyone else loses. All-or-nothing politics can lead to political instability, especially in new regimes. In addition, fixed terms of office are too inelastic; 'everything is rigid, specified, dated', wrote Bagehot (1867). As experience in the USA periodically reveals, the deadlock arising when executive and legislature disagree means that the political system may be unable to address pressing problems.

There is a danger, too, that presidents will grow too big for their boots. In the past, Latin American presidents have frequently amended the constitution so as to continue in office beyond their one- or two-term limits.

Even worse, a frustrated or ambitious president can turn into a dictator; presidential democracies are more likely than parliamentary democracies to disintegrate (Cheibub, 2002). The USA remains the world's only case of stable presidential government over the long term – an exception to admire but not, it seems, a model that can easily be replicated. Here, the judgement is to decide whether the presidential system's overall instability is inherent or simply an accident of geography; many presidential systems are found in historically volatile Latin America.

Parliamentary government

Unlike presidential systems, in which the chief executive is separate from the legislature and independently elected, the executive in parliamentary government is organically linked to the assembly (Figure 16.2). The government emerges from parliament and can be brought down by a vote of no confidence. Usually, ministers are drawn from the

assembly's ranks but, in some countries, there is no such convention and, in a few (such as Sweden), ministers must resign their seat in parliament (Box 16.3).

In nearly all cases, the executive can dissolve parliament and call fresh elections. If the paradox of presidentialism is executive weakness amid the appearance of strength, the puzzle of parliamentary government is to explain why effective government can still emerge from this mutual vulnerability of assembly and executive.

Parliamentary government
- The governing parties emerge from the assembly and can be dismissed from office by a vote of no confidence.
- The executive is collegial, taking the form of a cabinet (council of ministers) in which the prime minister (premier, chancellor) was traditionally only first among equals. The cabinet typically contains around two dozen members.
- A ceremonial head of state is normally separate from the post of prime minister.

Figure 16.2 Parliamentary government

In parliamentary government, the executive emerges from the assembly (most often in the form of a coalition) and remains accountable to it

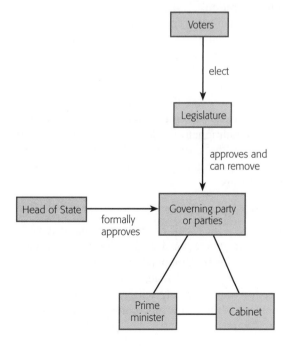

BOX 16.3

Compatibility rules

Can cabinet members also be members of parliament?	Examples
Yes, usually required	Ireland, United Kingdom
Yes	Denmark, Italy
No, incompatible	Belgium, Sweden

The solution to our puzzle is clear: party provides the necessary unifying device, bridging government and legislature in a manner that presidential systems are designed to prevent. Where a single party wields a parliamentary majority (as, historically, in Britain), government can be stable and decisive, perhaps excessively so. But the British model of single-party majority government, facilitated as it is by a plurality electoral system, is exceptional. In many parliamentary systems, the assembly is elected by proportional representation, a system which rarely results in a majority of seats for one party. The outcomes here are a coalition or a minority administration.

So, parliamentary government is as variable in operation as the presidential form. Just as the working of presidential government depends on whether the legislature is based on a two-party system (as in the USA), or a multiparty system (as in Brazil), so too does the parliamentary system have two variants, one based on majority government (e.g. as traditionally in the United Kingdom) and the other on either coalitions (e.g. Finland), or minority government (e.g. Denmark). We examine each of these forms.

Majority government

Britain was the classic example of parliamentary government based on a single ruling party with a secure majority. Although the 2010 election may presage long-term change, the plurality method of election has historically delivered a working majority in the House of Commons to a single party (see Chapter 11).

The leader of the majority party becomes prime minister (PM), selecting 20 or so parliamentary colleagues from the same party to form the cabinet. Where the American cabinet is marginal, the British cabinet is the formal lynchpin of the system. It is the focus of accountability to parliament and even the strongest PM cannot govern without its support. The cabinet meets in most weeks, and is chaired by the PM. The monarch now sits above the entire political process, meeting regularly with the PM but rarely, if ever, intervening in political decisions.

Government accountability to the House is tight. Nearly all cabinet ministers are drawn from, and remain, members of the Commons. All ministers, including the PM, must regularly defend their policies in the chamber; further, the opposition will demand a vote of no confidence whenever it senses an advantage from launching an attack. Should the government lose such a vote, it would be expected to resign, leading to a coalition, or the main opposition party taking power, or fresh elections.

However, the key to the system's stability is the party discipline that turns the cabinet into the master of the Commons, rather than its servant. The governing party spans the cabinet and the assembly, securing its domination of the parliamentary agenda. The cabinet is officially the top committee of state but it is also an unofficial meeting of the party's leaders. As long as senior party figures remain sensitive to the views of their backbenchers (and, often, even if they do not), they can control the Commons. The government does, indeed, emerge from its parliamentary womb but it dominates its parent from the moment of its birth.

How does the ruling party achieve this level of control? Each party has a Whip's Office to ensure that backbenchers (ordinary MPs) vote as its leaders require. Even without the attention of the whips, MPs will generally toe the party line if they want to become ministers themselves. In a strong party system such as Britain's, a member who shows too much independence is unlikely to win promotion. In extreme cases, MPs are thrown out of their party for dissent and are then unlikely to be re-elected by constituents for whom a party label is still key. Whatever their private views, it is in backbenchers' own interests to demonstrate public loyalty to their party.

Coalition and minority government

Many countries using parliamentary government elect their legislature by proportional representation, resulting in a situation where no single party gains a majority. Even single-member plurality elections no longer routinely deliver a majority government. In this situation, the tight link between the election result and government formation weakens, and government takes one of three main forms:

- a **majority coalition** in which two or more parties with a majority of seats join together in government. This is the most common form of rule across continental Europe; it characterizes Belgium, Finland, Germany, and the Netherlands in particular.

- a **minority coalition** or alliance. These are formal coalitions or informal alliances between parties which, even together, still lack a parliamentary majority. Minority coalitions have predominated in Denmark since the 1980s.

- a **single-party minority** government formed by the largest party. Single-party minority cabinets are common in Norway and Sweden.

Figure 16.3 shows the party composition of West European governments in the second half of the twentieth century. Majority coalitions were most frequent, followed by single-party minority governments, minority coalitions, and single-party majority governments.

Through both its statements and its silences, the constitution helps to account for these contrasts. Many constitutions explicitly specify the hurdles a new government must clear before taking office. As Box 16.4 shows, some constitutions (including most recent ones) demand that the legislature demonstrates majority support for a new government through a formal vote of investiture. Clearly, this requirement for a positive investiture vote by the assembly encourages the formation of a majority coalition with an agreed programme.

However, some constitutions do not require a majority vote for a new administration. In Sweden, for example, the proposed prime minister can form a government as long as no more than half the members of the *Riksdag* object (Bergman, 2000). The requirement is to avoid majority opposition rather than to command majority assent. In other countries, the constitution is entirely silent on the procedure for approving a new government. In these circumstances, the new administration takes office, and continues in power, until and unless it is voted down by the assembly. These less demanding conventions – a negative investiture vote, or none at all – facilitate the formation and survival of minority governments.

However, minority administrations often receive the support of other parties in parliament which, even outside office, can continue to influence legislation through their presence on parliamentary committees. These parliamentary support parties may even make an agreement with the governing party to offer their support in specific policy areas (Bale and Bergman, 2006). Such circumstances (which have become the norm in India, for instance) constitute a **parliamentary coalition** without a governing coalition. Some Green parties have succeeded in influencing environmental policy by this route.

Figure 16.3 Governments in Western Europe, 1945–99

Coalitions between parties which together possess a majority of seats in the assembly are by no means the only form of government in parliamentary systems. Minority administrations, whether by a single party or a coalition, are also common.

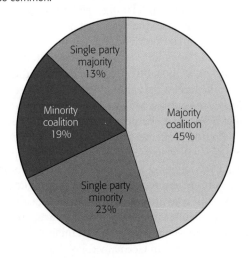

Notes: Based on 424 governments from 17 countries, including the UK. Non-party administrations (3 per cent) excluded.

Source: Adapted from Strøm and Nyblade (2007), table 32.1.

> A **parliamentary coalition** contains parties which agree to support the government in the assembly without necessarily participating in executive office.

At what stage do parties declare their preferred partners? On occasion, their vows precede the election, thus allowing voters to make a more informed judgement about the likely consequences of their own decisions. About one quarter of the governments formed in 20 parliamentary democracies between 1949 and 1995 were based on a pre-election coalition. Golder (2006) suggests these advance agreements secure a clear mandate for the government, even in the context of a proportional electoral system. They are an important exception to the thesis that, in proportional systems, voters are electing parliaments, rather than governments.

Most often, though, the party composition of government is decided after the election, through intricate negotiations between the leaders of the relevant parties. While this activity is under way, the outgoing government remains as a caretaker administration. On average, 30 days are needed before the new government takes office but much longer periods have been known: 208 days in the Netherlands (1977) and a record 541 days in Belgium (2010/11). Let us examine how the search for a new government proceeds during these interregnums.

Some constitutions specify a procedure which the parties are to follow in forming a government. This process often involves the head of state appointing an *informateur*, an experienced figure who explores the practical possibilities for the head of state. The *informateur* will most often recommend that the leader of the largest party be appointed *formateur*. The *formateur*'s task is to form an administration through negotiation, helping to legitimize the new administration that emerges. Figure 16.4 shows how this practice works in the typical case of Belgium.

The parties agreeing to go into coalition will next detail a joint programme in a lengthy public statement. As with constitutions, these package deals are often both opaque and lengthy: for instance, the agreement between the Christian Democrats and the Free Democrats in Germany following the 2009 election extended to 124 pages. These statements cover the policies to be pursued and the coalition's rules of conduct; for example, how it proposes to

---

BOX 16.4

Procedure for installing a government in parliamentary systems when no party possesses a majority of seats

	Description	Example
Positive investiture vote	To take office, a new government must obtain majority support in parliament	Spain, Finland
Negative investiture vote	A new government takes office unless voted down by a majority in parliament	Sweden
No investiture vote	No formal parliamentary vote is required before a new government takes office	Denmark

---

resolve disputes. Questions of office – which party obtains which ministry and whether that party alone determines the appointment – are also negotiated, with a party's bounty tightly reflecting its representation in parliament.

The compromises inherent in these deals mean that the rate of enactment of campaign pledges is somewhat lower in coalitions than in single party governments (Mansergh and Thomson, 2007). In a broader sense, though, coalitions tend to the centre, yielding a policy profile close to the median voter (see Chapter 12).

Types of coalition

So much for the formalities of coalition formation. What though are the political realities? In particular, why do some parties end up in a governing coalition while others – with an equal or even larger number of seats – remain on the sidelines?

It transpires that the most common type of coalition contains the smallest number of parties (typi-

Figure 16.4 Government formation in Belgium

Forming a government in European countries such as Belgium, where no party possesses a majority in parliament, is a highly structured and often lengthy process

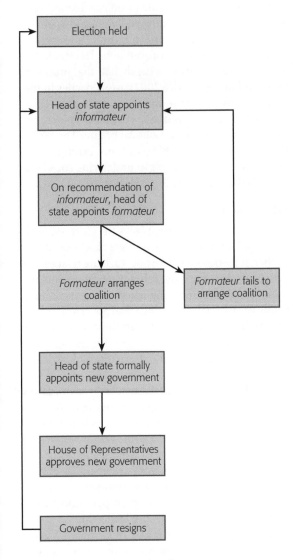

Source: Adapted from Deschouwer (2012).

BOX 16.5

Types of coalition government

Minimum (or minimal) winning	Contains the smallest number of parties which, together, can secure a parliamentary majority
Oversized (or surplus majority)	Contains more parties than the minimum winning coalition
Grand	Formed by the two leading parties, usually one from the left and the other from the right, which together command a substantial majority of seats
Connected	Only contains parties that are located next to each other on an ideological spectrum

Note: A coalition can be more than one type.

---

cally, two to four) needed to make a viable government. Party interest favours minimum winning coalitions (MWCs) because including additional parties in a coalition which already possesses a majority would simply dilute the number of posts and policy influence available to each participant. As Riker (1962, p. 47) succinctly wrote, when the resource to be shared out is fixed, 'participants create coalitions just as large as they believe will ensure winning and no larger'.

In addition, coalitions are usually based on parties with adjacent positions on the ideological spectrum. This test shapes which of many possible MWCs are chosen. In some Scandinavian countries, for example, coalitions usually draw exclusively on parties from within either the left-wing bloc or the right-wing bloc. Even in party systems lacking such well-defined blocs, the preference is still for connected coalitions – formed, that is, from parties adjacent to each other on an ideological and usually left–right scale.

Note that some parties, such as contemporary communist parties in Eastern Europe and extreme right-wing parties in Western Europe, are regarded as beyond the pale by the major players. These pariah parties fall outside the established party system and are effectively excluded from playing the coalition game.

The tendency for neighbours to cooperate benefits centre parties, which can jump either way. In Germany, for instance, the small liberal Free Democrat Party has participated in most coalitions, sometimes with the left-wing Social Democrats and, since 2009, with the more conservative Christian Democrats. Either coalition could be presented as ideologically coherent. Germany, however, also has some experience of grand coalitions between the two leading parties; these rare episodes marginalize smaller parties, such as the Free Democrats.

Occasionally, oversized coalitions emerge, containing more parties than are needed for a majority. These arrangements typically emerge when the partners are uncertain about the stability of their pact. An influential example is the five-party rainbow coalition, ranging from the conservative National Coalition to the Left Alliance, which governed Finland between 1995 and 2003 (Jungar, 2002). Oversized coalitions reflect the wise advice to keep your friends close but your enemies closer.

Durability of coalitions

We must address one final issue about coalitions. Such governments have frequently been condemned as unstable, not least by English-speaking critics of proportional representation. How valid is this charge? In a few countries, certainly, government duration has been measured in months: an average of five for the French Fourth Republic (1945–58) and eight for Italian governments (1948–89). In these over-cited examples, unstable coalitions certainly contributed to poor governance.

But, in most of Western Europe, coalitions typically last for several years (Strøm et al., 2008). The whole purpose of coalitions is to ensure political, if not always governmental, stability by incorporating parties and the interests they represent into the executive. With stability as an explicit goal, the political style is deliberately consensual and cautious. Coalitions require negotiation over policy and posts, but compromise is seen as a route to stability.

In some countries, additional conventions enhance durability. For example, coalition agreements in Austria, France, and the Netherlands typically include a clause stating that the partners will call an election if they dissolve the coalition. This election rule, as it is called, raises the price of dissolution and gives the partners an incentive to overcome the inevitable tensions in their relationship.

Germany offers a further device to enhance durability. The constructive vote of no confidence is a constitutional device requiring the assembly to select a new chancellor (prime minister) before it can dispose of the incumbent. This rule prevents parliament form bringing down a government without giving thought to its successor. It works: coalitions in Germany typically survive the full four years. The constructive vote of no confidence has also been adopted in Hungary, Israel, and Spain.

In post-communist Eastern Europe, however, coalitions have thus far proved to be less stable. Their average duration is barely half that found in Western Europe (Baylis, 2007). Most parties in the East have an uncertain social base and an unclear ideology. The result is fragile coalitions vulnerable to short-term shifts in the political breeze. The West European model of stable coalitions, carefully crafted to avoid any threat to underlying social stability, is difficult to replicate elsewhere.

Who governs?

Parliamentary government lacks the clear focus of the presidential system on a single chief executive. Rather, it involves a subtle and variable relationship between prime minister, cabinet, and government ministers. Box 16.6 distinguishes between cabinet, prime ministerial, and ministerial government. Examining the balance between these nodes in the governing network, and how they are changing over time, helps in appreciating the realities of parliamentary government.

For advocates of the parliamentary system, **cabinet government** is a key strength, encouraging more deliberation than occurs under a presidential format. When Olsen (1980, p. 203) wrote that 'a Norwegian prime minister is unlikely to achieve a position as superstar', many advocates of parliamentary government would have regarded his comment as praise. In theory, and sometimes in practice, parliamentary government involves collective leadership.

Finland provides a clear case of cabinet government. By law, the Finnish State Council is granted extensive decision-making authority. Both the prime minister and individual ministers are subject to constraints arising from Finland's complex multiparty coalitions. Prime ministers are primarily chairs of Council meetings, and it is at these meetings that decisions are reached and compromises made.

In many larger countries, the number and complexity of decisions means they cannot all be settled round the cabinet table. But scale of operation does not necessarily mean the end of cabinet government.

BOX 16.6

Location of decision-making in parliamentary government

	Description	Example
Cabinet government	Discussion in cabinet determines overall policy	Finland
Prime ministerial government	The PM is the dominant figure, dealing directly with individual ministers	Germany (chancellor democracy)
Ministerial government	Individual ministers operate with little direction from the PM or the cabinet	Italy

Rather, cabinet committees develop as important decision sites. These groups focus on specific areas such as the budget, legislation, or overall strategy. For example, there were 12 committees in New Zealand in 2012, including the Canterbury Earthquake Recovery group, and 8 in Canada, including the Committee on National Security. In addition to these standing committees, prime ministers also set up ad hoc committees to respond to specific issues such as labour disputes.

So, cabinet government, to the extent that it still exists, has often become government by the cabinet network, with the real decisions merely confirmed in the full meetings. Committees themselves largely ratify decisions agreed before the meeting through informal consultations, usually led by the relevant minister.

We move now to the middle row of Box 16.6: **prime ministerial government**. In contrast to cabinet government, the guiding principle here is hierarchy, rather than collegiality. Germany is an example, though the approach is known as 'chancellor democracy' in the country itself. The *Bundestag* (Germany's lower house) appoints a chancellor, not a party, and accountability to the *Bundestag* is mainly through the Chancellor's office. The chancellor answers to parliament; ministers

answer to the chancellor. The strong position of Germany's chief executive derives from the Basic Law which states that the 'chancellor shall determine, and be responsible for, the general policy guidelines'.

Although there is a danger of inventing a golden age of cabinet government, several commentators suggest that parliamentary executives are, in general, moving in the direction of prime ministerial government. The proposition is that prime ministers have ceased to be *primus inter pares* (first among equals) and, instead, have become president-ministers. Writing of Canada, Savoie (1999) suggests that in setting the government's agenda and taking major decisions, there is no longer any *inter* or *pares*, only *primus*. Similarly, Fiers and Krouwel (2005, p. 128) tell us that since the 1990s prime ministers in Belgium and the Netherlands have acquired more prominent and powerful positions, transforming these democracies into a kind of 'presidentialized' parliamentary system. King (1994) identified three factors at work here: increasing media focus on the premier, the growing international role of the chief executive, and the emerging need for policy coordination as governance becomes more complex. A substantial prime minister's office, employing around 100 people in the case of Canada, reflects these distinctive responsibilities and reinforces prime ministerial authority.

Ministerial government, the bottom row in Box 16.6, arises when ministers operate without extensive direction from either prime minister or cabinet. This decentralized pattern can emerge either from respect for expertise, or from the realities of coalition. Germany is an example of the importance attached to specialization. Although the chancellor sets the overall guidelines, the constitution goes on to say that 'each Federal Minister shall conduct the affairs of his department autonomously and on his own responsibility'. Ministers are appointed for their knowledge of the field and are expected to use their professional experience to shape their ministry's policy under the chancellor's guidance. So, Germany mixes two models, operating ministerial government within the framework of chancellor democracy.

In many coalitions, parties appoint their own leading figures to head particular ministries, again giving rise to ministerial government. In the Netherlands, for instance, the prime minister does not appoint, dismiss, or reshuffle ministers. Cabinet

BOX 16.7

Selecting the head of state in some parliamentary democracies

	Head of state	Method of selection	Tenure
Austria	President	Direct popular election by a two-round system	6 years
Germany	President	Election by a joint *Bundestag* and *Land* convention	5 years
India	President	Election by a college of federal and state assemblies	5 years
Italy	President	Election by a joint session of parliament and regional representatives	7 years
Spain	Monarch	Heredity (eldest male)	Life
United Kingdom	Monarch	Heredity (eldest child)	Life

members serve with, but certainly not under, the government's formal leader. In these conditions, the premier's status is diminished, with ministers owing more loyalty to their party than to either the prime minister or the cabinet. The chief executive is neither a chief nor an executive but, rather, a skilled conciliator. In India's multiparty coalitions, too, open defiance of the prime minister is far from unknown (Mitra, 2012, p. 583).

Heads of state and parliamentary government

One hallmark of a parliamentary system is, in Bagehot's classic analysis (1867), the distinction between the **dignified** and **efficient** aspects of government. Unlike presidential systems, which combine the offices of head of state and head of government, parliamentary rule separates the two positions. Dignified or ceremonial leadership lies with the head of state; efficient leadership is based on the premier. This separation of roles creates more time for prime ministers to concentrate on running the country.

How are heads of state selected? The position is either inherited (a monarchy), or elected (a presidency) (Box 16.7). At least in Europe and Asia, royal heads of state remain surprisingly numerous. Half the countries of Western Europe are constitutional monarchies, including Belgium, Denmark, the Netherlands, Spain, and the United Kingdom. In some former British colonies such as Canada, a governor general stands in for the monarch.

'In such constitutions there are two parts: ... first, those which excite and preserve the reverence of the population – the **dignified** parts, if I may so call them; and next the **efficient** parts – those by which it, in fact, works and rules ... Every constitution must first gain authority and then use authority; it must first win the loyalty and confidence of mankind, and then employ that homage in the work of government.' (Bagehot, 1867, p. 6)

Although monarchs are reluctant to enter the political arena in democratic times, royal influence can occasionally be significant, especially in eras of crisis and transition. In the 1970s, for instance, King Juan Carlos helped to steer Spain's move to democracy. The King of Belgium also played a conciliatory role in his country's long march to federal status.

Monarchies aside, most heads of state in parliamentary systems are elected, either by popular vote (e.g. Ireland), or by parliament (e.g. Israel). Alternatively, a special electoral college is used, often comprising the national legislature plus representatives from regional or local government (e.g. Germany).

Semi-presidential government

Presidential and parliamentary government provide pure models of the political executive. We can build on our discussion of these models in examining the semi-presidential executive. This format mixes both models to produce a distinct system with its own characteristics.

Specifically, **semi-presidential government** combines an elected president with a prime minister and cabinet accountable to parliament (Figure 16.5). Unlike the head of state in parliamentary systems, the president in a semi-presidential executive is in, rather than above politics. As a two-headed system, the semi-presidential executive creates a division of authority within the executive and creates the potential for struggle between president and prime minister.

The French political scientist Maurice Duverger (1980, p. 166) provided an influential definition of semi-presidentialism:

A political regime is considered semi-presidential if the constitution which established it combines three elements: (1) the president of the republic is elected by universal suffrage; (2) he possesses quite considerable powers; (3) he has opposite him, however, a prime minister and ministers who possess executive and governmental power and can stay in office only if the parliament does not show its opposition to them.

The 'quite considerable powers' of the president typically include special responsibility for foreign affairs, appointing the prime minister and cabinet, issuing decrees and initiating referendums, initiating and vetoing legislation, and dissolving the assembly. In theory, the president can offer leadership on foreign affairs, while the prime minister addresses the intricacies of domestic politics through parliament.

If the United States exemplifies the presidential system, the French Fifth Republic provides the archetype of the semi-presidential executive. The 1958 constitution establishing the new regime was designed to provide stable governance in the context of a political crisis caused by a divisive colonial war

> **Semi-presidential government**, or the dual executive, combines an elected president performing political tasks with a prime minister who heads a cabinet accountable to parliament. The prime minister, usually appointed by the president, is responsible for day-to-day domestic government, but the president retains an oversight role and responsibility for foreign affairs. Also, the president can usually take emergency powers.

Figure 16.5 Semi-presidential government

Semi-presidential government combines an elected president (who usually appoints the prime minister and can dissolve the legislature) with accountability of the prime minister and cabinet to the legislature

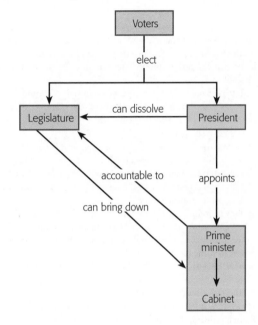

Note: Within semi-presidential government, Shugart and Carey (1992) distinguish between premier-presidential and president-parliamentary regimes. In the former, the cabinet is responsible to parliament; the president cannot dismiss ministers unilaterally, weakening the president. In the latter, the president as well as the assembly exerts authority over the cabinet's composition, strengthening the president.

in Algeria and a rebellious army. In addition, the unstable Fourth Republic, which had experienced 23 prime ministers in its short 12-year life, provided a model to avoid.

The new constitution created a presidency fit for the dominating presence of its first occupant, General Charles de Gaulle (President, 1959–69). De Gaulle saw himself as a national saviour, arguing that 'power emanates directly from the people, which implies that the head of state, elected by the nation, is the source and holder of that power' (Knapp and Wright, 2006, p. 53). In office, de Gaulle's imperious style developed the office to, and perhaps even beyond, its constitutional limits.

The president has been directly-elected since 1962, thus fully establishing the semi-presidential form.

FRANCE

LIBERAL DEMOCRACY

Form of government ■ a liberal democratic republic, headed by an elected president. The current republic, established in 1958, is the fifth republican regime since the revolution of 1789.

Legislature ■ the lower chamber, the National Assembly, contains 577 directly-elected members. The 348 members of the Senate are indirectly elected through local governments for a six-year term.

Executive ■ the semi-presidential executive combines a strong president, directly-elected for no more than two five-year terms, with a prime minister who leads a Council of Ministers accountable to the assembly. Ministers cannot be members of the assembly.

Judiciary ■ French law is based on the Napoleonic Codes (1804–11). The Constitutional Court has grown in significance during the Fifth Republic and, in 2008, acquired the power of judicial review.

Electoral system ■ a two-round system is used for both presidential and assembly elections, with a majority vote needed for victory on the first round.

Party system ■ left–right conflict remains a principle of French politics, though parties themselves have proved to be less durable. In the 2012 presidential election, François Hollande of the Socialist Party was elected in a run-off against the centre-right president, Nicolas Sarkozy.

Population (annual growth rate): 65.6 m (+0.5%)

World Bank income group: high income

Human development index (rank/out of): 20/187

Political rights score: ❶

Civil liberties score: ❶

Media status: free

Note: For interpretation and sources, see p. xvi.

Just how different is modern **FRANCE**? The case for French exceptionalism can be stated in three words: the French Revolution. The revolution of 1789 created a distinctive ethos within the country, centred on the idea of the nation. Expressed through a distinct language and culture, the nation remains the fundamental source of political authority.

The state is expected to stand above mere partial interests, defining the long-term national will. As with other states built on revolution – notably, the United States – France is an ideal, as well as a country. However, where American ideals led to pluralism, the French state is expected to take the lead in implementing the revolution's ideals of liberty, equality, and fraternity.

All citizens possess the same rights and obligations, and it is the state's task both to secure the rights and to extract the obligations.

As the country became more modern, urban, and industrial after 1945, so French uniqueness declined. Retreat from empire left France, as Britain, as a middle-ranking power with a new base in the European Union. The creation of a new regional level of governance within France reduced the state's traditional centralization. Immigration from North Africa moderated the country's homogeneity. Globalization challenged France's industrial base.

Such changes led Hayward (1994, p. 32) to conclude that 'the revolutionary impulse is exhausted'.

Yet, to portray France as just another democracy still seems imprudent. Public discourse continues to assume that the state must be capable of creating new jobs, while simultaneously protecting the security of full-time workers. Sovereignty is still presented as a cardinal virtue, with the result that globalization is seen more as a threat than an opportunity. Government spending remains exceptionally high. Dirigisme (state direction), suggests Wright (1997), has evolved, rather than disappeared.

Even if *l'exception française* is a myth, the legend itself still gives French political discourse its distinctive flavour.

SPOTLIGHT

The political executive in France

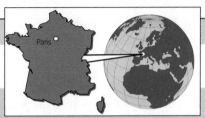

In France's semi-presidential executive the crucial relationship is between the president, on the one hand, and the prime minister and assembly, on the other. While the constitution may give control of foreign affairs to the president and reserve domestic policy to the prime minister, an interdependent world does not permit such pigeon-holing. France's relationship with the EU, for instance, encompasses both foreign and domestic affairs, complicating the decision-making process. Before one EU summit, Germany's chancellor insisted on meeting the French president and prime minister together, to speed negotiations. So, how does France's complex political executive operate?

Presidents and prime ministers need to work in harmony, a task made easier when the party in the Elysée Palace also has a majority in the assembly. This has been the case for most of the Fifth Republic. Indeed, the reduction of the president's term to five years was partly an attempt to coordinate presidential and parliamentary election terms, limiting the likelihood of **cohabitation**.

Cohabitation occurs in the semi-presidential executive when president and prime minister are drawn from different political camps. It intensifies competition between the two principals, and places the president in the awkward position of leading both the nation and the opposition.

When cohabitation does occur, as it has three times since 1986, presidential power tends to shrink. In these circumstances, prime ministers assert their constitutional duty to 'determine and direct the policy of the nation'. Crucially, though, cohabitation has not led to a crisis of the regime. The Fifth Republic has delivered the stability that its architects intended.

In the same way that the United States copes with power divided between the White House and Congress, so French experience confirms that the semi-presidential executive can provide stable government,

functioning resembles the American (rather than the British) equivalent;
■ ministers are given a detailed specification of their responsibilities on appointment and often come to the job with a background in its area, thus generating an expectation that they can function autonomously;
■ interventions by the prime minister and the president are often to resolve disputes, rather than to impose an overall agenda.

Cohabitation in the Fifth Republic

	President	Party	Prime minister	Party
1986–1988	François Mitterrand	Socialist	Jacques Chirac	Gaullist
1993–1995	François Mitterrand	Socialist	Edouard Balladur	Gaullist
1997–2002	Jacques Chirac	Gaullist	Lionel Jospin	Socialist

even when president and prime minister are drawn from different political blocs.

Beneath the president and prime minister, the government's day-to-day political work is carried out by 20 senior ministers, supported by deputy ministers and ministers of state. There are four main reasons, however, why this group lacks even the public collegiality displayed by members of the British cabinet:

■ most (though not all) governments in the Fifth Republic have been coalitions, with ministers drawn from more than one party;
■ the Council of Ministers (the cabinet), chaired by the president, is more ritual than discussion; its

Ministerial autonomy is further enhanced by limited accountability to the assembly (ministers cannot be members of parliament, though they do speak before it) and by a tradition of deferential treatment by the media, particularly on personal matters.

Further reading: Gaffney (2012), Knapp and Wright (2006), Lewis-Beck *et al.* (2012).

But more recent modifications have introduced slight limitations. In 2000, the presidential term was reduced from seven to five years, with a two-term limit following in 2008.

The constitution grants the French president extensive powers. For instance, the president is guarantor of national independence and the constitution, heads the armed forces, negotiates treaties, calls referendums, presides over the Council of Ministers, dissolves the National Assembly (but cannot veto legislation), appoints (but cannot dismiss) the prime minister, and appoints other ministers on the recommendation of the PM and dismisses them.

In pursuing these roles, the president is supported by a small political secretariat of around 60 people in the Elysée Palace (Stevens, 2003, p. 75). The first six presidents in the Fifth Republic sought to govern in expansive style, seeking to steer the ship of state, rather than just to arbitrate conflicts emerging among the crew. The seventh incumbent, François Hollande, may adopt more modest ambitions.

What of prime ministers in France's semi-presidential executive? Although they must countersign most presidential decisions, their main concern is domestic affairs, casually dismissed by de Gaulle as 'the price of milk'. Appointed by the president but accountable to parliament, the prime minister's task is rarely straightforward. He or she (Edith Cresson was PM 1991–92) formally appoints ministers and coordinates their day-to-day work, operating within the president's style and tone. Since the government remains accountable to parliament, much of the prime minister's work focuses on managing the National Assembly. The ability of the assembly to force the prime minister and the Council of Ministers to resign after a vote of censure provides the parliamentary component of the semi-presidential executive.

Some other countries with parliamentary traditions have also experimented with semi-presidential government. Because a strong president focused on international affairs contributes to an effective foreign policy, the format held particular appeal to European countries facing international difficulties. During the Cold War, Finland found a semi-presidential system particularly helpful in managing its sensitive relationship with the Soviet Union. And a dual executive also proved attractive to East European states in the immediate aftermath of com-munism's collapse. As international pressure receded, however, so the president's star tended to wane. In 2000, Finland modified its constitution to strengthen the parliamentary element. The semi-presidential executive has not threatened the pre-eminence of parliamentary government in Europe.

The executive of the European Union

Characteristically, the executive of the European Union does not map neatly onto any of the executive types – presidential, parliamentary, or semi-presidential – we have discussed. Nonetheless, its institutions are well-developed in comparison to mere intergovernmental organizations. Its unique structures merit discussion.

As we might expect for a confederal entity, the EU's executive is based on a balance between transnational and intergovernmental forces. The key executive body, the European Commission, represents the common European interest. However, the Council of the European Union (also known as the Council of Ministers) represents the member states and plays an increasingly important legislative and policy-making role. It is this blend of transnational (Commission) and intergovernmental (Council) ingredients which gives the EU executive its flavour.

Both the Commission and the Council perform legislative as well as executive functions. The Commission instigates legislative proposals, while the Council must approve them. So, the Council is sometimes seen as a second legislative chamber, representing the member states in the same way that Germany's state governments are directly represented in the *Bundesrat*. The sharp distinction drawn in many national constitutions between executive and legislative tasks is not matched in the EU. We examine the Commission and the Council, in turn.

The European Commission

The Commission is the EU's central executive body. According to the Maastricht Treaty (1992), it 'shall promote the general interest of the Union and take appropriate initiatives to that end'. Its structure, at least, resembles that of a national government in a parliamentary system. The Commission is headed by a president (the equivalent of a prime minister) who leads a college (cabinet) of commissioners (ministers). As with many national cabinets, the College meets weekly and reaches what are formally collective decisions. The 27 commissioners – one from each member state – operate with substantial autonomy and are supported by a small personal cabinet. In practice, the working method comes closer to the ministerial form of cabinet government, rather than the collegial, producing problems of coordination.

The Commission's 33,000 employees are the Union's civil servants; in that sense, the Commission forms an administrative bureaucracy, as well as a political executive. Although the Commission employs the vast majority of EU staff, it remains minute compared to national civil services. This fact reflects the EU's major role as a regulator, rather than as an executor. The Commission's job is to make regulations and oversee their execution, leaving implementation to member states.

Where the Commission does depart from the model of the parliamentary executive is in the manner of its appointment and the forms of its accountability. Rather than emerging from the European Parliament (EP), as we would expect from the parliamentary model, the president is nominated by the member states and only approved by the Parliament. Each member state then nominates a commissioner – typically a pro-European former minister from that country. Following hearings with the nominees, the EP then votes on the list as a whole. This process takes place after each five-yearly election to the Parliament. At root, then, appointments to the top level of the EU's executive arm reflect the Union's intergovernmental component, rather than its supranational component.

Again in contrast to parliamentary systems, the survival of the Commission is only loosely bound to its ability to maintain the parliament's confidence. Each College of Commissioners is expected to see out its five-year term, with a new Commission appointed after each parliamentary election. The EP is, however, empowered to censure the Commission as a whole. The right of censure, as with impeachment in presidential systems, provides a safety valve for difficult circumstances.

In pursuing the interests of the Union, the Commission possesses a substantial array of duties. It fulfils its function of promoting the common European interest by acting as guardian of the treaties, exclusively proposing legislation, managing the budget, overseeing the implementation of policy, and representing the EU externally.

Historically, the Commission provided the motor of European integration, particularly in developing the internal market in the 1980s. Now that the EU is more cautious about such grand initiatives, the Commission's drive has lessened, leading some to view it as a bureaucratic agent of the member states, rather than as a fully-functioning transnational executive (Magnette, 2005). Even so, the Commission undoubtedly remains a storehouse of expertise and an institution capable of transforming political will into administrative direction. Nugent (2010, p. 137) is surely justified in concluding that 'the Commission remains central and vital to the whole EU system'.

Council of the European Union

The intergovernmental Council of the European Union (Council of Ministers) is the major forum where the governments of the member states meet. Unlike the Commission, it is purely an intergovernmental body. The Council's responsibilities are to pass laws, in many areas jointly with the European Parliament; to coordinate the economic policies of the member states; to conclude international agreements; to approve the EU budget, jointly with the EP; to develop the EU's foreign and security policy; and to arrange for cooperation between member states in investigating cross-border crime (Europa, 2012).

The Council is a large forum in which varying groups of ministers from member states meet to formulate goals, agree policies, reach decisions, and issue statements. It meets in 10 different configurations, depending on the topic (e.g. economic and financial affairs). The relevant minister from each member state attends particular meetings, supported by officials from the home government. In total, the Council meets around 90 times a year, typically for all-day sessions which can contain over 100 participants, excluding interpreters. Decisions are reached by a qualified majority. The Council's president, supported by an extensive secretariat, seeks to build a consensus and inject coherence into the proceedings.

Contrary to the hopes of the Union's founders, the significance of the Council of the European Union has not faded as the EU has developed; on the contrary, its position has strengthened. Its legislative, strategic, and policy-making character, together with its focus on foreign policy and crime, give the Council a distinct position within the EU which both complements – and, to an extent, stands above – the Commission's more executive and administrative role.

The European Council

In addition to the Council of the European Union, the separate European Council, consisting of the heads of government and the Commission president, meets at least twice a year. The European Council is a political and intergovernmental summit intended to steer the Union's development and, especially, its foreign policy. The emergence of the European Council as a strategic forum has further strengthened the intergovernmental element of the EU, weakening (or, at least, supplementing) executive institutions such as the Commission.

Under the Treaty of Lisbon, the European Council appoints a President for a tenure of two-and-a-half years, renewable only once; the Council can also remove the incumbent. The first occupant, former Belgian prime minister Herman Van Rompuy, was appointed in 2009 for his skills as an internal conciliator, rather than as an outward-facing President of Europe.

The executive in authoritarian states

The central feature of the authoritarian executive is its lack of institutionalization. The leader seeks to concentrate power on himself and his supporters, not to distribute it among institutions. Jackson and Rosberg's idea of **personal rule** (1982), although developed in the context of African politics, travels widely through the non-democratic world. Politics takes precedence over government, and personalities matter more than institutions: a feast of presidents but a famine of presidencies.

The result of personal rule is often a struggle over succession, insufficient emphasis on policy and poor governance. In particular, the lack of a succession procedure (excepting hereditary monarchies) can create a conflict among potential successors not only after the leader's exit, but also in the run-up to it. Authoritarian leaders keep their job for as long as

> Jackson and Rosberg (1982, p. 19) define **personal rule** as 'a system of relations linking rulers not with the "public" or even with the ruled but with patrons, associates, clients, supporters and rivals who constitute the "system". The system is "structured" not by institutions but by the politicians themselves. The fact that it is ultimately dependent upon persons rather than institutions is its essential vulnerability'.

they can ward off their rivals. They must monitor threats and be prepared to neuter those who are becoming too strong. Politics comes before policy.

The price of defeat, furthermore, is high; politics can be a matter of life and death. When an American president leaves office, he can give well-paid lectures, or retire to his library to write his memoirs. Ousted dictators risk a harsher fate. By necessity, therefore, the governing style of non-democratic rulers inclines to the ruthless.

We will use post-colonial Africa and the Middle East to illustrate these themes, before turning to the rather more complex blend of leaders and institutions in communist and competitive authoritarian regimes.

Africa

Particularly in its most authoritarian phase before the 1990s, post-colonial Africa illustrated the importance of personal leadership in non-democratic settings. Leaders were adept at using the coercive and financial resources of the regime to reward their friends and punish their enemies. As an example, Sandbrook (1985) wrote this of Mobutu Sese Seko's rulership during his dictatorial tenure as President of Zaire (1965–97):

No potential challenger is permitted to gain a power base. Mobutu's officials know that their jobs depend solely on the president's discretion. Frequently, Mobutu fires cabinet ministers, often without explanation. Everyone is kept off balance. Everyone must vie for his patronage.

However, in post-colonial Africa, as in other authoritarian settings, personal rule was far from absolute. Inadequately accountable in a constitutional sense, many personal rulers were highly constrained by other political actors. These included the military, leaders of ethnic groups, landowners, the business class, the bureaucracy, multinational companies, and even factions in the leader's own court.

To survive, leaders had to distribute the perks of office so as to maintain a viable coalition of support. Enemies could be bought off by allowing them a share of the pie, but their slice must not become so large as to threaten the big man himself. Mobutu himself set out the ground rules: 'if you want to steal, steal a little in a nice way. But if you steal too much to become rich overnight, you'll be caught' (Gould, 1980, p. 485).

The Middle East

In the Middle East, personal rule remains central to those authoritarian regimes that survived the Arab Spring of 2011. Shahs, sheikhs, and sultans continue to rule oil-rich kingdoms in traditional patriarchal style. 'Ruling' rather than 'governing' is the appropriate term. In Saudi Arabia, for instance, advancement within the ruling family depends less on merit than on proximity to the family's network of advisers, friends, and guards. Public and private are interwoven, each forming part of the ruler's sphere. Government posts are occupied on good behaviour, as demonstrated by unswerving loyalty to the ruler's personal interests.

Such systems of personal rule have survived for centuries, limiting the development of strong institutions. But the Arab Spring also revealed the weaknesses of the format, as frustrated populations in several Arab states protested against the absence of opportunity in corrupt, conservative regimes headed by ageing autocrats.

Communist states

We might expect the institutions of government to have played a more central role in communist regimes. After all, these were administrative regimes par excellence, seeking to lead and transform society in a planned fashion.

Most communist states did have a clear structure of government, resembling the parliamentary form. But, in practice, the ruling communist party dominated the formal institutions of state. The party secretary often confirmed his supremacy by taking a state post, whether prime minister or president. However, power remained rooted in the party; if the top leader lost his position as party secretary, he was politically doomed.

Contemporary China both confirms and qualifies this notion of a party-dominated executive in communist states. As in other communist countries, the state is led by the party. But the party itself is divided into factions based on personality and patronage. It is these factions within the party which provide political glue, binding the actors together in a predictable but non-institutionalized way. The faction leaders serve as patrons, offering resources to their followers in exchange for their support. The faction then rises and falls with the political strength of its leader. Chinese politics has always been more fluid and personal than in other communist states; some past leaders have not occupied any formal positions at all, whether in the party or the government.

Thus, the Chinese case returns us to the theme of personal rule within the framework of a ruling party. In the party's factional environment, rising stars require cunning and patronage to prosper. Indeed, the evidence from China confirms that even this massive communist state can be ruled in a highly personal way. As Saich (2011, p. 83) observes:

Personal power and relations with powerful individuals are decisive throughout the Chinese political system. While this may decline as reforms become more institutionalized, most Chinese recognize that the best way to survive and flourish is to develop personal relationships (*guanxi*) with a powerful political patron.

Competitive authoritarian regimes

The characteristic form of the executive in competitive authoritarian regimes is presidential. This format provides a natural platform for leaders who seek to set themselves apart from – and above – all others. In such systems, the president operates without the full set of constitutional restraints which constrain the chief executive of a liberal democracy. Instead, the president uses his direct mandate from the people to cast a shadow over competing institutions such as the courts and the legislature without, however, reducing these bodies to token status. So, once again, we observe a form of personal rule.

This theme is illustrated by contemporary Russia. Formally, Russia is a semi-presidential regime arranged along French lines, with a directly-elected president coexisting with a chairman of the government (i.e. prime minister) who is nominated by the president and approved by the Duma (lower house).

In some minor respects, the Russian president's position is only slightly stronger than that of an American president. Both are limited to two four-year terms in office, but the Russian leader can stand again after a term out. Both are subject to impeachment but the threshold is more demanding in Russia: a two-thirds majority in both parliamentary chambers plus confirmation by the courts.

In reality, though, the Russian president can grasp the levers of power more easily than either his American or French equivalents. Under the 1993 constitution, the president acts as head of state, commander-in-chief, and guarantor of the constitution. In the latter capacity, he can suspend the decisions of other state bodies. He can also issue decrees, though these can be overridden by legislation. In contrast to most semi-presidential systems, the president is empowered to remove ministers without parliamentary consent; and does so.

Russia's president is also charged with 'defining the basic directions of the domestic and foreign policy of the state', and with 'ensuring the coordinated functioning and collaboration of bodies of state power'. These broad duties affirm Russia's long tradition of executive power, a norm which both predates and was reinforced by the communist era. Strong government is regarded as a necessary source of effective leadership for a large and sometimes lawless country.

Yet, even after completing his initial tenure as president in 2008 and taking up the office of prime minister, Vladimir Putin remained the pivotal figure. In cynically swopping jobs with Dmitry Medvedev, he created a natural experiment which showed power following the man. As president, Medvedev's influence seemed to be marginal compared with his predecessor. So, even in Russia, with its powerful state institutions centred on the Kremlin, a substantial measure of personal rule is superimposed on the institutions of state.

Discussion questions

- What difference would the introduction of parliamentary government make to politics in the United States?

- What difference would the introduction of presidential government make to politics in either the United Kingdom or your country (if parliamentary)?

- Is presidential or parliamentary government the most appropriate system for (a) new democracies, (b) divided societies?

- Why do most coalitions contain the smallest number of parties needed to secure a majority in the legislature?

- Have prime ministers become presidential and, if so, why?

- Does semi-presidential government provide the best of both worlds?

Further reading

R. Elgie, *Semi-Presidentialism: Sub-Types and Democratic Performance* (2011). This book examines how different forms of semi-presidentialism affect the quality and durability of democracy.

L. Han, ed., *New Directions in the American Presidency* (2011). Explores current themes in the study of the presidential system in the United States.

L. Helms, *Presidents, Prime Ministers and Chancellors: Executive Leadership in Western Democracies* (2005). A comparison of the political executive in Britain, Germany, and the United States.

A. Lijphart, ed., *Parliamentary versus Presidential Government* (1992). A classic collection of essays on parliamentary and presidential government.

T. Poguntke and P. Webb, eds, *The Presidentialization of Politics: A Comparative Study of Modern Democracies* (2005). An investigation of whether the operation of the executive has become more presidential in a range of liberal democracies.

K. Strøm, W. Müller and T. Bergman, eds, *Cabinets and Coalition Bargaining: The Democratic Life Cycle in Western Europe* (2008). A comparative examination of cabinet formation.

ONLINE RESOURCES AVAILABLE

Visit the companion website at **www.palgrave.com/politics/hague** to access additional learning resources, including multiple-choice questions, chapter summaries, web links and practice essay questions.

Chapter 17 The bureaucracy

The study of the **bureaucracy** focuses on the networks of central departments and public agencies that underpin the political executive. These networks provide advice to ruling politicians before policy is made and help to implement decisions once reached. The department secretary offering advice to the minister, the inspector checking tax returns, the health officer implementing a national anti-obesity strategy – all are part of the complex operation that is the public bureaucracy.

Traditionally, studies of the bureaucracy examined the permanent salaried officials employed in central government departments. These elite officials, and the ministries they occupy, remain of obvious importance, and the term 'bureaucracy' is sometimes confined to them. However, attention increasingly focuses on the wider governance beyond: in semi-independent agencies, local governments, and even the non-governmental organizations to which the delivery of public programmes is increasingly subcontracted. We refer to all public networks as comprising the bureaucracy; others employ such terms as 'public administration' or 'public management' to denote the study of the public sector in this wider sense. Whatever the labels, understanding the contemporary state, and following a career within it, requires a mental map of what are undoubtedly complex networks.

Evolution

To appreciate the modern bureaucracy, we must consider what preceded it. As with other aspects of government, the precursors varied between Europe and the New World. In Europe, clerical servants were originally agents of the royal household, serving under the personal instruction of the ruling monarch. Many features of modern bureaucracies – regular salaries, pensions, open recruitment – arose from a successful attempt to overcome this idea of public employment as personal service to the monarch.

> **Bureaucracy** is, literally, rule by officials. The word is used neutrally in this chapter to denote the organizations employing public officials and forming the public administration. However, the term has always carried critical overtones ('faceless bureaucrats') and is also specifically associated with Weber's model.

The evolution of royal households into twentieth-century bureaucracies was a massive transformation, intimately linked to the rise of the modern state. Today, we take the features of bureaucratic organization for granted, and even react against them, but in the early twentieth century the form was strikingly new: a phenomenon to be both admired and feared. The analysis presented by Max Weber exemplified this perspective, providing the tradi-

STUDYING . . .

BUREAUCRACY

- In liberal democracies, the contemporary public sector is a complex network encompassing not only government departments (ministries), but also non-departmental public bodies – such as regulatory agencies.

- The partial transition from bureaucracy as hierarchy to bureaucracy as network provides many opportunities to map these changes, to consider how they diffuse across countries, and to address their effects and effectiveness.

- The American, Norwegian and Swedish bureaucracies have long included independent agencies, providing experience from which other liberal democracies can learn. The European Union also offers a pure example of governance through regulation.

- That said, Weber's traditional model of bureaucracy remains the starting point for understanding bureaucracy, providing a base-line for subsequent thinking. Reforms in the Weberian heartland, such as Germany, have not matched those in the English-speaking world, but are not inconsequential and remain somewhat under-studied.

- Agency autonomy raises questions of accountability: how, how much, and how adequate? Studies here confront the reality of contemporary governance and, perhaps, an evolving conception of democracy in which the decision-making scope of government ministers is limited by agency autonomy (e.g. central banks)

- New public management (NPM) is no longer new but it remains an intriguing attempt to apply business-like practices in the public sector. Your assessment of NPM will be a litmus test for your overall perspective on how bureaucracies should operate.

- E-government is a more recent theme in public management. Its importance is debated but it clearly provides incentives for departments to collaborate, while also raising issues of surveillance, privacy, and data protection. E-government offers numerous opportunities for comparative research and lesson-drawing.

tional view of public administration as a disciplined hierarchy in which officials who have been recruited and promoted on merit systematically apply rules to the cases before them (Box 17.1).

Weber's central claim was that bureaucracy made administration more efficient, providing the means by which the techniques of modern industry and military organization could be brought to bear on civil affairs:

The fully developed bureaucratic apparatus compares with other organizations exactly as does the machine with non-mechanical modes of production. Precision, speed, clarity, knowledge of files, continuity, discretion, unity, strict subordination, reduction of friction and of material and personal costs – these are raised to the optimum point in the strictly bureaucratic administration (quoted in Kahlberg, 2005, p. 199).

While Weber's ideas proved to be highly influential in continental Europe, they carried less resonance in the New World. There, civil services developed in more pragmatic fashion. Lacking the European monarchical and state tradition, public management was initially considered to be a routine application of political directives. In the United States, the original philosophy was one of governance by the common man; almost every citizen, it was assumed, qualified for almost every public job.

The notion of a professional civil service was considered somewhat elitist and undemocratic.

This populist theory of bureaucracy conveniently underpinned the **spoils system**, a term deriving from the phrase 'to the victor, the spoils'. In the United States, the spoils system continued at least until 1883, when the Pendleton Act created a Civil Service Commission to recruit and regulate federal employees. In Canada, the merit principle was introduced in 1908 and adopted fully in the Civil Service Act, 1918. So, where a **merit system** had emerged in Europe in reaction to monarchy, in North America it supplanted spoils.

In a **spoils system**, elected politicians distribute government jobs to those with the foresight to support the winning candidate. In nineteenth-century America, for example, the election of a new president led to a virtually complete turnover of employees in what was then a small federal government. In contrast to this patronage-based approach, a **merit system** recruits public employees on ability as measured by competitive examination.

Weber's model imagines public service as professional and legalistic, rather than managerial and businesslike, in character. It remains significant, not least in Germany.

Western bureaucracies reached their zenith in the twentieth century. The depression and two world wars vastly increased government intervention in society. The welfare state, completed in Western and especially Northern European countries in the decades following World War II, required a massive bureaucratic apparatus to distribute grants, allowances, and pensions. By 1980, public employment accounted for almost one third of the total workforce in Britain and Scandinavia, though much of this expansion had taken place at local level.

However, the final quarter of the twentieth century witnessed declining faith in bureaucratic solutions. Where Weber had lauded the efficiency of the administrative machine, critics now judged civil servants to be engaged in unproductive games to increase the budgets and staff of their particular sections (Niskanen, 1971).

More generally, the policy-forming community in many liberal democracies has widened, diminishing any monopoly which civil servants directly

BOX 17.1

Max Weber on bureaucracy

The German sociologist Max Weber (1864–1920) conceived bureaucracy as a structured hierarchy in which salaried officials reach rational decisions by applying explicit rules to the facts before them. His model contains five features:

- bureaucracy involves a carefully defined division of tasks;
- authority is impersonal and decisions are reached by methodically applying rules to particular cases;
- people are recruited to serve in the bureaucracy based on proven (or, at least, potential) competence;
- officials who perform their duties competently possess secure jobs and salaries, and can expect promotion according to seniority and merit;
- the bureaucracy forms a disciplined hierarchy in which lower officials are subject to the authority of their superiors.

employed by the central government once exerted over policy advice. Instead, officials are encouraged to focus rather more on delivery – and, specifically, on the three Es of economy, efficiency, and effectiveness (Box 17.2). In the twenty-first century, therefore, senior civil servants must be skilled in the arts of governance, as well as government. Facing conflicting expectations derived from philosophies old and new, they must aim to:

- show flexibility while abiding by rules;

- deliver results, while working within set procedures;

- distil policy advice for ministers, while managing complex networks;

- act decisively, while consulting widely;

- help ministers realize political goals, while also remaining neutral.

This richer, multidimensional view of a top public official's task offers greater challenge, but also

The three Es: economy, efficiency and effectiveness

	Definition	Objective
Economy	Minimize inputs	Spend less
Efficiency	Achieve maximum output of goods and services for a given input	Spend well
Effectiveness	Ensure that policy achieves its goals	Spend wisely

Source: National Audit Office (2006).

greater satisfaction, for civil servants themselves than does Weber's more traditional, deterministic account.

Recruitment

Recruitment to bureaucracies has evolved in tandem with the development of the civil service itself. The shift from a spoils system to a merit system was a transition from recruitment by links with the ruler to open selection on merit. As such, it was a component in the transition from personal rule to the more abstract and, as Weber would have seen it, legalistic modern state.

Even though these reforms occurred in most democracies as long ago as the late nineteenth century, recruitment to the civil service remains a significant theme in public debate. Selection methods and employee profiles are scrutinized more carefully than in the private sector. Further, what counts as merit still varies between countries, revealing contrasting ideas of a civil servant's role. Here the main difference is between **unified** and **departmental** approaches. Britain exemplifies the unified (or generalist) tradition. Indeed, the United Kingdom pushes the cult of the amateur to extremes. Administration is seen as the art of judgement, born of intelligence and matured by experi-

ence. Specialist knowledge should be sought by bureaucrats but then treated with scepticism; experts should be on tap but not on top. A good administrator is expected to serve in a variety of departments and is considered more rounded for having done so. Given this philosophy, it is natural for recruits to be sought for the civil service as a whole, not for a particular department.

An alternative method of pursuing the unified approach is to recruit to a *corps* (body) of civil servants, rather than to a specific job in a ministry. France is an example of this somewhat complicated approach. It recruits civil servants through competitive examinations to such bodies as the Diplomatic Corps and the Finance Inspectorate. Although recruitment is to a specific *corps* with a specialized title, it is in reality as much an enrolment into an elite encompassing both public and private realms. Even within the civil service, more than one third of *corps* members are working away from their home *corps* at any one time. At its highest levels, the French bureaucracy is clearly generalist, albeit within a *corps* framework that makes a bow to specialized training.

Some unified civil services do stress one particular form of technical expertise: law. In many European countries with a codified law tradition, legal training remains common among higher bureaucrats. Germany is a leading and influential case (and one which provided the context for Weber's thinking). In Germany, most top civil servants are lawyers, compared with just 20 per cent in the United States, where the civil service tradition is departmental.

In a **unified** bureaucracy, recruitment is to the civil service as a whole, not to a specific job within it. Administrative work is conceived as requiring intelligence and education, rather than technical knowledge. By contrast, a **departmental** approach recruits people with technical backgrounds to a specific department or job.

How does a departmental (or specialist) system differ from the unified approach? In a departmental system, recruiters look for specialist experts for individual departments. The Finance Ministry will recruit economists and the Department of Health will employ staff with medical training. Recruitment is to particular posts, not to an elite civil service, or a *corps*. When staff depart, they often move to similar jobs in the private sector, rather than to different departments in government. The idea of a generalist civil servant pursuing a varied career in public service carries less resonance.

This emphasis on specific jobs and specialist expertise is common in countries with a weak state in which the administration lacks the status produced by centuries of service to pre-democratic rulers. The Netherlands, New Zealand, and the United States are examples. In the Netherlands, for instance, each department sets its own recruitment standards, usually requiring prior training and expertise in its own area. Once appointed, mobility within the civil service itself is limited; staff who remain in public service typically stay in the same department for their entire career (Andeweg and Irwin, 2009, p. 176). The notion of recruiting talented young graduates to an elite, unified civil service, or even to a *corps*, is weak or non-existent.

One issue in recruitment that led to some modification of strict selection on merit is **affirmative action**. The problem which this policy seeks to address is that, in liberal democracies, the typical senior civil servant is a male graduate from the dominant ethnic group and a middle- or upper-class family that was often itself active in public affairs (Aberbach *et al.*, 1981, p. 80). These findings disturb those who consider that the members of a bureaucracy should be representative of the wider population (Keiser, 2011).

A range of arguments support the thesis that a bureaucracy should reflect the social profile of the population. Broadly, these points match those advanced to promote descriptive representation in the legislature (see Chapter 15):

● civil servants whose work involves direct contact with specific groups will perform better at the job if they themselves belong to that group and literally speak the same language (e.g. Spanish-speakers in the USA);

● a public sector drawn from a range of religions and regions will encourage stability in divided societies;

● a diverse and representative bureaucracy, involving participation by all major social groups, will enhance the acceptability of decisions among the public at large;

● employment of minorities in the public sector will ripple through the labour market, including private companies;

● **positive discrimination** will only be needed for a transitional period because, once a representative bureaucracy is established to overcome the legacy of the past, it will maintain itself naturally as civil servants from minority groups become visible role models.

Affirmative action consists of policies designed to overcome the legacy of past discrimination against particular groups. One such policy is **positive discrimination** – applying lower recruitment standards to the members of disadvantaged groups.

In the 1960s and 1970s, considerable efforts were made in the United States to ensure that staff profiles matched those of the wider population. The stimulus here was an order by President Johnson, in 1965, that all government agencies must introduce affirmative action policies. Canadian governments, concerned since the early 1970s to improve recruitment from French-speakers, also extended their recruitment efforts. However, such schemes never achieved the same popularity in Western Europe, perhaps because they would have involved accepting the inadequacy of the constitutional requirement of neutrality imposed on some civil services. The Weberian philosophy of recruitment on merit was not to be moved. Even in the United States, positive discrimination was eventually restricted by the Supreme Court, and some states, including California, outlawed it altogether.

Those who are more sceptical of affirmative action suggest that the correct solution to under-representation lies in improving the qualifications of the under-represented groups through education. Furthermore, affirmative action (in the weaker sense of additional encouragement for minorities to apply for jobs) can be adopted without embracing positive discrimination.

The current philosophy is targets without quotas. Positive discrimination, in the sense of lower recruitment standards for groups subject to past discrimination, brings dangers of its own. First, those denied jobs just because they belong to a majority group naturally become resentful. Second, those who are accepted simply because they come from a minority background find themselves in an awkward position, lacking the confidence of colleagues recruited on a strict definition of merit.

Organization

Here, we examine the detailed organization of central government, looking at the cogs of the administrative machine. This section takes us to the heart of government, identifying the landmarks needed to map the elements of any particular state. Governance may be about the relationships between these elements but we cannot hope to understand the network without some appreciation of the nodes within it.

Although structures – and labels – vary by country, we can distinguish three main kinds of organization: departments, divisions, and non-departmental public bodies (Box 17.3).

Departments

Government departments (or ministries) form the centrepiece of modern bureaucracies. Here, we find the bodies pursuing the traditional tasks of government. In nearly all countries, a dozen or so established departments form the stable core of central government. The total number varies but is typically between 12 and 24. For instance, the United States has 15 departments, each headed by a secretary appointed by the president.

Most countries follow a similar sequence in introducing departments, giving effect to the expansion of the state (Figure 17.1). The first to be established are those performing essential state functions such as finance, law and order, defence, and foreign affairs. These ministries are often as ancient as the state itself. In the United States, for instance, the Department of State and the Treasury date from 1789. Subsequently, countries add extra ministries to deal with new functions, including agriculture, commerce, and labour. Later in the twentieth century come welfare departments dealing with social security, education, health, and housing. More recent additions include the environment and, in a few countries, security.

BOX 17.3

The organization of government: departments, divisions, and non-departmental public bodies

Department
An administrative unit, sometimes known as a ministry, over which a minister exercises direct management control. Usually structured as a formal hierarchy and often established by statute.

Division
An operating unit of a department, responsible to the minister but often with considerable independence in practice, especially in the USA. Also known as 'sections' and 'bureaus' – and 'departments' in countries where the larger unit is termed a 'ministry'.

Non-departmental public body
Operates at one or more removes from the government, in an attempt to provide management flexibility and political independence. Many powerful regulators – agencies – operate as non-departmental bodies.

Reflecting Weber's principles, the internal structure of departments is usually hierarchical (Figure 17.2). A single minister sits at the pinnacle, albeit often supported in large departments by junior ministers with divisional responsibilities. A senior civil servant, often known as the secretary or vice-minister, is responsible for administration and for providing the crucial bridge between political and bureaucratic levels.

In theory, ministers direct and public servants execute. Although no longer sufficient, hierarchical control by a minister remains an essential component of departmental oversight. However, in practice, the capacity of ministers to exert such control is conditioned by two other factors: the reach of political appointments and the use ministers make of personal advisers.

First, the greater the number of appointments made by a minister within a department, the easier it should be to impose a specific direction.

Figure 17.1 Founding of federal departments in Canada and the USA

As this comparison of Canada and United States illustrates, countries follow a broadly similar sequence in introducing departments

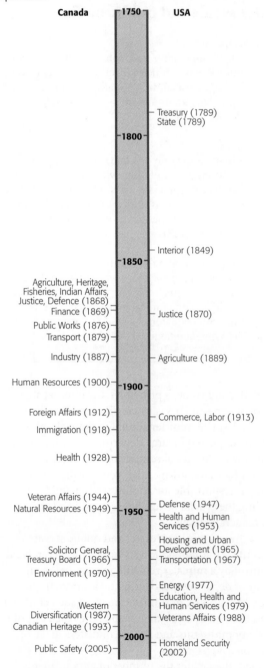

Note: Some departments (such as America's Defense Department) are an amalgamation of existing bodies (War – 1789, Navy – 1798).

Sources: Schmidt *et al.* (2012), table 14.1, Tardi (2002) pp. 302–3.

Recognizing that senior bureaucrats require political craft, many liberal democracies do now tend to staff important ministries with politically loyal and sympathetic civil servants. This practice, long familiar in Germany and Finland, has spread to other Western democracies (Peters and Pierre, 2004). Increasingly, politicians want civil servants who are, in Mrs Thatcher's famous phrase, 'one of us'.

Second, ministerial direction can also be aided by providing ministers with personal advisory staff. Because such advisers do not form part of the department's permanent staff, they can act as their minister's eyes and ears, reporting back on issues which might otherwise be lost in the official hierarchy. In New Zealand, every minister's office featured a political adviser by 2006 (Eichbaum and Shaw, 2007). Alternatively, as in France, ministers are aided by a cabinet. This is a group of about 15 to 20 people who form the ministers' personal advisory staff and work directly under their control (a cabinet in this sense of a ministerial advisory group is unconnected with the cabinet which stands at the pinnacle of parliamentary government).

Divisions

Departments are typically arranged into divisions or sections, each responsible for an aspect of the organization's work. Thus, an Education Department might include separate divisions for primary, secondary, and higher education. Divisions are the operating units of departments, the sections within which the work gets done. They are the workhorses of government, the store of its experience and, in practice, the site where many important decisions are reached. Divisions are the state's engine room.

In some democracies, divisions acquire added importance because they are partially autonomous from their parent department. The extreme case is the USA, whose bureaucracy is the great exception to Weber's principle of hierarchy in departments. Even in their formal structure, American departments are more like multinational corporations, containing many divisions (often called 'agencies' in the USA) jostling within a single shell. The departments are merely the wrapping around a collection of disparate divisions and it is these bureaus which form the main operating units of the federal government. For example, the Department of Health and

Figure 17.2 The structure of a typical government department

Government departments are hierarchical in organization, with the secretary (top civil servant) bridging the political and administrative levels

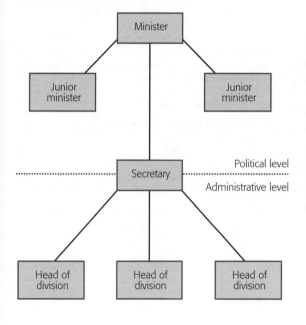

BOX 17.4

Operating divisions within the Department of Health and Human Services, USA, 2012

Administration for Children and Families

Administration on Aging

Agency for Toxic Substances and Disease Registry

Centers for Disease Control and Prevention

Centers for Medicare and Medicaid Services

Food and Drug Administration

Health Resources and Services Administration

Indian Health Service

National Institutes of Health

Substance Abuse and Mental Health Services

Source: Department of Health and Human Services (2012).

Human Services includes 11 operating divisions – called administrations, agencies, centres, and services – within its skin (Box 17.4). The autonomy of bureaus within American departments derives from their direct funding by Congress. It is a major and underestimated reason why American presidents experience such difficulty in imposing their will on Washington's administrative process.

Even in governments with more hierarchical departments, it would be naive to suppose that working practices correspond exactly to organization charts. Rarely does information move smoothly up and down the administrative pyramid. For instance, the many divisions in Germany's 14 federal ministries possess a concentration of expertise that enables them to block, or at least circumvent, reforms proposed from on high. A monopoly of knowledge creates the potential to neutralize change. In most liberal democracies, divisions within departments also possess their own ethos derived from long experience with their subject area. This entrenched in-house view breeds a natural cynicism

towards the latest political initiative, and helps to account for the frustration many ministers feel in steering their department in new directions.

Non-departmental public bodies

So far, we have considered government ministries and the divisions typically nested within them. But there is another type of public organization that is growing in importance: the non-departmental public body. The essential feature of these entities is that they operate at one remove from government departments, with a formal relationship of at least semi-independence. Such bodies occupy an ambivalent position, created and funded by the government; however, in contrast to divisions within a department, they are free from day-to-day ministerial control. Once appointed by the government, the members of such boards are expected to operate with considerable autonomy.

Throughout the democratic world, these non-departmental bodies are expanding in number, complicating not only the academic task of mapping government, but also the practical job of ensuring that the government as a whole acts coherently. Modern governance cannot be understood without delving deeper into the ecology of these non-departmental organizations.

COUNTRY PROFILE

JAPAN

Form of government ■ a parliamentary liberal democracy with a ceremonial emperor.

Legislature ■ ('Diet') the 480 members of the House of Representatives are elected for a four-year term. The smaller upper house, the House of Councillors, is less significant.

Executive ■ an orthodox parliamentary executive, with a cabinet and prime minister accountable to the Diet.

Judiciary ■ the 15-member Supreme Court possesses the power of judicial review under the 1946 constitution but has proved unassertive. Unusually, the Court's justices are directly appointed by the cabinet.

Electoral system ■ under the mixed-member majoritarian system, 300 members of the lower house are elected by plurality in single-member constituencies. The remainder are elected by the list system of proportional representation.

Party system ■ in 2012, the long dominant Liberal Democratic party (LDP) returned to office after suffering a resounding defeat in 2009. It replaced the Democratic Party of Japan. The nationalist Restoration Party won a significant number of seats in 2012.

Population (annual growth rate): 127.4 m (−0.07%)
World Bank income group: high income
Human development index (rank/out of): 12/187
Political rights score:
Civil liberties score: ②
Media status: free

Note: For interpretation and sources, see p. xvi.

Until 2009, **JAPAN** offered one of the few surviving cases of a dominant party system in a liberal democracy. Either alone or in coalition, the LDP governed Japan for all but 11 months between 1955 and 2009. During this period, as Scheiner (2006, p. 1) points out, the opposition was unable to mount an effective challenge, even though the LDP was unpopular with many voters.

How do we resolve this paradox of a party that was both successful and unpopular? The key lay in the LDP's willingness to use its control of an interventionist state to offer financial support and subsidies to those local areas which consistently elected the party's candidates. Japan's local governments depend heavily on central funding and voters possess a strong incentive to support the party that serves their local interests. This network worked especially well in rural areas, which are over-represented in parliament. The system was economically

inefficient, generating unnecessary bridges, roads, and dams throughout the land – and a large budget deficit for the state. The LDP's requirement for a steady flow of funds from the private sector also encouraged corruption.

In elections to the Diet in 2009, however, this elaborate political construction collapsed. The LDP's share of the party vote declined from 38 to 27 per cent, while its number of seats plummeted from 296 to 119. The LDP was replaced in office by the Democratic Party of Japan. However, the Democratic Party proved to be ineffective, enabling the LDP to return to power with a convincing victory in 2012.

For students of comparative politics, the LDP's defeat came as no great surprise. Throughout the democratic world, dominant parties have lost ground, falling victim to more independent electorates and to popular cynicism

about factionalism and corruption. The LDP had provided the political front behind which senior bureaucrats and industrial corporations had marshalled post-war economic recovery, creating what is now the world's third largest economy. However, an annual growth rate of 10 per cent in the 1960s declined to just 0.5 per cent per year between 1980 and 2012. Although the country coped relatively well with the global financial crisis, the LDP was by now dispirited, divided, and poorly-led. It experienced three changes of prime minister between 2006 and 2009.

Furthermore, a new electoral system introduced in 1996 meant that voters could no longer choose between different LDP candidates; a vote against the government now meant a vote for the opposition. Although the Democratic Party of Japan failed to offer a convincing policy alternative, it did not need to. In 2009, it was enough not to be the LDP.

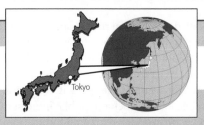

Tokyo

The bureaucracy in Japan

'The Japanese bureaucracy is probably more ballyhooed than any other bureaucracy in the world', write Rosenbluth and Thies (2012, p. 321). In particular, the civil service is usually accorded an important place in histories of the country's remarkably rapid economic growth in the 1950s and 1960s. How did the bureaucracy lead the development of the country's market economy?

Certainly, the bureaucracy as a whole remains relatively small, employing a lower proportion of the workforce than even the United States.

However, the Japanese civil service possesses high status and motivates its recruits with the thought of good post-retirement jobs in the private sector and local government. The bureaucracy attracts able male recruits through open competition. In 2009, for example, only 600 people of the 22,000 who took the entrance examination for the higher civil service were hired. Many successful candidates came from just one department: Tokyo University's Law School.

The philosophy of the bureaucracy is unified, rather than departmental, but movement between departments is rare. Each group of recruits forms a distinct cohort within a ministry, progressing through the hierarchy but with a smaller proportion achieving promotion to the next level; the convention is that staff should not expect to serve under anyone recruited later than they were. The system is competitive and demanding, but only highly-rewarding at the top levels.

As Johnson (1995, p. 68) wrote, senior bureaucrats form part of 'the economic general staff, which is itself legitimated by its meritocratic character'. The bureaucracy undoubtedly played a substantial role in post-war reconstruction. It was intertwined with the LDP – conservative in all but name – and big business. The professional economic bureaucracy – in particular, the Ministry of International Trade and Industry (MITI) – was a significant factor in Japan's success. As post-war reconstruction began, MITI targeted specific growth industries such as cameras, which were shielded from overseas competition until they became internationally successful.

Ministries of the Japanese government, 2012

Cabinet Office
Agriculture, Forestry and Fisheries
Defence
Economy, Trade and Industry
Education, Culture, Sports, Science
  and Technology
Environment
Finance
Foreign Affairs
Health, Labour and Welfare
Internal Affairs and
  Communications
Justice
Land, Infrastructure and Transport

Source: Prime Minister of Japan (2012).

MITI operated mainly through discussion and persuasion, thus reducing the risk of major mistakes, but it could rely when necessary on its influence over the allocation of what was then scarce capital.

In the post-war decades of high growth, Japan provided the pre-eminent example of how a small, merit-based bureaucracy, operating largely on the basis of persuasion, could guide rapid economic development within a mainly market framework.

In the 1990s, though, state-led deflation painted the bureaucracy in a harsher light. A few civil servants were involved in bribery cases; these scandals made some large companies more wary of hiring retired bureaucrats. More fundamentally, in a global economy civil servants could no longer offer the same strategic direction to industry, given that the largest companies now operated on a world scale and some overseas corporations had become established in Japan.

Reflecting these developments, as well as a desire to improve coordination, the central bureaucracy was reorganized in 2001, with the number of departments reduced from 22 to 12; the once-mighty MITI became part of a new ministry. The Japan Fair Trade Commission acquired a more extensive role in enforcing competition, signalling greater emphasis on the interests of consumers, rather than those of the large, export-oriented manufacturers which had emerged during Japan's high-growth phase.

Further reading: Kawabata (2007), Martin and Steel (2008), Rosenbluth and Theis (2012), Scheiner (2006).

Non-departmental public bodies include state-owned industries (known as 'government' or 'crown' corporations in North America), agencies delivering public services, agencies providing advice to government, and agencies charged with regulating an aspect of social life in which the public interest is at stake.

Why are non-departmental public bodies established? Why should ministers create entities over which they have limited control? They emerge for a wide range of reasons:

● to operate with more flexibility (and at lower cost) than would be acceptable for a ministry;

● to acknowledge the professional status and autonomy of their staff;

● as a response to short-term pressure to do something about a problem;

● to allow ministries to focus on policy-making;

● to provide protection from political interference in day-to-day operations.

From a governance perspective, regulatory agencies are the most important non-departmental bodies in contemporary liberal democracies. These agencies supervise natural monopolies (e.g. water supply) and such activities as adoption, broadcasting, elections, food standards, and nuclear energy. Regulatory agencies are increasing in number in nearly all liberal democracies, partly to balance risks which cannot be well-judged by the private sector. For example, weighing the benefits of introducing a new drug against the danger of side-effects is a task for public-minded experts, rather than for self-interested drug companies. Britain has embraced regulatory agencies with particular gusto; over 140 agencies, from the Food Standards Agency to Ofcom (the regulator of the communications industries), employ over 370,000 staff (Moran, 2011, p. 113, citing 1998 data).

The European Union, too, has achieved its policy objectives – in particular, moving towards a single market – through issuing regulations. In a sense, the EU is best labelled as the ERS – the European Regulatory State (Majone, 1996). The regulations its agencies issue in such areas as chemical and food

safety, competition, and telecommunications help to establish global standards (Bach and Newman, 2007).

But it is the United States that offers the best established system of independent regulatory agencies. The first such body there, the Interstate Commerce Commission, was created as early as 1887 (but abolished in 1995); other examples are the Federal Communications Commission and the Nuclear Regulatory Commission. The idea behind these bodies is that they should operate in a technical and non-political fashion. Despite their power to make, implement, and settle disputes about regulations in their sector, commissioners do not report to the president and can only be dismissed by the president for specific reasons set out in the law creating the agency. America's long experience here provides an interesting model (whether to emulate or avoid) for other liberal democracies as they develop their own regulatory frameworks.

In general terms, then, charting the non-departmental public bodies in any liberal democracy confirms the complexity of contemporary governance. The rise of regulatory agencies, in particular, gives the lie to any simplistic claims of a diminished role for the state. It also relates to the broader issue, discussed in Chapter 3, of whether professional influence on public policy is increasing as the decision-making scope of government ministers is increasingly circumscribed by non-departmental bodies.

Accountability

The relationship between politicians and senior administrators has always been sensitive. Traditionally, the problem was posed as one of ensuring political control over non-elected officials: how could civil servants be prevented from obstructing the goals of freely elected governments?

The problem of controlling bureaucratic power in a democracy was a particular concern for Max Weber. He identified the danger of public servants coming to dominate their elected masters, suggesting that:

under normal conditions, the power position of a fully developed bureaucracy is always overwhelming. The 'political master' finds himself in the position of the 'dilettante' who stands opposite the 'expert', facing the trained official who stands within the management of administration (quoted in Kahlberg, 2005, p. 211).

Today, Weber's observation is widely accepted. Commentators recognize that the bureaucracy's expertise, permanence, scale, and control of implementation mean that it is bound to be more than a mechanical conduit for political directives. Senior public employees – department secretaries, heads of divisions, chairs of non-departmental public bodies – are invariably in a position to influence and elaborate policy.

But contrary to Weber, the solution is not to regard public servants' policy-shaping as a subversion of the government's will. Given the rise of independent agencies, the contemporary response has been to reframe the issue as one of **accountability**, rather than control (Mulgan, 2003). Increasingly, the philosophy is to encourage civil servants to defend their behaviour after the fact, rather than to seek pre-emptive control over the actions themselves. In this way, accountability both acknowledges and potentially defuses Weber's fear of bureaucratic power – a neat move all round.

For example, Polidano (1998, p. 35) argues that in a complex environment, where most policy-making involves coordination between several ministries, straight-line accountability to a minister no longer suffices. He suggests that 'bureaucrats can be prevented from complying with ministerial directions, however legitimate those directions may be. Multiple accountabilities are an inescapable part of the reality of government'.

> **Accountability** can be used narrowly to refer to a reporting requirement ('to be called to account'), or more broadly as a synonym for responsibility ('to be held to account'). In the latter sense, to be accountable is to be held responsible for one's actions by, and often before, another body. This entity can express judgements about, and may be able to impose sanctions on, the actor.

Senior officials are accountable not only to ministers in their own department, but also to the prime minister, the finance ministry, and to the obligations inherent in agreements with other national, and even international, organizations. To take a specific example, 'the accountability system for deputy ministers [top civil servants] in Canada has been described as multiple, complex and at times contradictory' (Bourgault, 2002, p. 446). As elsewhere, the highest officials in Canada must march to many drums (Box 17.5).

For the highest officials, accountability extends beyond the private world or government to external bodies – notably, the legislature, judiciary, and ombudsman. We consider each in turn.

In the United States, bureaucrats have always been forthcoming in their appearances before the *legislature*; it is Congress, after all, that grants the appropriations. But even in Britain, where ministers alone were traditionally considered responsible to parlia-

---

BOX 17.5

Multiple accountabilities: deputy ministers (DMs, senior public officials) in Canada

Accountable to	Why?
Prime Minister	The PM appoints the DM
Minister	The DM is required to assist and serve the minister
Clerk of the Privy Council	The Clerk heads the Public Service and acts as the PM's DM
Treasury Board	DMs report to the Treasury Board on resource management
Public Services Commission	DMs report to the Public Services Commission on staffing issues
House of Commons committees	DMs give evidence to parliamentary committees
Committee of Senior Officials	COSO oversees performance appraisal of DMs

Source: Bourgault (2002), p. 438.

BOX 17.6

The European Ombudsman

- Investigates complaints about maladministration in the institutions and bodies of the European Union.
- Maladministration includes unfairness, discrimination, abuse of power, failure to reply, refusing information, and unnecessary delays.
- Any citizen or resident of a member state can complain.
- In 2010, the Ombudsman (with more than 70 staff) opened 323 inquiries on the basis of complaints and 6 on its own initiative.
- The Ombudsman forms part of the European Network of Ombudsmen, consisting of offices in 32 countries.
- The Ombudsman is appointed and regulated by the European Parliament.

Source: European Ombudsman (2012).

An **ombudsman** (grievance officer) is a public official appointed by the legislature to investigate allegations of maladministration in the public sector. These watchdogs originated in Scandinavia but have been emulated elsewhere, though often with more restricted jurisdiction, resources, and success.

be prepared to complain to them. So far, these conditions have rarely been met beyond Scandinavia (Ansell and Gingrich, 2003).

New public management

'Government is not the solution to the problem; government is the problem.' This famous declaration by Ronald Reagan was one inspiration behind new public management (NPM), a creed which swept through the Anglo-American world of public management in the final decade of the twentieth century.

Although no longer new, NPM remains of interest as a powerful critique of Weber's ideas about bureaucracy. It attracted many specialists who did not share the ideological perspective of Ronald Reagan; it was spoken of warmly by international bodies such as the Organisation for Economic Co-operation and Development; it led to radical change in the public sectors of Australia, Canada, the United Kingdom and especially New Zealand; and it provides the backdrop against which the less fervent reforms of the twenty-first century have developed.

The best way to approach NPM is to consider Osborne and Gaebler's *Reinventing Government* (1992), an exuberant statement of the new approach. Subtitled *How the Entrepreneurial Spirit is Transforming the Public Sector*, this American bestseller outlined 10 principles which it advised government agencies to adopt in order to enhance their effectiveness (Box 17.7). Whereas Weber's model of bureaucracy was based on ideas of efficiency drawn from the Prussian army, Osborne and Gaebler were inspired by the more freewheeling world of American business.

The authors cited with enthusiasm several examples of public sector organizations showing the required zeal. One was the California parks department that allowed managers to spend their budget on whatever they needed, without seeking approval

ment for the actions of their officials, civil servants now appear before select committees. Slowly and shyly, and still with a concern to avoid embarrassing their minister, British public officials are becoming willing to report in public on their work.

As with other areas of politics, the *judiciary* is also growing in importance as an external arena in which the bureaucracy can be called to account. Administrative law gives the judiciary a tool for checking bureaucratic decision-making, allowing the courts to overrule decisions that, for example, result from faulty procedures, or which violate natural justice (see Chapter 13).

The *ombudsman*, finally, is a more recent addition to the mechanisms of external scrutiny. Although this public watchdog was first introduced in Sweden in 1809, it was not emulated elsewhere until much later: 1919 in Finland, after 1945 in many other liberal democracies, and 1995 in the European Union (Box 17.6). Within countries, a single advocate may cover the entire public sector or, at the risk of reducing visibility and overlapping jurisdictions, separate commissioners may be appointed for specific areas. If they are to succeed, ombudsmen must be granted strong powers of investigation. In addition, the public must be aware of their existence and

BOX 17.7

Steer, don't row! Osborne and Gaebler's ten principles for improving the effectiveness of government agencies

- Promote competition between service providers.
- Empower citizens by pushing control out of the bureaucracy into the community.
- Measure performance, focusing not on inputs but, rather, on outcomes.
- Be driven by goals, not rules and regulations.
- Redefine clients as customers and offer them choices – between schools, training programmes, and housing options.
- Prevent problems before they emerge, rather than offering services afterwards.
- Earn money, rather than simply spend it.
- Decentralize authority and embrace participatory management.
- Prefer market mechanisms to bureaucratic ones.
- Catalyze all sectors – public, private, and voluntary – into solving community problems.

Source: Adapted from Osborne and Gaebler (1992).

for individual items of expenditure. Another was the public convention centre which formed a joint venture with private firms to bring in well-known entertainment acts, with each side sharing the risk and the profit.

The underlying theme was the gains achievable by giving pubic servants the flexibility to manage by results. And the significance of this empowerment, in turn, was the break it represented with Weber's view that the job of a bureaucrat was simply to apply fixed rules to cases. The role model for NPM was the entrepreneur, rather than the judge. For its supporters, NPM was public management for a new century; Weber's model was dismissed as history. Public administration, it was alleged, had been displaced by public management (Box 17.8).

In the history of NPM, New Zealand stands out as the pioneer. It achieved what was probably 'the most comprehensive and radical set of reforms of any Western democracy' (Pollitt and Bouckaert, 2011, p. 302). In the 1980s and 1990s, successive governments revolutionized the structure, management, and role of the public sector. As was typical for NPM, elite ideas provided the driving force. A remarkable coalition – business leaders, government economists, and senior politicians from both major parties – came together to force through unpopular but far from inconsequential reforms.

One particular feature of the New Zealand model was its massive use of contracts. This technique went far beyond the standard fare of using private firms to supply local services, such as refuse collection. Rather, it extended to engaging private suppliers in sensitive areas, such as debt collection. By such means, the number of civil servants, narrowly defined, was reduced from 88,000 in 1988 to 37,000 in 1994. Even though some people were simply reallocated to other segments of the public sector, this decline speaks to the radical nature of the reorganization.

In addition, contracts were introduced within New Zealand's public sector to govern the relationships between purchasers (e.g. the Transport Department) and providers (e.g. Transit New Zealand, responsible for roads). Contractual arrangements within the public sector were an additional step, and a more direct challenge to Weber's model, than simply contracting out services to the private sector.

What lessons can be learned from New Zealand's ambitious innovations in public administration?

BOX 17.8

Components of new public management

- Managers given more discretion but held responsible for results.
- Performance assessed against explicit targets.
- Resources allocated according to results.
- Departments unbundled into more independent operating units.
- More work contracted out to the private sector.
- More flexibility in recruiting and retaining staff.
- Costs cut in an effort to achieve more with less.

Source: Adapted from Hood (1996).

Mulgan (1997, p. 146) offered a balanced assessment:

The recent reorganization of the public service has led to greater clarity of government functions and to increased efficiencies in the provision of certain services to the public. At the same time, it has been expensive in the amount of resources consumed by the reform process itself and also in the added problems of coordination caused by the greatly increased number of individual public agencies.

Mulgan's conclusions may well apply beyond New Zealand. However, the wide-ranging and sometimes diffuse nature of NPM reforms precludes precise evaluation. Effects have varied by country, reform, and sector. The belief survives that citizens in receipt of public services should be treated differently from consumers in a market, with greater emphasis on accountability and the consistent application of explicit rules.

It seems more than likely that NPM was judged more fundamental for those who produce public services than for those who consume them. For instance, citizens may have been reconstructed as consumers by public servants without affecting the quality of their interaction with government at all. Still, the new thinking has surely changed mindsets and this cultural change has itself proved consequential:

For some commentators, the most significant evidence [of NPM effects] lives in the 'changed climate', the existence of 'new talk', and the promulgation of visions of privatization, marketization, participation, deregulation, and flexibility. In short, the crucial evidence is the growth of a 'new community of discourse' (Pollitt and Bouckaert, 2011, p. 156).

The fragmentation produced by NPM eventually led to a revived focus on **joined-up government**, or a **whole-of-government** approach. Improved coordination between specialized public agencies offered the prospect of greater coherence across government policy as a whole, and also the capacity for ministers in central departments to re-establish control over what happened in the field. These newer reforms reflected awareness that policy prob-

lems are linked: for instance, poverty and limited educational attainment.

Significantly, joined-up government made most progress in countries such as New Zealand, where NPM had permeated furthest. While it is tempting to use the whole-of-government approach to pronounce the death of NPM, Christensen and Lægreid (2007, p. 12) are probably more accurate in concluding that 'what we are seeing is a rebalancing or adjustment of the basic NPM model in a more centralized direction without any fundamental change'. That is, joined-up government may prove to be a development, rather than a repudiation, of NPM. At a deeper level, it represents the latest move in a perpetual battle within the public sector between decentralization in the search for initiative and centralization in pursuit of enhanced coordination. E-government is the prime example of the pursuit of integration in delivering public services.

> **Joined-up government**, or a **whole-of-government** approach, seeks to improve the coordination of public policy across agencies. The aim is to prevent policies from undermining each other, to align the organization of government with its actual tasks, and to provide citizens with seamless access to services.

E-government

'New public management is dead – long live digital era governance' (Dunleavy et al., 2006). The propositions underlying this rallying-cry are that **e-government** can drive efficiency gains in the public sector and require ministries to cooperate in providing an integrated electronic service to the public.

Overselling of NPM suggests caution in appraising

> **E-government** (digital era governance) is the use of information and communication technology (ICT) in providing public services. It can ease citizens' access, facilitate consultations by government, and enhance government surveillance of the population.

similar claims about e-government. Students applying for a government loan through their smartphone rather than by letter are unlikely to reappraise their entire relationship with the state. We must avoid technological determinism and also recognize that anticipated efficiency gains often dis-

Table 17.1 Top ten countries by e-government, 2012

E-government is most advanced in some high-income European democracies – notably, in Scandinavia – together with South Korea, the USA, and Singapore

Rank	Country
1	South Korea
2	Netherlands
3	United Kingdom
4	Denmark
5	USA
6	France
7	Sweden
8	Norway
9	Finland
10	Singapore

Note: Ratings are based not only on the development of government websites, but also on the national ICT infrastructure and overall education levels.

Source: UNPAN (2012).

appear as new channels supplement old ones without replacing them.

Still, ICT matters for government. At least for citizen-facing departments, there is surely something in the proposition that the ministry has become its website. Generally, ICT creates unprecedented opportunities for states to store, integrate, and analyze information about their populations. As with other political resources, these facilities can be used for purposes benign, malevolent, or both. E-government consumes substantial resources, has expanded considerably in most high-income democracies (Table 17.1), but clearly still has further to advance.

From the perspective of public management rather than political participation, e-government is said to involve four phases (Box 17.9). These stages can also be seen as different types of provision, rather than as distinct phases.

Information-only websites remain useful, not least for people who then seek further advice from, or want to engage in a transaction with, a public official in person. The comparison here is with consumers consulting a firm's website about features and price but completing the purchase in store. (Generally, e-government is partly driven by a per-

ception that people expect similar levels of electronic provision from government as from companies).

The final stage in Box 17.9, integration, is the most demanding and significant for the bureaucracy. In principle, all government services – from applying for a driving licence, to registering a business – can be accessed from one site, with a single registration and digital signature. But such portals, or electronic one-stop shops, are difficult to implement, requiring the integration of databases from several departments. It is worth noting here that the highly-detailed and coordinated nature of such work is far removed from the entrepreneurial activity expected of the new public manager.

Integration creates opportunities for public services to be more proactive. If your year of birth and address are available across government, then, as you move through life, the Transport Department can send you information about applying for a driving licence, the Interior Ministry can supply a voter registration form, and the Health Service can send home testing kits for age-related diseases. Similarly, linking school records to a national database of children could help to locate missing children who have moved elsewhere. In such ways, e-government can give effect to joined-up government.

Vision, nightmare, or both? Certainly, the integration of government databases involves an inherent loss of privacy and creates opportunities for misuse in response to unforeseen political developments

BOX 17.9

Stages of e-government

	Example
Information	Detailing a public service on a website
Interaction	Email; downloading forms
Transaction	Online applications
Integration	Accessing several services through a portal

Sources: Baum and Di Maio (2000); Montargil (2010).

(such as regime change) and the authorized or unauthorized transfer of data to third parties, including private companies and foreign states.

Furthermore, public suspicion of e-government is heightened by awareness that private electronic records – such as text messages, phone calls, and internet use – can also be accessed by government in response to security threats. Privacy and data protection codes, such as the European Union's comprehensive Directive on Data Protection (1998), offer only limited reassurance. Access to one's own personal records allows accuracy to be checked but does not prevent misuse.

In practice, the success of integrated e-government is likely to depend on the extent to which citizens trust their present and future governments. Cynical citizens may prefer personal information to be kept in departmental paper files, or even not to be recorded at all.

The bureaucracy in authoritarian states

As with the military, the bureaucracy is usually a more powerful force in non-democratic regimes. By definition, institutions of representation – elections, competitive parties, and freely organized interest groups – are weak, leaving more room for agencies of the state to prosper. A dictator can dispense with elections, or even with legislatures, but he cannot rule without officials to give effect to his will.

But the bureaucracy can be more than a dictator's service agency, not least in developing countries. Often in conjunction with the military, it can itself become a leading political force, claiming that its technical expertise and ability to resist popular pressure is the only route to long-term economic development. This assertion may have initial merit but, eventually, many bureaucracies in non-democratic regimes become bloated, over-politicized, and inefficient, acting as a drag on further progress. In the long run, bureaucratic regimes, as with military governments, become part of the problem rather than the solution.

Certainly, the bureaucracy has played a positive role in most authoritarian regimes experiencing rapid economic growth. In the 1950s and 1960s, it helped to foster economic modernization in several regimes in the Middle East and North Africa. In conjunction with the military and a strong national leader such as Gamal Abdel Nasser (President of Egypt, 1956–70), modernizing bureaucracies were able to initiate state-sponsored development, even against the opposition of conservative landowners.

O'Donnell (1973) introduced the term **bureaucratic authoritarianism** to describe Latin American countries which followed a similar course in the 1960s and 1970s. The bureaucracy ruthlessly pursued economic reform, with cover provided by repressive military leadership. The high-performing economies of East Asia, such as Indonesia and Malaysia, provide more recent examples of the contribution that the bureaucracy can make to development in largely authoritarian settings.

> **Bureaucratic authoritarianism** was a term coined by O'Donnell (1973) to describe regimes in which technocrats in the bureaucracy imposed economic stability within a capitalist framework under the protection of a military government. Such regimes repressed social movements. The concept was applied to Latin American countries such as Argentina and Brazil in the 1960s and 1970s.

But these instances of the bureaucracy instigating successful modernization are the exception. More often, the bureaucracy has inhibited, rather than encouraged, growth. The history of sub-Saharan Africa in the second half of the twentieth century provides a more sobering assessment of the role of bureaucracy in a non-democratic environment. After colonial rulers departed, authoritarian leaders used their control over public appointments as a political reward, denying the delicate distinction between politics and administration. This cavalier approach to public appointments extended to absorbing excess labour, especially among new graduates, into the administration. Public sector expansion was a method of buying support, or at least preventing the emergence of opposition.

The outcome was uncontrolled growth of the civil service. By the early 1990s, public employment accounted for most non-agricultural employment in Africa (B. Smith, 1996, p. 221). Once appointed, public employees found that ties of kinship meant that they were duty-bound to use their privileged positions to reward their families and ethnic group, producing further employment growth.

The fat bureaucracy that resulted proved incapable of acting as an effective instrument for development. Rather, the administrative class (for that is what it became) extracted resources from society for its own benefit – in that sense, continuing rather than replacing the colonial model. With the main source of national wealth (e.g. commodity exports) under state control, public employment became the highway to riches, creating a bureaucratic bourgeoisie. Only towards the end of the twentieth century, under pressure from international agencies, were attempts made to rein in the public sector through an emphasis on building **administrative capacity** (Turner and Hulme, 1997, p. 90).

> **Administrative capacity** refers to the bureaucracy's ability to address social problems through effective management and implementation of public policy.

Even where bureaucracy-led development did succeed, the formula often outlasted its usefulness. Several East Asian states discovered at the end of the twentieth century that public administrators are more effective at building industrial capacity than at managing a mature, open economy with an expanding services sector. In Indonesia, for example, the Asian financial crisis of the late 1990s exposed the extent to which investment patterns had been distorted by crony capitalism, with access to capital depending more on official contacts than on rates of return.

The position of the bureaucracy in totalitarian systems in some ways echoed its role in authoritarian regimes. But one key difference marked out administration in the communist form of totalitarian rule: its sheer scale. To achieve its theoretical mission of building a new society, the ruling party had to control all aspects of development, both economic and social, through the state. Most obviously, the private sector disappeared and the economy became an aspect of state administration.

In these circumstances, the party sought to pacify the bureaucracy in the same way that it controlled the armed forces: by controlling all major appointments. This goal was achieved through the *nomenklatura*, a mechanism that provided a powerful incentive for ambitious careerists to gain and retain a sound reputation within the party. The *nomenklatura* continues to this day in China, where the list contains millions of names (Manion, 2009, p. 435). By appointing people from the *nomenklatura* to jobs of any significance, the party's organization department retains control over careers.

> The *nomenklatura* (list of names) was a large panel of trusted individuals from which ruling communist parties appointed people to designated posts in the bureaucracy.

In discussion of competitive authoritarian regimes, the bureaucracy receives less attention than it deserves. The reason is understandable: such regimes are typically founded on a personal relationship between president and people. This implicit contract works against the strengthening of rule-governed institutions, including a Weberian bureaucracy. Competitive authoritarian regimes are political in nature, rather than bureaucratic.

Further, the rulers of hybrid regimes often present themselves in opposition to institutions such as the civil service. In Latin America, particularly, administrators frequently imitated the haughty remoteness of their long-gone colonial predecessors, producing a corrupt and unresponsive bureaucracy which provides a convenient target for populist politicians. Such rulers need enemies, and an inflexible civil service provides one. When the political leader of a competitive authoritarian regime can secure the financial benefits from natural resources such as oil, he can spend these resources on maintaining a viable political coalition through informal patronage, thus further weakening a Weberian civil service.

In Venezuela, for instance, Hugo Chávez introduced a new constitution in 1999 which defined the country's political system as 'democratic, participatory, elective, decentralized, responsible to the people, pluralist, based on term limits for elected officials and revocable mandates' (Alvarez, 2004, p. 152). The radical pretensions and inherent uncertainties of this new constitution contributed nothing to building an effective bureaucracy. Rather, the effect was to concentrate attention on the political realm – and on Chávez himself. His own local committees could distribute resources to his base in the shanty towns, securing a greater political gain than if the same resources were made available through a rule-based bureaucracy.

Russia's competitive authoritarian regime also shows an ambivalent relationship to the official bureaucracy (see profile, Chapter 8). Certainly, Russia's presidents have drawn on – rather than defined themselves in opposition to – the country's long tradition of state power. As Willerton (1997, p. 39) points out:

all past Russian political systems were characterised by a strong executive, with power concentrated on a small governing elite. An administrative bureaucracy supporting the political executive emerged under the Tatars [Turkic-speaking overlords of Russia, 1236–1452]. By the early eighteenth century Peter the Great had rationalised and professionalised that bureaucracy.

But in the post-communist era, securing control over these bureaucratic agencies required significant attention. In contrast to most liberal democracies, Russia never developed an integrated public bureaucracy with standard rules and merit-based appointments. Under communism, party and state became so intertwined that the collapse of the former came close to bringing down the latter. In the chaotic early years of post-communism, provision of public services inevitably devolved to the local level, fragmenting the administration of a large, diverse country.

The Civil Service Act (1995) did introduce more uniform provisions across the public sector, including for example a rigid grading structure, but the operation of Russia's bureaucracy still falls significantly short of Weber's standards. Even today, the legacy of inefficiency and corruption renders most of Russia's bureaucracy far less professional and responsive than, say, its American equivalent.

In an attempt to resolve these problems, Russia's post-communist presidents have developed a massive constellation of supervisory agencies, based in or reporting to the Kremlin. By 2009, the president's Executive Office contained 15 separate units, staffed in the main by loyal, competent, and reliable supporters. These offices include the Presidential Control Directorate which 'oversees and checks that federal laws, decrees, orders and other presidential decisions are enforced by the federal executive bodies of power, the regional authorities, and organizations' (President of Russia, 2009). Frequent reorganization of the Executive Office suggests that its success remains incomplete.

To some extent, however, such efforts are undermined by the very nature of elite politics in Russia's competitive authoritarian system. Clans of influential oligarchs operating in and around the Kremlin seek favourable business judgements in a manner which pays little heed to the requirements of transparent, rule-based governance.

Discussion questions

- Is positive discrimination the correct solution to the under-representation of specific groups in the public sector?

- What tests should determine whether provision of a public service should be outsourced to the private sector?

- Give examples of regulatory agencies in your country. Are, and should, they be politically accountable? How is, and how should, such accountability be achieved?

- How does, and how should, management in the public sector differ from the private sector?

- How effective is e-government in your country?

Further reading

R. Mulgan, *Holding Power to Account: Accountability in Modern Democracies* (2003). A thoughtful discussion of the concept of accountability.

P. Nixon, V. Koutrakou and R. Rawal, eds, *Understanding E-Government in Europe: Issues and Challenges* (2010). The mainly thematic chapters in this book examine the impact of information and communication technology on governance in Europe.

D. Osborne and T. Gaebler, *Reinventing Government: How the Entrepreneurial Spirit Is Transforming the Public Sector* (1992). Influential and enthusiastic advocacy of new public management.

B. Guy Peters, *The Politics of Bureaucracy: An Introduction to Comparative Public Administration*, 6th edn (2009). A widely-used comparative introduction to bureaucracy.

B. Guy Peters and J. Pierre, eds, *The Politicization of the Civil Service in Comparative Perspective* (2004). Country-based chapters address issues such as compensation, external appointments and partisanship in the bureaucracies of liberal democracies.

C. Pollitt and G. Bouckaert, *Public Management Reform – A Comparative Analysis: New Public Management, Governance, and the Neo-Weberian State*, 3rd edn (2011). A detailed analysis of changes in public management since 1980 in Australasia, Europe, and North America.

ONLINE RESOURCES AVAILABLE

Visit the companion website at **www.palgrave.com/politics/hague** to access additional learning resources, including multiple-choice questions, chapter summaries, web links and practice essay questions.

Chapter 18   The policy process

The task of policy analysis is to understand what governments do, how they do it, and what difference it makes (Dye, 2007). Where political science examines the organization of the political factory, policy analysis examines the products emerging from it. So, the focus is on the content, instruments, impact, and evaluation of public policy. The emphasis is downstream – on implementation and results, as much as upstream – on the institutional sources of policy.

Because analysts are concerned with improving the quality and efficacy of public policy, the subject exudes a practical air. Policy analysts want to know whether and why a policy is working, and how else its objectives might be pursued. Reflecting this interest, policy analysis is a subject that connects academic study with administrative practice.

What, then, is a **policy**? The concept is difficult to define precisely but, as a plan of action, a policy covers both an aim (say, to discourage obesity) and a series of decisions, past or future, designed to achieve the objective (e.g. reducing advertising of fast food). Policy can also take the form of explicit non-decisions: 'our policy is that nutritional choices should be left to the individual'.

> A **policy** is broader than a decision. It denotes an intention to make future decisions in accordance with an overall objective. At a minimum, a policy covers a bundle of decisions.

In understanding the policy process, it is important to avoid imposing rationality on a process that is often driven by political considerations, at least in high-profile sectors. Three points are noteworthy here:

● Public policies can be contradictory. Governments can subsidize tobacco growers while simultaneously running anti-smoking campaigns.

● Policies can be nothing more than window-dressing – an attempt to be seen to be doing something, but without any realistic expectation that the notional objective will be achieved.

● A policy statement may be a cover for acting in the opposite way. Leaders of low-income countries may dutifully inform international agencies of their support for a market economy, while simultaneously bringing major corporations under their political control.

In short, public policy is a part of, as much as an output of, politics. Policy and politics, we should remember, are words with the same root.

PUBLIC POLICY

- Studying public policy offers a distinctive perspective within the study of politics. It involves looking at what governments do, rather than the institutional framework within which they do it. Conducting projects in this area can provide useful insight if you are seeking a career in the public sector.

- Public policy can be studied in general terms or by examining specific policy sectors, such as education or defence. Models and concepts as reviewed in this chapter show their value when applied to particular sectors.

- Underlying much policy analysis is a concern with the quality and effectiveness of what government does. Hence, policy analysis provides an opportunity for applied and constructive work which asks 'How well?', rather than just 'Why?'

- There is always a danger of imagining policy-making as a rational process seeking precise goals. The incremental and garbage-can models offer a hearty dose of realism. Policy, it is always worth remembering, is embedded in politics; a statement of policy can be a cover for inaction.

- Breaking the policy process into its component stages, from initiation to evaluation, helps in analyzing and comparing policies. The later stages, implementation and evaluation, provide an interesting focus which is integral to policy analysis.

- Policy diffusion studies provide an opportunity to locate public policy in an international context. Analyzing the sequence in which a particular policy was introduced across countries is a useful exercise.

Models

In analyzing policy-making, scholars have developed three conceptions: the **rational** or synoptic model associated with Simon (1983); the **incremental** model developed by Lindblom (1979); and the **garbage-can** model, so named by Cohen *et al.* (1972). These accounts form an important part of the policy analysis tradition.

In evaluating these perspectives, and in looking at policy analysis generally, we must distinguish between accounts of how policy should be made and descriptions of how it actually is made. Moving from left to right across Box 18.1 is, in part, a transition from the former to the latter. The rational model seeks to elaborate what would be involved in rational policy-making without assuming that its conclusions are reflected in what actually happens. The incremental model, which views policy as a compromise between actors with ill-defined or even contradictory goals, can be seen either as an account

of how politics ought to proceed (namely, peacefully reconciling different interests), or as a description of how policy is made. The garbage-can model, finally, is concerned to highlight the considerable limitations of the policy-making process within many organizations; this perspective examines only what is, not what ought to be.

The lesson is that we should recognize the different functions these models perform, rather than presenting them as wholly competitive. This point will become clearer as we discuss each perspective.

The rational model

Suppose we are in charge of secondary education and have adopted a policy of seeking to improve students' performance. If we were to adopt a rational approach, we would first specify the outcomes sought, such as the proportion of students achieving a given qualification. Then, we would consider the most efficient means of maximizing that goal: would new schools, improved facilities, more teachers (or

BOX 18.1

Three models of policy-making

Rational model	Incremental model	Garbage-can model
Goals are set before means are considered	Goals and means are considered together	Goals are discovered through actions taken by the organization and are not specified separately
A good policy will achieve explicit goals	A good policy is one on which all the main actors agree	The garbage-can process does not resolve problems well, but choices are sometimes made
Analysis is comprehensive; all effects of all options are addressed	Analysis is selective; the object is acceptable policy, not the best policy	Little analysis; the organization acts, rather than decides
Theory is heavily used	Comparison with similar problems is heavily used	Trial and error, plus some memory of recent experiences, are used

some combination thereof) deliver the best results for a given expenditure?

So, this approach seeks to unpack the idea of rationality by examining how policy could develop from a systematic search for the most efficient means of achieving defined goals. Specifically, it requires policy-makers to:

- rank all their values;

- formulate specific options;

- check all the results of choosing each option against each value;

- select the alternative that achieves most values.

This is, of course, an unrealistic counsel of perfection. It requires policy-makers to foresee the unforeseeable and measure the unmeasurable. So, the rational model offers a theoretical yardstick, rather than a practical guide. Even so, techniques such as cost–benefit analysis (CBA) have developed in an attempt to implement aspects of the rational model, and the results of such analyses can at least discourage policy-making driven solely by political appeal (Boardman *et al.*, 2010).

Seeking to analyze the costs and benefits associated with each possible decision does have strengths, particularly when a choice must be made from a small set of options. Specifically, CBA brings submerged assumptions to the surface, benefiting those interests that would otherwise lack political clout. For instance, the benefit to the national economy from a new airport runway is factored in, not ignored by politicians overreacting to vociferous local opposition.

In addition, CBA discourages symbolic policy-making which addresses a concern without attempting anything more specific; it also contributes to transparent policy-making by forcing decision-makers to account for policies whose costs exceed benefits.

For such reasons, CBA has been formally applied to every regulatory proposal in the USA expected to have a substantial impact on the economy. It has also played its part in the development of risk-based regulation in the United Kingdom, under which many regulators seek to focus their efforts on the main dangers, rather than mechanically applying the same rules to all. The cost–benefit principle here is to incur expenditure where it can deliver the greatest reduction in risk (Hutter, 2005).

However, CBA, and with it the rational model of policy formulation, also possesses weaknesses. It underplays soft factors such as fairness and the quality of life. It calculates the net distribution of costs and benefits but ignores their distribution across social groups. It is cumbersome, expensive, and time-consuming. It does not automatically incorporate estimates of the likelihood that claimed benefits will, in fact, be achieved. In the real political world, the conclusions from CBA are often side-stepped. A CBA of CBA would not always yield positive results.

The incremental model

Let us return to our example of improving students' educational performance. Where the rational model starts with goals, the incremental approach starts with interests. A minister proceeding incrementally would consult with the various stakeholders: teachers' unions, parents' associations, educational researchers. A consensus acceptable to all interests might well emerge on how extra resources should be spent. The long-term goals of this expenditure might not be measured or even specified, but we would assume that a policy acceptable to all is unlikely to be disastrous. Such an approach is policy-making by evolution, not revolution; an increment is literally a small increase in an existing sequence.

The incremental model was developed by Lindblom (1979) as part of a reaction against the rational model. Rather than viewing policy-making as a systematic trawl through all the options, Lindblom judged that policy is continually remade in a series of minor adjustments, rather than as a result of a single, comprehensive plan. In reality, policy formulation rarely sails out on an open sea; mostly, it is a process of making minor adjustments to the existing direction.

Incrementalism represents what Lindblom calls the science of muddling through: what matters is that those involved should agree on policies, not objectives. Agreement can be reached on the desirability of following a particular course, even when objectives differ. Hence, policy emerges from, rather than precedes, negotiation with interested groups.

This approach may not lead to achieving grand objectives but, by taking one step at a time, it does at least avoid making huge mistakes. Yet, the model also reveals its limits in situations that can only be remedied by strategic action. As Lindblom (1979,

1990) himself came to recognize, incremental policy formulation deals with existing problems, rather than with avoiding future difficulties. It is politically safe, but unadventurous; remedial, rather than innovative. But the threat of ecological disaster, for instance, has arisen precisely from our failure to consider our long-term, cumulative impact on the environment. For the same reasons, incrementalism is better suited to stable high-income liberal democracies than to low-income countries seeking to transform themselves through development. It is pluralistic policy-making for normal times.

The garbage-can model

To understand the rather intriguing title of this model, we return to our example. How would the garbage-can model interpret policy-making to improve educational standards? The answer is that it would doubt the significance of such clear objectives. It would suggest that, within the government's education department, separate divisions and individuals engage in their own routine work, interacting through assorted committees whose composition varies over time. Low educational attainment may be a concern of some staff and solutions may be available elsewhere in the organization, perhaps in the form of people committed to computer-based learning, or a new way of teaching spelling. But whether participants with a solution encounter those with a problem, and in a way that generates a successful resolution, is hit and miss – as unpredictable and fluctuating as the arrangement of different types of garbage in a rubbish bin (Cohen *et al.*, 1972).

So, the garbage-can model presents a rather alarming image of decision-making. Where both the rational and incremental models offer some prescription, the garbage-can expresses the perspective of a jaundiced realist. Policy-making is seen as partial, fluid, chaotic, anarchic, and incomplete. Organizations are conceived as loose collections of ideas, rather than as holders of clear preferences; they take actions which reveal rather than reflect their preferences. To the extent that problems are addressed at all, they have to wait their turn and join the queue. Actions, when taken, typically reflect the requirement for an immediate response in a specific area, rather than the pursuit of a definite policy goal. At best, some problems are partly addressed some of the time. The organization as a whole displays limited overall rationality – and little good will come until we recognize this fact (Bendor et al., 2001).

This model can be difficult to grasp, a fact that shows how deeply our minds seek to impose rationality on the policy process, Large, decentralized, public organizations such as universities perhaps provide the best illustrations. Consider universities. On most campuses, decisions emerge from committees which operate largely independently. The energy-saving group may not know what instruments can achieve its goals: the engineering faculty, fully informed about appropriate devices, may not know that the green committee exists. The committee on standards may want to raise admissions qualifications; the equal opportunity group to lower them for members of minorities. Even within a single group, the position adopted may depend on which people happen to attend a meeting.

Government is of course a classic example of an entity that is both large and decentralized. It is not a single entity but, rather, an array of ministries and agencies. Several government departments may deal with different aspects of a problem, with none having an overall perspective. Or one department may be charged with reducing pollution while another works to attract investments in new polluting factories. By considering the garbage-can model, we can see why we should apply some scepticism to statements beginning, 'the government's policy is …'.

Clearly, the garbage-can model suggests that real policy-making is far removed from the rigours of rationality. Even on key issues, strong, sustained leadership is needed to impose a coherent response by government as a whole. Many presidents and prime ministers advocate joined-up government but few succeed in vanquishing the garbage-can. Often, rationality is a gloss paint applied to policy after it is agreed.

Stages

One way of thinking about the policy process is as a series of stages. Figure 18.1 distinguishes initiation, formulation, implementation, evaluation, and review. Of course, these divisions are more analytical

than chronological – meaning that, in the real world, they often overlap. So, again, we must keep a sharp eye on political realities and avoid imposing logical sequences on complex realities. Nonetheless, a review of these stages will help to elaborate the particular focus of policy analysis, including its concern with what, if anything, happens after a policy is agreed.

Initiation and formulation

Why did governments expand public welfare for the first three decades after 1945 and then at least stabilize provision by the century's end? Why did many Western governments take companies into public ownership after 1945 and then start selling them back to the private sector in the 1980s and 1990s? These are questions about policy initiation and formulation – about the decision to make (or reverse) policy in a particular area and then to develop specific proposals within that topic.

The question of where policy comes from admits of no easy answer. What we can say is that in liberal democracies much of the agenda bubbles up from below, delivered by bureaucrats in the form of issues demanding immediate attention. These requirements include the need to fix the unforeseen impacts of earlier decisions, leading to the notion of policy as its own cause (Wildavsky, 1979, p. 62). For example, once a highway is opened, additional action will be needed to combat the spillover effects of congestion, accidents, and pollution. Rather like legal decisions, public policy naturally tends to thicken over time; cases of withdrawal, such as the ending of prohibition in the United States, are less common. In addition, much political business, including the annual budget, occurs on a regular cycle, dictating attention at certain times. So, policymakers find that routine business always presses; in large measure, they respond to an agenda that drives itself.

Within that broad characterization, policy initiation does differ somewhat between the United States and European (and other party-led) liberal democracies. In the pluralistic world of American politics, success for a proposal depends on the opening of policy windows, such as the opportunities created by the election of a new administration. This policy window creates the possibility of innovation in a system biased against radical change.

Figure 18.1 Stages of the policy process

The policy process can be seen as consisting of five stages – albeit at the risk of suggesting a precise sequence unmatched by political reality

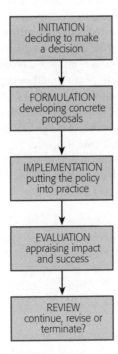

Thus, Kingdon (2010) suggests that **policy entrepreneurs** help to seize the moment. Like surfers, these initiators must ride the big wave by convincing the political elite not only of the scale of the problem, but also of the timeliness of their proposal for its resolution.

> **Policy entrepreneurs** are 'advocates for proposals or for the prominence of an idea' (Kingdon, 2010, p. 122). They exert influence by raising the profile of their pet topic (e.g. automobile safety); by framing how it is discussed (e.g. passengers before profits); and by showing how their existing ideas can be applied in fresh ways, to new areas and to current concerns (e.g. child seats).

From this perspective, interest group leaders succeed by linking their own preferred policies to a wider narrative; save the whale and you will be seen, rightly or wrongly, as concerned about the environment generally. Adopt our proposals for skills

training and you will be seen to be addressing the bigger question of economic competitiveness. However, policy openings soon close: the cycle of attention to a particular issue is short, as political debate and the public mood moves on.

The concepts of policy entrepreneur and policy window offer insight into the free-wheeling, competitive public discussion which governs policy initiation and formulation in the USA. However, these terms carry less resonance in the more structured, party-based democracies of Western Europe. Here, the political agenda is under firmer, if still incomplete, control. Party manifestos and coalition agreements set out an agenda for government in more explicit form than in the USA.

In the European Union, indeed, the policy agenda is formally the preserve of the supranational, non-party European Commission. This body is granted the sole right of initiation, enabling it to fulfil its commitment to integration. The Commission is naturally influenced by the broader political climate but Majone (2006, p. 231) can, nonetheless, make the formal legal point:

> The European Commission plays a very important role because of its monopoly of policy initiation. This monopoly has been granted by the founding Treaty and is carefully protected by the European Court of Justice. Hence, no national government can induce the Commission to make a specific proposal changing the status quo, unless that proposal also makes the Commission better off.

Such tight formal control of the policy agenda has few analogues in either parliamentary or presidential democracies.

Normally, policy-formers operate within a narrow range of options. They will seek solutions which are consistent with broader currents of opinion and previous policies within the sector. Compare American and British attitudes to medical care. In the United States, any health care reforms (including those achieved by President Obama) must respect the American preference for private provision. In Britain, by contrast, over 60 years' experience with the National Health Service has entrenched an expectation that medical care will be provided free at the point of care, and on a non-profit basis. Neither country could realistically adopt the other's approach, even if it were demonstrably superior. The general point is that policy formulation is massively constrained by earlier decisions.

Implementation

After a policy has been agreed, it must be put into effect – an obvious point, of course, except that much traditional political science stops precisely at the point where government reaches a decision, ignoring the myriad difficulties which arise in putting policy into practice. Probably the main achievement of policy analysis has been to direct attention to these problems of implementation. No longer can execution be dismissed with Woodrow Wilson (1887) as 'mere administration'. Policy is as policy does.

Turning a blind eye to implementation can still be politically convenient. Often, the political imperative is just to have a policy; whether it works, in some further sense, is neither here nor there. Coalition governments, in particular, are often based on elaborate agreements between parties on what is to be done. This bible must be obeyed, even if its commandments are expensive, ineffective, and outdated.

But there is a political risk in sleepwalking into implementation failure. For example, the British government's failure to prevent mad cow disease from crossing the species barrier to humans in the late 1980s was a classic instance of this error. Official committees instructed abattoirs to remove infective material from slaughtered cows but, initially, took no special steps to ensure these plans were carried out carefully. As a result of incompetence in slaughterhouses, the disease agent continued to enter the human food chain, killing over 170 people by 2012 (Ncjdrsu, 2012). The standing of the government of the day suffered accordingly.

We can distinguish two philosophies of implementation: top-down and bottom-up. The **top-down** approach represents the traditional view. Within this rather limited perspective, the question posed was the classical problem of bureaucracy: how to ensure political direction of unruly public servants. Elected ministers had to be able to secure compliance from departments already committed to pet projects of their own. Without vigilance from on high, sound policies would be hijacked by lower-level officials committed to existing procedures, thus diluting the impact of new initiatives (Hogwood and Gunn, 1984).

This top-down approach focused excessively on control and compliance. As with the rational model of policy-making from which it sprang, it was unrealistic, and even counter-productive. Hence the emergence of the contrasting **bottom-up** perspective, with its starting-point that policy-makers should seek to engage, rather than control, those who translate policy into practice. Writers in this tradition, such as Hill and Hupe (2002), ask: what if circumstances have changed since the policy was formulated? And what if the policy itself is poorly designed? Much legislation, after all, is based on uncertain information and is highly general in content. Often, it cannot be followed to the letter because there is no letter to follow.

> A **top-down** approach conceives the task of policy implementation as ensuring that policy execution delivers the outputs and outcomes specified by the policy-makers. By contrast, a **bottom-up** approach judges that those who execute policy should be encouraged to adapt to local and changing circumstances.

Many policy analysts now suggest that objectives are more likely to be met if those who execute policy are given not only encouragement and resources, but also flexibility. Setting one specific target for an organization expected to deliver multiple goals simply leads to unbalanced delivery. Only what gets measured, gets done.

Furthermore, at street level – the point where policy is delivered – policy emerges from interaction between local bureaucrats and affected groups. Here, at the sharp end, goals can often be best achieved by adapting them to local circumstances. For instance, education, health care, and policing must surely differ between the rural countryside and multicultural areas in the inner city. If a single national policy is left unmodified, its fate will be that of the mighty dragon in the Chinese proverb: no match for the neighbourhood snake.

Further, local implementers will often be the only people with full knowledge of how policies interact. They will know that, if two policies possess incompatible goals, something has to give. They will know the significant actors in the locality, including the for-profit and voluntary agencies involved in policy execution. Implementation is often a matter of building relationships between organizations operating in the field, an art which is rarely covered in central manuals. The twentieth-century American politician Tip O'Neill said 'all politics is local', a phrase that applies with particular force to policy implementation.

So, a bottom-up approach reflects an incremental view of policy-making in which implementation is seen as policy-making by other means. This approach is also attuned to the contemporary emphasis on governance, with its stress on the many stakeholders involved in the policy process. The challenge is to ensure that local coalitions work for the policy, rather than forming a conspiracy against it.

Evaluation

Just as policy analysis has increased awareness of the importance of policy implementation, so too has it sharpened the focus on evaluation. The task of policy evaluation is to work out whether a programme has achieved its goals and if so how efficiently and effectively.

Public policies, and the organizations created to put them into practice, lack the clear yardstick of profitability used in the private sector. How do we appraise a defence department if there are no wars and, therefore, no win–loss record? Which is the most successful police force: the one that solves the greatest number of crimes, or the one that has the fewest crimes to solve?

Evaluation is complicated further because, as we have seen, goals are often modified during implementation, transforming a failing policy into a different but more successful one. This 'mushiness of goals', to use Fesler and Kettl's phrase (2011, p. 287), means that policy-makers' intent is often a poor benchmark for evaluation. Few programmes have such a specific objective as President Kennedy's commitment in 1961 to land a man on the moon and return him safely to earth 'before the decade is out' (mission accomplished with five months to spare).

The question of evaluation has often been ignored by governments. Sweden is a typical case. In the post-war decades, a succession of Social Democratic administrations concentrated on building a universal welfare state without even conceiving of a need to evaluate the efficiency and effectiveness with which services were delivered by an expanding

bureaucracy. In France and Germany, and other continental countries where bureaucratic tasks are interpreted in legalistic fashion, the issue of policy evaluation still barely surfaces – often to the detriment of long-suffering citizens.

Yet, without some evaluation, governments are unable to learn the lessons of experience. In the United States, Jimmy Carter (President, 1977–81) did insist that at least 1 per cent of the funds allocated to any project should be devoted to evaluation; he wanted more focus on what policies achieved. In the 1990s, once more, evaluation began to return to the fore. For example, the Labour government elected in Britain in 1997 claimed a new pragmatic concern with evidence-based policy: what mattered, it claimed, was what worked. In some other democracies, too, public officials began to think, often for the first time, about how best to evaluate the programmes they administered.

> **Policy outputs** are what government does; **policy outcomes** are what government achieves. Outputs are the activity; outcomes are the effects, both intended and unforeseen. Outputs are measured easily enough: so many new prisons are built. Outcomes, such as a reduction in recidivism, are harder to pin down.

Evaluation studies distinguish between **policy outputs** and **policy outcomes**. Outputs are easily measured by quantitative indicators of activities: visits, trips, treatments, inspections. The danger is that outputs turn into targets; the focus becomes what was done, rather than what was achieved. So, outcomes – the actual results – should be a more important component of evaluation. The stated purpose of America's Government Performance and Results Act (1993) illustrates the distinction:

The Act seeks to shift the focus of government decision-making and accountability away from a preoccupation with the activities that are undertaken – such as grants dispensed or inspections made – to a focus on the results of those activities, such as real gains in employability, safety, responsiveness, or program quality. (GAO, 2009)

However, outcomes are tricky. They are easier to define than to measure; they are highly resistant to change and, as a result, the cost per unit of impact

BOX 18.2

Manipulating policy outcomes: the case of an employment service

Device	Definition	Example
Creaming	Give most help to the easiest clients	Focus on those unemployed clients who are most employable
Offloading	Keep difficult cases off the books, or remove them	Decline to take on unemployed people with mental health difficulties, or remove them from the list
Reframing	Re-label the category	Where plausible, remove unemployed people from the labour market by treating them as unemployable or disabled

Source: Adapted from Rein (2006).

can be extraordinarily high, with gains often proving to be only temporary. Further, even outcomes can be manipulated by agencies seeking to portray their performance in the best light. The devices available here include creaming, offloading, and reframing (Box 18.2).

With social programmes, in particular, a creaming process often dilutes the impact. For example, an addiction treatment centre will naturally find it easiest to reach those users who would have been most likely to overcome their drug use anyway. The agency will be keen to chalk up as successes cases to which it did not, in fact, make the decisive difference. Meanwhile, the hardest cases remain unreached. Just as regulated companies are usually in a position to outwit their regulator, so too do public agencies finesse measured outcomes using their unique knowledge of their policy sector.

The stickiness of social reality means that attempts to 'remedy the deficiencies in the quality of human life' can never be a complete success. Yet, they can be, and sometimes are, a total failure (Rossi *et al.*, 2003, p. 6). If our expectations of a policy's outcomes were more realistic, we might be less disappointed with limited results. So, we can understand why agencies evaluating their own programmes often prefer to describe their impressive outputs, rather than their limited outcomes.

Just as policy implementation in accordance with the top-down model is unrealistic, so judging policy effectiveness against specific objectives is often an implausibly scientific approach to evaluation. A more bottom-up, incremental approach to evaluation has therefore emerged. Here, the goals are more modest: to gather in the opinions of all the stakeholders affected by the policy, yielding a qualitative narrative, rather than a barrage of output-based statistics. As Parsons (1995, p. 567) describes this approach, 'evaluation has to be predicated on wide and full collaboration of all programme stakeholders including funders, implementers and beneficiaries'.

In such naturalistic evaluations, the varying objectives of different interests are welcomed. They are not dismissed as a barrier to objective scrutiny of policy. Unintended effects can be written back into the script, not excluded because they are irrelevant to the achievement of stated goals. This is a more pragmatic, pluralistic, and incremental approach. The stakeholders might agree on the success of a policy even though they disagree on the standards against which it should be judged. The object of a bottom-up evaluation can simply be to learn from the project, rather than to make uncertain judgements of success.

But there is a danger in these naturalistic evaluations. They can become games of framing, blaming, and claiming: politics all over again, with the most powerful stakeholder securing the most favourable write-up. To prevent the evaluation of a project from turning into an application for continued funding, evaluation studies benefit from external independent scrutiny.

Review

Once a policy has been evaluated, or even if it has not, the three possibilities are to continue, to revise, or to terminate. Most policies – or, at least, the functions associated with them – carry on with only minor revisions. Once a role for government is established, it tends to continue. But the agency charged with performing the function does change over time. In the United States, for instance, 426 separate agencies were established between 1946 and 1997 but most had been terminated by the end of the period, usually after a change of party in the White House (Lewis, 2002). So, the observation that there is nothing so permanent as a temporary government organization appears to be wide of the mark. Functions continue but the agencies performing them evolve, either because a task has been split between two or more agencies, or because previously separate functions have been consolidated into a single organization (Bauer *et al.*, 2012).

Yet, even if agency termination is surprisingly common, the intriguing question remains: why is policy termination so rare? Why does government as a whole seemingly prefer to adopt new functions than to drop old ones? Bardach (1976) suggests five reasons for the difficulties of policy termination:

- policies are designed to last a long time, creating expectations of future benefits;

- policy termination brings conflicts which leave too much blood on the floor;

- no one wants to admit the policy was a bad idea;

- policy termination may affect other programmes and interests;

- politics rewards innovation, rather than tidy housekeeping.

Instruments

So far, we have treated policy in a general way: goals are (sometimes) set; outputs are (often) achieved; outcomes are (occasionally) affected. But what are the instruments which give effect to policy? To put the question more broadly, how exactly do governments govern? The question is simple but useful, not least because a consideration of policy tools demonstrates the complexity of contemporary governance.

In thinking about the tools used to translate policy into practice, it is easy to overstate the importance of legislation and direct public provision. Certainly, parliament can establish a legal entitlement to a welfare benefit and then arrange for local governments to pay out the relevant sum to those who satisfy eligibility rules. The welfare states of Northern Europe developed in precisely this way and such state-administered mechanisms have generally proved to be popular with their electorates.

In reality, however, legislation and direct provision are just two of many policy instruments and by no means the most common. Even when a law is passed, it is increasingly fleshed out in lengthy and detailed delegated legislation issued by the sponsoring department.

A government's repertoire of policy instruments is, in fact, remarkably wide-ranging. The lengthy list in Box 18.3 is by no means comprehensive; more detailed catalogues extend to over 30 devices (Osborne and Gaebler, 1992).

Leaving aside the provision of services, policy instruments can be classified as sticks (sanctions), carrots (rewards), and sermons (information and persuasion) (Vedung, 1998). Sticks include traditional command and control functions: banning this, requiring that. Carrots include positive financial incentives such as taxation and subsidies. Sermons include that stalwart of agencies seeking to demonstrate their concern to all and sundry: the public information campaign.

In addition to these traditional tools, market-based instruments (MBIs) have emerged as an interesting addition to the repertoire of policy instruments. Such mechanisms as tradable permits and auctions are increasingly used in environmental policy as a way of ensuring that any pollution rights available within a government-set ceiling reach those producers who generate the greatest economic value from their polluting activity. These producers will be the ones willing to pay the highest price for their licence. In theory, MBIs resolve the conflict between regulation and markets; they aim to regulate by creating new, if in reality often imperfect, markets (Ruitenbeek *et al.*, 1999).

BOX 18.3

A selection of policy instruments: the example of tobacco

Command and control

Legislation	Authorizing the health department to take measures to limit passive smoking
Regulation	Banning tobacco consumption in restaurants
Public services	Funding public health clinics to provide smoking cessation sessions
Private services	Paying private agencies to run smoking cessation sessions

Finance

Taxation	Taxing tobacco products
Subsidy	Offering a rebate on purchases of nicotine replacement products

Advocacy

Information	Launching a publicity campaign about the harmful effects of smoking
Persuasion	Launching a publicity campaign to encourage people to stop smoking
Civil society	Creating and funding anti-smoking groups

Given a range of tools, how should policy-makers choose between them? In practice, instrument selection is strongly influenced by past practice in the sector, by national policy styles, and by political factors (e.g. an information campaign may be chosen for public visibility rather than effectiveness). Nonetheless, more technical criteria are available, including:

- effectiveness: will the instrument achieve its goals?

- efficiency: at what cost?

- equity: is it fair?

- appropriateness: does it fit the problem?

- simplicity: is it manageable?

Since most policies use a combination of tools, the overall configuration should also be addressed. Instruments should not exert opposite effects and they should form a sequence such that, for example, information campaigns come before direct regulation of behaviour (Salamon, 2002a).

Diffusion

Then, there were no speed limits, no seat belts, no nutritional labels, no restrictions on advertising cigarettes, no gender quotas for party candidates, no state subsidies for political parties. Now, there are. Most high-income countries have introduced broadly similar policies in these and many other areas – and often at a similar time. So, how did the developed world move in tandem from then to now? How does **policy diffusion** work (Dolowitz and Marsh, 1996; Rose, 2005)?

> **Policy diffusion** refers to the sequence in which programmes spread across countries. Policy transfer, policy learning, and lesson-drawing are similar terms, though policy diffusion carries fewer implications of an explicit process.

Policy diffusion has attracted attention as an example of international influence on national policy. Yet, cases where countries demonstrably emulate innovations from abroad remain thin on the ground. In theory, the whole world could be a laboratory for testing policy innovations; in practice, most policy-making still runs in a national groove. One puzzle, in fact, is to explain why convergence occurs without explicit emulation. In other words, why do high-income countries adopt broadly similar policies in the same time period without the self-aware learning from abroad that **policy convergence** suggests?

> **Policy convergence** is the tendency for countries' policies to become more alike. Note that convergence may occur in a specific sector without producing convergence overall because a country may be innovating in another sector, increasing divergence.

To begin, we review the general process of diffusion. Figure 18.2 shows the scheme proposed by Rogers (1962). It distinguishes between a few innovators, early adopters, the early and late majority, and a small number of laggards.

Although not designed with cross-national policy diffusion in mind, Rogers' analysis does allow us to interpret the spread of a particular policy and to ask why certain countries are innovators, either in a particular case, or in general. Innovation is perhaps most likely to emerge in high-income countries with the most acute manifestation of a specific problem; with the resources to commit to a new policy; and with the governance capacity to authorize and deliver. A new government with fresh ideas and a desire to make its mark is an effective catalyst.

Knill and Tosun (2012, p. 275) identify a series of factors encouraging policy convergence across nations (Box 18.4). Only one of these is direct learning and transfer from country to country, thus providing some clues as to how convergence can emerge with only limited lesson-drawing.

Of the factors listed in Box 18.4, independent problem-solving is surely one of the more significant contributors to convergence. As countries modernize, they develop similar problems calling for a policy response. At an early stage of development, for example, issues such as urban squalor, inadequate education, and the need for social security force themselves onto the agenda. The problems of development come later: obesity, for example, or the social cost of care for the elderly. In national responses to such difficulties, we often observe policy-making in parallel, rather than by diffusion.

Figure 18.2 The diffusion of innovations

In analyzing how new ideas percolate through the units in a social system (such as countries in the world), Rogers distinguished between innovators, early adopters, the early majority, the late majority, and laggards (non-adopters excluded)

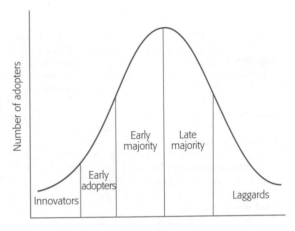

Source: Adapted from Rogers (1962).

BOX 18.4

Mechanisms of policy convergence

	Comment
Independent problem-solving	As countries develop, similar problems emerge, often resulting in similar policies
International agreements	Countries seek to comply with international laws, regulations, and standards
International competition	Policies providing an economic or political advantage will be replicated elsewhere
Policy learning	Explicit lesson-drawing (can occur even when no competitive advantage ensues)

Note: Coercion and conditionality (e.g. adopt our policies in exchange for our aid) are additional mechanisms.

Source: Adapted from Knill and Tosun (2012), table 11.5.

SWEDEN

LIBERAL DEMOCRACY

Form of government ■ a unitary parliamentary democracy with a monarch serving as ceremonial head of state.

Legislature ■ the 349-member *Riksdag* ('meeting of the realm') plays a full part in the legislative process, supported by 15 influential committees. The parliament has been unicameral since 1971.

Executive ■ the government is headed by a prime minister who chairs weekly meetings of the cabinet.

Constitution and judiciary ■ the constitution consists of four entrenched laws: the Instrument of Government, the Act of Succession, the Freedom of the Press Act, and the Fundamental Law on Freedom of Expression. The Supreme Court is traditionally restrained.

Electoral system ■ the *Riksdag* is elected for a four-year term by party list proportional representation, with an additional tier of seats used to enhance proportionality. The national vote threshold to secure seats is 4 per cent.

Party system ■ the Social Democrats were historically the leading party, sharing their position on the left with the Left (formerly communist) Party and the Greens. However, a centre–right coalition (led by the conservative Moderates and including the Centre Party, the Christian Democrats, and the Liberals) has governed the country since 2006.

Population (annual growth rate): 9.1 m (+0.2%)	
World Bank income group: high income	
Human development index (rank/out of): 10/179	
Political rights score: ❶	
Civil liberties score: ❶	
Media status: free	

Note: For interpretation and sources, see p. xvi.

SWEDEN offers a high quality of life to its citizens. In particular, it combines a high standard of living with a comparatively equal distribution of income, demonstrating with other Scandinavian countries that mass affluence and limited inequality are compatible. Average life expectancy is more than two years higher than in the USA.

The country's economic strengths are considerable. As the CIA (2012) notes, 'aided by peace and neutrality for the whole of the 20th century, Sweden has achieved an enviable standard of living under a mixed system of high-tech capitalism and extensive welfare benefits. It has a modern distribution system, excellent internal and external communications, and a skilled labor force'.

Yet, these strengths have been achieved with a relatively equal income distribu-

tion. The factors limiting income dispersion include:

■ a universal welfare system offering generous benefits;
■ targeted support for groups vulnerable to poverty;
■ relatively low differences in pre-tax incomes;
■ a progressive income tax (Palme, 2006).

Social and political stability has also contributed to Sweden's economic performance. This stability, in its turn, reflects limited internal diversity. Swedish is the foremost language, with Sami- and Finnish-speaking minorities; the dominant religion is Lutheran. A traditionally generous asylum policy has strengthened minorities from such countries as Syria and Iraq, but the national culture con-

tinues to emphasize equality and tolerance.

Lacking strong national, religious, and ethnic divisions, the party system has been based around class and the left–right dimension. 'In no other country', wrote Bergström (1991, p. 8), 'has the basic left–right scale accounted for so much of the party structure and electoral behaviour'. In particular, Sweden has exemplified the traditional five-party Scandinavian pattern of communist, social democratic, centre, liberal, and conservative parties. Since the 1990s, the Greens and Christian Democrats have also achieved a place in the *Riksdag*. The Social Democrats traditionally led this party system, gaining support from the large public sector, as well as the traditional working class.

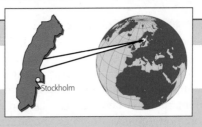

The policy process in Sweden

In an influential analysis, Richardson et al. (1982) classified countries by their policy style – their preferred way of making policy. The first of the two major dimensions in this scheme is whether a government seeks to anticipate problems, or merely to react to them, fire brigade-style. The second dimension is whether, in forming policy, a government attempts to reach a consensus through discussion with organized groups or, alternatively, is inclined to impose its decisions on society. Examining Sweden through this lens, Richardson et al. (1982) characterized the country's policy style as anticipatory and consensus-seeking. Is this interpretation still valid and how is it implemented in Swedish governance?

Anton's depiction (1969, p. 94) of Swedish policy-making as 'open, rationalistic, consensual and extraordinarily deliberative' remains fundamentally correct, from a comparative perspective. In one sense, the accuracy of this description is surprising, since Sweden is a small unitary state with sovereignty firmly based on a unicameral parliament. On this potentially centralized foundation, however, Sweden has developed an elaborate negotiating democracy which is culturally and institutionally secure.

One factor sustaining Sweden's distinctive policy process is the compact size and policy focus of the 12 departments of central government. Less than 5,000 staff are employed at these ministries. Their core task is to 'assist the government in supplying background material for use as a basis for decisions and in conducting inquiries into both national and

international matters' (Regeringskansliet, 2009).

Most technical issues, and the services provided by the extensive welfare state, are contracted out to over 300 public agencies and to local government. This division of tasks requires extensive collaboration between public institutions, and is sustained by high levels of transparency and trust.

of comments received). The bill is then discussed in parliament, not least in one of the *Riksdag*'s committees, where it may be modified before reaching the statute book.

This rather slow policy-making method is highly rational (in that information is collected and analyzed), but also incremental (in that organized opponents of the proposal are given ample opportunity to voice their concerns).

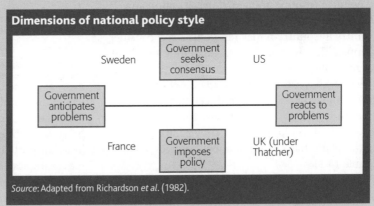

Dimensions of national policy style

Source: Adapted from Richardson *et al.* (1982).

Committees of enquiry (also known as 'commissions') are the key device facilitating policy deliberation. Typically, the government appoints a committee to research a topic and present recommendations. Committees usually comprise a chair and advisers but can include opposition members of parliament; some enquiries are carried out by an individual person. The commission consults with relevant interests and political parties. Next, its recommendations are published and discussed further. The relevant ministry then examines the report and, if appropriate, issues a government bill (which is presented with a summary

There are downsides. Extensive deliberation may contribute to bland policy. In addition, the strong emphasis on policy formulation may be at the expense of insufficient focus on implementation. Still, the style is distinctively Swedish – and offers a useful yardstick against which to compare the less measured policy-making style found in other liberal democracies.

Further reading: Lewin (2006), Lindvall and Rothstein (2006), Miles (2013).

Even if the response in one country is influenced by policy innovations elsewhere, it is still the need to respond to domestic problems that drives policy.

In addition, policy convergence can result from conformity to international agreements. The thicket of international laws, regulations, and standards is a common influence on states, encouraging convergence. These norms, covering everything from the design of nuclear reactors to protection of prisoners' rights, are facilitated and monitored by intergovernmental organizations. Certainly, global standards may be voluntary and may themselves be shaped by the strongest states; that is, by the standard-makers, rather than the standard-takers. Even so, international norms are an additional factor encouraging policy convergence.

Even without formal international regulation, international competition itself generates pressures to emulate winning policies. If privatization and deregulation are seen to benefit the economy of country A, country B may (and only may) consider comparable reforms. Here, an expanding supply of league tables produced by international bodies provides benchmarks nudging governments in the direction favoured by the producer. In the competition for foreign direct investment, for instance, what government would want to occupy a lowly position in the World Bank's ease of doing business table? (Table 18.1)

Note, however, that there is more than one way to skin a rabbit. In seeking overseas investment, some governments emphasize workforce quality (a race to the top), while others give priority to low labour costs (a race to the bottom). Competition generates similar pressures but not identical policies; rather, it encourages countries to exploit their natural advantages, yielding divergence, rather than convergence.

The final row of Box 18.4, direct policy learning, is perhaps the weakest mechanism of policy diffusion. Domestic constraints limit the capacity for policy emulation. Governments do not select from a full slate of options but must operate in the context of national debates and their own past decisions. So, tweaking is more common than innovating. Overseas models are only likely to be considered seriously when the domestic agenda seems to be incapable of resolving a problem. Even then, the search will not be global but, rather, will focus on similar or neighbouring countries with which the receiving country

Table 18.1 Top ten countries by ease of doing business, 2011

The World Bank's ease of doing business index ranks economies based on 10 areas, including ease of starting a business, registering property, and securing an electricity supply. Such tables are prepared to encourage reform in countries scoring poorly.

Rank	Country
1	Singapore
2	New Zealand
3	United States
4	Denmark
5	Norway
6	United Kingdom
7	South Korea
8	Iceland
9	Ireland
10	Finland

Source: Doing Business (2012).

has a long-standing and friendly relationship. Furthermore, policies themselves often evolve in the process of diffusion; they are translated, rather than just transported. Even if a government does cite overseas examples, it may be to justify a policy adopted for domestic political reasons. In general, governments find learning more difficult than do individuals and (in this case) we should resist the temptation to draw comparisons between the two.

Of course, lesson-drawing can be negative as well as positive. Models to avoid are generally more visible than those worthy of emulation. Germany's hyper-inflation in the 1920s, and Japan's lost decades of the 1990s and 2000s, continue to influence economic policy-makers throughout the developed world. Similarly, few countries have shown a desire to reproduce Britain's National Health Service, with its delivery of medical care through a gigantic nationalized industry controlled by a government minister.

One conclusion, perhaps, is that we should think in terms of the diffusion of ideas, rather than policies, across nations. Even if policies remain attached to national anchors, at least for stronger states, ideas know no boundaries. They are inveterate travellers.

Policy agendas (where do we need policy?) and frames (how should we think about this area?) are often transnational in character and refined by discussions in international organizations. Ideas provide a climate within which national policies are made, whether or not national policy-makers are aware of this influence. In public policy, as in politics generally, ideas matter even if their influence is difficult to analyze on other than a case-by-case basis.

The policy process in authoritarian states

Compared with liberal democracies, policy analysis is less important to understanding the politics of authoritarian regimes and illiberal democracies. Nonetheless, it is important to appreciate the reasons for, and implications of, this characterization.

The central theme in the policy process of many non-democratic regimes is the subservience of policy to politics. Often, the key task for non-elected rulers is to play off domestic political forces against each other so as to ensure their own continuation in office, an art developed to its highest level by the cautious ruling families of the Middle East. Uncertain of their own long-term survival in office, authoritarian rulers may want to enrich themselves, their family, and their support group while they remain in control of the state's resources. These tasks of political survival and personal enrichment are hardly conducive to orderly policy development; rather, they demand a lack of transparency in policy presentation. As Hershberg (2006, p. 151) says:

To be successful, policies must reflect the capabilities – encompassing expertise, resources and authority – of the institutions and individuals charged with their implementation. Those capabilities are more likely to be translated into effective performance in environments characterized by predictable, transparent and efficient procedures for reaching decisions and for adjudicating differences of interest.

But it is precisely these 'predictable, transparent and efficient procedures' that non-democracies are often unable to supply. Frequently, opaque patronage is the main political currency; the age-old game of creating and benefiting from political credits works against clear procedures of any kind. The result is a conservative preference for the existing rules of the game, an indifference to policy and a lack of interest in national development. As Chazan *et al.* (1999, p.171) note in discussing Africa, 'patriarchal rule has tended to be conservative: it propped up the existing order and did little to promote change. It required the exertion of a great deal of energy just to maintain control'.

In addition, rulers may simply lack the ability to make coherent policy. As a group, authoritarian rulers are less well-educated than the leaders of liberal democracies. This weakness was especially common in military regimes whose leaders frequently lacked formal education and managerial competence. The generals sometimes seized power in an honest attempt to improve public policy-making but then discovered that good governance required skills they did not possess.

Policy inertia is therefore the standard pattern under authoritarian rule. Stagnation is reinforced when, as in many of the largest non-democracies, the rulers engage in **rent-seeking**, often using their control over natural commodities such as oil or rare minerals as their main source of revenue. In these circumstances, the government need not achieve the penetration of society required to collect taxes, expand the economy, and develop human capital. Rather, a stand-off of mutual distrust develops between rulers and ruled, creating a context which is incompatible with the more sophisticated policy initiatives found in many liberal democracies. In the absence of effective social policy at national level, problems of poverty, welfare, and medical care are addressed locally, if at all.

Rent-seeking occurs when people aim to obtain an income from selling a scarce resource without adding real value. Examples include government officials taking bribes to provide a licence to a company, or a passport to a citizen. In such cases, civil servants sell their capacity to exercise discretion. Rent-seeking benefits both buyer and seller, but imposes a hidden tax on the economy and society.

In addition, the absence of an extensive network of voluntary associations and interest groups in authoritarian states prevents the close coordination between state and society needed for effective policy-making and implementation. The blocking mechanism here is fear among rulers as much as the ruled. Saich (2011, p. 223) identifies these anxieties in the case of China's party elite:

While it is true that public discourse is breaking free of the codes and linguistic phrases established by the party-state, it is also clear that no coherent alternative vision has emerged that would fashion a civil society. From the party's point of view, what is lurking in the shadows waiting to pounce on any opening that would allow freedom of expression is revivalism, religion, linguistic division, regional and non-Han ethnic loyalties.

As always, however, it is important to distinguish between different types of authoritarian government. At one extreme, many military and personal rulers demonstrated immense concern about their own prosperity but none at all for their country's, leading to a policy shortage. At the other extreme, modernizing regimes whose ruling elite displayed a clear sense of national goals and a secure hold on power followed long-term policies, especially for economic development. Examples include Asia's developmental states (such as pre-democratic Korea) and some communist regimes.

Yet, even in communist states, planning eventually yielded economic stagnation. Communism may have been an ideology of transformation but, once the early revolutionary zeal was exhausted in countries such as the Soviet Union, the rulers' political security trumped policy development. As in many non-communist authoritarian regimes, the dominance of politics over policy, and a relationship of suspicion between state and society, resulted in inertia, decay, and collapse.

China is, of course, the major exception. It survives as an authoritarian regime partly because it pursues policies leading to rapid economic development. The capacity of the party's top leadership in Beijing to form and implement coherent policy in the world's most populous country is a remarkable achievement. It owes much to political flexibility, the country's authoritarian tradition, and the legitimacy the regime has derived from economic growth.

The leadership's sensitivity to public concerns, unusual in authoritarian regimes, is seen not only in the achievement of economic development but also in attempts to limit its inegalitarian consequences. For example, the party's 2006 programme, Building a Harmonious Society, sought to reduce income inequality, improve access to medical care for rural-dwellers and urban migrants, extend social security, and contain the environmental damage from industrialization (Saich, 2009). Such goals are clear and explicit.

In competitive authoritarian regimes, the policy process falls between liberal democracies and authoritarian states. On the one hand, these regimes inherently lack the strong institutions, legal framework, and detailed connections with society that permit the policy processes found in liberal democracies. On the other hand, competitive authoritarian states cannot simply retreat from policy in the manner of, say, military regimes. There are elections to be won and popular dreams to be fed. Poverty and inequality generate the hope of a better life and leaders must make an attempt to deliver.

So, in Russia, after the initial chaotic transition from communism, the country's rulers achieved considerable policy successes. A body of law was established which provided a more predictable environment for business investment. A recentralization of power encouraged the more uniform application of a newly-codified legal system. The tax-take improved, offering an improvement in public revenues with the prospect of further gains. Social policy became more coherent, with a 'controversial 2005 reform that replaced the bulk of Soviet-era privileges (free or subsidised housing, transportation, medicine and the like for pensioners, students and others) with supposedly equivalent cash payments' (Twigg, 2005, p. 219).

But, as in other competitive authoritarian states, policy-making in post-communist Russia remains subject to the political requirements of the ruling elite. The business environment has become more predictable but industrialists who pose a political threat to the president still find that numerous rules and regulations are invoked selectively against them. The state has disposed of many enterprises but rent-seeking continues; indeed, the government has tightened its control over the key resources of oil and gas. In 2006, for example, Russia's government provided its allies in charge of state-owned companies with a greater share of the Sakhalin-2 oil field in Siberia by simply rewriting the contract with Royal Dutch Shell. Six years later, BP sold its Russian oil interests to a state-run group. Political and economic power remain tightly interwoven, precluding – at the highest level – uniform policy implementation.

As in other rent-seeking states, public control of export commodities enables the Russian elite to sustain its own position even if it neglects the development of closer connections with the Russian population. Social problems such as poverty, alcoholism, violent crime, and rural depopulation remain deep-rooted. Despite the attempt to modernize social policy, for many impoverished Russians the transition from communism must appear as a move from an authoritarian welfare state to an authoritarian state full stop.

As in many poor countries, even-handed policy implementation is impossible because many public officials are so poorly paid that corruption remains an essential tool for making ends meet. It may be true that sunlight is the best disinfectant but the improved policy process enabled by an escape from corruption and rent-seeking cannot be achieved simply by calling for more transparency. The dilemma is that transparency flows naturally from broad-based economic development, but such development itself requires a reduction in corruption. Countries in this position must pull themselves up by their own bootstraps – and this can be done.

Discussion questions

- Why does policy often fail to achieve its objectives?

- Which policy instruments are likely to be most effective in reducing (a) obesity, and (b) drug addiction?

- Give examples of rent-seeking in your country.

- Apply the garbage-can model of policy-making to your university. How accurate is the fit?

- Where in the Spotlight figure on Sweden (p. 355) would you locate (a) your country, and (b) China?

- Can you identify any public policies in your country which were (a) adapted from, or (b) influenced by, policies in other countries?

Further reading

T. Birkland, *An Introduction to the Policy Process: Theories, Concepts and Models of Public Making*, 3rd edn (2010). A thematic introduction to public policy with a particular focus on policy stages.

P. Eliadis, M. Hill and M. Howlett, eds, *Designing Government: From Instruments to Governance* (2005). This book provides a detailed examination of policy instruments.

C. Knill and J. Tosun, *Public Policy: A New Introduction* (2102). A thematic overview of the public policy literature, emphasizing theories and concepts.

B. Guy Peters, *American Public Policy: Promise and Performance*, 9th edn (2012). A wide-ranging text covering both the policy process and specific policy sectors in the USA.

R. Rose, *Learning from Comparative Public Policy: A Practical Guide* (2005). An influential examination of how countries can learn from each other about the successes and failures of policy initiatives.

P. Sabatier, ed., *Theories of the Policy Process*, 2nd edn (2007). Chapters cover theories of the policy process including the multiple streams framework, punctuated equilibrium theory, and the advocacy coalition perspective.

ONLINE RESOURCES AVAILABLE

Visit the companion website at **www.palgrave.com/politics/hague** to access additional learning resources, including multiple-choice questions, chapter summaries, web links and practice essay questions.

Chapter 19 Comparative methods

How do we find out about political systems, processes and behaviour? Books such as this are replete with accounts of research findings but the methods used to create these results sometimes receive less attention. This final chapter provides an introduction to the main research strategies used in comparative politics. Our goal is neither to repeat the discussion of broad theoretical approaches in Chapter 5, nor to cover highly specific techniques such as interviewing (Halperin and Heath, 2012). Rather, we hope that some of the strategies discussed here will be relevant to students planning comparative projects of their own.

We begin with the widely-used technique of the case study before proceeding to explicitly comparative methods, both qualitative and quantitative. We conclude by discussing how a historical dimension can be incorporated into political research.

Case studies

Case study is one of the most widely used strategies in political research, providing the lion's share of articles published in journals of comparative politics (Hull, 1999). Such studies combine a qualitative investigation of a specific topic, using all the techniques appropriate for that subject, with a link to wider themes in the study of politics.

One key to a successful case study is to be clear what the study is a case of. By its nature, a case is an instance of a more general category. To conduct such a study is therefore to undertake an investigation with significance beyond its own boundaries. Lawyers study cases which are taken to illustrate a wider legal principle. Physicians study a case of a particular ailment because they want to learn how to treat similar instances in the future. To return to politics, an account of the Japanese election of 2009 which does not venture beyond the topic itself is a study, not a case study. But an analysis which takes this election as an example of the fall of a previously dominant party (the Liberal Democrats) is a case study.

So, a case study adds value by offering a detailed illustration of a theme of wider interest, turning history and journalism into political science (Box 19.1). For instance, we could take the United States as an example of presidential government, Canada as an illustration of federalism, and Ireland as a case of a country employing the single transferable vote.

By their nature, case studies are multi-method, using the range of techniques in the political scientist's tool kit. The kit includes:

- reading the academic literature;
- examining secondary documents;

COMPARATIVE METHODS

- Studying the strategies used in comparative political research helps in appreciating how research is conducted within the field and also assists in planning comparative projects of one's own.

- There is no single formula for conducting comparative political research. Many worthwhile studies in the field adopt the pragmatic tactic of just getting on with it. There is no point in forcing a study into an artificial framework if doing so impoverishes the study itself.

- But, even if only as background, it is valuable to be aware of both the potential of comparison (Chapter 1) and its limitations (this chapter). Beyond that, researchers can select from a suite of techniques, many of which are also used in other fields.

- Just as comparison is used in many fields of study, in and beyond politics, so too can it be used with units of analysis other than countries. For example, considerable research compares states in the USA.

- Even if not strictly comparative, case studies are a flexible device for placing a specific project in a broader comparative context. The existence of different types of case study enables this method to be used with greater precision.

- When comparative projects seek to examine the relationship between two or more factors, it is worth considering the most similar and most different designs. Unlike case studies, these designs are inherently comparative.

- Statistical analysis, even of a straightforward kind, helps in describing the characteristics of countries and trends within them. Comparative projects, such as the International Social Survey Programme, provide opportunities for comparative statistical analysis.

- History is arguably under-used in comparative political research. Current cases can be compared with past examples, and developments over time can be compared across countries. Here, the ideas of path dependence, critical junctures, and slow-moving causes can be helpful.

- scrutinizing primary sources;

- conducting interviews with participants and other observers in the country, organization, or other unit under scrutiny;

- experiencing and visiting the unit under study.

In other words, scholars of cases engage in 'soaking and poking, marinating themselves in minutiae' (King *et al.*, 1994, p. 38). They aim to provide a description which is both rounded and detailed, a goal which Geertz (1973) called 'thick description'. This multiple methods approach contrasts with more specific and explicit techniques seeking to understand the matter in hand though a single lens, such as a statistical analysis, or an experiment. Unlike statistical analysis, which seeks to identify relationships between variables measured across a series of observations, case analysis aims to identify how a range of factors interact in the context of the example under scrutiny.

Case studies possess broad significance by definition, but this added value can be acquired in various ways. Box 19.2 outlines five types of case study. A case can be useful because it is representative, prototypical, deviant, exemplary or critical (or a combination of these).

Of these designs, the **representative case** is the most common. It is the workhorse of case studies, as useful as it is undramatic. Often researchers will use their own country as a representative example. For

---

BOX 19.1

Some research designs in politics

	Number of cases	Case-, variable- or process-centred?	Strategy
Case study	One	Case	Intensive study of a single instance with wider significance
Qualitative comparison (small-*N*)	A few	Case	Qualitative comparison of a few instances
Quantitative analysis (large-*N*)	Many	Variable	Searches for causes by making statistical assessments of the relationships between variables
Historical analysis (small-*N*)	One	Process	Often, tracing the process leading to a known outcome

Note: N means the number of cases.

---

instance, researchers may be interested in coalition formation in general, but choose to study in detail how governments form in their homeland. The home country is the research site but the hope is that the results will contribute to broader understanding. A collection of representative case studies can provide the raw material for generalization by other scholars taking a wider approach.

By contrast, a **prototypical case** is chosen not because it is representative but because it is expected to become so. As Rose (1991a, p. 459) puts it, 'their present is our future'. The point here is that studying a pioneer can help in comprehending a phenomenon which is growing in significance elsewhere. In the nineteenth century, the French scholar Alexis de Tocqueville (1835, ch. 1) studied America because of his interest in the new politics of democracy. He wrote, 'my wish has been to find there [in the USA] instruction by which we [in Europe] may ourselves profit'. De Tocqueville regarded the United States as a harbinger of democracy and therefore a guide to Europe's own future. Another example of a prototypical case would be studying Tunisia as the first instance of the Arab Spring, or the political impact of social media by examining the country where such communications facilities are used most widely.

The purpose of a **deviant case** study is very different. Here, we deliberately seek out the exceptional and the untypical, rather than the norm: the countries which remain communist, or which are still governed by the military, or which seem to be immune from democratizing trends. Deviant cases are often used to tidy up our understanding of exceptions and anomalies: why does India contradict the thesis that democracy presupposes prosperity? Why did tiny Switzerland adopt a federal architecture when many federations are found in large countries? Why did turnout stay high in Denmark even as it fell elsewhere (Elkit *et al.*, 2005)?

Deviant cases always attract interest and, by providing a contrast with the norm, enhance our understanding of typical examples. But since the exceptional tends to the exotic, the danger is overstudy. Comparative politics should be more than a collection of curios.

Exemplary cases are archetypes that generate the category of which they are taken, in a somewhat circular way, as representative. For instance the French Revolution altered the whole concept of revolution, reconstructing the idea as a progressive, modernizing force. In this way, the French Revolution made possible all the modern revolutions which followed. In similar fashion, the American presidency does far

BOX 19.2

Some types of case study

	Definition	Example
Representative	Typical of the category	Coalition government in Finland
Prototypical	Expected to become typical	The United States as a pioneering democracy
Deviant	The exception to the rule	India as stable democracy in a poor country
Exemplary	Creates the category	The French Revolution
Critical	If it works here, it will work anywhere	Promoting democracy in Afghanistan

Further reading: Yin (2004, 2013).

more than illustrate the presidential system of government: it is the model which influenced later creations of similar systems, notably in Latin America. While an exemplar is often defined as a case to be emulated, in research design the term refers more neutrally to an influential example which illustrates the essential features of a phenomenon. An exemplary case is often, but need not be, prototypical.

Finally, a **critical case** (also known as a 'crucial case') enables a proposition to be tested in the circumstances least favourable to its validity. The logic is simple: if true here, then true everywhere. For instance, if we find that political participation is low among a sample of politics students, we can be fairly sure that it will be more limited still among students of other subjects. Thus, a small survey of politics students might permit inferences about a wider population without the expense of sampling the larger group. In this way, critical case studies can be highly efficient, providing exceptional returns on the research investment. However, the pay-off comes with risk: a critical case design builds a potential for generalization into a single investigation but involves a bet that the relevant proposition will, in fact, be confirmed in the conditions least favourable to its validity.

In the absence of overarching theory, case studies are the building blocks from which we construct our understanding of the political world. In a similar way to judges in common law systems, political scientists (and politicians more so) usually proceed by comparing cases, rather than by making deductions

from first principles. In consequence, much comparative political analysis takes the form not of relating cases to abstract theory but, rather, simply of drawing analogies between the cases themselves. For instance, how did the process of state-building differ between post-colonial states of the twentieth century and the states of early modern Europe? What are the similarities and differences between the Russian and Chinese revolutions? Why does the plurality electoral system produce a two-party system in the USA but a multiparty system in India? As we will see in the next section, a comparison of cases can create space for a broader understanding.

Comparative studies

A comparative design is well-established in politics, more so than in most disciplines. As we saw in Chapter 1, comparison pays dividends: it broadens our understanding of the political world, leads to improved classifications, and gives potential for explanation and even prediction. At the same time, of course, the breadth of the approach brings its own difficulties (Box 19.3). So, here we continue our discussion of the comparative approach by examining these potential pitfalls.

Understanding meaning

We should remember that the meaning of an action depends on the conventions of the country con-

The difficulties of comparison

- The 'same' phenomenon can mean different things in different countries, creating difficulties in comparing like with like.
- Globalization means that countries cannot be regarded as independent of each other, thus reducing the effective number of cases available for testing theories.
- Any pair of countries will differ in many ways, meaning we can never achieve the experimenter's dream of holding all factors constant apart from the one the impact of which we wish to test.
- The countries selected for study are often an unrepresentative sample, limiting the significance of the findings.

cerned. Comparing like with like is not always as straightforward as it seems. For instance, styles of political representation vary across nations. Where Nigerian politicians seek to impress by acts of flamboyant extravagance (such as seducing their competitors' female companions), Swedish politicians set out to affirm their very ordinariness. The same goal of impressing constituents is achieved by culturally specific means. What works in Lagos would be disastrous in Stockholm, and what succeeds in Stockholm would be met with apathy in Lagos.

Similarly, when members of a legislature vote against their party's line, the consequences can range by country from complete indifference to expulsion from the party. What appears to be the same act carries varying significance. Meaning depends on context.

So, before we begin any cross-national comparison we should ensure that we understand the relevant cultural codes of the countries we are studying. Failure here results in cultural imperialism, in which the meaning of an action in our home country is incorrectly projected onto other societies.

Globalization

Globalization poses a considerable challenge to comparative political research, understood as the comparison of separate states (Teune, 2010). Although 193 'independent' countries belonged to the United Nations by 2011, in reality these states

were interdependent, or even dependent. Countries learn from, copy, compete with, influence and even invade each other in a constant process of interaction. States did not develop independently; rather, the idea of statehood diffused outwards from its proving ground in Europe.

The major transitions of world history – industrialization, colonialism, decolonization, democratization – unfolded on a world stage. In that sense we inhabit one global system, rather than a world of independent states. Green (2002, p. 5) puts the point well when he says the world is arranged 'as if national polities are in fact cells of a larger entity with a life all its own'. The implication is that we should study this larger organism, rather than comparing its component parts as if they were unconnected.

Specific institutional forms also reflect diffusion. The presidential system in Latin America was imported from the United States; the ombudsman was a device copied from Sweden. The development of international organizations, from the United Nations to the European Union, also creates a newer layer of governance to which all member states must react.

Why do these links constitute a pitfall for students of comparative politics? They do not invalidate comparative analysis; indeed, they permit studies comparing the impact of an international factor on different countries, thus bridging the study of international and comparative politics. But interdependence does create technical difficulties for statistical analysis. Treating countries as independent entities artificially inflates the effective sample size in statistical research, resulting in exaggerated confidence in the significance of the results obtained (Tilly, 1997). To put the point more intuitively, treating countries as separate can lead to false inferences if in reality they are all subject to a common external influence, such as a colonial power.

Too many variables, too few countries

This is a major problem for those who conceive of comparative politics as a version of the experimenter's laboratory, in which researchers patiently seek to isolate the impact of a single variable. Even with 193 sovereign states, it is impossible to find a country which is identical to another in all respects except for that factor (say, its electoral system) whose effects we wish to detect. For this reason, political comparisons can never be as precise as laboratory experiments. We simply do not have sufficient countries to serve that purpose.

To make the same point from another angle, we will never be able to test all possible explanations of a political difference between countries. For example, why was New Zealand particularly sympathetic to introducing the private sector into the running of its public services during the 1990s? Perhaps the strength of the reforms reflected the pro-market thinking of the country's political and business elite (Boston *et al.*, 1995). Or perhaps the public sector in New Zealand was vulnerable to reform because, unlike many democracies in continental Europe, its structure was not protected by the constitution and civil law codes (Hood, 1996).

Here, we have two potential explanations for New Zealand's distinctiveness, one based on ideology and the other on law. Both interpretations are broadly consistent with the facts. But we have no way of isolating which factor is decisive. Ideally, we would want to discover whether the public sector had been reformed in a country identical to New Zealand except that only one of these two factors applied. But there is no such country; we have run out of cases.

In such circumstances, we can of course resort to asking hypothetical 'What if …?' questions. What would the outcome have been in New Zealand had its reforming elite confronted an unsympathetic legal framework? Would public sector reform still have proceeded? We should not shy away from such **counterfactuals**, for they must form part of any attempt to estimate the impact of unique events. To help us in this task, Tetlock and Belkin (1996) have developed useful guidelines for judging the plausibility of any particular counterfactual. However, by definition, the outcome of such thought experiments can never be tested against reality.

> A **counterfactual** is a thought experiment speculating on possible outcomes if a particular factor had been absent from a process, or an absent factor had been present. What would our world be like if Hitler had died in a car crash in 1932, or if his invasion of Russia had succeeded (Rosenfeld 2005)? If there had been no World War II, would there still be a European Union, and what form would it take?

Selection bias

We turn finally to a more technical, but nonetheless significant, difficulty in comparative research. **Selection bias** is at issue whenever the units of study (such as countries, democracies, or electoral systems) are chosen other than randomly. In these circumstances, the danger is that the units studied are unrepresentative of the wider population and, in consequence, results cannot be generalized to the broader category from which the cases are drawn. Given the rarity of random sampling in qualitative comparisons, the point is not so much to eliminate such bias as to be aware of its presence.

This danger often emerges as an unintended result of haphazard selection. For example, we choose to study those countries which speak our language, or which have good exchange schemes, or which we feel are safe to visit. As a result, large and powerful countries are studied more intensively than small and powerless ones, even though large states are untypical. By contrast, countries in which it is difficult to conduct research receive insufficient attentions. For example, Goode (2010) suggests that competitive authoritarian regimes such as Russia are under-studied because of the political sensitivity of conducting research in such domains. The result of such biases in selection is that published work is unrepresentative of all countries.

> **Selection bias** arises when selected cases and variables are unrepresentative of the wider class from which they are drawn. For instance, studies of English-speaking democracies are unrepresentative of all democracies; studies of communist parties that remain in power are untypical of ruling communist parties in the twentieth century.

One virtue of statistical designs covering a large number of countries is that they reduce the risk of selection bias. Indeed, when a study covers all current countries, selection bias disappears – at least, so long as generalization is restricted to the contemporary world. But, alas, the problem may just resurface in another form, through an unrepresentative selection of variables, rather than countries. To appreciate this version of selection bias, consider an illustration. Much statistical research in comparative politics relies on existing data collected by governments and international bodies with different interests from our own. The priorities of these organizations are often economic, rather than political. So, the availability of data means that financial and economic variables receive more attention and politics runs the risk of being treated as a branch of economics. The variables available to us are an unrepresentative selection of those with which we would like to work.

A particularly important form of selection bias comes from examining only positive cases, thus eliminating all variation in the phenomenon we seek to explain. Because this is a common, noteworthy, and avoidable mistake, it deserves special consideration. King *et al.* (1994, p. 129) explain the problem:

The literature is full of work that makes the mistake of failing to let the dependent variable vary; for example, research that tries to explain the outbreak of wars with studies only of wars, the onset of revolutions with studies only of revolutions, or patterns of voter turnout with interviews only of non-voters.

The problem here is that when only positive cases are studied, conclusions about the causes and consequences of the phenomenon are ruled out. Contrast is needed to give variation, so that we can then consider what factors distinguish times of war from times of peace, periods of revolution from periods of stability, and abstainers from voters.

Even without variation in the dependent variable, we can still identify common characteristics of the cases. For example, we may find that revolutions are always preceded by war, or that all non-voters are cynical about politics. However, we have no contrast to explore and explain. We do not know whether the conditions associated with revolution often exist without triggering a revolution, or whether the political cynicism we find among abstainers is equally prevalent among those who do turn out on election day (Geddes, 2003). Put differently, war may be a necessary condition of revolution (no revolution in the absence of war) without being a sufficient condition (whenever there is a war, revolution follows).

Survivorship bias is a particular form of selection bias. This issue arises when non-survivors of a temporal process are excluded, leading to biased results. Studying contemporary communist states or military governments as representative of the entire class of such regimes (past as well as present) is an error because those that survived may differ systematically from those that disappeared.

For instance, given that some federations fail, we should ask not only whether current federations are successful, but also what proportion of all federations, past and present, survive and prosper. In general, we should not treat those who complete a journey as typical of those who started out, for to do so would be to ignore the casualties along the way. In designing our research, we should look through both ends of the telescope – at starters as well as finishers, at casualties as well as survivors.

Qualitative comparisons

Implementing a comparative design involves making either qualitative or quantitative comparisons, or a blend of the two. In this section, we examine qualitative comparison, turning to quantitative analysis later.

Qualitative comparison falls between case studies and statistical analysis, consisting of small-N studies concentrating on the intensive examination of an aspect of politics in a few countries (or other units such as provinces). Most often, the number of countries is either two (a paired or binary comparison), or three (a triangular comparison). The concern with predefined aspects of the cases explains why George (1969) calls this method 'structured, focused comparison'. Countries are usually selected to introduce variation into the dependent variable, thus overcoming an inherent limit of the single case study.

To illustrate the technique, consider two examples using paired comparison. First, Kudrle and Marmor (1981) compared the growth of social security programmes in the United States and Canada. They sought to understand Canada's higher levels of spending and programme development, concluding that the elements of left-wing ideology and conservative paternalism found there were the key contrasts with the USA.

Second, Heclo (1974) compared the origins of unemployment insurance, old age pensions, and earnings-related supplementary pensions in Britain and Sweden. In both countries, Heclo concluded, the bureaucracy was the main agent of policy formulation. In contrast to Kudrle and Marmor – and, indeed, to most qualitative comparisons – Heclo sought to explain a similarity, rather than a difference, between the countries examined.

Qualitative comparisons such as these have proved to be a success story of comparative politics. As with case studies, they remain sensitive to the details of particular countries but, in addition, they demand the intellectual discipline inherent in the comparative enterprise. The dimensions of comparison must be addressed, similarities and differences identified, and an effort made to account for the contrasts observed. For these reasons, qualitative comparisons allow research findings to cumulate, whereas the reports of case studies often languish in their covers.

How should countries be selected for a qualitative comparison? A common strategy is to select countries which, although differing on the factor of interest, are otherwise similar. This is the **most similar** design. With this approach, we seek to compare countries which are as similar as possible in, say, their history, culture, and government institutions, so that we can clearly rule out such common factors as explanations for the particular difference for which we wish to account.

Kurdle and Marmor's study of Canada's higher social security spending compared with the USA is a typical application of this 'most similar' method. Another example would be to investigate why Britain managed a more peaceful transition to democracy than Germany. This study would examine a contrast between two states which are nonetheless comparable as large countries with a shared European heritage.

> A **most similar** design takes similar countries for comparison on the assumption, as Lipset (1990, p. xiii) put it, that 'the more similar the units being compared, the more possible it should be to isolate the factors responsible for differences between them'. By contrast, the **most different** design seeks to show the robustness of a relationship between two factors by demonstrating its validity across diverse settings (Przeworski and Teune, 1970).

However, even with a 'most similar' design, many factors will remain as possible explanations for an observed difference and, usually, there will be no decisive way of testing between them. The problem of too many variables and too few countries cannot be sidestepped; in practice, much of the value of a qualitative comparison lies in the journey, rather than the destination.

A **most different** design follows a different track. Here, we seek to test a relationship by discovering whether it can be observed in a range of countries with contrasting histories, cultures, and so on. If so, our confidence that the relationship is real, and not due to the dependence of both factors on an unmeasured third variable, will increase (Peters, 1998).

For example, Rothstein (2002) examined the evolution of social and political trust in two contrasting democracies, Sweden and the United States, assuming that any trends shared between these two different countries should also be observable in other democracies. In a similar way, if we were to find that the plurality method of election is associated with a two-party system in each of the diverse group of countries employing that electoral system, our confidence in the robustness of the relationship between plurality elections and a two-party system would increase. In addition to its role in qualitative comparisons, the most different design is also the basis of much statistical research, to which we now turn.

Quantitative comparisons

In political research, quantitative comparison or statistical analysis is now less common than at the height of the behavioural era but it remains a significant and worthwhile strand. Statistical analysis is inherently comparative but possesses strong conventions. In this section, we outline some of these principles without attempting a full guide to techniques (for which, see Pennings *et al.*, 2006).

Simple counts provide an underrated beginning. As Miller (1995) says, asking the plain question 'How many of them are there?' is worthwhile. For instance: how many federations are there? How many states are democratic? What is the probability that an authoritarian regime in 1980 has become democratic today? Such questions must be answered, if we are to achieve a comparative understanding of the political world. Just as straightforward case studies can contribute more to

The **dependent variable** is the factor for which we wish to account; for example, party voted for. The **independent variable** is the factor believed to influence the dependent variable; for example, level of education.

comparative politics than elaborate attempts at theory testing, so descriptive counts can provide more useful results than sophisticated statistical analyses.

In contrast to the techniques reviewed so far, the quantitative approach is based on variables, rather than cases. When we move beyond straightforward counting, the object is usually to explore the extent to which variables or factors co-vary, such that knowing a country's score on one variable (for instance, its literacy rate) allows us to predict its score on another (for instance, its electoral turnout). In such analyses, one variable is **dependent**, while the others are **independent** or explanatory. Examples of such work in comparative politics include tests of the following hypotheses:

● the more educated a population, the higher its proportion of postmaterialists;

● the higher a person's social status, the greater his or her participation in politics;

● the more affluent a country, the more likely it is to be a liberal democracy;

● presidential government is less stable than parliamentary government.

To illustrate the statistical approach, consider an example. Figure 19.1 is a scatterplot showing the relationship between the number of members in a national assembly (the dependent variable) and a country's population, within the 10–60 million range (the independent variable) The graph reveals a **positive correlation**: the larger the population, the larger the assembly.

The **correlation** coefficient measures the accuracy with which we can predict from one statistical variable to another. A **positive** correlation means that scores on the variables go up (or down) in tandem. A **negative** correlation means that a high score on one variable is associated with low scores on the other.

However, the content of the graph can be summarized more precisely. This is achieved by calculating a **regression line**: the line giving the best fit to the data. This line, also shown in Figure 19.1, is defined by a formula linking the two variables. In this case, the equation reveals that, on average, the size of an assembly increases by about seven members for each increment of 1 million in a country's population. Given such an equation, which also gives a base estimate for assembly size given a notional population of zero, we can use the population of any particular country to predict its assembly size.·

The **regression line** is the line of best fit in a scatterplot. **Outliers** are the observations furthest away from the value predicted by the regression line.

One important virtue of a regression equation is that it allows us to identify **outliers** or off-the-line cases. The larger the difference between the predicted and the actual assembly size, the greater the need for additional explanation, thus providing a link to deviant case analysis. In our example, Cuba's National Assembly of People's Power is far larger than would be expected for a country with a population of 11 million.

How can we account for this outlier? The answer is probably that communist states adopted large assemblies as a way of reducing any threat they might pose to the party's power. Such an interpretation offers a plausible starting point for further investigation, giving us a case selection strategy in which the case is nested within a statistical framework (Lieberman, 2005).

The value of quantitative comparisons is that they can provide precise summaries of large amounts of data using standard techniques whose application can be checked by other researchers. But, as always, interpretation is the difficult part, requiring attention to two main dangers. First, a strong correlation between two variables may arise simply because both depend on a third, unmeasured factor. In such cases, there is no relationship of cause and effect. For example, a correlation between proportional representation (PR) and multiparty systems might arise because both factors emerge in divided societies, not because PR itself increases the number of parties. Or a correlation between ethnic minority status and abstention at elections might arise because both

Figure 19.1 Population and assembly size, 2012, showing the line of best fit and highlighting two outliers

A regression line summarizes the relationship between two variables. Here, the dependent variable is assembly size and the independent variable is population. Outliers, here Cuba and Colombia, can also be identified.

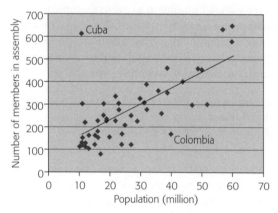

Note: For bicameral assemblies, the size of the lower chamber is used.

Sources: IPU (2012); CIA (2012).

factors are concentrated among the poor, not because ethnic status itself reduces turnout.

In principle, the solution to this problem of **spurious correlation** is simple: include all relevant variables in the analysis, for advanced statistical techniques can, to an extent, control for such problems. In practice, however, not all relevant variables will be known and spurious correlation is a continuing danger. Note, though, that even a spurious correlation may be a practical (if risky) basis for prediction.

> A **spurious correlation** is one which arises because both factors depend on a third variable. For instance, the relationship between the proportion of immigrants in an area and its crime rate may be spurious because poverty is the real cause of crime, and both immigration and crime are high in poor areas.

The second issue in interpreting statistical results is that, even if a relationship is genuine, the direction of causation remains to be established. Take an example. Suppose we find that liberal democracies secure higher rates of economic growth than authoritarian regimes. We still face a problem of interpretation. Does the correlation arise because democracy facilitates economic growth, or because a high rate of growth fosters a stable democracy? A case can be made either way, or both; by itself a statistical correlation will not provide the answer. In itself, a correlation does not show the direction of causation.

Worthwhile quantitative comparisons can be made even when the variables take the form of categories (e.g. yes/no), rather than numerical scores. For example, are federations less likely than unitary states to develop welfare states? Is proportional representation linked to coalition government? Are non-Muslim countries more likely to be democratic than Islamic countries? Here, we are dealing with categories, rather than numerical scales: a country is either a federation or not, a government is either a coalition or not. In these circumstances, a straightforward cross-tabulation is the qualitative equivalent of the scatterplot in Figure 19.l. Correlation-like statistics can nonetheless be calculated for such tables (Pennings *et al.*, 2006).

Historical analysis

Most studies in politics – and in comparative politics, especially – focus on the contemporary world; in the main, we leave history to the historians. But this division of labour is, of course, arbitrary; today's present is tomorrow's past. Political science can, and perhaps should, make more use of the past as a treasure trove of additional cases, whether of rare events such as genocide and revolution or of particular episodes that exemplify, challenge, or refine existing theories. History can enlarge our database, enabling us in particular to employ the most different design to examine the robustness of findings across distinct time periods.

Quarrying the past by political scientists in this way is rather different from the approach adopted by traditional historians. According to the German historian Leopold von Ranke (1795–1886), history 'merely wants to show how essentially things happened'. For von Ranke (1824, p. iv), 'a strict representation of facts, be it ever so narrow, and unpoetical, is, beyond doubt, the first law'. From this perspective, the obligation of historians is to present the past in its own terms – as a narrative pieced together from primary sources. Many political scientists, however, would be concerned with the past as a source of generalization; in other words, with case studies, rather than studies.

The further and more interesting question, though, is how students of politics should understand temporal sequences as such. That is, how can we make the transition from taking snapshots of the present – the traditional focus of most political research – to developing moving pictures of change over time? This section addresses this question, beginning with the specific notion of an analytic narrative and then introducing some broader ideas which help us to locate politics in time.

The **analytic narrative** (Bates *et al.*, 1998) is a design that seeks to combine the historian's concern with telling the story with the political scientist's interest in explaining outcomes. The task of an analytic narrative, typically located in the rational choice framework, is to show how actors' interests and understanding create strategies which, interacting over time, generate the outcome of interest. In contrast to a case study, an analytic narrative is necessarily concerned with sequence; however, it does not aim to provide a comprehensive, rounded description of events. Rather, the goal is to identify the key factors driving towards the outcome.

> An **analytic narrative** attempts to integrate historical and political science methods. It examines how a particular sequence of moves, made by calculating actors aware of the options available to them, generates a particular result (Bates *et al.*, 1998).

Two examples will help to clarify the design. First, Weingast (1998) shows how slavery was maintained in the USA until the Civil War by a balance between Northern and Southern interests – both within parties and in the Senate as a whole. According to Weingast, this balance provided an equilibrium in which even Northerners lacked strong incentives to advance anti-slavery initiatives. So, here we have two actors – Northerners and Southerners – interacting over time to yield a stable situation in which Northerners opposed to slavery were nonetheless prepared to accept it.

Second, Bates (1998) narrates the birth, life, and death of the International Coffee Organization (ICO, 1962–89). He seeks to explain why the government of a coffee-consuming nation – the USA – supported a body which was essentially a cartel of coffee producers. The answer involves a range of actors, including producers, roasters, and bureaucrats. Their interactions during the Cold War produced and maintained an equilibrium – in the form of the ICO – until the balance was destroyed by shifts in market taste and by the emergence of new producers who declined to join the organization.

Although analytic narratives provide a way of examining politics over time, broader approaches are still needed. Pierson (2004) brings together some terms for thinking about politics in the context of time; this vocabulary renders explicit our often submerged thoughts about political change. We will introduce each notion in Box 19.4.

We begin with path dependence. A political process is **path dependent** when its outcome depends on earlier decisions; that is, the destination depends on the route. Path dependence implies an emphasis on history generally and branching points specifically. By contrast, path independence means that all roads lead to Rome; the same destination will be reached, irrespective of the route. Path independence implies an emphasis on underlying structures and resources rather than historical sequences.

Consider an example. The result of a football game is path dependent if the first score is vital; it is path independent if the better team is sure to win in the end, no matter who scores first. To take a more political illustration, the outcome of a war is path dependent if a particular battle proves decisive; it is path independent if the stronger side is sure to win eventually, whatever the result of a specific confrontation.

It is important to recognize that much political research imagines path independence. If all rich countries are liberal democracies, tracing the process by which a particular wealthy nation became democratic would not cast light on the general relationship. If all wealthy states end up as democracies, whatever their political starting point, we should concentrate on why affluent countries select democracy in and dictatorship out. In short, when an outcome is inevitable, we should look for underlying causes; in these circumstances, historical narratives can describe the route, but not account for the destination.

Process tracing involves identifying and describing the historical sequence linking a cause to an effect.

BOX 19.4

History matters: politics in time

	Definition	Example
Path dependence	The outcome of a process is not inevitable but depends on initial decisions which lead down a particular path	Britain's decision after World War II to adopt a tax-funded health system, free at the point of service, was a choice that set the country on a one-way road of socialized medicine
Critical juncture	A turning point which establishes interests, structures or institutions persisting through time	The constitutional convention which established the USA
Sequencing	The order of events, not merely their occurrence, affects the outcome	Communist regimes which introduced economic reform before political liberalization (e.g. China) were more likely to survive than those beginning the reform process with political change (e.g. the USSR)
Slow-moving cause	An influence which changes slowly but, over a long period, dramatically	The gradual expansion of education eventually creates a demand for freedom

Source: Adapted from Pierson (2004).

For example, what were the steps leading from Hitler's anti-Semitism to the Holocaust? Through what mechanisms does defeat in war lead to a change of regime? Process tracing reconnects political science with history.

Often, however, the outcome is far from predetermined. It is here that the concepts of critical junctures, sequences, and slow-moving causes provide tools for thinking about how the political past influences the political present.

Critical junctures, for example, can initiate a path dependent process. These key moments clear a new path that continues to be followed long after the juncture itself has passed. During the critical phase (often, a moment of crisis), all options really are on the table and history is, indeed, written. Revolutions are one example; constitutional conventions another.

Once the new order has consolidated, however, politics settles down and the choices realistically available to decision-makers shrink. The revolutionary generation gives way to pragmatic operators of the new regime. As ideas are displaced by institutions, so the constitution as choice is supplanted by the constitution as constraint.

By dividing history into critical and normal eras, we arrive at a plausible perspective on the old debate about whether people make their own history. The answer is perhaps that they do, but only occasionally. That is, critical junctures are rare choice points in which human agency really can be decisive for the long term.

Ideas, in particular, rise to prominence during critical junctures. In normal times, much political discussion is what Schmidt (2002, p. 252) calls 'cheap talk', expressing negotiating positions which defend established interests. But, sometimes, the existing stock of ideas becomes incapable of responding to a shift in circumstances, creating pressures for established procedures to be revised or completely rethought. A country may experience economic decline; a party, a fall in votes; a trade union, a collapse in membership. Suddenly, ideas that had previously received scant consideration find themselves at the centre of the table. When disintegration threatens, new thoughts are urgently needed.

Sequencing, the order in which events unfold, can help to account for path dependence. For example, in European countries where trade unions developed before socialism became a full-blooded ideology (notably, Britain), the labour movement took on a moderate reformist character. But where Marxist thought was already established, as in France, communist unions developed a more radical political agenda. So, whether trade unions emerged before or after the onset of Marxism helps to explain whether particular European countries developed a reformist or radical labour movement. The outcome was not predetermined but, rather, depended on the sequence of events.

In a similar way, the order in which government departments are created influences their contemporary status. Those created earliest (such as the finance and justice ministries) typically constitute the core of government, with later ministries (such as environment and transport) occupying a more peripheral position. Thus, the functioning of the central government is likely to be incompletely understood if this historical sequence is ignored and all departments are treated as equal in status.

One form of 'sequence' is a conjuncture in which separate events occur at the same time, enlarging their political impact. The collision of World War I with the emergence of working-class socialism, or of the Vietnam War with the student movement, generated political effects which were greater than would have been the case had these events unfolded separately. These confluences are typically made by history; they are another contributor to path dependence.

Slow-moving causes, finally, are processes that unfold over a long period. Examples include modernization and technological advance, the spread of education, and the growth of the mass media. Such processes often need to reach a **threshold** before exerting a visible, dramatic effect. The emergence of students as a force in national politics, for instance, can be explosive, but this rapid onset may reflect decades of gradual expansion in higher education. A critical mass is needed before the student voice becomes so strong that it can be ignored no longer.

> A **threshold** is a level or tipping point above which a variable begins to exert a critical effect. The point at which sliding snow turns into an avalanche is an illustration. In politics, the number of women representatives in an assembly may need to reach a critical mass before the increase exerts significant impact on how the chamber operates.

Similarly, the election of the first member of an ethnic minority to the legislature will usually indicate that long-run changes in attitudes to minorities have passed a threshold at which their representation becomes a practical possibility. But minority representation in parliament may need to cross another threshold before the institution itself begins to change its procedures and policies.

When thresholds are involved, long-term but otherwise slow-moving causes need to be understood historically. Contemporary explosions have long fuses and political scientists need to search into the past to uncover them.

Discussion questions

■ For what topics could your country serve as a representative case study?

■ 'Affluence breeds democracy.' Identify a deviant case for this proposition and account for the exception.

■ What challenges does globalization pose for comparative politics?

■ Devise (a) a most similar, and (b) a most different design to identify the effects of one type of electoral system.

■ How does the study of politics differ from the study of history?

■ Give an example of (a) path dependence, (b) a critical juncture, (c) a slow-moving cause.

Further reading

B. Geddes, *Paradigms and Sand Castles: Theory Building and Research Design in Comparative Politics* (2003). Sage advice on research strategies in comparative politics.

A. George and A. Bennett, *Case Studies and Theory Development in the Social Sciences* (2004). Examines the role of case studies in social science research, including politics.

S. Halperin and O. Heath, *Political Research: Methods and Practical Skills* (2012). An exceptionally clear introduction to qualitative and quantitative research methods in politics.

P. Pennings, H. Keman, and J. Kleinnijenhuis, *Doing Research in Political Science: An Introduction to Comparative Methods and Statistics*, 2nd edn (2006). Introduces statistical methods in the context of comparative politics.

B. Guy Peters, *Comparative Politics: Theory and Methods* (1998). A detailed examination of theory and strategy in comparative politics.

P. Pierson, *Politics in Time: History, Institutions and Social Analysis* (2004). A thoughtful discussion of the relationship between history and political analysis.

R. Yin, *Case Study Research: Design and Methods*, 5th edn (2013). A standard source on conducting case studies, using examples from a range of disciplines.

ONLINE RESOURCES AVAILABLE

Visit the companion website at **www.palgrave.com/politics/hague** to access additional learning resources, including multiple-choice questions, chapter summaries, web links and practice essay questions.

References

These references, and those from the previous editions, are listed by chapter on the companion website.

A

Aardal, B. and Binder, T. (2011) 'Leader Effects and Party Characteristics', in *Political Leaders and Democratic Election,* ed. K. Aarts, A. Blais and H. Schmitt (Oxford: Oxford University Press) pp. 108–26.

Aarts, K., Blais, A. and Schmitt, H. (eds) (2011) *Political Leaders and Democratic Elections* (Oxford: Oxford University Press).

Aberbach, J., Putnam, R. and Rockman, B. (1981) *Bureaucrats and Politicians* (Cambridge, MA: Harvard University Press).

Abramowitz, A. (1988) 'An Improved Model for Predicting Presidential Election Outcomes', *PS: Political Science & Politics* (21) 843–7.

Abramowitz, A. (2010) 'Ideological Realignment among Voters', in *New Directions in American Political Parties*, ed. J. Stonecash (New York: Routledge) pp. 126–47.

Adams, J., Green, J. and Milazzo, C. (2012) 'Has the British Public Depolarized Along with Political Elites? An American Perspective on British Public Opinion', *Comparative Political Studies* (45) 507–30.

Adeney, K. and Wyatt, A. (2010) *Contemporary India* (Basingstoke: Palgrave Macmillan).

Adman, P. (2009) 'The Puzzle of Gender-Equal Political Participation in Sweden: The Importance of Norms and Mobilization', *Scandinavian Political Studies* (32) 315–36.

Akkerman, T. (2012) 'Comparing Radical Right Parties in Government: Immigration and Integration Policies in 9 Countries, 1966–2010', *West European Politics* (35) 511–29.

Albrecht, H. (2008) 'The Nature of Political Participation', in *Political Participation in the Middle East*, ed. E. Lust-Okar and S. Zerhouni (Boulder, CO: Lynne Rienner) pp. 15–32.

Albuquerque, A. de (2012) 'On Models and Margins: Comparative Media Models Viewed from a Brazilian Perspective', in *Comparing Media Systems Beyond the Western World*, ed. D. Hallin and P. Mancini (New York: Cambridge University Press) pp. 72–95.

Albritton, R. (2006) 'American Federalism and Intergovernmental Relations', in *Developments in American Politics 5*, ed. G. Peele *et al.* (Basingstoke: Palgrave Macmillan) pp. 124–45.

Allison, G. (1971) *Essence of Decision: Explaining the Cuban Missile Crisis* (Boston, MA: Little, Brown).

Allison, G. and Zelikow, P. (1999) *Essence of Decision: Explaining the Cuban Missile Crisis* (New York: Longman).

Almond, G. (1993) 'The Study of Political Culture', in *Political Culture in Germany*, ed. D. Berg-Schlosser and R. Rytlewski (New York: St. Martin's Press) pp. 13–26.

Almond, G. and Verba, S. (1963) *The Civic Culture* (Princeton, NJ: Princeton University Press).

Alonso, S. and Ruiz-Rufino, R. (2007) 'Political Representation and Ethnic Conflict in New Democracies', *European Journal of Political Research* (46) 237–67.

Alonso, S., Keane, J. and Merkel, W. (eds) (2011) *The Future of Representative Democracy* (Cambridge: Cambridge University Press).

Alter, K. (2008) 'The European Court and Legal Integration: An Exceptional Story or Harbinger of the Future?' in *The Oxford Handbook of Law and Politics*, ed. K. Whittington, R. Kelemen and G. Caldeira (Oxford: Oxford University Press) pp. 209–28.

Alter, K. (2009) *The European Court's Political Power: Selected Essays* (New York: Oxford University Press).

Althaus, S. (2003) *Collective Preferences in Democratic Politics: Opinion Surveys and the Will of the People* (New York: Cambridge University Press).

Altman, D. (2011) *Direct Democracy Worldwide* (New York: Cambridge University Press).

Alvarez, A. (2004) 'State Reform Before and After Chávez's Election', in *Venezuelan Politics in the Chávez Era: Class, Polarization and Conflict*, ed. S. Ellner and D. Hellinger (Boulder, CO: Lynne Rienner) pp. 147–60.

Álvarez-Rivera, M. (2009) 'Elections to the German Bundestag', *Election Resources on the Internet*, http://electionresources.org/de/, accessed 22 November 2009.

American National Election Studies (2012) *Data Center*, http://www.electionstudies.org, accessed 15 May 2012.

Anderson, B. (1983) *Imagined Communities: Reflections on the Origins and Spread of Nationalism* (London: Verso).

Andeweg, R. and Irwin, G. (2009) *Governance and Politics of the Netherlands*, 3rd edn (Basingstoke: Palgrave Macmillan).

Ansell, C. and Gingrich, J. (2003) 'Reforming the Administrative State', in *Democracy Transformed? Expanding Political Opportunities in Advanced Industrial Democracies,* ed. B. Cain, R. Dalton and S. Scarrow (New York: Oxford University Press) pp. 164–91.

Ansolabehere, S. (2006) 'Voters, Candidates and Parties' in *The Oxford Handbook of Political Economy*, ed. B. Weingast and D. Wittman (Oxford: Oxford University Press) pp. 29–49.

Anton, T. (1969) 'Policy-Making and Political Culture in Sweden', *Scandinavian Political Studies* (4) 82–102.

Apter, D. (1965) *The Politics of Modernization* (Chicago: University of Chicago Press).

Arendt, H. (1970) *On Violence* (London: Allen Lane).

Aristotle (1962 edn) *The Politics,* trans. T. Sinclair (Harmondsworth: Penguin).

Armitage, D. (2005) 'The Contagion of Sovereignty: Declarations of Independence since 1776', *South African Historical Journal* (52) 1–18.

B

Bach, D. and Newman, A. (2007) 'The European Regulatory State and Global Public Policy', *Journal of European Public Policy* (14) 827–46.

Bache, I. and Flinders, M. (eds) (2004) *Multi-Level Governance* (Oxford: Oxford University Press).

Bachrach, P. and Baratz, M. (1962) 'The Two Faces of Power', *American Political Science Review* (56) 941–52.

Bagehot, W. (1867) [1963 edn] *The English Constitution* (London: Fontana).

Bale, T. and Bergman, T. (2006) 'Captives No Longer, But Servants Still? Contract Parliamentarianism and the New Minority Governance in Sweden and New Zealand', *Government and Opposition* (41) 422–49.

Bale, T. and Dunphy, R. (2011) 'In from the Cold? Left Parties and Government Involvement since 1989', *Comparative European Politics* (9) 269–91.

Baldwin, N. (2012) *Legislatures of Small States: A Comparative Study* (Abingdon: Routledge).

Barber, B. (1995) *Jihad vs McWorld* (New York: Ballantine Books).

Barber, J. (1992) *The Pulse of Politics: Electing Presidents in the Media Age* (New Brunswick, NY: Transaction Books).

Bardach, E. (1976) 'Policy Termination as a Political Process', *Policy Sciences* (7) 123–31.

Bates, R. (1998) 'The International Coffee Organization: An International Institution' in *Analytic Narratives*, ed. R. Bates, A. Greif, M. Levi, J.-L. Rosenthal and B. Weingast (Princeton, NJ: Princeton University Press) pp. 194–230.

Bates, R., Greif, A., Levi, M., Rosenthal, J.-L. and Weingast, B. (eds) (1998) *Analytic Narratives* (Princeton, NJ: Princeton University Press).

Bauer, G. and Tremblay, M. (eds) (2011) *Women in Executive Power: A Global Overview* (Abingdon: Routledge).

Bauer, M., Jordan, A., Green-Pedersen, C. and Héritier, A. (eds) (2012) *Dismantling Public Policy: Preferences, Strategies, and Effects* (Oxford: Oxford Universty Press).

Baum, C. and Di Maio, A. (2000) *Gartner's Four Phases of E-Government* (Stanford, CT: Gartner).

Bayat, A. (2010) *Life as Politics: How Ordinary People Change the Middle East* (Stanford, CA: Stanford University Press).

Baylis, T. (2007) 'Embattled Executives: Prime Ministerial Weakness in East Central Europe', *Communist and Post-Communist Studies* (40) 81–106.

BBC News (2009) *Obama Speaks of Hopes for Africa*, http://www.news.bbc.co.uk, accessed 8 August 2009.

Beckman, L. (2007) 'The Professionalization of Politicians Reconsidered: A Study of the Swedish Cabinet, 1917–2004', *Parliamentary Affairs* (60) 66–83.

Beetham, D. (2004) 'Freedom as the Foundation', *Journal of Democracy* (15) 61–75.

Bell, D. (2012) 'The Real Meaning of the Rot at the Top of China', *Financial Times*, 24 April, p. 11.

Bell, S. and Hindmoor, A. (2009) *Rethinking Governance: The Centrality of the State in Modern Society* (Cambridge: Cambridge University Press).

Bellamy, R. (2008) *Citizenship: A Very Short Introduction* (Oxford: Oxford University Press).

Bendor, J., Moe, T. and Shorts, K. (2001) 'Recycling the Garbage Can: An Assessment of the Research Program', *American Political Science Review* (95) 169–90.

Bennett, W. Lance (2005) 'Social Movements beyond Borders: Understanding Two Eras of Transnational Activism', in *Transnational Protest and Global Activism*, ed. D. della Porta and S. Tarrow (Lanham, MD: Rowman & Littlefield) pp. 203–26.

Bentley, A. (1908) *The Process of Government* (Chicago, IL: University of Chicago Press).

Benz, A. and Broschek, J. (eds) (2012) *Federal Dynamics: Continuity, Change and the Varieties of Federalism* (Oxford: Oxford University Press).

Berger, S. and Compston, H. (eds) (2002) *Policy Concertation and Social Partnership in Western Europe: Lessons for the 21st Century* (Oxford: Berghahn).

Bergman, T. (2000) 'Sweden: When Minority Cabinets Are the Rule and Majority Coalitions the Exception', in *Coalition Governments in Western Europe*, ed. W. Müller and K. Strøm (New York: Oxford University Press) pp. 192–230.

Bergström, H. (1991) 'Sweden's Politics and Party System at the Crossroads', *West European Politics* (14) 8–30.

Berry, W., Berkman, M. and Schneiderman, S. (2000) 'Legislative Professionalism and Incumbent Reelection: The Development of Institutional Boundaries', *American Political Science Review* (94) 859–74.

Best, H. and Cotta, M. (2000) *Parliamentary Representatives in Europe, 1848–2000* (Oxford: Oxford University Press).

Betz, H.-G. (1994) *Radical Right-Wing Populism in Western Europe* (Basingstoke: Macmillan).

Beyers, J., Eising, R. and Maloney, W. (eds) (2009) *Interest Group Politics in Europe: Lessons from EU Studies and Comparative Politics* (London: Routledge).

Bickerton, J. and Gagnon, A.-G. (2011) 'Regions', in *Comparative Politics*, 2nd edn, ed. D. Caramani (Oxford: Oxford University Press) pp. 275–91.

Binderkrantz, A. (2005) 'Interest Group Strategies: Navigating Between Privileged Access and Strategies of Pressure', *Political Studies* (53) 694–715.

Bipartisan Policy Center (2012) *2012 Voter Turnout*, http://www.bipartisanpolicy.org, accessed 3 December 2012.

Birkland, T. (2010) *An Introduction to the Policy Process: Theories, Concepts and Models of Public Policy Making*, 3rd edn (Armonk, NY: M.E. Sharpe).

Bischof, R. (2012) 'Britain needs better rather than less regulation', *Financial Times*, September 10.

Bittner, A. (2011) *Platform or Personality? The Role of Party Leaders in Elections* (Oxford: Oxford University Press).

Blackstone, W. (1765–9) [1832 edn] *Commentaries on the Laws of England*, 4 books (New York: W. E. Dean).

Blais, A., Massicotte, L. and Dobrzynska, A. (1997) 'Direct Presidential Elections: A World Summary', *Electoral Studies* (16) 441–55.

Blais, A., Dobrzynska, A. and Massicotte, L. (2003) *Why is Turnout Higher in Some Countries than in Others* (Ottawa, Ontario: Elections Canada).

Blaydes, L. (2011) *Elections and Distributive Politics in Mubarak's Egypt* (New York: Cambridge University Press).

Boardman, A., Greenburg, D., Vining, A. and Weimer, D. (2010) *Cost–Benefit Analysis: Concepts and Practice*, 4th edn (Upper Saddle River, NJ: Prentice Hall).

Bogdanor, V. (2009) *The New British Constitution* (London: Hart).

Boix, C. (2003) *Democracy and Redistribution* (Cambridge: Cambridge University Press).

Boix, C. (2011) 'Democracy, Development and the International System', *American Political Science Review* (105) 809–28.

Bolleyer, N. (2012) 'New Party Organization in Western Europe: Hierarchies, Stratarchies and Federations', *Party Politics* (18) 315–36.

Bonneau, C. and Hall, M. (2009) *In Defense of Judicial Elections* (New York: Routledge).

Borchert, J. and Zeiss, J. (eds) (2003) *The Political Class in Advanced Democracies* (Oxford: Oxford University Press).

Borón, A. (1998) 'Faulty Democracies? A Reflection on the Capitalist "Fault Lines"', in *Fault Lines of Democracy in Post-Transition Latin America*, ed. F. Agüero and J. Stark (Coral Gables, FL: University of Miami) pp. 41–66.

Börzel, T. and Sedelmeieir, U. (2006) 'The EU Dimension in European Politics', in *Developments in European Politics*, ed. P. Heywood, E. Jones, M. Rhodes and U. Sedelmeier (Basingstoke and New York: Palgrave Macmillan), pp. 54–70.

Boston, J., Martin. L., Pallot, J. and Walsh, P. (eds) (1995) *Reshaping the State: New Zealand's Bureaucratic Revolution* (Oxford: Oxford University Press).

Boucek, F. (2012) *Factional Politics: How Dominant Parties Implode or Stabilize* (Basingstoke: Palgrave Macmillan).

Bourgault, J. (2002) 'The Role of Deputy Ministers in Canadian Government', in *The Handbook of Canadian Public Administration*, ed. C. Dunn (Don Mills, Ontario: Oxford University Press) pp. 430–49.

Bourgault, L. (1995) *Mass Media in Sub-Saharan Africa* (Bloomington, IN: Indiana University Press).

Bowler, S. and Donovan, T. (2002) 'Democracy, Institutions and Attitudes about Citizen Influence on Government', *British Journal of Political Science* (32) 371–90.

Brans, M., De Winter, L. and Swenden, W. (eds) (2009) *The Politics of Belgium: Institutions and Policy Under Bipolar and Centrifugal Federalism* (London: Routledge).

Bratton, M. (1998) 'Second Elections in Africa', *Journal of Democracy* (9) 51–66.

Braun, D. with Walti, A., Bullinger, A.-B. and Ayrton, R. (2003) *Fiscal Policies in Federal States* (Burlington, VT: Ashgate).

Bräutigam, D., Fjeldstad, O.-H. and Moore, M. (2008) *Taxation and State-Building in Developing Countries: Capacity and Consent* (Cambridge: Cambridge University Press).

Breslin, S. (2004) 'Capitalism with Chinese Characteristics: The Public, the Private and the International', *Working Paper No. 104*, Asia Research Centre (Perth: Murdoch University).

Brewer, M. (2008) *Party Images in the American Electorate* (New York: Routledge).

Brewer, M. (2010) 'Strategic Maneuvers: Political Parties and the Pursuit of Winning Coalitions in a Constantly Changing Electoral Environment', in *New Directions in American Political Parties*, ed. J. Stonecash (New York: Routledge) pp. 22–43.

Brewer, P., Aday, S. and Gross, K. (2003) 'Rallies All Round: The Dynamics of System Support', in *Framing Terrorism: The News Media, the Government and the Public*, ed. P. Norris, M. Kern and M. Just (New York: Routledge) pp. 229–54.

Brewer-Carías, A. (2010) *Dismantling Democracy in Venezuela: The Chávez Authoritarian Experiment* (New York: Cambridge University Press).

Broder, D. (1972) *The Party's Over: The Failure of Politics in America* (New York: Harper and Row).

Brooker, P. (2009) *Non-Democratic Regimes: Theory, Government and Politics*, 2nd edn (Basingstoke: Palgrave Macmillan).

Brooks, S. (2012) *Canadian Democracy: An Introduction*, 7th edn (Don Mills, Ontario: Oxford University Press).

Brooks, T. (2008) 'Is Plato's Political Philosophy Anti-Democratic?', in *Anti-Democratic Thought*, ed. E. Kofmel (Exeter: Imprint Academic) pp. 17–33.

Brown, A. (ed.) (2004) *The Demise of Marxism-Leninism in Russia* (Basingstoke: Palgrave Macmillan).

Bryce, J. (1919) *The American Commonwealth*, Vol. 1 (London: Macmillan).

Bryce, J. (1921) *Modern Democracies*, Vol. 2 (New York: Macmillan).

BSA (British Social Attitudes) (2012) *Information System*, http://www.britsocat.com, accessed 16 May 2012.

Budge, I. (2006) 'Identifying Dimensions and Locating Parties: Methodological and Conceptual Problems', in *Handbook of Party Politics*, ed. R. Katz and W. Crotty (Thousand Oaks, CA: Sage) pp. 422–34.

Bull, M. and Newell, J. (2005) *Italian Politics: Adjustment under Duress* (Cambridge: Polity).

Burgess, M. (2006) *Comparative Federalism: Theory and Practice* (London: Routledge).

Burgess, M. (2012) *In Search of the Federal Spirit: New Theoretical and Empirical Perspectives in Comparative Federalism* (Oxford: Oxford University Press).

Burke, E. (1774) [1975 edn] 'Speech to the Electors of Bristol', in *Edmund Burke on Government, Politics and Society*, ed. B. Hill (London: Fontana) pp. 156–8.

Burke, J. (2010) 'The Institutional Presidency', in *The Presidency and the Political System*, 9th edn, ed. M. Nelson (Washington, DC: CQ Press) pp. 341–66.

Bush, G. (2005) 'New Zealand: A Quantum Leap Forward?', in *Comparing Local Governance: Trends and Developments*, ed. B. Denters and L. Rose (Basingstoke: Palgrave Macmillan) pp. 174–92.

Butler, D. (1989) *British General Elections Since 1945* (Oxford: Blackwell).

Butler, D. and Stokes, D. (1971) *Political Change in Britain: Forces Shaping Electoral Choice* (Harmondsworth: Penguin).

C

Cabinet Office (2008) *The National Security Strategy of the United Kingdom: Security in an Interdependent World*, http://interactive.cabinetoffice.gov.uk, accessed 20 December 2008.

Calhoun, C. (1997) *Nationalism* (Buckingham: Open University Press).

Calhoun, J. (1851) [2007 edn] *Disquisition on Government*, ed. H. Cheek (South Bend, IN: St Augustine's Press).

Calleros-Alarcón, J. (2008) *The Unfinished Transition to Democracy in Latin America* (New York: Routledge).

Campbell, A., Converse, P., Miller, A. and Stokes, D. (1960) *The American Voter* (New York: Wiley).

Canel, E. (1992) 'Democratization and the Decline of Urban Social Movements in Uruguay: A Political Institutional Account', in *The Making of Social Movements in Latin America: Identity, Strategy and Democracy*, ed. A. Escobar and S. Alvarez (Boulder, CO: Westview) pp. 276–90.

Carey, J., Niemi, R., Powell, L. and Moncrief, G. (2006) 'The Effects of Term Limits on State Legislatures: A New Survey of the 50 States', *Legislative Studies Quarterly* (31) 105–34.

Carlyle, T. (1840) [1908 edn] *On Heroes, Hero-Worship, and the Heroic in History* (London: Dent).

Carothers, T. (2004) *Critical Mission: Essays on Democracy Promotion* (Washington, DC: Carnegie Endowment for International Peace).

Carty, K. (2002) 'Canada's Nineteenth-Century Cadre Parties at the Millennium', in *Political Parties in Advanced Industrial Democracies*, ed. P. Webb, D. Farrell and I. Holliday (Oxford: Oxford University Press) pp. 131–52.

Carty, K. (2004) 'Parties as Franchise Organizations: The Stratarchical Organizational Imperative', *Party Politics* (10) 5–24.

Case, W. (1996) 'Can the "Halfway House" Stand? Semi-Democracy and Elite Theory in Three Southeast Asian Countries', *Comparative Politics* (28) 437–64.

CAWP (Center for American Women and Politics) (2012) *Gender Differences in Voter Turnout*, http://www.cawp.rutgers.edu, accessed 31 May 2012.

Center for Responsive Politics (2012) *The Money behind the Elections*, http://www.opensecrets.org, accessed 2 December 2012.

Chabal, P. and Daloz, J.-P. (2006) *Culture Troubles: Politics and the Interpretation of Meaning* (London: Hurst).

Chari, R., Murphy, G. and Hogan, J. (2010) *Regulating Lobbying: A Global Comparison* (Manchester: Manchester University Press).

Chazan, N., Lewis, P., Mortimer, R., Rothchild, D. and Stedman, S. (1999) *Politics and Society in Contemporary Africa*, 3rd edn (Boulder, CO: Lynne Rienner).

Chehabi, H. and Linz, J. (eds) (1998) *Sultanistic Regimes* (Baltimore, MD: Johns Hopkins University Press).

Cheibub, J. (2002) 'Minority Governments, Deadlock Situations and the Survival of Presidential Democracies', *Comparative Political Studies* (35) 284–312.

Chen, J. and Malhotra, N. (2007) 'The Law of 1/n: The Effect of Chamber Size on Government Spending in Bicameral Legislatures', *American Political Science Review* (101) 657–76.

Chesterman, S., Ignatieff, M. and Thakur, R. (eds) (2005) *Making States Work: State Failure and the Crisis of Governance* (New York: United Nations University Press).

ChinaToday.com (2009) *Communist Party of China*, http://www.chinatoday.com, accessed 18 April 2009.

Christensen, T and Lægreid, P. (2007) 'Theoretical Approach and Research Questions', in *Transcending New Public Management: The Transformation of Public Sector Reforms*, ed. T. Christensen and P. Lægreid (Farnham: Ashgate) pp. 1–16.

CIA (Central Intelligence Agency) (2012) *The World Factbook*, https://www.cia.gov/cia/publications/factbook/index.html, accessed on various dates.

Cigler, C. and Loomis, B. (eds) (2012) *Interest Group Politics*, 8th edn (Washington: Congressional Quarterly Press).

Clark, S. (1995) *State and Status: The Rise of the State and Aristocratic Power in Western Europe* (Montreal and Kingston: McGill-Queen's University Press).

Clayton, C. and Gillman, H. (1999) 'Beyond Judicial Decision Making', in *The Supreme Court in American Politics: New Institutionalist Approaches*, ed. C. Clayton and H. Gillman (Lawrence, KS: University Press of Kansas) pp. 1–12.

Coase, R. (1960) 'The Problem of Social Cost', *Journal of Law and Economics* (3) 1–44.

Cohen, M., March, J. and Olsen, J. (1972) 'A Garbage Can Model of Organizational Choice', *Administrative Science Quarterly* (17) 1–25.

Colebatch, H. (1998) *Policy* (Buckingham: Open University Press).

Colomer, J. (ed.) (2004a) *Handbook of Electoral System Choice* (Basingstoke: Palgrave Macmillan).

Colomer, J. (2004b) 'The Strategy and History of Electoral System Choice', in *Handbook of Electoral System Choice*, ed. J. Colomer (Basingstoke: Palgrave Macmillan) pp. 3–80.

Common Cause (2012) *About Us* (Washington, DC: Common Cause), http://www.commoncause.org, accessed 28 June 2012.

Conley, P. (2001) *Presidential Mandates: How Elections Shape the National Agenda* (Chicago: University of Chicago Press).

Conradt, D. (2008) *The German Polity*, 9th edn (New York: Longman).

Corbett, R., Jacobs, F. and Shackleton, M. (2011) *The European Parliament*, 8th edn (London: John Harper).

Corbridge, S., Harriss, J. and Jeffrey, C. (2012) *India Today: Economy, Politics and Society* (Cambridge: Polity).

Corner, J. and Pels, D. (eds) (2003) *Media and the Restyling of Politics: Consumerism, Celebrity, Cynicism* (London: Sage).

Corrigan, B. and Brader, T. (2011) 'Campaign Advertising: Reassessing the Impact of Campaign Ads on Political Behavior', in *New Directions in Campaigns and Elections*, ed. S. Medvic (New York: Routledge) pp. 79–97.

Cotta, M. and Best, H. (eds) (2007) *Democratic Representation in Europe: Diversity, Change and Convergence* (Oxford: Oxford University Press).

Cotta, M. and Verzichelli, L. (2007) *Political Institutions in Italy* (Oxford: Oxford University Press).

Cox, G. and Morgenstern, S. (2002) 'Latin America's Reactive Assemblies and Proactive Presidents', in *Legislative Politics in Latin America*, ed. S. Morgenstern and B. Nacif (New York: Cambridge University Press) pp. 446–68.

Creveld, M. van (1999) *The Rise and Decline of the State* (Cambridge: Cambridge University Press).

Crick, B. (2005) *In Defence of Politics*, 5th edn (London: Continuum).

Cronin, T. and Genovese, M. (2012) *The Paradoxes of the American Presidency*, 4th edn (New York: Oxford University Press).

Cross, W. and Blais, A. (2012a) *Politics at the Centre: The Selection and Removal of Party Leaders in the Anglo Parliamentary Democracies* (Oxford: Oxford University Press).

Cross, W. and Blais, A. (2012b) 'Who Selects the Party Leader?' *Party Politics* (18) 127–50.

Cross, W. and Katz, R. (eds) (2013) *The Challenges of Intra-Party Democracy* (Oxford: Oxford University Press).

Crotty, W. (2006) 'Party Transformations: The United States and Western Europe', in *Handbook of Party Politics*, ed. R. Katz and W. Crotty (Thousand Oaks, CA: Sage) pp. 499–514.

Crouch, H. (1996) *Government and Society in Malaysia* (Ithaca, NY: Cornell University Press).

Cummings, S. (2005) *Kazakhstan: Power and the Elite* (London: I. B. Tauris).

Curran, J. and Seaton, J. (2009) *Power Without Responsibility: The Press and Broadcasting in Britain*, 7th edn (London: Methuen).

D

Dahl, R. (1957) 'The Concept of Power', *Behavioral Science* (2) 201–15.

Dahl, R. (1961) *Who Governs? Democracy and Power in an American City* (New Haven, CT: Yale University Press).

Dahl, R. (1970) *After the Revolution? Authority in a Good Society* (New Haven, CT: Yale University Press).

Dahl, R. (1989) *Democracy and its Critics* (New Haven, CT: Yale University Press).

Dahl, R. (1993) 'Pluralism', in *The Oxford Companion to Politics of the World*, ed. J. Krieger (New York: Oxford University Press) pp. 704–7.

Dahl, R. (1998) *On Democracy* (New Haven, CT: Yale University Press).

Dahl, R., Shapiro, I. and Cheibub, J. (eds) (2003) *The Democracy Sourcebook* (Cambridge, MA: MIT Press).

Dahl, R. and Tufte, E. (1973) *Size and Democracy* (Stanford, CA: Stanford University Press).

Dahlerup, D. (ed.) (2006) *Women, Quotas, and Politics* (New York: Routledge).

Dalton, R. (1994) *The Green Rainbow: Environmental Groups in Western Europe* (New Haven, CT: Yale University Press).

Dalton, R. (2008a) *Citizen Politics: Public Opinion and Political Parties in Advanced Industrial Democracies,* 5th edn (Washington, DC: CQ Press).

Dalton, R. (2008b) 'Citizenship Norms and the Expansion of Political Participation', *Political Studies* (59) 76–98.

Dalton, R. and Gray, M. (2003) 'Expanding the Electoral Marketplace', in *Democracy Transformed? Expanding Political Opportunities in Advanced Industrial Democracies*, ed. B. Cain, R. Dalton and S. Scarrow (New York: Oxford University Press) pp. 23–44.

Dalton, R. and Klingemann, H.-D. (2007) 'Preface', in *The Oxford Handbook of Political Behaviour*, ed. R. Dalton and H.-D. Klingemann (Oxford: Oxford University Press) pp. vii–viii.

Dalton, R. and Sickle, A. van (2005) *The Resource, Structural and Cultural Bases of Protest* (Center for the Study of Democracy, University of California, Irvine).

Dalton, R. and Wattenberg, M. (2000) *Politics without Partisans: Political Change in Advanced Industrial Democracies* (New York: Oxford University Press).

Dalton, R., McAllister, I. and Wattenberg, M. (2000) 'The Consequences of Partisan Dealignment', in *Parties without Partisans: Political Change in Advanced Industrial Democracies*, ed. R. Dalton and M. Wattenberg (New York: Oxford University Press) pp. 37–63.

Darcy, R., Welch, S. and Clark, J. (1994) *Women, Elections and Representation*, 2nd edn (Lincoln, NE: University of Nebraska Press).

Darnstädt, T. (2012) 'Ruling Shows Court's Weakness in EU Matters', *Speigel Online International*, http://www.spiegel.de, accessed 7 December 2012.

Denters, B. and Klok, P.-J. (2005) 'The Netherlands: In Search of Responsiveness', in *Comparing Local Governance: Trends and Developments,* ed. B. Denters and L. Rose (Basingstoke: Palgrave Macmillan) pp. 65–82.

Denters, B. and Rose, L. (eds) (2005) *Comparing Local Governance: Trends and Developments* (Basingstoke: Palgrave Macmillan).

Denver, D., Carman, C. and Johns, R. (2012) *Elections and Voters in Britain*, 3rd edn (Basingstoke: Palgrave Macmillan).

Department of Health and Human Services (2012) *About HHL,* http://www.hhs.gov, accessed 2 November 2012.

Derbyshire, J. and Derbyshire, L. (1999) *Political Systems of the World* (Oxford: Helicon).

Deschouwer, K. (2005) 'The Unintended Consequences of Consociational Federalism: The Case of Belgium', in *Power Sharing: New Challenges for Divided Societies*, ed. I. O'Flynn and D. Russell (London: Pluto Press) pp. 92–106.

Deschouwer, K. (2012) *The Politics of Belgium: Governing a Divided Society*, 2nd edn (Basingstoke: Palgrave Macmillan).

Desfor Edles, L. (1998) *Symbol and Ritual in the New Spain* (Cambridge: Cambridge University Press).

DGB (Confederation of German Trade Unions) (2012) *Structure and Tasks*, http://www.dgb.de, accessed 1 October 2012.

DHS (Department of Homeland Security) (2011) *FY 2012: Budget in Brief*, http://www.dhs.gov, accessed 28 October 2011.

Diamond, L. (1992) 'Economic Development and Democracy Reconsidered', in *Re-examining Democracy: Essays in Honor of Seymour Martin Lipset*, ed. G. Marks and L. Diamond (Thousand Oaks, CA: Sage) pp. 93–131.

Dicey, A. (1885) [1959 edn] *Introduction to the Study of the Law of the Constitution,* 10th edn (London: Macmillan).

Dickson, B. (2007) 'Integrating Wealth and Power in China: The Communist Party's Embrace of the Market Sector', *China Quarterly* (192) 827–54.

Dodd, L. and Oppenheimer, B. (eds) (2012) *Congress Reconsidered,* 10th edn (Washington, DC: Congressional Quarterly Press).

Dogan, M. and Pelassy, G. (1990) *How to Compare Nations* (Chatham, NJ: Chatham House).

Doing Business (World Bank) (2012) *Measuring Business Regulations*, http://www.doingbusiness.org, accessed 12 October 2012.

Dollery, B., Garcea, J. and LeSage, E., Jr (eds) (2008) *Local Government Reform: A Comparative Analysis of Advanced Anglo-American Countries* (New York: Routledge).

Dolowitz, D. and Marsh, D. (1996) 'A Review of the Policy Transfer Literature', *Policy Studies* (44) 343–57.

Donaldson, R. (2004) 'Russia', *Journal of Legislative Studies* (10) 230–49.

Dooley, B. and Baron, S. (eds) (2001) *The Politics of Information in Early Modern Europe* (New York: Longman).

Downs, A. (1957) *An Economic Theory of Democracy* (New York: Harper).

Duch, R. and Stevenson, R. (2008) *The Economic Vote: How Political and Economic Institutions Condition Electoral Results* (New York: Cambridge University Press).

Duerst-Lahti, G. (2002) 'Knowing Congress as a Gendered Institution: Manliness and the Implications of Women in Congress', in *Women Transforming Congress*, ed. C. Rosenthal (Norman, OK: University of Oklahoma Press) pp. 20–49.

Dunleavy, D., Margetts, H., Bustow, S. and Tinkler, J. (2006) 'New Public Management is Dead – Long Live Digital Era Governance', *Journal of Public Administration Research and Theory* (16) 467–94.

Duverger, M. (1954) [1970 edn] *Political Parties* (London: Methuen).

Duverger, M. (1980) 'A New Political System Model: Semi-Presidential Government', *European Journal of Political Research* (8) 165–87.

Dye, T. (2007) *Understanding Public Policy*, 12th edn (Englewood Cliffs, NJ: Prentice-Hall).

E

Eagleton, T. (1991) *Ideology: An Introduction* (London: Verso).

Easton, D. (1965) *A Systems Analysis of Political Life* (New York: Wiley).

Eberle, J. (1990) 'Understanding the Revolutions in Eastern Europe', in *Spring in Winter: The 1989 Revolutions*, ed. G. Prins (Manchester: Manchester University Press) pp. 193–209.

Eckersley, R. (2011) 'Representing Nature', in *The Future of Representative Democracy*, ed. S. Alonso, J. Keane and W. Merkel (Cambridge: Cambridge University Press) pp. 236–57.

Eichbaum, C. and Shaw, R. (2007) 'Ministerial Advisers, Politicization and the Retreat from Westminster: The Case of New Zealand', *Public Administration* (85) 569–87.

Eigen, L. and Siegel, J. (1993) *The Macmillan Dictionary of Political Quotations* (New York: Macmillan).

Eijk, C. van der and Franklin, M. (2009) *Elections and Voters* (Basingstoke: Palgrave Macmillan).

Elazar, D. (1996) 'From Statism to Federalism: A Paradigm Shift', *International Political Science Review* (17) 417–30.

Eley, G. and Suny, R. (1996) 'From the Moment of Social History to the Work of Cultural Representation', in *Becoming National: A Reader*, ed. G. Eley and R. Suny (New York: Oxford University Press) pp. 3–37.

Elgie, R. (ed.) (1999) *Semi-Presidentialism in Europe* (Oxford: Oxford University Press).

Elgie, R. (ed.) (2001) *Divided Government in Comparative Perspective* (Oxford: Oxford University Press).

Elgie, R. (ed.) (2003) *Political Institutions in Contemporary France* (Oxford: Oxford University Press).

Elgie, R. (2011) *Semi-Presidentialism: Sub-Types and Democratic Performance* (Oxford: Oxford University Press).

Eliadis, P., Hill, M. and Howlett, M. (eds) (2005) *Designing Government: From Instruments to Governance* (Montreal and London: McGill-Queen's University Press).

Elkit, J., Svensson, P. and Togeby, L. (2005) 'Why is Voter Turnout Not Declining in Denmark?', paper prepared for delivery at the *Annual Meeting of the American Political Science Association*, Washington, DC.

Elster, J. (1989) *Nuts and Bolts for the Social Sciences* (Cambridge: Cambridge University Press).

Endersby, J., Petrocik, J. and Shaw, D. (2006) 'Electoral Mobilization in the United States', in *Handbook of Party Politics*, ed. R. Katz and W. Crotty (Thousand Oaks, CA: Sage) pp. 316–36.

Engels, F. (1844) [1999 edn] *The Condition of the Working Class in England in 1844*, ed. D. McLellan (Oxford: Oxford University Press).

Erikson, R., Mackuen, M. and Stimson, J. (2002) *The Macro Polity* (Cambridge: Cambridge University Press).

Esman, M. (1996) 'Diasporas and International Relations', in *Ethnicity*, ed. J. Hutchinson and A. Smith (Oxford: Oxford University Press) pp. 316–20.

Esmer, Y. and Pettersson, T. (2007) 'The Effects of Religion and Religiosity on Voting Behavior' in *The Oxford Handbook of Political Behavior*, ed. R. Dalton and H.-D. Klingemann (Oxford: Oxford University Press) pp. 481–503.

Eulau, H. (1963) *The Behavioral Persuasion in Politics* (New York: Random House).

Europa (2012) *The European Commission*, http://www.europa.eu, accessed 28 October 2012.

European Ombudsman (2012) *European Ombudsman*, http://www.ombudsman.europa.eu, accessed 11 January 2012.

Evans, A., Jr (2005) 'A Russian Civil Society?', in *Developments in Russian Politics 6*, ed. S. White, Z. Gitelman and R. Sakwa (Basingstoke: Palgrave Macmillan) pp. 96–113.

Evans, G. and de Graaf, N. (eds) (2012) *Political Choice Matters: Explaining the Strength of Class and Religious Cleavages in Cross-National Perspective* (Oxford: Oxford University Press).

Ezrow, N. and Frantz, E. (2011) *Dictators and Dictatorships: Understanding Authoritarian Regimes and Their Leaders* (New York: Continuum).

F

Falconer, C. (2006) 'History', *Judicial Appointments Commission*, http://www.judicialappointments.gov.uk, accessed 4 August 2006.

Farcau, B. (1994) *The Coup: Tactics in the Seizure of Power* (Westport, CT: Praeger).

Farnen, R. and Meloen, J. (eds) (2000) *Democracy, Authoritarianism and Education* (Basingstoke: Macmillan).

Farr, J. (1995) 'Remembering the Revolution: Behavioralism in American Politics Science' in *Political Science in History: Research Programs and Political Traditions*, ed. J. Farr, J. Dryzek and S. Leonard (New York: Cambridge University Press) pp. 198–224.

Farrell, D. (2011) *Electoral Systems: A Comparative Introduction*, 2nd edn (Basingstoke: Palgrave Macmillan).

Fesler, J. and Kettl, D. (2011) *The Politics of the Administrative Process*, 5th edn (Washington, DC: CQ Press).

Fiers, S. and Krouwel, A. (2005) 'The Low Countries: From "Prime Minister" to President-Minister', in *The Presidentialization of Politics: A Comparative Study of Modern Democracies*, ed. T. Poguntke and P. Webb (Oxford: Oxford University Press) pp. 128–58.

Finer, S. (1966) *Anonymous Empire: A Study of the Lobby in Great Britain* (London: Pall Mall).

Finer, S. (1970) *Comparative Government* (Harmondsworth: Penguin).

Finer, S. (1997) *The History of Government from the Earliest Times*, 3 vols (Oxford: Oxford University Press).

Finnemore, M. (1996) *National Interests in International Society* (Ithaca, NY: Cornell University Press).

Fiorina, M. (1981) *Retrospective Voting in American National Elections* (New Haven, CT: Yale University Press).

Fish, S. and Kroenig, M. (2009) *The Handbook of National Legislatures: A Global Survey* (New York: Cambridge University Press).

Fisher, J. and Eisenstadt, T. (2004) 'Comparative Party Finance: What Is To Be Done?' *Party Politics* (10) 619–26.

Fishkin, J. (1991) *Democracy and Deliberation: New Directions for Democratic Reform* (New Haven, CT: Yale University Press).

Fishkin, J. (2011) *When the People Speak: Deliberative Democracy and Public Consultation* (New York: Oxford University Press).

Flammang, J., Gordon, D., Lukes, T. and Smorsten, K. (1990) *American Politics in a Changing World* (Pacific Grove, CA: Brooks/Cole).

Foley, M. (1999) 'In Kiev They Fine a Journalist $1m and Cut Off All the Phones', *The Times*, 2 April, p. 45.

Folkes, A. (2004) 'The Case for Votes at 16', *Representation* (41) 101–6.

Foweraker, T., Landman, T. and Harvey, N. (2003) *Governing Latin America* (Cambridge: Polity).

Fox, R. and Ramos, J. (2012a) 'Politics in the New Media Era', in *iPolitics: Citizens, Elections and Governing*, ed. R. Fox and J. Ramos (New York: Cambridge University Press) pp. 1–21.

Fox, R. and Ramos, J. (eds) (2012b) *iPolitics: Citizens, Elections and Governing* (New York: Cambridge University Press).

Franklin, M. (1992) 'The Decline of Cleavage Politics', in *Electoral Change: Responses to Evolving Social and Attitudinal Structures in Western Countries,* ed. M. Franklin, T. Mackie and H. Valen (Cambridge: Cambridge University Press) pp. 383–405.

Franklin, M. (2004) *Voter Turnout and the Dynamics of Electoral Competition in Established Democracies* (Cambridge: Cambridge University Press).

Franklin, M. and Webber, T. (2010) 'American Electoral Practices in Comparative Perspective', in *The Oxford Handbook of American Elections and Political Behavior*, ed. J. Leighley (Oxford: Oxford University Press) pp. 667–84.

Freedom House (2011) *Freedom in the World,* http://www.freedomhouse.org, accessed on various dates.

Friedrich, C. (1937) *Constitutional Government and Politics* (New York: Harper).

Frolic, B. (1997) 'State-Led Civil Society' in *Civil Society in China,* ed. T. Brook and B. Frolic (Armonk, NY: M. E. Sharpe) pp. 46–67.

Fukuyama, F. (1992) *The End of History and the Last Man* (New York: Free Press).

Fukuyama, F. (2004) *State Building: Governance and World Order in the Twenty-First Century* (Ithaca, NY: Cornell University Press).

Fuller, G. (2002) 'The Future for Political Islam', *Foreign Affairs* (81) 48–60.

Fuller, L. (1969) *The Morality of Law* (New Haven, CT: Yale University Press).

Fund for Peace (2011) *Failed States Index,* http://www.fundforpeace.org, accessed 9 October 2011.

G

Gaffney, J. (2012) *Political Leadership in France: From Charles de Gaulle to Nicolas Sarkozy* (Basingstoke: Palgrave Macmillan).

Gagnon, A.-G. and Tully, J. (eds) (2001) *Multinational Democracies* (Cambridge: Cambridge University Press).

Gallagher, M., Laver, M. and Mair, P. (2011) *Representative Government in Modern Europe: Institutions, Parties, and Governments*, 5th edn (Maidenhead: McGraw-Hill).

Gallagher, M. and Mitchell, P. (eds) (2005) *The Politics of Electoral Systems* (Oxford: Oxford University Press).

Gallie, W. (1956) 'Essentially Contested Concepts', *Proceedings of the Aristotelian Society* (56) 157–97.

Gallup (2012) *Election Polls – Accuracy Record in Presidential Elections,* http://www.gallup.com, accessed 21 September 2012.

Gamble, A. (2009) *The Spectre at the Feast: Capitalist Crisis and the Politics of Recession* (Basingstoke: Palgrave Macmillan).

Gandhi, J. (2008) *Political Institutions under Dictatorship* (New York: Cambridge University Press).

GAO (General Accountability Office) (2009) *Reports on the Government Performance and Results Act*, http://www.gao.gov, accessed 11 August 2009.

Gates, L. (2010) *Electing Chávez: The Business of Anti-Neoliberal Politics in Venezuela* (Pittsburgh, PA: University of Pittsburgh Press).

Geddes, B. (2003) *Paradigms and Sand Castles: Theory Building and Research Design in Comparative Politics* (Ann Arbor, MI: University of Michigan Press).

Geertz, C. (1973) [1993 edn] 'Thick Description: Toward an Interpretative Theory of Culture', in *Interpretation of Cultures*, ed. C. Geertz (London: Fontana) pp. 1–33.

Geissel, B. and Newton, K. (eds) (2012) *Evaluating Democratic Innovations: Curing the Democratic Malaise* (Abingdon: Routledge).

Gellner, E. (1983) *Nations and Nationalism* (Oxford: Blackwell).

George, A. (1969) 'The Operational Code: A Neglected Approach to the Study of Political Leaders and Decision-Making', *International Studies Quarterly* (13) 190–222.

George, A. and Bennett, A. (2004) *Case Studies and Theory Development in the Social Sciences* (Cambridge, MA: MIT Press).

Gerth, H. and Mills, C. Wright (1948) *From Max Weber* (London: Routledge & Kegan Paul).

Geys, B. (2006) 'Explaining Voter Turnout: A Review of Aggregate-Level Research', *Electoral Studies* (25) 637–63.

Gheissari, A. (ed.) (2009) *Contemporary Iran: Economy, Society, Politics* (New York: Oxford University Press).

Giese, K. (2012) 'The Austrian Agenda Initiative: An Instrument Dominated by Political Parties' in *Citizens' Initiatives in Europe: Procedures and Consequences of Agenda-Setting by Citizens*, ed. M. Setälä and T. Schiller (Basingstoke: Palgrave Macmillan) pp. 175–92.

Ginsborg, P. (2003) *A History of Contemporary Italy: Society and Politics, 1943–1988* (Basingstoke: Palgrave Macmillan).

Girard, P. (2006) *Paradise Lost: Haiti's Tumultuous Journey from Pearl of the Caribbean to Third World Hotspot* (Basingstoke: Palgrave Macmillan).

Gitelman, Z. (2005) 'The Democratization of Russia in Comparative Perspective', in *Developments in Russian Politics 6*, ed. S. White, Z. Gitelman and R. Sakwa (Basingstoke: Palgrave Macmillan) pp. 241–56.

Gleeson, B. and Steele, W. (2012) 'Cities' in *Contemporary Politics in Australia: Theories, Practices and Issues*, ed. R. Smith, A. Vromen and I. Cook (Melbourne: Cambridge University Press) pp. 320–31.

Golder, S. (2006) 'Pre-Election Coalition Formation in Parliamentary Democracies', *British Journal of Political Science* (36) 193–212.

Goldstone, J., Kaufmann, E. and Toft, M. (eds) (2012) *Political Demography: How Population Changes Are Reshaping International Security and National Politics* (New York: Oxford University Press).

Goldthorpe, J. (1999) 'Modelling the Pattern of Class Voting in Britain, 1964–92', in *The End of Class Politics: Class Voting in Comparative Context*, ed. G. Evans (Oxford: Oxford University Press) pp. 59–82.

Goode, J. (2010) 'Redefining Russia: Hybrid Regimes, Fieldwork, and Russian Politics', *Perspectives on Politics* (8) 1055–75.

Goodin, R. and Klingemann, H.-D. (1996) 'Political Science: The Discipline' in *A New Handbook of Political Science*, ed. R. Goodin and H.-D. Klingemann (New York: Oxford University Press) pp. 3–49.

Goodwin, J. and Jasper, J. (2003) 'Editors' Introduction', in *The Social Movements Reader: Cases and Concepts*, ed. J. Goodwin and J. Jasper (Oxford: Blackwell) pp. 3–7.

Goren, P. (2012) *On Voter Competence* (New York: Oxford University Press).

Gott, R. (2011) *Hugo Chávez and the Bolivarian Revolution*, 2nd edn (London: Verso).

Gould, D. (1980) 'Patrons and Clients: The Role of the Military in Zaire Politics', in *The Performance of Soldiers as Governors*, ed. I. Mowoe (Washington, DC: University Press of America) pp. 473–92.

Graber, D. (2009) *Mass Media and American Politics*, 8th edn (Washington, DC: CQ Press).

Graber, M. (2008) 'Constitutional Law and American Politics' in *The Oxford Handbook of Law and Politics*, ed. K. Whittington, R. Kelemen and G. Caldeira (Oxford: Oxford University Press) pp. 300–20.

Green, D. (ed.) (2002) *Constructivism and Comparative Politics* (Armonk, NY: M.E. Sharpe).

Green, D. and Shapiro, I. (1994) *Pathologies of Rational Choice Theory: A Critique of Applications in Political Science* (New Haven, CT: Yale University Press).

Green, J. (2010a) *The Eyes of the People: Democracy in an Age of Spectatorship* (New York: Oxford University Press).

Green, J. (2010b) 'Gauging the God Gap: Religion and Voting in US Presidential Elections' in *The Oxford Handbook of American Elections and Political Behavior*, ed. J. Leighley (Oxford: Oxford University Press) pp. 433–49.

Green, S., Hough, D. and Miskimmon, A. (2011) *The Politics of the New Germany*, 2nd edn (Abingdon: Routledge).

Greenwood, J. (2011) *Interest Representation in the European Union*, 3rd edn (Basingstoke: Palgrave Macmillan).

Gregorian, V. (2004) *Islam: A Mosaic, Not a Monolith* (Washington, DC: Brookings Institution Press).

Grugel, J. (2002) *Democratization: A Critical Introduction* (Basingstoke: Palgrave Macmillan).

Guardian, The (2012) *The World's Top 10 Newspaper Websites*, http://www.guardian.co.uk, accessed 25 May 2012.

Guarnieri, C. (2003) 'Courts as an Instrument of Horizontal Accountability: The Case of Latin Europe', in *Democracy and the Rule of Law*, ed. J. Maravall and A. Przeworski (New York: Cambridge University Press) pp. 223–41.

Guarnieri, C. and Pederzoli, P. (2002) *The Power of Judges: A Comparative Study of Courts and Democracy*, trans. C. Thomas (Oxford: Oxford University Press).

Guehenno, J.-M. (1995) *The End of the Nation-State* (Minneapolis, MN: University of Minnesota Press).

Guo, G. (2007) 'Organizational Involvement and Political Participation in China', *Comparative Political Studies* (40) 457–82.

Gunther, R. and Montero, J. (2009) *The Politics of Spain* (Cambridge: Cambridge University Press).

Gunther, R., Montero, J. and Botella, J. (2011) *Democracy in Modern Spain* (New Haven, CT: Yale University Press).

Gurr, T. (1980) *Why Men Rebel* (Princeton, NJ: Princeton University Press).

H

Hacker, J. and Pierson, P. (2010) *Winner-Take-All Politics: How Washington Made the Rich Richer – And Turned Its Back on the Middle Class* (New York: Simon & Schuster).

Haerpfer, C., Bernhagen, P., Inglehart, R. and Welzel, C. (eds) (2009) *Democratization* (Oxford: Oxford University Press).

Hallin, D. and Mancini, P. (2004) *Comparing Media Systems: Three Models of Media and Politics* (Cambridge: Cambridge University Press).

Hallin, D. and Mancini, P. (eds) (2012) *Comparing Media Systems Beyond the Western World* (Cambridge: Cambridge University Press).

Halperin, S. and Heath, O. (2012) *Political Research: Methods and Practical Skills* (Oxford: Oxford University Press, 2012).

Hamilton, A. (1788a) [1970 edn] *The Federalist*, No. 70, intro W. Brock (London: Dent) pp. 357–63.

Hamilton, A. (1788b) [1970 edn] *The Federalist*, No. 84, intro W. Brock (London: Dent) pp. 436–45.

Hamilton, A. (1788c) [1970 edn] *The Federalist*, No. 45, intro W. Brock (London: Dent) pp. 233–8.

Hamilton, A. (1788d) [1970 edn] *The Federalist*, No. 51, intro W. Brock (London: Dent) pp. 263–7.

Hamilton, A. (1788e) [1970 edn] *The Federalist*, No. 62, intro W. Brock (London: Dent) pp. 314–20.

Hamilton, A. (1788f) [1970 edn] *The Federalist*, No. 69, intro W. Brock (London: Dent) pp. 350–6.

Hamilton, R. (1987) 'The Elements of the Concept of Ideology', *Political Studies* (35) 18–38.

Hammerstad, A. (2011) 'Population Movement and Its Impact on World Politics', in *Issues in 21st Century World Politics*, ed. M. Beeson and N. Bisley (Basingstoke: Palgrave Macmillan) pp. 238–50.

Han, L. (ed.) (2011) *New Directions in the American Presidency* (New York: Routledge).

Hancock, M. and Krisch, H. (2008) *Politics in Germany* (Washington, DC: CQ Press).

Hansard Society (2012) *Audit of Political Engagement 9: The 2012 Report*, http://www.hansardsociety.org.uk, accessed 28 May 2012.

Hansen, M. (1999) *The Athenian Democracy in the Age of Demosthenes* (Norman, OK: University of Oklahoma Press).

Hansen, R. and Weil, P. (eds) (2002) *Dual Nationality, Social Rights and Federal Citizenship in the U.S. and Europe* (New York: Berghahn).

Hardin, R. (2006) *Trust* (Cambridge: Polity).

Hare, T. (1873) *The Election of Representatives, Parliamentary and Municipal*, 4th edn (London: Longmans, Green, Reader & Dyer).

Harrop, M. and Miller, W. (1987) *Elections and Voters: A Comparative Introduction* (London: Macmillan).

Hartley, T. (2010) *The Foundations of European Law*, 7th edn (Oxford: Clarendon Press).

Hartlyn, J. (1998) 'The Trujillo Regime in the Dominican Republic', in *Sultanistic Regimes*, ed. H. Chehabi and J. Linz (Baltimore, MD: Johns Hopkins University Press) pp. 85–112.

Hay, C., Lister, M. and Marsh, D. (2005) *The State: Theories and Issues* (Basingstoke: Palgrave Macmillan).

Hayward, J. (1994) 'Ideological Change: The Exhaustion of the Revolutionary Impulse', in *Developments in French Politics,* ed. R. Hall, J. Hayward and H. Machin (London: Macmillan) pp. 15–32.

Hazan, R. (2002) 'Candidate Selection', in *Comparing Democracies 2: New Challenges in the Study of Elections and Voting,* ed. L. LeDuc, R. Niemi and P. Norris (Thousand Oaks, CA: Sage) pp. 108–26.

Hazan, R. and Rahat, G. (2010) *Democracy within Parties: Candidate Selection Methods and Their Political Consequences* (Oxford: Oxford University Press).

Heater, D. (1999) *What is Citizenship?* (Cambridge: Polity).

Heclo, H. (1974) *Modern Social Policies in Britain and Sweden* (New Haven, CT: Yale University Press).

Heclo, H. (1978) 'Issue Networks and the Executive Establishment', in *The New American Political System,* ed. A. King (Washington, DC: American Enterprise Institute) pp. 87–124.

Heffernan, R., Cowley, P. and Hay, C. (eds) (2011) *Developments in British Politics 9* (Basingstoke: Palgrave Macmillan).

Held, D. (2006) *Models of Democracy,* 3rd edn (Cambridge: Polity).

Hellinger, D. (2003) 'Political Overview: The Breakdown of *Puntofijismo* and the Rise of *Chavismo*', in *Venezuelan Politics in the Chávez Era: Class, Polarization and Conflict,* ed. S. Ellner and D. Hellinger (Boulder, CO: Lynne Rienner), pp. 27–54.

Helms, L. (2005) *Presidents, Prime Ministers and Chancellors: Executive Leadership in Western Democracies* (Basingstoke: Palgrave Macmillan).

Hellwig, T. (2010) 'Elections and the Economy' in *Comparing Democracies 3: New Challenges in the Study of Elections and Voting,* ed. L. LeDuc, R. Niemi and P. Norris (Thousand Oaks, CA: Sage) pp. 184–201.

Herb, M. (1999) *All in the Family: Absolutism, Revolution and Democracy in the Middle Eastern Monarchies* (Albany, NY: State University of New York Press).

Herb, M. (2005) 'Princes, Parliaments, and the Prospects for Democracy in the Gulf', in *Authoritarianism in the Middle East,* ed. M. Posusney and M. Angrist (Boulder, CO: Lynne Rienner) pp. 169–92.

Herbst, J. (2001) 'Political Liberalization in Africa after 10 Years', *Comparative Politics* (33) 357–75.

Herbst, S. (1998) *Reading Public Opinion: How Political Actors View The Political Process* (Chicago: University of Chicago Press).

Hershberg, E. (2006) 'Technocrats, Citizens and Second-Generation Reforms: Colombia's Andean Malaise', in *State and Society in Conflict: Comparative Perspectives on the Andean Crisis,* ed. P. Drake and E. Hershberg (Pittsburgh, PA: University of Pittsburgh Press) pp. 134–56.

Hetherington, M. (2004) *Why Trust Matters: Declining Political Trust and the Demise of Political Liberalism* (Princeton, NJ: Princeton University Press).

Heywood, A. (2012) *Political Ideologies: An Introduction,* 5th edn (Basingstoke: Palgrave Macmillan).

Heywood, P. (1995) *The Government and Politics of Spain* (Basingstoke: Macmillan).

Hibbs, D., Jr (2006) 'Voting and the Macroeconomy' in *The Oxford Handbook of Political Economy,* ed. B. Weingast and D. Wittman (Oxford: Oxford University Press) pp. 565–86.

Hibbs, D., Jr (2012) *Obama's Re-election Prospects under "Bread and Peace" Voting in the 2012 US Presidential Election,* http://www.douglas-hibbs.com, accessed 5 December 2012.

Hill, L. (2002) 'On the Rightness of Compelling Citizens to "Vote": The Australian Case', *Political Studies* (50) 80–101.

Hill, M. and Hupe, P. (2002) *Implementing Public Policy: Governance in Theory and Practice* (Thousand Oaks, CA: Sage).

Hillygus, D. (2010) 'Campaign Effects on Vote Choice' in *The Oxford Handbook of American Elections and Political Behavior,* ed. J. Leighley (Oxford: Oxford University Press) pp. 326–45.

Hindmoor, A. (2010) 'Rational Choice' in *Theory and Methods in Political Science,* 3rd edn, ed. D. Marsh and G. Stoker (Basingstoke: Palgrave Macmillan) pp. 42–59.

Hirschl, R. (2004) *Towards Juristocracy: The Origins and Consequences of the New Constitutionalism* (Cambridge, MA: Harvard University Press).

Hirschl, R. (2008) 'The Judicialization of Politics' in *The Oxford Handbook of Law and Politics,* ed. K. Whittington, R. Kelemen and G. Caldeira (Oxford: Oxford University Press) pp. 119–41.

Hix, S. and Hoyland (2012) *The Political System of the European Union,* 3rd edn (Basingstoke: Palgrave Macmillan).

HMG (Her Majesty's Government) (2010) *A Strong Britain in an Age of Uncertainty: Britain's National Security Strategy* (London: Stationery Office).

Hobbes, T. (1651) [1968 edn] *Leviathan,* ed. M. Oakeshott (Toronto: Crowell-Collier).

Hogwood, B. and Gunn, L. (1984) *Policy Analysis for the Real World* (Oxford: Oxford University Press).

Holbrook, T. (1996) *Do Campaigns Matter?* (Thousand Oaks, CA: Sage).

Holmberg, S. and Oscarsson, H. (2011) 'Party Leader Effects on the Vote' in *Political Leaders and Democratic Elections,* ed. K. Aarts, A. Blais and H. Schmitt (Oxford: Oxford University Press) pp. 35–51.

Holmes, L. (1997) *Postcommunism: An Introduction* (Cambridge: Polity).

Hood, C. (1996) 'Exploring Variations in Public Management Reform in the 1990s', in *Civil Service Systems in Comparative Perspective,* ed. H. Bekke, J. Perry and T. Toonen (Bloomington, IN: Indiana University Press) pp. 268–87.

Hood, C., James, O., Scott, C., Jones, G. and Travers, T. (1999) *Regulation Inside Government: Waste-Watchers, Quality Police and Sleaze-Busters* (Oxford: Oxford University Press).

Hood, C., Rothstein, H. and Baldwin, R. (2004) *The Government of Risk: Understanding Risk Regulation Regimes* (New York: Oxford University Press).

Hooghe, L. and Marks, G. (2001) *Multilevel Governance and European Integration* (Lanham, MD: Rowman & Littlefield).

Hooghe, L., Marks, G. and Schakel, A. (2010) *The Rise of Regional Authority: A Comparative Study of 42 Democracies* (Abingdon: Routledge).

Horowitz, D. (2002) 'Constitutional Design: Proposals versus Processes', in *The Architecture of Democracy: Constitutional Design, Conflict Management and Democracy* (New York: Oxford University Press) pp. 15–36.

Horowitz, D. (2006) 'Constitutional Courts: Primer for Decision-Makers', *Journal of Democracy* (17) 125–37.

House of Commons Procedure Committee (2009) *Written Parliamentary Questions*, http://www.publications.parliament.uk, accessed 11 December 2012.

Hrebenar, R. (1997) *Interest Group Politics in America*, 3rd edn (Englewood Cliffs, NJ: Prentice-Hall).

Hughes, M. (2011) 'Intersectionality, Quotas, and Minority Women's Political Representation Worldwide', *American Political Science Review* (105) 604–20.

Hull, A. (1999) 'Comparative Political Science: An Inventory and Assessment since the 1980s', *Political Science and Politics* (32) 117–24.

Huntington, S. (1968) *Political Order in Changing Societies* (New Haven, CT: Yale University Press).

Huntington, S. (1970) 'Social and Institutional Dynamics of One-Party Systems', in *Authoritarian Politics in Modern Society: The Dynamics of Established One-Party Systems*, ed. S. Huntington and C. Moore (New York: Basic Books) pp. 3–47.

Huntington, S. (1991) *The Third Wave: Democratization in the Late Twentieth Century* (Norman, OK: University of Oklahoma Press).

Huntington, S. (1993) 'Clash of Civilizations', *Foreign Affairs* (72) 22–49.

Huntington, S. (1996) *The Clash of Civilizations and the Making of World Order* (New York: Simon & Schuster).

Hutter, B. (2005) 'Risk Management and Governance', in *Designing Government: From Instruments to Governance*, ed. P. Eliadis, M. Hill and M. Howlett (Montreal: McGill-Queen's University Press) pp. 303–21.

I

IDEA (International Institute for Democracy and Electoral Assistance) (2006) *Engaging the Electorate: Initiatives to Promote Voter Turnout From Around the World*, http://www.idea.int, accessed 13 June 2006.

IDEA (International Institute for Democracy and Electoral Assistance) (2008) *Direct Democracy*, http://www.idea.int, accessed 17 April 2009.

IDEA (International Institute for Democracy and Electoral Assistance) (2012) *Political Finance Regulations Around the World: An Overview of the International IDEA Database*, http://www.idea.int, accessed 21 September 2012.

Ignazi, P. (2006) *Extreme Right Parties in Western Europe* (Oxford: Oxford University Press).

IMF (International Monetary Fund) (2011) *World Economic Outlook: September 2011*, http://www.imf.org, accessed 6 October 2011.

Immigrant Voting Project (2012) *Current Immigrant Voting Rights*, http://www.immigrantvoting.org, accessed 5 July 2012.

Inglehart, R. (1971) 'The Silent Revolution in Europe: Intergenerational Change in Post-Industrial Societies', *American Political Science Review* (65) 991–1017.

Inglehart, R. (1990) *Culture Shift in Advanced Industrial Society* (Princeton, NJ: Princeton University Press).

Inglehart, R. (1997) *Modernization and Postmodernization: Cultural, Economic and Social Change in 43 Societies* (Princeton, NJ: Princeton University Press).

Inglehart, R. (1999) 'Postmodernization Erodes Respect for Authority, but Increases Support for Democracy', in *Critical Citizens: Global Support for Democratic Governance*, ed. P. Norris (New York: Oxford University Press) pp. 236–56.

Inglehart, R. (2000) 'Political Culture and Democratic Institutions', paper prepared for the *Annual Conference of the American Political Science Association*, Washington, DC.

Inglehart, R. and Welzel, C. (2005) *Modernization, Cultural Change and Democracy: The Human Development Sequence* (Cambridge: Cambridge University Press).

Inglehart, R. and Welzel, C. (2010) 'Changing Mass Priorities: The Link between Modernization and Democracy', *Perspectives on Politics* (8) 551–67.

Internet World Stats (2011) *Internet Usage Stats: The Big Picture*, http://www.internetworldstats.com, accessed 24 April 2009.

Inwood, G. (2012) *Understanding Canadian Federalism: An Introduction to Theory and Practice* (Don Mills, Ontario: Pearson Education Canada).

IOM (International Organization for Migration) (2010) *World Migration Report* (Geneva: IOM).

Ipsos-Mori (2008) *Hansard Society: Audit of Political Engagement 6*, http://www.ipsos-mori.com, accessed 7 April 2009.

IPU (Inter-Parliamentary Union) (2012) *Parline Database on National Parliaments*, http://www.ipu.org, accessed on various dates.

Ivaldi, G. (2006) 'Beyond France's 2005 Referendum on the European Constitutional Treaty', *West European Politics* (29) 47–69.

Iyengar, S., Peters, M. and Kinder, D. (1982) 'Experimental Demonstrations of the "Not-So-Minimal" Consequences of Television News Programs', *American Political Science Review* (76) 848–58.

J

Jackson, K. (1994) 'Stability and Renewal: Incumbency and Parliamentary Composition', in *The Victorious Incumbent: A Threat to Democracy?* ed. A. Somit, R. Wildenmann and B. Boll (Aldershot: Dartmouth) pp. 251–77.

Jackson, R. (1990) *Quasi-states: Sovereignty, International Relations and the Third World* (Cambridge and New York: Cambridge University Press).

Jackson, R. (2007a) *Sovereignty: The Evolution of an Idea* (Cambridge: Polity).

Jackson, R. (2007b) 'Sovereignty and its Presuppositions: Before 9/11 and After', *Political Studies* (55) 297–317.

Jackson, R. and Rosberg, C. (1982) *Personal Rule in Black Africa: Prince, Autocrat, Prophet, Tyrant* (Berkeley, CA: University of California Press).

Jahn, D. (2011) 'Concerning Left and Right in Comparative Politics: Towards a Deductive Approach', *Party Politics* (17) 745–65.

Jamieson, K. and Waldman, P. (2003) *The Press Effect: Politicians, Journalists and the Stories that Shape the Political World* (New York: Oxford University Press).

Janis, I. (1982) *Groupthink: Psychological Studies of Policy Decisions and Fiascoes*, 2nd edn (Boston, MA: Houghton Mifflin).

Jasiewicz, K. (2003) 'Elections and Voting Behaviour', in *Developments in Central and East European Politics 3*, ed. S.

White, J. Batt and P. Lewis (Basingstoke: Palgrave Macmillan) pp. 173–89.

Jayal, N. (2007) 'Situating Indian Democracy', in *Democracy in India*, ed. N. Jayal (New Delhi: Oxford University Press) pp. 1–50.

Johnson, C. (1995) *Japan: Who Governs? The Rise of the Developmental State* (New York: Norton).

Johnson, D. (ed.) (2009) *Campaigning for President: Strategy and Tactics, New Voices and New Techniques* (New York: Routledge).

Jones, J. (2005) *Entertaining Politics: New Political Television and Civic Culture* (Lanham, MD: Rowman & Littlefield).

Jordan, A., Wurzel, R. and Zito, A. (2005) 'The Rise of "New" Policy Instruments in Comparative Perspective: Has Governance Eclipsed Government?', *Political Studies* (53) 477–96.

Joseph, W. (ed.) (2010) *Politics in China: An Introduction* (New York: Oxford University Press).

Joyce, P. (2002) *The Politics of Protest: Extra-Parliamentary Politics in Britain since 1970* (Basingstoke: Palgrave Macmillan).

Judge, D. and Earnshaw, D. (2008) *The European Parliament*, 2nd edn (Basingstoke: Palgrave Macmillan).

Jungar, A.-C. (2002) 'A Case of a Surplus Majority Government: The Finnish Rainbow Coalition', *Scandinavian Political Studies* (25) 57–83.

K

Kahlberg, S. (ed.) (2005) *Max Weber: Readings and Commentary on Modernity* (Oxford: Blackwell).

Kaldor, M. (2007) *Human Security* (Cambridge: Polity).

Katz, R. (1997) *Democracy and Elections* (New York: Oxford University Press).

Katz, R. and Crotty, W. (eds) (2006) *Handbook of Party Politics* (Thousand Oaks, CA: Sage).

Katz, R. and Mair, P. (1995) 'Changing Models of Party Organization and Party Democracy: The Emergence of the Cartel Party', *Party Politics* (1) 5–28.

Kavalski, E. and Zolkos, M. (eds) (2008) *Defunct Federalisms: Critical Perspectives on Federal Failure* (New York: Routledge).

Kavanagh, D. and Butler, D. (2005) *The British General Election of 2005* (Basingstoke: Palgrave Macmillan).

Kavanagh, D. and Cowley, P. (2010) *The British General Election of 2010* (Basingstoke: Palgrave Macmillan).

Kawabata, E. (2007) *Contemporary Government Reform in Japan* (Basingstoke: Palgrave Macmillan).

Keane, J. (2009) *The Life and Death of Democracy* (London: Simon & Schuster).

Kearns, D. (1976) *Lyndon Johnson and the American Dream* (New York: Harper & Row).

Keiser, L. (2011) 'Representative Bureaucracy' in *The Oxford Handbook of American Bureaucracy*, ed. R. Durant (Oxford: Oxford University Press) pp. 714–37.

Kelley, S. (1983) *Interpreting Elections* (Princeton, NJ: Princeton University Press).

Kelso, A. (2011) 'Changing Parliamentary Landscapes' in *Developments in British Politics 9*, ed. R. Heffernan, P. Cowley and C. Hay (Basingstoke: Palgrave Macmillan) pp. 51–69.

Kernell, S. (2006) *Going Public: New Strategies of Presidential Leadership*, 4th edn (Washington, DC: CQ Press).

Kerrouche, F. (2006) 'The French *Assemblée Nationale*: The Case of a Weak Legislature', *Journal of Legislative Studies* (12) 336–65.

Key, V. (1966) *The Responsible Electorate* (Cambridge, MA: Harvard University Press).

King, A. (1994) 'Ministerial Autonomy in Britain', in *Cabinet Ministers and Parliamentary Government*, ed. M. Laver and K. Shepsle (Cambridge: Cambridge University Press) pp. 203–25.

King, A. (2002a) 'Conclusions and Implications' in *Leaders' Personalities and the Outcomes of Democratic Elections*, ed. A. King (Oxford: Oxford University Press) pp. 210–221.

King, A. (ed.) (2002b) *Leaders' Personalities and the Outcomes of Democratic Elections* (Oxford: Oxford University Press).

King, G., Keohane, R. and Verba S. (1994) *Designing Social Inquiry: Scientific Inference in Qualitative Research* (Princeton, NJ: Princeton University Press).

King, S. (2007) 'Sustaining Authoritarianism in the Middle East and North Africa', *Political Science Quarterly* (122) 433–60.

Kingdon, J. (2010) *Agendas, Alternatives and Public Policy*, updated 2nd edn (New York: Longman).

Kingsley, J. (1944) *Representative Bureaucracy* (Yellow Springs, OH: Antioch).

Kirchheimer, O. (1966) 'The Transformation of the Western European Party Systems', in *Political Parties and Political Development*, ed. J. LaPalombara and M. Weiner (Princeton, NJ: Princeton University Press) pp. 177–200.

Kissinger, H. (2001) 'The Pitfalls of Universal Jurisdiction', *Foreign Affairs* (80) 86–98.

Kitschelt, H. (2007) 'Growth and Persistence of the Radical Right in Post-Industrial Democracies: Advances and Challenges in Comparative Research', *West European Politics* (30) 1176–1206.

Kittilson, M. and Schwindt-Bayer, L. (2012) *The Gendered Effect of Electoral Institutions: Political Engagement and Participation* (New York: Oxford University Press).

Klapper, J. (1960) *The Effects of Mass Communication* (New York: Free Press).

Kleinfeld, R. (2006) 'Competing Definitions of the Rule of Law', in *Promoting the Rule of Law Abroad: In Search of Knowledge*, ed. T. Carothers (Washington, DC: Carnegie Endowment for International Peace) pp. 31–74.

Knapp, A. and Wright, V. (2006) *The Government and Politics of France*, 5th edn (London: Routledge).

Knill, C. and Tosun, J. (2012) *Public Policy: A New Introduction* (Basingstoke: Palgrave Macmillan).

Knutsen, O. (1996) 'Value Orientations and Party Choice: A Comparative Study of the Relationship between Five Value Orientations and Voting Intention in Thirteen West European Democracies', in *Wahlen und Politische Einstellungen in Westlichen Demokratien*, ed. O. Gabriel and W. Falter (Frankfurt: Peter Lang) pp. 247–319.

Knutsen, O. (2006) *Class Voting in Western Europe: A Comparative Longitudinal Study* (Lanham, MD: Lexington).

Knutsen, O. (2007) 'The Decline of Social Class?' in *The Oxford Handbook of Political Behaviour*, ed. R. Dalton and H.-D. Klingemann (Oxford: Oxford University Press) pp. 457–80.

Kommers, D. (2006) 'The Federal Constitutional Court: Guardian of German Democracy', *Annals of the American Academy of Political and Social Science* (603) 111–28.

Kopecky, P. (2006) 'Political Parties and the State in Post-Communist Europe: The Nature of Symbiosis', *Journal of Communist Studies and Transition Politics* (22) 251–73.

Kornhauser, W. (1959) *The Politics of Mass Society* (Glencoe, IL: Free Press).

Kostadinova, T. (2002) 'Do Mixed Electoral Systems Matter? A Cross-National Comparison of Their Effects in Eastern Europe', *Electoral Studies* (21) 23–34.

Kreiss, D. (2012) *Taking Our Country Back: The Crafting of Networked Politics from Howard Dean to Barack Obama* (New York: Oxford University Press).

Kriesi, H. (2012) 'Direct Democracy: The Swiss Experience' in *Evaluating Democratic Innovations: Curing the Democratic Malaise*, ed. B. Geissel and K. Newton (Abingdon: Routledge) pp. 39–55.

Krook, M. (2007) 'Candidate Gender Quotas: A Framework for Analysis', *European Journal of Political Research* (46) 367–94.

Krook, M. (2009) *Quotas for Women in Politics: Gender and Candidate Selection Reform Worldwide* (New York: Oxford University Press).

Krouwel, A. (2003) 'Otto Kirchheimer and the Catch-All Party', *West European Politics* (26) 23–40.

Kudrle, R. and Marmor, T. (1981) 'The Development of Welfare States in North America', in *The Development of Welfare States in Europe and America*, ed. P. Flora and A. Heidenheimer (New Brunswick, NJ: Transaction) pp. 187–236.

Kühn, Z. (2006) 'The Judicialization of European Politics', in *Developments in European Politics*, ed. P. Heywood, E. Jones, M. Rhodes and U. Sedelmeier (Basingstoke: Palgrave Macmillan) pp. 216–36.

Kuklinski, J. and Peyton, B. (2007) 'Belief Systems and Political Decision Making', in *The Oxford Handbook of Political Behaviour*, ed. R. Dalton and H.-D. Klingemann (Oxford: Oxford University Press) pp.45–64.

Kulik, A. (2007) 'Russia's Political Parties: Deep in the Shadow of the President', in *When Parties Prosper: The Uses of Electoral Success*, ed. K. Lawson and P. Merkl (Boulder, CO: Lynne Rienner) pp. 27–42.

L

Lachapelle, R. (2009) 'The Diversity of the Canadian Francophonie', *Statistics Canada*, http://www.statcan.gc.ca, accessed 13 August 2012.

Lakatos, I. (1978) *The Methodology of Scientific Research Programmes: Philosophical Papers* Vol. 1, ed. J. Worrall and G. Curie (Cambridge: Cambridge University Press).

Landes, R. (2002) *The Canadian Polity: A Comparative Introduction*, 6th edn (Scarborough, Ontario: Prentice-Hall Canada).

Lange, M. (2009) *Lineages of Despotism and Development: British Colonialism and State Power* (Chicago: University of Chicago Press).

Langman, L. (2006) 'The Social Psychology of Nationalism', in *The Sage Handbook of Nations and Nationalism*, ed. G. Delanty and K. Kumar (London: Sage) pp. 71–83.

Lasswell, H. (1936) *Politics: Who Gets What, When, How?* (New York: McGraw-Hill).

Laver, M. (1983) *Invitation to Politics* (Oxford: Martin Robertson).

Lawson, K. (2001) 'Political Parties and Party Competition', in *The Oxford Companion to Politics of the World*, 2nd edn, ed. J. Krieger (New York: Oxford University Press) pp. 670–3.

Lazarsfeld, P. and Merton, R. (1948) [1996 edn] 'Mass Communication, Popular Taste and Organized Social Action', in *Media Studies: A Reader*, ed. P. Marris and S. Thornham (Edinburgh: Edinburgh University Press) pp. 14–24.

Le Cheminant, W. and Parrish, J. (eds) (2011) *Manipulating Democracy: Democratic Theory, Political Psychology and Mass Media* (New York: Routledge).

LeDuc, L., Niemi, R. and Norris, P. (eds) (2010) *Comparing Democracies 3: New Challenges in the Study of Elections and Voting* (Thousand Oaks, CA: Sage).

Leites, N. (1960) *American Foreign Policy* (London: George Allen).

Lelieveldt, H. and Princen, S. (2011) *The Politics of the European Union* (Cambridge: Cambridge University Press).

Lesch, A. (2004) 'Politics in Egypt', in *Comparative Politics Today: A World View*, 8th edn, ed. G. Almond, G. Bingham Powell, K. Strøm and R. Dalton (New York: Longman) pp. 581–632.

Levitsky, S. and Way, L. (2010) *Competitive Authoritarianism: Hybrid Regimes After the Cold War* (New York: Cambridge University Press).

Levy, J. (2006) 'The State Also Rises: The Roots of Contemporary State Activism', in *The State After Statism: New State Activities in the Age of Liberalization*, ed. J. Levy (Cambridge, MA: Harvard University Press) pp. 1–30.

Lewin, L. (2004) 'Sweden: Introducing Proportional Representation from Above', in *Handbook of Electoral System Choice*, ed. J. Colomer (Basingstoke: Palgrave Macmillan) pp. 265–78.

Lewin, L. (2006) *Ideology and Strategy: A Century of Swedish Politics* (New York: Cambridge University Press).

Lewis, D. (2002) 'The Politics of Agency Termination: Confronting the Myth of Agency Termination', *Journal of Politics* (64) 89–120.

Lewis-Beck, M., Nadeau, R. and Bélanger, E. (2012) *French Presidential Elections* (Basingstoke: Palgrave Macmillan).

Lewis-Beck, M., Norpoth, H., Jacoby, W. and Weisberg, H. (2008) *The American Voter Revisited* (Ann Arbor, MI: University of Michigan Press).

Lewis-Beck, M. and Stegmaier, M. (2007) 'Economic Models of Voting' in *The Oxford Handbook of Political Behavior* (Oxford: Oxford University Press) pp. 518–37.

Lichbach, M. (2009) 'Thinking and Working in the Midst of Things: Discovery, Explanation and Evidence in Comparative Politics', in *Comparative Politics: Rationality, Culture and Structure*, 2nd edn, ed. M. Lichbach and A. Zuckerman (New York: Cambridge University Press) pp. 18–71.

Lichbach, M. and Zuckerman, A. (eds) (2009) *Comparative Politics: Rationality, Culture and Structure*, 2nd edn (New York: Cambridge University Press).

Lieberman, E. (2005) 'Nested Analysis as Mixed-Method Strategy for Comparative Research', *American Political Science Review* (99) 435–52.

Liebman, B. (2007) 'China's Courts: Restricted Reform', *China Quarterly* (191) 620–38.

Lijphart, A. (1968) *The Politics of Accommodation: Pluralism and Democracy in the Netherlands* (Berkeley, CA: University of California Press).

Lijphart, A. (1977) *Democracy in Plural Societies: A Comparative Exploration* (Berkeley, CA: University of California Press).

Lijphart, A. (1979) 'Religious vs Linguistic vs Class Voting: The Crucial Experiment of Comparing Belgium, Canada, South Africa and Switzerland', *American Political Science Review* (73) 442–58.

Lijphart, A. (ed.) (1992) *Parliamentary versus Presidential Government* (Oxford: Oxford University Press).

Lijphart, A. (1999) *Patterns of Democracy: Government Forms and Performance in Thirty Six Countries* (New Haven, CT: Yale University Press).

Lijphart, A. (2000) 'The Future of Democracy: Reasons for Pessimism but also Some Optimism', *Scandinavian Political Studies* (23) 265–72.

Lijphart, A. (2002) 'The Evolution of Consociational Theory and Consociational Practices, 1965–2000', *Acta Politica* (37) 11–20.

Lin, N. and Erickson, B. (eds) (2008) *Social Capital: An International Research Program* (New York: Oxford University Press).

Lindblom, C. (1959) 'The Science of Muddling Through', *Public Administration* (19) 78–88.

Lindblom, C. (1979) 'Still Muddling, Not Yet Through', *Public Administration Review* (39) 517–26.

Lindblom, C. (1990) *Inquiry and Change: The Troubled Attempt to Understand and Shape Society* (New Haven, CT: Yale University Press).

Lindvall, J. and Rothstein, B. (2006) 'Sweden: The Fall of the Strong State', *Scandinavian Political Studies* (29) 47–63.

Linn, S., Nagler, J. and Morales, M. (2010) 'Economics, Elections, and Voting Behavior' in *The Oxford Handbook of American Elections and Political Behavior*, ed. J. Leighley (Oxford: Oxford University Press) pp. 375–96.

Linz, J. (1975) [2000 edn] *Totalitarian and Authoritarian Regimes* (Boulder, CO: Lynne Rienner).

Linz, J. and Stepan, A. (1996) *Problems of Democratic Transition and Consolidation: Southern Europe, South America, and Post-Communist Europe* (Baltimore, MD: Johns Hopkins University Press).

Linz, J. and Valenzuela, A. (eds) (1994) *The Failure of Presidential Democracy* (Baltimore, MD: Johns Hopkins University Press).

Lippman, W. (1922) *Public Opinion* (London: Allen & Unwin).

Lipset, S. (1959) 'Some Social Requisites of Democracy: Economic Development and Political Legitimacy', *American Political Science Review* (53) 69–105.

Lipset, S. (1960) [1983 edn] *Political Man* (New York: Basic Books).

Lipset, S. (1990) *Continental Divide: The Values and Institutions of the United States and Canada* (New York: Routledge).

Lipset, S. and Rokkan, S. (1967) 'Cleavage Structures, Party Systems and Voter Alignments', in *Party Systems and Voter Alignments*, ed. S. Lipset and S. Rokkan (New York: Free Press) pp. 1–65.

Listhaug, O. and Grønflaten, L. (2007) 'Civic Decline? Trends in Political Involvement in Norway, 1965–2001', *Scandinavian Political Studies* (30) 272–99.

Lively, J. (1991) 'Sièyes, Emmanuel Joseph', in *The Blackwell Encyclopaedia of Political Thought*, ed. D. Miller (Oxford: Blackwell) pp. 475–6.

Locke, J. (1690) [1970 edn] *Two Treatises of Government*, ed. P. Laslett (Cambridge: Cambridge University Press).

Loewenberg, G., Squire, P. and Kiewit, D. (eds) (2002) *Legislatures: Comparative Perspectives on Representative Assemblies* (Ann Arbor, MI: University of Michigan Press).

Loughlin, J., Hendriks, F. and Lidström, A. (eds) (2011) *The Oxford Handbook of Local and Regional Democracy in Europe* (Oxford: Oxford University Press).

Lowenstein, D. (2006) 'Legal Regulation and Protection of American Parties', in *Handbook of Party Politics*, ed. R. Katz and W. Crotty (Thousand Oaks, CA: Sage) pp. 456–70.

Lucassen, G. and Lubbers, M. (2011) 'Who Fears What? Explaining Far-Right-Wing Preference in Europe by Distinguishing Perceived Cultural and Economic Ethnic Threats', *Comparative Political Studies* (45) 547–74.

Lukes, S. (2005) *Power: A Radical View*, 2nd edn (Basingstoke: Palgrave Macmillan).

Lust-Okar, E. and Zerhouni, S. (eds) (2008) *Political Participation in the Middle East* (Boulder, CO: Lynne Rienner).

Lutz, D. (2007) *Principles of Constitutional Design* (New York: Cambridge University Press).

Lynch, M. (2011) 'After Egypt: The Limits and Promise of Online Challenges to the Authoritarian Arab State', *Perspectives on Politics* (9) 301–10.

M

Macedo, S., Berry, J., Alex-Assensoh, Y., Brintnall, M. and Campbell, D. (2005) *Democracy at Risk: How Political Choices Undermine Citizen Participation, and What We Can Do About It* (Washington, DC: Brookings).

Mackenzie, G. and Labiner, J. (2002) *Opportunity Lost: The Rise and Fall of Trust and Confidence in Government after September 11* (Washington, DC: Center For Public Service, Brookings Institution), http://www.brookings.edu/gs/cps, accessed 15 April 2006.

Mackenzie, W. (1958) *Free Elections: An Elementary Textbook* (London: Allen & Unwin).

Macpherson, C. (1977) *The Life and Times of Liberal Democracy* (Oxford: Oxford University Press).

Maddex, R. (2007) *Constitutions of the World*, 3rd edn (Washington, DC: CQ Press).

Madhukar, S. and Nagarjuna, B. (2011) 'Inflation and Growth Rates in India and China: A Perspective of Transition Economies', *IPEDR* (4) 489–92.

Madison J. (1781) [1970 edn] 'The Federalist, No. 51', in *The Federalist or, The New Constitution*, intro. W. Brock (London: Dent) pp. 263–7.

Magnette, P. (2005) *What Is the European Union? Nature and Prospects* (Basingstoke: Palgrave Macmillan).

Magone, J. (2008) *Contemporary Spanish Politics*, 2nd edn (London: Routledge).

Magyar, K. (1992) 'Military Intervention and Withdrawal in Africa: Problems and Perspectives', in *From Military to Civilian Rule*, ed. C. Danopoulos (London: Routledge) pp. 230–48.

Mahler, G. (2007) *Comparative Politics: An Institutional and Cross-National Approach*, 5th edn (Upper Saddle River, NJ: Pearson).

Mahoney, C. and Baumgartner, F. (2008) 'Converging Perspectives on Interest-Group Research in Europe and America', *West European Politics* (31) 1253–73.

Mahoney, J. (2003) 'Knowledge Accumulation in Comparative Historical Research: The Case of Democracy and Authoritarianism', in *Comparative Historical Analysis in the Social Sciences*, ed. J. Mahoney and D. Rueschmeyer (New York: Cambridge University Press) pp. 337–72.

Mahoney, J. and Rueschmeyer, D. (eds) (2003) *Comparative Historical Analysis in the Social Sciences* (New York: Cambridge University Press).

Mahoney, J. and Thelen, K. (2010) 'A Theory of Gradual Institutional Change' in *Explaining Institutional Change: Ambiguity, Agency and Power*, ed. J. Mahoney and K. Thelen (New York: Cambridge University Press) pp. 1–37.

Mainwaring, S. (1992) 'Presidentialism in Latin America', in *Parliamentary versus Presidential Government*, ed. A. Lijphart (Oxford: Oxford University Press) pp. 111–17.

Mainwaring, S. and Shugart, M. (eds) (1997) *Presidentialism and Democracy in Latin America* (New York: Cambridge University Press).

Mair, P. (1994) 'Party Organizations: From Civil Society to the State', in *How Parties Organize: Change and Adaptation in Party Organizations in Western Democracies*, ed. R. Katz and P. Mair (Thousand Oaks, CA: Sage) pp. 1–22.

Mair, P. (1996) 'Comparative Politics: An Overview', in *A New Handbook of Political Science*, ed. R. Goodin and H. Klingemann (Oxford: Oxford University Press) pp. 309–35.

Mair, P. (2006) 'Cleavages', in *Handbook of Party Politics*, ed. R. Katz and W. Crotty (Thousand Oaks, CA: Sage) pp. 371–5.

Mair, P. (2008) 'The Challenge to Party Government', *West European Politics* (31) 211–34.

Mair, P. (2009) 'Left-Right Orientations', in *The Oxford Handbook of Political Behavior*, ed. R. Dalton and H.-D. Klingemann (Oxford: Oxford University Press) pp. 206–22.

Mair, P. and van Biezen, I. (2001) 'Party Membership in Europe, 1980–2000', *Party Politics* (7) 5–22.

Maisel, L. Sandy and Berry, J. (eds) (2010) *The Oxford Handbook of American Political Parties and Interest Groups* (Oxford: Oxford University Press).

Majone, G. (1996) *Regulating Europe* (London: Routledge).

Majone, G. (2006) 'Agenda Setting', in *The Oxford Handbook of Public Policy*, ed. M. Moran, M. Rein and R. Goodin (Oxford: Oxford University Press) pp. 228–50.

Maloney, W. (2009) 'Interest Groups and the Revitalization of Democracy', *Representation* (45) 277–88.

Mammone, A. and Veltri, G. (eds) (2010) *Italy Today: The Sick Man of Europe* (London: Routledge).

Mandelbaum, M. (2007) *Democracy's Good Name: The Rise and Risks of the World's Most Popular Form of Government* (New York: PublicAffairs).

Manion, M. (2009) 'Politics in China', in *Comparative Politics Today: A World View*, 9th edn, ed. G. Almond, G. Bingham Powell, R. Dalton and K. Strøm (New York: Pearson Longman) pp. 418–65.

Mansergh, L. and Thomson, R. (2007) 'Election Pledges, Party Competition and Policy Making', *Comparative Politics* (39) 311–30.

Manza, J. and Uggen, C. (2008) *Locked Out: Felon Disenfranchisement and American Democracy* (New York: Oxford University Press).

March, D. and Olsen, J. (1984) 'The New Institutionalism: Organizational Factors in Political Life', *American Political Science Review* (78) 734–49.

Marsh, D. and Rhodes, R. (eds) (1992) *Policy Networks in British Government* (Oxford: Oxford University Press).

Marsh, D. and Stoker, G. (2010a) 'Introduction' in *Theory and Methods in Political Science*, 3rd edn, ed D. Marsh and G. Stoker (Basingstoke: Palgrave Macmillan) pp. 1–12.

Marsh, D. and Stoker, G. (eds) (2010b) *Theory and Methods in Political Science*, 3rd edn (Basingstoke: Palgrave Macmillan).

Marshall, T. (1987) [2004 edn] 'The Constitution: A Living Document', in *Judges on Judging: Views from the Bench*, ed. D. O'Brien (Washington, DC: CQ Press) pp. 178–82.

Martin, S. and Steel, G. (eds) (2008) *Democratic Reform in Japan: Assessing the Impact* (Boulder, CO: Lynne Rienner).

Marx, K. and Engels, F. (1845/6) *The German Ideology*, http://www.marxists.org, accessed 9 August 2009.

Marx, K. and Engels, F. (1848) [1967 edn] *The Communist Manifesto*, intro. G. Stedman Jones (Harmondsworth: Penguin).

Matland, R. and Studlar, D. (2004) 'Determinants of Legislative Turnover: A Cross-National Analysis', *British Journal of Political Science* (34) 87–108.

Matthews, T. (1989) 'Interest Groups', in *Politics in Australia*, ed. R. Smith and L. Watson (Sydney: Allen & Unwin) pp. 211–27.

Mayer, K. (2011) 'The Presidential Power of Unilateral Action', in *The Oxford Handbook of the American Presidency*, ed. G. Edwards III and W. Howell (Oxford: Oxford University Press) pp. 427–54.

Mayhew, D. (1991) *Divided We Govern: Party Control, Lawmaking and Investigations, 1946–1990* (New Haven, CT: Yale University Press).

Mazzoleni, G. (1987) 'Media Logic and Party Logic in Campaign Coverage: The Italian General Election of 1983', *European Journal of Communication* (2) 81–103.

McAllister, I. (2002) 'Calculating or Capricious? The New Politics of Late Deciding Voters' in *Do Political Campaign Matter? Campaign Effects in Elections and Referendums*, ed. D. Farrell and R. Schmitt-Beck, pp. 22–41.

McAllister, I. (2003) 'Australia: Party Politicians as a Political Class', in *The Political Class in Advanced Democracies*, ed. J. Borchert and J. Zeiss (Oxford: Oxford University Press) pp. 26–44.

McAllister, I. and Studlar, D. (2002) 'Electoral Systems and Women's Representation: A Long-Term Perspective', *Representation* (39) 3–14.

McCargo, D. (2012) 'Partisan Polyvalence: Characterizing the Political Role of Asian Media', in *Comparing Media Systems Beyond the Western World*, ed. D. Hallin and P. Mancini (New York: Cambridge University Press) pp. 201–23.

McCaughan, M. (2004) *The Battle of Venezuela* (London: Latin America Bureau).

McChesney, R. (1999) *Rich Media, Poor Democracies* (Urbana, IL: University of Illinois Press).

McDonnell, D. and Newell, J. (2011) 'Outsider Parties in Government in Western Europe', *Party Politics* 17 (443–52).

McEldowney, J. (2009) 'Administrative Law', in *The Concise Oxford Dictionary of Politics*, 3rd edn, ed. I. McLean and A. Macmillan (Oxford: Oxford University Press).

McFarland, A. (2010) 'Interest Group Theory', in *The Oxford Handbook of American Political Parties and Interest Groups*, ed. L. Maisel and J. Berry (Oxford: Oxford University Press) pp. 37–56.

McFaul, M. (2005) 'The Electoral System', in *Developments in Russian Politics 6*, ed. S. White, Z. Gitelman and R. Sakwa (Basingstoke: Palgrave Macmillan) pp. 61–79.

McGarry, J. and O'Leary, B. (2006) 'Consociational Theory, Northern Ireland's Conflict and its Agreement – Part 1', *Government and Opposition* (41) 43–63.

McGregor, R. (2010) *The Party: The Secret World of China's Communist Rulers* (London: Allen Lane).

McKay, D. (1999) *Federalism and European Union: A Political Economy Perspective* (Oxford: Oxford University Press).

McKay, D. (2009) *American Politics and Society*, 7th edn (Chichester: Wiley).

McLean, I. (1989) *Democracy and New Technology* (Cambridge: Polity).

Medvic, S. (ed.) (2011) *New Directions in Campaigns and Elections* (New York: Routledge).

Meguid, B. (2008) *Party Competition between Unequals: Strategies and Electoral Fortunes in Western Europe* (New York: Cambridge University Press).

Melleuish, G. (2002) 'The State in World History: Perspectives and Problems', *Australian Journal of Politics and History* (48) 322–35.

Melvin, N. (2000) *Uzbekistan: Transition to Authoritarianism on the Silk Road* (Reading: Harwood).

Meredith, M. (2006) *The Fate of Africa: From the Hopes of Freedom to the Heart of Despair* (New York: Public Affairs).

Michels, R. (1911) [1962 edn] *Political Parties* (New York: Free Press).

Mickiewicz, E. (2008) *Television, Power and the Public in Russia* (New York: Cambridge University Press).

Migdal, J. (2001) *State in Society: Studying How States and Societies Transform and Constitute One Another* (New York: Cambridge University Press).

Milbrath, L. and Goel, M. (1977) *Political Participation: How and Why Do People Get Involved in Politics*, 2nd edn (Chicago, IL: Rand McNally).

Miles, L. (2013) *The New Politics of Sweden* (London: Bloomsbury).

Mill, J. S. (1859) [1982 edn] *On Liberty* (Harmondsworth: Penguin).

Mill, J.S. (1861) [1991 edn] 'Considerations on Representative Government', in *Collected Works of John Stuart Mill*, Vol. 19, ed. J. O'Grady and B. Robson (Toronto: University of Toronto Press) pp. 371–577.

Miller, R. (2005) *Party Politics in New Zealand* (South Melbourne, Victoria: Oxford University Press).

Miller, W. (1991) *Media and Voters: Audience, Content and Influence of Press and Television at the 1987 General Election* (Oxford: Clarendon Press).

Miller, W. (1995) 'Quantitative Methods', in *Theory and Methods in Political Science*, ed. D. Marsh and G. Stoker (Basingstoke: Macmillan) pp. 154–72.

Mills, C. Wright (1956) *The Power Elite* (New York: Oxford University Press).

Mitra, S. (2011) *Politics in India: Structure, Process and Policy* (Abingdon: Routledge).

Mitra, S. (2012) 'Politics in India' in *Comparative Politics Today*, 10th edn, ed. G. Bingham, Powell, R. Dalton and K. Strøm (Glenview, IL: Pearson) pp. 568–615.

Moestrup, S. and Elgie, R. (eds) (2005) *Semi-presidentialism outside Europe* (London: Routledge).

Möller, T. (2007) 'Sweden: Still a Stable Party System?', in *When Parties Prosper: The Uses of Electoral Success*, ed. K. Lawson and P. Merkl (Boulder, CO: Lynne Rienner) pp. 27–42.

Montargil, F. (2010) 'E-Government and Government Transformation: Technical Interactivity, Political Influence and Citizen Return', in *Understanding E-Government in Europe: Issues and Challenges*, ed. P. Nixon, V. Koutrakou and R. Rawal (Abingdon: Routledge) pp. 61–77.

Moore, Barrington, Jr (1966) *Social Origins of Dictatorship and Democracy: Lord and Peasant in the Making of the Modern World* (Boston, MA: Beacon Press).

Moran, M. (2003) *The British Regulatory State: High Modernism and Hyper-Innovation* (Oxford: Oxford University Press).

Moran, M. (2011) *Politics and Governance in the UK*, 2nd edn (Basingstoke: Palgrave Macmillan)

Moran, M., Rein, M. and Goodin, R. (eds) (2006) *The Oxford Handbook of Public Policy* (Oxford: Oxford University Press).

Morel, L. (2007) 'The Rise of "Politically Obligatory" Referendums: The 2005 French Referendum in Comparative Perspective', *West European Politics* (30) 1041–67.

Morgenstern, S. (2012) *Patterns of Legislative Politics: Roll-Call Voting in Latin America and the United States* (New York: Cambridge University Press).

Morlino, L. (2010) 'Authoritarian Legacies, Politics of the Past and Quality of Democracy in Southern Europe: Open Conclusions', *South European Society and Politics* (15) 507–29.

Morlino, L. (2012) *Changes for Democracy: Actors, Structures, Processes* (Oxford: Oxford University Press).

Mosca, G. (1896) [1939 edn] *The Ruling Class* (New York: McGraw-Hill).

Mueller, J. and Stewart, M. (2011) *Terror, Security, and Money: Balancing the Risks, Benefits, and Costs and Homeland Security* (Oxford: Oxford University Press).

Mughan, A. (2000) *Media and the Presidentialization of Parliamentary Elections* (Basingstoke: Palgrave).

Mulgan, R. (1997) *Politics in New Zealand*, 2nd edn (Auckland: Auckland University Press).

Mulgan, R. (2003) *Holding Power to Account: Accountability in Modern Democracies* (Basingstoke: Palgrave Macmillan).

Müller, W. and Strøm, K. (eds) (2000a) *Coalition Governments in Western Europe* (Oxford: Oxford University Press).

Müller, W. and Strøm, K. (2000b) 'Coalition Governance in Western Europe', in *Coalition Governments in Western Europe*, ed. W. Müller and K. Strøm (Oxford: Oxford University Press) pp. 559–92.

Muñoz, H. (2006) 'The Growing Community of Democracies', in *Democracy Rising: Assessing the Global Challenge*, ed. H. Muñoz (Boulder, CO: Lynne Rienner) pp. 1–8.

Munro, W. (1925) *The Governments of Europe* (New York: Macmillan).

Murrie, M. (2006) 'Broadcasters Getting Online, Staying On Air', *eJournal USA* (11), http://usinfo.state.gov/journals/itgic/0306/ijge/ijge0306.htm, accessed 28 April 2006.

N

National Audit Office (2006) *The Role of the National Audit Office,* http://www.nao.org.uk, accessed 12 November 2006.

Ncjdrsu (National CJD Research and Surveillance Unit) (2012) *Creutzfeldt-Jakob Disease in the UK,* http://www.cjd.ed.ac.uk, accessed 16 December 2012.

Nef, J. (2003) 'Public Administration and Public Sector Reform in Latin America', in *Handbook of Public Administration,* ed. B. Guy Peters and J. Pierre (Thousand Oaks, CA: Sage) pp. 523–35.

Negretto, G. (2008) 'Political Parties and Institutional Design: Explaining Constitutional Choice in Latin America', *British Journal of Political Science* (39) 117–39.

Nelson, M. (ed.) (2009) *The Presidency and the Political System,* 9th edn (Washington, DC: CQ Press).

Neustadt, R. (1991) *Presidential Power and the Modern Presidents: The Politics of Leadership from Roosevelt to Reagan* (New York: Free Press).

Newell, J. (2010) *The Politics of Italy: Governance in a Normal Country* (Cambridge: Cambridge University Press).

Newton, K. (2006) 'May The Weak Force Be With You: The Power of the Mass Media in Modern Politics', *European Journal of Political Research* (45) 209–34.

Nicholson, P. (1990) 'Politics as the Exercise of Force', in *What is Politics?,* ed. A. Leftwich (Cambridge: Polity) pp. 41–52.

Niskanen, W. (1971) *Bureaucracy and Representative Government* (Chicago: Aldine, Atherton).

Nixon, P., Koutrakou, V. and Rawal, R. (eds) (2010) *Understanding E-Government in Europe: Issues and Challenges* (Abingdon: Routledge).

Norpoth, H. (1992) *Confidence Regained: Economics, Mrs Thatcher, and the British Voter* (Ann Arbor, MI: University of Michigan Press).

Norris, P. (1999a) 'The Growth of Critical Citizens and Its Consequences', in *Critical Citizens: Global Support for Democratic Governance,* ed. P. Norris (New York: Oxford University Press) pp. 257–72.

Norris, P. (ed.) (1999b) *Critical Citizens: Global Support for Democratic Governance* (New York: Oxford University Press).

Norris, P. (2000) *A Virtuous Circle: Political Communication in Postindustrial Societies* (Cambridge: Cambridge University Press).

Norris, P. (2009) 'New Feminist Challenges to the Study of Political Engagement', in *The Oxford Handbook of Political Behavior,* ed. R. Dalton and H.-D. Klingemann (Oxford: Oxford University Press) pp. 724–41.

Norris, P. (2011) *Democratic Deficit: Critical Citizens Revisited* (Cambridge: Cambridge University Press).

Norris, P. and Inglehart, R. (2011) *Sacred and Secular: Religion and Politics Worldwide,* 2nd edn (Cambridge: Cambridge University Press).

Norton, P. (ed.) (1990) *Legislatures* (Oxford: Oxford University Press).

NRA (National Rifle Association) (2012) *A Brief History of the NRA,* http://www.nra.org, accessed 9 September 2012.

Nugent, N. (2010) *The Government and Politics of the European Union,* 7th edn (Basingstoke: Palgrave Macmillan).

O

Oates, S. (2005) 'Media and Political Communication', in *Developments in Russian Politics* 6, ed. S. White, Z. Gitelman and R. Sakwa (Basingstoke: Palgrave Macmillan) pp. 114–29.

O'Brien, K. (2008) *Reform without Liberalization: China's National People's Congress and the Politics of Institutional Change* (New York: Cambridge University Press).

O'Connor, K., Sabato, L. and Yanus, A. (2011) *Essentials of American Government: Roots and Reform* (New York: Longman).

O'Donnell, G. (1973) *Modernization and Bureaucratic Authoritarianism: Studies in South American Politics* (Berkeley, CA: California University Press).

O'Donnell, G. (1994) 'Delegative Democracy', *Journal of Democracy* (5) 55–69.

O'Donnell, G. (2003) 'Horizontal Accountability: The Legal Institutionalization of Mistrust', in *Democratic Accountability in Latin America,* ed. S. Mainwaring and C. Welna (New York: Oxford University Press) pp. 34–54.

O'Donnell, G. and Schmitter, P. (1986) *Transitions from Authoritarian Rule: Tentative Conclusions about Uncertain Democracies* (Baltimore, MD: Johns Hopkins University Press).

O'Donnell, G., Schmitter, P. and Whitehead, L. (eds) (1986) *Transitions from Authoritarian Rule: Comparative Perspectives* (Baltimore, MD: Johns Hopkins University Press).

OECD (Organisation for Economic Co-operation and Development) (2011) *OECD.Stat Extracts,* http://stats.oecd.org, accessed on various dates.

OECD (Organisation for Economic Co-operation and Development) (2011) *50th Anniversary Vision Statement,* http://www.oecd.org, accessed 11 October 2011.

Ohr, D. and Oscarsson, H. (2011) 'Leader Traits, Leader Image, and Vote Choice', in *Political Leaders and Democratic Elections,* ed. K. Aarts, A. Blais and H. Schmitt (Oxford: Oxford University Press) pp. 187–219.

Olsen, J. (1980) 'Governing Norway: Segmentation, Anticipation and Consensus Formation', in *Presidents and Prime Ministers,* ed. R. Rose and E. Suleiman (Washington, DC: American Enterprise Institute) pp. 203–55.

Olsen, J. (2009) 'Democratic Government, Institutional Autonomy and the Dynamics of Change', *West European Politics* (32) 439–65.

Olson, D. (1994) *Legislative Institutions: A Comparative View* (New York: M.E. Sharpe).

Onuf, N. (1989) *World of Our Making: Rules and Rule in Social Theory and International Relations* (Columbia, SC: University of South Carolina Press).

Opello, W. and Rosow, S. (2004) *The Nation-State and Global Order: A Historical Introduction to Contemporary Politics,* 2nd edn (Boulder, CO: Lynne Rienner).

Orren, K. and Skowronek, S. (1995) 'Order and Time in Institutional Study: A Brief for the Historical Approach', in *Political Science in History: Research Programs and Political Traditions,* ed. J. Farr, J. Dryzek and S. Leonard (New York: Cambridge University Press) pp. 296–317.

Osborne, D. and Gaebler, T. (1992) *Reinventing Government: How the Entrepreneurial Spirit Is Transforming the Public Sector* (London: Penguin).

Ostrogorski, M. (1902) *Democracy and the Organisation of Political Parties* (London: Macmillan).

Ottaway, M. (2003) *Democracy Challenged: The Rise of Semi-Authoritarianism* (Washington, DC: Carnegie Endowment for International Peace).

Owen, R. (1993) 'The Practice of Electoral Democracy in the Arab East and North Africa: Some Lessons from Nearly a Century's Experience', in *Rules and Rights in the Middle East*, ed. E. Goldberg, R. Kasaba and J. Migdal (Seattle, WA: University of Washington Press) pp. 17–40.

Owen, R. (2004) *State, Power and Politics in the Middle East*, 3rd edn (London and New York: Routledge).

P

Page, E. and Wright, V. (eds) (2006) *From the Active to the Enabling State: The Changing Role of Top Officials in European Nations* (Basingstoke: Palgrave Macmillan).

Paine, T. (1791/2) [1984 edn] *Rights of Man* (Harmondsworth: Penguin).

Palme, J. (2006) 'Income Distribution in Sweden', *Japanese Journal of Social Security Policy* (5) 16–26.

Palmer, G. and Palmer, M. (2004) *Bridled Power: New Zealand's Constitutional Government* (South Melbourne: Oxford University Press).

Palmer, M. (2003) *Breaking the Real Axis of Evil: How to Oust the World's Last Dictators by 2025* (Lanham, MD: Rowman & Littlefield).

Panebianco, A. (1988) *Political Parties: Organization and Power* (Cambridge: Cambridge University Press).

Park, H. (1976) 'Changes in Chinese Communist Ideology', in *Comparative Communism: The Soviet, Chinese and Yugoslav Models*, ed. G. Bertsch and T. Ganschow (San Francisco: W. H. Freeman) pp. 144–50.

Parkin, F. (2002) *Max Weber*, revised edn (London: Routledge).

Parsons, C. (2010) 'Constructivism', in *Theory and Methods in Political Science*, 3rd edn, ed. D. Marsh and G. Stoker (Basingstoke: Palgrave Macmillan) pp. 80–98.

Parsons, T. (1967) 'On the Concept of Political Power', in *Sociological Theory and Modern Society*, ed. T. Parsons (New York: Free Press) pp. 286–99.

Parsons, W. (1995) *Public Policy: An Introduction to the Theory and Practice of Policy Analysis* (Aldershot: Edward Elgar).

Pateman, C. (1970) *Participation and Democratic Theory* (Cambridge: Cambridge University Press).

Pateman, C. (2012) 'Participatory Democracy Revisited', *Perspectives on Politics* (10) 7–19.

Paulsen, B. (2007) 'The Question of Roles and Identities in Public Administration', *Public Administration* (30) 469–90.

Pennings, P., Keman, H. and Kleinnijenhuis, J. (2006) *Doing Research in Political Science: An Introduction to Comparative Methods and Statistics*, 2nd edn (London: Sage).

Peregudov, S. (2001) 'The Oligarchical Model of Russian Capitalism', in *Contemporary Russian Politics: A Reader*, ed. A. Brown (Oxford and New York: Oxford University Press) pp. 259–68.

Peréz-Liñán, A. (2006) 'Evaluating Presidential Runoff Elections', *Electoral Studies* (25) 129–46.

Peretti, T. (2001) *In Defence of a Political Court* (Princeton, NJ: Princeton University Press).

Perlmutter, A. (1981) *Modern Authoritarianism* (New Haven, CT: Yale University Press).

Peters, B. Guy (1998) *Comparative Politics: Theory and Methods* (New York: New York University Press).

Peters, B. Guy (2009) *The Politics of Bureaucracy: An Introduction to Comparative Public Administration*, 6th edn (New York: Routledge).

Peters, B. Guy (2011) 'Approaches in Comparative Politics', in *Comparative Politics*, 2nd edn, ed. D. Caramani (Oxford: Oxford University Press) pp. 37–49.

Peters, B. Guy (2012) 'The United States of America', in *Government Agencies: Practices and Lessons from 30 Countries*, ed. K. Verhoest, S. van Thiel, G. Bouckaert and P. Lægreid (Basingstoke: Palgrave Macmillan) pp. 69–76.

Peters, B. Guy (2012) *American Public Policy: Promise and Performance*, 9th edn (Washington, DC: CQ Press).

Peters, B. Guy and Pierre, J. (eds) (2004) *The Politicization of the Civil Service in Comparative Perspective: A Quest for Control* (London: Routledge).

Peterson, D., Grossback, L., Stimson, J. and Gangl, A. (2003) 'Congressional Response to Mandate Elections', *American Journal of Political Science* (47) 411–26.

Petracca, M. (1992) 'The Rediscovery of Interest Group Politics', in *The Politics of Interests: Interest Groups Transformed*, ed. M. Petracca (Boulder, CO) pp. 3–31.

Pharr, S. and Putnam, R. (eds) (2000) *Disaffected Democracies: What's Troubling the Trilateral Countries?* (Princeton, NJ: Princeton University Press).

Phillips, A. (1995) *The Politics of Presence* (Oxford: Oxford University Press).

Pierce, J. (2007) *Inside the Mason Court Revolution: The High Court of Australia Transformed* (Durham, NC: Carolina Academic Press).

Pierre, J. (2011) *The Politics of Urban Governance* (Basingstoke: Palgrave Macmillan).

Pierson, P. (2004) *Politics in Time: History, Institutions and Social Analysis* (Princeton, NJ: Princeton University Press).

Poguntke, T. and Webb, P. (eds) (2005) *The Presidentialization of Politics: A Comparative Study of Modern Democracies* (Oxford: Oxford University Press).

Polidano, C. (1998) 'Why Bureaucrats Can't Always Do What Ministers Want: Multiple Accountabilities in Westminster Democracies', *Public Policy and Administration* (13) 35–50.

Polity IV Project (2011) *Global Report 2011: Conflict, Governance and State Fragility*, http://www.systemicpeace.org, accessed 14 February 2011.

Pollitt, C. and Bouckaert, G. (2011) *Public Management Reform: A Comparative Analysis*, 3rd edn (Oxford: Oxford University Press).

Porta, D. della and Diani, M. (1999) *Social Movements: An Introduction* (Oxford: Blackwell).

Posusney, M. (2005) 'The Middle East's Democracy Deficit in Comparative Perspective', in *Authoritarianism in the Middle East: Regimes and Resistance*, ed. M. Posusney and M. Angrist (Boulder, CO: Lynne Rienner) pp. 1–20.

President of Russia (2009) *President of Russia*, http://www.kremlin.ru, accessed 11 November 2009.

President of the United States (2002) *National Security Strategy of the United States of America* (Washington, DC), http://www.whitehouse.gov, accessed 5 January, 2006.

Prillaman, W. (2000) *The Judiciary and Democratic Decay in Latin America: Declining Confidence in the Rule of Law* (Westport, CT: Praeger).

Prime Minister of Japan (2012) *Ministries and Other Organizations,* http://www.kantei.go.jp, accessed 9 August 2012.

Pryor, K. (2003) *A National State of Confusion* (New York: Salon.com), http://dir.salon.com/story/opinion/feature/2003/02/06/iraq_poll/index.html, accessed 2 May 2006.

Przeworski, A. (1991) *Democracy and the Market: Political and Economic Reforms in Eastern Europe and Latin America* (New York: Cambridge University Press).

Przeworski, A. and Teune, H. (1970) *The Logic of Comparative Social Inquiry* (New York: Wiley).

Przeworski, A., Alvarez, M., Cheibub, J. and Limongi, F. (2000) *Democracy and Development: Political Institutions and Well-Being in the World, 1950–1990* (New York: Cambridge University Press).

Psephos (2012) *Adam Carr's Election Archive,* http://psephos.adam-carr.net, accessed on various dates.

Pulzer, P. (1967) *Political Representation and Elections in Britain* (London: George Allen & Unwin).

Putnam, R. (1976) *The Comparative Study of Political Elites* (Englewood Cliffs, NJ: Prentice-Hall).

Putnam, R. (1993) *Making Democracy Work: Civic Traditions in Modern Italy* (Princeton, NJ: Princeton University Press).

Putnam, R. (2000) *Bowling Alone: The Collapse and Revival of American Community* (New York: Simon & Schuster).

Putnam, R. (ed.) (2002) *Democracies in Flux: The Evolution of Social Capital in Contemporary Society* (New York: Oxford University Press).

Putnam, R. and Goss, K. (2002) 'Introduction', in *Democracies in Flux: The Evolution of Social Capital in Contemporary Society*, ed. R. Putnam (New York: Oxford University Press) pp. 3–20.

Putnam, R., Pharr, S. and Dalton, R. (2000) 'What's Troubling the Trilateral Countries?', in *Disaffected Democracies: What's Troubling the Trilateral Countries?*, ed. S. Pharr and R. Putnam (Princeton, NJ: Princeton University Press) pp. 3–30.

Pye, L. (1995) 'Political Culture', in *The Encyclopaedia of Democracy,* ed. S. Lipset (London and New York: Routledge) pp. 965–9.

Q

Qualter, T. (1991) 'Public Opinion', in *The Blackwell Encyclopaedia of Political Science,* ed. V. Bogdanor (Oxford: Blackwell) p. 511.

Qvortrup, M. (2005) *A Comparative Study of Referendums: Government by the People,* 2nd edn (Manchester: Manchester University Press).

Qvortrup, M. (2008) 'Citizen Initiated Referendums (CIRs) in New Zealand: A Comparative Appraisal', *Representation* (44) 69–78.

R

Raadschelders, J., Toonen, T. and van der Meer, F. (eds) (2007) *The Civil Service in the 21st Century: Comparative Perspectives* (Basingstoke: Palgrave Macmillan).

Rahat, G. (2007) 'Candidate Selection: The Choice before the Choice', *Journal of Democracy* (18) 157–71.

Rainer, H. and Siedler, T. (2006) 'Does Democracy Foster Trust?' *ISER Working Paper 2006–31* (Colchester: University of Essex).

Ranke, L. von (1824) [1887 edn] *Histories of the Latin and Teutonic Peoples from 1494 to 1514* (London: Chiswick Press).

Rasch, B. (2004) 'Parliamentary Government', in *Nordic Politics: Comparative Perspectives,* ed. K. Heidar (Oslo: Universitetsforlaget) pp. 127–41.

Regeringskansliet (Government Offices of Sweden) (2009) *How the Government and Government Offices Function,* http://www.regeringen.se, accessed 6 August 2009.

Rein, M. (2006) 'Reforming Problematic Policies', in *The Oxford Handbook of Public Policy,* ed. M. Moran, M. Rein and R. Goodin (Oxford: Oxford University Press) pp. 389–405.

Reith, J. (1949) *Into the Wind* (London: Hodder & Stoughton).

Remington, T. (2011) *Politics in Russia,* 7th edn (Upper Saddle River, NJ: Prentice-Hall).

Renan, E. (1882) [1990 edn] 'What is a Nation?' in *Becoming National: A Reader,* ed. G. Eley and R. Suny (New York: Oxford University Press) pp. 42–55.

Renwick, A. (2010) *The Politics of Electoral Reform: Changing the Rules of Democracy* (Cambridge: Cambridge University Press).

Reynolds, A., Reilly, B. and Ellis, A. (2005) *Electoral System Design: The International IDEA Handbook* (Stockholm: International Institute for Democracy and Electoral Assistance), http://www.idea.int, accessed 11 June 2006.

Rhodes, R. (1996) 'The New Governance: Governing without Government', *Political Studies* (44) 652–67.

Richardson, J., Gustafsson, G. and Jordan, G. (1982) 'The Concept of Policy Style', in *Policy Styles in Western Europe,* ed. J. Richardson (London: Allen & Unwin) pp. 1–16.

Riches, W. (2010) *The Civil Rights Movement: Struggle and Resistance,* 3rd edn (Basingstoke: Palgrave Macmillan).

Riker, W. (1962) *The Theory of Political Coalitions* (New Haven, CT: Yale University Press).

Riker, W. (1975) 'Federalism', in *The Handbook of Political Science,* Vol. 5, ed. F. Greenstein and N. Polsby (Reading, MA: Addison-Wesley) pp. 93–172.

Riker, W. (1990) 'Political Science and Rational Choice', in *Perspectives on Positive Political Economy,* ed. J. Alt and K. Shepsle (New York: Cambridge University Press) pp. 182–97.

Riker, W. (1996) 'European Federalism: The Lessons of Past Experience', in *Federalizing Europe? The Costs, Benefits and Preconditions of Federal Political Systems,* ed. J. Hesse and V. Wright (Oxford: Oxford University Press) pp. 9–24.

Riker, W. and Ordeshook, P. (1973) *Introduction to Positive Political Theory* (Englewood Cliffs, NJ: Prentice-Hall).

Rodriguez, D. (2008) 'Administrative Law', in *The Oxford Handbook of Law and Politics,* ed. K. Whittington, R. Kelemen and G. Caldeira (Oxford: Oxford University Press) pp. 340–59.

Rogers, E. (1962) *Diffusion of Innnovations* (New York: Free Press).

Rohde, R. and Barthelemy, M. (2011) 'The President and Congressional Parties in an Era of Polarization', in *The Oxford Handbook of the America Presidency,* ed. G. Edwards, III and N. Howell (Oxford: Oxford University Press) pp. 289–310.

Rokkan, S. (1970) *Citizens, Elections, Parties* (New York: McKay).

Rosanvallon, P. (2008) *Counter-Democracy: Politics in an Age of Distrust* (Cambridge: Cambridge University Press).

Rose, L. (2004) 'Local Government and Politics', in *Nordic Politics: Comparative Perspectives,* ed. K. Heidar (Oslo: Universitetforlaget) pp. 164–82.

Rose, R. (1989) *Politics in England: Change and Persistence,* 5th edn (London: Macmillan).

Rose, R. (1991) 'Comparing Forms of Comparative Analysis', *Political Studies* (39) 446–62.

Rose, R. (2005) *Learning from Comparative Public Policy: A Practical Guide* (Abingdon: Routledge).

Rose, R. and Urwin, D. (1969) 'Social Cohesion, Political Parties and Strains in Regimes', *Comparative Political Studies* (2) 7–67.

Rosenbluth, E. and Thies, M. (2012) 'Politics in Japan', in *Comparative Politics Today: A World View,* 10th edn, ed. G. Bingham Powell, R. Dalton and K. Strøm (New York: Pearson Longman) pp. 294–333.

Rosenfeld, G. (2005) *The World Hitler Never Made: Alternate History and the Memory of Nazism* (Cambridge: Cambridge University Press).

Ross, C. (2010) 'Reforming the Federation', in *Developments in Russian Politics* 7, ed. S. White, R. Sakwa and H. Hale (Basingstoke: Palgrave Macmillan) pp. 152–70.

Ross, M. (2009) 'Culture in Comparative Political Analysis', in *Comparative Politics: Rationality, Culture and Structure*, ed. M. Lichbach and A. Zuckerman (New York: Cambridge University Press) pp. 134–61.

Rossi, P., Freeman, H. and Lipsey, M. (2003) *Evaluation: A Systematic Approach,* 7th edn (Thousand Oaks, CA: Sage Publications).

Rothstein, B. (1996) 'Political Institutions: An Overview', in *A New Handbook of Political Science*, ed. R Goodin and H.-D. Klingemann (Oxford: Oxford University Press) pp. 205–22.

Rothstein, B. (2002) 'Sweden: Social Capital in the Social Democratic State', in *Democracies in Flux: The Evolution of Social Capital in Contemporary Society*, ed. R. Putnam (New York: Oxford University Press) pp. 289–332.

Rothwell, D. (1986) 'Risk-Taking and Polarization in Small Group Communication', *Communication Education* (35) 182–7.

Rottinghaus, B. (2011) 'The Presidency and Congress', in *New Directions in the American Presidency*, ed. L. Han (New York: Routledge) pp. 83–102.

Rousseau, J.-J. (1755) [1988 edn] *Rousseau's Political Writings*, ed. A. Ritter and J. Bondanella (New York: Norton).

Rousseau, J.-J. (1762) [1913 edn] *The Social Contract* (New York: Dutton).

Roy, O. (1994) *The Failure of Political Islam* (London: I. B. Tauris).

Rubin, E. and Feeley, M. (2008) 'Federalism and Internationalism', *Publius* (38) 167–91.

Rucht, D. (2007) 'The Spread of Protest Politics', in *The Oxford Handbook of Political Behavior*, ed. R. Dalton and H-.D. Klingemann (Oxford: Oxford University Press) pp. 708–23.

Ruitenbeek. J., Seroa de Motta, R. and Huber, R. (1999) *Market-Based Instruments for Environmental Policymaking in Latin America and the Caribbean: Lessons from Eleven Countries* (Washington, DC: World Bank).

Russell, B. (1938) *Power: A New Social Analysis* (London: Allen & Unwin).

S

Sabatier, P. (ed.) (2007) *Theories of the Policy Process,* 2nd edn (Boulder, CO: Westview).

Sadurski, W. (2005) *Rights before Courts: A Study of Constitutional Courts in Postcommunist States of Central and Eastern Europe* (Dordrecht: Springer).

Safire, W. (1993) *Safire's New Political Dictionary* (New York: Random House).

Saich, A. (2011) *Governance and Politics of China,* 3rd edn (Basingstoke: Palgrave Macmillan).

Saikal, A. (2003) *Islam and the West: Conflict or Cooperation?* (Basingstoke: Palgrave Macmillan).

Sait, E. (1938) *Political Institutions: A Preface* (New York: Appleton-Century).

Sakwa, R. (2011) *The Crisis of Russian Democracy: The Dual State, Factionalism and the Medvedev Succession* (Cambridge: Cambridge University Press).

Salamon, L. (2002a) 'The New Governance and the Tools of Public Action: An Introduction', in *The Tools of Government: A Guide to the New Governance*, ed. L. Salamon (New York: Oxford University Press) pp. 1–47.

Salamon, L. (ed.) (2002b) *The Tools of Government: A Guide to the New Governance* (New York: Oxford University Press).

Sandbrook R. (1985) *The Politics of Africa's Economic Stagnation* (Cambridge: Cambridge University Press).

Sanders, D., Ward H., Marsh, D. and Fletcher, T. (1987) 'Government Popularity and the Falklands War: A Reassessment', *British Journal of Political Science* (18) 281–313.

Sartori, G. (1976) *Parties and Party Systems: A Framework for Analysis* (Cambridge: Cambridge University Press).

Sartori, G. (1994) *Comparative Constitutional Engineering: An Inquiry into Structures, Incentives and Outcomes* (London: Macmillan).

Sauvé, J.-M. (2010) *The French Administrative Jurisdictional System*, Speech to the Australia Administrative Appeals Tribunal Conference, Hunter Valley, 4 March 2010.

Savoie, D. (1999) *Governing from the Centre: The Concentration of Power in Canadian Politics* (Toronto: University of Toronto Press).

Scarrow, S. (ed.) (2002) *Perspectives on Political Parties: Classic Readings* (Basingstoke: Palgrave Macmillan).

Scarrow, S. (2006) 'Party Subsidies and the Freezing of Party Competition: Do Cartel Mechanisms Work?', *West European Politics* (29) 619–39.

Scarrow, S. and Gezgor, B. (2010) 'Declining memberships, changing members? European political party members in a new era', *Party Politics* (16) 823–43.

Schabas, W. (2011) *An Introduction to the International Criminal Court*, 4th edn (Cambridge: Cambridge University Press).

Schattschneider, E. (1942) *Party Government* (New York: Farrar & Rinehart).

Schattschneider, E. (1960) *The Semisovereign People* (New York: Holt, Rinehart, Winston).

Schedler, A. (ed.) (2006) *Electoral Authoritarianism: The Dynamics of Unfree Competition* (Boulder, CO and London: Lynne Rienner).

Scheiner, E. (2006) *Democracy without Competition in Japan: Opposition Failure in a One-Party Dominant State* (New York: Cambridge University Press).

Schepereel, J. (2010) 'European Culture and the European Union's "Turkey Question"', *West European Politics* (33) 810–29.

Schmidt, S., Shelley, M., Bardes, B. and Ford, L. (2012) *American Government and Politics Today*, 2011–12 edn (Boston, MA: Wadsworth).

Schmidt, V. (2002) *The Futures of European Capitalism* (New York: Oxford University Press).

Schmidt-Beck, R. and Farrell, D. (2002) 'Do Political Campaigns Matter? Yes, but It Depends', in *Do Political Campaigns Matter? Campaign Effects in Elections and Referendums,* ed. D. Farrell and R. Schmitt-Beck (London: Routledge) pp. 183–93.

Schmitter, P. (2011) 'Diagnosing and Designing Democracy in Europe', in *The Future of Representative Democracy*, ed. S. Alonso, J. Keane and W. Merkel (Cambridge: Cambridge University Press) pp. 191–211.

Scholzman, K. (2010) 'Who Sings in the Heavenly Chorus? The Shape of the Organized Interest System', in *The Oxford Handbook of American Political Parties and Interest Groups*, ed. L. Sandy Maisel and J. Berry (Oxford: Oxford University Press) pp. 425–50.

Schöpflin, G. (1990) 'Why Communism Collapsed', *International Affairs* (66) 3–17.

Schudson, M. (1998) *The Good Citizen: A History of American Civic Life* (Cambridge, MA: Harvard University Press).

Schumpeter, J. (1943) *Capitalism, Socialism and Democracy* (London: Allen & Unwin).

Scott, J. (1985) *Weapons of the Weak: Everyday Forms of Peasant Resistance* (New Haven, CT: Yale University Press).

Scott, W. (2007) *Institutions and Organizations: Ideas and Interests*, 3rd edn (London Oaks, CA: Sage).

Segal, J. and Spaeth, H. (2002) *The Supreme Court and the Attitudinal Model Revisited* (New York: Cambridge University Press).

Semetko, H. and Scammell, M. (eds) (2012) *The Sage Handbook of Political Communication* (London: Sage).

Sen, A. (2011) 'Quality of Life: India vs. China', *New York Review of Books*, 12 May, http://www.nybooks.com, accessed 19 April 2012.

Seyd, P. and Whiteley, P. (2002) *New Labour's Grassroots: The Transformation of the Labour Party Membership* (Basingstoke: Palgrave Macmillan).

Shapiro, M. (1987) 'Review of Rasmussen's "On Law and Policy in the European Court of Justice: A Comparative Study in Judicial Policy-Making"', *American Journal of International Law* (81) 1007–11.

Shapiro, M., and Stone Sweet, A. (2002) *On Law, Politics and Judicialization* (Oxford: Oxford University Press).

Sharlet, R. (2005) 'In Search of the Rule of Law', in *Developments in Russian Politics 6*, ed. S. White, Z. Gitelman and R. Sakwa (Basingstoke: Palgrave Macmillan) pp. 130–47.

Shepherd, R. (2006) 'The Denim Revolt that Can Rid Europe of Tyranny', *Financial Times,* 17 March 2006, p. 19.

Shepsle, K. (2006) 'Rational Choice Institutionalism', in *The Oxford Handbook of Political Institutions*, ed. R. Rhodes, S. Binder and B. Rockman (Oxford: Oxford University Press) pp. 23–38.

Shin, M. and Agnew, J. (2008) *Berlusconi's Italy: Mapping Contemporary Italian Politics* (Philadelphia, PA: Temple University Press).

Shirk, S. (ed.) (2011) *Changing Media, Changing China* (New York: Oxford University Press).

Shively, W. (2011) *Power and Choice: An Introduction to Political Science,* 13th edn (New York: McGraw-Hill).

Shugart, M. and Carey, J. (1992) *Presidents and Assemblies: Constitutional Design and Electoral Dynamics* (New York: Cambridge University Press).

Shugart, M. and Wattenberg, M. (eds) (2000) *Mixed-Member Electoral Systems: The Best of Both Worlds* (New York: Oxford University Press).

Silvia, S. and Schroeder, W. (2007) 'Why Are German Employers' Associations Declining? Arguments and Evidence', *Comparative Political Studies* (40) 1433–59.

Simon, H. (1983) *Reason in Human Affairs* (Oxford: Blackwell).

Skocpol, T. (1979) *States and Social Revolutions: A Comparative Analysis of France, Russia and China* (New York: Cambridge University Press).

Skocpol, T. (2003) 'Doubly Engaged Social Science: The Promise of Comparative Historical Analysis', in *Comparative Historical Analysis in the Social Sciences*, ed. J. Mahoney and D. Rueschmeyer (New York: Cambridge University Press) pp. 407–28.

Slaughter, A.-M. (2003) 'Governing the Global Economy through Government Networks', in *The Global Transformations Reader,* 2nd edn, ed. D. Held and A. McGrew (Cambridge: Polity) pp. 189–203.

Slaughter, A.-M. (2004) *A New World Order* (Princeton, NJ: Princeton University Press).

Smilde, D. and Hellinger, D. (eds) (2011) *Venezuela's Bolivarian Democracy: Participation, Politics and Culture under Chávez* (Durham, NC: Duke University Press).

Smith, A. (2009) *Ethno-symbolism and Nationalism: A Cultural Approach* (London: Routledge).

Smith, A. (2010) *Nationalism*, 2nd edn (Cambridge: Polity)

Smith, B. (1996) *Understanding Third World Politics* (London: Macmillan).

Smith, G. (2010) 'Legal Reform and the Dilemma of Rule of Law' in *Developments in Russian Politics 7*, ed. S. White, R. Sakwa and H. Hale (Basingstoke: Palgrave Macmillan) pp. 135–51.

Solomon, P. (2007) 'Courts and Judges in Authoritarian Regimes', *World Politics* (60) 122–45.

Sørensen, G. (2004) *The Transformation of the State: Beyond the Myth of Retreat* (Basingstoke: Palgrave Macmillan).

Sparks, A. (2009) *Beyond the Miracle: Inside the New South Africa* (Chicago: University of Chicago Press).

Spiller, P. and Gely, R. (2008) 'Strategic Judicial Decision-Making', in *The Oxford Handbook of Law and Politics*, ed. K. Whittington, R. Kelemen and G. Caldeira (Oxford: Oxford University Press) pp. 34–45.

Srebeny, A. and Khiabany, G. (2010) *Blogistan: The Internet and Politics in Iran* (London: I.B. Tauris).

Statistics Canada (2001) *2001 Census of Canada,* http://www12.statcan.ca, accessed 15 December 2006.

Steinberger, P. (2004) *The Idea of the State* (Cambridge: Cambridge University Press).

Steinmo, S. (2003) 'The Evolution of Policy Ideas: Tax Policy in the Twentieth Century', *British Journal of Politics and International Relations* (5) 206–36.

Stepan, A. (2001) *Arguing Comparative Politics* (Oxford: Oxford University Press).

Stepan, A., Linz, J. and Yadav, Y. (2011) *Crafting State-Nations: India and Other Multinational Democracies* (Baltimore, MD: Johns Hopkins University Press).

Steven Fish, M. (2011) *Are Muslims Distinctive? A Look at the Evidence* (New York: Oxford University Press).

Stevens, A. (2003) *Government and Politics of France*, 3rd edn (Basingstoke: Palgrave Macmillan).

Stevens, A. (2007) *Women, Power and Politics* (Basingstoke: Palgrave Macmillan).

Stevenson, G. (2009) *Unfulfilled Union: Canadian Federalism and National Unity*, 5th edn (Montreal: McGill-Queen's University Press).

Stimson, J. (2004) *Tides of Consent: How Public Opinion Shapes American Politics* (New York: Oxford University Press).

Stimson, J. (2009) 'Perspectives on Representation', in *The Oxford Handbook of Political Behavior*, ed. R. Dalton and H.-D. Klingemann (Oxford: Oxford University Press) pp. 850–61.

Stoker, G. and Marsh, D. (2010) 'Introduction', in *Theory and Methods in Political Science*, 3rd edn, ed. D. Marsh and G. Stoker (Basingstoke: Palgrave Macmillan) pp. 14–29.

Stokes, D. (1966) 'Some Dynamic Elements of Contests for the Presidency', *American Political Science Review* (60) 19–28.

Stokes, W. (2005) *Women in Contemporary Politics* (Cambridge: Polity).

Stone, D. (2001) *Policy Paradox: The Art of Political Decision Making*, rev. edn (New York: Norton).

Stonecash, J. (2005) *Political Parties Matter: Realignment and the Return of Partisan Voting* (Boulder, CO: Lynne Rienner).

Stonecash, J. (2010a) 'Changing American Political Parties', ed. J. Stonecash, in *New Directions in American Political Parties* (New York: Routledge) pp. 3–10.

Stonecash, J. (ed.) (2010b) *New Directions in American Political Parties* (New York: Routledge, 2010).

Stone Sweet, A. (2000) *Governing with Judges: Constitutional Politics in Europe* (Oxford: Oxford University Press).

Street, J. (2011) *Mass Media, Politics and Democracy*, 2nd edn (Basingstoke: Palgrave Macmillan).

Strøm, K. and Nyblade, B. (2007) 'Coalition Theory and Government Formation', in *The Oxford Handbook of Comparative Politics*, ed. C. Boix and S. Stokes (Oxford: Oxford University Press) pp. 782–804.

Strøm, K., Müller, W. and Bergman, T. (eds) (2008) *Cabinets and Coalition Bargaining: The Democratic Life Cycle in Western Europe* (New York: Oxford University Press).

Stubager, R. (2010) 'The Development of the Education Cleavage: Denmark as a Critical Case', *West European Politics* (33) 505–33.

Sundberg, J. (2002) 'The Scandinavian Party Model at the Crossroads', in *Political Parties in Advanced Industrial Democracies*, ed. P. Webb, D. Farrell and I. Holliday (Oxford: Oxford University Press) pp. 181–216.

Svolik, M. (2008) 'Authoritarian Reversals and Democratic Consolidation', *American Political Science Review* (102) 153–68.

T

Tardi, G. (2002) 'Departments and Other Institutions of Government', in *Canadian Public Administration*, ed. C. Dunn (Don Mills, Ontario: Oxford University Press) pp. 281–304.

Tarrow, S. (2005) *The New Transnational Activism* (New York: Cambridge University Press).

Tarrow, S. (2011) *Power in Movement: Social Movements and Contentious Politics*, 3rd edn (New York: Cambridge University Press).

Tetlock, P. and Belkin, A. (1996) *Counterfactual Thought Experiments in World Politics* (Princeton, NJ: Princeton University Press).

Teune, H. (1995a) 'Preface', *Annals of the American Academy of Political and Social Sciences* (540) 8–10.

Teune, H. (1995b) 'Local Government and Democratic Political Development', *Annals of the American Academy of Political and Social Sciences* (540) 11–23.

Teune, H. (2010) 'The Challenge of Globalization to Comparative Research,' *Journal of Comparative Politics* (3) 4–19.

Thomas, C. and Hrebenar, R. (2009) 'Comparing Lobbying Across Liberal Democracies: Problems, Approaches and Initial Findings,' *Journal of Comparative Politics* (2) 131–42.

Thomas, S. (2005) 'Introduction', in *Women and Elective Office*, 2nd edn, ed. S. Thomas and C. Wilcox (New York: Oxford University Press) pp. 3–25.

Tilly, C. (1975) 'Reflections on the History of European State-Making', in *The Formation of National States in Western Europe*, ed. C. Tilly (Princeton, NJ: Princeton University Press) pp. 3–83.

Tilly, C. (1978) *From Mobilization to Revolution* (Reading, MA: Addison-Wesley).

Tilly, C. (1997) 'Means and Ends of Comparison in Macrosociology', *Comparative Social Research* (16) 43–53.

Tilly, C. (2004) *Social Movements, 1768–2004* (Boulder, CO: Paradigm Publishers).

Tilly, C. (2011) *Power in Movement: Social Movements and Contentious Politics*, 3rd edn (New York: Oxford University Press, 2011).

Tocqueville, A. de (1835) [1966 edn] *Democracy in America* (New York: Vintage Books).

Tocqueville, A. de (1856) [1954 edn] *The Ancien Regime and the Revolution in France* (London: Fontana).

Tracey, M. (1998) *The Decline and Fall of Public Service Broadcasting* (Oxford: Oxford University Press).

Tremewan, C. (1994) *The Political Economy of Social Control in Singapore* (Basingstoke: Palgrave Macmillan).

Tripp, A. and Kang, A. (2008) 'The Global Impact of Quotas', *Comparative Political Studies* (41) 338–61.

Tschentscher, A. (2004) *China Constitution* (International Constitutional Law Project), http://www.oefre.unibe.ch, accessed 16 August 2006.

Tsebelis, G. (2002) *Veto Players: How Political Institutions Work* (Princeton, NJ: Princeton University Press).

Tsebelis, G. and Money, J. (1997) *Bicameralism* (Cambridge and New York: Cambridge University Press).

Turner, M. and Hulme, D. (1997) *Governance, Administration and Development* (London: Macmillan).

Twigg, J. (2005) 'Social Policy in Post-Soviet Russia', in *Developments in Russian Politics 6*, ed. S. White, Z. Gitelman and R. Sakwa (Basingstoke: Palgrave Macmillan) pp. 204–20.

U

UN DESA (United Nations, Department of Economic and Social Affairs) (2010) *World Population Prospects, The 2010 Revision*, http://esa.un.org, accessed 5 October 2011.

UNESCO (United Nations Educational, Scientific and Cultural Organization) (2002) *Universal Declaration on Cultural Diversity*, http://www.unesco.org, accessed 14 April 2006.

UNHCR (United Nations High Commission for Human Rights) (1966) *United Nations Covenant on Civil and Political Rights*, http://www.unhcr.ch, accessed 9 February 2006.

United Nations (2009) *Growth in United Nations Membership, 1945–2009*, http://www.un.org, accessed 1 August 2009.

United Nations Development Programme (UNDP) (2009) *Human Development Report*, http://hdr.undp.org, accessed 3 April 2009.

United States Elections Project (2011) *Voter Turnout*, http://elections.gmu.edu, accessed 18 December 2011.

United States Elections Project (2012) *2012 Early Voting Statistics*, http://elections.gmu.edu, accessed 11 November, 2012.

UNPAN (United Nations Public Administration Programme) (2012) *E-Government Survey*, http://www.unpan.org, accessed 15 August 2012.

usfederalbudget.us (2012) *Government Spending: The Details*, http://www.usfederalbudget.us, accessed 13 August 2012.

V

Valentino, B. (2004) *Final Solutions: Mass Killing and Genocide in the 20th Century* (Ithaca, NY: Cornell University Press).

Vanhanen, T. (1997) *Prospects of Democracy: A Study of 172 Countries* (London: Routledge).

Vedung, E. (1998) 'Policy Instruments: Typologies and Theories', in *Carrots, Sticks, and Sermons: Policy Instruments and Their Evaluation*, ed. M.-L. Bemelmans-Videc, R. Rist and E. Vedung (New Brunswick, NJ: Transaction) pp. 21–52.

Verba, S. (1987) *Elites and the Idea of Equality: A Comparison of Japan, Sweden and the United States* (Cambridge, MA: Harvard University Press).

Verba, S., Nie, N. and Kim, J. (1978) *Participation and Political Equality: A Seven-Nation Comparison* (New York: Cambridge University Press).

Verba, S., Scholzman, K. and Brady, H. (1995) *Voice and Equality: Civic Voluntarism in American Politics* (Cambridge, MA: Harvard University Press).

Vibert, F. (2007) *The Rise of the Unelected: Democracy and the New Separation of Powers* (Cambridge: Cambridge University Press).

Voerman, G. and Schurr, W. van (2011) 'Dutch Political Parties and their Members' in *Party Membership in Europe: Exploration into the Anthills of Party Politics*, ed. E. van Haute (Brussels: Editions de l'Université de Bruxelles) pp. 57–94.

Volgy, T., Fausett, E., Grant, K. and Rodgers, S. (2006) 'Ergo Figo: Identifying Formal Intergovernmental Organizations', *Working Papers Series in International Politics*, Department of Political Science, University of Arizona, http://www.us.arizona.edu, accessed 27 September 2012.

Vreese, C. de (2010) 'Campaign Communication and Media', in *Comparing Democracies 3*, ed L. LeDuc, R. Niemi and P. Norris (Thousand Oaks, CA: Sage) pp. 118–40.

W

Waldron, J. (2007) *Law and Disagreement* (Oxford: Oxford University Press).

Walker, J. (1991) *Mobilizing Interest Groups in America: Patrons, Professionals and Social Movements* (Ann Arbor, MI: University of Michigan Press).

Walpole, S. (1881) *The Electorate and the Legislature* (London: Macmillan).

WAN (World Association of Newspapers) (2011) *World Press Trends*, http://www.wan-press.org, accessed 9 September 2012.

WARC (World Advertising Research Center) (2009) *Media Use in Spain*, http://www.warc.com, accessed 7 September 2009.

Warleigh, A. (1998) 'Better The Devil You Know? Synthetic and Confederal Understandings of European Integration', *West European Politics* (21) 1–18.

Washington, G. (1796) [2002 edn] 'Farewell Address to Congress', in *Perspectives on Political Parties: Classic Readings*, ed. S. Scarrow (New York: Palgrave Macmillan) pp. 45–8.

Waters, M. (2000) *Globalization*, 2nd edn (London: Routledge).

Watts, R. (2008) *Comparing Federal Systems*, 3rd edn (Montreal: McGill–Queen's University Press).

Watson, G. (2011) 'Monti's Team', *Corriere della Sera*, 16 November, http://www.corriere.it, accessed 12 November 2012.

Wattenberg, M. (2000) 'The Decline of Party Mobilization', in *Parties without Partisans*, ed. R. Dalton and M. Wattenberg (New York: Oxford University Press) pp. 64–76.

Wattenberg, M. (2011) 'US Party Leaders: Exploring the Meaning of Candidate-Centred Politics' in *Political Leaders and Democratic Elections*, ed. K. Aarts, A. Blais and H. Schmitt (Oxford: Oxford University Press) pp. 76–90.

Watts, R. (2005) 'Comparing Forms of Federal Partnerships', in *Theories of Federalism: A Reader*, ed. D. Karmis and W. Norman (New York: Palgrave Macmillan) pp. 233–54.

Way, L. (2011) 'Comparing the Arab Revolts: The Lessons of 1989', *Journal of Democracy* (22) 17–27.

Weale, A. (2007) *Democracy*, 2nd edn (Basingstoke: Palgrave Macmillan).

Weaver, R. and Rockman, B. (eds) (1993) *Do Institutions Matter? Government Capabilities in the United States and Abroad* (Washington, DC: The Brookings Institution).

Webb, P., Farrell, D. and Holliday, I. (eds) (2002) *Political Parties in Advanced Industrial Democracies* (Oxford: Oxford University Press).

Weber, M. (1905) [1930 edn] *The Protestant Ethic and the Spirit of Capitalism* (London: Allen & Unwin).

Weber, M. (1918) [1990 edn] 'The Advent of Plebiscitarian Democracy', in *The West European Party System*, ed. P. Mair (Oxford: Oxford University Press) pp. 31–7.

Weber, M. (1921–22) [1978 edn] *Economy and Society: An Outline of Interpretive Sociology*, ed. G. Roth and C. Wittich (Berkeley, CA: University of California Press).

Weber, M. (1922) [1957 edn] *The Theory of Economic and Social Organization* (Berkeley, CA: University of California Press).

Weber, M. (1923) [1946 edn] 'The Social Psychology of the World Religions', in *From Max Weber: Essays in Sociology*, ed. and trans. H. Gerth and C. Wright Mills (New York: Oxford University Press) pp. 267–301.

Wehner, J. (2006) 'Assessing the Power of the Purse: An Index of Legislative Budget Institutions', *Political Studies* (54) 767–85.

Weiler, J. (1994) 'A Quiet Revolution: The European Court of Justice and its Interlocutors', *Comparative Political Studies* (26) 519–34.

Weingast, B. (1998) 'Political Stability and Civil War: Institutions, Commitment and American Democracy', in R. Bates, *Analytic Narratives* (Princeton, NJ: Princeton University Press) pp. 148–93.

Weissberg, R. (2002) *Polling, Policy and Public Opinion: The Case Against Heeding 'The Voice of the People'* (Basingstoke: Palgrave Macmillan).

Welzel, C. and Inglehart, R. (2009) 'Political Culture, Mass Beliefs, and Value Change', in *Democratization*, ed. C. Haerpfer, P. Bernhagen, R. Inglehart and C. Welzel (Oxford: Oxford University Press) pp. 127–44.

Wendt, A. (1999) *Social Theory of International Politics* (Cambridge: Cambridge University Press).

West, D. and Orman, J. (2003) *Celebrity Politics* (Upper Saddle River, NJ: Prentice-Hall).

Wheeler, D. and Mintz, L. (2012) 'New Media and Political Change: Lessons from Internet Users in Jordan, Egypt, and Kuwait', in *iPolitics: Citizens, Elections, and Governing in the New Internet Era*, ed. R. Fox and J. Ramos (Cambridge University Press) pp. 259–87.

White, S. (2005a) 'The Political Parties', in *Developments in Russian Politics 6*, ed. S. White, Z. Gitelman and R. Sakwa (Basingstoke: Palgrave Macmillan) pp. 80–95.

White, S. (2005b) 'Russia: The Authoritarian Adaptation of an Electoral System', in *The Politics of Electoral Systems*, ed. M. Gallagher and P. Mitchell (Oxford: Oxford University Press) pp. 313–32.

White, S. (2007) 'Russia's Client Party System', in *Party Politics in New Democracies*, ed. P. Webb and S. White (Oxford: Oxford University Press) pp. 21–52.

White, S. (2011) *Understanding Russian Politics* (Cambridge: Cambridge University Press).

White, S., Hale, H. and Sakwa, R. (eds) (2009) *Developments in Russian Politics 7* (Basingstoke: Palgrave Macmillan).

White House (2006) *National Security Strategy, March 2006*, http://www.whitehouse.gov, accessed 24 August 2006.

Whiteley, P. (2011) 'Is the Party Over? The Decline of Party Activism and Membership Across the Democratic World', *Party Politics* (17) 21–44.

Whiteley, P. (2012) *Political Participation in Britain: The Decline and Revival of Civic Culture* (Basingstoke: Palgrave Macmillan).

Whittington, K., Kelemen, R. and Caldeira, G. (eds) (2008) *The Oxford Handbook of Law and Politics* (Oxford: Oxford University Press).

Wiarda, H. (ed.) (2004) *Authoritarianism and Corporatism in Latin America - Revisited* (Gainesville, FL: University Press of Florida).

Wigbold, H. (1979) 'Holland: The Shaky Pillars of Hilversum', in *Television and Political Life*, ed. A. Smith (London: Macmillan) pp. 191–231.

Wildavsky, A. (1979) *The Art and Craft of Policy Analysis* (Boston, MA: Little, Brown).

Wilde, R. (2007) *Territorial Administration by International Organizations* (Oxford: Oxford University Press).

Willerton, J. (1997) 'Presidential Power', in *Developments in Russian Politics,* ed. S. White, A. Pravda and Z. Gitelman (London: Macmillan) pp. 35–60.

Willerton, J. (2005) 'Putin and the Hegemonic Presidency', in *Developments in Russian Politics 6*, ed. S. White, Z. Gitelman and R. Sakwa (Basingstoke: Palgrave Macmillan) pp. 18–39.

Williams, R. (1962) *Communications* (Harmondsworth: Penguin).

Wilson, G. (2003) *Business and Politics: A Comparative Introduction,* 3rd edn (London: Macmillan).

Wilson, W. (1885) *Congressional Government* (Boston, MA: Houghton Mifflin).

Wilson, W. (1887) 'The Study of Administration', *Political Science Quarterly* (2) 197–222.

Winter, L. and Brans, M. (2003) 'Belgium: Political Professionals and the Crisis of the Party State', in *The Political Class in Advanced Democracies*, ed. J. Borchert and J. Zeiss (Oxford: Oxford University Press) pp. 45–66.

Wlezien, C. (2010) 'Election Campaigns' in *Comparing Democracies 3: Elections and Voting in the 21st Century*, ed. L. Leduc, R. Niemi and P. Norris (Thousand Oaks, CA: Sage) pp. 98–117.

Wood, B (2011) 'Presidents and the Political Agenda', in *The Oxford Handbook of the American Presidency*, ed. G. Edwards III and W. Howell (Oxford: Oxford University Press) pp. 108–32.

Wood, G. (1993) 'Democracy and the American Revolution', in *Democracy: The Unfinished Journey, 508 BC to AD 1993*, ed. J. Dunn (Oxford: Oxford University Press) pp. 91–106.

World Bank (1997) *World Development Report: The State in a Changing World* (Oxford: Oxford University Press).

World Bank (2011) *How We Classify Countries*, http://data.worldbank.org/about/country-classification, accessed 9 October 2011.

Wright, V. (1997) 'La Fin du Dirigisme?', *Modern and Contemporary France* (5) 151–5.

Y

Yin, R. (ed.) (2004) *The Case Study Anthology* (Thousand Oaks, CA: Sage).

Yin, R. (2013) *Case Study Research: Design and Methods,* 5th edn (Thousand Oaks, CA: Sage).

Z

Zakaria, E (2003) *The Future of Freedom: Illiberal Democracy at Home and Abroad* (New York: Norton).

Zelikow, P. (2011) 'The Global Era and The End of Foreign Policy', *Financial Times,* 17 August, p. 9.

Zijderveld, A. (2000) *The Institutional Imperative: The Interface of Institutions and Networks* (Amsterdam: Amsterdam University Press).

Index